Introduction to
Special Education

Introduction to
Special Education

SECOND EDITION

James E. Ysseldyke
University of Minnesota

Bob Algozzine
The University of North Carolina at Charlotte

HOUGHTON MIFFLIN COMPANY   Boston

Dallas   Geneva, Illinois   Palo Alto   Princeton, New Jersey

Printed in the U.S.A.
Library of Congress Catalog Card Number: 89–80974
ISBN: 0–395–35811–6

ABCDEFGHIJ–VH–9543210–89

Cover photograph © Paul Elledge.

Part- and chapter-opening photo credits: Part 1, p. 2, © Richard Hutchings/PR; Chapter 1, p. 5, © John Winthrop School, Bridgeport, Conn., © Maureen Fennelli/Comstock; Chapter 2, p. 38, © Gilbea Dupuy/Black Star; Part 2, p. 74, © Michael Weisbrot and Family; Chapter 3, p. 77, © Michael Weisbrot and Family; Chapter 4, p. 113, © Alan Carey/The Image Works; Chapter 5, p. 159, © Michael Weisbrot and Family; Chapter 6, p. 194, © Meri Houtchens-Kitchens/The Picture Cube; Part 3, p. 236, © Spencer Grant/Monkmeyer Press Photo Service; Chapter 7, p. 239, © Paul Conklin; Chapter 8, p. 278, © Emilio Mercado/Jeroboam; Part 4, p. 304, © Kathy Sloane/Jeroboam; Chapter 9, p. 307, © Susan Lapides; Chapter 10, p. 355, © Suzanne Arms Wimberly/Jeroboam; Chapter 11, p. 387, © Stephen McBrady Studios; Part 5, p. 424, © Barrerra/TexaStock; Chapter 12, p. 427, © David M. Grossman; Chapter 13, p. 464, © Evan Johnson/Jeroboam.

Excerpts from the following material have been reprinted by permission of the publishers:

"Ever Wonder How Stevie Wonder Reads His Mail?" reprinted by permission of Stevie Wonder, Steveland Morris Music, Burbank, CA, and Xerox Corporation, Stamford, CT.

Friedman, J., and Gallo, N., "Steve Largent Has Caught More Passes Than Anyone, But Without His Home Team He'd Be Incomplete," *People Weekly*, November 20, 1988, pp. 77–80. Reprinted with permission.

Adapted from James J. Gallagher, *Teaching the Gifted Child*, 3rd edition. Copyright © 1985 by Allyn and Bacon, Boston. Used by permission.

"Language Disabilities in the School-Age Child," in G.H. Shames & E. Wiig (Eds.), *Human Communication Disorders* (Columbus, OH: Merrill), pp. 282–283. Reprinted by permission of the publisher.

"Minnesota Standards for Services to Gifted and Talented Students," pp. 2–3, April 22, 1988. St. Paul, MN: Minnesota State Advisory Council for the Gifted and Talented. Reprinted by permission.

From Michael Rogers, "Technology: More Than Wheelchairs," *Newsweek*, April 24, 1989. © 1989, *Newsweek*, Inc. All rights reserved. Reprinted by permission.

Contents

***Preface* xiv**

PART **one**

Special Education Today 2

1 *The Foundations of Special Education* 5

DEFINING SPECIAL EDUCATION 8
   What Is Special Education? 9
   How Did Special Education Come to Be? 9
   Why Do Students Receive Special Education? 12
   Who Receives Special Education? 13
   Window on Practice 14
   How Many Students Receive Special Education? 17
   How Are Students Assigned to Special Education? 20
   Window on Practice 22
   What Special Services Do Exceptional Students Receive? 24
   Where Are Exceptional Students Taught? 25
   How Old Are Exceptional Students? 26
DIVERSITY IN SPECIAL EDUCATION 28
   The Students 29

Educational Settings 32
WHAT WE THINK ABOUT SPECIAL EDUCATION 33

2 *The Legal Basis for Special Education 38*

DEFINITIONS 41
    Constitutional Provisions 42
    Laws 42
    Regulations and Guidelines 44
    Court Rulings 44
    Professional Standards and Codes of Ethics 44
    Teachers and the Law 45
LEGISLATION 45
    Section 504 of the Rehabilitation Act of 1973 46
    Public Law 94–142 47
    Public Law 99–457 58
    Window on Practice *60*
LITIGATION 61
    Court Action Before Public Law 94–142 61
    Court Action After Public Law 94–142 65
THE ROLE OF PARENTS 70
WHAT WE THINK ABOUT THE LEGAL BASIS FOR SPECIAL EDUCATION 71

PART *two*
Exceptional Students 74

3 *Perspectives on Exceptionality 77*

DEFINING NORMALITY AND ABNORMALITY 78
    Statistical Standards 81
    Medical Standards 82
    Social Standards 83
REACTIONS TO EXCEPTIONALITY 85
    The Nature of the Exceptionality 85
    Window on Practice *86*
    The Cause of the Exceptionality 88
    The Effect of Labels 89
    The Context in Which Exceptionality Occurs 92
PERCEIVING EXCEPTIONALITY 95
    Expectations 95

Window on Practice 96
Expectations and Performance 98
Expectations and Academic Performance 101
Expectations and Social Behaviors 102
The View from Outside 103
WHAT WE THINK ABOUT EXCEPTIONALITY 107

4 *High-prevalence Categories of Exceptionality* 113

STUDENTS WITH LEARNING DISABILITIES 115
  Definition 115
  History 117
  Prevalence 121
  Characteristics 123
  Window on Practice 130
STUDENTS WHO ARE GIFTED AND TALENTED 132
  Definition 132
  History 135
  Prevalence 137
  Characteristics 137
  Window on Practice 142
STUDENTS WITH SPEECH AND LANGUAGE PROBLEMS 145
  Definition 145
  History 147
  Prevalence 148
  Characteristics 148
PRACTICAL CONSIDERATIONS IN TEACHING STUDENTS IN HIGH-
PREVALENCE CATEGORIES 152
WHAT WE THINK ABOUT HIGH-PREVALENCE CONDITIONS 156

5 *Moderate-prevalence Categories of Exceptionality* 159

STUDENTS WITH MENTAL RETARDATION 161
  Definition 161
  History 162
  Window on Practice 166
  Prevalence 169
  Characteristics 171
STUDENTS WHO ARE EMOTIONALLY DISTURBED 175
  Definition 175
  History 177
  Prevalence 178

Characteristics 180
Window on Practice *182*
PRACTICAL CONSIDERATIONS IN TEACHING STUDENTS IN MODERATE-
PREVALENCE CATEGORIES 185
WHAT WE THINK ABOUT MODERATE-PREVALENCE CONDITIONS 188

6   *Low-prevalence Categories of Exceptionality 194*

STUDENTS WITH ORTHOPEDIC HANDICAPS AND OTHER HEALTH
IMPAIRMENTS 197
Definitions 197
History 198
Prevalence 199
Major Conditions 199
Characteristics 206
Window on Practice *208*
STUDENTS WHO ARE MULTIHANDICAPPED 210
Definition 210
History 211
Prevalence 211
Characteristics 213
STUDENTS WHO ARE HARD OF HEARING AND DEAF 213
Definition 213
History 215
Prevalence 215
Characteristics 215
Window on Practice *220*
STUDENTS WHO ARE VISUALLY HANDICAPPED 222
Definition 222
History 224
Prevalence 225
Characteristics 225
STUDENTS WHO ARE DEAF AND BLIND 227
History 227
Prevalence 228
Characteristics 228
PRACTICAL CONSIDERATIONS IN TEACHING STUDENTS IN LOW-
PREVALENCE CATEGORIES 228
Eliminate Barriers 229
Improve Communication 230
Foster Independence 231
WHAT WE THINK ABOUT LOW-PREVALENCE CONDITIONS 232

PART **three**

Practicing Special Education 236

7 *Delivering Services to Students with Special Needs 239*

CLASSIFICATION IN SPECIAL EDUCATION 241
    Objectives 241
    Window on Practice 242
    A Brief History of Classification Practices 245
    Current Classification Practices 247
CONCEPTS GUIDING PLACEMENT DECISIONS 250
    Least Restrictive Environment 251
    Window on Practice 253
    Mainstreaming 254
SPECIAL EDUCATION PROGRAMS 258
    Settings and Services 258
    Organizing Programs 259
ISSUES IN DELIVERING SERVICES 267
    Cascade of Services 267
    The Regular Education Initiative 270
    Early Intervention 273
    Vocational Education and Transition Services 274
WHAT WE THINK ABOUT DELIVERING SERVICES TO STUDENTS WITH
SPECIAL NEEDS 275

8 *Professionals in Special Education 278*

REGULAR EDUCATION TEACHERS 280
SPECIAL EDUCATION TEACHERS 281
    Instructional Consultant 283
    Itinerant Teacher 284
    Resource Room Teacher 284
    Self-contained Special Class Teacher 284
    Clinical Teacher 285
    Window on Practice 286
    Homebound Teacher 288
RELATED SERVICES PERSONNEL 289
    Counselor 289
    School Psychologist 289
    Educational Diagnostician 291
    Occupational Therapist 291

Physical Therapist 291
Speech-Language Pathologist 291
Audiologist 292
School Social Worker 293
ADMINISTRATORS 293
Superintendent of Schools 293
Window on Practice *294*
Director or Coordinator of Special Education 296
Supervisor of Specific Service Components 296
Building Principal 296
OTHER PROFESSIONALS 296
SUPPLY AND DEMAND 297
PROFESSIONAL ORGANIZATIONS 298
WHAT WE THINK ABOUT PROFESSIONALS IN SPECIAL EDUCATION 301

PART **four**

Teaching Exceptional Students *304*

9 *Assessment Practices in Special Education 307*

ASSESSMENT FOR DECISION-MAKING PURPOSES 309
Screening and Referral 309
Eligibility, Classification, and Placement 310
Instructional Planning 311
Progress Evaluation 311
Program Evaluation 313
Decision-making Practices 314
COLLECTING ASSESSMENT DATA 318
Methods for Collecting Data 318
Behaviors Sampled by Assessment 323
STANDARDS FOR GOOD ASSESSMENT PRACTICES 341
Reliability: Is Performance Consistent? 341
*Representativeness: Does the Instrument Adequately Sample
the Behavior? 341*
Window on Practice *342*
*Validity: Does a Procedure Measure What It Is Supposed
to Measure? 344*
ASSUMPTIONS UNDERLYING ASSESSMENT PRACTICES 345
Major Assumptions 345
Further Considerations 349
WHAT WE THINK ABOUT ASSESSMENT 352

10 *Effective Instruction 355*

COMPONENTS OF EFFECTIVE INSTRUCTION 357
    Planning Instruction 357
    Window on Practice *358*
    Managing Instruction 365
    Delivering Instruction 367
    Evaluating Instruction 374
    Window on Practice *380*
APPLICATION OF EFFECTIVE INSTRUCTION 381
WHAT WE THINK ABOUT EFFECTIVE INSTRUCTION 383

11 *Teaching Exceptional Students 387*

SPECIAL PURPOSES FOR INSTRUCTION 389
INDIVIDUALIZED EDUCATION PROGRAMS 393
SPECIAL LEARNING NEEDS 397
SPECIAL TEACHING METHODS 399
    Behavior Therapy 399
    Precision Teaching 401
    Ability Training 402
    Direct Instruction 402
    Cognitive Skills Training 403
    Counseling Therapy 404
    Learning Strategies Training 405
    Cooperative Learning 405
    Peer-directed Learning 405
    Social Skills Training 407
SPECIAL INSTRUCTIONAL ADAPTATIONS 408
    For Communication 408
    Window on Practice *410*
    For Mobility 415
WE REMEMBER TEACHERS 418
WHAT WE THINK ABOUT TEACHING EXCEPTIONAL STUDENTS 419

P A R T *five*

The Social Context for Special Education 424

12 *The Social, Political, and Economic Realities of
Special Education 427*

THE CONDITION OF EDUCATION 428
SOCIAL FACTORS AND SPECIAL EDUCATION 431
  Window on Practice 432
  How Do Social Values Influence Policy? 433
  How Are Ethnic Origin and Treatment Related? 435
POLITICAL FACTORS AND SPECIAL EDUCATION 439
  How Do Political Values Influence Policy? 439
  Window on Practice 440
  How Do People Who Are Handicapped Achieve Rights? 441
  How Are Categories and Eligibility Criteria Determined? 443
ECONOMIC FACTORS AND SPECIAL EDUCATION 445
  Who Pays for Special Education Services? 446
  How Are the Monies Allocated? 449
  What Are the Costs of Special Education? 452
  Are We Doing This the Right Way? 457
WHAT WE THINK ABOUT THE SOCIAL, POLITICAL, AND ECONOMIC
REALITIES OF SPECIAL EDUCATION 459

13 *Exceptional People and Society* *464*

THE CHANGING ROLES OF PARENTS AND FAMILIES 467
  Window on Practice 468
SPECIAL EDUCATION IS CHANGING 471
  Early Childhood Intervention 472
  Cultural Diversity and Special Education 474
  Technology and Special Education 476
  Regular Education and Special Education 478
WHAT HAPPENS AFTER SCHOOL? 482
  Who Leaves Special Education? 482
  What Happens to Exceptional People in Society? 487
  Where Do People with Handicaps Live? 489
WHAT WE HAVE LEARNED ABOUT SPECIAL EDUCATION 493

***Appendix A Professional Associations Relevant to
        Special Education 498***

Appendix B Commonly Used Tests 508

***Appendix C Council for Exceptional Children Code
        of Ethics 521***

***Appendix D Council for Exceptional Children Policy
        on Standards for Professional Practices in
        Special Education 522***

References 524

Glossary 536
Author Index 545
Subject Index 549

Preface

Audience and Purpose

For many people reading this text, the words *special education* will evoke
strong images. Some images may derive from intensely personal recollec-
tions or experiences, others may reflect professional aspirations or knowledge acquired about exceptional individuals. Whatever the source, those
images are often powerful reminders of why people choose to pursue a career in special education or seek to learn more about exceptional individuals. In this text, we aim to engage the novice student's personal motivation
for studying special education and bolster it with in-depth knowledge of
the principles, practices, and wide-ranging influences that inform the education of students with special learning needs.

   Introduction to Special Education offers an overview of the field of
special education geared to those who are preparing to work with exceptional students, including regular and special educators, counselors, psychologists, and other related professionals, and parents. As an introductory text, it provides the first-time student with fundamental information
on definitions of terms commonly used in the field, characteristics of individuals in each category of exceptionality, laws and legal cases affecting
the delivery of services to exceptional individuals, the full range of settings
in which exceptional students are served, and principles of effective instruction and practices that promote informed decision making throughout teaching. In helping the reader understand the impact of society on exceptional individuals, the text explores the subtle factors that impinge on
exceptional people's personal performance, self-image, and integration in

school and the community and examines the key areas in which changes are occurring in the lives of exceptional people. In its breadth and depth of coverage, the text seeks to enlighten readers with information that will enable them to approach their work as knowledgeable, dedicated, and open-minded professionals.

Organization of the Text

Coverage of special education and exceptional students is presented in thirteen chapters and divided into five parts.

Part One, "Special Education Today," is a foundation for the text. Chapter 1 defines basic terms and introduces major topics covered in depth in the text. Chapter 2 analyzes the laws and court cases affecting the development of special education and general treatment of exceptional individuals in our society.

Part Two, "Exceptional Students," considers exceptionality in terms of the expectations used to define it and presents considerable information about the categories of exceptionality covered in the Education for All Handicapped Children Act. Chapter 3 focuses on standards used to make judgments about exceptional behavior and devotes substantial discussion to the role that expectations play in influencing perceptions of exceptionality. Given the realities of practicing special education today, professionals need to know basic information about the characteristics of individuals in each category of exceptionality. Chapters 4, 5, and 6 provide extensive coverage of the categories of exceptionality, organized according to degree of prevalence. Each chapter includes definitions, historical perspectives, prevalence data, characteristics, and practical considerations for teaching exceptional students. Chapter 4 focuses on the high-prevalence categories of exceptionality: learning disabilities, giftedness and talent, and speech and language problems. In Chapter 5, the moderate-prevalence categories—mental retardation and emotional disturbance—are discussed. Chapter 6 considers the low-prevalence categories: orthopedic handicaps and other health impairments, multiple handicaps, hearing impairments, and visual impairments.

In Part Three, "Practicing Special Education," we focus on the delivery of services to exceptional students. In Chapter 7, we discuss classification practices and the specific settings in which exceptional learners are taught. Coverage includes substantive discussion of the two major concepts—*least restrictive environment* and *mainstreaming*—that guide decisions about placing exceptional students. The chapter also examines the key issues influencing delivery of services in special education today. In Chapter 8, we describe the professionals and organizations involved with exceptional individuals, and include information pertaining to certification and licensing requirements.

Part Four, "Teaching Exceptional Students," provides essential information on effective teaching. Chapter 9 focuses on decisions educators make about students based on information collected during assessment, and offers useful coverage of guidelines for conducting assessment and considerations that help define what assessment should be. Chapter 10 examines the principles that make education work for all students. All teachers must plan, manage, deliver, and evaluate instruction, and this chapter considers the effective implementation of those aspects of good teaching that apply to all students. Chapter 11 covers the instructional variables that characterize special education in its examination of the purposes of special education and in-depth discussion of the function of the individualized education program. In addition, the chapter considers common instructional techniques that educators use to meet the special learning needs of exceptional students.

External factors that affect the day-to-day practice of special education and the lives of exceptional individuals are examined in Part Five, "The Social Context of Special Education." Chapter 12 provides in-depth coverage of the critical ways in which social attitudes, politics, and economics influence the development of policies that directly affect the treatment, education, housing, employment, and integration of exceptional individuals in our society. Chapter 13 considers the key areas in which changes are occurring in the lives of exceptional individuals and in the practice of special education.

Features of the Text

The text includes the following features to help students grasp content and apply their knowledge:

- **Focusing Questions** open each chapter to highlight important topics that students should understand after they have finished reading.
- **Checkpoints** provide brief summaries of major topics at regular intervals in each chapter.
- **Windows on Practice** offer an enhanced perspective on issues affecting special education and include profiles of exceptional individuals, family members, and practitioners of special education.
- **"What We Think About. . ."** sections at the end of each chapter serve as a forum for our observations about topics covered in the text.
- **Summaries** at the end of chapters review major concepts discussed in text and help students study content.

- **Activities** and **Suggested Readings** are provided at the end of each chapter to stimulate class discussions and to encourage review and extension of text material.

- A **Glossary** at the end of the text offers readers definitions of all key terms that appear in boldface type in text.

The text also features two teachers who bring to life for readers the experiences of professionals who work with exceptional students. Kim, a fifth-grade regular classroom teacher, and Larry, a secondary special education teacher, appear in examples interacting with their students and demonstrating concepts discussed in text.

Four appendixes at the end of the book include useful resource material: a directory of professional associations in special education, the code of ethics of the Council for Exceptional Children (CEC), CEC's policy statement on standards for professional practices in special education, and a list of tests commonly used by educators in assessing students.

Instructional Components That Accompany the Text

Student Handbook The handbook provides students with many opportunities for demonstrating their understanding of course content and for practicing what they have learned. Each chapter in the handbook is divided into four sections. The first section presents a brief overview of material covered in the corresponding text chapter and a list of key concepts for students to identify as they read the chapter. The study questions included in the second section are cross-referenced to the page on which they are discussed in the text. Activities in the third section enable students to demonstrate their grasp of content and apply their knowledge through outside research and projects. The last section is a list of key terms that students are asked to define. The handbook also includes five multiple-choice practice tests that correspond to coverage in each of the text's five parts to help students prepare for examinations.

Videotape A fifteen-minute videotape entitled "Window on Practice" effectively shows the major themes of the text by portraying a day in the life of Lynn Wilcox, a special education supervisor in a rural cooperative in Nebraska.

Instructor's Resource Manual This teaching aid provides supplementary material including chapter overviews, objectives for teaching key concepts, teaching tips, additional readings, a guide to using the Student Handbook, and a guide to using the videotape, "Window on Practice."

Test Bank   Multiple-choice test items and short answer questions are included in the Test Bank.

MicroTest   This is an interactive computerized version of the Test Bank.

Transparencies   An extensive set of overhead transparencies in one and two colors features figures from the text and highlights key concepts covered in the chapters.

Acknowledgments

We received lots of advice from our colleagues as we prepared the text. Their reviews at various stages helped shape the text and we are grateful for their constructive suggestions:

Stephen Aloia, California State University at Fullerton

Dana Anderson, Furman University, Greenville, South Carolina

Linnae Anderson, Kishwaukee College, Malta, Illinois

John Beattie, University of North Carolina at Charlotte

Susan Bertram, Hood College, Frederick, Maryland

Joan Bildman, Adelphi University, Garden City, New York

Lin Douglas, Central Washington University, Ellensburg

Patricia Edwards, University of Maine, Orono

W. Floyd Elliott, Texas A & I University, Kingsville

Joseph George, Columbus College, Columbus, Georgia

Victor S. Lombardo, West Virginia College of Graduate Studies, Institute

Larry Maheady, Michigan State University, East Lansing

James McBride, University of South Alabama, Mobile

Irene Melvin, Capital University, Columbus, Ohio

Vicki Phillips, Kentucky Department of Education

Sr. LeAnn Probst, St. Mary of the Plains College, Dodge City, Kansas

L. Lawrence Riccio, Trinity College, Washington, D.C.

Sam Rust, Central Washington University, Ellensburg

Judith Schapiro, Old Dominion University, Norfolk, Virginia

Keith Stearns, Illinois State University, Normal

Timothy Miles Sturm, Lyndon State College, Lyndonville, Vermont

Jackie Wessels, Augustana College, Rock Island, Illinois

Dan White, Abilene Christian University, Abilene, Texas

We'd also like to thank Martha Thurlow, who prepared the test questions, and Jim Shriner, who coauthored the Student Handbook.

Finally, the professional assistance provided by the editors and staff at Houghton Mifflin has been invaluable in preparing this text. Our work has been improved by their efforts.

James E. Ysseldyke
Bob Algozzine

Introduction to
Special Education

one

Special Education Today

Special education is a complex service delivery system for meeting the special learning needs of exceptional students. Individuals receive special education services because parents, teachers, and other professionals believe they need them to achieve their fullest potential. We begin this text with chapters in which we answer commonly asked questions about special education and analyze the legal basis for special education.

In Chapter 1, as a foundation for the rest of the text, we define special education, discuss how it came to be, describe students who receive special education, and consider the services they receive and where they receive them. We also examine diversity in special education because we think people should find out early that the field is not just a set of clear-cut rules or categories of people who are exceptional.

Special education does not occur in a vacuum, and the influence of legislation and litigation has become central to meeting effectively the special learning needs of exceptional students. In Chapter 2, we describe major federal legislation and court action prior to and after the passage of Public Law 94–142, the Education for All Handicapped Children Act, as a basis for understanding the practice of special education today.

1

The Foundations
of Special Education

FOCUSING QUESTIONS

- What is the goal of special education?
- How have laws and court decisions expanded educational alternatives for students with special needs?
- Why has the number of students categorized as learning disabled increased significantly during the past ten years?
- How are students declared eligible for special services?
- How does the regular classroom teacher participate in the prereferral and postreferral stages of the special education process?
- How do cultural diversity and geography influence who receives special education?

K IM IS A FRIEND OF OURS. PRACTICALLY ALL OF HER adult life, she has wanted to be or has been a teacher. The enthusiasm Kim showed many years ago in her education classes in college is still evident in her teaching today. She loves the variety in teaching, she loves helping students of all different types to grow and develop. And she's a good teacher, concerned about her fifth-grade students and informed (through professional associations and journals) about current practices in education. We've written this book for people like Kim.

As a student in this course, you probably share Kim's concern for students and her excitement about teaching. You may be taking this course to learn to teach in general education classes or in special education classes or as part of your training to work in some other special service profession. You undoubtedly have questions. What is special education? How is special education different from regular education? Who receives special education services? How are students declared eligible for special education? Why do we have special education? In this book, we discuss the practices that are shaping special education today. We believe regular and special class teachers should share responsibility for educating *all* students. We think a central concern for teachers is how to help one another educate students with special learning needs. We believe special education is a dynamic field, that it is different today than it was several years ago, and we expect it to continue to change. To help you understand this field, we describe the system that has evolved as parents, teachers, and other professionals work together to provide educational experiences for students with special learning needs.

Darryl is one of Kim's students. Whatever the level or kind of work that Kim assigns him, Darryl demonstrates superior academic performance. He works hard, sometimes redoing an assignment after the final grade has been recorded. Most of his classmates look to Darryl for academic, athletic, social, and emotional leadership during the school day. Kim finds teaching Darryl a challenge; he keeps her actively involved in staying up to date in her content areas of instruction.

Marti is another one of Kim's students. Marti always seems to be behind. Yet she is a joy to have in class, talkative and funny. Many of her classmates enjoy helping Marti because she appreciates that help so much. And Kim often derives that same satisfaction from working with Marti.

Kim was prepared to teach students with special learning needs like Darryl and Marti. In her training program, she took courses in which she learned how to modify her teaching to accommodate the individual differences that are common in most classrooms. But now and again she has a student whose special needs make teaching difficult. Bobby is one of those students. He comes from a home where both parents are alcoholics. He does not trust adults and often takes out his anger with them on his classmates. When he is not physically disrupting the class, Bobby is "entertaining" his classmates with stories, songs, or animal noises. The rules that are important to many of Kim's students (asking permission to leave the room, raising a hand to ask a question or offer information) are not the rules Bobby uses to structure his life. The things that many of Kim's students do in school to get her attention (finishing their work quickly, sharing stories) are not the things that Bobby does to get attention. Bobby's behavior in school is neither expected nor accepted by his teacher or classmates.

Phyllis is also a challenge, not because of what she does, but because of what she does not do. Phyllis was born blind. She needs special help with many of the ordinary things children are expected to do in school. Kim has to consider Phyllis's visual functioning when she plans activities for her.

Kim is a regular education teacher, but some of her students also receive special education. Kim believes, as we do, that most students—whatever their special needs—can be taught in regular classrooms. If you teach, your classroom will probably contain students like those whom Kim teaches. Providing special assistance to students who need it is one of the reasons that many of us become teachers.

Kim's friend Larry is also a teacher. He teaches in one of the high schools in the town where Kim lives. Larry became a teacher because he wanted to help people with special needs. Sandy is one of Larry's students. He is an exceptional athlete, with awards in football, basketball, and baseball. He would like to go to college, but his academic abilities are not commensurate with his athletic performances. Sandy spends about two hours a day in Larry's classroom working on his reading and mathematics skills, and he is making considerable progress. Janet also goes to Larry's room for special instruction one period a day. She is working on her study skills. Just like the other teachers in his school, Larry teaches five periods a day and has one planning period. His "basic skills" classes help students learn to read, write, and do math better. His "learning strategies" classes help students develop skills they can use when they return to their other academic classes. He also teaches one class of students who have social and emotional problems. Larry relates well to older students, and he loves teaching special education students in high school.

Larry and Kim teach students of different ages in different educational settings. Although Larry is a special education teacher, he faces the same concerns about his students as do other high school teachers. All teenagers worry about what their friends think about them, their social lives, and their futures. Kim deals with these concerns too, but to a lesser extent. She is more concerned that her students accept those who have special needs, that her exceptional students continue to be integrated into regular education classes, and that all her students develop the basic skills they need to succeed in school. Even though Kim and Larry teach in different settings, the types of students and the ways they teach are similar. For example, they both structure their teaching to accommodate their students' individual differences. They both use information from tests and classroom observations to plan instruction and to evaluate the effects of that instruction. And they both have to deal with discipline in the classroom to be effective teachers.

There was a time when students of all ages and capabilities were educated in a single classroom. In many communities, the one-room schoolhouse disappeared because it became more and more difficult for a single teacher to meet the diverse needs of a large number of students. Educators believed that grouping students by age and by subject matter would make teaching them a little easier. A by-product of this thinking was separate classes for students with special needs. This parallel system of regular and special classes continues today. Is it effective? We don't think so. We believe that regular and special education experiences should be blended together as much as possible, that students with special needs should receive all or part of their education in regular classrooms.

DEFINING SPECIAL EDUCATION

When our students ask questions about special education, they tell us they are trying to "get a handle" on the material we are teaching, to define the concepts we are presenting. All of us use questions to shape our impressions of new experiences. We use them here to introduce the foundations of special education.

Special education is evidence of society's willingness to recognize and respond to the individual needs of students and the limits of regular school programs to accommodate those needs.
(© Jean-Claude Lejeune/Stock, Boston)

What Is Special Education?

Education is the process of learning and changing as a result of schooling and other experiences. **Special education** is instruction designed for students with special learning needs. Some of these students have difficulty learning in regular classrooms; they need special education to function in school. Others generally do well in regular classrooms; they need special education to help them master additional skills to reach their full potential in school. Special education is evidence of society's willingness to recognize and respond to the individual needs of students and the limits of regular school programs to accommodate those needs. We have more to say about teaching exceptional students in Chapter 11.

How Did Special Education Come to Be?

If we were writing a fairy tale about special education, we would begin it like this: "Once upon a time, there was no special education. . . ." In the United States today, almost 4.5 million students receive some form of special education. They are being taught in a variety of instructional environments designed to meet their unique learning needs by specially trained teachers. How did this complex system evolve?

Compulsory school attendance began in this country around 1850; by 1916, children in every state were required to attend school. Although requiring students to go to school was probably a good idea, making it happen was not easy. For one thing, many families were not convinced that school was the best place to receive an education. (In fact, today a growing number of families educate their children at home.) Another issue was deciding what to do with students once they were in school. The class-graded system that exists today was one solution to the problem of structuring the school day. Early educators reasoned that students should be taught specific content and that the content could best be organized into graded units.

Students with special learning needs always have been (and always will be) a part of the educational system in America. But before they were required to attend school, they did not attract much attention. Progressive social policy brought them to school. When traditional graded units failed to transmit content to these students, or when teachers and other school personnel argued that the presence of exceptional students was interfering with the training of other students and hindering the education of the exceptional students themselves, physicians and early special educators developed a formal alternative to the regular education system.

Early public educational programs offered two primary choices: Students were taught in a lock-step graded class or in an ungraded special class. Early administrators believed that special education classes were clearinghouses for students who would be going to institutions for physically, mentally, or morally "deviant" members of society.

Today, special education is a sophisticated series of educational alternatives that is a handicapped student's right. In 1975, President Gerald Ford signed into law the **Education for All Handicapped Children Act** (Public Law 94–142)—the first compulsory special education law. It guaranteed handicapped students and their parents certain rights, and it placed specific responsibilities on people who organize and deliver special education services. In brief, the law mandates the following:

- A free, appropriate public education for handicapped students between ages 3 and 21
- Well-planned school programs tailored to meet students' unique learning needs
- Protection of the rights of handicapped students under the same legal provisions that protect the rights of nonhandicapped students (due process)
- The right of exceptional students to have decisions made about them in an unbiased manner
- Educational environments like those provided nonexceptional students

Gifted and talented students have special learning needs in areas requiring functional use of intelligence and artistic ability. About 3 percent of the general public is classified in this category.

(© Michael Weisbrot and Family)

Public Law 94–142 was needed to protect the rights of students with handicaps because they were not always treated the same as their nonhandicapped peers in school. The law guarantees to handicapped students the rights that other students have long enjoyed; it protects them from educational policies that discriminate against people with handicaps.

There was a time when placement in a special class meant the end of a student's normal educational and social experiences. Once assigned to special classes, students often remained in those classes for their entire school careers. Moreover, students were placed in special classes on the recommendation of one teacher or on the basis of their performance on one test. This system produced special class enrollments in which minority students were heavily overrepresented. And there were problems with the programs themselves. Some institutions and special schools were substituting harsh discipline for the educational services exceptional students needed. Parents and professionals, arguing that these practices did not reflect sound educational policy or equality of opportunity, lobbied for laws that mandated change. Their legacy is the system of special education you will learn about in this book.

Why Do Students Receive Special Education?

Students receive special education services because parents, teachers and other professionals, and sometimes the students themselves believe those services will help them achieve their fullest potential in school. Different students have different special needs. Some need help dealing with the social and psychological problems they face as a result of their exceptionality. Many gifted students, for example, feel isolated from their classmates. Special education programs not only challenge them intellectually, but also can help them deal with their feelings of alienation.

Other exceptional students need special services because of what they are not able to do, because some handicapping condition limits their ability to learn in the typical educational program. Students who are blind, for example, must be taught to read in braille. Students who cannot hear need instruction in a manual sign language or some other special communication system. These students also face social and psychological problems. They have to learn to cope with not only the challenge of their handicapping condition, but also other people's reactions to their condition. And for many students whose special needs mean learning in separate educational settings, there's the added knowledge that their educational experiences are not like those of other people:

> With very rare exceptions, today's adults with disabilities who recall segregated facilities, separate classes, or home instruction cannot say enough about how inadequate was their academic training. They compare their education with that of siblings or neighbors who were not disabled and speak only of the gaps. For example, they mention subjects, such as science, that they never studied, maps they never saw, field trips they never took, books that were never available, assignments that were often too easy, expectations of their capacity (by nearly all teachers) that were too low. (Asch, 1989, p. 183)

In many countries, those with disabilities or handicaps are entitled to special services. The special education system that exists in the United States today has its roots in the methods used to treat disabled and handicapped people in Europe and Scandinavia more than one hundred years ago. That system entitles exceptional students to a free, appropriate public education. Federal laws now make it illegal to discriminate against people because they are handicapped or disabled. This means that people cannot be denied an education or a job because of a handicapping condition. It also means that records are kept of the types and numbers of handicapped students receiving special education in this country. Federal law does not require states to provide special education to gifted and talented students, so the number of those students receiving special education services does not appear in annual reports to Congress. Several states, however, have passed laws mandating special services for this group of exceptional students.

Who Receives Special Education?

Exceptional students are those who are handicapped or disabled and those who are gifted and talented. These students differ from nonexceptional students in the ways they perform tasks used to measure school achievement. We believe the similarities between exceptional and nonexceptional students far exceed their differences. We recognize, however, that some of the differences are central to success in school, and so form the basis for the concern of teachers, parents, and students themselves.

Today, most states organize their special education departments along categorical lines. A *category* is simply a name assigned to a group of exceptional students. Although the names of the categories vary slightly from state to state, special education generally is provided to students within each of the following groups:

- *Blind or visually handicapped.* These students have special learning needs in areas requiring functional use of vision. Less than 1 percent of the school-age population is classified in this category.
- *Deaf or hard of hearing.* These students have special learning needs in areas requiring functional use of hearing. Less than 1 percent of the school-age population is classified in this category.
- *Deaf and blind.* These students have special learning needs in areas requiring functional use of hearing and vision. Less than 1 percent of the school-age population is classified in this category.
- *Orthopedically or other health impaired.* These students have special learning needs in areas requiring functional use of hands, arms, legs, feet, and other body parts. Less than 1 percent of the school-age population is classified in these two categories.
- *Mentally retarded.* These students have special learning needs in areas requiring functional use of intelligence and adaptive behavior. About 1.4 percent of the school-age population is classified in this category.
- *Gifted and talented.* These students have special learning needs in areas requiring functional use of intelligence and artistic ability. About 3 percent of the school-age population is classified in this category.
- *Learning disabled.* These students have special learning needs in areas requiring functional use of listening, speaking, reading, writ-

*Window
on
Practice*

MY SON, BENJAMIN, IS eight and one-half years old and he is physically and mentally handicapped. For the past six years he has progressed through various areas of special educational services with varying degrees of separation from the rest of the educational world. Most of his schooling has been in settings where he had little or no contact with so-called "normal" children.

Last year in School District 287, he experienced some ventures into the community, such as weekly bowling, swimming, and field trips. His class had regular activities with a second grade. This year, in addition to these activities, he spends about half his school day in the first grade and is expected to participate to the best of his ability. He is not a mere visitor.

When I first learned that Ben would be joining the class, I was afraid that it was just a patronizing gesture on the part of the teacher and the students. Also, because he cannot do the academic work, I didn't feel there would be any great benefit for him. I was wrong on both accounts.

In the two months Ben has been in the classroom, I have come to think of this experience differently. He has actually picked up some early academic skills like paying attention and using the materials. More importantly, he has increased his social awareness. He knows when people are trying to communicate with him and he knows he has a lot of control over how the project will get done.

His interactions with other children have changed. He has always been afraid of his younger brother (with good cause) and totally ignored other children unless they came into his personal space. Anyone entering his space was subject to severe objections from Ben. He is now tolerant of contact with his brother. He observes other children with caution, but there seems to be some curiosity mixed with fear.

Ben's first grade experience is also linked to the larger community. When we meet his classmates in public they are eager to introduce him to their families. It is interesting to see how much more comfortable the kids are than their parents. I realize that Ben is somewhat of a novelty to them but that is not all bad. They are very matter-of-fact about his differences and their special attention to him seems to stem from concern rather than curiosity. I feel that both Ben and his first grade classmates have benefited from this experience and the long-term gains will be even greater, not only for them but for the whole community.
Katherine Marfield
November 1988

It's been my greatest pleasure having Ben Marfield as my part-time student in first grade this year. The children view him as I do: a classmate who goes to another teacher for special help for some of the day.

His aide is a warm, sensitive person with much expertise, and the two of them are encouraged to join us in as many activities as they wish.

The children treat him as they do their full time classmates, with kindness and respect.

Whatever positive changes may occur in Ben's life because of our time together, the lives of the rest of us have been enhanced in far greater measure.
Luanne Lescarbeau
First Grade Teacher

Some years ago I saw a Walt Disney cartoon entitled "Ben and Me." It depicted a small field mouse who lived in Benjamin Franklin's breast pocket, negotiating a written pact with Ben about his housing arrangements. He prompted Ben's writing of the pact, at his ear and at his elbow, word for word. I, the viewer, saw it as a fantasy depiction of Ben Franklin struggling over and perfecting the wording of the Preamble to the U.S. Constitution. The mouse saw it as the writing of his new contract with his landlord for a mutual life of liberty and the pursuit of happiness.

So it is with Ben Marfield and me in Mrs. Lescarbeau's first grade classroom, Washburn Elementary in Bloomington. We enter the classroom, participate in the classroom and leave the classroom, together, with Ben always in the foreground and me at his ear, or at his elbow, helping, urging, prompting, cajoling and praising.

Ben begins his class time on the floor with the other first graders for 15–20 minutes of sharing time. There are always children in front, behind and on either side of him, everyone at the same eye level. At first he wasn't so sure he approved. Then he began to bear it. Now he looks disappointed when they leave him and return to their desks.

He then spends the next hour at his own desk working on handwriting, math and reading. Mrs. Lescarbeau treats him exactly like all the other students, and includes him at all the appropriate times. She expects no more and no less of him than he is presently able. He has not yet needed a reminder for leaving his seat without permission but he has been reprimanded for pulling out his hearing aid and throwing it across the room. She believes in accepting the student where he/she is now—

not where he/she is "supposed" to be. When Ben is working at his desk, I become the mouse in our story. I guide, encourage or push Ben to get working on his daily "preamble."

We are with the class at least two and a half hours a day. At first, I stayed completely in the background, even sitting behind him instead of sitting beside him. Then I moved to his side to help in manual guidance as well as in verbal guidance. He is accustomed to my presence and is becoming much more aware of the different inflections or levels in my voice. I also stayed in the background as far as the other children were concerned. I wanted Ben to be the reason we were there—front and center. Now I converse with and/or help any child who requests it and I usually coax them to stand in front of me to ask their questions. That way the children and Ben get to look at each other.

I feel that Ben's integration into the first grade is a huge success. He has come from tears about my absence from view, fear of other children close to him, and the total refusal to cooperate with manual guidance, to an eagerness to be in the room, very little worry, and acceptance of manual guidance. I give 10% of the credit to my conviction that Ben deserves to be there, 90% of the credit to Mrs. Lescarbeau, the teacher who feels every child has the right to learn, and 100% of the credit to the children who think that the only thing that's different about Ben is that he's not in the room all day.

Ben and me, we'll perfect that preamble yet.
Ann Romstad
Special Education Paraprofessional

Source: *Steven Dahlstrom, "From the Inside Looking Out," Reflections. . . Movement toward the Community, Spring 1989, pp. 1–2. Published by the Department of Educational Psychology, Institute for Disabilities Studies, University of Minnesota, Minneapolis, MN 55414. Reprinted with permission.*

Public Law 94–142—the Education for All Handicapped Children Act—guarantees students and their parents free, appropriate public education for all handicapped students between ages 3 and 21 in educational environments like those provided non-exceptional students.

(© Michael Weisbrot and Family)

ing, reasoning, and arithmetic skills. About 5 percent of the school-age population is classified in this category.

■ *Emotionally disturbed.* These students have special learning needs in areas requiring functional use of social and emotional skills. About 1 percent of the school-age population is classified in this category.

■ *Language impaired.* These students have special learning needs in areas requiring functional use of language and communication skills. About 2.5 percent of the school-age population is classified in this category.

■ *Multihandicapped* or *severely impaired.* These students have special learning needs in more than one area requiring functional use of skills. Less than 1 percent of the school-age population is classified in this category.

Some states have a consultant or supervisor who is responsible for one group of exceptional students. In these states, local school districts usually organize their special education programs along categorical lines. Other states have a single administrator who is responsible for all groups of exceptional students. In these states, local programs are organized differently, with most special needs students receiving some part of their education in regular classes.

Although some states (New Jersey, for one) are moving toward non-categorical organization, only two states (Massachusetts and South Dakota) do not use categories as the basis for organizing their special education systems (Table 1.1). We provide detailed information on each of the categories of special education in Chapters 4, 5, and 6.

Checkpoint

- *Special education is instruction designed for students with special learning needs.*

- *The Education for All Handicapped Children Act (Public Law 94–142) entitles handicapped individuals between the ages of 3 and 21 to special education services. (Special services for gifted and talented students are provided by state and local laws.)*

- *Students receive special education services because parents, teachers, and other professionals, and the students themselves believe those services will help them achieve their fullest potential in school.*

- *Exceptional students can be handicapped or disabled, or gifted and talented.*

- *Most states group exceptional students and organize their special education systems by categories.*

How Many Students Receive Special Education?

Nearly 4.5 million students receive special education services in school or community settings in the United States every year. That number is roughly equivalent to the number of full-time undergraduates in four-year colleges and universities in this country. In fact, it is about the same as the combined population of North Dakota, South Dakota, Montana, Nevada, Idaho, and Wyoming, and exceeds the population of each of thirty-two states.

The number of exceptional students receiving special education services has increased steadily in recent years (Figure 1.1). The handicapped student population rose from 3.7 million to over 4.4 million between 1977 and 1987; in a decade, more than 712,000 new students were identified as needing special education. As shown in Table 1.2, the average rate of increase during those years was almost 2 percent a year. This substantial increase (19 percent) in the number of students enrolled in special education classes occurred at the same time that enrollment in general education fell by almost 6 percent.

The source of the growth is generally attributed to increases in students classified as learning disabled. Reasons for growth in this category

Table 1.1
Categories of Exceptionality Used in the United States

State / Territory

Categories	Alabama	Alaska	Arizona	Arkansas	California	Colorado	Connecticut	Delaware	District of Columbia	Florida	Georgia	Hawaii	Idaho	Illinois	Indiana	Iowa	Kansas	Kentucky	Louisiana
Autistic [3]		x					x	x		x		x							x
DEAF [1]		x		x			x	x				x	x						x
DEAF-BLIND [1]	x			x			x	x	x	x	x	x	x				x	x	x
EARLY CHILDHOOD SPECIAL EDUCATION [2]		x		x								4		x		x			4
Gifted/Talented [3]	x	x	x				x		x					x				x	x
HARD OF HEARING [1]		x		x			x		x			x							x
Hearing Impaired/Disordered/Handicapped [3]	x		x	x	x		x			x	x		x	x	x	x	x	x	
Homebound/Hospitalized [3]		x								x									x
MENTALLY RETARDED [1]		x		x											x				
Mentally Impaired/ Disabled/Handicapped [3]			x						x	x		x				x	x		
Educable (Mild) [3]	x		x		x					x	x	x		x				x	x
Trainable (Moderate) [3]	x		x		x					x	x	x		x				x	x
Severe/ Profound [3]	x		x		4					x	x	x		x				x	x
MULTIHANDICAPPED [1]	x			x															x
Multiply Impaired/Handicapped [3]		x	x	x	x		x							x	x			x	
Severely/Profoundly (Multiply) Impaired/Handicapped [3]												x				x	x		
ORTHOPEDICALLY IMPAIRED [1]	x	x		4	x		x		x		4	x							4
Physically Impaired/Disabled/Handicapped [3]						4			x		x		x	x	x	x		x	
OTHER HEALTH IMPAIRED [1]	x	x		x	x		x	x	x		x	x	4	x			x	x	x
SERIOUSLY EMOTIONALLY DISTURBED [1]	4	x	x	x	x	4	4	4	x	4	4				x			x	x
Behaviorally Impaired/Disordered [3]						4						x		x		x	x		x
Emotionally Disturbed/Handicapped [3]	4								4		x		x	4					
SPECIFIC LEARNING DISABILITIES [1]	x			x	x			x	x	x	x						x		
Learning Disabled/Impaired/Handicapped [3]		x	x				x	x					x	x	x	x		x	x
SPEECH-LANGUAGE IMPAIRED [1]	x	x	x	x	x		4	x	x	x		x	x	x				x	x
Speech-Language Disabled/Disordered/Handicapped [3]						x						x							4
Communication Disorder/Handicap [3]						x										x			
VISUALLY HANDICAPPED [1]		x		x	x	x						4		x				x	4
Visually Impaired [3]	x	x		x			x	x	x	x		x	x		x	x			

Note: (1) P.L. 94–142 category; (2) P.L. 99–457 category; (3) nonfederal category; (4) category reported but not the same as P.L. 142 category, P.L. 99–457 category, or nonfederal categories reported.

Source: Adapted from J. E. Garrett and Nettye M. Brazil, "Categories of Exceptionality: A Ten-Year Follow Up." Unpublished manuscript, 1989. Reprinted with permission.

State/Territory

	Maine	Maryland	Massachusetts	Michigan	Minnesota	Mississippi	Missouri	Montana	Nebraska	Nevada	New Hampshire	New Jersey	New Mexico	New York	North Carolina	North Dakota	Ohio	Oklahoma	Oregon	Pennsylvania	Rhode Island	South Carolina	South Dakota	Tennessee	Texas	Utah	Vermont	Virginia	Washington	West Virginia	Wisconsin	Wyoming	Off. of Indian Progs.	American Samoa	Guam	Palau	Puerto Rico	Saipan	Virgin Islands
				x	x		x							x	x				x					x	x	x		x											
	x	x						x			x			x			x			x							x	x	x						x	x	x	x	x
	x	x		x	x	x	x	x			x				x	x				x	x		x	x	x		x	x	x				x		x		x	x	x
				4	x		4				4	4	4		4	4												x	4	4					x		x	x	x
					x				x			x			x	x				x	x	x		x					x						x				
	x	x			x				x		4	x	4		x					x				4	x		x	x					x		x	x	x	x	
				x	x	x	x		x			x			x	x	x		x	x	x			x			x		x	x	x		x		x	x	x	x	x'
																							x											x					
	x				x						x			x		x		4	x							4								x			x	x	
		x					x	x			x		x										x	x					x	x	x	x		x	x	x			
				x		x			x			x					x	x	x	x				4			x	x											
				x		x			x			x					x	x	x	x				4			x	x											
				x		x			x				4				x	x	x					4			x	x											
	x	x			x	x	x	x		x					x			x					x		x		x		x	x			x	x	x	x	x	x	x
					x						x	x	x	x		x							x								x								
			x															x					x		x														
	x	x		x	x	x	x			x	x	x	x	x			x	x	x	x	x	x			x	x	x	x	x	x		x	x	x	x	x	x	x	x
	x	x		x	x	x	x		x			x		x	x	x	x	x	x	x	x	x		x			x	x	x	x	x	x		x	x	x	x	x	x
	x	x		x	x		x	x	x			x	4		x	x	x	x	x	x	x			x			x	x	x	x	4		x		x	x	x	x	x
		x		x	x				x			x			x	x		x	x	x	x			x				x	x	4		x			x	x	x		
	x				x		x		x			x			x		4		4				x				x			x		x		x					
				4	4	x		x			x	x	x									4			x					x		x		x	x				
		x		x	x			x		x	4			x	x	x				x				x		x	x	x	x	x		x	x		x	x	x		
	x				x	x	x		x			x	x				x	x	x	x				x			x			x		x		x					x
	x	x		x	x			x	x		x			x	x	x		x	x	x				x			x	x				x		x	x	x	x	x	x
				x	x		x		x		x									x	x		x			x				x	x			x					
									x		x														x			x	x										
		x			x		x	x	x	x	x				x				x					x	x		x	x		x	4					x	x		
	x			x		x	x			x	x	x	x		x	x	x	x				x	x			x	x			x		x	x					x

(Category labels printed vertically within the table: "Children in need of special services" (beneath Massachusetts), "Children in need of special assistance/prolonged assistance" (beneath South Dakota), "Special needs students" (beneath Guam).)

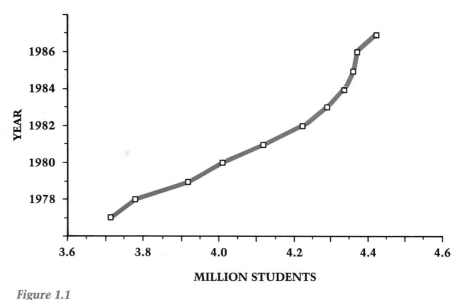

Figure 1.1
Recent Growth in Handicapped Student Population
Source: U.S. Department of Education (1988). *To assure the free appropriate public education of all handicapped children: Tenth annual report to Congress on the implementation of the Education of the Handicapped Act* (Washington, D.C.: U.S. Department of Education).

include a desire not to stigmatize students with other labels, the need created by legal actions to reclassify students previously labeled mentally retarded, and the desire to obtain supplemented instruction for students in need when other alternatives (such as Title I) were becoming less available (Singer & Butler, 1987).

The growing number of students in special education programs means that plenty of new teaching positions have been created in the field. Using a conservative average of fifteen students for each special class teacher, about forty-seven hundred new teachers were needed each year from 1977 to 1987. The growth in enrollment also has created problems for school personnel who have to decide how to pay for expanding programs. The costs of educating exceptional students sometimes compete with the costs of educating students in regular programs.

How Are Students Assigned to Special Education?

Special education is a service delivery system. Students who need special education must be declared eligible for its services before those services can be provided in public school programs. This is different than the way it

Table 1.2
Number of Handicapped Students in the United States, Ages 3 to 21

Year	Total Number of Students	Number of New Students	Rate of Increase (%)
1977	3,708,913	—	—
1978	3,777,286	68,373	1.84
1979	3,919,073	141,787	3.75
1980	4,036,219	117,146	2.99
1981	4,177,689	141,470	3.51
1982	4,233,282	55,593	1.33
1983	4,298,327	65,045	1.54
1984	4,341,399	43,072	1.00
1985	4,362,968	21,569	0.50
1986	4,370,244	7,276	0.17
1987	4,421,601	51,357	1.18
1988	4,494,280	72,679	1.60
Average		71,397	1.76

Note: Beginning in 1984–85, the number of handicapped children reported reflects revisions of state data received by the U.S. Office of Special Education Programs following the July 1 grant date and includes revisions received by October 1. Previous reports provided data as of the grant award date.

Source: U.S. Department of Education (1989). *To assure the free appropriate public education of all handicapped children: Eleventh annual report to Congress on the implementation of the Education of the Handicapped Act.* (Washington, D.C.: U.S. Department of Education).

works in general education, where students are provided free public education between the ages specified in each state's laws.

Some exceptional children are identified before they enter school. Others are identified after they start school, their difficulty or outstanding progress in the regular education program evidence of their special needs. There is an emphasis today on **mainstreaming** exceptional students— wherever possible, keeping them in the regular classroom. This means that teachers try to accommodate students with special needs in their regular classes before placing them in special classes. The process of requesting information to decide if a student is eligible for special services is called **referral.** Finding ways to keep exceptional students in regular classrooms is called **prereferral intervention.** If this intervention does not help the student, the formal special education process begins.

When you think about how students receive special education, picture a three-stage process:

1. Determining eligibility

Window on Practice

ALL OF US WHO HAVE HAD the opportunity to attend a school within our neighborhood can most likely recall the friends we made and the feeling of belonging that we had during our school-age years. However, children's views of the benefits of neighborhood schooling provide a refreshing and uniquely honest perspective on some of the reasons why having the opportunity to go to a neighborhood school is something that can't be taken for granted. Third, fourth, fifth and sixth graders at Edison School in Stickney, Illinois offered the following comments when asked about the benefits of neighborhood schools.

"I'm glad I have a neighborhood school so I can play at the playground and play ball and roller skate at the playground. I can walk with friends so you won't get home late."

Shannon, Third Grade

"It is nice to go to a neighborhood school because it is in your neighborhood and it's your school and maybe because your friends go and you don't want to be left alone and go to a different school. That's what I think."

Tammy, Fourth Grade

"I like going to a neighborhood school because my friends go there. You're not with some kids you don't know and who live miles apart."

Mike, Sixth Grade

"What I like about it is that everybody kind of knows everybody, and you don't have to go a long way to visit friends you make and you don't have to get up earlier to go on a hot, stuffy bus."

Zipporah, Fifth Grade

"I like going to a neighborhood school because: my friends live close to me. Everybody knows each other. We're all friends!"

Terry, Fifth Grade

"Your friends live close to you, so it's easy to play with them."

Melinda, Fifth Grade

"If the school has an event, you don't have to worry about having to get a ride from your mom or dad. In a neighborhood school, you usually have friends that go to your school."

Tim, Sixth Grade

"At a neighborhood school, you don't have to take the bus and you could play after school and you could help the teacher after school. In a neighborhood school, a lot of parents know each other, and you get to walk to school and it is good for your legs."

Corry, Third Grade

"Your mom will know the other kids' moms."

Crystal, Third Grade

"Your friends are in the same town."

Robert, Fourth Grade

"I like going to a neighborhood school because all of your friends are right around. You know where everyone is, and if there's a parent-teacher conference, your parents don't have to drive for an hour just to get to school."

Michelle, Sixth Grade

"You're so lucky to have your friends beside you."

Christy, Fourth Grade

"I like my neighborhood school because it's cool!"

Jack, Fourth Grade

Source: *Howard P. Blackman, "Students Speak Out on the Benefits of Neighborhood Schools," Total Integration Neighborhood Schools, 1989, p. 8. Published by La Grange Area Department of Special Education, 1301 West Cossitt Avenue, La Grange, IL 60525. Reprinted with permission. Dr. Blackman is executive director of the La Grange Area Department of Special Education and is a member of the President's Committee on Mental Retardation.*

2. Delivering special instruction
3. Evaluating progress.

The first stage—determining eligibility—begins when students progress unusually quickly or slowly at home or at school, or sometimes when teachers feel that students can't learn in a regular classroom setting without special help. A team of professionals gathers information and uses it to decide whether a student is eligible for special services. A key factor here is the extent to which the student performs like others. For example, differences in physical abilities (seeing, hearing, moving) are the basis for assigning students to several categories of exceptionalities.

In the second stage of the process, the student receives individualized instruction from trained professionals. Once a team of professionals decides that a student is eligible for special education and will profit from specially designed instruction, and the student's parents give their consent, service delivery begins. What happens during this stage varies with the nature of the individual's special needs. A formal document, the **individualized education program (IEP)**, serves as a guide for this phase of the process. The IEP describes in writing

- the student's present levels of functioning in areas considered important for success in school.
- the annual goals and short-term objectives of the student's special education experiences.
- the services to be provided and the extent of regular programming.
- the starting date and expected duration of special education services.
- evaluation plans for use on at least an annual basis to monitor the effectiveness of the individual's special education program. A more detailed description of the components of an IEP is provided in Chapter 11.

The third stage of the special education process is evaluation. The student's progress is evaluated to determine the need for continuing, changing, or concluding special services. A student who is handicapped must be evaluated at least once a year. Every three years, a formal reevaluation is necessary to determine if a student is still eligible for special services. Students can be removed from special programs any time they have shown sufficient progress.

Kim and the other regular classroom teachers in her school play an important role in the special education process (Table 1.3, Figure 1.2). They often are the first to notice that a student's performance is different from that of other class members. They gather information and try alternative

Table 1.3

How the Regular Classroom Teacher Participates in Special Education Decision Making

Prereferral Stage: Regular Education Process

The teacher notices that a student is performing differently from most of the other students in the class.

The teacher checks with other teachers to verify his or her observations, then checks with the student's parents to eliminate special circumstances at home that might explain the exceptional performance.

The teacher tries different methods of instruction (prereferral interventions) to identify the nature of the problem, and gathers information about the student's performance in other areas.

The teacher decides the prereferral intervention was effective and continues to use instructional modifications to provide special education in the regular classroom.

The teacher decides the student's performance is sufficiently different to warrant special services, and refers the student to the school's special education support team.

Postreferral Stage: Special Education Process

The teacher reviews the results of individual psychological and educational testing, then consults with other team members and compares the student's performance to established criteria for eligibility for special education.

The teacher offers an opinion about the appropriate placement for the student.

The teacher cooperates with other team members in providing special services and evaluating their effectiveness.

teaching techniques (prereferral intervention). They also collect information that is used to decide whether a student is eligible for special education services. In Kim's school, regular classroom teachers are a part of the team that makes the decision about how to educate a student who is exceptional. They also are involved in all individual progress and program evaluations.

What Special Services Do Exceptional Students Receive?

Today, special education is a complex system for meeting the special learning needs of exceptional students. Three types of assistance are generally available: direct services, indirect or consultative services, and related services.

- **Direct services** are provided by working with students themselves to correct or compensate for the conditions that have caused them to fall behind in school or to enrich or accelerate the progress they are making in school. Teaching a deaf student to use sign language, a learning disabled student to read using a special method of instruction, or a gifted fourth-grader to do algebra are examples of direct services provided by teachers.

- **Indirect or consultative services** are provided by working with classroom teachers and others who work with exceptional students over a period of time to help meet the needs of the students. Helping a teacher identify the best method for teaching a student with learning disabilities to read or showing a teacher how to reposition a student who is physically handicapped are examples of indirect services provided by teachers and other professionals.

- **Related services** are provided by specially trained personnel directly (to students) or indirectly (to those who work with exceptional students). Related services include psychological testing and counseling, school social work, educational/occupational therapy, adapted physical education, school health services, and transportation.

The types of services students receive as part of their special education program vary according to the level of their learning needs.

Where Are Exceptional Students Taught?

Public Law 94–142 mandates a "free, appropriate public education" for handicapped students. Central to this provision of the law is the concept of **least restrictive environment (LRE)**. Special education students should be educated in environments that are as much like normal—least restrictive—as possible.

This does not mean that all students with handicaps must be placed in regular classrooms. It does mean, however, that these students should spend as much time as possible in regular classes, ideally with their special needs met by indirect or consultative services. Some students may spend most of their time in the regular classroom, leaving only for direct or related services. Still others may spend the bulk of their time in special education classes, attending regular classes for certain types of instructional activities (perhaps music or art).

Even when students require full-time special services, there are different degrees of "restrictiveness." Some students spend all their time in special education classrooms. Some, because of illness or other medical problems, are educated in hospitals or at home. And some are taught in residential (institutional) settings, in classes run and staffed by personnel from local school districts. In the most restrictive setting, students live in

Students who receive special education services are of different sexes and come from different racial groups, categorical groups, geographical regions, and socioeconomic levels of society.
(© Alan Carey 1987/The Image Works)

a residential school or institution and are taught by staff members of that school or institution.

The guiding principle here is to move those with handicaps into less restrictive settings as much as possible. The goal is to maximize opportunities for these students to spend time and interact with their peers who are not handicapped. For more details on settings in which exceptional students are taught, see Chapter 7.

Participation in the regular classroom is a form of equal opportunity for students with special needs. It gives them a chance to share in experiences that are there as a matter of course for those who are not handicapped. And those experiences are what really make their education "special."

How Old Are Exceptional Students?

Recent government figures indicate that more nine-year-olds receive special education services than any other age group. The reason for this has to do with the demands school makes on this age group. Through the third grade, students are not expected to function as independently as they are during and after the fourth grade. Faced with new demands, students' skill deficiencies become evident. Teachers are more likely to refer students who do not read well, follow directions, or complete assignments independently when most of their classmates are demonstrating these skills.

The recent growth in enrollment in special education programs is reflected in the number of students at each age level receiving services. The percentages of six- to seventeen-year-olds and eighteen- to twenty-one-year-olds have increased steadily over the last ten years. For example, approximately 7.5 percent of six- to seventeen-year-olds received special education services during the 1978–79 school year; almost 9 percent were being served ten years later. The rate of service in the population 18 years old and older more than doubled, from 0.6 percent to 1.27 percent, during this same period.

Although the rate of service among older students has grown, the actual number of students in special education programs falls dramatically after age 16. Older students do not stay in school. In fact, about 25 percent of handicapped students between the ages of 16 and 21 drop out of school.

Because early intervention programs in the public schools are relatively new, the number of three- to five-year-olds in those programs is relatively small. Although that number did grow between 1978 and 1988, so did the general population of young children. This means we find just asmall change in the percentage of preschool children served. Figure 1.3 shows the percentage of students served in different age groups between the 1976–77 and 1986–87 school years.

Checkpoint

- ■ *The number of students receiving special education has increased steadily in recent years.*

- ■ *Students who need special education must be declared eligible for its services before those services can be provided in public school programs.*

- ■ *Special education is a three-stage process: (1) determining eligibility, (2) delivering instruction, and (3) evaluating the student's progress.*

- ■ *Regular classroom teachers are an integral part of the special education team.*

- ■ *The types of services (direct, indirect, or related) students receive as part of their special education program vary according to the level of their learning needs.*

PREREFERRAL STAGE: REGULAR EDUCATION PROCESS

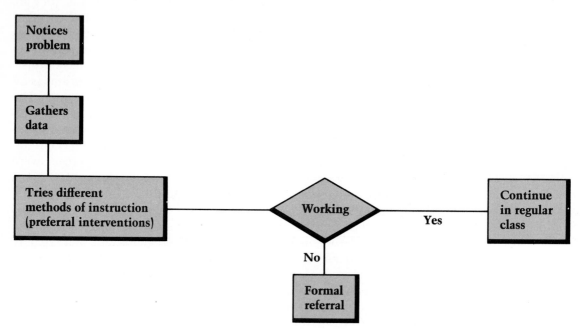

Figure 1.2
How the Regular Classroom Teacher Participates in Special Education Decision Making

- *Public Law 94–142 mandates that students with special needs must be taught in the least restrictive environment.*
- *More nine-year-olds receive special education services than any other age group.*

DIVERSITY IN SPECIAL EDUCATION

Special education seems to be a neat, orderly approach to helping students with special needs. It uses categories to organize students and curriculum. It sets criteria for eligibility. It defines each student's educational goals in a rational way.

But it's unfair to teach you about special education without also teaching you about the diversity that is part and parcel of it. Many of the con-

POSTREFERRAL STAGE: SPECIAL EDUCATION PROCESS

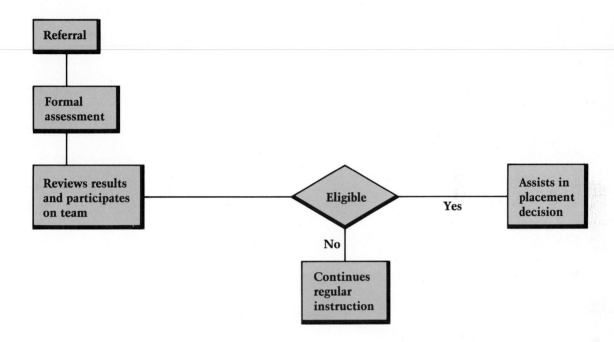

cepts that are central to special education (categories, related services) are defined differently in different places. Moreover, no matter how convenient categories are; they mask both the similarities among students in different groups and the individual differences among students in the same groups. Then there are all the different teaching methods and environments to think about. Understanding this diversity, the many different students and the many different ways special education is practiced, is central to understanding special education today.

The Students

Not all students who need special education services receive them, and those who do receive them are of different sexes and come from different racial groups, categorical groups, geographical regions, and socioeconomic levels of society. Also, the proportions of these groups in the population of students with special needs does not necessarily reflect their proportions in the general population. For example, 51 percent of students ages 3 through 21 who are enrolled in school are male, yet twice as many males as

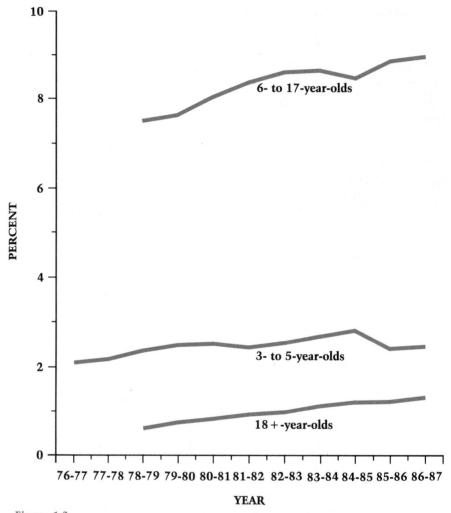

Figure 1.3

Percentage of Children Served under EHA-B by Age Group, School Years 1976–77 to 1986–87

Note: Data are not available for children age 6 and under prior to 1978–1979. Percentage is based on population counts compiled by the U.S. Bureau of the Census.

Source: U.S. Department of Education (1988). *To assure the free appropriate public education of all handicapped children: Tenth annual report to Congress on the implementation of the Education of the Handicapped Act* (Washington, D.C.: U.S. Department of Education), p. 19, Figure 9.

females are enrolled in special education programs. Seventy-five percent of the national school enrollment is white, but white students make up only 71 percent of the special education enrollment. Black students make

A central provision of Public Law 94–142 is the concept of least restrictive environment: special education students should be educated in environments that are as much like normal as possible.
(© Michael Weisbrot and Family)

up 16 percent of public school enrollment and 21 percent of the enrolled students in special education programs.

Many students do not receive special education because they are not in school. Nationally, about 10 percent of students drop out of school each year. Dropout rates for some ethnic groups are much higher. For example, recent government figures indicate that 15 percent of blacks, 20 percent of Hispanics, and 22 percent of Native Americans leave school without finishing. We said earlier that about 25 percent of handicapped students drop out of school. While very few (7 percent) of students who are deaf and blind drop out, a large number (40 percent) of students who are emotionally disturbed leave high school before finishing. And while less than 5 percent of handicapped students drop out in some areas (for example, Connecticut, Delaware, Washington, D.C.), more than 40 percent drop out in others (New Hampshire, New York, Tennessee).

Variation is also evident in the numbers of different types of exceptional students who receive special education services and in the numbers of specific types served in different states. For example, more students with learning disabilities are served than almost all other groups of exceptional students combined. About 90 percent of exceptional students are called learning disabled, mentally retarded, emotionally disturbed, or language impaired. Less than 1 percent are categorized deaf or blind or physically impaired. Twice as many students with learning disabilities are educated

Table 1.4
How Many Students Are Exceptional?

Category	Basis for Exceptionality	Demographics*
Blind or visually handicapped	Performance on vision tests	<1% Range: <1–1%
Deaf or hard of hearing	Performance on hearing tests	1% Range: 1–2%
Deaf and blind	Performance on hearing and vision tests	<1% Range: 0–1%
Orthopedically impaired	Performance on physical or medical tests	1% Range: 1–3%
Other health impaired	Performance on physical or medical tests	1% Range: 1–3%
Mentally retarded	Performance on mental tests and judgments about adaptive behavior	14% Range: 4–34%
Gifted/talented	Performance on mental tests	4%** Range: 1–10%
Learning disabled	Performance on achievement tests	47% Range: 28–64%
Emotionally disturbed	Judgments about behavior	9% Range: 1–27%
Language impaired	Performance on language tests	23% Range: 12–38%
Multihandicapped or severely impaired	Performance on physical, medical, or other tests	<1% Range: 0–3%

* Figures represent average percentages of handicapped students across fifty states and the range of variation among states.

** Percentage of the school-age population.

in some states as are educated in neighboring states. Table 1.4 lists the percentages of exceptional students by categories in the United States today.

Educational Settings

According to Public Law 94–142, exceptional students must be educated in the least restrictive environment. In recent years, this has meant that most exceptional students have received special education and related services in schools with their nonhandicapped peers. Here, too, we find variation in the extent to which students in different categories are placed in specific settings. For example, although about 65 percent of students with language impairments are served in regular classrooms, fewer than 10 percent of students who are mentally retarded, emotionally disturbed, or deaf and blind are served there. Most students who are mentally retarded (55 percent) are served in separate classes; as are at least 35 percent of those who are emotionally disturbed and multihandicapped; but less than 25 percent of students who are learning disabled, visually handicapped, or deaf and blind are placed in special classes.

Learning environments also vary in different states (Table 1.5). For example, fewer than 10 percent of children ages 3 to 21 are served in regular classes in nine states, but more than 30 percent are served in regular classes in twenty-five states. Less than 10 percent of students with learning disabilities are served in separate classes in seventeen states, but less than 10 percent of students with speech impairments are placed in these settings in thirty-seven states. Overall, very few deaf, blind, and physically impaired students are served in separate facilities, but some states use this option much more than others. More than twice as many learning disabled students are educated in regular classes in some states than are educated in the same setting in neighboring states.

Checkpoint	■ *Despite the structure of the special education system, there is great diversity among students, educational settings, and instructional practices.*
	■ *Differences among students with special needs exist across gender groups, racial groups, categorical groups, geographical regions, and socioeconomic levels.*
	■ *There are differences in the extent to which students in various groups are placed in different educational settings.*

WHAT WE THINK ABOUT SPECIAL EDUCATION

Special education is many things to many people. To parents, it promises help, a means for their child to reach his or her full potential. And as members of the special education team, it brings them into the decision-making process, giving them a say in how their child is served.

Exceptional students usually react to special education differently at different stages of the process. Initially, they think that *special* means different in a bad way, that the services are a kind of punishment for their inability to do certain things. But if their individualized programs help them

Table 1.5
Where Students Receive Special Education

Setting	Description of Placement	Demographics*
Regular class	Receive special education and related services less than 21% of the school day	26% Range: 0–72%
Resource room	Receive special education and related services at least 21% but not more than 60% of the school day	41% Range: 8–73%
Separate class	Receive special education and related services more than 60% of the school day	24% Range: 8–40%
Separate school	Receive special education and related services in a building that houses special education classes only	4% Range: <1–15%
Private school	Receive special education and related services in school run by a nonpublic agency	2% Range: <1–11%
Residential school	Receive special education and related services in a facility that also serves as a residence	<1% Range: 0–5%
Correctional setting	Receive special education and related services in a setting controlled by a legal agency	<1% Range: 0–2%
Homebound	Receive special education and related services at home	<1% Range: 0–3%

* Figures represent average percentages of handicapped students across fifty states and the range of variation among states.

Source: U.S. Department of Education (1988). *To assure the free appropriate public education of all handicapped children: Tenth annual report to Congress on the implementation of the Education of the Handicapped Act* (Washington, D.C.: U.S. Department of Education), p. B45, Table BC1.

master academic, social, and personal skills, their negative feelings about special education begin to fall away.

For teachers, special education is simply a method for dealing with students whose learning needs are different in some way. For administrators, caught up in arranging class schedules, transportation, and conferences, it's a logistical nightmare.

And what about special educators? Some insist that special education is a separate system for educating exceptional students. But most disagree. Special education is a process for helping students with special learning needs, and that process must be an integral part of the general education system. All students—both exceptional and nonexceptional—are more alike than they are different. They need to interact, to share experiences. The importance of that interaction for exceptional students is clear: To learn to act in expected ways, they must be exposed to expected behaviors. But it is equally important for those who are not exceptional. With that interaction comes an understanding of how little differences matter, of how much alike all people are. And with that understanding comes acceptance.

Our feelings about the special education process have shaped the form of this book, making it different from other introductory textbooks. Where those books are organized around the categories of exceptional students, this book focuses on educational practices. In choosing this organization, we do not mean to downplay the importance of the categories to contemporary practice. As we've indicated, most states currently organize their special education programs along categorical lines. And we believe most will continue to do so because it's convenient.

We chose to do this book differently because we believe that categorical distinctions offer little help in deciding how to teach students with special learning needs. Teaching is a decision-making process. To teach exceptional students is to make decisions about them, and most of those decisions have little to do with a student's category of exceptionality. When we collect information about a student, the process generally is the same whether the student is exceptional or not. When we present information in class, we don't change that information for different students.

We've organized your introduction to special education around the concepts and practices that we believe are central to the field that has captured our interest for most of our professional lives. As we travel on an educational journey through the foundations, the people, and the practices of this exciting profession, we rely on our own and others' experiences teaching, learning from, and working with exceptional students across the country. We are glad you're going with us, and we hope you enjoy the trip.

Summary

1. Special education addresses the special learning needs of students, to help them reach their full potential in school.
2. Public Law 94–142 protects the rights of students with handicaps, guaranteeing them an "appropriate public education."
3. The categories in special education represent different kinds of learning needs.

4. The number of students receiving special education has increased steadily in recent years; today, close to 4.3 million handicapped students are enrolled in special education programs.
5. Students with special needs must be declared eligible for services before those services can be provided in public school programs.
6. The types of services students receive as part of a special education program vary according to the level of their special needs.
7. The law mandates that students with special needs be taught in the least restrictive environment.
8. Despite structured categories and educational plans, special education is a diverse field.
9. The belief that all students are more alike than they are different is shaping contemporary practices in special education today.

Activities

1. Interview three people. Ask them to define *special education* and to give you one or two examples of students they believe should be provided special services.
2. Make a list of the kinds of handicapping conditions for which students in your state are eligible to receive special education services. Identify how your state's department of education defines each of these conditions.
3. Start a scrapbook of newspaper and magazine articles about exceptional people and their educational experiences.
4. Consult any general introductory special education textbook and list the definitions the author gives of *special education* and *exceptional students.*
5. Ask several of your professors how they define *disability, handicap,* and *gifted and talented students.* Have them describe the behaviors they use to tell the difference among these concepts.

Suggested Readings

Algozzine, B., & Ysseldyke, J. (1987). Questioning discrepancies: Retaking the first step twenty years later. *Learning Disability Quarterly, 10,* 301–313.

> *The authors challenge the common practice of defining learning disabilities on the basis of discrepancies between ability and achievement. They demonstrate that it is relatively common to find large discrepancies among children who are not formally identified as learning disabled. The article argues that definitional issues in special education have been addressed in the wrong way.*

Davis, W. E. (1989). The regular education initiative debate: Its promises and problems. *Exceptional Children, 55,* 440–446.

The most intense issue receiving attention in the special education professional literature at the time this textbook was prepared was the regular education initiative (REI) debate. Davis examines the arguments about this issue, identifies specific problems and issues related to the REI debate, and suggests strategies for overcoming perceived obstacles and improving dialogue.

Greer, J. V. (1988). Cultural diversity and the test of leadership. *Exceptional Children, 55,* 199–201.

Greer describes the cultural diversity of our schools and the promise of this diversity for leadership in the profession of special education.

Hallahan, D. P., & Kauffman, J. M. (1977). Labels, categories, behaviors: ED, LD, and EMR reconsidered. *Journal of Special Education, 11,* 139–149.

The authors argue that there are few functional differences in the behaviors of children labeled emotionally disturbed, learning disabled, and educable mentally retarded. They offer valid criticisms of labeling and categorizing children.

Lipsky, D. K., & Gartner, A. (1989). *Beyond separate education: Quality education for all.* Baltimore: Paul H. Brookes.

The authors compiled a set of original articles that argue that all exceptional people are entitled to effective educational programs. Included are chapters on the passage of Public Law 94–142, a history of effective school research, and the thoughts of students who have received special services.

Reynolds, M. C., & Balow, B. (1972). Categories and variables in special education. *Exceptional Children, 38,* 357–366.

The authors describe the negative nature of the categories and labels (impaired, disordered, disturbed) used to identify exceptional students.

2

The Legal Basis for Special Education

FOCUSING QUESTIONS

- What impact have legislation and court rulings had on current practice in special education?

- What are the specific provisions of Section 504 of the Rehabilitation Act of 1973?

- How have the provisions of Public Law 94–142 changed the nature of instructional planning, evaluation procedures, and educational environment for exceptional students?

- What is an individualized family service plan?

- What effect did court cases in the years preceding the enactment of Public Law 94–142 have on the form of the law?

- What is the emphasis of recent court decisions pertaining to special education?

- What role have parents of children with handicaps played in changing the delivery of special services?

*I*F YOU ASKED ONE HUNDRED DIRECTORS OF SPECIAL EDU-cation why special education services exist in their school districts, more than half probably would answer that state and federal laws require them. And if you asked specific questions—like "Why do you try to educate nonhandicapped students and students who have handicaps in the same classes?" "Why do you allow parents to challenge proposed changes in their child's educational program?" "Why do you make extensive efforts to conduct evaluations that are not racially or culturally biased?" "Why do school personnel write individualized education programs for students who are handicapped?"—again, most probably would say that state and federal laws require these actions.

Over the last twenty-five years, the courts and federal and state legislatures have become deeply involved in the process of schooling, and educators have been compelled to comply with an increasing number of court rulings and laws. Court decisions have focused on equal protection for exceptional students. In early cases this meant the right to treatment (education) and due process; in recent cases, focus has shifted to the methods of testing students and assigning them to special education classes.

People use the courts to settle disputes or to achieve rights. Courts develop rules of conduct, but they do so in piecemeal fashion and only after parties in a lawsuit have presented sound legal arguments. Rule-making bodies (legislatures, government agencies), on the other hand, do not have to wait for litigants to argue their cases. They can respond directly to changes in public opinion and social policy. "When, among other reasons, problems need a broader solution than courts can provide, or they affect many people, lawmakers enact statutes and administrators promulgate regulations that have comprehensive effect" (Bersoff, 1979, p. 7). For example, if a group of parents of children who are mentally retarded believes that their children are being excluded from school programs, the parents go to court to compel the schools to include the children. When many parents in many states start taking legal action on the same issue—including children who are mentally retarded in public school classes—and when that action reflects a shift in public opinion, Congress may pass a law that says that all mentally retarded children have the right to attend school.

The fundamental principle that underlies both litigation and legislation on the rights of students who are exceptional is the equal protection clause of the U.S. Constitution. The Fourteenth Amendment specifies that "no State shall make or enforce any law which shall abridge the privileges or immunities of citizens of the United States; nor shall any State deprive any person of life, liberty, or property, without due process of law; nor deny to any person within its jurisdiction the equal protection of the laws." It was the civil rights movement that pushed the equal protection clause onto national and state agendas. And it was the court decisions and laws that addressed the rights of minorities and women that had enormous impact on the laws protecting the rights of people who are handicapped.

In this chapter we examine three laws that have had important effects on the practice of special education today: Section 504 of Public Law 93–112 (the Rehabilitation Act of 1973), Public Law 94–142 (the Education for All Handicapped Children Act), and Public Law 99–457 (the 1986 Amendments to the Education for All Handicapped Children Act). We also look at the influence of several major court cases. Finally, we discuss the ways in which parents have become increasingly involved in the education of their children who are exceptional.

Over time, special education has undergone radical change as a result of judicial and legislative actions. It is important to recognize that the situation is a dynamic one. People talk about *the* law; but the law is always changing. Practices that were followed yesterday may be illegal today. Procedures that are required today may be replaced by others tomorrow. Laws, rules, and regulations change as society's social and economic priorities change. Still, despite the evolutionary nature of the process, at any time the specific laws, practices, and procedures that govern education are expected to reflect the broad principles of freedom and equality that society, through the Constitution, has agreed on. As we write this text—even as you read it—Congress, state legislatures, and the courts are shaping public policy in special education by making and interpreting laws that affect how students are treated in our schools.

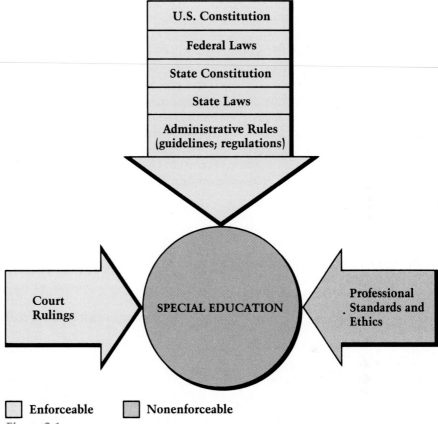

Figure 2.1
The Legal Basis for Special Education

DEFINITIONS

Practices in special education today have been shaped in good part by national and state constitutions and laws, administrative regulations and guidelines, court rulings, and the standards and ethics of the profession. The relationship among these elements is shown in Figure 2.1.

Federal and state constitutions set forth broad political principles that guide the lawmaking process at both national and state levels. Administrative rules and regulations usually are written to clarify laws; they have the force of law. Notice that as we move down the list, we are moving from general to specific. The U.S. Constitution (in the Fourteenth Amendment) makes a broad guarantee of equal protection. In one application of that guarantee, legislators have taken *equal protection* to mean "equal opportunity in education," mandating that all students have the right to free, appropriate public education. The law defines certain elements of that education; others it leaves to local school districts to clarify in the form of specific regulations and guidelines.

The courts interpret the laws and regulations and guidelines in light of the Constitution and precedent (earlier related judicial decisions). Theoretically, the courts are not lawmaking bodies. But their rulings can change existing law, in effect giving them the power to make new laws. These rulings have had significant impact on the practice of special education.

Professional standards and codes of ethics are not laws, and they do not have the force of law. But they do affect the ways in which educators conduct themselves with all students, including students who are exceptional.

Constitutional Provisions

The basis for all law in the United States is the Constitution. Public laws, practices, and procedures must be consistent with the Constitution; when they are not, the courts usually intervene to modify them.

Nowhere in the Constitution does it say that children have a right to be educated; education is a state, not a federal, responsibility. But if states mandate public education for their citizens—and today all states do—they must provide public education that is consistent with the provisions and principles embodied in the U.S. Constitution. For example, if a state establishes schools, then those schools must give all students an equal opportunity to learn. Schools cannot refuse to educate students, nor can they segregate students on the sole basis of race, religion, gender, or handicapping condition because constitutional provisions prohibit it.

State constitutions contain provisions mandating that children and adolescents be educated, and they must be consistent with the federal constitution. If state rules, regulations, and guidelines are inconsistent with state constitutions, the courts intervene to modify those regulations and guidelines.

Administrative rules relevant to special education are written by personnel in federal and state departments of education. These professionals have the large and difficult task of writing guidelines and regulations that are practical, reasonable to implement, and consistent with state and federal constitutions.

Laws

Federal and state legislation is by far the most important influence on the delivery of special education services. There are two kinds of federal laws

Section 504 of the Rehabilitation Act of 1973 protects the civil rights of people with handicaps and prohibits institutions like schools from excluding people because they have handicaps.
(© David Strickler/ Monkmeyer Press Photo Service)

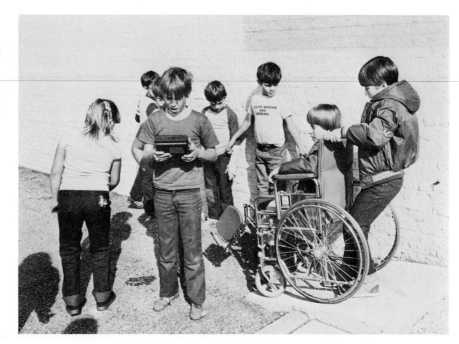

that define the ways in which schools must educate exceptional students: program laws and civil rights laws. **Program laws** make funds available to government agencies and school districts for the delivery of services. Public Law 94–142 is a program law. It makes funds available to states and school districts to provide special education services to students who are handicapped. The law outlines certain procedures for delivery of services; programs that want to receive funds must comply with those procedures.

Civil rights laws are not tied to program funds; these laws must be adhered to even in the absence of funds. For example, Section 504 of the Rehabilitation Act of 1973 (Public Law 93–112) protects the civil rights of people with handicaps. It prohibits institutions like schools and colleges from excluding people simply because they have handicaps.

State laws that pertain to education are wide ranging. They affect school attendance (most states have laws mandating that all persons between specified ages must attend school), suspension, and inclusion of exceptional students. Because the laws differ from state to state, definitions of *exceptional students* vary from state to state, as do procedures for their identification and instruction.

Schools and educators must comply with federal and state laws. Those who do not, risk losing federal funding for programs and litigation.

Regulations and Guidelines

Federal laws governing the education of students with handicaps are administered by the Office of Special Education and Rehabilitative Services within the U.S. Department of Education. At the state level, various agencies are responsible for administering programs for students with handicaps, although usually the agency in charge is located within the office of the commissioner of education or secretary of education. Program administrators write regulations for putting laws into practice. **Regulations** are relatively specific rules about how states and districts should operate; they have the force of law.

Sometimes laws and even regulations are ambiguous, subject to different interpretations. To make procedures consistent, program personnel write **guidelines.** Although guidelines do not have the force of law, they are important; they often are used in court cases to define standards of best practice.

Court Rulings

The courts are mediators, balancing the rights of the public (parents and students) and the rights of the state (schools). When parents of students with handicaps believe that their children's civil rights are being denied, they can take legal action. Often that action is specific to one student: A case is brought by parents to protect the rights of their own child. But legal action can be brought on behalf of a number of people with similar claims. This is called a **class action suit.**

Court decisions have changed the practice of special education. The substantive issue in most of these decisions is equal opportunity or equal protection of the law. These cases often are called *civil rights cases* because litigants are arguing about the civil rights (and equal protection) of the plaintiffs.

Professional Standards and Codes of Ethics

Professional standards and codes of ethics have indirect influence on the practice of special education. The standards that bear most directly on that practice are the Standards for Professional Practice published by the Council for Exceptional Children (CEC). These standards identify instructional responsibilities, behavioral management techniques, the amount of instruction and supervision required to perform support services, responsibilities to parents, and advocacy standards. They also define criteria for professional employment, professional development, and intra- and interprofessional behavior. The CEC Code of Ethics defines broad principles that special educators are responsible for upholding and advancing. (The

CEC Standards for Professional Practice and Code of Ethics are in Appendix A.)

For the most part, in special education as in general education, professional standards and ethical codes are not enforceable; they do not have the power of law. But this does not mean that they are not important. Although a school district would not take legal action against a teacher for unethical conduct, it probably would take formal action to dismiss the teacher.

Teachers and the Law

You probably are in this class because you plan to teach or work in the field of education. Why, then, are we talking about constitutions and laws and court decisions? There are two reasons for understanding the legal basis for special education. Constitutional provisions, laws, and related litigation drive current practices. The kinds of services we offer students with special needs today are more a product of law than of new ways to teach. Where and how those services are delivered are primarily a function of legislation and judicial interpretation. To understand current practice, we must understand the laws that govern that practice.

Understanding here is also a form of protection. Laws are there to be followed. When they're not followed, state education agencies, school districts, even teachers get sued.

Checkpoint

- *Federal and state constitutions give us broad principles of law.*
- *Congress and state legislatures apply those principles in specific laws, to guarantee individual rights.*
- *Government agencies write regulations and guidelines that refine the provisions of laws.*
- *The courts interpret the laws, often changing them in the process.*
- *Professional standards and ethical codes define and direct the behavior of those who work with exceptional students.*
- *Understanding the legal basis of special education is critical to an understanding of current practices in the field.*

LEGISLATION

The history of legislation to provide services for people with handicaps dates back over 160 years. Before 1950, most laws were directed at providing institutional care or rehabilitative services. For example, in the nineteenth century, legislation was enacted to fund asylums, hospitals, and institutions for those with physical and mental handicaps. In the first half of the twentieth century, laws were passed to support vocational rehabilitation for disabled war veterans, and counseling and job placement for citizens with physical handicaps. In the 1950s, the focus of legislation began to change. Although state and community facilities continued to be funded, there was a new emphasis on research and training, vocational education, assessment, and special education services.

Table 2.1 lists key federal statutes affecting persons with disabilities. As you read through it, notice how newer laws build on older ones. In the sections that follow, we examine three of the most important of these laws.

Section 504 of the Rehabilitation Act of 1973

Section 504 of the Rehabilitation Act of 1973, which was finally adopted in 1977, prohibits discrimination against people who are handicapped.

> No otherwise qualified handicapped individual shall, solely by reason of his handicap, be excluded from the participation in, be denied the benefits of, or be subjected to discrimination in any program or activity receiving federal financial assistance.

Notice that Section 504 is a program law. Noncompliance means the loss of federal funds.

Another important provision of Section 504 is **architectural accessibility,** the removal of steps and other barriers that limit the participation of people with handicaps. The law does not require that every building be barrier free, or that every method of transportation be accessible to those who are handicapped. Instead, it demands equal access to programs and services. If band concerts are held in one building on campus, that building must be accessible to those who are handicapped, so that they, like their nonhandicapped peers, have the opportunity to attend concerts. And if a college or university does not make that building barrier free, any federal funds it receives can be cut off. The law says that all programs and services must be accessible. A college does not have to make every building barrier free, but it does have to offer at least one section of every class in a building that is barrier free.

Section 504 also mandates the provision of auxiliary aids (readers for students who are blind, interpreters for students who are deaf) for those with impaired sensory, manual, or speaking skills. This does not mean that a school must provide these services at all times; it simply means that it cannot exclude students for failing to have an appropriate aid present.

Most of the provisions of Section 504 were incorporated into and expanded in the Education for All Handicapped Children Act of 1975. But Section 504 is broader than Public Law 94–142; in one sense its provisions are not restricted to a specific age group or to education. It is the law most often cited in court cases involving employment of people who are handicapped and appropriate education in colleges and universities for students who are handicapped. Also, the accessibility provisions of the law have removed the architectural barriers that limited the full participation of those with handicaps in school and community functions.

Public Law 94–142

On November 29, 1975, President Gerald R. Ford signed Public Law 94–142. The law mandated a free, appropriate public education for handicapped students between the ages of 3 and 21. Its objectives were

1. to assure that all children with handicaps have available to them a free appropriate public education;
2. to assure that the rights of children with handicaps and their parents are protected;
3. to assist States and localities to provide for the education of children with handicaps; and
4. to assess and assure the effectiveness of efforts to educate children with handicaps.

The Education for All Handicapped Children Act is a program law that came about because parents, advocacy groups, and professionals were dissatisfied with certain conditions and brought them to the attention of legislators. Among other things, Congress found that

- more than 8 million handicapped children (from birth to age 21) were living in the United States, and that more than half of them were not receiving an appropriate education.
- more than 1 million handicapped children were excluded entirely from the educational system, and that many others were enrolled in regular education classes where, because their handicaps were undetected, they were not learning as much as could be expected.
- families were being forced to find services outside the public schools because the educational services within the schools were inadequate.

Table 2.1
Legislative History of Key Statutes Affecting Persons with Disabilities

Category and Law	Public Law	
	Date Signed	Number
Education		
Elementary and Secondary Education Act:		
ESEA Amendments of 1965	4/11/65	89–10
Education Amendments of 1972	6/23/72	92–31B
Education Amendments of 1976	9/12/76	94–482
Education Amendments of 1978	11/1/78	95–561
Education of the Handicapped Act:		
Captioned Films for the Deaf Act	10/19/65	89–258
Elementary and Secondary Education Act Amendments of 1966	11/3/66	89–750
ESEA Amendments of 1967	1/2/68	90–247
ESEA Amendments of 1970	4/13/70	91–230
Education Amendments of 1974	8/21/73	93–380
Handicapped Children's Early Education Assistance Act		90–538
Education for All Handicapped Children Act of 1975	11/29/75	94–142
Authorizing Education Programs for Handicapped Persons through FY 1982	6/17/77	95–49
Education of the Handicapped Amendments of 1983	12/2/83	98–199
Education of the Handicapped Amendments of 1986	10/8/86	99–457
Education of the Deaf Act of 1986	8/4/86	99–371
Handicapped Programs Technical Amendments Act of 1988	11/7/88	100–630
Vocational Education Act	12/18/63	88–210
Carl D. Perkins Vocational Education Act	10/19/84	98–524
Job Training Partnership Act	10/13/82	97–300
Health		
Social Security Act:		
Intermediate Care Amendments of 1971	12/28/71	92–223
Social Security Benefit Increase	7/1/72	92–336
Maternal and Child Health Amendments	7/10/72	92–345
Maternal and Child Health Amendments	6/1//73	93–53

Table 2.1 *cont.*
Legislative History of Key Federal Statutes Affecting Persons with Disabilities

	Public Law	
Category and Law	Date Signed	Number
To provide for reimbursement for rural health clinic services under the Medicare and Medicaid programs	12/13/73	95–210
Community Mental Health Centers Act:		
Mental Retardation Facilities and Community Mental Health Centers Construction Act of 1963	10/31/63	88–164
Mental Retardation Facilities and Community Mental Health Centers Construction Act of 1965	8/4/65	89–105
To provide grants for construction of community mental health centers	3/13/70	91–211
Comprehensive State Mental Health Planning Act of 1986	11/14/86	99–660
Public Health Service Act:		
Comprehensive Health Planning and Public Health Services Amendments of 1966 "Partnership for Health"	11/3/66	89–749
Establishment of National Eye Institute	8/16/68	90–489
Health Services and Facility Amendments of 1968	10/15/68	90–574
National Advisory Commission on Multiple Sclerosis Act	10/25/72	92–563
National Health Planning and Resources Development Act of 1974	1/4/75	93–641
National Arthritis Act of 1974	1/4/75	93–640
Special Health Revenue Sharing Act	7/29/75	94–63
Social Security Disability Benefits Reform Act of 1984	10/9/84	98–460
Employment Opportunities for Disabled Americans Act	11/10/86	99–643
National School Lunch and Child Nutrition Act of 1974	6/30/74	93–326
National School Lunch and Child Nutrition Act Amendments of 1977	11/10/77	95–166
Omnibus Drug Enforcement Education and Control Act	10/14/86	99–470

Table 2.1 *cont.*
Legislative History of Key Federal Statutes Affecting Persons with Disabilities

	Public Law	
Category and Law	Date Signed	Number
Rights		
Elimination of Architectural Barriers to Physically Handicapped	8/12/68	90–480
To ensure that certain federally constructed facilities be constructed so as to be accessible to persons with physical handicaps	3/5/70	91–205
Rights of the Blind and Other Physically Handicapped in the District of Columbia	10/21/72	92–515
Rehabilitation Amendments of 1973	9/26/73	93–112
Rehabilitation Amendments of 1974	12/7/74	93–516
Developmentally Disabled Assistance and Bill of Rights Act	10/4/75	94–103
Education for All Handicapped Children Act of 1975	11/29/75	94–142
Child Abuse Prevention and Treatment and Adoption Reform Act of 1984	10/9/84	98–457
Protection and Advocacy for Mentally Ill Individuals Act of 1986	10/30/85	99–139
Education of the Handicapped Amendments of 1986	10/8/86	99–457
Rehabilitation Act Amendments of 1986	10/21/86	99–506
Developmental Disabilities Assistance and Bill of Rights Amendments of 1987	10/29/87	100–146
Protection and Advocacy for Mentally Ill Individuals Amendments Act of 1988	10/20/88	100–509
Civil Rights Restoration Act		100–259
Developmental Disabilities:		
Mental Retardation Facilities and Community Mental Health Centers Construction Act of 1963	10/31/63	88–164
Mental Retardation Facilities and Community Mental Health Centers Construction Act of 1965	8/4/65	89–105
Mental Retardation Amendments of 1967	12/4/67	90–170
Authorizing funds for increased facilities for mental retardation programs	10/30/69	91–517
Developmentally Disabled Assistance and Bill of Rights Act	10/4/75	94–103

Table **2.1** *cont.*
Legislative History of Key Statutes Affecting Persons with Diabilities

Category and Law	Public Law	
	Date Signed	Number
Head Start Act:		
Economic Opportunity Amendments of 1972	9/19/72	92–424
Community Services Act of 1974	1/4/75	93–644
Head Start Act of 1981	8/13/81	97–35
Technology-Related Assistance for Individuals with Disabilities Act of 1988	8/19/88	100–407
Vocational Rehabilitation		
Vocational Rehabilitation Act Amendments of 1966	11/8/66	89–333
Vocational Rehabilitation Amendments of 1967	10/3/67	90–99
Vocational Rehabilitation Amendments of 1968	7/7/67	90–391
To extend for 1 year the authorization for various programs under the Vocational Rehabilitation Act	1/31/77	91–610
Rehabilitation Amendments of 1973	9/26/73	93–112
Rehabilitation Act Amendments of 1974	12/7/74	93–516
Handicapped Programs Technical Amendments Act of 1988	11/7/88	100–630

Source: Clearinghouse on the Handicapped, Office of Special Education and Rehabilitative Services, U.S. Department of Education and Rehabilitative Services, *Summary of Existing Legislation Affecting Persons with Disabilities* (Washington, DC: U.S. Government Printing Office, 1988).

The lawmakers believed that special education could make a difference, that with special education services these children would stand a better chance of achieving their potential. And they believed that it was in the national interest to fund programs to meet the needs of students who were handicapped.

The law sets forth a number of procedures; states that do not comply with them cannot receive federal funds. Specifically, the law requires each state to have a plan that fully describes the policies and procedures used to ensure a free, appropriate education for all handicapped students between the ages of 3 and 21, and to have procedures in place for identifying all handicapped students.

The law makes several very specific provisions about the education of handicapped students. For example, wherever possible, handicapped students must be taught in regular classrooms, along with their nonhandicapped peers. Also, tests and other evaluation devices used to decide the nature of a student's handicap must be both racially and culturally fair.

We talk about four specific areas of the law below, to give you a perspective on the magnitude of this landmark legislation. As you read, think about how these provisions affect the work of special education teachers, general education teachers, school psychologists, administrators, counselors, speech-language pathologists, and all the other people who work with students who are exceptional.

Individualized Education Program Provisions
A central concept to the law is the individualized education program. As we said in Chapter 1, an IEP is a written document that describes

- the student's present levels of functioning.
- the annual goals and short-term objectives of the program.
- the services to be provided and the extent of regular programming.
- the starting date and expected duration of services.
- evaluation procedures and criteria for monitoring progress.

The IEP is the product of a thorough evaluation that begins with information about the child gathered from parents, teachers, and formal and informal assessments, and often ends with a review by a team of professionals. The law states that the instructional goals specified in an IEP must be *measurable*—observable and based on performance. Figure 2.2 shows the IEP of a fifth-grader with learning disabilities in reading, math, and language skills. Notice that assessment results are specified, along with long- and short-term goals, and a description of the services to be provided.

Why was a formal plan necessary? What were lawmakers thinking when they drafted the IEP provision? First, they recognized the need for a mechanism to keep track of the students' progress. Second, special educators had convinced them that outcomes would be better if school personnel had specific objectives for students, a plan of where they were going and how they were going to get there, and a method for evaluating the extent to which students were meeting individual goals.

PL 94–142 reaffirms the Fourteenth Amendment's guarantee of due process for handicapped students by giving parents the right to examine their child's records and have independent evaluations of their child.
(© Lila Weisbrot/ Michael Weisbrot and Family)

The IEP has had a profound effect on the activities of teachers, school psychologists, and other school personnel. Students must be assessed by a multidisciplinary team, and that assessment must form the basis of students' individual instructional programs. These programs can be carried out in a variety of settings (general education classes, self-contained classes, homes, separate schools), and teachers (both in general and special education) are expected to provide instruction that ties in with the goals specified in the IEP.

Due Process Provisions

The Fourteenth Amendment guarantees the citizens of the United States due process of law. Public Law 94–142 reaffirms that guarantee for handicapped students. The law gives their parents, guardians, or parent surrogates the right to examine their child's records. It also gives them the right to independent evaluations of their child. Whenever a school proposes or refuses to initiate or change the identification, evaluation, or placement of a child, the parents must receive prior written notice (in their native language, if at all possible). Parents have a right to challenge the school's decision at an impartial hearing. If they are not satisfied with the findings of the hearing, in most states they can appeal the decision to the state education agency, and from there to the civil courts.

At a due process hearing, parents have several rights: the right to counsel and/or experts in special education; the right to present evidence,

Figure 2.2
An Individualized
Education Program

INDIVIDUALIZED EDUCATION PROGRAM

<u> 11/11/90 </u>
Date

STUDENT: Last Name   First   Middle

		5.3	8-4-80

School of Attendance   Home School   Grade Level   Birthdate/Age

School Address   School Telephone Number

Child Study Team Members

LD Teacher
Case Manager

Homeroom
Name   Title

Parents
Name   Title

Facilitator
Name   Title

Name   Title

Speech
Name   Title

Name   Title

Summary of Assessment Results

IDENTIFIED STUDENT NEEDS: *Reading from last half of DISTAR II — present performance level*

LONG-TERM GOALS: *To improve reading achievement level by at least one year's gain. To improve math achievement to grade level. To improve language skills by one year's gain.*

SHORT-TERM GOALS: *Master Level 4 vocabulary and reading skills. Master math skills in basic curriculum. Master spelling words from Level 3 list. Complete Units 1-9 from Level 3 curriculum.*

MAINSTREAM MODIFICATIONS

White copy—Cumulative folder   Golden rod—Case manager
Pink copy—Special teacher   Yellow copy—Parent

Description of Services to Be Provided

Type of Service	Teacher	Starting Date	Amt. of time per day	OBJECTIVES AND CRITERIA FOR ATTAINMENT
SLD Level III	LD teacher	11-11-90	2½ hrs.	Reading: will know all vocabulary through the "Honeycomb" level. Will master skills as presented through Distar II. Will know 123 sound-symbols presented in "Sound Way to Reading." Math: will pass all tests at basic 4 level. Spelling: 5 words each week from Level 3 list. Language: will complete Units 1-9 of the grade 4 language program. Will also complete supplemental units from "Language Step by Step."

Mainstream Classes	Teacher	Amt. of time per day	OBJECTIVES AND CRITERIA FOR ATTAINMENT
		3½ hrs.	Out-of-seat behavior: sit attentively and listen during mainstream class discussions. A simple management plan will be implemented if he does not meet this expectation. Mainstream modifications of Social Studies: will keep a folder in which he expresses through drawing the topics his class will cover. Modified district social studies curriculum. No formal testing will be made. An oral reader will read text to him, and oral questions will be asked.

The following equipment, and other changes in personnel, transportation, curriculum, methods, and educational services will be made: _Distar II Reading Program, Spelling Level 3, "Sound Way to Reading" Program, Vocabulary tapes_

Substantiation of least restrictive alternatives: _The planning team has determined the student's academic needs are best met with direct SLD support in reading, math, language, and spelling._

ANTICIPATED LENGTH OF PLAN _1 yr._ The next periodic review will be held: _____ May 1991 _____
DATE/TIME/PLACE

- ☒ **I do approve this program placement and the above IEP**
- ☐ **I do not approve this placement and/or the IEP**
- ☐ **I request a conciliation conference**

_____
PARENT/GUARDIAN

_____
Principal or Designee

cross-examine, and compel the attendance of witnesses; and the right to a written or taped record of the hearing. These due process rights apply to civil court actions as well as agency hearings and court actions.

At one time, the practice of testing children and making changes in their educational placement without their parents' knowledge or consent was widespread. Parents had little or no input in their child's education. The due process provisions of Public Law 94–142 bring parents into the system; they give parents an opportunity to be involved, to understand and question what the schools are doing with their child.

Protection in Evaluation Procedures Provisions

The protection in evaluation procedures (PEP) provisions of Public Law 94–142 address assessment practices. Those practices must be fair, with no racial or cultural bias.

> Procedures to assure that testing and evaluation materials and procedures utilized for the purposes of evaluation and placement of handicapped children will be selected and administered so as not to be racially or culturally discriminatory. Such materials or procedures shall be provided and administered in the child's native language or mode of communication, unless it clearly is not feasible to do so, and no single procedure shall be the sole criterion for determining an appropriate educational program for a child. (Section 615–5C)

There are specific rules and regulations for the implementation of the PEP provisions:

- A "full and individual evaluation" of a student's needs must be made before the student is placed in a special education program.
- Tests must be administered in the child's native language or other mode of communication.
- Tests must be valid for the specific purpose for which they are used.
- Tests must be administered by "trained personnel" following the instructions provided by their producer.
- Tests and other evaluation materials must be relevant to specific areas of educational needs, not designed to yield a single general IQ score.
- The results of tests administered to students who have impaired sensory, manual, or speaking skills must reflect aptitude or achievement, not the impairment.
- Special education placement cannot be determined on the basis of a single procedure.

■ Evaluations for special education placement must be made by a multidisciplinary team, including at least one teacher or other specialist with "knowledge in the area of suspected disability."

■ Students must be assessed in all areas related to their suspected disability, including general health, vision, hearing, behavior, general intelligence, motor abilities, academic performance, and language abilities.

The PEP provisions were included in Public Law 94–142 to address abuses in the assessment process. In the background testimony for this law, it was asserted that children were being tested with unfair tests, instruments that were in languages other than their primary languages and that included items from cultures other than those to which the children had been exposed. It was argued that "there oughta be a law" to stop these abuses. The product of that argument was the PEP provisions.

Least Restrictive Environment Provisions

Public Law 94–142 also specifies that handicapped students be educated in the least restrictive environment (LRE). States must have policies and procedures in place to ensure that handicapped students, including those in public or private institutions or other care facilities, are educated with children who are not handicapped, that students are removed from the regular education environment only when the severity of a handicap is such that instruction in regular classes with the use of supplementary aids and services is not effective (Section 612–5).

The LRE provisions reflect the generally held belief that students are better off and demonstrate better development when they spend as much time as possible interacting with their nonhandicapped peers. And they reflect the generally held belief that if students can learn in an environment that is relatively nonrestrictive, then they can live and work in that environment as they get older.

A Summary

Current practice in special education is driven in large part by state and federal laws that mandate services for exceptional students. The intent of Public Law 94–142 was massive educational reform for students with handicaps. Its major provisions target different stages in the three-stage process that characterizes special education: (1) deciding who to serve, (2) deciding how to serve those students, and (3) deciding whether the services have done any good. The due process and protection in evaluation procedures provisions obviously relate to the first stage, determining eligibility. They attempt to reduce the problems inherent in deciding who should receive special education. The IEP and least restrictive environment provi-

PL 99–457 extends the right to a free, appropriate public education to all handicapped children ages 3 through 5 and provides for early intervention for children from birth through age 2 who are at risk of substantial delay in development.

(© Michael Weisbrot and Family)

sions target the second stage, treatment practices. And all the provisions address aspects of progress evaluation, the third stage of the process. Of course, passing a law in no way guarantees that changes will occur in the ways the law directs. Interpretation of the law—by the courts—influences the effect the law has on practice.

Public Law 99–457

In 1986 Congress amended Public Law 94–142, extending all rights and protections of the law to preschoolers with handicaps. Effective in the 1990–91 academic year, all states that apply for funds under Public Law 94–142 must provide free, appropriate public education to all handicapped children ages 3 through 5.

At the same time, as part of Public Law 99–457, the 1986 Amendments to the Education for All Handicapped Children Act, Congress established a new state grant program for infants and toddlers with handicaps. Eligible for **early intervention** are children from birth through age 2 who are delayed in development or at risk of substantial delay in development. The states have the authority to specify the criteria for deciding who to serve.

To receive the federal funds that are available as part of Public Law 99–457, states must have an agency that administers the services and an interagency coordinating council to help develop programs and services. By the 1990–91 academic year, statewide early intervention systems must be in place, providing all eligible infants and toddlers with multidisciplinary assessments, individualized programs, and case management services.

The law specifies that each school district use a multidisciplinary assessment to develop an **individualized family service plan (IFSP)** for each child. The IFSP must include

- a statement of the child's present level of cognitive, social, speech and language, and self-help development.
- a statement of the family's strengths and needs related to enhancing the child's development.
- a statement of the major outcomes expected for the child and family.
- criteria, procedures, and timelines for measuring progress.
- a statement of the specific early intervention services necessary to meet the unique needs of the child and family, including methods, frequency, and intensity of service.
- projected dates for initiation and expected duration of services.
- the name of the person who will manage the case.
- procedures for transition from early intervention into a preschool program.

Checkpoint

- *Section 504 of the Rehabilitation Act of 1973 declared illegal the discrimination against people who are handicapped solely on the basis of their handicap. It mandates the inclusion of exceptional people in public programs and the removal of architectural barriers that limit the accessibility of public programs to people who are handicapped.*
- *Public Law 94–142 mandates a free, appropriate education for all handicapped students between the ages of 3 and 21.*
- *Among other things, Public Law 94–142 provides for individualized education programs, due process, protection in evaluation procedures, and education in the least restrictive environment.*
- *Public Law 99–457 extended the protections of the Education for All Handicapped Children Act to infants and toddlers.*
- *An important component of early intervention is the individualized family service plan.*

Window on Practice

*T*HE FIRST CIRCUIT COURT of Appeals, in a decision that could affect handicapped children nationwide, ruled recently that public school systems are mandated by federal law to provide education for all handicapped children regardless of how little they might benefit from it.

The 51-page decision, written by Appeals Court Judge Hugh Bownes, reversed a decision by a district court in New Hampshire. The district court had ruled that a severely retarded and handicapped child, Timothy W., was too disabled to gain anything from a special education program.

But the decision by the three-member appellate panel said that the 1975 Education for All Handicapped Children Act "mandates an appropriate public education for all handicapped children, regardless of the level of achievement that such children might attain."

Advocates for the handicapped said the ruling cleared the way for hundreds of severely disabled children around the country to continue receiving an education. Had the court ruled differently, many children would have been denied that opportunity, they said.

But the decision drew sharp criticism from public school officials, who argued that to provide such a public education would impose a substantial burden on school systems and taxpayers.

The ruling arose from a 1974 complaint filed by Timothy W. in US District Court in New Hampshire, alleging that his rights under both New Hampshire state law and federal law had been violated by the Rochester, N.H., School District when it concluded the boy was not eligible for special education.

In later hearings, Timothy's mother and therapists testified he could hear, see bright light, and respond to music, touching and talking. But a developmental pediatrician testified he "did not have educational needs and could not benefit from an education."

The case continued until July 15, 1988, when the district court ruled that federal law mandates that a determination must first be made as to whether or not a child may benefit from special education in order to receive it. The court concluded Timothy W. was ineducable.

However, on May 25, 1989, the federal appelate judges said the law does not call for such a preliminary determination. "A school district has a duty to provide an educational program for every handicapped child in the district, regardless of the severity of the handicap," the judges wrote.

The judges remanded the decision to the district court, until the school district develops a "suitable individualized education program" for Timothy W. The school district will pay damages.

In Rochester, school superintendent Raymond Yeagley said the cost of providing a special education for Timothy would be a financial burden to the school system and "a lot of money for taxpayers."

He added the decision would force the school system to shift resources from students who could benefit from an education and focus on less capable students.

Similar concerns were echoed in Washington by the National School Boards Association, which filed a brief in support of the Rochester school district. Gwendolyn Gregory, the group's deputy general counsel, said that school boards around the country are overburdened with demands for special education programs.

"School districts are getting to the point they are asked to do everthing, and spend more on education services than education," said Gregory. She added that the decision could expand a school's liability for a host of medical services, such as physical therapy, that could be considered education.

In New Hampshire, attorney Ronald K. Lospennato, who represented Timothy W. and the Disabilities Rights Center, hailed the decision. "It simply reinforces what the Education Act said all along—that all handicapped children are entitled to an education. They shouldn't have to fight to get in the school door."

Source: Elizabeth Neuffer, "US Appeals Court Rules That Schools Must Educate Handicapped Children," *The Boston Globe,* May 25, 1989, p. 53. Reprinted courtesy of *The Boston Globe.*

LITIGATION

Change in special education typically arises from change in public policy, from legislation, or from litigation (Burrello & Sage, 1979). Some of the court cases that have had a direct and significant effect on special education are listed in Table 2.2. Most of these cases were heard in the state court. Since Public Law 94–142 was passed, the U.S. Supreme Court has gotten involved in just five cases.

Court Action Before Public Law 94–142

Court action before the enactment of Public Law 94–142 in 1975 focused on the individual's right to a free, appropriate public education and on guidelines for the states to follow in educating students. The cornerstone of this litigation was set in 1954, when the U.S. Supreme Court, in *Brown* v. *Board of Education,* ruled that separate schools for black and white students are inherently unequal and therefore unconstitutional. The parents of handicapped students who later sued school systems for the denial of equal protection in assessment and assignment of their handicapped children to allegedly inferior educational settings based their legal arguments on the decision in *Brown.*

Other issues addressed by the courts before Public Law 94–142 was passed included ability grouping based on test performance, the notion that children are persons under the Constitution and have civil rights, the exclusion of students with handicaps from schools, the misclassification of minority and non-English speaking children, and the exclusion of retarded students from schools. In separate cases, the courts ruled that the exclusion of students labeled as behavior problems, mentally retarded, emotionally disturbed, or hyperactive is unconstitutional; that it is illegal to group students by ability ("track") based on their performance on standardized tests; that all handicapped children have the right to a "constructive" education; that assessment tests must be in a student's primary

Table 2.2
Primary Rulings in Court Cases Relevant to Special Education

Case	Ruling
Watson v. *City of Cambridge* (1893)	A student can be expelled for "disorderly conduct or imbecility."
Beattie v. *State Board of Education* (1919)	Students who are physically handicapped can be excluded from school when their presence has a "depressing and nauseating effect" on other students.
Brown v. *Board of Education* (1954)	Segregation in schools is illegal because it denies equal protection and equal opportunity (U.S. Supreme Court).
Hansen v. *Hobson* (1967)	Ability grouping (tracking) based on pupil performance on standardized tests, as employed in the Washington, D.C., schools, is unconstitutional, violating both due process and equal protection.
Tinker v. *Des Moines Independent School District* (1969)	Children are "persons" under the Constitution and have civil rights independent of their parents (U.S. Supreme Court).
Diana v. *State Board of Education* (1970)	In a consent decree, the state of California agreed <ul><li>that all children whose primary language is not English should be tested in both their primary language and English.</li><li>to eliminate "unfair verbal items" from tests.</li><li>to reevaluate all Mexican-American and Chinese students enrolled in EMR classes using only nonverbal items and testing them in their primary language.</li><li>to develop IQ tests reflecting Mexican-American culture and standardized only on Mexican-Americans.</li></ul>
Covarrubias v. *San Diego Unified School District* (1971)	A consent decree establishing the right of plaintiffs to monetary damages for misclassification.
Lemon v. *Bossier Parish School Board* (1971)	Ability grouping is unconstitutional.
Ordway v. *Hargraves* (1971)	Exclusion from school of pregnant students is unconstitutional.

Table 2.2 *cont.*
Primary Rulings in Court Cases Relevant to Special Education

Case	Ruling
Martella v. *Kelley* (1972)	Juveniles held in noncriminal custody have a right to treatment.
Mills v. *Board of Education* (1972)	■ Exclusion of students labeled as having behavior problems, mentally retarded, emotionally disturbed, or hyperactive is unconstitutional.
	■ Any handicapped child has a right, under equal protection, to a "constructive education," including appropriate specialized instruction.
	■ Due process of law requires a hearing before exclusion from, termination of, or classification into a special program.
Pennsylvania Association for Retarded Children v. *Commonwealth of Pennsylvania* (343 F. Supp. 279, 1972)	In a consent decree, Pennsylvania was enjoined from excluding mentally retarded students from the state's schools. The state agreed to engage in extensive child-find activities.
Meriken v. *Cressman* (1973)	■ The use of personality tests in a study of potential drug abusers is an invasion of privacy.
	■ Personality tests lack the necessary technical adequacy to identify "the right students."
Goso v. *Lopez* (1974)	Due process is required before students are suspended or expelled from school.
Hairston v. *Drosick* (1974)	Exclusion of handicapped children from the regular classroom without procedural safeguards is a violation of their constitutional rights as well as of the Rehabilitation Act of 1973.
Wyatt v. *Stickney* (1971; 1974)	Mentally retarded individuals committed to a state school have a right to adequate treatment (education).
Washington v. *Davis* (1976)	When actions result in a discriminatory outcome, one can assume discriminatory intent.
Frederick L. v. *Thomas* (1976; 1977)	Philadelphia schools must engage in massive screening and follow-up

Table 2.2 *cont.*
Primary Rulings in Court Cases Relevant to Special Education

Case	Ruling
	evaluation designed to locate and serve students with learning disabilities.
Panitch v. *State of Wisconsin* (1977)	A long delay in implementing a state law designed to give equal education to the handicapped is sufficient indication of "intentional discrimination," in violation of the equal protection clause.
Lora v. *New York City Board of Education* (1978)	■ The process of evaluating students to determine if they should enter "special day schools" for emotionally disturbed students violates students' rights to treatment and due process. ■ To the extent that students are referred to largely racially segregated schools, there is a denial of equal opportunity in violation of Title VI. ■ New York City's monetary problems do not excuse violation of students' rights.
Larry P. v. *Riles* (1979)	■ The California State Department of Education cannot use intelligence tests to place black students in EMR classes. ■ Schools in California must eliminate the disproportionate placement of black students in EMR classes. ■ Schools in California must reevaluate all black students currently enrolled in EMR classes.
PASE v. *Hannon* (1980)	Intelligence tests are not biased against black students, and so are appropriate for use in placing black students in EMR classes.
Board of Education of Hendrick Hudson School District v. *Rowley* (1982)	It is not necessary for a school district to provide a sign language interpreter in the classroom as part of a deaf child's education program. Schools do not have to develop handicapped students' maximum potential; they must grant them access to educational opportunities.

Table 2.2 *cont.*
Primary Rulings in Court Cases Relevant to Special Education

Case	Ruling
Irving Independent School District v. *Tatro* (1983)	School personnel must provide related services that enable a handicapped child to remain at school during the day.
Smith v. *Robinson* (1984)	Attorney's fees are not reimbursable under Public Law 94–142.
Burlington School Committee v. *Department of Education* (1985)	Reimbursement for private school tuition is an appropriate form of relief for a court to grant.
Honig v. *Doe* (1988)	School officials cannot unilaterally decide to expel or suspend students who are handicapped.

Source: Adapted from J. Ysseldyke and B. Algozzine, *Critical Issues in Special and Remedial Education.* Boston: Houghton Mifflin Co., 1982, pp. 215–217.

language (in California); and that students who are mentally retarded have the right to attend schools with students who are not retarded.

Many of the findings in these cases had a direct effect on the form of Public Law 94–142. For example, one of the key settlement issues in *Diana* v. *State Board of Education* was that students had the right to be tested in their primary language. This later was specified in Public Law 94–142.

Court Action after Public Law 94–142

The courts are not lawmaking bodies; they interpret laws that have already been passed. Legislation serves "as a springboard to future litigation, as parties seek to define, implement, and enforce its provisions. Federal and state statutes may evoke what may be called 'second generation' issues" (Bersoff, 1979, p. 103). The cases that followed the enactment of Public Law 94–142 challenged the procedures by which schools assess and make placement decisions about students with handicaps or potential handicaps.

The best known of these cases—*Larry P.* v. *Riles*—was rendered by a California state court in 1979. The initial complaint was filed in 1971 on behalf of a single plaintiff. The case eventually became a class action suit, extended on behalf of all black children in California who had been or might be wrongfully placed and maintained in special classes for the educable mentally retarded (EMR) on the basis of intelligence tests. The defendant in the case was Wilson Riles, California's superintendent of public instruction. The plaintiffs challenged the placement process and, specifically, the use of standardized intelligence tests in the decision-mak-

Cases following PL 94–142 challenged the procedures by which schools assess and place students with handicaps, eliminating the disproportionate enrollment of children from minority groups in special classes.

(© Michael Weisbrot and Family)

ing process, contending that IQ tests were biased and discriminated against black children. As evidence the plaintiffs cited the disproportionate number of black students in special classes.

The case went through several appeals, but finally was decided in favor of the plaintiffs. In outlining his "remedy," Judge Robert F. Peckham addressed two specific problems: abuses in testing and the disproportionate enrollment of black children in special classes for the educable mentally retarded.

- The state of California was prohibited from using, permitting the use of, or approving the use of any standardized intelligence test for identifying black EMR children or placing them in special classes for the educable mentally retarded.
- The schools were ordered to monitor or eliminate disproportionate placement of black students in EMR classes in California.
- The schools were ordered to reevaluate every black child currently identified as educable mentally retarded, without using standardized intelligence tests.

Judge Peckham concluded his opinion with this:

Whatever the future, it is essential that California's educators confront the problem of the widespread failure to provide an adequate education to underprivileged minorities such as the black children who brought this lawsuit. Educators have too often been able to rationalize inaction by blaming educational failure on an assumed intellectual inferiority of disproportionate numbers of black children. That assumption without validation is unacceptable, and it is made all the more invidious when "legitimized" by ostensibly neutral, scientific I.Q. scores. (495 F. Supp. 96, 109–110 (N.D. Cal. 1979))

The issue of bias in assessment was not settled by *Larry P.*; it continues to be debated in the nation's courtrooms. In *PASE* v. *Hannon* (1980), a class action suit was brought by Parents in Action on Special Education on behalf of "all black children who have been or will be placed in special classes for the educable mentally handicapped in the Chicago school system." Plaintiffs observed that although 62 percent of the enrollment of the Chicago public schools was black, black students comprised 82 percent of the enrollment in classes for the educable mentally handicapped. The plaintiffs claimed that the misassessment of children was caused by racial bias in standardized intelligence tests.

Here the judge ruled in favor of the school system, stating that he could find little evidence that the tests were biased. The ruling was clearly contrary to *Larry P.* As a direct result of these two cases, the assessment processes in California and Illinois are very different. In California, IQ tests are not used in the process of classifying students as mentally retarded; in Illinois, they are.

Two other cases—*Frederick L.* v. *Thomas* (1976, 1977) and *Lora* v. *New York City Board of Education* (1978)—addressed legal issues of critical importance to special education. Although these cases were decided by federal district courts and affect the law only in Pennsylvania and New York, respectively, their rulings have persuasive power in other state courts.

Frederick L. v. *Thomas* was a class action suit. The parents of learning disabled students charged that the Philadelphia school district was not providing their children with an appropriate education. They accused the school district of denying services to significant numbers of students with learning disabilities. The schools argued that some eligible students had not been referred and were being served appropriately in regular classrooms. The court ordered the school district to conduct "massive screening and follow-up individual psychological evaluations" to identify students with learning disabilities.

Lora v. *New York City Board of Education* was a class action suit brought by black and Hispanic students who claimed that their statutory right to a free, appropriate public education in the least restrictive environment had been violated by the city of New York. The students, who were identified as emotionally disturbed, had been segregated in separate schools and facilities. Judge Weinstein, in his opinion, held that (1) the process used in New York City to evaluate students to determine whether they should enter "special day schools" violated students' right to treatment and due process; (2) to the extent that students were referred to largely racially segregated schools, there was a denial of equal educational opportunity in violation of Title VI of the U.S. Civil Rights Act; and (3) New York City's fiscal problems did not excuse violation of the students' rights. Here, too, the schools were ordered to conduct more extensive assessment and evaluation. The decisions in *Frederick L.* and *Lora* forced the school systems to spend more money on assessment and to change current practices.

Recently the Supreme Court has been involved in defining and clarifying the meaning of *appropriate education* as mandated by Section 601c of Public Law 94–142. In *Board of Education of Hendrick Hudson School District* v. *Rowley* (1982), the Court overturned a lower-court ruling that had required a school to provide an interpreter for a deaf student. The case began when Amy Rowley's parents asked the school to provide a sign language interpreter in their deaf daughter's class on a full-time basis. The school was providing speech therapy, use of a hearing aid, and a tutor for one hour a day, and had offered sign language instruction to those of Amy's teachers who wanted it. But the school refused to put an interpreter in Amy's classroom. The Supreme Court ruled that the school was acting within its rights. In writing the decision for the Court, Justice William Rehnquist stated that schools do not have to develop the maximum potential of students who are handicapped; that it was the intent of the law to give students *access* to educational opportunities.

In *Irving Independent School District* v. *Tatro* (1984), the issue was the responsibility of a school to provide a medical procedure, in this case catheterization, to a handicapped child. Chief Justice Warren Burger, writing for the majority, reasoned that

> a service that enables a handicapped child to remain at school during the day is an important means of providing the child with the meaningful access to education that Congress envisioned. . . . Services like CIC [clean intermittent catheterization, which involves washing a small metal tube called a catheter, inserting the catheter in the bladder to allow urine to drain, pulling the catheter out, and wiping the bladder region] that permit a child to remain at school during the day are not less related to the effort to educate than are services that enable the child to reach, enter, or exist in the school. (104 S. Ct. 3371 (1984)).

He went on to say that catheterization, because it can be carried out by a school nurse, is a related service, not a medical service. Schools are not required to provide medical services that have to be administered by a physician (with the exception of some assessment and diagnostic services); but they must provide services that can be carried out by a school nurse.

A third case heard by the Supreme Court involved the payment by school districts of tuition and fees for students who are handicapped to attend private schools. In *Burlington School Committee v. Department of Education* (1985), the lower courts asked the Supreme Court for a ruling on the meaning of appropriate education. Michael Panaco, a first-grader with a specific learning disability, was enrolled in a private school because his parents contended that he was not receiving an education that met his unique needs in the local public school. The Court noted that "where a court determines that a private placement desired by the parents was proper under the Act and that an IEP calling for placement in a public school was inappropriate, it seems clear beyond cavil that appropriate relief include[s] . . . placing the child in a private school" (p. 231). The Court ruled that the most important element of Public Law 94–142 is an appropriate educational program, wherever it takes place.

Court actions take time. For example, the *Burlington* case took eight years. They also cost a lot of money. Parents who go to court on behalf of their child incur extensive legal fees. It is not surprising, then, that the fourth case heard by the Supreme Court involved the issue of responsibility for legal fees. In *Smith* v. *Robinson* (1984), the school district had agreed to place Thomas Smith, a youngster with cerebral palsy and physical and emotional handicaps, in a day treatment program at a hospital in Rhode Island. After a period of time, the school district informed the parents that the Rhode Island Department of Mental Health, Retardation and Hospitals would have to take over the expense of the program. The state supreme court ruled that the duty of funding the educational program rested with the local school, not the state. The parents appealed the case to a federal district court and, in addition, asked for payment of attorney's fees. The district court agreed with the parents, but the court of appeals did not. The Supreme Court ruled that parents are responsible for paying attorney's fees.

So the Supreme Court had ruled that parents could be reimbursed for private school tuition but not for attorney's fees. In 1986 Congress settled the issue by passing the Handicapped Children's Protection Act, an amendment to Public Law 94–142. The amendment specified that courts could award attorney's fees to parents who win in current proceedings or in cases that began after July 4, 1984 (coincidentally, the date that the rulings in both *Tatro* and *Smith* were read by the Supreme Court). Parents have the right to collect for attorney's fees. However, they must work in good faith to try to settle their case. Also there are specific conditions under which parents are not entitled to recover attorney's fees.

In *Honig* v. *Doe* (1988), the Supreme Court reaffirmed the decision of a lower court that schools cannot exclude handicapped students, specifically those who have emotional handicaps, because of their behavior. The case involved the suspension of two students who were receiving special education services in the San Francisco School District. The students (called John Doe and Jack Smith in the decision) had been expelled for different reasons:

Student Doe had been placed in a developmental center for handicapped students. While attending school, he assaulted another student and broke a window. When he admitted these offenses to the principal he was suspended for five days. The principal referred the matter to the school's student placement committee with the recommendation that Doe be expelled. The suspension was continued indefinitely as permitted by California state law, which allowed suspensions to extend beyond five days while expulsion proceedings were being held.

Student Smith's individualized education program (IEP) stated he was to be placed in a special education program in a regular school setting on a trial basis. Following several incidences of misbehavior the school unilaterally reduced his program to half-day. His grandparents agreed to the reduction; however, the school district did not notify them of their right to appeal. A month later Smith was suspended for five days when he made inappropriate sexual comments to female students. In accordance with California law Smith's suspension was also continued indefinitely while expulsion proceedings were initiated by the school placement committee. (Yell, in press)

The case went through several levels of courts, eventually ending up in the Supreme Court. Justice William Brennan, writing for the majority, stated that schools cannot unilaterally exclude disabled students. When placement is being debated, the child must remain in the current educational setting unless school officials and parents agree otherwise. The decision left a number of questions unanswered (Yell, in press): In what ways can handicapped students be disciplined? How should the schools deal with students who are a danger to themselves or others but whose parents do not consent to removal?

Checkpoint	■ *Litigation following enactment of Public Law 94–142 has centered on abuses in testing for placement purposes and unfair practices in special education.*
	■ *In five recent cases, the U.S. Supreme Court has tried to refine the definitions of* appropriate education *and* related services, *has dealt with parents' recovery of private school tuition and attorney's fees, and has addressed the placement of exceptional students pending evaluation.*

THE ROLE OF PARENTS

Parents have been the primary movers in obtaining civil rights for exceptional students. Much of the legislation and most of the court rulings that have changed the practices of special education are a product of parents' working to redress problems with the education their children were receiving. Parents have banded together to form advocacy groups, acting on behalf of students who are handicapped.

In recognition of the role parents have played in shaping special education, they have become an integral part of the process, sharing with other team members in making decisions about their children's learning.

WHAT WE THINK ABOUT THE LEGAL BASIS FOR SPECIAL EDUCATION

The U.S. Constitution was written to protect the citizens of this country. It describes broad rights that must be upheld by the laws of the country. Administrative regulations and guidelines take the general directives in those laws and refine them. Further refinement comes through the state and federal courts, in the process of interpreting the laws.

Constitutional provisions, legislation, administrative rules, and litigation have had tremendous impact on the field of special education. Much of current practice in the field has been shaped by them. This means that the changes we see today in special education are less a product of new teaching techniques and new research findings and new technologies than of new laws or interpretations of those laws.

What effect does this legal basis for special education have on those who work with exceptional students? As a practical matter, most of the changes have meant extra work for special educators—keeping detailed records, filling out forms, meeting with other team members. Then there's the legal responsibility that has attached itself not only to school districts and schools, but also to educators.

But think for a minute about the lawmaking process. That process draws on all kinds of information and opinion in the drafting of new legislation. Here, new teaching techniques and research findings and technologies are examined. Here, parents and educators and psychologists are heard. The end product tends to find a balance between what has come before and what is possible, dished up with a healthy portion of common sense and common decency. And that product—the laws that shape special education—has immeasurably improved the delivery of special services to exceptional students.

Summary

1. Federal and state legislation in America determine who goes to school, where schooling takes place, how long students must attend school, and what services are provided by the schools.

2. Constitutional provisions offer broad principles; laws apply those principles to specific cases; and regulations and guidelines define the ways in which laws are implemented. Court rulings interpret laws. And professional standards and ethics describe the behavior of those working in a field. All of these elements have had an impact on special education.

3. Program laws make funds available to a program; the failure to comply with those laws can mean the loss of funding. Civil rights laws are not linked to funding; the failure to comply with them can mean legal action.

4. Section 504 of the Rehabilitation Act of 1973 prohibits discrimination based solely on an individual's handicap and mandates access to publicly funded programs and activities for those with handicaps.

5. Specific provisions in Public Law 94–142 mandate individualized education programs, due process, protection in evaluation procedures, and the least restrictive environment for students with handicaps.

6. Public Law 99–457 extends the rights and protections of Public Law 94–142 to handicapped youngsters from ages 3 to 5, and establishes early intervention programs for infants and toddlers with handicaps.

7. The individualized family service plan—a provision of early intervention programs—functions much like an IEP but includes a description of the family's needs and services as well as those of the child.

8. Court decisions that influenced passage of Public Law 94–142 supported the individual's right to a free, appropriate education and created guidelines for the state to follow in educating students.

9. Since the enactment of Public Law 94–142, court cases have focused on the procedures by which schools assess and make placement decisions about exceptional students.

10. Parents—acting as their children's advocates—have been a driving force for change in special education. And today, they are a part of the special education team, participating in the decision-making process.

Activities

1. Obtain a copy of Public Law 94–142 and read it. Make a list of the things school personnel must do in order to comply with the law.

2. Go to your library and locate a summary of one of the cases listed in Table 2.2. Write a report in which you list the plaintiffs, the defendants, and the nature of the complaint, then describe the arguments made by each side and the court's decision.

3. Contact your state department of education or an administrator in your local school district. Ask for a copy of the guidelines for provision of services to infants and toddlers with handicaps. Discuss in class the ways in which this legislation will affect teacher training.

Suggested Readings

Abeson, A., & Zettel, J. (1977). The end of the quiet revolution: The Education for All Handicapped Children Act of 1975. *Exceptional Children, 44*, 115–128.
> *A review of the major factors leading up to passage of Public Law 94–142. The authors also cover the main provisions of the act.*

Ballard, J., & Zettel, J. (1977). Public Law 94–142 and Section 504: What they say about rights and protections. *Exceptional Children, 44*, 177–185.
> *A review of the similarities and differences between two major pieces of legislation that affect students with handicaps.*

Bersoff, D. (1979). Regarding psychologists testily: Legal regulation of psychological assessment in the public schools. *Maryland Law Review, 39*, 27–120.
> *A review of major legislation and litigation affecting the testing practices of psychologists.*

Exceptional Children, 52 (1986).
> *This entire issue is devoted to litigation and special education. Leading special educators describe and interpret the findings in* Frederick L. *v.* Thomas, Lora *v.* New York City Board of Education, Larry P. *v.* Riles, Board of Education *v.* Rowley, Irving Independent School District *v.* Tatro, *and* Smith *v.* Robinson.

Smith, B. (Ed.). (1988). *Mapping the future for children with special needs: PL 99–457.* Iowa City, IA: University of Iowa.
> *A comprehensive description of P.L. 99–457, and a look at implications of this legislation for delivery of appropriate educational services to infants, toddlers, and preschool children who are handicapped.*

Yell, M. 1989. *Honig* v. *Doe:* The suspension and expulsion of handicapped students. *Exceptional Children, 56*, 60–69.
> *Procedures for disciplining students who are handicapped are not addressed in P.L. 94–142. Yell describes the recent Supreme Court ruling in* Honig v. Doe, *and in doing so describes the role of educators in the suspension and expulsion of students who are handicapped. He also offers recommendations for school district policies on discipline.*

sequence ditto.
you received three presents
three boxes.
What would you like to find in them?
Draw a picture showing what you would
like to find and what you would do with
them.
Write a sentence to tell about the
picture.
Stuffed animal

two

Exceptional Students

Categories of exceptionality are the central features of most federal, state, and local special education programs. In developing opinions about this system of delivering services, it is important to consider the bases for exceptionality and the views people who are exceptional have about themselves as well as the views others have about exceptional children. Information about the categories of special education is also important in learning about special education.

In Chapter 3, we discuss statistical, medical, and social standards for defining normality and exceptionality. We also talk about factors that influence reactions to exceptionality and views people hold about what it means to be exceptional. In Chapters 4, 5, and 6, we describe the categories of exceptionality: high-prevalence categories (learning disabilities, giftedness and talent, and speech and language problems), moderate-prevalence categories (mental retardation and emotional disturbance), and low-prevalence categories (orthopedic handicaps and other health impairments, multihandicaps, hearing impairments, and visual impairments).

3

Perspectives
on Exceptionality

FOCUSING QUESTIONS

■   What standards do special educators use to define normality?

■   What factors influence our reactions to exceptionality?

■   What are the advantages and disadvantages of labeling exceptional students?

■   What is the relationship between expectations and behavior?

■   How do expectations and attributions affect the performance of exceptional students?

■   What are the special challenges faced by the parents of exceptional children?

■   What is the special responsibility of those who teach exceptional students?

MOST PEOPLE HAVE STANDARDS ON WHICH THEY make judgments about others. These standards are based on experience and often change, depending on specific circumstances. Studying how people define normality helps us understand the foundations of special education because definitions of normality serve as the basis for judgments about whether someone is exceptional and what it means to be exceptional.

Special education exists because there are individual differences in the ways students perform the wide variety of tasks necessary to function from day to day in school. The decision whether a student requires special education is based in good part on the ways in which the student is different from his or her classmates. We recognize the need for making these decisions, but we want them to be made carefully because we have seen the profound effects they can have on people's lives.

In this chapter, we focus on the factors that influence our perceptions of normality and exceptionality. We also consider the ways in which people react to exceptionality in others as well as how exceptional individuals feel about those reactions. Our objective here is twofold: to help you form a personal point of view on exceptionality and understand the impact that point of view can have on exceptional students.

DEFINING NORMALITY AND ABNORMALITY

Would you consider people with blond hair less intelligent than people with brown or black hair? Would you use the word *abnormal* to describe

Normality is a relative concept: We make judgments about what is normal based on perceptions and past experiences and tempered by the situation.

(© Laima Druskis/ Jeroboam)

someone who prefers milk in his coffee? Is it abnormal to wash your hands twenty-five times a day? Is it normal to refrain from eating for five days or to laugh during a religious ceremony? Behaviors or characteristics, in and of themselves, are neither normal nor exceptional. They generate actions or reactions by others who judge them to be so.

Normality is a relative concept: It depends not only on our perception of normal, but also on the circumstances. Our perceptions are formed through experiences, and our judgments are based on those perceptions tempered by the situation.

Normality, then, is not an absolute. A person is considered normal in our society or in school as long as he or she behaves in ways that the majority of others do or in ways that parents, teachers, or principals think of as normal.

The decisions we make about exceptional people before, during, and after school are based in large measure on what we know about normal development. For example, by the age of 3, most children have been toilet trained, their attention spans have developed enough to listen to stories, and they use their vocabularies of about 200 words to carry on conversations. By 4, most children are running, jumping, and riding tricycles, and have the fine motor skills to cut with scissors, do puzzles, and make things. Youngsters this age also are beginning to understand the concept of numbers. By the time they enter first grade, most children have started to learn from books and to play for long periods of time with their peers. Well-developed speech and language skills mark the early school years. By the end of fourth grade, most youngsters can read, write, do math, and solve problems proficiently. By the time they enter middle or junior high school, their independent learning skills are developed and many of the social skills they will have as adults are in place.

Parents and teachers and other professionals use their knowledge of normal developmental phases to make decisions about the special learning needs of students. A two-year-old who is beginning to use a few words to get what he wants is normal; a two-year-old who speaks in full sentences is exceptional. What about a fourth-grader who is not reading fluently? Normal or abnormal? It depends. Most of us would agree that the behavior is not normal. But if the child just moved to this country and does not speak English as a first language, the behavior might very well be normal. Or if the child experienced a series of traumatic events in earlier grades, again the behavior might be normal. Our judgment of a behavior, then, depends not only on the behavior, but also on the circumstances in which we find it.

As professionals refine their definitions of normality, they often assign names to behaviors that are not normal. In special education, these names are categories of exceptionality. Although some characteristics overlap, each category represents a discrete cluster of symptoms. Special educators use both conceptual definitions and operational criteria to define categories of exceptionality. **Conceptual definitions** are the generally agreed-on ideas that shape a category. For example, the most common conceptual definition of mental retardation is "significantly subaverage general intellectual functioning existing concurrently with deficits in adaptive behavior and manifested during the developmental period" (Grossman, 1973, p. 1). It tells us that people who score poorly on intelligence tests and who do not adapt well in society may be mentally retarded. **Operational criteria** are the standards we use to make judgments about an exceptional behavior. The operational criteria for mental retardation specify the levels of subaverage intellectual functioning (that is, specific IQ scores) and the levels of deficits in adaptive behavior that should be used to identify individuals who are mentally retarded.

The operational criteria used with any conceptual definition should be both universal and specific: All individuals who meet the definition should be included in it, and the definition should apply to one specific group of individuals. For example, if an IQ score of 90 to 110 is considered normal, then the intelligence of all individuals with IQ scores in this range is considered normal. If the intelligence of some individuals with IQ scores of 98 is not considered normal, then the criterion is not being applied universally. And if the intelligence of some individuals with IQ scores of 89 is

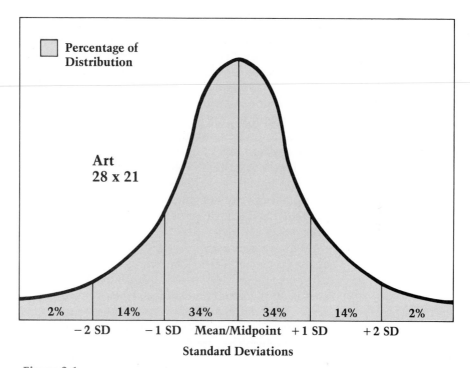

Figure 3.1
Normal Curve

considered normal, then the criterion is not being applied specifically, to this group. In special education, determining whether a student is eligible for special education services can be confusing when the criteria used in the identification process are not applied universally and specifically.

Decisions about normality rest on evaluations of the extent to which individual differences vary from accepted standards. These standards, which we use as operational criteria in the decision-making process, are based on statistical, medical, and social norms. In some cases, research data support the decision. Many times, physical or medical information provides a basis for evaluating skills, characteristics, and behaviors. And decisions about normality also are made using conventional wisdom, public opinion, and other socially accepted standards, values, and norms.

Statistical Standards

Statistics track performance, giving us information we need to distinguish between exceptionality and normality. Many human behaviors and characteristics fall into a pattern of distribution that forms a bell shape (Figure 3.1). This symmetrical distribution is called the *normal curve*.

The shape of the normal curve is exactly the same on either side of its midpoint, so we can predict the area between points on the curve. The midpoint is the mean (arithmetic average) of the curve. The degree to which occurrence of a behavior or characteristic differs from the mean is expressed in standard deviation (SD) units, each of which contains a fixed percentage of cases above and below the mean.

For example, the scores of high school students on the College Board examinations are normally distributed. The average score is 500: Half the students score higher than 500 and half score lower. If the standard deviation for these scores is 100, then 68 percent of the scores will be between 1 standard deviation below the mean and 1 standard deviation above the mean, or between 400 and 600. This information helps us interpret a student's score. It also helps us predict how a population of students will do on the tests.

The normal curve gives us a numerical basis for making decisions about the probability of something—a behavior or characteristic—happening. Special educators use these standards in defining exceptionality, focusing on the small percentage of cases at either side of the curve. For example, the definition of *mental retardation* is based on the idea that intelligence is normally distributed in the general population. In this context, IQ scores that are 2 standard deviations below the average on intelligence tests are used to identify students who are retarded. Giftedness also is defined in terms of performance on intelligence tests. Here scores 2 standard deviations above the mean indicate exceptionality.

Medical Standards

In medicine, normality means the presence of normal signs or the absence of disease symptoms. The medical standard for normal human body temperature is 98.6 degrees. It was arrived at by evaluating many "healthy" people. Temperatures above or below that point are one indicator of illness. In the same way, doctors use blood tests to check for abnormal levels of body chemicals, the symptoms of certain diseases or health problems. And standards in blood pressure, respiration rate, and pulse rate are used to determine physical well-being.

Genetic abnormalities, prenatal problems, infections, physical trauma, all can cause special learning needs. You probably remember from high school biology that normal cells contain forty-six chromosomes. Any deviation from this standard number produces physical and biological abnormalities. More than one hundred genetic disorders have been identified. One of them, **Down syndrome**, causes retardation. Most people with the condition have forty-seven chromosomes instead of forty-six. Postnatal German measles, encephalitis, and other infectious diseases also can cause retardation if they occur during critical periods of development.

Anoxia (insufficient oxygen to the fetus during the birth process) destroys brain cells, producing cerebral palsy, mental retardation, or other exceptional conditions. Malnutrition and lead paint poisoning are physical traumas that increase the risk of mental retardation.

Family medical history also can be helpful in the diagnosis of a handicapping condition. Some conditions tend to occur more frequently within families. For example, the risk of schizophrenia in the general population is about one in one hundred; it is eight times higher in siblings and forty-four times higher in identical twins. The mother's age at the birth of the child is another important factor. More than 50 percent of children with Down syndrome are born to mothers over age 35.

Medical standards give us a benchmark against which to gauge exceptionality. The logic of using these standards to determine who or what is exceptional is appealing. Specific symptoms appear to be associated with specific problems. But most exceptional students are identified through other means.

Social Standards

Sociologists, psychologists, anthropologists, and educators often define normality in terms of a society's or subculture's code of behavior. Certain behaviors are expected as part of "normal" schooling. Many of these behaviors are written down or otherwise made clear in the form of *explicit rules.* But schools also operate with a set of *implied rules,* rules that are unwritten but that students must conform to no less than to explicit rules. For example, students are expected to demonstrate competence in basic skills (reading, writing, math) by the end of the third grade. Not being able to read, write, or compute to accepted or adopted standards is a form of exceptional behavior, as is performing above those standards.

Research has found high rates of mental illness in inner-city areas. This finding has led some to conclude that community attitudes and standards play a part in how we define normality. Others believe that abnormal behaviors are learned by associating with people who have abnormal lifestyles. Certainly what we know about the person being judged influences at least our initial reaction to that individual's behavior. We expect the younger brothers and sisters of a legendary class clown to act up in class, and we expect the siblings of a gifted student to do well.

Teachers play an important role in defining exceptionality, both in terms of their expectations for students and in terms of their difficulty handling specific behaviors. Because teachers are individuals and because they are working with individual students, we can't say with certainty how they will respond to their exceptional students. But we do know that in the course of elementary school, 50 to 60 percent of students are perceived to have behavior problems by at least one teacher. We also know that boys are

Teacher-pleasing behaviors such as compliance and self-control are less likely to be displayed by boys, who tend to be aggressive, noncompliant, and active—behaviors that some teachers have problems handling.
(© Michael Weisbrot and Family)

less likely to show teacher-pleasing behaviors (self-control, being prepared for class, complying with teachers' requests); instead, they tend to be aggressive, noncompliant, and active—behaviors that teachers are more likely to have problems handling.

Of all the standards used to judge normality, social standards are the most subjective. For example, some teachers believe students should be quiet during school; and others believe students should actively communicate about their assignments and work together on them. You may recall the confusion created by two teachers with different expectations in your own school career. Regardless of the basis used to decide if someone is normal or exceptional, the reactions others have to the person being judged are central to developing a perspective on exceptionality.

Checkpoint

- *Studying how people define normality helps us understand the foundations of special education because definitions of normality serve as the basis for judging whether a student is exceptional.*

- *A person is considered normal as long as he or she behaves in ways that the majority of others do or in ways that parents, teachers, or principals believe are normal.*

- *Special educators use conceptual definitions and operational criteria to define categories of exceptionality.*

- *Numbers and other mathematical data often are used to support the decisions made about exceptional students.*

- *Medical information is another basis for judging the normality of skills, characteristics, and behaviors.*

> ■ *Codes of behavior, community standards, and teachers' expectations and values play an important role in determining the nature of students' behavior.*

REACTIONS TO EXCEPTIONALITY

How do you react to people who are exceptional? Do you look away from the woman in a wheelchair? Do you speak loudly to the blind man who asks you for directions on campus? Are you surprised when your friend who's brilliant in math misspells a word? It's not unusual to be embarrassed by a handicapping condition, to assume that one sensory impairment means another, or to expect that being gifted and talented extends to all aspects of life. The problem is that these typical reactions to exceptionality have enormous impact on the behaviors of those who are exceptional. They force them to deal, not only with the exceptional condition itself, but also with what the condition means to others.

Our reactions to exceptionality—our own or that of others—is influenced by four factors: the nature of the exceptionality, its cause, the label assigned to it, and the environment in which it occurs.

The Nature of the Exceptionality

All of us respond in different ways to the things around us. Certain things are more important to some of us than others. For some, a defeat on the basketball court may be just another loss; for others, it may be a critical casualty in a Cinderella season. We react to exceptional conditions in much the same way. Some of us are uncomfortable with those who have a physical disability; others are put off, not by physical impairments, but by mental or emotional ones. And some have difficulty interacting with those whose handicaps are pronounced.

Because exceptional people are all unique individuals, it makes no sense to tell you how to act around them. And because you are a unique individual, it makes it difficult for us to predict how exceptional people will interact with you. But we can tell you one thing: Although exceptional people are different in some ways, they are more like you than not. It is important to understand the differences and to respond to them matter-of-factly; it is more important to recognize the similarities, to treat those with exceptionalities as you would any person.

RECENTLY, I CAME ACROSS a newspaper article about Stephen Hawking, the well-known astrophysicist who has ALS, or Lou Gehrig's disease. He is severely disabled. Physically, that is. He commented that he was lucky to have chosen a career that is primarily mental work, that he had a wonderfully supportive wife and family, and that his colleagues have been unfailingly helpful. "Fortunately," he said, "my disability hasn't been a serious handicap."

My guess is that, at some point in our lives each of us has wondered about what it means to be disabled. Maybe we have a friend who had polio, or a neighbor who has a child with a hearing loss, or a high school classmate who was injured in Vietnam, or a cousin who has cerebral palsy, or an officemate whose new baby was born with spina bifida.

Perhaps we have noticed the feelings that come up for us when we are with someone with a disability—when we walk past a woman putting her wheelchair in the backseat of her car, when we enter an elevator where several deaf adults are involved in a sign language conversation, when we watch the Special Olympics on TV, or when we check out at the corner market and the owner's son who has Down Syndrome carries out our bags.

Because we live in a society that has rigid standards for appearance and performance and that places a high value on independence, it is hard for us to imagine that the lives of persons with disabilities can be full and satisfying. In fact, in the literature on family adjustment to a child with disabilities, the most common framework for disability is that of a tragic event. Is it possible that there are other ways to think about what a disability means to an individual, to his or her family, and to society at large?

Let's start by considering the difference in meaning between the words disability and handicap. Traditionally, disability refers to an actual diagnosed medical condition, while handicap refers to the extent to which it impairs someone's functioning.

The degree to which a disability handicaps an individual depends on many factors. Hill (1949) provides a way to understand a crisis that is very helpful in explaining how the same disability can affect people in such different ways. He calls the model the ABCX Model. In this framework, A is the stressor event, B is the resources that an individual/ family have to bring to bear on the crisis, C is the personal meaning that the individual/family gives to the event, and X is the resulting level of crisis. Let's use Stephen Hawking's experience to see how this model applies.

A, the stressor event is ALS disease. Among the resources (B) he has to bring to bear on the situation are strong support from his family and his colleagues, the type of work he does, and his previous accomplishments and stature in the field. The personal meaning he gives the event (C) is, to paraphrase his wife, "Stephen doesn't give in to his disability and we don't give in to him." In other words, his interpretation of his condition is that it is one that can be handled. The resulting level of crisis (X) for this individual with ALS disease is mediated by the considerable resources he has, and by the personal meaning that he attributes to the disease ("I can handle this"). Another individual with the same condition who has fewer resources and/or who views the disability in a different way would have a very different outcome.

It is surprising to realize how influential the meaning that individuals give to their disability is to their ultimate functioning in the world. In fact, the rehabilitation literature suggests that the personal meaning assigned is the most powerful predictor of long-term adjustment to disability, more powerful even than the type of disability one has or the severity of the condition. Thus, how an individual feels about him/herself is one of the most important aspects in his/her adjustment to disability.

In looking at our own beliefs about disability, what has been our contact with persons who have physical or mental differences? What feelings do these experiences evoke in us? Can we learn to separate how we feel about a disability from the individual who has the condition? Are we willing to re-evaluate our views in light of what persons with disabilities have to teach us?

"The deaf are not ready yet to function in the hearing world" are words that forever changed Gallaudet College and caused a whole nation to re-examine its beliefs about persons with hearing impairments. Intuitively, all of us—lay persons and professionals in the field—understood the depth of the students' feelings and the correctness of their position. Perhaps it is the hearing world that has not been ready to live with persons who are different from ourselves. Are we ready to listen?

Adults with disabilities often say it is the attitudinal, rather than the architectural barriers that are the hardest to overcome. Now that P.L.

99-457 greatly expands the possibility of services for young disabled children and their families, it's time to take the next step: to re-examine our views of disability, to tackle the attitudinal barriers, and to develop a framework that empowers families to love their children unconditionally, and enables children to reach their fullest potential.

> Children can learn to live with a disability. But they cannot live well without the conviction that their parents find them utterly loveable. . . . If the parents, knowing about his (the child's) defect love him now, he can believe that others will love him in the future. With this conviction, he can live well today and have faith about the years to come. (Bettelheim, 1972)

What framework would empower children and families to have the conviction Bettelhiem speaks of? I posed this question to my friend Marsha Saxton, a counselor of persons with disabilities, an author (1987) about women's issues and disability, and an adult with a physical handicap. She said that such a new view would acknowledge that disability involves a loss of some capacity, that it is usually accompanied by some objective hardships, and that it is an equally valid, fully human lifestyle.

We know that a child's self-esteem develops both from within—the child's own sense of competence—and from without—the approval he receives from others. Because cultural beliefs affect how families feel, and how families feel affect children, we are compelled to look again at society's beliefs about disability—to look again within ourselves.

Source: *Linda Gilkerson, "A Fully Human Life," in* Family Resource Coalition Report, 2, *1988. Published by the Family Resource Coalition, 230 North Michigan Ave., Chicago, IL 60601, (312) 726–4750. Reprinted by permission.*

Our reaction to exceptionality—our own or that of others—is influenced by four factors: the nature of the exceptionality, its cause, the label assigned to it, and the environment in which it occurs.

(© Bob Daemmrich/ The Image Works)

The Cause of the Exceptionality

Infections, physical trauma, prenatal problems, genetic abnormalities, environmental problems, and many other factors can cause a handicapping condition. Often the cause of an exceptionality influences the way people respond to it. **Organic impairments**—physical problems that are out of the individual's control—seem more acceptable than **functional impairments**—problems that have no known cause but that appear to be controllable. For example, most of us do not mind being held up in traffic by a person crossing the street in a wheelchair; however, we react very differently to somebody who deliberately slows us down. And most of us are more willing to help a person who can't do something than a person who simply refuses to do it.

That our perceptions about the cause of an abnormal behavior influence our own behavior toward the person who exhibits the abnormal behavior was supported by at least one research project. In a psychological experiment, undergraduate students indicated they would give milder electric shocks to a person they believed was organically retarded than to a person they thought was normal or mentally ill (with no organic cause evident).

The Effect of Labels

Labels are cues that help organize our knowledge, perceptions, and behavior. They carry with them certain expectations—some good, some bad. These expectations can change the relationships between those who are labeled and those who are not.

Change comes here in three stages (Figure 3.2). In Stage 1, an individual exhibits a behavior and is labeled in some way on the basis of that behavior. In Stage 2, the reactions of those around the individual reflect the cues they pick up from the label. Again, these reactions carry with them certain expectations. In Stage 3, the individual responds to these expectations, often behaving in ways that fulfill them.

What is important here is that those around the labeled individual are responding to the label and the biases (for good or bad) that are part and parcel of the label, not to the individual. And the individual's behavior in the third stage is a response to those expectations and biases.

The effects of labels on exceptional students have received considerable attention (Table 3.1). In one analysis of studies in which the label *mentally retarded* was evaluated, MacMillan, Jones, and Aloia (1974) concluded that labeling does not have a detrimental effect. Guskin, Bartel, and MacMillan (1976) closed their discussion of the effects of labeling from the view of the labeled child by stating that there is no simple predictable consequence of labeling for the individual. Algozzine and Mercer (1980), in a review of the research, concluded that different kinds of effects have been shown in studies that manipulated various special education labels. In another book, we reported on research in which the label *mentally retarded* was examined, and concluded that labels are powerfully biasing stimuli (Ysseldyke & Algozzine, 1982).

Those who question the appropriateness of assigning labels to students do so on the basis of their beliefs that the students are treated differently after they are labeled. These opinions come from research that has illustrated that teachers expect students labeled mentally retarded to perform poorly in reading, writing, and mathematics, students labeled emotionally disturbed to be disruptive and difficult to teach, and students labeled learning disabled to perform poorly on a complex visual-motor task. Deciding whether labels are good or bad is difficult because research supports both opinions.

Table 3.1
Studies of the Effects of Labeling

Investigator	Label(s) Studied	Method of Investigation	Outcome
Foster & Ysseldyke (1976)	Learning disability (LD), emotional disturbance (ED), mental retardation (MR), normal	Hypothetical and videotaped presentations	More negative expectations for MR than LD or ED; however, all special categories were viewed less favorably than normal.
Severance & Gasstrom (1977)	Mentally retarded versus non–mentally retarded	Varied descriptions of a child's performance to show success or failure at a puzzle	Ability, effort, and level of task difficulty were perceived differently for labeled versus nonlabeled students.
Dembo, Yoshida, Reilly & Reilly (1978)	Educable mentally retarded versus educationally handicapped	Naturalistic study in which teacher-pupil classroom interactions were analyzed	No differential interaction patterns were evident within different types of special classes.
Sutherland & Algozzine (1979)	Learning disability versus normal	Experiment in which undergraduate students taught child labeled *learning disabled* or *normal*	Performance of normal fourth-grade children was affected by labels assigned before an instructional session.
Elliot & Argulewicz (1983)	Normal versus learning disabled	Ratings scale scores of labeled and nonlabeled students were compared for students in different ethnic groups	Differences were found in ethnicity but not as a function of label assigned to student.
Schloss & Schloss (1984)	Mentally retarded, deaf, normal	Asked employers about type and level of training they anticipated for different employees	More intrusive training was believed necessary for those who were labeled *retarded* than for normal or deaf individuals.
Goldsmith & Schloss (1986)	Deaf versus not handicapped	Case study presented to school psychologists for diagnosis and treatment recommendations	Diagnostic group overshadowed the decisions made by the psychologists.
Minner et al. (1987)	Learning disabled, physically handicapped	Case studies of labeled and nonlabeled students	Nonlabeled and "physically handicapped" students were placed in gifted programs more often than students labeled *learning disabled*.

Table 3.1 *(cont.)*
Studies of the Effects of Labeling

Investigator	Label(s) Studied	Method of Investigation	Outcome
Algozzine, Algozzine & Morsink (1988)	Educable mentally retarded, learning disabled, emotionally disturbed	Naturalistic study of classroom inter-actions	No differences were found in teacher behaviors as a function of categorical placement of student.

There are several studies that support the idea that labeling does not affect exceptional students or those who interact with them, but the findings in each case were blurred by the presence of behaviors or characteristics that contradicted the labels. For example, Gottlieb (1974) showed fourth-grade children a videotape of "classmates" labeled *mentally retarded* or *normal,* and concluded that the labels did not affect the children. But the tape also showed "competent" and "incompetent" behavior. It is not clear, then, that the labels had no effect; more likely the students were influenced more by degrees of competence than by the labels. Aloia (1975) found that undergraduate students learning to be teachers were not influenced by labels. But here, the influence of physical signs may have masked the effect of the labels. Yoshida and Meyers (1975) gave teachers a videotape in which a child's performance improved over four sets of trials. The teachers were told that they were participating in a teacher judgment experiment and were asked to predict how the child would perform in the future. An analysis of the results indicated that the teachers saw an improvement in performance and that no labeling effects were present. Of course, in light of the improved performance, the label *mentally retarded* may have been less believable.

These studies do not tell us that labels have no effect on exceptional students and those around them. But they do indicate that a hierarchy of influence is operating in some cases, that at times students' competence or physical characteristics seem to have more influence than the names we give to their conditions.

Despite the effects labeling can have on exceptional students, state agencies often require it and many professionals believe it is necessary to obtain funding for special programs. There is some evidence that the availability of funds may be the source of labeling, not the result of it. Nelson (1983) used financial, demographic, and socioeconomic data to investigate the relationship between labeling students and providing programs. The availability of financial resources led to labeling more students as handicapped.

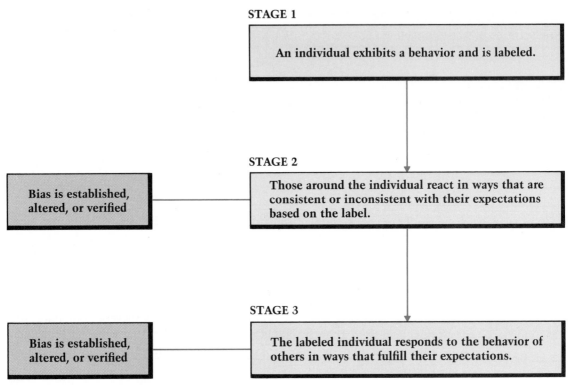

Figure 3.2
The Effects of Labels on Interpersonal Relationships

Deciding whether the effects of labeling students are positive or negative is not easy. There are many factors at work here (Table 3.2). Certainly exceptional students need special services. If the educational system requires that these students be labeled before they can receive those services, then we understand why people are labeled. But if the students, their parents, their peers, and their teachers act differently because they are labeled, then we understand why people don't want to be labeled and why others don't want to label them.

The Context in Which Exceptionality Occurs

Predicting reactions to specific behaviors (or physical characteristics) is not a simple task. Similar behaviors evoke both similar and different reactions. For example, the extent to which disruptive behavior is tolerated by teachers varies widely. Students who are outspoken in class may be encouraged, tolerated, or punished by different teachers. Moreover, teachers'

Table 3.2
The Pros and Cons of Labeling

Advantages	Disadvantages
Being labeled creates a basis for people to be more compassionate to one another.	Being labeled creates a basis for a poor self-concept and dependent behavior.
Labels make it easier for professionals to communicate.	Labels reduce professionals' expectations of what a person can do.
Being labeled creates special funding opportunities.	Being labeled uses money that could be spent on other services.
Labels give the special needs of exceptional people greater visibility.	Labels hurt the exceptional person's chances of being treated normally.
Being labeled creates opportunities for special treatment.	Being labeled reduces opportunities for normal school experiences.
Being labeled focuses attention on people's special strengths, on what they can do.	Being labeled focuses attention on people's general weaknesses, on what they cannot do.

responses are likely to depend on the particular type of disruptive behavior under consideration. Some teachers may permit students to speak out in class, but they have difficulty coping with students who are withdrawn and uncomfortable participating in class discussions. Other teachers may prefer their students to behave quietly and to listen attentively—they can't handle aggressive, candid students. When it comes to interpersonal interactions, making meaningful predictions about what will happen when we do something differently than others would like us to do is very difficult. Goffman (1963) described the importance of context this way:

> It is possible for signs which mean one thing to one group to mean something else to another group, the same category being designated but differently characterized. For example, the shoulder patches that prison officials require escape-prone prisoners to wear can come to mean one thing to guards, in general negative, while being a mark of pride for the wearer relative to his fellow prisoners. (p. 46)

Teachers respond differently to certain features of their students; they handle different behaviors in different ways. An understanding of the role context plays in our reactions to exceptional students is critically important to our definition of what it means to be exceptional.

Checkpoint   ■   *Our reactions to exceptionality are influenced by the nature of the condition, its cause, the label we assign to it, and the context in which it occurs.*

*Point
of
View*

MILO AND TOCK WALKED up to the door, whose brass name plate read simply "THE GIANT," and knocked.

"Good afternoon," said the perfectly ordinary-sized man who answered the door.

"Are you the giant?" asked Tock doubtfully.

"To be sure," he replied proudly. "I'm the smallest giant in the world. What can I do for you?"

"Are we lost?" said Milo.

"That's a difficult question," said the giant. "Why don't you go around back and ask the midget?" And he closed the door.

They walked to the rear of the house, which looked exactly like the front, and knocked at the door, whose name plate read "THE MIDGET."

"How are you?" inquired the man, who looked exactly like the giant.

"Are you the midget?" asked Tock again, with a hint of uncertainty in his voice.

"Unquestionably," he answered. "I'm the tallest midget in the world. May I help you?"

"Do you think we're lost?" repeated Milo.

"That's a very complicated problem," he said. "Why don't you go around to the side and ask the fat man?" And he, too, quickly disappeared.

The side of the house looked very like the front and back, and the door flew open the very instant they knocked.

"How nice of you to come by," exclaimed the man, who could have been the midget's twin brother.

"You must be the fat man," said Tock, learning not to count too much on appearance.

"The thinnest one in the world," he replied brightly; "but if you have any questions, I suggest you try the thin man, on the other side of the house."

Just as they suspected, the other side of the house looked the same as the front, the back, and the side, and the door was again answered by a man who looked precisely like the other three.

"What a pleasant surprise!" he cried happily. "I haven't had a visitor in as long as I can remember."

"How long is that?" asked Milo.

"I'm sure I don't know," he replied. "Now pardon me; I have to answer the door."

"But you just did," said Tock.

"Oh yes, I'd forgotten."

"Are you the fattest thin man in the world?" asked Tock.

"Do you know one that's fatter?" he asked impatiently.

"I think you're all the same man," said Milo emphatically.

"S-S-S-S-S-H-H-H-H-H-H-," he cautioned, putting his finger up to his lips and drawing Milo closer. "Do you want to ruin everything? You see, to tall men I'm a midget, and to short men I'm a giant; to the skinny ones I'm a fat man, and to the fat ones I'm a thin man. That way I can hold four jobs at once. As you can see, though, I'm neither tall nor short nor fat nor thin. In fact, I'm quite ordinary, but there are so many ordinary men that no one asks their opinion about anything. Now what is your question?"

Source: *From pp. 110–114 of* The Phantom Tollbooth. *Copyright © 1961 by Norton Juster. Reprinted by permission of Random House, Inc., and Wm. Collins Sons & Co., Ltd.*

The behavior and needs of exceptional people often are a function of how they are perceived by themselves and others.
(© Don Hogan Charles/NYT Pictures)

■ *Although labels may be a necessary first step in receiving special education services, they affect the behavior of exceptional students and those around them.*

■ *We cannot predict teachers' reactions to specific behaviors or physical characteristics because their tolerance varies.*

PERCEIVING EXCEPTIONALITY

Being exceptional means many different things. Not all exceptional people are alike, and few are treated the same way. Often their behavior and needs are a function of how they are perceived by themselves and others.

Expectations

At times, all of us have had difficulty measuring up to standards we set for ourselves or that were set for us by others. Exceptional people also have to deal with expectations, but the difficulties they face are sometimes tougher to overcome. An **expectation** is simply a prediction about an event or action. Expectations give us a framework in which to organize our experiences. Our experiences help us form expectations for our own behavior and

WHEN I WAS IN COLLEGE, Paul, a grad student, was writing a paper. He asked me, "How do you think blindness will affect your employability?"

"I suppose it has to be a factor, " I said. "But if I am good enough, it shouldn't matter all that much."

The following year, a grad student myself, I found Paul's notes. He had interviewed every blind student on the campus and without exception, without experience, we had made similar responses to his questions. There was a file card for each of us. The last one with Paul's name bore a single line of braille: "It's shit to be blind."

Because I had never looked at it that way, because that was in a world before I had children or wrote computer programs that blow up, the use of the strong language startled me profoundly. The thought—the idea—was new. I considered deeply for six weeks what Paul in his supposed privacy had written, and at length decided that he was right.

In his book, *Blindness: What It Is and How to Live with It*, Father Richard Carroll defines the greatest areas of lack for a newly blinded individual as communication and mobility, and it is, I think, valid to say that for a congenitally blinded person this is also true.

Most blind people talk too loud because they can't see the person they are talking to and can't tell if he is hearing them. Their facial expressions are at best not communicative and sometimes downright misleading. (My daughter sometimes asks why I look so sad.) Even though they usually speak clearly, blind people don't move their mouths a lot when they talk. It is almost impossible for a deaf person to lipread a blind person.

The idea that I was to look at the eyes of someone speaking with me was at first bizarre, and I still forget to do it much of the time. It seems natural to me to direct my eyes toward the place where the sound is coming from, the mouth, rather than some indefinite place above the sound. Knowing if someone is talking to you is a problem that goes both ways. The blind person doesn't know, and the sighted person doesn't know if the blind person knows. Sighted persons do not use names when speaking to people and do not speak when they enter a room. They stand by a blind person and expect to be recognized or ask a direct question to one person in a group and don't realize that the blind person won't know to whom the question is addressed.

A blind kid doesn't know that he must not pick his nose in public, or pull his hangnails until they bleed, or scratch himself or even touch himself in some places, or inform himself about other people and things by touching or sniffing them. If parents of a blind child intend him to live a normal life, it is absolutely imperative that they define for him which actions are and which are not socially correct, and that they constantly evaluate his behavior for him. If the child ever hopes to be "one of the guys," he absolutely must learn how important it is for him to appear as much like them as he possibly can.

The world is made of, by, and for people who can see. When shopping, a blind person cannot select a peach or find the notepaper. A kid cannot go buy soda or candy, and a teenager can just forget about sneaking cigarettes or beer from his parents. He can't operate a candybar or a soda machine. No way he can go independently through the line at the cafeteria or graciously pour a friend a glass of water. Eating is difficult and keeping food from sliding off the edge of a plate or off a fork is sometimes impossible. If I didn't enjoy it so much, I would forego the hassle altogether.

Crossing streets is an extremely stressful necessity. You go forward when the traffic beside you goes forward. Sometimes cars move forward prior to doing a right turn on red. Often the up curb is a different height from the down curb; sometimes one or both curbs are not there at all. Unlike sighted people, blind people must not cross against the light. Cars are often silent, and more often swift. Learning to hold your temper when sighted people take you across the street is another problem. I've been pushed across streets that I did not want to cross. I've been told, "I will help you," (unasked) and had my cane hand grasped thereby rendering the cane useless for me because it didn't touch the ground. Short of being truly rude (and next time I might really need the help), there is nothing to do but try to accept as help what is meant to be help, instead of responding to the indignity as it is.

Like the sighted traveler in a blizzard, the blind person wishing to move from one place to another is woefully short of information about his surroundings. He may be walking north, seeking south, wandering in the proverbial circle, or standing perfectly still three feet from his objective—a miss being as good as a mile. The skills necessary for independent travel are not easily developed. The blind child must learn how to trip but not fall, to listen for cars and people and bicycles, to get lost and retrace his path exactly until he is back to familiar territory, to be always attentive not only to where he is going but also to where he has been. Experience—the more, the better—will teach him. Before I went to kindergarten, I walked alone

the two blocks to the store. At eight I walked the mile to my girlfriend's house to play. Last month I missed the bus and had to carry my 6-month-old baby the two miles to the doctor for her routine checkup. It wasn't fun, but we arrived safely and no one at the office knew there had been a problem.

It is important to me to be self-reliant. The person who arouses another's pity is not, after all, the person who arouses another's respect—and I choose to be respected. The person who is cared for is not the one who is given responsibility—and I choose to be responsible. For the handicapped person as well as the nonhandicapped person, life is a continuum of choices—to choose to be pleased with a gift, to choose to do the difficult task, to choose not to be offended. Learning to make the right choices begins in infancy. The choice that is "natural" is usually the easy choice instead of the best choice. It is the parent who stands between the child—any child—and inability. It is the parent who must make the right choices and accept responsibility for the pain they cause. The demand on parents is especially great when the child is handicapped. Wishing to offer only that which gives joy, they work to spare him not only those hurts his handicap might cause, but also those that a normal child would meet, robbing him not only of childhood, but of a self-reliant adulthood as well. The good parent never says, "You can't do that because you are blind." He says, maybe, "Be careful."

It is difficult, almost impossible, to view oneself as a useful, contributing human being when society as a whole is so sure you are inept. You fight the little battles—the cop-out battles—constantly (to sew on a button, to pay your bills on time, to

(continued)

jump rope or run or ice skate or ride a bike or win at Trivial Pursuit or dress like the other guys), but these are small compared to the real battle, the one for self-esteem. Honestly, I am not physically as good as a sighted person. Honestly, my baby is not as potentially safe in my care as in the care of someone who can see. Honestly, I can't drive my children to parties, choose their clothes, judge the length of their hair, evaluate their handwriting. I can't even go to the grocery store without help. Do I feel sorry for myself? Nobody does it better. But defining the problem is the first step toward solving it, and one can use self-pity as an aid to definition. I don't recommend it, but handicapped people aren't saints—they're just people with handicaps—and everybody feels

sorry for himself sometimes. Knowing I am inferior and trying to face it with patience and courage is a constant, wearying task. I try harder—always— than the other guy, because to appear equal I must be better. I don't (usually) blame someone or something else when things go wrong, because when you blame outside sources for a problem, the solution is out of your hands.

Paul was right, of course: being blind is no picnic, not even remotely fun sometimes, absolutely not something a person can "overcome" or "compensate for." But I can live with it, can even respect myself for having the courage to live with it, and most of the time—only most of the time—believe that the world is a better place because I am here.

Source: *From a selection by Ann Byrne in* The Parental Voice *(unpublished manuscript) by Robert Holzberg and Sara Walsh (eds.). Reprinted by permission.*

for that of others (Figure 3.3). How we've done something in the past shapes our expectations about how well we will do it in the future. If we've done well, we expect to do well; if we've done poorly, we usually expect to do poorly. Past performance and the expectations based on that performance also shape our current behavior. Most of us enjoy the things we do well, and most of us avoid the activities that we don't expect to do well.

Expectations also affect how others interpret our actions and how they treat us. If teachers want and expect students to speak out in class, they encourage that behavior; if they expect students to sit back and listen, they encourage that behavior.

Expectations and Performance

One of the earliest attempts to explain the relationship between expectations and performance was made by Julian B. Rotter (1954). Building on the work of Clark Hull, Edward L. Thorndike, and other psychologists, Rotter suggested that people act in certain ways because their actions lead

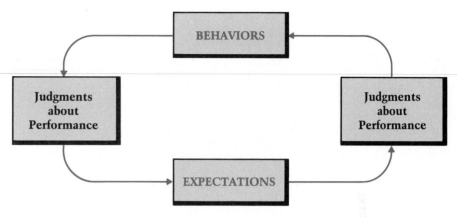

Figure 3.3
Expectations and Behaviors: The Cycle of Influence

to outcomes that are valued. He believed that expectations are powerful inducements for behavior.

Look at these test items:

1. In the figure below, if the average of the length of segments *xy* and *yz* is 1.5, what is the length of *yz*?

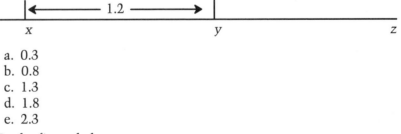

    a. 0.3
    b. 0.8
    c. 1.3
    d. 1.8
    e. 2.3

2. In the figure below, *x* + *y* =

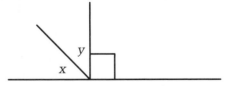

    a. 360 degrees.
    b. 180 degrees.
    c. 90 degrees.
    d. 150 degrees.
    e. 45 degrees.

3. If $1/2x + 2 = B$, then $2x + 2 =$
    a. $2B$.
    b. $2B - 2$.
    c. $4B$.
    d. $4B - 2$.
    e. $4B - 6$.

4. $$\frac{1}{1000} + \frac{3}{10} + \frac{5}{100} =$$

    a. 0.135.
    b. 0.153.
    c. 0.315.
    d. 0.351.
    e. 3.510.

5. If the sum of the positive integers x and y is 12, the value of x can equal all of the following except
    a. $5y$.
    b. $4y$.
    c. $3y$.
    d. $2y$.
    e. y.

How well do you think you could do them? How many could you complete in five minutes? Do you think you could do better if you had more time? Do you think you could do better with some practice? Your answers reflect your expectations, and those expectations are based on your experiences.

Expectations are general or specific. *General expectations* are based on experiences in similar situations; they are more global in nature than *specific expectations,* which relate primarily to experiences in particular situations. Many teachers base their expectations for how well their students will perform in different academic areas on class records. A teacher who expects a student who reads poorly to write poorly is demonstrating a generalized expectation. A teacher who believes that a student will do poorly in math because the student has done poorly in math before is demonstrating a specific expectation.

Like all of us, exceptional people hold expectations for themselves. Those expectations are based on past performance, but they also are influenced by the expectations of others. In the following quote, a man thought to be retarded describes his frustration with what others think about him.

> I don't believe that anyone from the hospital has it easy outside. There's problems from being in that place [the institution]. I mean with people you meet. They take me as if I'm not a smart person. That's what makes me so

provoked. And I mean they act like I don't understand things, which I do understand things. . . . Sometimes I'd rather be dead than have people act like I'm not a smart person. (Edgerton, 1967, p. 206)

This man believes that people respond, not to him, but to the institution where he has been. Their expectations of how he should act influence his behavior.

Attributions also are used to explain behavior. An **attribution** is the reason assigned to why somebody does something. Four common reasons are ability, effort, task difficulty, and luck. Ability and effort are *internal*, under the individual's control; task difficulty and luck are *external*, beyond the individual's control.

Attributions play an important role in self-image, in our definition of personal success and failure. We are more likely to improve at a task if we assign an external attribution (task difficulty, luck) to our failure to carry it out well in the past. In fact, this is characteristic of high achievers. Low achievers, on the other hand, tend to assign their failures to their ability or effort, and their successes to the nature of the task or luck. We find this same pattern among students with learning disabilities.

Our attributions, like our expectations, are shaped in part by the attributions others assign to our behavior. We recently observed several classes in Kim's school for one of our research projects. Ashley had been having trouble in math. The teacher returned a math quiz on which Ashley had earned a B+. At the top of the paper, she had written, "Gee, it must be your lucky day." In the same class, the teacher returned a perfect paper to Courtney with this comment: "This is a good job, Courtney. I guess it was too easy for you." Clearly, the teacher had her own expectations for Ashley and Courtney, and she attributed their performances to luck and her perception of the difficulty of the task. It's not hard to imagine the effect of her comments on these students. It's also not hard to imagine what the effect would have been if she had written "Gee, you must have worked hard to earn this B+, Ashley," or "This was a good job, Courtney; this was a difficult quiz, and you did it perfectly."

Expectations and attributions—our own and others—influence performance. Teachers have a special responsibility here to recognize the effect of their expectations and attributions on their students, and to encourage and reinforce positive behaviors through the feedback they give their students.

Expectations and Academic Performance

A number of factors have been shown to influence teachers' expectations of their students. For example, a student's appearance, race, gender, classroom behavior, even the achievements of older siblings affect teachers' expectations. And those expectations influence the ways in which teachers and pupils interact.

It's not surprising that category labels (*emotionally disturbed, learning disabled, blind, deaf, gifted*) play a part in shaping teachers' expectations of their students. Most of us believe that students who are gifted will do well on most tasks, and that students who are mentally retarded will do poorly. These beliefs and others like them affect students' personal expectations and, most important, their performance. Teachers' expectations become a *self-fulfilling prophecy*, influencing the students' own expectations and behaviors. This can be a good thing when teachers' expectations are high; but it can be very damaging when they are not.

The literature describes case after case of exceptional students who have been held back academically by the low expectations of others. Here are two of them:

> The . . . circumstances under which many deaf persons learned and began using sign language has had its impact on the language and on the level of linguistic sophistication of many sign language users. The signs themselves often tell a story about the frustrations of ineffective education. For example, one composite sign stands for "Too many big words." There are signs that indicate negative self-image, such as "dummy" and "pea-brain," and deaf people often apologize to hearing persons or to more educated deaf persons with comments such as "Me dummy—know nothing." (Becker & Jauregui, 1985, p. 27)

> Pat, who emigrated to this country from South America at age 9, said that most of her elementary and junior high school years were spent in special education courses that were far too easy. Comparing special education with mainstream classes, she said: "In ninth grade I had four special education classes. They were very, very easy. I told my mother I wanted out. Now that I'm in all mainstreamed classes, even homeroom, I don't think I'm favored because I'm disabled. I have to work for my grades. Some other disabled kids are passed along." (Asch, 1989, p. 188)

Expectations and Social Behaviors

We've been talking about the effect of expectations on the academic achievement of exceptional students. Expectations also have a strong influence on the social behaviors of those who are exceptional.

In his book *The Cloak of Competence* (1967), Edgerton described the life experiences of a group of people who had been released from a large institution. Although the book appeared over twenty years ago, we think much of what these people had to say still has relevance today. Throughout the book, for example, is evidence of the kind of "passing" that is part of the social behavior of many exceptional people.

I don't like to read. It hurts my eyes. I'd rather watch TV. (p. 131)

When I try to get a job they always ask me where I'm from. I don't tell no-body I'm from there [the hospital]—I say I'm just an outsider like anybody, but I've been working in the East. (p. 151)

You know old [another ex-patient]. He's always putting on. He went and got these books at the junk shop for ten cents a piece, and now he's got 'em all over his place like he was some kind of millionaire. Well, I went and got me some books too, real classy ones, I paid a dollar for some of 'em. Got all kinds, I think they look real nice. (p. 159)

The powerful impact of being exceptional is also illustrated in the words of a middle-aged mother of four children:

I never had an interpreter when I went to the hospital for my children's births. The first time I was really scared . . . I didn't know what was hap-pening. No one told me what to expect. Later on, when the kids were get-ting older, I struggled with writing notes back and forth to the kids' doctors and school counselors. It was a waste of time. I never understood what peo-ple were trying to tell me. . . . When a child was sick, I never knew just how serious it was, or what I could do if one of them was having trouble in school. I get angry just thinking about it. (Becker & Jauregui, 1985, p. 29)

Often those with handicaps avoid social contacts or use defensive cov-ering to reduce the likelihood of having to deal with other people socially. Some use a hostile bravado to protect themselves in social interactions.

Research into the social interactions, self-concept, peer acceptance, and general social communications skills of those with learning disa-bilities sheds some light on the difficulties these and other exceptional individuals experience in interpersonal relationships. For example, in conversations, they are more hostile and less cooperative than their non-handicapped peers. And those with learning disabilities are less skilled in starting and maintaining conversations with their peers, and less able to sustain a dominant speaker role.

The evidence is clear that the perceptions and interactions of excep-tional people are affected by their condition. It is also clear that those around them—peers, teachers, and parents—often allow the exceptional condition to affect their expectations for and behavior toward these people.

The View from Outside

We know that the behaviors of those with exceptionalities are shaped in large part by the reactions of those around them—their peers, their teach-ers, and their parents. How does the behavior of their classmates affect ex-

Parents' characteristics and expectations for their children influence how they respond to having an exceptional child.

(© Meri Houtchens-Kitchens/The Picture Cube)

ceptional students? In what ways do teachers influence the performance of these students? How do parents respond to having an exceptional child?

Our knowledge of what classroom teachers think about exceptional students comes from a number of natural and contrived experiments.

- Classroom teachers rate specific groups of exceptional students less favorably than normally achieving students on measures of personal and social adjustment.
- Teachers interact differently with students in different special education categories.
- Teachers rate students lower in terms of social skills and academic potential when those students have been labeled with a handicap.

Two sources give us information on the parents of children who are exceptional. The first is the parents themselves, in their descriptions of what it's like to have a special child. The second is studies in which parents' characteristics, thoughts, and expectations for their children are sampled. Both are revealing.

It is common for parents to deny that anything is wrong with their child. Often they go from one doctor to the next, looking for a different diagnosis, or they isolate themselves and their child from social interactions. Some parents feel guilty, angry, and afraid, which affects their interactions with each other, their exceptional child and any other children, and their friends and coworkers.

In a work that describes the positive contributions the exceptional child often makes to the family, Ferguson and Asch (1989) point out that having an exceptional child complicates family and interpersonal relationships:

> The "message" of this section is not that parents rejoice in the disabilities of their children. . . . No parent narrative expresses pleasure about the opportunity to deal with a child's physiological limitations. Nor is the message that many parents eventually reach some golden stage of adjustment called "acceptance" by some social workers and psychologists. The limitations of any disability are too much embedded in the biases of the culture to allow some simple acquiescence to the latest professional version of "biology of destiny." The narratives repeatedly express anger, frustration, and resentment not at fate, but at the unnecessary burdens they and their children face because of social attitudes and behavior toward disabilities. (p. 113)

One of the most frustrating aspects of having an exceptional child is collecting the information necessary to make reasoned decisions about medical treatment, education, and available programs. Parents often turn to doctors for help with their handicapped children, but doctors are "notoriously unschooled about nonmedical services" (Gorham, 1975, p. 522). Although parents must give permission for information to be released to (and by) diagnostic personnel, they often are not allowed to read it themselves. When parents are told the best place for the child is the community, they often find there are no placements available. When they are told to institutionalize their child, they find that institutions are the least equipped placements of all. It is not surprising, then, that parents are angry, intimidated, confused, exasperated, frightened, and frustrated, and that they are aggressive advocates of special education.

Despite the difficulties, having an exceptional child can be rewarding. Steve Largent, a professional football player, described how life changed for his family when his son, Kramer, was born.

> That was on Nov. 11, 1985, perhaps the best and worst evening of Steve Largent's life. "I always cry at the births of my children because I get so emotional," he says. "I was making jokes, feeling happy, when the doctor said to me, 'Uh, oh, we've got a problem.'" The newborn had an exposed spinal cord—spina bifida. The possible consequences included paralysis and retardation.
>
> "I was crushed," Largent says. "I broke down, went into a corner and wept. Then I heard Terry [Largent's wife] say, 'God planned Kramer. Having him in our lives will be one of the greatest things that ever happened to us.'"

The day after Kramer was born, he underwent surgery to close his spine. Bowel and bladder problems are common with spina bifida, but so far Kramer has not developed any. Although he must use crutches for longer distances, the 3-year-old can already walk across a room unaided, and doctors say he may eventually gain full use of his legs. "He's been a blessing for me," says Largent. "When you have someone like Kramer, you think about all the things people have to overcome, and it makes you more sympathetic. His brothers and sisters are very protective of him, but they play rough and tumble, too."

With a whoop, Kramer gets up off the floor and toddles unsteadily toward his father. "That's it!" Largent cries. "That's just great, Kramer!" The boy begins to totter, and his father grabs him just in time. Largent is accustomed to spectacular receptions, but it is clear from his expression that, to his way of thinking, this catch ranks as one of his finest. (Friedman & Gallo, 1988, p. 80)

Ferguson and Asch (1989) suggest that four themes emerge in the writings of parents of children with disabilities: They shelter their children from the world; they pretend, often through silence and denial, that nothing is wrong; they try to find ways to "fix" the disabilities or minimize the difference of those that cannot be fixed; or they minimize the impact of the exceptionality while working to ensure their child has a full life. These reactions seem reasonable to us. We think parents always have the best interests of their child in mind as they adjust to an exceptionality. Although there's no question the adjustment is difficult, the testimony of their children tells us how important that adjustment is.

In thinking about the writings of disabled adults and reflecting on my own life, I can give my parents high marks. They did not deny that I was blind, and did not ask me to pretend that everything about my life was fine. They rarely sheltered. They worked to help me behave and look the way others did without giving me a sense that to be blind—"different"—was shameful. They fought for me, and then with me, to ensure that I lived as full and as rich a life as I could. For them, and consequently for me, my blindness was a fact, not a tragedy. It affected them but did not dominate their lives. Nor did it dominate mine. (Ferguson & Asch, 1989, p. 118).

Parents of those who are gifted share some of the concerns of parents of other exceptional children. They also have their own special concerns:

Zelda's mother worries that her daughter may be socially ostracized or isolated as a result of negative peer-group reaction to her intellectual gifts. This is a particularly sensitive issue to Zelda's mother, who never was very popular herself and does not wish her only daughter to face the same loneliness that she had had to endure. . . . Sam's mother has very different anxieties. Will Sam turn against her or will he be embarrassed by her lack of education when he himself becomes an educated young man? She will strive for him because she believes so deeply that education is a way for

Sam to achieve success in the world, but she often wonders, late at night, as to whether she is not helping him reach his goal at the expense of losing him psychologically. . . . Laura's parents . . . wonder if she follows a career in dance or music whether she can maintain a traditional or reasonable life-style, or whether she will be drawn off by persons who will lead her into increasingly atypical patterns of behavior. (Gallagher, 1985, pp. 403–404)

Studies of parents of exceptional children focus on their attitudes and expectations. Researchers have found that parents of children with learning disabilities hold negative views about their children. They describe them as more difficult to talk to, more anxious, and less able to control themselves than their nonhandicapped siblings. The parents of these children also tend to attribute success less to ability and more to luck, and failure more to a lack of ability and less to bad luck than do parents of children who are not learning disabled. Analyses of tape-recorded interactions between mothers and their children show that parents use different kinds of language when they talk to a handicapped child. Finally, mothers of exceptional children generally hold less favorable opinions about their children's experiences in school.

Checkpoint

- *Expectations are predictions about an event or action; they are a framework within which we organize our experiences.*

- *General expectations are based on previous experience in similar situations; specific expectations relate primarily to experience in particular situations.*

- *Attributions are the reasons we assign to why somebody does something.*

- *Because teachers' expectations affect students' own expectations and performance, they become a self-fulfilling prophecy.*

- *Expectations affect both the academic and social behaviors of exceptional students.*

- *The parents of exceptional children must deal with all the emotions of having an exceptional child and with all the special needs of that child.*

WHAT WE THINK ABOUT EXCEPTIONALITY

What does it mean to be exceptional? There is no simple answer to this question. Exceptional people are individuals, each unique. Their exceptionality may give them a common challenge, but they are not all alike.

We believe the concepts of normality and exceptionality are relative. Behaviors, in and of themselves, are neither normal nor exceptional. They generate actions or reactions by which others judge them to be normal or exceptional.

Our perspective on normality is based on the belief that there are no standards for many of the concepts that shape our lives. Data that have been collected on the prevalence of a behavior or characteristic in the population can be useful as a reference to the group that supplies them. But normality is always a relative concept regardless of the context in which it is evaluated.

In our writings, we have talked at length about the negative effects of labeling people. We believe it is wrong to stereotype students. We understand that labels can be a passport to special services. But we are angry and frustrated when we see people responding, not to the individual, but to the label.

A handicap (real or perceived) can be both a promise and a burden. For many, their only hope for a full life is classification and subsequent special education. But the costs of classification can be high, when public recognition leads to changed interpersonal interactions, discrimination, and rejection.

Teachers have a special responsibility to exceptional students. Their expectations shape their students' own expectations and behaviors. When they base those expectations, not on what a student can do, but on what a label implies that student can do, they do the student a grave injustice. Exceptional students are people first. Yes, in some ways they are different. But each of us is different in some ways. It is very wrong to allow an exceptional condition to be the source of lowered expectations and differential treatment in school.

Summary

1. Normality is a relative concept that depends, not only on our perception of normal, but on the context in which we make our judgment.
2. A person is considered normal in our society or in school as long as he or she behaves in ways that the majority of others do or in ways that parents, teachers, or principals think of as normal.
3. Conceptual definitions are the generally agreed-on ideas that shape a special education category.
4. Operational criteria are the standards we use to make judgments about an exceptional behavior; they must be both universal and specific.

5. We use statistical standards to keep track of the performance of others and to make comparisons that distinguish exceptionality from normality.
6. In medicine, normality is defined as the presence of normal signs or the absence of disease symptoms.
7. Sociologists, psychologists, anthropologists, and educators often define normality in terms of a group's code of behavior.
8. The nature of the exceptionality, its perceived cause, its label, and the environment in which it occurs all influence the actions and reactions of and to exceptional people.
9. Although labeling is a first step in providing special services, the labels themselves can and do change the relationships of those who are labeled with those around them.
10. Expectations are predictions for our own behavior and for how others will act or behave toward us.
11. Expectations are based on experience (past performance) and have strong impact on our future behaviors.
12. General expectations are based on previous experience in similar situations; specific expectations relate primarily to experience in particular situations.
13. Attributions are the reasons (ability, effort, task difficulty, luck) assigned to why somebody does something.
14. Attributions play an important part in the definition of personal success and failure for exceptional students.
15. Because teachers' expectations affect students' own expectations and performance, they become a self-fulfilling prophecy.
16. Expectations affect both the academic and social behaviors of exceptional students.
17. The parents of exceptional children must accept the fact of the exceptionality, then deal with the day-to-day problems of raising an exceptional child.
18. Teachers' expectations should reflect what their students are capable of doing, not what the students' labels imply they can do.

Activities

1. Interview either a handicapped adolescent or the parent of a handicapped child. Ask about his or her experiences in school and in society. Specifically, investigate the ways in which others interact with the handicapped student.
2. Interview one of your classmates. Have the person tell you all the characteristics he or she associates with a specific label (like *gifted* or *emotionally disturbed*).

3. Find a newspaper or magazine article on a handicapped person. List the ways in which the behaviors of that person are described.

Suggested Readings

Anderson, W., Chitwood, S., & Hayden, D. (1982). *Negotiating the special education maze: A guide for parents and teachers.* Englewood Cliffs, NJ: Prentice-Hall.
> *A teacher, a parent of a disabled student, and a parent-training specialist prepared this easy-to-read guide describing the major decisions faced by parents and teachers when considering special education as an alternative for an exceptional student. The guide discusses referral, school records, individualized education programs, and due process rights, and provides many practical checklists.*

Baum, D. D. (1981). *The human side of exceptionality.* Baltimore: University Park Press.
> *Explores handicapping conditions through the use of popular literature. The book contains over forty articles that have appeared in popular magazines, covering a wide range of handicapping conditions. The articles reveal the effects of handicapping conditions in the home, school, and community.*

Biklen, D., Ferguson, D., & Ford, A. (Eds.). (1989). *Schooling and disability.* Chicago: University of Chicago Press.
> *Some of today's most controversial issues related to educating students with disabilities are discussed in the yearbook of the National Society for the Study of Education. Reformulating the system for providing special education to exceptional students is the central theme of this collection of essays.*

Blatt, B. (1981). *In and out of mental retardation: Essays on educability, disability, and human policy.* Baltimore: University Park Press.
> *A description of the ways those who are mentally retarded are treated in the United States.*

Buck, P. S. (1950). *The child who never grew.* New York: John Day.
> *The author gives a brief account of her efforts to find institutional care for her mentally retarded child.*

Fine, M., & Asch, A. (Eds.). (1988). *Women with disabilities: Essays in psychology, culture, and politics.* Philadelphia: Temple University Press.
> *This book grew out of a personal friendship between the editors, and the political commitment they had made to feminism and disability rights. It is a collection of essays from activists in varied academic disciplines. The editors' objective was to shift the image*

of girls and women with disabilities from one of passiveness and weakness to one incorporating passion and strength; it was accomplished very well.

Foster, G. G., Ysseldyke, J. E., & Reese, J. (1975). I wouldn't have seen it if I hadn't believed it. *Exceptional Children, 41,* 469–473.

> *The authors report the results of an experiment in which teachers were shown videotapes of normal children, but were told that the children were handicapped. The teachers rated the children as handicapped. The authors use the finding to emphasize the importance of preconceived notions on teachers' expectations for the behaviors of students.*

Frank, J. P. (1951). *My son's story.* New York: Knopf.

> *A father's account of what it meant to him and his wife when they discovered that their baby was neurologically impaired and would always be intellectually handicapped.*

Gottlieb, J. (1974). Attributes toward retarded children: Effects of labeling and academic performance. *American Journal of Mental Deficiency, 79,* 268–273.

> *The author describes the extent to which other children are influenced by the labels assigned to retarded children. He also describes the extent to which children are influenced by the actual academic performance of retarded students.*

Jones, R. (1972). Labels and stigma in special education. *Exceptional Children, 38,* 553–564.

> *The author summarizes the results of studies on more than ten thousand children to show that (1) children reject the labels* culturally deprived *and* culturally disadvantaged *as applied to themselves, (2) acceptance of these labels is associated with more negative attitudes toward school, (3) teachers hold lower expectations for children labeled* disadvantaged, *(4) students who are educable mentally retarded report a stigma associated with special class placement, and (5) teachers have few strategies for managing stigmas in special classes.*

Jablow, M. M. (1982). *Cara: Growing with a retarded child.* Philadelphia: Temple University Press.

> *A mother's account of what it means to live and grow with an exceptional child.*

Keller, H. (1911). *The story of my life.* Garden City, NY: Doubleday, Page.

> *Helen Keller's autobiography, describing her rich intellectual and emotional development. Without vision or hearing, she used her senses of touch, taste, and smell to help her communicate with others.*

Turnbull, H., & Turnbull, A. (Eds.). (1979). *Parents speak out: Views from the other side of a two-way mirror.* Columbus, Ohio: Charles E. Merrill.

A compilation of personal experiences of families who have had a handicapped child. Parents describe their difficulties in obtaining professional services for their child and the problems they have had raising their child.

4

High-prevalence Categories of Exceptionality

FOCUSING QUESTIONS

■ Why is there so much controversy over the definitions of exceptional conditions and the criteria used to identify students with those conditions?

■ How do we explain the variation among states in the number of students receiving special education services for learning disabilities, giftedness and talent, and speech and language impairments?

■ Despite the debate surrounding the definition of learning disabilities, educators agree on the kinds of students who show special needs in this area. What criteria do they use?

■ What distinction can be made between students who are gifted and students who are talented?

■ What characteristic is universal among students with communication disorders?

■ What is the difference between speech and language impairments?

*T*HE MAJORITY OF STUDENTS WHO RECEIVE SPECIAL education services in schools are identified as learning disabled, gifted and talented, or speech and language impaired. Of the 4.5 million students identified as handicapped and served during the 1987–88 school year, 47 percent (1.9 million) were considered learning disabled, and 23 percent (about 1 million) were labeled speech and language impaired. Local school districts and state departments of education do not routinely report to the U.S. Department of Education the numbers of gifted and talented students who receive special education services. A report published in 1987 by the Council of State Directors of Programs for the Gifted indicated that about 1.6 million students receive special education services in gifted and talented programs. Of all students who attend U.S. public schools, about 5 percent are considered learning disabled, 4.2 percent are identified as gifted and talented, and 2.5 percent are identified as speech and language impaired (U.S. Department of Education, 1989). These students receive special education services because of their unique educational needs. Most receive those services in general education classrooms, but some are taught for part or all of the school day in different "pull-out" programs.

In this chapter we talk about these three high-prevalence categories and the kinds of criteria used to assign students to them. We begin with standard definitions and describe the controversy that surrounds those definitions and the ways in which they have changed to reflect changes in the field and current practice. Even though several of the federal definitions are problematic, and states experience difficulty putting the definitions into practice, states must use the federal definitions or those that will specify an "equivalent population" if they are to receive funds for special education services. In our discussion of definitions you will note that since special education is an ever-changing, dynamic profession, state department of education personnel are continually attempting to establish more educationally relevant definitions of categories. And advocacy groups are continually debating definition criteria and advising state and federal education personnel about how the categories ought to be defined.

Next we look at the history of services for students in each of these categories. Then we examine prevalence figures—the number of students being served in each category and the percentage that number represents in the school-age population. Finally, we examine the characteristics that are attributed to these students in the areas of cognition, academic skills, physical skills, social/emotional/behavioral skills, and communication.

STUDENTS WITH LEARNING DISABILITIES
Definition

Puzzling is a term teachers use to describe students with learning disabilities. They tell us that these students look entirely normal, seem intelligent, carry on intelligent conversations—that they don't appear to be any different than other students. Yet these students have difficulty doing certain tasks—not all things—in school. Some have difficulty reading; others perform poorly in spelling; still others make frequent mistakes in math. Teachers tell us that these students are very hard to teach—that they simply do not learn in the same ways or as easily as others their age. They tell us that these students have special needs and are not easy to teach in large classes in which most other students perform reasonably well. They tell us that modifying instruction so that these students can profit from teaching is an intricate process.

To qualify for program funds, the states must have a means for identifying exceptional students. Defining any exceptionality is not easy. And the process becomes even more difficult when the condition is as complex as this one. Most states base their description of learning disabilities on the definition that was published in the *Federal Register* (December 29, 1977) after Public Law 94–142 was passed. According to that definition, the term

> "children with specific learning disabilities" means those children who have a disorder in one or more of the basic psychological processes involved in understanding or in using language, spoken or written, which disorder may manifest itself in imperfect ability to listen, think, speak, read, write, spell, or to do mathematical calculations. Such disorders

Students with learning disabilities don't appear to be any different than other students, but they have difficulty doing certain tasks—not all things—in school.
(© Michael Weisbrot and Family)

include such conditions as perceptual handicaps, brain injury, minimal brain dysfunction, dyslexia, and developmental aphasia. Such term does not include children who have learning problems which are primarily the result of visual, hearing, or motor handicaps, of mental retardation, of emotional disturbance, or of environmental, cultural, or economic disadvantage. (p. 65803)

In that same issue of the *Federal Register*, the U.S. Department of Education specified the criteria to be used in identifying students with learning disabilities:

1. A team may determine that a child has a specific learning disability if:
   a. The child does not achieve commensurate with his or her age and ability levels in one or more of the following areas when provided with learning experiences appropriate for the child's age and ability levels: oral expression, listening comprehension, written expression, basic reading skill, reading comprehension, mathematics calculation, or mathematics reasoning.
   b. The team finds that a child has a severe discrepancy between achievement and intellectual ability in one or more of the same areas listed in the preceding statement.

2. The team may not identify a child as having a specific learning disability if the severe discrepancy between ability and achievement is primarily the result of:
   a. a visual, hearing, or motor handicap
   b. mental retardation
   c. emotional disturbance
   d. environmental, cultural, or economic disadvantage. (p. 65803)

In the next section we examine the conflict that has surrounded the definition of learning disabilities. Although they may not agree on that definition, most special educators do agree on the kinds of students who show special needs in this area:

- These students show a significant discrepancy between their academic ability and achievement. In practice a student usually has to earn a reasonably high score on an intelligence test and a reasonably low score on an achievement test to be considered learning disabled.
- Their difficulties stem from a **process disorder,** a neurological impairment that interferes with the students' ability to learn. The cause of that disorder must be beyond the control of the individual student and his or her parents and cannot be the result of inappropriate instruction or insufficient opportunity to learn.
- Learning disabilities are not caused by other handicapping conditions, although they can appear with other conditions.
- Without special education services, these students continue to do poorly in school.

History

Because their condition was not recognized formally until the early 1960s, schools did not have special classes or services for students with learning disabilities. Some of these students did receive services, but in classes for those who were emotionally disturbed or mentally retarded. Others were served by remedial reading teachers. Still others were called brain injured, neurologically impaired, perceptually handicapped, dyslexic, or aphasic, their labels a function of the professional group attending them. For example, physicians called the students they worked with brain injured or neurologically impaired; educators talked about students with perceptual handicaps or hyperkinetic behavior disorder; speech and language professionals referred to the students as dyslexic or developmentally aphasic.

The history of learning disabilities as a category of special needs had its beginnings in the early work of those who conducted clinical research on mentally retarded children and adults who were brain injured (called *endogenous retardation*) and in clinical work with children who had language and reading problems. Kurt Goldstein, Hans Werner, and Alfred Strauss were pioneers in the field. Goldstein studied soldiers who suffered traumatic head injuries during World War I. Werner and Strauss did extensive research at the Wayne County Training School in Detroit. They described the characteristics of two kinds of brain-injured children: those who appeared to be mentally retarded and those who had experienced a traumatic head injury (an auto accident, a fall, a gunshot wound). Their research produced a list of behavioral characteristics that differentiated between those with and those without brain injuries:

- Excessive motor activity
- Hyperactivity
- Awkwardness and consistently poor motor performance
- Erratic behavior
- Poor organization
- High distractibility
- Faulty perceptions (like reversals)

The tests that were constructed to assess the behavioral characteristics of brain-injured children often are used today in the diagnosis of learning disability. The characteristics identified by Werner and Strauss also are used today to describe children with learning disabilities.

In the 1930s and 1940s clinical psychologists, educators, and reading teachers began to apply the research of Goldstein, Werner, Strauss, and Laura Lehtinen to clinical work with children who were experiencing academic difficulties.

- Samuel Orton was a neurologist who believed that lack of cerebral dominance was a cause of language disorders. (In normal individuals either the left or right side of the brain has dominance in controlling specific functions.)
- Grace Fernald established a clinic at UCLA where she perfected remedial reading and spelling techniques.
- Samuel Kirk developed a test, the Illinois Test of Psycholinguistic Abilities, for use in describing language functioning and developing remedial programs.
- Cruickshank focused his efforts on the study of brain-injured children, specifically children with cerebral palsy.
- Getman, Marianne Frostig, Newell Kephart, and Ray Barsch focused on the correlation of perceptual disorders and developed remedial procedures ranging from optometric eye exercises, tracing and copy-

ing patterns, and differentiating figure from background in a puzzle, to making angels in the snow.

Lerner (1989) links this early work to the later recognition of learning disabilities:

> Strauss and his coworkers laid the foundation for the field of learning disabilities by (1) perceiving a homogeneity in a diverse group of children who had been misdiagnosed by specialists, misunderstood by parents, and often discarded by society; (2) planning and implementing educational settings and procedures to teach such children successfully; and (3) alerting many professions to the existence of a new category of exceptional children. (p. 34)

Kirk was the first to use the term *learning disability* formally, at a meeting in Chicago in 1963. That meeting was attended by parents whose children were experiencing academic difficulties, who in other ways appeared normal, and who had been labeled dyslexic, brain injured, perceptually handicapped, neurologically impaired, and aphasic. These parents wanted to form a common organization and were searching for a name to identify their group. Kirk gave them that name. The Association for Children with Learning Disabilities (ACLD), known today as the Learning Disabilities Association (LDA), was founded.

Since 1963, debate in the profession has centered on the meaning of *learning disability*, the criteria that should be used to identify students who are learning disabled, and the kinds of students who should be considered eligible for special education services under this category.

Arriving at a definition of *learning disabilities* has been a special problem. The federal definition (see pages 115–116) has met with major criticism. Some question its language. All of us, they claim, have an "imperfect ability" in some area or another. Are we all learning disabled? Others argue that process disorders are difficult to assess, and that it is difficult to differentiate those with learning disabilities from those who are culturally disadvantaged, emotionally disturbed, mildly mentally retarded, or just slow learners. And others insist that scores on intelligence tests are not a valid criterion, that they focus on a single area of disability and are systematically biased against students who earn low scores on intelligence tests.

Dissatisfaction with the federal definition led to formation of the National Joint Committee for Learning Disabilities (NJCLD), a group made up of representatives from the major professional organizations in the field. In 1981 the committee proposed this definition of learning disabilities:

> *Learning disabilities* is a generic term that refers to a heterogeneous group of disorders manifested by significant difficulties in the acquisition and use

of listening, speaking, reading, writing, reasoning, or mathematical abilities. These disorders are intrinsic to the individual and presumed to be due to central nervous system dysfunction. Even though a learning disability may occur concomitantly with other handicapping conditions (e.g., sensory impairment, mental retardation, social and emotional disturbance) or environmental influences (e.g., cultural differences, insufficient/inappropriate instruction, psychogenic factors), it is not the direct result of those conditions or influences. (Hammill, Leigh, McNutt, & Larsen, 1981, p. 336)

Three years later the Learning Disabilities Association adopted a definition that extends beyond academic performance:

Specific learning disabilities is a chronic condition of presumed neurological origin which selectively interferes with the development, integration, and/or demonstration of verbal and/or nonverbal abilities. Specific learning disabilities exists as a distinct handicapping condition in the presence of average to superior intelligence, adequate sensory and motor systems, and adequate learning opportunities. The condition varies in its manifestations and in degree of severity. Throughout life the condition can affect self-esteem, education, vocation, socialization, and/or daily living activities.

Most recently, a study group appointed by the National Institutes of Health (NIH) used the NJCLD definition as the basis of a new definition that encompasses social skills and expresses the relationship between learning disabilities and attention deficit disorder. (We've used italics to highlight portions that are changed from the NJCLD definition.)

Learning disabilities is a generic term that refers to a heterogeneous group of disorders manifested by significant difficulties in the acquisition and use of reading, writing, reasoning, or mathematical abilities, *or of social skills.* These disorders are intrinsic to the individual and presumed to be due to central nervous system dysfunction. Even though a learning disability may occur concomitantly with other handicapping conditions (e.g., sensory impairment, mental retardation, social and emotional disturbance), with *socioenvironmental* influences (e.g., cultural differences, insufficient/inappropriate instruction, psychogenic factors), *and especially with attention deficit disorder, all of which may cause learning problems, a learning disability* is not the direct result of those conditions or influences. (Silver, 1988)

Several questions crop up again and again in the debate over a definition of learning disabilities. Should process disorders, socioenvironmental influences, and attention deficit disorder be a part of that definition? And can students who have other exceptional conditions (like mental retardation, emotional disturbance, blindness, or giftedness) also be learning disabled? Some have tried to address this lack of unity by suggesting that there is more than one kind of learning disabled student.

In recent definitions, *learning disabilities* is described as a "generic term," a "heterogeneous group of disorders." This wording implies that there are *subtypes* of learning disabled children. For example, Kirk and Chalfant (1984) describe two subtypes: those who evidence **academic learning disabilities** in reading, arithmetic, spelling, and writing, and those who evidence **developmental learning disabilities,** disorders or dysfunctions in the processes or abilities necessary to acquire academic skills (attention, memory, perceptual-motor functioning, perception, thinking, language). James McKinney and his colleagues describe seven subtypes of learning disabled students: those with (1) attention deficits, (2) conduct problems, (3) withdrawn behavior, (4) low positive behavior, (5) global behavior problems, and (6) and (7) two types of normal behavior with elevated scores on certain trait measures (McKinney, 1987; McKinney & Speece, 1986).

Although subtyping may be a way out of the definition maze, it is a relatively arbitrary process. We find it difficult to use and misleading to teachers.

Prevalence

Learning disabilities is the most prevalent exceptional condition. About 5 percent of the school-age population is considered learning disabled. Of the over 4.4 million students who received services under Public Law 94-142 during the 1986–87 school year, 47 percent (1.9 million students) were identified as learning disabled.

Because the states use different definitions and criteria to determine eligibility, these figures may be misleading. Table 4.1 lists the percentage of students in each state who were identified as learning disabled and received special education services during the 1987–88 academic year. Notice the variation in the number of students identified and served in each state. The percentages range from lows of 2.4 in Georgia, 3.1 in Wisconsin, and 3.4 in Kentucky, to highs of 7.3 in New Jersey, 7.8 in Delaware, and 9.5 in Rhode Island.

Table 4.2 shows the number of students classified learning disabled according to federal counts from the 1976–77 school year (the first year these counts were made) to the 1986–87 school year.

During that time, there was a 142 percent increase in the number of students served. This remarkable increase—the number more than doubled over an eleven-year period—has not occurred with any other condition. In fact, the total number of students enrolled in special education has increased only slightly over the last decade. This means that growth in

Table 4.1
Students Identified as Learning Disabled and Receiving Special Education Services in the 1987–88 School Year, by State

State	Percent	State	Percent
Alabama	3.93	Montana	5.17
Alaska	6.73	Nebraska	4.78
Arizona	5.19	Nevada	5.23
Arkansas	5.39	New Hampshire	5.70
California	5.31	New Jersey	7.34
Colorado	4.36	New Mexico	4.93
Connecticut	6.92	New York	6.05
Delaware	7.82	North Carolina	4.12
District of Columbia	3.76	North Dakota	4.61
Florida	4.80	Ohio	4.26
Georgia	2.41	Oklahoma	4.89
Hawaii	4.16	Oregon	5.57
Idaho	5.02	Pennsylvania	4.78
Illinois	5.89	Rhode Island	9.46
Indiana	3.90	South Carolina	4.36
Iowa	4.82	South Dakota	4.49
Kansas	4.21	Tennessee	5.40
Kentucky	3.41	Texas	5.24
Louisiana	3.26	Utah	4.40
Maine	5.15	Vermont	5.56
Maryland	6.69	Virginia	5.12
Massachusetts	6.11	Washington	4.60
Michigan	4.20	West Virginia	5.74
Minnesota	5.29	Wisconsin	3.09
Mississippi	5.20	Wyoming	5.38
Missouri	5.56		

Source: U.S. Department of Education. (1989). *Eleventh annual report to Congress on the implementation of Public Law 94-142: The Education for All Handicapped Children Act.* Washington, DC: U.S. Department of Education, p. A-37.

the category of learning disabilities has occurred while the number of students in other categories has fallen.

There are several explanations for the rapid growth in the number of students with learning disabilities. In 1983 the National Association of State Directors of Special Education attributed the increase to (1) improved procedures for identifying and assessing students, (2) liberal eligibility criteria, (3) social acceptance/preference for the learning disabled classification, (4) cutbacks in other programs and lack of general education alternatives for children who experience problems in the regular classroom, and (5) court rulings. The 1988 *Annual Report to Congress* noted that the

Table 4.2
Students Identified as Learning Disabled Each Academic Year from 1976–77 to 1986–87

Year	Number of Students	Year	Number of Students
1976–77	797,212	1982–83	1,745,871
1977–78	969,423	1983–84	1,818,308
1978–79	1,135,559	1984–85	1,839,292
1979–80	1,281,379	1985–86	1,872,339
1980–81	1,468,014	1986–87	1,926,097
1981–82	1,627,344		

1985–86 school year saw a leveling off of numbers identified but that once again numbers are sharply increasing. That fluctuation is attributed by Department of Education officials to the tightening of criteria by states and school districts during 1985–86 and then the increasing numbers of students who were found to meet the tightened criteria during 1986–87.

Another explanation for the significant increase in the number of students labeled learning disabled offers a better interpretation of trends in school and society as well as research findings on the issue. Fewer students today are meeting the standards set for them in general education. These students need help, and the only way (or the best way) to get them that help is to classify them learning disabled.

Characteristics

Sometimes it seems as though a deficiency in any human characteristic is thought to indicate or be the result of a learning disability. In Table 4.3 we've listed some of the terms used to describe students who are learning disabled. Read through the table. In many cases, two conflicting terms are listed. For example, while some professionals argue that students who are learning disabled are hyperactive, others argue that they are hypoactive (inactive). These students are said to perseverate (continue working at a task beyond a reasonable time), but they also are described as distractible. Some claim that learning disabled students have difficulty getting to sleep and that they sleep very little; others insist that they sleep too much. Obviously, there's little consensus on the characteristics of the condition. Do note, though, that most of the terminology associated with this condition is negative. It has led to negative stereotyping.

Part of the problem lies in the lack of consensus in the definition of learning disabilities. And part of the problem lies in the nature of the exceptionality itself. It is very difficult to measure the kinds of deficiencies

The number of learning disabled students doubled in a decade because of improved identification and assessment procedures, liberal eligibility criteria, social acceptance/preference for the learning disability classification, lack of general education alternatives, and court rulings.

(© Michael Weisbrot and Family)

and disorders that are characteristic of students with learning disabilities. This leaves a good deal of latitude in the diagnosis of learning disabilities. Given that learning disabilities are thought to be caused by deficits or disorders within children (process disorders), rather than by the way the children have been raised or educated, the label has become an attractive one. Parents would much rather have their youngster called learning disabled than mentally retarded or emotionally disturbed.

From the late 1960s to the early 1980s, most of the research in the field focused on describing the characteristics of students called learning disabled. These descriptions usually were based on test performance. As more tests were developed and new names were given to them, researchers claimed to discover new kinds of learning disabilities: auditory sequential memory disabilities, grammatic closure deficits, body image disorders, manual expression dysfunctions, figure-ground pathology. We can't tell you exactly what these conditions are. All we can say is that students who supposedly show these disorders have scored poorly on tests that test authors say measure these disorders.

During the same period researchers tried to show that the test performances of students with learning disabilities were measurably different than those of other groups of students. They were unable to do so.

In the sections that follow, we describe the traits and characteristics commonly attributed to students who are learning disabled. But we want

Table 4.3
Terms That Are Used in the Professional Literature to Describe Students with Learning Disabilities and That Lead to Inappropriate Stereotypes

brain injured	hyperactive
conceptually confused	hypersensitive
confused	hypoactive
daydreaming	immature
disordered in auditory association	impulsive
disordered in auditory sequential memory	inattentive
disordered in language processing	lacks gross motor skills
disordered in social perception	language impaired
disordered in visual sequential memory	math disordered
disruptive	negative
distractible	overly energetic
erratic	perceptually disordered
has auditory closure deficit	perceptual motor impaired
has body image problem	perseverative
has difficulty differentiating figure from ground	processing disordered
has learned helplessness	reading disabled
has listening deficit	spelling disordered
has low frustration tolerance	unmotivated
has negative impulse control	unstable
has sequencing problem	

you to recognize that these are nonspecific traits. That is, we believe, and research supports our contention, that learning disabled students do not differ systematically from other kinds of students on these characteristics.

Cognitive

Most educators argue that learning disabled students show average or above-average intelligence. Others insist that students can be both learning disabled and mentally retarded, as long as they show a significant discrepancy between ability and achievement. Students with learning disabilities do show specific cognitive (thinking) deficits or disorders, among them memory deficits, attention deficits, perceptual disorders, and the failure to develop and use cognitive strategies.

Both visual and auditory memory deficits have been found in students with learning disabilities. Their difficulty remembering can interfere with their development of reading and language skills.

Attention is a critical component of learning. To learn, students must pay attention to what is going on in the classroom—to what the teacher

It is difficult to measure the kinds of deficiencies and disorders that are characteristic of students with learning disabilities.

(© Smiley/TexaStock)

says, to the book they are reading, to the task at hand. Research documents that students who are learning disabled have difficulty coming to attention, focusing attention, and sustaining attention.

Often distractibility goes hand in hand with hyperactivity. The American Psychiatric Association (1987) now describes a disorder called *attention deficit-hyperactivity disorder* (AD-HD), which manifests itself in inappropriate (developmentally) levels of inattention, impulsiveness, and hyperactivity. Associated with these characteristics are low self-esteem, mood instability, low frustration tolerance, academic underachievement, and temper tantrums. The disorder is said to be common, occurring in as many as 3 percent of children. The diagnostic criteria the American Psychiatric Association recommends be used to identify this disorder are listed in Table 4.4.

Perceptual disorders also are common among learning disabled students. Students can have difficulty distinguishing left from right (left-right orientation), differentiating figure from ground, identifying patterns (pattern discrimination), body image difficulties, recognizing symbols, and associating sounds with symbols (auditory association). But professionals have not been able to develop adequate measures of these disorders or to show that perceptual problems are specific to those with learning disabilities.

Table 4.4
Diagnostic Criteria for Attention Deficit–Hyperactivity Disorder

A. A disturbance of at least six months during which at least eight of the following are present:

   1. Often fidgets with hands or feet or squirms in seat (in adolescents, may be limited to subjective feelings of restlessness)
   2. Has difficulty remaining in seat when required to do so
   3. Is easily distracted by extraneous stimuli
   4. Has difficulty awaiting turn in games or group situations
   5. Often blurts out answers to questions before they have been completed
   6. Has difficulty following through on instructions from others (not due to oppositional behavior or failure of comprehension), e.g., fails to finish chores
   7. Has difficulty sustaining attention in tasks or play activities
   8. Often shifts from one uncompleted activity to another
   9. Has difficulty playing quietly
   10. Often talks excessively
   11. Often interrupts or intrudes on others, e.g., butts into other children's games
   12. Often does not seem to listen to what is being said to him or her
   13. Often loses things necessary for tasks or activities at school or at home (e.g., toys, pencils, books, assignments)
   14. Often engages in physically dangerous activities without considering possible consequences (not for the purpose of thrill seeking), e.g., runs into street without looking

B. Onset before the age of seven.

C. Does not meet the criteria for a Pervasive Developmental Disorder.

Criteria for severity of Attention Deficit–Hyperactivity Disorder:

Mild: Few, if any, symptoms in excess of those required to make the diagnosis and only minimal or no impairment in school or social functioning.

Moderate: Symptoms of functional impairment intermediate between "mild" and "severe."

Severe: Many symptoms in excess of those required to make the diagnosis and significant and pervasive impairment in functioning at home and school and with peers.

Source: Reprinted with permission from the *Diagnostic and Statistical Manual of Mental Disorders* (3rd ed., rev.) (pp. 52–53). Copyright 1987 American Psychiatric Association.

Learning disabled children are said to fail to develop and use the cognitive strategies necessary to learning, such as organizing learning tasks and learning how to learn. "Normal" learners employ a set of self-monitoring and self-regulating strategies in learning; it is thought that these are absent or deficient in students who are learning disabled. These students are said to lack awareness of the skills, strategies, and steps that are necessary to solve problems or complete tasks, and have difficulty evaluating the effectiveness of what they do.

Kirk and Chalfant (1984) identify two kinds of cognitive disorders: in problem solving and in concept formation. Students who have a disorder in problem solving have difficulty analyzing and synthesizing information, and therefore have a tough time adapting to new situations. Those who exhibit difficulties in concept formation have trouble classifying objects and events (for example, they may not recognize that a beagle and a Siamese cat are both animals).

Students with learning disabilities can show deficits or disorders in almost any area of cognitive functioning. Notice that we use that word *can*. Not all learning disabled students demonstrate cognitive difficulties, and different students demonstrate different kinds of difficulties. It would be nice if we could categorize students neatly, but it's just not possible. These are individuals, each unique. And although tests may pinpoint similarities among students, they can't begin to reflect all the many differences among them. Adding to the confusion are the different terms and definitions used to describe the cognitive characteristics of students with learning disabilities.

It is important that you grasp a critical distinction at this point, a distinction we repeat again and again as we talk about the kinds of characteristics attributed to specific groups of exceptional children. Many of the students who experience significant learning disabilities or disorders *do* demonstrate many of the characteristics we've described above. But, not all students who exhibit learning disabilities show these characteristics. And many children who have no difficulty whatsoever learning in school evidence one or more of the characteristics we've described, as do many of the students who are considered mentally retarded, emotionally disturbed, speech and language impaired, deaf, and blind. These characteristics are neither universal (evidenced by everyone who is said to be learning disabled) nor specific (evidenced only by students who are said to be learning disabled). You cannot say that "all students who are learning disabled perseverate, McGillicuddy perseverates, therefore McGillicuddy is learning disabled." This kind of stereotypic thinking just does not make sense. In order to teach effectively, you must be able to separate the behavior or characteristic from the exceptionality, to respond to your students as individuals.

Academic

Students with learning disabilities typically do not perform as well in school as their teachers or parents expect them to perform (on the basis of

their experience working with the student, or the student's past performance or performance on an intelligence test). This is the primary characteristic of learning disability. Students who evidence other characteristics
(like cognitive disorders, attention deficits, perceptual problems, and fine
motor coordination difficulties) usually are not considered learning disabled if their performance in school is adequate. There is considerable debate about just how poorly a student must perform before the student is
considered learning disabled. This debate raises other interesting (mostly
philosophical rather than practical) questions: Can gifted children be
learning disabled? Can a child be both retarded and learning disabled?

Many students do not profit from their experiences in school. Many
perform poorly in reading, mathematics, and spelling. One of the major
challenges educators face is identifying among them those who are learning disabled and eligible for special education.

Physical

Students with learning disabilities look like students who do not have
learning disabilities. But they can be clumsy and awkward. And some lack
fine motor coordination. Many of the tests used by schools to screen for
learning disabilities include copying and tracing exercises to spot students
who need remediation in physical areas.

It generally is assumed that students who evidence learning disabilities have some degree of neurological impairment. Nearly all definitions
of learning disabilities include reference to internal causation. Probably
the most extensive review of evidence for the biological origins of learning
disabilities was conducted by Gerald Coles (1988), who argues that there is
no evidence for neurological dysfunction as a cause of learning disabilities
or a characteristic of learning disabled children. He goes on to say that "the
very existence of this condition has been virtually unproven, with only the
shakiest of evidence reported" (p. xii) and that "after decades of research it
still has not been demonstrated that disabling neurological dysfunctions
exist in more than a minuscule number of these children" (p. xii).

Social/Emotional/Behavioral

The government's definition of learning disabilities (see pages 115–116)
excludes difficulties caused by social or emotional conditions. If a student's difficulties stem primarily from social or emotional problems, the
student usually is thought to be emotionally disturbed or behaviorally disordered. But the most recent definition of learning disabilities—the one
developed by the NIH (see page 120)—includes deficits or disorders in social skills as a learning disability. Students with learning disabilities appear to show differing degrees of social and emotional problems as a result
of those disabilities. McKinney (1987) described subtypes of learning dis-

*Window
on
Practice*

I WENT IN THE LD PROGRAM when I was in second grade. A lot of times I wondered why I was put in there, but I think I know the answer to that now. When I was small, I didn't have many kids to play with. I didn't like to talk to anybody. I was kind of shy; you could say I was a Mama's boy. Anyway, when I was in school, I hardly talked to anyone. The teacher tried to get me to do something and I didn't want to do it. So they called people in and had me evaluated. They thought I was slow—real slow—and so they put me in the LD program. I didn't think that was right. I felt ashamed to be in the LD program because of the way people would tease me about it. People had the idea that we were retarded and treated us like we had a disease. Even other teachers were saying, "Well, he's in the special education program and I don't think he can do that." I got so depressed sometimes. I'd start hiding my books, lying about what class I was in, dodging classes, doing anything to stop it.

When I got into sixth grade, I decided that I wanted to make a change, so I started reading books, magazines, newspapers, anything I could get my hands on. It was really hard, but I stuck with it. I was determined to learn how to read and I was determined to stop people from picking on me because I couldn't read. When I did finally start reading a little better, and getting better and better, I still had a problem—they were still picking on me. I thought to myself, "I know I can read pretty good. Why are they still picking on me?" In ninth grade I realized that the only reason those kids were picking on me was because I was still ducking and hiding who I really was.

I was hiding when I walked into my special education class with my special education teacher and the other special education students. While I was hiding, people were looking and wondering, "Who is that? Why is he hiding?" When I stopped doing that and stopped lying about which class I was in and which teacher I had, I found that the teasing leveled off. When I got into tenth grade, it stopped completely. Nobody said anything because I wasn't ducking and hiding.

One of the biggest problems I've had to deal with is not being allowed to choose what classes I wanted to take. I always had a teacher who'd sit there and fill out my sheet for me. In the ninth grade I wanted to take algebra, but I wasn't allowed to. I didn't complain much, but I wasn't quite as informed about certain things then as I am now. I transferred to another high school when I entered the tenth grade. One day we had an assembly and they were talking about requirements for college. I realized I had none of the required classes, especially in math and foreign language. When I found I wouldn't be able to go to college if I didn't have the classes that I had wanted to choose, I got really mad. In eleventh grade I complained. Thank God for Ms. Hines, my special education teacher now. She was about the only teacher who really listened to me and I'm glad of that. Teachers need to be a little more lenient when they come down on students picking their classes. They need to allow students to choose which classes they want to take. If it doesn't work out, they can always pull you out of those classes. That's how I feel. That's what it's all about—a chance.

Anthony Wolfe is in the eleventh grade at Terry Sanford Senior High School in Fayetteville, North Carolina.

abled students who show conduct problems, low positive behavior, withdrawn behavior, and global behavior problems. Kirk and Chalfant (1984) argue that the cognitive deficits experienced by learning disabled students, especially those who have difficulty in problem solving, lead to difficulty in adapting to new situations or responding appropriately in social situations. At least some students with learning disabilities have a hard time getting along with their peers and classmates. Many of the social and emotional behaviors shown by learning disabled students are the same as the behaviors shown by those who are emotionally disturbed, mentally retarded, or speech and language impaired, or who perform poorly in school but otherwise are considered normal. Remember, these characteristics are neither universal nor specific.

Communication

"Language disorders are the most common disabilities noted at the preschool level. Generally, the child does not talk, does not talk like older brothers and sisters did at a similar age, or does not respond adequately to directions or verbal statements" (Kirk & Gallagher, 1989, p. 190). In older children, we find difficulty listening, speaking, defining words, and formulating linguistic constructions. These are *oral language* difficulties. We also find *written language* difficulties, problems with written expression.

Some of the most important work being done by educational researchers involves **pragmatic language disorders,** disorders that interfere with students' understanding of language. There is a growing contention in the literature that students who show pragmatic language disorders are learning disabled and that students who are learning disabled have pragmatic language disorders.

Checkpoint

■ *Although conflict surrounds the definition of learning disabilities and the criteria used to determine who is learning disabled, educators agree that these students do not perform as well in school as they could, that their difficulties stem from an internal cause, that they can have other disorders in addition to learning disabilities, and that they need special education services.*

■ *There is a good deal of variation among the states in the number of students identified and served in this category.*

■ *Although many characteristics are attributed to students with learning disabilities, and students who are learning disabled do demonstrate many of them, there are no characteristics that are universal and specific to the condition.*

STUDENTS WHO ARE GIFTED AND TALENTED
Definition

Many students in Kim's and Larry's schools are very smart, but some have been formally identified as **gifted and talented.** The term *gifted* usually is used to refer to people with intellectual or cognitive gifts; the term *talented* usually is used to refer to people who show outstanding performance in a specific dimension of skill (music, art, athletics). In most individuals there is a positive relationship between giftedness and talent (Kirk & Gallagher, 1989).

The category gifted is not defined in Public Law 94–142. The Gifted and Talented Children's Education Act of 1978 (Public Law 95–561) gives the states financial incentives to develop programs for students who are gifted and talented. The legislation includes the following definition:

> The term "gifted and talented" means children and, whenever applicable, youth who are identified at the preschool, elementary, or secondary level as possessing demonstrated or potential abilities, that give evidence of high performance capability in areas such as intellectual, creative, specific academic, or leadership ability, or in the performing and visual arts, and who by reason thereof require services or activities not ordinarily provided by the school.

Most state departments of education now have a coordinator for gifted and talented programs, and most have formal guidelines for the provision of services to gifted and talented students. Following enactment of Public Law 95–561, a federal agency—the Office of Gifted and Talented Students—was created. In 1982 that office was disbanded. The federal government now gives money to the states for this and thirty or so other programs in the form of block grants. State education agencies decide whether to spend any of the money on programs for gifted students, and how much to spend.

State department of education personnel write their own definitions and criteria for identifying students who are gifted and talented. In some states, definition and criteria combine both gifted and talented; in others, the two groups are distinct. For example, here's the definition Maryland uses for gifted and talented students:

> An elementary or secondary student who is identified by professionally qualified individuals as having outstanding abilities in the area of
>
> > general intellectual capabilities;
> > specific academic aptitudes; or
> > the creative, visual or performing arts.

A gifted and talented student needs different services beyond those normally provided by the regular school programs in order to develop his potential.

Louisiana defines gifted and talented separately:

Gifted children and youth are those who possess demonstrated abilities that give evidence of high performance in academic and intellectual aptitude.

Talented is possession of demonstrated abilities that give evidence of high performance in visual and/or performing arts.

There is one other difference between these definitions. The Maryland definition specifically includes the concept of educational need; the Louisiana definitions do not. This concept is prominent in other state definitions, criteria, and regulations. For example, the *Minnesota Standards for Services to Gifted and Talented Students* (1988) lists the characteristics of gifted and talented students and describes the educational need related to each characteristic. The standards also include descriptions of individual students who are gifted and talented, as examples of the kinds of students who should be identified.

Chu. Now a high school student, this Vietnamese immigrant came to the United States at age nine. He learned to speak English. His fifth grade teacher noticed his artistic and musical abilities and he was encouraged to develop these talents. Chu loved designing intricate paper patterns and enjoyed learning. His teacher noticed a very mature sense of humor. Although new to the English language, his humor was dry and he understood the nuances of language missed by many of his age-peers. He was particularly advanced in mathematics and was fascinated with computers.

Encouraged by a mentoring teacher in junior high, Chu succeeded in learning to program a computer and won three national contests sponsored by a national computer firm. There were outlets for his talent. His coursework included independent study and frequent communication with his teacher/mentor who shared his interest in computers. Chu's interest in economics was sparked by a community volunteer who sought him out and provided additional support.

His exceptional ability in computer science was supported by individualized attention at his school. Chu was lucky. The high school in his attendance area has a technology focus. The mentoring teacher happened to share his interest and donated her free time to work with him. The community volunteer heard about Chu and wanted to help. He needed support, the tools to learn, an educational climate which recognized and valued his talent, and outlets for his work. His talent in computer science was appropriately matched with his school program. At the heart of this program was the mentoring teacher who devised an individualized plan to challenge him.

Annette. Annette is a highly creative and artistic fifth grader. Her family is very supportive, although they are somewhat bewildered by her disorganized, erratic approach to school work in contrast to her sister, who is well organized and a "teacher pleaser."

Her greatest skills and most intense interests are in art and writing. Annette draws incessantly, often instead of doing assignments. She seldom takes the initiative to write a story, although when she receives a writing assignment, she begins with gusto and proceeds far beyond normal expectations. She does not cooperate with all school tasks. She complains about "old facts" (things she already knows), and she is excited by new information.

Annette's life is marked by passionate involvement with drawing, creative fantasy, and a wide interest in a variety of subjects. Her peers respect her drawing skills and sense of humor. Her passionate discourses command their attention, but she is not a sought-after playmate. She changes the rules of the game to use her creativity and her peers regard this action as cheating. Annette lacks athletic skill.

She has been identified for a gifted and talented program designed to challenge her abilities. Annette's classroom teacher also provides special challenges which involve her artistic and creative ability.

Elmer. When he entered kindergarten Elmer was reading at a third grade level. In mathematics he was able to read numbers in the trillions and he could add and subtract. He took pride in recalling populations and land sizes around the world. His kindergarten teacher provided him with more difficult work in reading and mathematics. Elmer still thought kindergarten was a waste of his time.

His kindergarten year was also a year in which he formed his opinion on abortion, divorce, world peace, and war. Elmer became depressed and talked about wishing he were dead.

Elmer was withdrawn from school and his mother taught him for first and second grade. At the end of second grade, his family moved to a new school district which would provide an individualized plan and allow for some acceleration. At his new school he was given a battery of achievement tests and scored consistently at the eighth and ninth grade levels.

Currently a fourth grader, Elmer is enrolled in science and mathematics classes with eighth graders. His language arts instruction is provided with a tutor. He attends the remaining classes with other fourth graders. His mental health began to improve when he began to receive a more correct academic diet.

However, Elmer still notes many days of feeling bad about himself and the world. He is very introspective. He receives less encouragement and fewer pats on the back than other children. People assume that someone with his ability has it "all together." His parents continue to be concerned about his mental health. They have arranged for psychological counseling and have actively sought an intellectual peer for him. Elmer is an "at risk" student and his psychological and cognitive growth continue to be a serious concern. (pp. 2–3)

History

The Ancient Greeks, in their efforts to fully develop the ablest among their population, were the first to establish programs for students with intellectual gifts. Public schools in the U.S. did not have formal programs for gifted and talented students until the first intelligence tests were developed. One of the first intelligence tests in the United States was the Stanford-Binet Intelligence Scale, developed by Louis Terman and Maude Merrill in 1916. In describing the objective of the test, Terman talked about giftedness and gifted people—those who scored in the top 2 percent of the population. Over time, this was operationalized as a score above 130. Today, that criteria—a score above 130 on an intelligence test—is used by most educators to define giftedness.

In 1972 an effort was made to broaden the concept of giftedness. In a report to Congress, Sidney Marland, the U.S. commissioner of education, offered this definition of gifted and talented children:

> Those identified by professionally qualified persons, who, by virtue of outstanding abilities, are capable of high performance. These are children who require differentiated educational programs and services beyond those normally provided by the regular program in order to realize their contribution to self and society. Children capable of high performance include those with demonstrated and/or potential ability in any of the following areas:
>
> 1. General intellectual ability
> 2. Specific academic aptitude
> 3. Creative or productive thinking
> 4. Leadership ability
> 5. Visual and performing arts. (p. 10)

Since Terman's early work, professionals have debated the definition of giftedness and the specific criteria used in identifying students as gifted. These debates are much like the debates that surround the definitions and criteria used to identify other exceptional students. Among the issues in question are the importance of leadership ability, the distinction between ability and *potential* ability, and the age at which giftedness can be identified.

Historically, gifted and talented students have been served through three kinds of educational approaches: enrichment, acceleration, and separation. **Enrichment** means enhancing the educational experiences of students without changing the setting in which they are educated. Early efforts to educate gifted and talented students consisted entirely of enrichment programs. One of the earliest was established in the Cleveland public schools in 1922. Students identified as gifted or talented stayed in the regular classroom, in the same grade as their agemates, but were given advanced work or extra work.

Enrollment in programs for the gifted and talented historically was based on IQ test performance, but the concept of giftedness has expanded beyond intellectual ability to include those who are talented and creative.
(© Rhoda Sidney/ Monkmeyer Press Photo Service)

Today enrichment can mean more than within-class tinkering with the curriculum. Students who are gifted can attend special programs at other schools, or they can enroll early in university programs. In many states, for example, high school students who are gifted and talented are allowed to take courses at colleges and universities. Others participate in after-school coursework at the university in mathematics. And some school districts conduct summer programs in which students take advanced coursework or receive enrichment experiences.

Gifted students also have been treated by **acceleration**, sometimes called *double promotion* or *skipping a grade.* Here we change curriculum or level by changing placement, instead of modifying within placement. "Flexible promotion" was the first of the three approaches to be used, beginning in 1867, in the St. Louis public schools.

Finally, there is **separation.** Gifted students sometimes, not often, are placed in **self-contained classes.** This kind of pull-out approach assumes that the students have similar characteristics and will profit from similar treatment. (This same approach is taken by private schools, which usually conduct extensive screening before admitting students.) Sometimes pull-out programs consist of separate schools. The first public school for gifted students was established in Worcester, Massachusetts, in 1901. Special programs for gifted students increased significantly in the 1950s, in response to the Russian launching of Sputnik.

Enrollment in programs for gifted and talented students historically has been based on performance on intelligence tests. This practice has shifted over time, with efforts to expand the concept of giftedness beyond intellectual ability to include those who are talented and creative.

Prevalence

Of the approximately 38 million students who attend elementary and secondary schools in the United States, about 2.3 percent are formally identified as gifted and talented. During the 1986–87 school year, 1,664,113 gifted and talented students received special education services. In some states services are mandated; in others they are discretionary. Look at Table 4.5. Notice the variation among the states in the number of students who are identified as gifted and talented. And notice the variation in the percentage of each state's enrollment, from 0.7 percent in North Dakota to 9.9 percent in New Jersey. We believe this variation is a function of differences in the states' definitions, regulations, criteria, and resources. It is these differences (not chemicals in the water!) that account for the variation in adjacent states (9.9 percent in New Jersey, 4.6 percent in New York, and 4.7 percent in Pennsylvania).

Characteristics

In the sections that follow we describe the characteristics typically associated with giftedness and talent. Before you go on, however, look at Table 4.6. It lists some of the terms typically used to describe students who are gifted and talented. Notice that almost all of them are positive, unlike the terms associated with learning disabilities and other handicapping conditions.

Cognitive

Gifted students are quick to understand abstract symbols (concepts like diffusion, justice, homogeneity, and positivism) and the complex relationships among the symbols they learn (like balance, symbiosis, photosynthesis, and equality). They are able to generalize quickly and accurately (Newland, 1976). This is very important because *all* learning involves generalization. Although children, adults, even animals generalize in the process of learning, gifted students do so more quickly and more extensively, on the basis of fewer experiences.

One of the cognitive traits regularly associated with giftedness is creativity. There has been much discussion about whether or not creativity is an intellectual trait. Some children and adolescents who earn high scores on intelligence tests also earn high scores on measures of creativity. But creativity is not a characteristic of all gifted students, and not all those who

Table 4.5
Gifted and Talented Programs and Students Receiving Services in Public
Elementary and Secondary Schools in the 1986–87 Academic Year, by State

State	Gifted and Talented Programs		Gifted and Talented Students	
	Mandated	Discretionary	Receiving Services	As a Percent of Enrollment
Alabama	x		16,834	2.3
Alaska	x		3,854	3.7*
Arizona	x		20,000	3.4*
Arkansas	x		19,928	4.6
California		x	219,073	5.1
Colorado	x		—	—
Connecticut	†		19,000	4.1
Delaware	††		3,815	4.1
Florida	x		47,463	3.0
Georgia	x		38,000	3.5
Hawaii			15,193	9.2
Idaho	x		2,510	1.2
Illinois		x	86,000	4.0
Indiana		x	27,800	2.9
Iowa	x		8,600	1.8
Kansas	x		11,786	3.0
Kentucky	x		25,000	3.9
Louisiana	x		14,000	1.9
Maine	x		—	—
Maryland		x	54,000	8.1
Massachusetts		x	—	—
Michigan		x	119,708	7.5
Minnesota		x	55,171	7.9
Mississippi		x	14,145	2.8
Missouri		x	16,000	2.0
Montana		x	4,500	2.9
Nebraska		x	19,000	7.1
Nevada		x	5,321	3.3
New Hampshire			—	—
New Jersey		x	111,190	9.9
New Mexico	x		5,063	1.8
New York	x		125,000	4.6
North Carolina	x		62,329	4.5
North Dakota		x	1,365	0.7
Ohio		x	50,000	2.8
Oklahoma	x		38,084	6.4
Oregon		x	15,338	3.6
Pennsylvania	x		78,000	4.7
Rhode Island		x	5,200	3.9
South Carolina	x		35,264	5.8

Table 4.5 *(cont.)*
Gifted and Talented Programs and Students Receiving Services in Public
Elementary and Secondary Schools in the 1986–87 Academic Year, by State

| State | Gifted and Talented Programs | | Gifted and Talented Students | |
	Mandated	Discretionary	Receiving Services	As a Percent of Enrollment
South Dakota	x		4,791	3.8
Tennessee	x		13,852	1.7
Texas		x	113,000	3.5
Utah		x	22,000	5.5
Vermont			—	—
Virginia	x		81,741**	8.5
Washington		x	21,708	2.9
West Virginia	x		10,787	3.1
Wisconsin	x		—	—
Wyoming		x	2,700	2.7

* Data for the 1985–86 academic year.
† Legislation mandates only that all gifted and talented students be identified.
†† Delaware does not mandate for services to gifted and talented students, but it has gifted programs in all districts.
** Fiscal year 1986.
x Legislation has been passed.
— Data not available.

Source: Council of State Directors of Programs for the Gifted, *The 1987 State of the States Gifted and Talented Education Report.* (This table was prepared in November 1987.)

perform well on measures of creativity also perform well on intelligence tests.

J. P. Guilford (1959, 1972) is a psychologist whose research on the concepts of intelligence and creativity has helped distinguish between the two traits. Guilford describes two kinds of thinking: divergent and convergent. Those who perform well on measures of **divergent thinking** are creative. They demonstrate *fluency* (produce many words, associations, phrases, and sentences), *flexibility* (offer a variety of ideas and alternative solutions to problems), *originality* (use rare responses and unique words), and *foresight* (see alternative solutions ahead of time). Those who perform well on measures of **convergent thinking** (reasoning, memory, and classification) show high academic aptitude. The traits can be independent or overlap. Most often, they overlap: Those who perform well on measures of creativity also perform well on traditional aptitude measures.

Joseph Renzulli has repeatedly challenged school personnel to broaden their thinking about giftedness and has added to the concept of giftedness the notion of *task commitment.* In 1979 he described giftedness as the

Table 4.6
Terms That Are Used in the Professional Literature to Describe Students Who
Are Gifted and Talented and That Lead to Inappropriate Stereotypes

abstract thinker	intuitive
advanced comprehension	less willing to cooperate
bookish	or compromise
cooperative	motivated
creative	natural leader
daydreamer	persistent
divergent thinker	precocious
disruptive	prefers to think in generalities
erratic	problem solver
evaluative	responsible
flexible	self-critical
good memory	spontaneous
happy-go-lucky	sensitive
highly verbal	understands quickly
high tolerance for ambiguity	unmotivated
immature	willing to take mental and
intelligent	emotional risks

intersection of three cognitive traits: above-average ability, creativity, and task commitment (Figure 4.1). According to Renzulli, a major characteristic of individuals who are gifted is a consistently high level of performance on tasks.

Academic

Not all gifted individuals perform well in school. In fact, a major line of national research has addressed the problem of gifted students who perform very poorly in school or drop out of school. It has been argued that students who are gifted often drop out of school because they are not challenged or motivated to perform well in school, that these students learn to underachieve. The paradox is that students usually are not formally identified as gifted and provided special education services unless they perform well academically. In most states students have to be performing significantly above grade level academically, in addition to earning high scores on intelligence tests, to be considered gifted.

Students who are gifted and talented do not perform at high levels in all school subjects. For example, it repeatedly has been shown that students who are gifted perform especially well on measures of paragraph meaning, social studies, and science, but that their performance on measures of mathematics are more often at or slightly above grade level. This finding

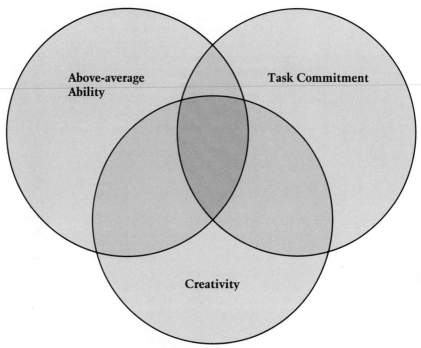

Figure 4.1
Renzulli's Three-ring Conception of Giftedness
Source: J. Renzulli (1979), p. 10. Copyright © 1979 by the National/State Leadership
Training Institute of the Gifted and the Talented. (N/S-LTI-G/T), Office of the Superin-
tendent of Ventura County Schools, Ventura, California. Reprinted by permission.

makes sense. Many children learn to read independent of school; once they
learn basic decoding skills, they can read very high level text. Most students' progress in mathematics is limited by their exposure to or formal instruction in mathematics skills. Gallagher (1985) explained the observed
difference in performance this way:

> Once the basic skills of reading have been learned, there are almost no ad-
> ditional barriers that need to be surmounted before the youngsters can go
> ahead, often on their own, in rapidly improving their breadth of knowledge
> and skill. Their performance on achievement tests, linked to reading, re-
> quires no further learning of skills.
>
> However, in the area of arithmetic, achievement is measured by the
> student's ability to progress through a series of a well-defined hierarchy of
> skills. Thus, the third-grade child, in order to attain a score in arithmetic
> computation at the sixth-grade level, would not necessarily have to have
> great depth of mathematical knowledge but merely knowledge of such
> arithmetic operations as subtraction of fractions or long division. (p. 39)

*Window
on
Practice*

A S A TODDLER, WAYNE Whitney delighted in solving mental arithmetic problems. By the time he entered school, he was intrigued by logarithms and higher numbers. At age 12, Wayne scored 780 on the mathematics portion of the Scholastic Aptitude Test and 660 on the verbal section, earning a combined score achieved by only 1 percent of the country's college-bound high school seniors.

By all accounts, Wayne, now 15, is an exceptional student.

Only one in 10,000 12-year-olds received top scores on the college board exam and fewer than 400 students in the United States per year are capable of that level of mathematical reasoning, according to Julian C. Stanley, director of the Study of Mathematically Precocious Youth at Johns Hopkins University.

"Wayne is, perhaps, the best student I've seen in 18 years of teaching secondary school physics," said Richard Shapiro, a teacher at Medfield High School in Massachusetts, where Wayne will enter his senior year in the fall. "I've had other students who have excelled on the SAT test, with perfect 800 scores. They were brilliant, but they could not go beyond what they were taught. Wayne can look a step beyond."

Nevertheless, Wayne lives in a state that will spend only $750,000 this year on programs for the gifted and talented. He lives in a country that led the world in the development of technology, but does not have a cohesive national policy for improving basic education or increasing math and science literacy. Moreover, federal support of exceptionally gifted students such as Wayne has been spotty, at best. . . .

Today, programs for the gifted vary from state to state. In Massachusetts, state funding decreased from $1 million in 1986 to $750,000 in 1988. . . .

Some states spend more.

Florida will spend $69 million this year for gifted and talented programs in its 67 county school districts. In 1987, Georgia and Pennsylvania spent $23 million each. Connecticut appropriated $4.5 million and Ohio poured $11.9 million into programs, according to the Council of State Directors for Programs for the Gifted.

In a recent study, the council found that 18 states do not fund such programs. . . .

Wayne Whitney was a baby when his mother, Patricia, a mathematician, began playing number games with him. As he grew older, the games became more complex.

"He had a fascination with numbers at an early age," Patricia Whitney recalled. "We started with counting and went on to adding and then to multiplying. It was a natural progression." . . .

At Medfield High School, Wayne Whitney completed the most advanced mathematics course available after taking a three-week advanced calculus class at Skidmore College last summer.

He has studied logic, probability, symmetry and numbers theory on his own as part of an independent study program. Even so, there are drawbacks.

"Most of the stuff I did in math class, I found pretty simple. In the advanced placement calculus class, the pace was pretty slow," Wayne said in an interview.

"The independent study was a way to do more, but I know I don't do as much work on it as I would if there was someone to report to."

A serious youth who also likes history, debating and politics, Wayne said the Medfield school system has tried to accommodate him by permitting him to move faster through its sequence of mathematics courses.

Still, he said, "No one's really keeping me back, but no one's urging me to go forward either. So, I don't always do as much as I could. Ideally, it would be better if one of the teachers had a free period and could work with me one-on-one."

Although he qualifies for admission to college, Wayne and his parents decided that he should complete another year of high school.

For the most part, the Whitneys rely heavily on summer college programs and courses.

"For some reason, there is a real stigma associated with being gifted," said Patricia Whitney. "Some people feel that having special programs for the gifted is a form of elitism, but all children benefit from these programs."

Specialists say that although some students have the aptitude for outstanding achievement, their potential can only be nurtured by providing specially targeted educational experiences and highly trained teachers. Unfortunately, most gifted programs do not make the grade.

"When you look at programs for the gifted, what you find—if you find anything—are programs in which the kids are getting enrichment. Typically, these programs are undifferentiated and not well targeted," said psychologist David Henry Feldman, director of the Jessie Smith Noyes Foundation at Tufts University.

He believes students of Wayne's caliber should be identified early and then paired with a mathematician or scientist who can provide one-on-one instruction.

Feldman, who has worked closely with gifted youth for many years, says large numbers of talented youngsters from poor and working-class families are not being identified. Gifted minority students from low-income families and depressed neighborhoods represent the largest reservoir of underdeveloped talent, he said.

"Every once in a while you'll hear stories about an immigrant child who has done extraordinarily well," Feldman said. "The truth, of course, is that the child has parents who practically killed themselves trying to make sure that he'd do well. . . . That's great, but we really need to ask ourselves why we've made no real effort to identify these children early on."

Others say that the pace at which algebra, geometry, trigonometry and calculus is being taught in most American schools is extremely slow for the gifted student.

"There is no suitable way to while away class hours when you already know much of the material and you can learn the rest almost instantaneously as it is first presented," said Julian C. Stanley of Johns Hopkins University. "Boredom, frustration and habits of gross inattention are usually the result."

Source: *Diane E. Lewis, "Gifted, Talented—and Underserved," The Boston Globe, July 5, 1989, pp. 1, 12. Reprinted courtesy of The Boston Globe.*

Physical

Many people believe that those who are gifted are gangly, awkward, and physically uncoordinated. There is no evidence for this stereotype. Terman and Oden (1951), reporting the results of their fifty-year longitudinal study of gifted children, stated that "the average member of our group is a slightly better physical specimen than the average child" (p. 23). Yet gifted students are not always physically different than other students. Gallagher (1985) illustrates this point well:

> If the approximately three million children of twelve years of age were lined up on the interstate highway from New York, they could form a line extending all the way to Chicago. If a teacher then drove from New York to Chicago, he could get a reasonably good picture of the physical characteristics of the children. Suppose that the youngsters whom we have called academically gifted children tied red bandanas around their necks; we could then get some general impression of whether, *on the average,* they tended to be larger or heavier than the other children without bandanas.
>
> If someone came to the teacher after this interesting drive and asked him . . . what he thought about the physical characteristics of gifted children, the teacher might very well say, "Well, I thought they were a little bit heavier than the other children." At the same time, however, the teacher would remember the very thin, scrawny boy east of Toledo who, although he had a red bandana around his neck, didn't fit the general statement that the teacher had just made. (pp. 32–33)

Social/Emotional/Behavioral

"It is not meaningful from the standpoint of the teacher to talk about the social abilities of gifted children or the emotional adjustment of gifted children, because gifted children vary so widely in these characteristics" (Gallagher, 1985, p. 21). Yet here too we find stereotypes of those who are gifted. Most prevalent is the idea that students who are gifted are "eggheads" who do not get along well with their peers and classmates. We think of them as isolated, even "weird." Terman and his colleagues, though, found that students who are gifted are popular and enjoy relatively high social status.

There are no social, emotional, or behavioral characteristics that are universal and specific to students who are gifted and talented. But these students do have unique needs that teachers must recognize and work toward meeting. Heward and Orlansky (1988) describe the affective needs of students who are gifted, including the need to be stimulated through association with peers and through interaction with adult models. Students who are gifted also must learn to accept their own abilities, to accept their role as producers of knowledge and creative products. And they need to develop habits of inquiry and intellectual independence. It is not uncommon for students who are gifted and who are not sufficiently challenged by their teachers and educational experiences to isolate themselves or to do just enough in school to get by, to save themselves the difficulty of meeting their teachers' and parents' expectations.

Communication

Newland (1976) described psychological peerness in communication as a characteristic of gifted individuals. Students who are gifted and talented typically communicate at a higher level than their agemates, and tend to associate with others who communicate "at their level." You've heard groups of adolescents talking. They carry on conversations about similar topics at different levels. Suppose the topic is money. One group might be talking about whether they will ever make enough money to be able to afford that great jacket in the window at Macy's. Another group might be discussing the ways in which the laws of supply and demand affect the availability of goods. It's important for you to understand that students seek their own level in communicating with other students. This has an effect on natural social groupings in and across classrooms—something to remember when you group students for instructional purposes.

Checkpoint	■ *Gifted and talented students demonstrate outstanding general academic aptitude, high-level specific aptitudes, creative ability, or ability in the performing and visual arts.*
	■ *The category usually is defined to include students who evidence potential abilities and skills as well as demonstrated abilities and skills.*
	■ *There is much debate about how best to identify those who are gifted and talented, and considerable variation among the states in the number of students served.*
	■ *Although many characteristics are attributed to students who are gifted and talented, there is no one profile of giftedness.*

STUDENTS WITH SPEECH AND LANGUAGE PROBLEMS

The third largest group of students who are eligible for special education services is those with speech and language problems. This group makes up about 23 percent of handicapped students. The students in this group have communication disorders, speech or language problems that interfere significantly with their ability to communicate.

Definition

The most commonly cited definition of **communication disorder** was developed by the American Speech-Language-Hearing Association (ASHA) in 1976:

Communication disorders are impairments in articulation, language, voice, or fluency. Hearing impairment may be classified as a communication disorder when it impedes the development, performance, or maintenance of articulation, language, voice, or fluency. (p. 26)

Speech disorders are not the same thing as language disorders.

Speech is abnormal when it deviates so far from the speech of other people that it calls attention to itself, interferes with communication, or causes the speaker or his listeners to be distressed. (Van Riper and Emerick, 1984, p. 34)

There are three kinds of speech disorders: disorders of articulation, voice, and fluency. The ASHA (1982) has developed formal definitions of each:

- *Articulation disorder* is defined as "the abnormal production of speech sounds" (p. 949). When a youngster says, "The wabbit wan don the woad," he or she is using spoken language appropriately but is not producing sounds correctly.
- *Voice disorder* is defined as "the absence or abnormal production of vocal quality, pitch, loudness, resonance, and/or duration" (p. 949). Individuals with voice disorders sometimes sound very hoarse, or speak very loudly or in a very high or low pitch.
- *Fluency disorder* is defined as "the abnormal flow of verbal expression, characterized by impaired rate and rhythm which may be accompanied by struggle behavior" (p. 949). The most common fluency disorder is stuttering. There are approximately 17 million stutterers worldwide—2 million in the United States. At one time, stuttering was attributed to psychological problems. Although this explanation has not been entirely cast aside, researchers suspect that a combination of factors—biological, psychological, and environmental—predispose a person to stutter. New evidence suggests that stuttering may be involuntary, caused by a physiological breakdown of brain mechanisms or possibly by excessive tension in the vocal cords.

The ASHA (1982) also defines three kinds of language disorders:

A language disorder is the impairment or deviant development of comprehension and/or use of a spoken, written, and/or other symbol system. The disorder may involve (1) the form of language (phonologic, morphologic, and syntactic systems), (2) the content of language (semantic system), and/or (3) the function of language in communication (pragmatic system) in any combination.

1. Form of Language
   a. *Phonology* is the sound system of a language and the linguistic rules that govern the sound combinations [speech sounds].
   b. *Morphology* is the linguistic rule system that governs the structure of words and the construction of word forms from the basic elements of meaning.
   c. *Syntax* is the linguistic rule governing the order and combination of words to form sentences, and the relationships among the elements within a sentence [word order and sentence structure].
2. Content of Language
   a. *Semantics* is the psycholinguistic system that patterns the content of an utterance, intent and meanings of words and sentences.
3. Function of Language
   a. *Pragmatics* is the sociolinguistic system that patterns the use of language in communication which may be expressed motorically, vocally, or verbally [social use of language]. (pp. 949–950)

The states use a number of criteria to identify students with communication disorders. In practice, however, most are identified by their performance on tests of language.

History

The best-known story about a person with a speech disorder is that of the Greek orator and political leader, Demosthenes. He went down to the ocean, filled his mouth with pebbles, and shouted over the waves to cure his stuttering. In the eighteenth and nineteenth centuries, children with speech and language disorders usually were treated at clinics and hospitals. In 1908, the first public school class for children with speech disorders was established in New York. By 1910 the Chicago public schools were hiring "speech correction teachers." And by the early 1920s most large-city school systems had speech correction teachers on staff. In 1925 professionals in this field met and formed the American Academy of Speech Correction, known today as the American Speech-Language-Hearing Association.

Most students with speech and language problems are educated in the regular classroom. Until the early 1980s, it was common to pull out these students for special services. Speech-language pathologists removed students from classrooms and gave them brief periods of speech and language therapy. In the last few years, however, we've seen a shift from direct to indirect services. Increasingly, speech-language pathologists work with general and special education teachers to devise ways to facilitate speech and language development in the classroom, for all students, not just for those with speech or language difficulties.

Speech-language pathologists work with general and special education teachers to facilitate speech and language development for all students and not just those with speech or language difficulties.

(© Michael Weisbrot and Family)

Public Law 95-561, the Education Amendments of 1978, has significantly affected the development of services for students with speech and language disorders. The law expanded the definition of *basic skills* to include listening and speaking skills and provided federal support for programs and services that improved speaking and listening skills for all children.

Prevalence

Students with speech and language problems are the second largest group of handicapped students; they are the third largest group of exceptional students. During the 1987–88 school year, a total of 946,904 children were served. This is 23 percent of all students considered handicapped; it is 2.5 percent of all students who attend school. Over the past ten years, the number of students with communication disorders has been relatively constant, falling slightly.

Here, too, we find variation from state to state in the number of students identified and receiving services. The figures range from a low of 1.0 percent in New York to a high of 4.9 percent in New Jersey (Table 4.7).

Characteristics

In their counts, state departments of education do not differentiate students with speech problems from those with language problems. Yet students with speech problems sometimes demonstrate different characteristics than those with language problems. Wherever possible, we call

Table 4.7
Students Identified as Having Speech and Language Problems and Receiving
Special Education Services in the 1987–88 School Year, by State

State	Percent	State	Percent
Alabama	2.73	Montana	2.43
Alaska	2.64	Nebraska	3.00
Arizona	1.97	Nevada	1.70
Arkansas	1.67	New Hampshire	1.54
California	2.11	New Jersey	4.94
Colorado	1.51	New Mexico	3.57
Connecticut	2.28	New York	1.00
Delaware	1.71	North Carolina	2.28
District of Columbia	1.49	North Dakota	3.16
Florida	3.54	Ohio	2.96
Georgia	1.84	Oklahoma	2.99
Hawaii	1.29	Oregon	2.68
Idaho	1.65	Pennsylvania	3.37
Illinois	3.45	Rhode Island	2.24
Indiana	3.91	South Carolina	2.97
Iowa	2.19	South Dakota	3.31
Kansas	2.71	Tennessee	3.30
Kentucky	3.76	Texas	1.93
Louisiana	2.52	Utah	2.11
Maine	2.68	Vermont	3.43
Maryland	3.75	Virginia	2.57
Massachusetts	3.72	Washington	1.67
Michigan	2.23	West Virginia	3.31
Minnesota	2.14	Wisconsin	1.75
Mississippi	3.50	Wyoming	2.71
Missouri	3.44		

Source: U.S. Department of Education. 1989. *Eleventh annual report to Congress on the
implementation of Public Law 94-142: The Education for All Handicapped Children Act.*
Washington, DC: U.S. Department of Education, p. A-37.

attention to those differences in our discussion here. Table 4.8 lists some of
the terms used to describe students with speech and language impairments.

Cognitive
There are two schools of thought about the extent to which students who
have speech and language problems show cognitive difficulties. According
to one of them, some students do have cognitive difficulties; they perform
poorly on intelligence tests, particularly on verbal intelligence tests. And
their development of cognitive skills (identifying similarities among objects or concepts, understanding sentences and words)—which is heavily

Table 4.8
Terms That Are Used in the Professional Literature to Describe Students with
Speech and Language Problems and Lead to Inappropriate Stereotypes

aggressive	impulsive
anxious	irritable
asocial	language delayed
competitive	language deviant
confused	language disordered
daydreamer	rigid
developmentally aphasic	shrewd
disfluent	shy
disruptive	stubborn
distractible	submissive
erratic	unintelligent
frustrated	unmotivated
immature	uses baby talk

dependent on language—is hampered by their language problems. The competing view holds that students with language disorders have normal or average intellectual functioning but appear deficient because their language problems affect their performance on intelligence tests that sample large doses of verbal behavior.

It may be that language difficulties cause cognitive difficulties, or it may be that cognitive difficulties cause language difficulties. The research is not clear. Language difficulties sometimes cause cognitive difficulties, and cognitive difficulties sometimes cause language difficulties. The close relationship between language and cognitive development can make it difficult to decide where a student's actual needs are.

Academic

School is a verbal-symbolic environment. Throughout the school years, especially in kindergarten and first grade, academic performance is highly dependent on students' skill in listening, following directions, and comprehending. Students are expected to understand and act in response to verbal symbols and spoken language. Students who have speech and language problems usually experience difficulties in reading, social studies, language arts, and other subjects that depend heavily on understanding and using language.

Physical

Individuals with certain conditions—cerebral palsy, cleft palate or other kinds of oral-facial disorders, mental retardation—may experience speech and language difficulties as well as physical problems. But for most students who are speech impaired there is no specific correspondence between physical appearance or functioning and speech or language functioning.

Social/Emotional/Behavioral

Communication is a social function. Students with speech and language difficulties, by the nature of their difficulties, often call attention to themselves. When a student's speech or language is obviously different from his or her peers, teachers, adults, and those peers behave differently toward the student. They may pay more attention to the way in which the student says something than to what the student says. And at times others may ridicule an individual whose speech is noticeably different, which can cause emotional problems. Students who have speech and language difficulties may withdraw from social situations, be rejected in social situations, and ultimately suffer from a loss of self-confidence.

Communication

The characteristics of students with communication disorders are a function of the kind of disorder. For example, students with articulation disorders mispronounce words or parts of words; they have difficulty being understood. But the nature of the problem can be very different for different students. Diane's articulation problem may be one of omitting sounds; Sam's, one of distorting sounds.

Voice disorders can appear in quality, loudness, or pitch. At times the disorder is of such magnitude that the student's speech irritates teachers and other students. You can imagine what it's like to have a "squeaky-voiced" kid in a classroom, or a member of the "loud" family.

Students with fluency disorders demonstrate interruptions in the timing or rhythm of their speech, which can frustrate both speaker and listener.

Students with language disorders may demonstrate difficulty combining sounds to form words or combining words to form structurally correct sentences. They also may have difficulty in what we call *language usage*, in motoric, vocal, or verbal expression, or in the sociology of language—that is, in communicating their intent and meaning effectively.

Checkpoint

- *Students with speech and language problems have difficulties that interfere significantly with communication.*
- *There are four areas in which communication can be impaired: articulation, language, voice, and fluency.*
- *A language disorder affects the form, content, or function of language.*

- *The number of students served in this category varies significantly from state to state.*
- *Although many characteristics are attributed to students with speech and language problems, none are universal and specific.*

PRACTICAL CONSIDERATIONS IN TEACHING STUDENTS IN HIGH-PREVALENCE CATEGORIES

All exceptional students are more like than unlike normal students. No behaviors or characteristics are specific to the high-prevalence conditions of exceptionality. You've learned that students with learning disabilities are not all alike. And you've learned that variations exist among students who are gifted and those who have speech and language disorders. It is therefore very difficult to specify a set of teaching techniques or activities unique to various groups. However, the behaviors these students evidence do have specific instructional implications. Certain instructional techniques are effective with students who are distractible or with students who comprehend new material at a more rapid rate than their classmates. In Chapters 10 and 11 we share with you a set of practical considerations in teaching students who fit the descriptions of high-prevalence conditions discussed in this chapter.

The one characteristic universal to students with learning disabilities is poor academic performance. Teaching methods that are effective in improving the academic performance of a student with learning disabilities are central to instructional efforts. Following are some considerations found effective with these students.

- Seat students in the front of the room and use visual aids (e.g., maps, slides) with lectures. Provide a written outline for each unit being studied. Summarize key points before, during and after a lesson.
- Use audio tapes of lectures for individual instruction and review. Prepare written outlines and notes to accompany any taped presentations.
- Have students work together as much as possible. Make one member of the group responsible for copying assignments, another responsible for summarizing class presentations, and another responsible for review.
- Use mnemonic devices to help students memorize specific content.

- Give short written assignments and oral tests whenever possible.

- Use visual cues when referring to objects in the room and during instructional units (e.g., outline of lesson written on board or hand-out).

- Use prompts and cues, spaced reviews, and overlearning to help students retain what they are learning. Prompts and cues include saying the first letter of a word a student is having trouble remembering or physically assisting a student performing a fine-motor act such as cutting, coloring, or writing. Spaced reviews involve providing practice activities over a period of time after a student learns a new skill rather than only immediately after completing an instructional unit. Overlearning is repeated drill and practice beyond the point where acceptable levels of mastery have been achieved.

- Have classmates take notes for a peer with special learning needs and have the exceptional student transcribe the notes after the oral presentation.

- Vary the form and style of presentations provided during instructional lessons. Use models, demonstrations, diagrams, tapes, films, and slides as well as oral lectures.

- Develop alternative forms for independent seat work. Encourage students to select assignments at the appropriate level of difficulty relative to amounts of work that are required for successful, timely completion.

A variety of classroom adaptations are available for teaching students who are gifted. Gallagher (1985) has noted that school personnel need to make efforts to change the instructional environment of students who are gifted in order to bring them into contact with other gifted students. Commonly used methods for adapting the learning environment for students who are gifted are illustrated below (Gallagher, 1985):

- *Enrichment in the Regular Classroom.*   The classroom teacher provides special materials and lessons to help gifted and talented students. Students remain in the classroom for the school day.

- *Consultant Teacher.*   A specially trained teacher serves as a consultant to the classroom teacher in providing appropriate lessons and instruction for gifted students. Will meet periodically with many teachers.

- *Resource Room.*   Gifted and talented students attend a resource room for a small part of the day and do special projects under the supervision of a teacher especially trained in working with gifted and talented students.

- *Mentor.*   Persons with special skills who work in the community and are not members of the school staff work individually, or in small groups, with gifted and talented students. Example: a scientist or musician tutors a student a few hours a week in their own specialty.

- *Independent Study.*   The gifted and talented students are trained in how to choose and carry out an independent study project under the supervision of appropriately trained personnel. Example: the study of traffic patterns in a local community as part of a transportation unit.

- *Special-Interest Classes.*   Special classes are established in specific content fields (e.g., symbols, logic, Egyptian history, creative writing, etc.) and are offered to students who have a special interest and would volunteer for the additional experience. Content often attractive to gifted students.

- *Special Classes.*   Gifted and talented students receive basic instruction from a specially trained teacher in self-contained or special subject area classes (math or science, with other gifted and talented students). Students must demonstrate eligibility before participating.

- *Special Schools.*   Entire school may be devoted to special instructional methods and content for gifted and talented students. Students must demonstrate eligibility before participating. Special schools in art or mathematics would be examples.

The following more specific alterations in the content and form of classroom instruction also have been suggested as effective when teaching these students (cf. Clark, 1979; Gallagher, 1985).

- Vary the breadth and depth of content presentations and expectations. For example, students studying the American Revolution can conduct independent research and then discuss another revolution.

- Vary the tempo or pace of content presentations and expectations. For example, a student can accelerate within specific curriculum areas, such as taking algebra in the fifth grade.

- Vary the kind of content presentations and expectations. For example, provide a new curriculum unit focusing on using measurement in space or economic leaders of early America.

- Use curriculum compacting as content adaptation. First, provide a brief description of the basic material to be covered. Then, describe activities that guarantee mastery of basic content. Finally, provide enrichment activities in content areas in which basic skills are mastered. Identify what should be learned, verify that it has been learned, and develop special activities to use the knowledge.

- Emphasize problem solving and problem finding to encourage creative use of knowledge that has been acquired. *Problem solving* is the selection and use of an existing solution from among a set that is known. *Problem finding* is the detection of the need for a new solution by comparing what is known with what works in different situations.

■ Ask content area teachers for special materials such as games or activities that can be used as enrichment with specific subject matter.

■ Ask teachers to suggest alternative classroom activities, materials, and instructional units that will vary depth, pace, and kind of instruction that is being provided.

The kinds of instructional tactics used with students who have speech and language problems vary as a function of the nature of the specific disorder. When interventions are carried out by speech and language pathologists, they will vary on the basis of the orientation and preferred teaching approach of the therapist. This is especially true when a speech and language pathologist is working with a student who shows an articulation disorder. We do not provide you with a set of practical considerations in working with these students. It is common practice, though, for speech and language professionals to provide such suggestions to general and special education teachers.

Teachers should work to facilitate good communication among students. When students make errors, the teacher can correct them by rephrasing. For example, consider the following conversation between a teacher and student:

Student: Yesterday I builded a dog house, and tomorrow I finished it.
Teacher: That's right, yesterday you *built* a dog house, and tomorrow you *will finish* it.

Wiig (1982) provides a number of practical considerations in working with students who evidence speech and language disorders.

1. Follow normal developmental sequences and schedules.
   a. Teach unfamiliar vocabulary and language concepts (semantics) in the order in which they normally develop.
   b. Teach word formation and sentence structure and transformation rules (morphology and syntax) in the order in which they are normally acquired.
   c. Emphasize the communication functions (informing, controlling, feeling, ritualizing, and imagining) relevant to the youngster's development and educational and social setting.
   d. Teach levels of the functions in the order in which they are normally acquired.
2. Consider principles of learning and reinforcement in carrying out the intervention objectives.
   a. Provide *distributed* rather than *massed* practice to facilitate retention.
   b. Provide opportunities for generalization and transfer of acquired skills in curriculum tasks and social contexts.

      c. Provide positive reinforcement and select appropriate rewards and reward schedules to accelerate learning and facilitate retention.

  3. Arrange early personal success for the student.

      a. Teach words, sentence structures and transformations, and communication functions that are most important for the child and contribute most to her/his success in academic or vocational settings or in social and interpersonal interactions.

      b. Begin with the words, sentence structures and transformations, and communicate functions that are easiest to learn on the basis of either length, complexity, or frequency.

      c. Begin with the words, sentence structures and transformations, and communication functions that are emerging or that the child uses correctly some or most of the time.

  4. Consider the impact of specific language and communication deficits on learning potential, acceptance by others, psychosocial development and adjustment, communication effectiveness, and self-realization.

      a. Begin with vocabulary and language concepts and sentence structures and transformations which contribute the most to the youngster's learning potential and communication effectiveness.

      b. Emphasize the communication functions and levels of the functions which contribute the most to the youngster's acceptance in interactions with peers and adults and contribute the most to overall communicative effectiveness. (pp. 282–283)

WHAT WE THINK ABOUT HIGH-PREVALENCE CONDITIONS

There *are* students who demonstrate specific learning disorders, gifts and talents, and speech and language problems. But within each group, there is tremendous diversity. This is why we've always been more comfortable talking about students' behaviors than about their conditions.

    Students' behaviors in class have important implications, both for them and for the nature of instruction. Some students are highly distractible, others have specific difficulties remembering what they have been taught, still others need to be challenged. Teachers must take these factors into account when they plan instruction, manage classrooms, and teach. Although behaviors have specific implications for teachers, categorical distinctions do not. They offer little help in deciding how to teach students with special learning needs.

    In Chapter 3, we introduced the concepts of universality and specificity to help you understand exceptional behaviors. There are characteristics that are evidenced by all students who are members of one of the specific categories described in this chapter. Students who are learning disabled do not perform in school at the level professionals and parents have reason to believe they can perform. Those who are gifted and talented demonstrate outstanding performance or potential in academics, art, or music. Those who have speech and language disorders have significant difficulty communicating with others. But there are no characteristics that are specific to these conditions. Recognizing that behaviors or characteristics are not condition-specific will help you think in terms of behaviors, not conditions, when you are teaching exceptional students.

Summary

1. Of the eleven categories of exceptional children served in most states, three are high-prevalence categories: learning disabilities, gifted and talented, and speech and language disorders.
2. Learning disabilities and speech and language problems are identified in Public Law 94-142 as handicapping conditions. The law defines these conditions but does not specify the criteria that the states must use when identifying members of the categories.
3. The Gifted and Talented Children's Education Act of 1978 (Public Law 95-561) gives states financial incentives to develop programs for students who are gifted and talented. The states develop the criteria used in identifying those students who receive special education services.
4. State departments of education vary considerably in their definitions of high-prevalence categories and in the criteria they use to identify students who are learning disabled, gifted and talented, and speech and language impaired.
5. There is considerable variation among the states in the number of students who are served in these high-prevalence categories.
6. There are characteristics that are universal to each of the conditions described in this chapter, but none of them is specific to these conditions.
7. Teachers need to think more about the specific behaviors that students demonstrate than about their condition or category.

Activities

1. Go to any of the general textbooks on learning disabilities, giftedness and talent, and speech and language disorders, and make a list of the characteristics said to be demonstrated by students who are members of each category. (This activity comes up again in the next two chapters.)
2. Ask a classroom teacher whether students who are not in a high-prevalence category of exceptionality ever demonstrate the characteristics you listed in Activity 1. For example, ask whether emotionally disturbed students ever demonstrate any of the characteristics you listed for students with learning disabilities.

3. In a professional journal (for example, the *Journal of Learning Disabilities, Learning Disability Quarterly,* or *Learning Disabilities Research*), find two research studies in which learning disabled students were used as subjects. Describe how the subjects are described in each of the studies. Are there characteristics that you would have to know in order to repeat the study exactly but that are missing from the description? State similarities and differences in the characteristics listed and identify any missing information.

4. Obtain a copy of the criteria used in your state to identify students as gifted and talented. Then list the things you would do (tests you would administer, skills you might ask the student to demonstrate) to help you decide whether a student is gifted and talented and has special learning needs. Describe how you would make that judgment.

Suggested Readings

Algozzine, B., & Ysseldyke, J. E. (1983). Learning disabilities as a subset of school failure: The oversophistication of a concept. *Exceptional Children, 50,* 242–246.

> *The authors argue that learning disabilities has become a category of low achievement. They report the results of a comparison of students identified as learning disabled and students who are low achieving in school. They found few differences in the performance of the students on the tests.*

Kavale, K., & Forness, S. (1987). *The science of learning disabilities.* Boston: College Hill Press.

> *This text is a summary of much of the research literature on specific learning disabilities.*

Lerner, J. (1989). *Learning disabilities,* 5th ed. Boston: Houghton Mifflin.

> *This basic introduction to learning disabilities discusses definitions, history, characteristics, and instructional approaches to be used with students called learning disabled.*

Newland, T. E. (1979). *The gifted in socioeducational perspective.* Englewood Cliffs, NJ: Prentice-Hall.

> *An in-depth analysis of giftedness from developmental and socioeducational perspectives.*

Shames, G. H., & Wiig, E. H. (1982). *Human communication disorders.* Columbus, OH: Merrill.

> *An introduction to the profession of speech-language pathology and audiology. The reader is given an overview of human communication and the many impairments that can inhibit development of effective communication.*

5

Moderate-prevalence Categories of Exceptionality

FOCUSING QUESTIONS

- How is mental retardation defined?

- How do we define *adaptive behavior?*

- What role did professionals play in changing the treatment of those who are mentally retarded or emotionally disturbed?

- In what ways have medical and social advances affected the prevalence of mental retardation in the school-age population?

- How do we distinguish between the cognitive deficits of students who are mentally retarded and those of students who are learning disabled?

- What is the usual process by which students are identified as emotionally disturbed?

- What impact have lifespan issues (living and working in the community) had on programs for high school students who are mentally retarded or emotionally disturbed?

W HEN WE TALK TO TEACHERS AND THOSE WHO ARE preparing to become teachers about exceptional students, they think most often of students who are physically handicapped, mentally retarded, and emotionally disturbed. They tell us that the term *exceptional students* conjures up visions of students in wheelchairs, students who are severely mentally retarded, and students who act out.

In point of fact, these are not the most prevalent groups of exceptional students. In the last chapter you learned that the majority of students who are exceptional are learning disabled, gifted and talented, or speech and language impaired. Students with physical handicaps are a low-prevalence group; we talk about them in the next chapter. Here we look at students who are retarded or emotionally disabled, two handicapping conditions that occur with moderate prevalence. Together these two conditions are evidenced by about 2.4 percent of students who attend school, and by about 24 percent of students who are handicapped.

This chapter is organized like Chapter 4. Our discussions of mental retardation and emotional disturbance begin with definitions and a history of educational services for students with these conditions. Then we look at the prevalence of the conditions. Finally, we examine the characteristics attributed to students who are mentally retarded or emotionally disturbed.

STUDENTS WITH MENTAL RETARDATION
Definition

The states use a number of different terms to label students who are mentally retarded: *mentally retarded, educationally retarded, educationally handicapped, mentally handicapped, students with significantly limited intellectual capability.* And some states deliver services to students who are mentally retarded without formally labeling them, on a noncategorical basis (we talk more about this arrangement in Chapter 7).

Mental retardation is formally defined in federal rules and regulations:

> *Mentally retarded* means significantly subaverage general intellectual functioning concurrently with deficits in adaptive behavior and manifested during the developmental period, which adversely affects a child's educational performance. (*Federal Register*, August 23, 1977; Code of Federal Regulations, 1977)

This definition is identical to the one published by the American Association on Mental Deficiency (AAMD) (Grossman, 1983)—with one important exception.* The AAMD definition does not stipulate that the condition must adversely affect educational performance. If you read the professional literature, the definition you will come across most often is the one specified by the AAMD.

The first part of this definition—"significantly subaverage intellectual functioning"—usually is translated as a score of 70 or less on an intelligence test. The second part of the definition—that the individual also must demonstrate "deficits in adaptive behavior"—is the more important requirement; it is also the more subjective measure. Whenever we try to define adaptive behavior we come up against the same variables that make defining normal behavior a difficult process. The decision about the extent to which a person's behavior is adaptive is a subjective one; it depends largely on the standards of the individuals making the judgment and the environment to which the student is expected to adapt. There is no definition of adaptive behavior in the federal rules, but generally it refers to the way in which an individual functions in his or her social environment. The AAMD defines **adaptive behavior** as

> the effectiveness or degree with which the individual meets the standards of personal independence and social responsibility expected of his/her age and cultural group. (Grossman, 1983, p. 1)

Because expectations for different age groups vary, so do the criteria used to identify deficits in adaptive behavior at different ages. Grossman

* Today the AAMD is known as the American Association on Mental Retardation (AAMR).

(1983) linked the criteria to developmental stages: During *infancy and early childhood,* deficits appear in

- the development of sensorimotor skills.
- communication skills (including speech and language).
- self-help skills.
- socialization (development of the ability to interact with others).

During *childhood and early adolescence,* deficits appear in all the areas listed above and/or

- application of basic academic skills in daily life activities.
- application of appropriate reasoning and judgment in mastery of the environment.
- social skills (participation in group activities and interpersonal relationships).

During *late adolescence and adult life,* deficits appear in all the areas listed above and/or

- vocational and social responsibilities and performance.

The adaptive-behavior criterion is critical for identifying students who are mentally retarded. School-age individuals who function adequately outside school are not considered mentally retarded, even if they perform poorly on intelligence tests.

For educational purposes, distinctions usually are made among mild, moderate, severe, and profound mental retardation, generally based on performance on general intelligence tests (Table 5.1).

Students who are mildly mentally retarded sometimes are called *educable mentally retarded.* Most of the states that offer special education services for these students use IQ scores between 50 and 70 to determine eligibility. Moderately retarded students sometimes are called *trainable mentally retarded.* Those who are severely or profoundly retarded are dependent on others for care.

History

In early Greek society, infants were examined by a council of elders. If they were weak or disabled, they were left to die in the mountains. In early Roman society, children who were blind, deaf, or mentally dull were thrown by their parents into the Tiber River. Throughout early European and

Table 5.1
Levels of Retardation, by IQ Score

Level	IQ Range
Mild mental retardation	50–55 to 70
Moderate mental retardation	35–40 to 50–55
Severe mental retardation	20–25 to 35–40
Profound mental retardation	Below 20 or 25

Source: H. J. Grossman, ed., *Classification in mental retardation.* Washington, DC: American Association on Mental Retardation, 1983, p. 13. Reprinted by permission.

Asian history, people who were thought to be retarded were excluded from society.

Treatment Advocacy

Change in the treatment of those with mental retardation came from the work of professionals who demonstrated that these people could be helped, and argued for humane treatment. Jean Marc Gaspard Itard was a French physician. In 1798 a boy was found living with wolves in the woods near Aveyron. Itard worked with the boy to rehabilitate him, and was in part successful.

In 1843 Dorothea Dix gave a famous speech to the Massachusetts legislature decrying the inhumane treatment in institutions for the retarded or insane. In 1848 Edouard Seguin, Itard's pupil, moved to the United States and advocated specific methods for treating youngsters who were retarded. These methods involved "a good diagnosis and a treatment according to the findings of the diagnosis" (1846, p. 537) and relied on physical (motor and sensory) training, intellectual (speech and academic) training, and moral (socialization) training.

The nation's first residential school for individuals with mental retardation was established in 1859 in South Boston. It was called the Massachusetts School for Idiotic and Feebleminded Youth. Treatment was restricted to this kind of institution until 1896, when the first public school day classes for mentally retarded pupils were started in Providence, Rhode Island.

In 1950 the National Association for Retarded Citizens (NARC) was formed, and the group began to press for special education and other services for retarded individuals. In 1972 a state affiliate of that organization, the Pennsylvania Association for Retarded Citizens (PARC), sued the Pennsylvania Department of Education, claiming denial of services to retarded children. Based on the decision in *PARC* v. *Commonwealth of Pennsylvania*, the state's school districts were forced to locate, assess, and plan an appropriate educational program for mentally retarded children

In the United States today people with handicaps are less likely than in the past to be institutionalized and placed in special classes and more likely to participate fully in the community.

(© Maureen Fennelli/ Comstock)

who had been excluded from school. The decision in *PARC* was one of the primary forces behind enactment of Public Law 94–142.

Through litigation and the activity of advocacy groups (among them, the Association for Retarded Citizens, the Council for Exceptional Children, and The Association for the Severely Handicapped) and individuals (among them, the Kennedys and Hubert Humphrey), treatment and services for students classified mentally retarded have improved dramatically.

The treatment of retarded people throughout history has been characterized by genocide, sterilization, inhumanity, exclusion, and institutionalization. But in the United States today we are witnessing a slow but steady shift away from institutionalization and placement in special classes toward fuller participation in school and the workplace. An example: In 1989 the La Grange Area Department of Special Education (LADSE), a cooperative educational unit made up of sixteen school districts in the Chicago metropolitan area, began a program to integrate students with disabilities into regular education. All students, regardless of disability, have the opportunity to attend their neighborhood school, in classes with their agemates. Every effort is being made to provide special education and supportive services within the regular classroom, to maximize the benefits of special and adapted instruction for all students. Dr. Howard Blackman, the executive director of LADSE, explained the philosophy underlying the program: "I believe that this type of program also reinforces the values that our communities hold, namely that people with disabilities are valued citizens who make meaningful contributions to our communities, and therefore have the right, just like all others, to be included in every part of the community, especially the neighborhood school" (LADSE, 1989, p. 3).

Major Themes in the History of Mental Retardation

Seymour Sarason and John Doris (1979) identify four major themes in the history of mental retardation:

- Mental retardation is a concept that has no meaning outside the context of social and cultural history.
- The history of mental retardation has been shaped by evolving public policies.
- Over time, the treatment of mental retardation reflects society's changing views about residential institutions.
- Mental retardation is a social invention that society chooses to diagnose and manage.

We use these themes to trace the history of treatment and education of students with mental retardation.

First, Sarason and Doris state that "the shifting definitions and management of mental retardation are not understandable in terms of the 'essence' of the 'condition' but rather in terms of changing social values and conditions" (p. 417). Our concept of mental retardation, then, has meaning only in a social context. Over time, factors in American society have influenced how we think about retardation and its causes, and how we treat the "condition." For example, immigration, industrialization, slavery, religious conflict, urbanization, high technology, all have influenced the way we think about people and their intellectual abilities.

Researchers have shown conclusively a high correlation between poverty and mental retardation that is reflected in the composition of classes for students who are mentally retarded. In the professional literature, the terms *psychosocial disadvantage* and *cultural familial retardation* appear often. Children who grow up in environments where resources and experiences are limited can develop intellectually at a very slow rate. Poor children as a group tend to earn lower scores on intelligence tests, one criterion for placement in classes for students who are mentally retarded. The end product is classes comprised heavily of youngsters from poor families. As we've come to recognize the relationship between test scores and economic status (and that has taken a very long time—longer in some communities than in others), our thinking about mental retardation has changed, as has our thinking about the factors that cause retardation.

MY PERSPECTIVE ON having a daughter with Down syndrome is unique. When I moved to Buffalo, New York, pregnant with my first child, my husband and I rented an apartment in a duplex downstairs from another couple who were also expecting their first child. In the short weeks before I gave birth, I became best friends with that other expectant mother, Lucy, and we looked forward to raising our children together. Little did we suspect that one month after my daughter Keller was born with Down syndrome, her son Michael would also be born with Down syndrome. Thus, my experience and attitude are colored by the fact that I have never felt alone or isolated as I know many parents of children with disabilities must feel. My friendship with Lucy has given me strength to take on more challenges than I might have taken on alone.

In our house Down syndrome was the norm. Keller was enrolled in an early intervention program, but I continued to treat her as a regular part of the family. At times I behaved as if I didn't realize she was different. When I went out, she went out. When she did something really goofy looking, I would laugh or get embarrassed. I had to keep my sense of humor and a kid with Down syndrome can be a source of real entertainment. Don't think for a second that I don't love my daughter with all my heart, but a part of loving her is accepting that she can bring me as much joy and laughter as any child brings to a parent.

When it came time for Keller to begin school, I looked at all the options our school system had to offer and, frankly, they were too segregated for me. Keller has always been treated as a regular member of our neighborhood. She had been functioning beautifully in our family, church, and the world in general. I was never quite happy with the separation in her preschool special education setting. No matter how much attention was heaped on her by teachers and professionals, it didn't make up for the fact that she wasn't included in the mainstream. How would she recognize normal and appropriate behavior if she was segregated from her peers? In the long run, I don't want her to be given special attention. I want her to be accepted and to meet her full potential. I didn't want to be the parent of a child with disabilities before I gave birth to Keller, but now I can't imagine my life without her. I suspected other people would feel about her the same way that I do if given the chance.

That's about all the rationale we had when Lucy and I asked our neighborhood school to give integration a chance for our kids starting kindergarten. It was not easy getting everyone to buy the idea, but we finally managed. Nor has it been easy to implement. The program has been in place for a year and I can't tell you how surprised and pleased I am with its success. Keller started writing her name spontaneously on her school work because all the other kids in the class did. She's learning age-appropriate independence and has impressed her teachers with how mature she has become. She's motivated to learn from her peers. She's been invited to birthday parties, friends call her on the phone, and her teacher reports she is quite popular in the class. It's a success for everybody involved: Keller and Michael, their classmates, their classmates' parents, the teachers, and the school in general.

I didn't know what a good idea integration would be until it happened. But then I didn't know what a good idea it would be having Keller as a member of our family. It's a good thing I wasn't given a chance to argue why I couldn't handle being the parent of a child with Down syndrome because I might have missed the opportunity to experience one of my greatest joys. And I'm not going to let our schools and school children miss the joy of knowing Keller and Michael either.

Charlotte Vogelsang is cofounder of Parent Network, an organization in Buffalo, New York, that advocates for handicapped children.

Second, in the United States, the concept of mental retardation and the treatment of those considered retarded show the influence of tremendous change in public policy. At first, those considered mentally retarded were simply excluded from school. Only through legislation and litigation did mentally retarded individuals gain their constitutional rights, and this only in the last twenty years. Through the early 1970s, many mentally retarded students were segregated in dehumanizing institutions or separated from the educational mainstream if and when they attended school. They were stigmatized with perjorative labels—*idiot, imbecile, moron, feeble-minded, fool, simpleton*—that hurt their opportunities to become socially and economically independent.

Third, the treatment of individuals who are mentally retarded reflects society's changing views and policies about the institutions that serve them. Since 1975 we have had laws mandating that retarded students be placed in the least restrictive environment. The laws reflect significant changes in social policy, changes that came about largely because parents and advocacy groups fought for them.

Sarason and Doris's fourth major theme is simply that "mental retardation is never a thing or a characteristic of an individual, but rather a social invention stemming from time-bound societal values and ideology that make diagnosis and management seem both necessary and socially desirable" (p. 417). As you think about the definition of mental retardation, the places where mentally retarded children are raised and educated, and the ways in which students with mental retardation are taught, compare the changes in the field with the ongoing evolution of values, ideologies, and attitudes in society at large.

Two things happen when someone is identified as mentally retarded: First, the person becomes eligible for treatment that should help develop skills and competencies; second, the person is removed from specific situations, from regular classrooms or even from society. Over time, our ideas about who should be treated and who we are willing to tolerate have changed. With that change has come change in the treatment of those who are mentally retarded.

The Evolution of a Definition of Mental Retardation

Like the definitions of other handicapping conditions, the definition of mental retardation has changed over time, more in response to social, political, and economic pressures than in response to advances in the ways in which people with mental retardation are treated or educated. Early definitions emphasized medical or biological aspects of the condition. For example, in 1937 mental retardation was defined as

> a state of incomplete mental development of such a kind and degree that the individual is incapable of adapting himself to the normal environment of his fellows in such a way to maintain existence independently of supervision, control, or external support. (Tredgold, 1937, p. 4)

In 1959, the AAMD offered two classifications of mental retardation (Heber, 1959). One, a medical classification, defined mental retardation as "a manifestation of some underlying disease process or medical condition." The other, a behavioral classification, defined mental retardation as "subaverage intellectual functioning associated with deficiencies in adaptive functioning."

In 1961 that definition was revised:

> Mental retardation refers to subaverage general intellectual functioning which originates during the developmental period and is associated with impairment in adaptive behavior. (Heber, 1961, p. 3)

And in 1973, it was revised again:

> Mental retardation refers to significantly subaverage general intellectual functioning existing concurrently with deficits in adaptive behavior, and manifested during the developmental period. (Grossman, 1973, p. 5)

There are subtle yet historically important differences in these definitions. Notice the word *significantly* in the later definition. Before 1973, students who scored below 85 on an intelligence test were considered retarded; beginning in 1973, however, the criterion was lowered to scores below 70. Before 1973, subaverage intellectual functioning had to occur in association with deficits in adaptive behavior; beginning in 1973, students had to demonstrate deficits in both intellectual functioning and adaptive behavior.

These changes came about more in response to social and political considerations than in response to advances in educating retarded students. In the mid- to late 1960s, classes for mentally retarded students were populated very heavily by minority (mostly black) students who were from poor families. Professionals, parents, and advocacy groups expressed concern about what was perceived as the overrepresentation of minority students.

The label *mentally retarded* also was thought to stigmatize the students, limiting their future educational and employment opportunities.

The change in the IQ criterion led to the removal of a large number of minority students from the ranks of those with mental retardation. Many of these students were no longer eligible for special education services. Some were returned to regular classrooms, where they experienced academic difficulties. Some experienced success. There is evidence to suggest that others continued to be placed in separate environments (classes or schools), but were reclassified learning disabled (Tucker, 1980).

Prevalence

Of the 4.5 million students considered handicapped during the 1987–88 school year, 601,288 were categorized mentally retarded. This number represents about 15 percent of handicapped students, and about 1.4 percent of all students who attend school. Over time there has been a significant drop in the number of students labeled mentally retarded, from an incidence of nearly 1 million in 1976–77 to 601,288 in 1987–88.

There is variation among the states in the percentage of the school-age population identified as mentally retarded and receiving special education services. The overall rate of identification is 0.95 percent. As Table 5.2 shows, the rate in the states varies from highs of 3.74 percent in Alabama and 3.47 percent in Massachusetts to lows of 0.35 percent in Alaska and 0.47 percent in California.

The decreasing prevalence of mental retardation over time is in part a function of medical and social advances in treating the factors that cause retardation. There are five general causes of mental retardation (American Psychiatric Association, 1987):

- Hereditary factors (inborn errors of metabolism, genetic abnormalities, chromosomal abnormalities). Down syndrome, a chromosomal abnormality, is the best known of these.
- Alterations of embryonic development due to maternal ingestion of toxins (alcohol, drugs), infections (maternal rubella), cerebral malformation, or unknown causes.
- Pregnancy and perinatal problems (prematurity, trauma, fetal malnutrition).
- Physical disorders acquired in childhood (lead poisoning, infections, traumas, brain disease).
- Environmental influences (psychosocial deprivation, sensory deprivation, severe neglect, malnutrition, complications of severe mental disorders).

Table 5.2
Students Identified as Mentally Retarded and Receiving Special Education
Services in the 1986–87 School Year, by State

State	Percent	State	Percent
Alabama	3.74	Montana	0.72
Alaska	0.35	Nebraska	1.56
Arizona	0.82	Nevada	0.56
Arkansas	2.67	New Hampshire	0.52
California	0.47	New Jersey	0.50
Colorado	0.59	New Mexico	0.66
Connecticut	0.75	New York	0.84
Delaware	1.29	North Carolina	1.91
District of Columbia	1.16	North Dakota	1.19
Florida	1.40	Ohio	2.63
Georgia	2.11	Oklahoma	1.94
Hawaii	0.70	Oregon	0.72
Idaho	1.21	Pennsylvania	2.00
Illinois	1.40	Rhode Island	0.65
Indiana	2.01	South Carolina	2.47
Iowa	2.13	South Dakota	1.18
Kansas	1.37	Tennessee	1.64
Kentucky	2.82	Texas	0.73
Louisiana	1.19	Utah	0.77
Maine	1.55	Vermont	1.71
Maryland	0.74	Virginia	1.24
Massachusetts	3.47	Washington	0.94
Michigan	1.12	West Virginia	2.45
Minnesota	1.44	Wisconsin	0.60
Mississippi	1.77	Wyoming	0.61
Missouri	1.88		

Source: U.S. Department of Education. (1989). *Eleventh annual report to Congress on the implementation of Public Law 94–142: The Education of the Handicapped Act.* Washington, DC: U.S. Government Printing Office, p. A-37.

A German measles vaccine has made major inroads in preventing maternal rubella, one cause of mental retardation in children. Phenylketonuria, an inherited metabolic disorder that can cause retardation, is being treated through diet. Efforts to educate women about the importance of good prenatal care have reduced the incidence of fetal malnutrition. And with an understanding of the environmental influences on retardation have come programs to improve conditions for those who are culturally disadvantaged.

An interesting point: The prevalence of mental retardation due to known biological causes is similar among children of all social and eco-

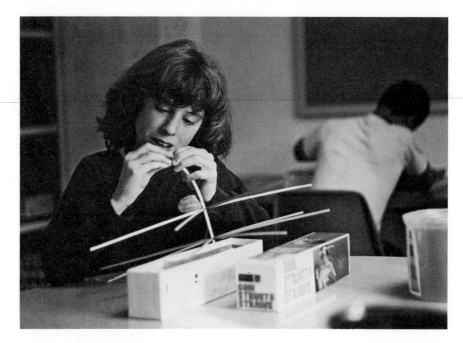

Hereditary factors as well as environmental influences are among the general causes of mental retardation.

(© Elizabeth Crews/ Stock, Boston)

nomic classes, except that certain causative factors, like prematurity and lead poisoning, are linked to poverty and lower social status. In cases in which no specific biological cause can be identified, mental retardation is evidenced by far more students from low than from high socioeconomic environments.

Characteristics

Early researchers in the field focused much of their effort on describing the characteristics of students with mental retardation. So there's a long list of characteristics said to be evidenced by these students (Table 5.3). In addition, mental retardation can be a secondary condition, coexisting with another exceptionality. And there is considerable overlap between the kinds of characteristics said to be evidenced by students with mental retardation and those attributed to students with learning disabilities or behavior disorders. For example, students who are mentally retarded and those who are learning disabled are said to demonstrate attentional, memory, motor, and information-processing disorders. Students who are mentally retarded and those who are emotionally disturbed are said to be anxious, to have temper tantrums, and to be overly aggressive, disruptive, dependent, and impulsive. It is almost impossible, then, to identify characteristics that are universal or specific to students who are mentally retarded. And

---

Table 5.3
Terms Used in the Professional Literature to Describe Students Who Are
Mentally Retarded

apathetic	inattentive
anxious	language delayed
concrete	language disordered
confused	limited
daydreamer	perseverative
disruptive	rigid
distractible	slow
easily manipulated	socially unaware
erratic	stubborn
forgetful	unintelligent
frustrated	unmotivated
immature	unstable
impulsive	withdrawn

---

note that *all* of the terms listed in Table 5.3 are negative terms that lead to
negative stereotypic thinking about those who are mentally retarded.

Cognitive

By definition, students with mental retardation show delayed cognitive
functioning. A low score or set of scores on one or more intelligence tests is
a diagnostic criterion of the condition and its severity. Students who are
mentally retarded are said to be slow to generalize and conceptualize and to
have very weak comprehension skills. They are said to demonstrate limited short-term memory and to have difficulty in discrimination, sequencing, and identifying analogies. These cognitive deficits are considered the
primary cause of their academic difficulties.

Academic

Students with mental retardation perform poorly academically, but at a
level commensurate with what we would expect on the basis of the scores
they earn on intelligence tests. This is one distinction between students
who are mentally retarded and those who are learning disabled. (Remember, students with learning disabilities show a discrepancy between their
scores on intelligence tests and achievement tests.) Still another distinction is in the breadth of deficient performance. Those who are mentally retarded typically perform poorly in all (or at least the majority of) academic
subject areas; students who are learning disabled often demonstrate specific areas of academic difficulty.

Physical

Some students who are mentally retarded do appear physically different from other students. Usually their retardation is a product of genetic, rather than environmental, factors. Nearly all of the genetic syndromes that result in mental retardation leave the individual with physical symptoms. For example, those who have Down syndrome usually have a rounder face and shorter limbs than others their age, and suffer heart, eye, respiratory, or ear problems.

Klinefelter's syndrome is a combination of physical abnormalities that typically result from aberrations in the sex chromosomes (the male has an extra X chromosome). These abnormalities become apparent only at and after puberty, and can include gynecomastia (development of female secondary sex characteristics), small testes, poor hair growth, and mental retardation. *Microcephaly* literally means "smallness of the head"; this too can be a physical sign of mental retardation. Finally, *neurofibromatosis* (von Recklinghausen's disease) is characterized by nerve tumor formation that can involve many parts of the body. If brain or spinal tissue becomes involved, mental retardation can result.

Social/Emotional/Behavioral

Researchers have not been able to identify social and emotional characteristics that are specific to students who are mentally retarded, probably because each student is unique and interindividual variation is considerable, both in level of retardation and in the kinds of characteristics evidenced. By definition, individuals who are mentally retarded exhibit socially inappropriate behaviors; often they are both socially and emotionally immature. Inappropriate behaviors, antisocial behaviors, and odd mannerisms can lead others to reject those with mental retardation.

Individuals who are severely or profoundly retarded have difficulty with independent living and self-direction; often they must be cared for throughout their lives.

Communication

Conceptual development and language are closely related. Individuals who show delayed cognitive functioning typically show delayed development of language and communication skills.

Students who are mentally retarded may have difficulty expressing themselves well enough to be understood. This is especially true of those who are severely or profoundly retarded. Those who are mildly retarded may demonstrate delayed comprehension, receptive, or expressive language.

Researchers have not been able to identify social and emotional characteristics that are specific to students who are mentally retarded.

(© Robert Houser/ Comstock)

Checkpoint

- *Students who are mentally retarded demonstrate significantly subaverage intellectual functioning and deficits in adaptive behavior, which adversely affect school performance.*

- *For educational purposes, distinctions usually are made among mild, moderate, severe, and profound mental retardation.*

- *Advances in the treatment and education of people who are mentally retarded have come largely through the work of groups and individuals who advocated for humane treatment within society and schools.*

- *About 1 percent of the school-age population is identified as mentally retarded and receives special education services.*

- *The characteristic common to all students with mental retardation is low performance on cognitive measures.*

- *There are no characteristics that are evidenced only by students who are mentally retarded.*

STUDENTS WHO ARE EMOTIONALLY DISTURBED
Definition

Students who are severely emotionally disturbed are listed in Public Law 94–42 as eligible for special education services. Although the states define and describe **emotional disturbance** in different ways, most use the federal definition:

> The term means a condition exhibiting one or more of the following characteristics over a long period of time and to a marked degree, which adversely affects educational performance:
>
> (a) an inability to learn which cannot be explained by intellectual, sensory, or health factors;
> (b) an inability to build or maintain satisfactory interpersonal relationships with peers and teachers;
> (c) inappropriate types of behavior or feelings under normal circumstances;
> (d) a general pervasive mood of unhappiness or depression; or
> (e) a tendency to develop physical symptoms or fears associated with personal or school problems.
>
> The term includes children who are schizophrenic or autistic. The term does not include children who are socially maladjusted, unless it is determined that they are seriously emotionally disturbed. (Education of Handicapped Children, *Federal Register*, Section 121a5, 1977)

In 1981, autistic children were moved from this category to other health impaired. The basis for the change was the contention that autism is a biological condition, not an emotional disturbance. This, like so many of the changes that have taken place in special education in recent years, was the product of parent and group advocacy efforts.

Here, too, we are dealing with a condition whose definition is subjective. That is, there are no hard-and-fast rules for diagnosing emotional disturbance. Consider the case of Susan, who seems unhappy most of the time at school. Her classmates say she's in a "rotten mood" and avoid her. How do we judge the extent to which Susan's unhappiness is "general" and "pervasive"? And what about Luis, a third-grader who doesn't get along well with his classmates or his teachers? Is he showing "an inability to build or maintain satisfactory interpersonal relationships"?

There is much debate over the standards that are used in deciding whether students are disturbed. That debate focuses on the difficulty of measuring abstractions. What constitutes "good" mental health? How do we determine frequency? How do we tell whether a student's behavior is the product of emotional disturbance, mental retardation, or a learning disability?

Observation is very important here. Typically teachers, school psychologists, and counselors gather data over a relatively long period of time before deciding whether a student is emotionally or behaviorally disturbed. But these observations are limited by time and setting. Behaviors judged normal at one time in one educational setting may be judged abnormal at another time, in another setting.

Although they may disagree about the extent to which certain behaviors are disturbed or disturbing, classroom teachers do agree on one thing: that students who disrupt classes should be educated elsewhere.

While some debate the criteria, others have been dealing with the term *emotional disturbance*. The Council for Children with Behavior Disorders (CCBD), a division of the Council for Exceptional Children, issued a position paper in 1985 in which it argued that the term *behaviorally disordered* should be used instead of *emotionally disturbed*. Its argument was based on the following contentions:

- The term *behaviorally disordered* is not associated exclusively with any particular theory of causation, while the term *emotionally disturbed* usually is associated with a psychoanalytic theoretical perspective, a perspective that assumes inner causation and prescribes psychoanalytic interventions.
- The term affords a more comprehensive assessment of the population.
- The term is less stigmatizing than the term *emotional disturbance*.
- The term is more representative of the kinds of students served under Public Law 94–142.

That same year, Congress commissioned a study to look at whether a change in terminology was in order. The report concluded that there was no compelling reason to change the terminology and that a change would not affect the number of children served, the nature of services offered, or the stigma associated with the label. We use both terms interchangeably.

Students who are severely aggressive or withdrawn usually are easy to identify, but most students who are emotionally disturbed do not display dramatic indicators. They are vulnerable to a particular teacher's tolerance for and ability to redirect their behavior. In essence, to be labeled emotionally disturbed (or behavior disordered), a student must do something that bothers someone else (usually a parent or a teacher), then must be identified as disturbed or disordered by a sanctioned labeler (a physician, psychiatrist, psychologist, social worker, judge, or the police). These labelers try to be objective but differ in their perceptions of the seriousness of various be-

Students who are severely aggressive or withdrawn usually are easy to identify, but most students who are emotionally disturbed do not display dramatic indicators.

(© Judith D. Sedwick/The Picture Cube)

haviors and of the abnormality of specific behaviors, and in their views of how behaviors should be treated and whether it is necessary to understand the causes of behaviors before treatment begins.

History

Deviance, whether intellectual or behavioral, has always been a social and political issue. Just as conceptions of mental retardation and the treatment of those who are mentally retarded have changed over time, conceptions of emotional disturbance and the treatment of the condition have changed, largely as a function of changes in social values. Like the concept of mental retardation, the concept of emotional disturbance is inextricably linked to the social, economic, and political history of the United States. In fact, the histories of the two conditions are very similar.

In pre-Biblical times, those whose behavior was strange or bizarre were thought to be possessed by demons. Throughout history, these people were put to death, incarcerated, institutionalized, excluded from the educational mainstream, and stigmatized.

As with mental retardation, many of the advances made in the education and treatment of individuals with behavior disorders can be attributed to professional advocacy. Until the early nineteenth century those with emotional disturbances were excluded from schools; they were placed in institutions or were educated at home by their parents (if they were educated at all). Services improved slightly after Dix's impassioned speech on the deplorable treatment of people in institutional settings. That speech contributed to change at a time when all kinds of institutions were being reformed—poorhouses, jails, orphanages, and asylums.

By the early 1900s, treatment procedures in asylums were based largely on the concept of *moral treatment*:

> Although moral treatment was never clearly defined, its orientation promoted the development of a definite therapeutic system. Practitioners of moral treatment paid much attention to the social, psychological, and physical well-being of their patients. The moral therapist "acted towards his patients as though they were mentally well. He believed that kindness and forebearance were essential in dealing with them. He also believed firmness and persistence in impressing on patients the idea that a change to more acceptable behavior was expected." (Bockhoven, 1963, p. 76, cited in Cullinan, Epstein, & Lloyd, 1983, p. 16)

In 1908 Clifford Beers wrote *A Mind That Found Itself*, in which he described his recovery from a mental breakdown and the shoddy treatment he received in three institutions. In 1909, largely in response to Beers's book, the National Committee for Mental Hygiene was formed and began to advocate for the humane treatment of individuals said to be emotionally disturbed.

Model schools have played an important role in the development of treatment and educational services for students with behavior disorders (Coleman, 1986). Over time, two kinds of treatment centers have emerged: School systems developed separate structures (usually separate schools but recently separate classes within a school) where students considered disturbed or disordered can be treated or educated; and the court system in conjunction with the social welfare system has created centers, institutions, and private schools where students considered disturbed, delinquent, or behavior disordered can be sent (often by court order).

Prevalence

Short-term behavior problems are evidenced by most children and adolescents. Most students in our introductory classes are surprised to learn that the prevalence of emotional disturbance is relatively low. Of the nearly 4.2 million students identified and served as handicapped during the 1987–88 academic year, 374,730 were called emotionally disturbed. This represents 9.1 percent of those labeled and served as handicapped, and about 1 percent of the general school-age population. The prevalence of emotional disturbance has been relatively constant over the last ten years.

Table 5.4

Students Identified as Emotionally Disturbed and Receiving Special Education Services in the 1987–88 School Year, by State

State	Percent	State	Percent
Alabama	0.84	Montana	0.42
Alaska	0.48	Nebraska	0.94
Arizona	0.64	Nevada	0.56
Arkansas	0.10	New Hampshire	0.91
California	0.25	New Jersey	1.29
Colorado	1.67	New Mexico	1.11
Connecticut	2.64	New York	1.74
Delaware	2.34	North Carolina	0.81
District of Columbia	0.94	North Dakota	0.41
Florida	1.34	Ohio	0.43
Georgia	1.60	Oklahoma	0.24
Hawaii	0.42	Oregon	0.57
Idaho	0.25	Pennsylvania	1.05
Illinois	1.59	Rhode Island	1.04
Indiana	0.45	South Carolina	1.05
Iowa	1.34	South Dakota	0.49
Kansas	1.07	Tennessee	0.29
Kentucky	0.46	Texas	0.74
Louisiana	0.50	Utah	2.58
Maine	2.05	Vermont	0.71
Maryland	0.57	Virginia	0.79
Massachusetts	2.28	Washington	0.55
Michigan	1.34	West Virginia	0.73
Minnesota	1.51	Wisconsin	1.33
Mississippi	0.05	Wyoming	0.51
Missouri	1.03		

Source: U.S. Department of Education. (1989). *Eleventh annual report to Congress on the implementation of Public Law 94–142: The Education of the Handicapped Act.* Washington, DC: U.S. Government Printing Office, p. A-37.

There is considerable variation from state to state in the percentage of the school-age population identified as emotionally disturbed. In Table 5.4 we list the percentages by state, for the 1987–88 school year. Prevalence figures range from a high of 2.64 percent in Connecticut to a low of 0.05 percent in Mississippi.

The prevalence of behavior disorders is related to gender and age. About 80 percent of the students referred for psychoeducational evaluation as potentially emotionally disturbed are boys. Relatively few cases of emotional disturbance are reported in the early grades; there is a sharp increase and peak in the middle grades, then a drop beginning in junior high and continuing through high school.

An issue that is generating considerable discussion today is the contention that schools are underidentifying students who are emotionally disturbed. This controversy has given some states the impetus to develop definitions that are more relevant educationally, systematic procedures for identification, and alternative service delivery models (among them, school-based mental health services).

Characteristics

Students demonstrate many different behaviors, and they are said to demonstrate many different kinds of behavior disorders. And the magnitude of behaviors exhibited differs. We skimmed the professional literature to identify terms associated with emotional disturbance or behavior disorders. They are listed in Table 5.5. Notice that many of the terms used to describe students who are emotionally disturbed also are used to describe students who are learning disabled and mentally retarded. Note once again that all of the terms are negative.

Cognitive
Many cognitive deficiencies are attributed to students with emotional or behavioral disorders. These students are said to have poor memory and short attention spans, and to be preoccupied, overly active, and anxious, among other things.

Most students identified as emotionally disturbed or behavior disordered score in the low 90s on intelligence tests, although the scores of individual students cover the entire range.

Academic
Most emotionally disturbed or behaviorally disordered students do not do as well academically as we would expect based on their scores on intelligence tests (Kauffman, 1985). In fact, when students evidence a significant disparity between the level at which they perform on intelligence tests and the level at which they perform on achievement tests, practitioners question whether an emotional disturbance or a learning disability is the primary cause of the students' difficulties.

Emotional problems are correlated with or associated with academic problems, but the relationship is not necessarily causal. Emotional problems can lead to academic problems. When students are suffering emotionally, they can become very preoccupied and simply not attend well to academics. Students who demonstrate behavior and emotional problems in school may be subjected to disciplinary actions (suspension, expulsion), which in turn limit their time in school and exposure to academics. And

Table 5.5
Terms Used in the Professional Literature to Describe Students Who Are
Emotionally Disturbed

aggressive	immature
aloof	impulsive
annoying	inattentive
anxious	irritable
attention seeking	jealous
avoidant	manic
compulsive	negative
daydreams	obsessive
depressed	passive
delinquent	preoccupied
destructive	restless
disruptive	rowdy
distractible	schizoid
disturbing	self-conscious
erratic	tense
frustrated	truant
has short attention span	unmotivated
hostile	unsocialized
hyperactive	withdrawn

academic difficulties can lead to emotional problems. When students do not perform well academically, their perceptions of their own self-worth suffer. They can become withdrawn or aggressive. Students who receive low grades may give up and begin acting out. And, of course, independent factors (life stressors like parental divorce, a move, loss of a parent or sibling) can lead students to experience both academic and emotional problems.

Physical
Most students with behavior disorders are physically like other students. The exceptions are those with **psychosomatic complaints** (in which the physical illness actually is brought on by or associated with the individual's emotional state). Students who have serious physical disorders can develop behavior disorders, especially when a physical disorder leads others to act negatively toward a student and the student develops low feelings of self-worth.

Social/Emotional/Behavioral
This is the major area in which emotionally disturbed students are said to differ from others. Again, hundreds of specific kinds of social or emotional

MY NAME IS SHANNON C2 and I am a survivor. I am the middle child of three kids from a divorced family. As a child, I was abused sexually by a neighbor. I can remember my behaviors changing as the abuse was going on. I became more angry and violent toward males and did not care about my appearance. I never talked about the abuse to anyone—parents, peers, teachers, no one. It was something that was to be kept a secret, something I felt ashamed about.

I remember the transition into junior high school as being very difficult and scary for me. My dad entered law school around this time and was hardly ever home. My memories of when he was home are of his emphasis on "all work and no play." It seemed when my dad wasn't fighting with my mom, he was fighting with me and my sisters. I also remember feeling as if I did not fit in with my peers at this time. Their concerns were on dating and slumber parties and mine were on what it would be like when I got home. My grades at this point started to suffer. I went from a student who basically made all high grades to one who started receiving failing marks. At no point did a teacher of mine ever ask me if something was wrong.

At the beginning of my freshman year in high school, my parents were planning to get a divorce and my dad moved out of the house. The breakup of my parents was very traumatic for me. I lost all concentration and energy in school. My days were spent wondering and worrying about what was going to happen to me and my family. I fell into a deep depression. Sometimes I would go to my classes and just sleep all day. Some days I would doodle in half of my classes and cry in the other half. I remember sitting in my algebra class and just crying. I tried to keep the crying to myself, but I ended up hyperventilating. My teacher came over and asked me if I wanted to go to the restroom. He did not ask me if I needed to talk, go to the counselor, or just simply needed help. On another day, when I was once again crying, this same teacher came over and patted me twice on the back without ever saying a word. Was what I was going through really that bad?

As my freshman year went on, my depression grew even deeper. I began to see my life as hopeless and worthless and I also felt helpless and powerless over my parents' divorce. I felt scared and could not see things as ever getting better, so I started trying to kill myself. I would make one attempt a week to kill myself. As I look back now, I remember having all the classic signs of suicide, yet not one of my teachers ever asked me how I was doing. Did they just not care? Or did they just not know, understand, or recognize the key signs?

At the end of my freshman year, I again attempted suicide, but this time I was caught by a family member. The next day I was admitted to a children's psychiatric hospital. While I stayed there, my parents' divorce became final and my mom received a job transfer to another part of the state 200 miles away. When I was discharged from the hospital, I went to a new home, a new town, a new school. The community was small and rural. I received counseling once a week, at a small outpatient counseling facility. My school counselor and teachers were aware of my having been in a psychiatric hospital. I had to face a thing called stigmas. I was called "crazy," "psycho," "loonbin," and "crackpot" by my peers. Even with my teachers and family there were labeling comments. These were very hard to deal with. No one ever told me that they weren't true, and after hearing them for awhile my self-esteem sank even lower. I began to believe these stigmas. I felt as if I would be institutionalized the rest of my life or that I was only destined to be a bag lady.

My grades remained low and my depression wasn't getting any better. After two years of just trying to make it through the day, I began to get real tired and hopeless again. I remember feeling so alone. I once again tried to kill myself and was placed back in the same psychiatric hospital where I had been two years earlier.

After eight and a half months at the hospital, I was released and returned to my home. After being gone for so long, it was difficult readjusting to my family, my school, and my peers. I found that the stigmas were still there. Nothing had changed. Somehow I managed to graduate, which seemed to be a shock for my peers and some of my teachers, as they never thought that a "crazy person" could do this.

Presently, I am 21 years old and a junior at a university majoring in Human Services. I am also a grateful recovering alcoholic. The stigmas from high school and a feeling of aloneness continued as I entered college. The pressures of college life and education, combined with my own growing self-doubts as to any truths in those stigmas overwhelmed me. I came to the point where I used alcohol to mask and numb every feeling and memory I had. For two years, I bounced between surviving and being numb.

To my surprise, both my professor/adviser and my supervisor at the time seemed to actually care about me. They would ask me how I was doing, if I was okay, if I needed anything. They did not shy away from me when I was depressed; instead, they would ask me what was going on and actually talk and listen to me. This was scary for me because no adult figure in my life, outside of my family and a handful of hospital personnel, ever took the time to see how I was or even who I was. It was with the support of my professor/adviser and my supervisor that I was able to achieve sobriety.

Today, I have been able to come to terms with my past. However, when I get real tired and stressed, it is very easy for me to relive and feel those stigmas and remember how I was treated in school. It seems as if this will be something I will always have to deal with.

I was lucky—I survived. But does life for every kid with an emotional disorder have to be as difficult as mine was?

Source: *Shannon C2 is a student at Northern Kentucky University and works at a runaway shelter.*

behaviors are said to characterize this population of students. For example, these students are said to be passive, sluggish, depressed, disruptive, fixated, verbally abusive, too orderly, too conforming, disorderly, attention seeking, self-injurious, isolated, irresponsible, disobedient, preoccupied, shy, withdrawn, secretive, bossy, aggressive, hypersensitive, jealous, dependent, impulsive, compulsive, delinquent, psychotic, truant, noncompliant, and negative.

Some professionals have tried to organize the long list of behaviors said to characterize emotionally disturbed students by developing alternative

Research points to two major kinds of behavior disorders: environmental conflict (behavior putting the child into conflict with others) and personal disturbance (behavior interfering with the child's personal development).

(© Jean-Claude Lejeune/Stock, Boston)

classification systems (subtypes). For example, one system describes conduct disorders, personality disorders, mood disorders, learning problems, neuroses, and psychoses. Another divides students with emotional disturbances into those who *externalize* (take out their problems on others and on society) and those who *internalize* (keep problems to themselves and blame themselves for their difficulties).

Patterson (1964) studied 7- to 12-year-old boys who were referred to a guidance clinic for emotional problems. He proposed five types of behavior problems: aggressive, hyperactive, withdrawn, anxious, and immature. Quay and Peterson (1975) identified four types of behavior disorders based on teachers' ratings of students on a behavior checklist: conduct problems, personality problems, inadequacy-immaturity, and socialized delinquency.

Much of the research points to two major kinds of behavior disorders:

■ *Environmental conflict*, "in which the student evidences behavior that irritates, harms, disrupts, or otherwise puts the child into conflict with individuals or groups in his or her environment" (Cullinan, Epstein, & Lloyd, 1983, p. 129).

■ *Personal disturbance*, "behavior that concerns others because it interferes with the child's personal development and/or indicates serious emotional distress" (Cullinan, Epstein & Lloyd, 1983, p. 129).

Finally, the behavioral characteristics of these students are specified in the definition of emotional disturbance: an inability to learn, an inability to build or maintain satisfactory interpersonal relationships, inappropriate types of behavior or feelings, a general pervasive mood of unhappiness or depression, and a tendency to develop physical symptoms or fears.

Communication

There are no characteristics having to do with communication that are universal or specific to those with mild emotional disturbance. Students who are severely disturbed, especially those considered psychotic, do demonstrate abnormal language and communication skills. Many never speak, while others develop language and speech disorders like *echolalia* (parrot-like imitation of speech), illogical or disorganized speech, and inadequate comprehension of verbal instructions.

Checkpoint

- *Students are labeled emotionally disturbed when their behaviors lead others to refer them to a sanctioned labeler, who identifies them and declares them eligible for special education services.*

- *All students who are emotionally disturbed demonstrate behaviors that bother others, but there are no characteristics specific to students who are emotionally disturbed.*

- *There are two major kinds of behavior disorders: environmental conflict (behaviors that lead to conflict with other individuals or groups) and personal disturbance (behaviors that concern others because they interfere with the student's personal development or indicate emotional distress).*

PRACTICAL CONSIDERATIONS IN TEACHING STUDENTS IN MODERATE-PREVALENCE CATEGORIES

Students who are mentally retarded and emotionally disturbed show considerable diversity and variability. No behaviors or characteristics are specific to the two conditions; students differ in their experiences, educational history, temperament, self-perception, and expectations. Individuals also vary in the severity of the problems they exhibit. Teaching strategies must be tailored to these individual differences. Teachers must treat the behaviors exhibited by the students rather than the conditions. For this reason we do not provide a set of recipes of interventions for students with mental retardation and emotional disturbance. There are, however, practical considerations for dealing with students who evidence cognitive impairments and who behave in ways that teachers and others find disturbing.

The educational implications of cognitive impairment or emotional disturbance differ as a function of the severity of impairment students evidence. For example, the goal for individuals with mild retardation and disturbance is total normal functioning. For those with severe impairments, the goal of teachers and parents is to enable the individuals to help themselves with their daily needs and to care for themselves as much as possible.

The kinds of teaching techniques and strategies that work for students who are nonhandicapped will work for students who are mildly retarded. The students do not learn in different ways, though they may learn at slower rates. Regular or special class teachers who teach students with mild retardation should structure learning situations so that ambiguities are kept at a minimum. In teaching basic skills, for example, the teacher should analyze what is being taught by breaking down complex skills into their component parts, making sure all parts are taught, and carefully sequencing instruction.

Much attention should be given to helping students who are mildly or moderately retarded achieve functional literacy. The teacher must develop basic skills in reading and mathematics and direct instruction in communication and socialization. These students need very specific instruction in written and oral communication activities like writing letters, completing job applications, and using the phone properly. They need specific instruction in socialization skills like grooming, dancing, sex education, alcohol use, and drug abuse. Socialization training might extend to the development of good work habits like cooperation, punctuality, and persistence.

At the junior and senior high school levels much of the curriculum for students with mild and moderate retardation consists of prevocational and vocational training. Students need instruction in choosing jobs that fit their interests and skills and in techniques for finding and maintaining a job and managing the financial resources that come from employment. Specific attention should be given to instruction that facilitates transition from school to work environments.

The curriculum for students who are severely or profoundly retarded is largely one of instruction in self-help and self-care activities. These may include mobility training, education in toileting, grooming, dressing, and personal hygiene.

Rizzo and Zabel (1988) list four key issues in educating students with personality problems:

(1) the establishment of an environment in which the characteristics and needs of the individual child are of foremost importance and never mindlessly subjugated to routines, schedules, and the requirements of orderly institutional functioning; (2) a clear recognition that these children are inhibited in functioning by intense anxiety, fearfulness, or depressed mood,

and not by desires to be stubborn, willful, or manipulative; (3) a commitment to education through the active and intentional rewarding of successful ventures rather than inattention to nonproblem children or through punishment of curiosity, exploration, experimentation, and hesitant ventures; and (4) explicit, consistent, but gentle pressure toward assertiveness, self-exploration, and self-acceptance (p. 108).

Those who teach students with personality problems must provide students with support, reassurance, protection, and avoidance of criticism and confrontation.

Many of those with emotional disturbance evidence conduct disorders. Conduct disorders are learned behaviors, so the instructional approach should help students unlearn problem behaviors and learn new ways of behaving appropriately. We find it difficult to convince teachers that a key ingredient in teaching students with conduct disorders is a teacher who keeps his or her cool. Those who teach students with conduct disorders must develop the kind of self-control, consistency of attitude and behavior, and commitment expected of the students they teach. Teachers develop these skills over time. Algozzine (1989) provides an entire compendium of activities teachers can use to manage problem behaviors. We provide here four illustrations of behavior problems and the activities teachers can practice to manage them.

One problem that teachers confront on a regular basis is students who talk in class. When students obviously are not talking about the content of instruction, teachers may try the following interventions.

- Look at the students so that they know that you see them.
- Direct a question to someone nearby the talking students. That focuses attention to the noisy area of the class but doesn't put the talking students on the spot and make a scene in class.
- Physically move toward that part of the room—perhaps not all the way, but close enough. From that vantage point, look directly at the students who are talking.
- Speak to the students privately before or after class. Tell them their talking distracts you and other students and ask them to please refrain.

Teachers are sometimes confronted with students who sleep in class, do homework from another class, or in some way just are not paying attention. In such cases, it is helpful to do the following:

- Address a question to a student next to the one not paying attention. That directs your and everyone else's attention to that part of the room. The students may feel the focus and rejoin the class.

- Direct lots of eye contact to the problem area and move toward the student.

- Break the class into small discussion groups or in some other way vary the method of presenting material.

- Speak to the student privately. In some cases the student and the class may be better served if the student stays at home and sleeps in comfort.

- Stop lecturing and quietly contemplate (for at least 30 seconds) the topic you are about to address.

Students sometimes miss deadlines, come to class late, and are otherwise lax in matters of self-discipline. When these things occur, teachers can do the following:

- Design the class so that there are logical consequences resulting from these behaviors. If the policy is not to accept late papers, then don't accept them except under the most extraordinary circumstances and then in private.

- Regularly meet your deadlines. Start and finish class on time. If you say tests will be graded and returned by Friday, then get them back to students on Friday.

Students sometimes challenge teachers' authority, asking loaded questions like "Why do you make the tests so hard?" When this happens, consider following these suggestions:

- Honestly answer the question, explaining (not defending) your instructional objective. If the student continues to press, table the discussion until later and then continue it with the student in private.

- Take an active role in explaining your expectations for students. Be sure they understand that you have their best interests in mind when you expect them to demonstrate high levels of competence.

WHAT WE THINK ABOUT MODERATE-PREVALENCE CONDITIONS

Large numbers of students experience significant developmental delays and emotional or behavioral problems, but in most states they must be assessed and formally identified before they can be served. The identification process takes time and effort. Is it worth it?

Precise distinctions between the mildly handicapping conditions of learning disabilities, mild or educable mental retardation, and emotional disturbance are regarded as absolutely essential by some constituencies and, just as absolutely, irrelevant by other constituencies. All would agree that making such distinctions is a complex, time-consuming activity. (Reschly, 1987, p. 36)

We have never found it very helpful to distinguish among categories for students who are mildly handicapped. As you will learn in Chapter 9, the assessment tools available are not precise enough to make fine-line distinctions, teachers tell us they can't really distinguish between categories of mildly handicapped students, and the instructional strategies that have been shown to be effective work across categories. We have long advocated a major shift in the efforts of school personnel, away from spending time and energy on differentiating among categories to spending that time and energy on meeting the needs of students with developmental and emotional difficulties.

Large numbers of students have academic and behavior problems. We see them in the classroom; we read about them in the papers. The evidence of those problems is overwhelming. For example:

- Most recent research indicates that about 13 percent of seventeen-year-olds and 40 percent of minority youth are functionally illiterate.
- Since 1979, there has been a 31 percent increase in the number of children living in poverty; in urban schools more than half of all students are poor, and the dropout rate is 30 percent.
- Over 1 million children a year experience the divorce or separation of their parents. About one-third of high school seniors have lived with a divorced parent.
- Approximately 1.7 million documented reports of child maltreatment were collected by the American Association for Protecting Children in 1984. An estimated 1,000 children die each year from abuse and neglect. In a recent Carnegie Foundation survey of 22,000 teachers, 89 percent said there were abused or neglected children at their schools.
- Nearly 60 percent of high school seniors report that they have used illicit drugs.
- In 1987 in New York there were more than three hundred instances in which students stabbed, punched, or otherwise assaulted public school teachers.

- In 1988, 22 percent of black boys, 7 percent of black girls, 34 percent of white boys, and 15 percent of white girls reported that they had been in trouble with the police during the past year.

- The age at which serious crimes are being committed is falling. For example, 25 percent of serious crimes in Minnesota during 1985 were committed by individuals under age 18.

- Many teenagers are unhappy with their lives. In a Minnesota Mental Health Survey conducted in 1987, nearly 20 percent of males and females described themselves as "sad, discouraged, and hopeless" or said they were depressed. More than 20 percent were "dissatisfied with their personal lives."

- Suicide is more frequent among teenagers than ever before. In the same survey, 2.3 percent of males and 5.6 percent of females said they had attempted suicide within the past year.

- Dropout rates for students with mild handicapping conditions are as high as 65 percent in large urban school districts. Students served in programs for emotional or behavioral disorders typically have dropout rates higher than students in any other category of handicap.

We believe that students who demonstrate significant developmental delays and emotional problems need large doses of help from school personnel. We believe that the practice of sorting students into categories, and the time spent doing so, are largely unnecessary.

Students who develop academically and socially at a rate that is much slower than their agemates have considerable difficulty in school. And they give teachers extra work. It is important that classroom instruction be at a level that is appropriate for the learners. Most classroom activities are organized to fit the development of typical or average students at an age or grade level. When students function at a level significantly below average, teachers must modify or adapt instruction to their level. By identifying these students as mentally retarded, teachers are able to get them the special education services they need.

In the past students who were mentally retarded were removed from regular classrooms and schools; today they are increasingly being integrated into the regular classroom. But that integration depends on the severity of the retardation. Those with very significant developmental delays are still being educated in separate classes.

Students with severe behavior disorders are a particular challenge for regular and special education teachers. These students can be very demanding. But increasingly educators are recognizing the benefits of spending time and exerting effort to modify the behavior of these students or the classroom environment to enable the students to spend more time in the classroom.

Significant developmental, emotional, and behavior problems do not suddenly go away when students get older. They need to be addressed throughout the individual's life. Work is an area of special concern. Large numbers of students with mental retardation and emotional disturbance become adults who are unemployed and underemployed. The problems are not new, but they are gaining increased attention.

> The significant societal and personal costs associated with the unemployment and underemployment of these youth have raised the issue to the level of national priority. . . . There is considerable evidence to suggest that these individuals will not make any major gains in the world of work unless there is a concentrated effort to identify and introduce interventions that will lead to their employment. Focusing upon transition from school to work, as a national priority, will begin to impact on efforts to employ youth with handicaps who are conspicuously absent from the workplace. (Rusch & Phelps, 1987, pp. 487, 491)

Some people with severe intellectual and emotional disabilities lose their jobs because they lack social skills or demonstrate inappropriate behaviors. Instruction in secondary school programs for students with intellectual and emotional difficulties, then, must address both occupational preparation and social skills training. More and more, parents and advocacy groups are insisting that students have real work experience before they leave school (Wehman, 1987). And increasingly we see secondary school programs focusing on job training, career planning, the transition from school to work, and training in the specific social skills that will facilitate employment and community adjustment.

Finally, we think it's important for you to realize that schools cannot operate alone in meeting the needs of students who demonstrate mental retardation or behavior disorders. They must work together with social and community agencies—church groups, community mental health agencies, developmental achievement centers, and Easter Seal Society centers, for example. We talk more about the collaboration of schools and agencies in Chapters 7 and 8.

Summary

1. About 2.4 percent of the school age population is identified as either mentally retarded (1.4 percent) or emotionally disturbed (1.0 percent).
2. Students who are mentally retarded earn low scores on intelligence tests, demonstrate behaviors that are not appropriate to their age and culture, and perform poorly in school.
3. Most schools further classify students who are mentally retarded as either mildly (educable), moderately (trainable), severely, or profoundly retarded.

4. Students labeled emotionally disturbed have demonstrated behaviors that bothered someone enough so that the students were referred to a sanctioned labeler who formally identified them and declared them eligible for special education services.
5. Early treatment for both mental retardation and emotional disturbance was in institutions or asylums, where individuals were often simply cared for, not educated.
6. Over time educational programs for students who are mentally retarded or emotionally disturbed were developed in separate schools and classes; today most students who demonstrate mild conditions receive their education in the regular classroom.
7. There are no characteristics specific to students with mental retardation or those with behavior disorders.
8. The curriculum today for high school students with mental retardation or emotional disturbance must cover career planning, social skills training, and the transition from school to work.

Activities

1. Go to any of the general textbooks on mental retardation and emotional disturbance, and make a list of the characteristics said to be demonstrated by students who are members of each category.
2. Look in the yellow pages of your local phone book for social service agencies that serve individuals who are mentally retarded or emotionally disturbed. Call and ask about the kinds of services they provide and how they work with school personnel to meet the needs of students.
3. Read an issue of the *American Journal on Mental Retardation, Education and Training of the Mentally Retarded*, or *Mental Retardation*. Identify ten characteristics attributed to students who are mentally retarded. Then look over an issue of *Behavior Disorders*, the *Journal of Abnormal Child Psychology*, or *Child Development*. List ten characteristics attributed to students who are behaviorally disordered. In class, discuss the overlap you and your classmates find in the characteristics attributed to students who evidence the two conditions.
4. In one of the journals listed in Activity 2, find a treatment or intervention used with students who are mentally retarded or emotionally disturbed. Then indicate the extent to which you believe the treatment or intervention would work with students who are identified as learning disabled.

Suggested Readings

MacMillan, D. (1982). *Mental retardation in school society.* Boston: Little, Brown.

*This general textbook on mental retardation includes extensive
detail on definition, the history of treatment and educational practices, causes, syndromes, classification, and characteristics.*

Reschly, D. J., & Jipson, F. J. (1976). Ethnicity, geographic locale, age,
sex, and urban-rural residence as variables in the prevalence of mild retardation. *American Journal of Mental Deficiency 81,* 154–161.

*The article describes the ways in which and the extent to which
ethnicity, geographic locale, age, sex, and residence affect the prevalence of mild mental retardation.*

Rizzo, J. V., & Zabel, R. H. (1988). *Educating children and adolescents
with behavioral disorders.* Boston: Allyn & Bacon.

*Rizzo and Zabel describe basic issues in the study of behavioral
disorders in children and adolescents; specific types of behavioral
disorders; and models of intervention, educational planning, and
service delivery for this population.*

Sarason, S. B., & Doris, J. (1979). *Educational handicap, public policy,
and social history: A broadened perspective on mental retardation.*
New York: Free Press.

*Sarason and Doris describe how the concept of mental retardation
has changed over time and how the changing character of the field
reflects changes in the larger society. They examine the relationship between mental retardation and immigration policy, poverty,
and the growth of universal compulsory education. And they offer
a thorough critique of current government policy on the education
of students who are mentally retarded.*

6

Low-prevalence Categories of Exceptionality

FOCUSING QUESTIONS

■ In recent years there has been increased interest in low-prevalence conditions of exceptionality. Why?

■ In what ways are orthopedic handicaps and other health impairments alike and different?

■ How do other health impairments affect academic performance?

■ What is the effect of a single handicap versus the effect of that same handicap appearing in combination with another?

■ What four factors influence the academic performance of students who are deaf or hearing impaired?

■ Why is it important for teachers to know the age at which their students became deaf or blind?

■ What are the educational implications of sensory handicaps?

O F THE TEN CATEGORIES OF EXCEPTIONALITY SPECIFIED in Public Law 94–142, we've discussed learning disabilities and speech and language impairments (high-prevalence conditions) and mental retardation and emotional disturbance (moderate-prevalence conditions). In this chapter we look at the rest—orthopedic impairments, other health impairments, multiple handicaps, hearing impairments, visual impairments, and deafness and blindness—all low-prevalence conditions.

During the 1987–88 school year, just 253,679 students received services in these six categories (Table 6.1 lists the percentage of students identified in each of the six low-prevalence categories, by state). This represents only about 5 percent of the students who are handicapped, and about 0.6 percent of the school-age population.

Despite their low prevalence, there has been heightened interest in these conditions over the past few years, and heightened activity in the fields of medicine and education to prevent and treat them. Improved medical care has increased the longevity of those with serious illness, adding to the visibility of their conditions. Also, the work of parents and advocacy groups has been especially intense on behalf of those with low-prevalence conditions. The same legal and legislative initiatives that have had an impact on the delivery of services to those with high- and moderate-prevalence conditions have affected the education and treatment of those with low-prevalence conditions. And those initiatives have brought these students into general education settings, increasing their visibility and

Table 6.1
Students Identified with Low-prevalence Conditions and Receiving Special Education Services in the 1987–88 School Year, by State

State	Ortho-pedically Impaired (percent)	Other Health Impaired (percent)	Multi-handi-capped (percent)	Hard of Hearing and Deaf (percent)	Visually Handi-capped (percent)	Deaf-Blind (percent)
Alabama	0.06	0.08	0.13	0.13	0.06	0.00
Alaska	0.11	0.11	0.25	0.14	0.03	0.00
Arizona	0.09	0.06	0.19	0.16	0.06	0.00
Arkansas	0.03	0.05	0.12	0.12	0.04	0.00
California	0.14	0.28	0.10	0.15	0.05	0.00
Colorado	0.14	0.00	0.50	0.13	0.05	0.01
Connecticut	0.05	0.07	0.16	0.14	0.09	0.00
Delaware	0.23	0.12	0.07	0.22	0.07	0.03
District of Columbia	0.08	0.10	0.17	0.06	0.02	0.01
Florida	0.12	0.14	0.00	0.09	0.05	0.00
Georgia	0.06	0.02	0.00	0.11	0.04	0.00
Hawaii	0.19	0.05	0.12	0.12	0.04	0.00
Idaho	0.10	0.09	0.02	0.16	0.03	0.00
Illinois	0.20	0.08	0.09	0.18	0.07	0.00
Indiana	0.06	0.01	0.09	0.12	0.06	0.00
Iowa	0.19	0.00	0.11	0.15	0.04	0.01
Kansas	0.10	0.04	0.12	0.14	0.06	0.01
Kentucky	0.07	0.04	0.16	0.13	0.07	0.00
Louisiana	0.11	0.15	0.10	0.15	0.06	0.00
Maine	0.17	0.16	0.47	0.15	0.05	0.00
Maryland	0.08	0.11	0.38	0.17	0.08	0.01
Massachusetts	0.13	0.20	0.33	0.20	0.08	0.01
Michigan	0.22	0.01	0.09	0.15	0.05	0.00
Minnesota	0.16	0.06	0.00	0.19	0.04	0.00
Mississippi	0.12	0.00	0.05	0.09	0.03	0.00
Missouri	0.10	0.04	0.05	0.10	0.04	0.01
Montana	0.09	0.11	0.16	0.13	0.09	0.01
Nebraska	0.25	0.00	0.14	0.16	0.06	0.00
Nevada	0.07	0.06	0.16	0.08	0.04	0.00
New Hampshire	0.08	0.16	0.14	0.13	0.06	0.00
New Jersey	0.06	0.04	0.50	0.11	0.04	0.00
New Mexico	0.16	0.03	0.21	0.14	0.05	0.01
New York	0.08	0.12	0.32	0.14	0.05	0.00
North Carolina	0.08	0.17	0.11	0.16	0.05	0.00
North Dakota	0.08	0.07	0.00	0.12	0.05	0.01
Ohio	0.20	0.00	0.21	0.12	0.05	0.00
Oklahoma	0.05	0.03	0.20	0.12	0.04	0.01
Oregon	0.22	0.18	0.00	0.20	0.07	0.00

Table 6.1 *(cont.)*
Students Identified with Low-prevalence Conditions and Receiving Special Education Services in the 1987–88 School Year, by State

State	Ortho-pedically Impaired (percent)	Other Health Impaired (percent)	Multi-handi-capped (percent)	Hard of Hearing and Deaf (percent)	Visually Handi-capped (percent)	Deaf-Blind (percent)
Pennsylvania	0.09	0.00	0.00	0.18	0.08	0.00
Rhode Island	0.12	0.14	0.04	0.12	0.05	0.00
South Carolina	0.11	0.02	0.06	0.15	0.06	0.00
South Dakota	0.14	0.07	0.30	0.25	0.04	0.02
Tennessee	0.10	0.21	0.15	0.16	0.10	0.00
Texas	0.11	0.25	0.11	0.12	0.06	0.00
Utah	0.06	0.07	0.29	0.15	0.06	0.00
Vermont	0.12	0.14	0.13	0.19	0.04	0.01
Virginia	0.06	0.05	0.12	0.11	0.06	0.00
Washington	0.12	0.38	0.22	0.18	0.03	0.00
West Virginia	0.10	0.02	0.00	0.11	0.07	0.00
Wisconsin	0.06	0.02	2.14	0.02	0.03	0.00
Wyoming	0.15	0.22	0.06	0.21	0.05	0.00

Source: U.S. Department of Education. (1989). *Eleventh annual report to Congress on the implementation of Public Law 94–142: The Education of the Handicapped Act.* Washington, DC: U.S. Government Printing Office, p. A-37

interest in their conditions. Finally, the high costs of educating and treating these students has policymakers and educators examining programs and services.

STUDENTS WITH ORTHOPEDIC HANDICAPS AND OTHER HEALTH IMPAIRMENTS

In this section we examine two low-prevalence conditions: orthopedic handicaps and other health impairments.

Definitions

Federal rules and regulations define **orthopedic handicap** as an

> impairment which adversely affects a child's educational performance. The term includes impairments caused by congenital anomaly (e.g. clubfoot, absence of some member, etc.), impairments caused by disease (e.g. poliomyelitis, bone tuberculosis, etc.), and impairments from other causes (e.g. cerebral palsy, amputations, and fractures or burns which cause contractures. (*Federal Register*, August 23, 1977, p. 42478)

Other health impairment

means (i) having an autistic condition which is manifested by severe communication and other developmental and educational problems; or (ii) having limited strength, vitality or alertness, due to chronic or acute health problems such as a heart condition, tuberculosis, rheumatic fever, nephritis, asthma, sickle cell anemia, hemophilia, epilepsy, lead poisoning, leukemia, or diabetes, which adversely affects a child's educational performance. (*Federal Register*, 1981, 46, p. 3866)

These conditions are similar in that both are caused by disease or defect (*congenital anomaly* means "birth defect"). The primary difference between them is that orthopedic impairments involve muscle or bone, and affect movement and mobility.

The terms *orthopedic handicap* and *other health impairment* tell us little about the educational needs of students. But they do describe conditions that usually can be identified objectively. Arthritis, tuberculosis, sickle-cell anemia, and epilepsy, for example, are physical illnesses that can be diagnosed by medical tests. Arthritis is a measurable inflammation of the joints that limits movement and makes it painful. Tuberculosis is caused by a bacterium that we can test for. Sickle-cell anemia is easy to identify by the shape of the individual's red blood cells (sickle shaped), which impair circulation and result in chronic illness, long-term complications, and premature death. Epilepsy is a brain disorder that causes seizures. We can measure its effects.

History

There is a widely held belief that early societies murdered those with serious physical disabilities, that infanticide (the killing of infants) and euthanasia (the killing or allowing the death of people who suffer from painful or incurable diseases) were common practices. This was not necessarily so. Different societies treated these individuals in different ways (Scheerenberger, 1983). For example, there is little evidence of infanticide in Egypt and none among the ancient Hebrews, yet the Greeks practiced infanticide on a broad scale. Ancient Romans actually mutilated children to increase their value as beggars.

But there is a common thread here. Throughout history, those with physical disabilities have been mistrusted, devalued, ignored, exploited, and deprived. Often their treatment was a product of superstition and fear. It was thought, for example, that those with epilepsy had been possessed by demons; to protect itself, society excluded them.

Change came slowly, at first in response to society's needs, not to any special or new understanding of physical disabilities. During the Middle Ages, the high mortality rate created a labor shortage in certain areas of Europe that led to the limited acceptance of people with disabilities (Edmonson, 1988). It was not until the nineteenth century—the era of moral treatment (see Chapter 5)—that the question of how these people were being treated was raised. At one time it was assumed that any abnormality present at birth was passed from parents to their children (Nuffield, 1988). Advances in medicine have helped us understand the causes of physical and other health impairments. And with that understanding have come efforts to prevent and treat these conditions.

The Rehabilitation Act of 1973 was a milestone in the history of the education and treatment of individuals with orthopedic and other health impairments (see Chapter 2). It recognized society's role in limiting the opportunities of those with physical disabilities and set out to right several wrongs. The law mandated that public facilities and transportation must be accessible to those with handicaps, and declared it illegal to discriminate against people solely on the basis of a handicapping condition.

With changes in technology, science, politics, and society have come new opportunities for those with physical and other health impairments. And they are seizing those opportunities and using them to adapt to their environment, to care for themselves, to learn, to work, in ways that many once thought impossible.

Prevalence

During the 1987–88 school year, 47,409 students were classified orthopedically handicapped; that is 1.1 percent of handicapped students (see Table 6.1 for the breakdown by state) and about 0.12 percent of the school-age population. In the late 1970s and early 1980s, there was a significant drop in the number of students considered orthopedically handicapped, due in large part to the introduction of the multihandicapped category. There was a slight increase from 1982 to 1985, but the number has been dropping since. Today the population is roughly a third of what it was in the 1977–78 academic year.

In the 1987–88 school year, about 0.11 percent of the school-age population and 1.1 percent of the population of students with handicaps was served in the category other health impaired. A total of 45,865 students were identified in this category. Here, too, we find a drop (by 33 percent) in the number of students served since 1977. And again, part of that decrease is due to students being reclassified multiply handicapped.

Major Conditions

In most cases we are able to identify the specific conditions underlying orthopedic or other health impairments. These conditions fall into three major groups: neurological disorders, orthopedic disorders, and other health conditions.

Neurological disorders affect the brain or spinal cord; they may be genetic, be due to infection or injury, or stem from unknown causes.

(© Spencer Grant/The Picture Cube)

Neurological Disorders

Neurological disorders affect the brain or spinal cord. Some are genetic; others are due to infection or injury; still others stem from unknown causes.

Cerebral Palsy   Cerebral palsy is actually a group of neuromuscular disorders that result from prenatal, perinatal, or postnatal damage to the central nervous system (the brain and spinal cord). There are three major types of cerebral palsy—spastic, athetoid, and ataxic—although the disorder sometimes occurs in mixed form.

■ *Spastic cerebral palsy* is the most common, occurring in 70 percent of those who have the disorder. In its mildest form, spastic cerebral palsy can be detected only by a careful neurological examination. Severe spasticity leaves the individual rigid, with muscles tense and contracted.

■ *Athetoid cerebral palsy* occurs in approximately 20 percent of those who have the disorder. The condition results in involuntary movements—grimacing, writhing, sharp jerks—that impair voluntary movements.

■ *Ataxic cerebral palsy* is the rarest form, occurring in about 10 percent of those who have cerebral palsy. Its characteristics include disturbed balance, lack of coordination, hypoactive reflexes, constant involuntary movement of the eyeballs, muscle weakness, tremor, lack of leg movement during infancy, and a wide gait as the child begins to walk.

Up to 40 percent of those with cerebral palsy are also mentally retarded; about 25 percent have seizure disorders; and about 80 percent have impaired speech. Cerebral palsy cannot be cured.

Epilepsy Epilepsy is a condition that affects 1 to 2 percent of the population. It is characterized by recurring seizures. Petit mal seizures occur most often in children 6 to 14 years old and usually consist of a brief loss of consciousness (the eyes blink or roll, the child stares blankly, and the mouth moves slightly). Each petit mal seizure lasts from one to ten seconds. Grand mal seizures typically begin with a loud cry, brought on by air rushing through the vocal cords. The person falls to the ground, losing consciousness; the body stiffens, then alternately relaxes and stiffens again. Tongue biting, loss of bowel control, labored breathing, temporary cessation of breathing followed by rapid breathing, and blue to purple coloring of the skin can result. Grand mal seizures generally last for several minutes. Although they can be frightening, they are not dangerous. Undiagnosed seizures can be mistaken for daydreaming or temper tantrums. Epilepsy can be controlled by drugs.

Paralysis Many forms of paralysis are caused by traumatic injuries to the central nervous system, the result of car or motorcycle accidents, gunshot wounds, or falls.

Spina Bifida This is a birth defect that has to do with the development of the embryonic neural tube (the structure from which the brain and spinal cord develop) during the first trimester of pregnancy. One or more vertebrae push the spinal contents out, in an external sac. Usually the defect occurs in the lower back area, but it can occur at any point along the spine. Treatment is a function of the severity of the condition. An individual with a minor disorder may require no treatment and may be able to lead essentially a normal life. The most serious form of the condition is myelomeningocele. Here, a saclike structure that contains spinal cord membranes, spinal fluid, and a portion of the spinal cord protrudes over the spinal column. The condition usually is corrected surgically but results in some neurological impairment.

Head Trauma   Head trauma can result in neurological impairments that necessitate special education services. Head injuries can range in severity from concussions, from which most individuals recover in twenty-four to forty-eight hours, to cerebral contusions (bruising of brain tissue) and skull fractures. A skull fracture is considered a neurological condition because of possible brain damage, a more serious problem than the fracture itself. Skull fractures are classified according to both severity and location, and their effects can range from minor to severe.

Polio   Poliomyelitis is an acute communicable disease caused by the polio virus. The disease can be very mild (no apparent symptoms) to severe (paralysis, muscular atrophy, even fatal paralysis). Polio was first recognized in the mid-1800s and became epidemic in Norway and Sweden in 1905. The incidence of polio in North America, Europe, Australia, and New Zealand peaked during the 1940s and early 1950s. A vaccine developed by Dr. Jonas Salk became available in 1955 and effectively eliminated the disease. The Sabin vaccine, which can be taken orally and is more than 90 percent effective, is now the vaccine of choice. Today it is hard to appreciate how frightening polio once was. Still, occasional outbreaks of the disease occur, usually among groups who have not been immunized. The most recent in the United States was in 1979, among Pennsylvania's Amish population.

Orthopedic Disorders

Orthopedic handicaps limit muscular movement and mobility. Like other handicapping conditions, orthopedic handicaps differ in their severity. Students who evidence mild impairments can function very well in general education classrooms with little or no special help. Those with very severe disabilities may need special furniture or devices, or the help of trained personnel.

Muscular Dystrophy   Muscular dystrophy is actually a group of birth disorders in which the skeletal muscles progressively atrophy; there are no neurological or sensory defects. There are four main forms of muscular dystrophy:

- *Pseudohypertrophic (Duchenne's) type* accounts for about 50 percent of cases and is found only in boys. The disease usually is diagnosed when the child begins to walk. The disorder is progressive: By the time they are teenagers, most of those who have the condition are in wheelchairs. Few live more than ten to fifteen years from the onset.

- *Facioscapulohumeral (Landouzy-Dejerine) type* occurs in both sexes and weakens the shoulders and arms more than the legs. This form usually appears before age 10 but can start during adolescence. Early symptoms include the inability to pucker or whistle, and abnormal facial movements when laughing or crying. The disease is slower to progress than Duchenne's type, and many who have the condition live a normal life.

- *Limb-girdle dystrophy (juvenile dystrophy or Erb's disease)* follows a slow course and often causes only slight disability. Usually the disease begins between ages 6 and 10. Muscle weakness appears first in the upper arms and pelvis. Other symptoms include poor balance, a waddling gait, and an inability to raise the arms.
- *Mixed dystrophy* generally occurs between ages 30 and 50, affects all voluntary muscles, and causes rapidly progressive deterioration.

At this time there is no treatment to stop the progressive impairment associated with muscular dystrophy. Those who have the condition most often are helped by orthopedic appliances (crutches, walkers, and wheelchairs), exercise, and physical therapy.

Juvenile Rheumatoid Arthritis   This is a disorder of the tissues that connect bones; there is no known cause. There are three major types of juvenile rheumatoid arthritis: systemic (Still's disease or acute febrile type), polyarticular, and pauciarticular. In the systemic form, the individual develops sudden fevers, rashes, chills, an enlarged spleen and liver, and swollen, tender, and stiff joints. Students with arthritis usually require only mild forms of special education intervention. Those who have severe forms of the disease may be incapacitated for long periods of time and require homebound instruction.

Osteogenesis Imperfecta   This is a hereditary disorder that leaves the child or adolescent with very brittle bones. The disease occurs in two forms. In the rarer, fractured bones are present at birth, and the infant usually dies within a few weeks. In the other form (called *osteogenesis imperfecta tarda*), the child develops fractures after the first year of life. Preventing injury is the most common form of treatment. Depending on the severity of the condition, children with this disorder either do not participate in contact sports or wear protective devices (pads, helmets) when they do.

Multiple Sclerosis   Multiple sclerosis is a disease of older adolescents and adults. Because students who are handicapped are now entitled to a free, appropriate education until age 21, you may come across this condition among your students.

Multiple sclerosis is a disease in which the membranes of the brain and spinal cord progressively deteriorate. Those with multiple sclerosis have periods of severe incapacity and periods of remission, when symptoms are relieved and they can lead active lives.

Osteomyelitis   Inflammation of the bone marrow occurs more often in children than adults, and much more often in boys than girls. Usually it is the result of an infection coupled with trauma. It begins when a child is bruised in some way and at the same time has an infection. The infection finds a home in the hematoma (swelling) caused by the injury, then spreads through the bone to other parts of the body. In children, the most common infections are in the bones of the arms and legs. Osteomyelitis also can result in underdeveloped bones.

Legg-Calve-Perthes Disease   This disease affects the head of the femur, the upper bone in the leg. Interrupted blood flow causes the head of the bone to degenerate; a new head forms that is misshapen, usually flattened. The disease occurs most often in boys ages 4 to 10. Those who have the disease show a persistent limp that becomes more severe over time. The disease can interfere with participation in typical classroom activities.

Missing Limb   Sometimes, because of an accident or illness that requires amputation, a student is missing one or more arms or legs. A student also can be born missing entire limbs or parts of limbs. If the condition interferes significantly with performance in school, the student may require special education services.

Other Health Conditions

Any disease that interferes with learning can make students eligible for special services. This includes the diseases we describe below as well as cancer, tuberculosis, AIDS, rheumatic fever, sickle-cell anemia, asthma, diabetes, and nephritis. Students whose problems are primarily due to alcoholism or drug abuse cannot be classified health impaired or any other handicapping condition. Alcoholism and drug abuse are related problems, not disabilities.

Autism   The National Society for Children and Adults with Autism (1978) defined autism as a biological syndrome (a complex combination of biological symptoms) manifested before 30 months of age and including disturbances of (1) developmental rates and/or sequences, (2) responses to sensory stimuli, (3) speech, language, and cognitive capacities, and (4) capacities to relate to people, events, and objects. All of the stated characteristics must be present for the diagnosis to be applied.

   Until 1981 autism was included in the definition of emotional disturbance, but in that year the Secretary of Education moved autism from the federal definition of emotional disturbance to the category of other health

Since autism was first brought to public attention in 1943, professionals have debated the extent to which the disorder is a biological condition or the result of family, environmental, or psychosocial factors.

(© Sven Martson/ Comstock)

impaired. The decision to change categories was made in consultation with the National Society for Autistic Children and the National Institute for Neurological and Communicative Disorders and Stroke and was based on evidence that autism was biologically rather than psychologically caused. The 1981 shift in categories reflects the recurrent debate among professionals about autism. Since Kanner, a psychiatrist at Johns Hopkins University, first brought the disorder to public attention in 1943, professionals have debated the extent to which autism is a biological condition or the result of family, environmental, or psychosocial factors. There is agreement that this is a complex, pervasive developmental disorder.

Heart Disorders   Heart disorders are not uncommon among students. Some of the disorders are congenital; others are the product of inflammatory heart disease (myocarditis, endocarditis, pericarditis, rheumatic heart disease). Some students have heart valve disorders; others have disorders of the blood vessels. Very recently, students are returning to school following heart transplants. When heart disorders or the medication necessary to treat them interfere with a student's ability to participate in normal activities, special education intervention may be called for.

Craniofacial Anomalies   Microcephaly, hydrocephaly, cleft lip, and cleft palate are forms of craniofacial anomalies, defects of the skull and face. One effect of microcephaly and hydrocephaly can be mental retardation (see Chapter 5). Conditions that involve the mouth or jaw usually result in some form of speech impairment. Craniofacial anomalies are evidenced by many of the students who receive special education services. They are especially significant because they affect the ways in which people react to handicapped individuals (see Chapter 3).

Fetal Alcohol Syndrome   This condition is evidenced by babies born to mothers who drink alcoholic beverages before and during pregnancy. Children born with fetal alcohol syndrome have low birth weight and height, have unusual facial features, and are mentally retarded. Some also have heart problems and varied learning problems.

Cystic Fibrosis Cystic fibrosis is a hereditary disease that affects the lungs and pancreas. Those who have cystic fibrosis have recurrent respiratory problems and spend time out of school. The disease is progressive; few survive beyond age 20.

Hemophilia   Hemophilia is a hereditary disease in which the blood clots very slowly or not at all. The disorder is transmitted by a sex-linked recessive gene and nearly always occurs in males. Those who have hemophilia bleed excessively from minor cuts and scrapes and suffer internal bleeding when they are bruised. Students with hemophilia should be protected from contact sports and school activities in which they might suffer a physical injury, but normal physical exercise should be encouraged.

Characteristics

Students who are orthopedically handicapped or other health impaired do not demonstrate a set of common characteristics. Their behaviors and characteristics are usually specific to their particular impairment.

Cognitive

The cognitive characteristics of students with orthopedic handicaps or other health impairments are specific to the particular disease or injury they exhibit. For example, some physical illnesses (cretinism, phenylketonuria, Down syndrome) often cause mental retardation. Students who have a disorder or injury that causes mental retardation receive special education services typically received by students who are mentally retarded. In the same way, students whose illness or injury causes learning disorders usually are classified learning disabled. An exception here is when a physical condition is so stigmatizing that school personnel choose to label a student *physically handicapped* and place the student with others who are physically handicapped. School personnel must determine the primary disorder and provide services under the label assigned to that disorder. Students who are both mentally retarded and physically impaired or who are both learning disabled and physically impaired can be categorized multihandicapped.

When a condition does not result in mild, moderate, or severe retardation, the student usually is classified orthopedically handicapped or other health impaired, depending on the classification process used in the school district. These labels do not identify specific cognitive characteristics. In fact, students with motor or speaking difficulties often have no cognitive impairments. This is true, for example, in the case of cerebral palsy.

Academic

Students with orthopedic handicaps and other health impairments are more likely than nonhandicapped students to experience academic difficulties. The problems are not always a function of academic skills, but of limited opportunities to learn that translate into limited academic achievement. School attendance is a major consideration for some students. For example, students with asthma are absent about 10 percent of the time (Creer, Marion, & Harm, 1988). Those who have orthopedic impairments may have their school day interrupted by physical and occupational therapy services. Students with other health impairments may not be able to last a full day at school, or may miss school for long periods of time. When students' opportunities to participate in class are limited, they miss academic content.

Increasingly, medical and educational personnel are becoming concerned about the ways in which allergies and medications affect academic performance. For example, the most commonly prescribed asthma medication is correlated with inattentiveness, hyperactivity, drowsiness, and withdrawn behavior (Furakawa et al., 1984; McLoughlin et al., 1983). There is considerable research under way on this topic, but the findings to date do not show a clear relationship between allergies and academic performance or between various medications and academic performance.

Physical

The physical symptoms evidenced by students with orthopedic conditions and other health impairments are specific to their conditions. We can't begin to describe all of the physical symptoms demonstrated by students who have physical disorders. This is a very heterogeneous group: No one case is like another.

But we can say that physical disabilities are the primary difficulties faced by students with orthopedic handicaps or other health impairments. For some, their disorders mean chronic illness, weakness, and pain; for others, these symptoms are present only during acute phases. Some students with physical disabilities develop extraordinary physical strength. Wit-

*Window
on
Practice*

STEPHEN W. HAWKING, considered one of the world's most brilliant physicists, is trapped in a body that doesn't work.

The Oxford-born Hawking, 47, is confined to a wheelchair, paralyzed by a progressive and incurable motor-neuron ailment known as Lou Gehrig's disease. He cannot speak. But perish the thought that the gentleman has been incapacitated.

This conversation, though excruciatingly slow, happens as Hawking answers detailed questions by pecking out answers on a computer with his three functioning fingers.

Suggest that he is a spiritual being and Hawking makes it clear he does not believe in "a personal God." But the depth and clarity of his spirit shine through his answers, which are sometimes sad, sometimes funny.

Hawking's intellect has been compared to that of Albert Einstein. He holds the Lucasian professorship of mathematics at Cambridge University, the chair once held by Isaac Newton. His book, "A Brief History of Time: From the Big Bang to Black Holes," continues to be a best seller.

Hawking earned his bachelor's degree in physics from Oxford University in 1962 and his doctorate in theoretical astronomy from Cambridge in 1966. Now based in London, he has been married to Jane Wilde since 1965; they have three children.

"I get embarrassed when people say I have courage. It is not as if I have had a choice and have chosen the more difficult alternative. I have simply followed the only course open to me.

"I have been very lucky. My condition has not affected my ability to do what I've always wanted to do: physics.

"I have been lucky to get more help than most people in my position. So I have not needed so much determination. It is the less fortunate who have to be 'determined' to keep going.

"I don't enjoy parties much unless they are with people I know. It is difficult, with strangers, to be more than one of the wonders of modern technology with my computer system. The reaction of strangers to my system is generally: 'Oooh! Aaah!'

"It's true my illness has given me time to think. But I'm afraid that much of it is about physics, and that is boring. The rest I like to keep private.

"You say that I've been quoted as saying my illness has enhanced my career.

"That is a misquote. My illness has not helped my career. But it has not been too serious a handicap.

"It prevents me from doing some things—like writing long equations. It has the compensation of keeping me off committees and involvement in undergraduate teaching.

"Yes, a sense of humor is important. The world would be a pretty awful place if one took it seriously.

"I'm not bitter. I might have been bitter if I had been less fortunate. But I have been successful in my work. I have a beautiful family and I have written a best seller.

"One can't hope for much more.

"Like Einstein, I don't believe in a personal God. I study the beginning of the universe because I want to know where we come from. I think this interest in our origin is shared by most people.

"What do I think death is?

"I think death is like the breaking down of a computer. No one has suggested an afterlife for computers.

"I'm not afraid of death. I have lived with the prospect of an early death for half my life. But I'm in no hurry to die. I still have a lot I want to do.

"I don't think I have more imagination than many people. It's just that I can concentrate my imagination on physics.

"I always feel I am in a race against time, like I am now. But I think it has nothing to do with my condition. It's just that I have more things to do than time to do them.

"I'm glad it's not the other way around.

"I have to go now.

"Goodbye! Goodbye!"

Source: *Marian Christy, "Physicist Handicapped—Not Incapacitated,"* The Boston Sunday Globe, *June 4, 1989, p. A12. Reprinted courtesy of the* Boston Globe.

ness the outstanding athletic achievements and upper-body strength of students who are wheelchair users.

Social/Emotional/Behavioral

There are no specific social or emotional behaviors associated with orthopedic handicaps and other health impairments. The social and emotional behaviors that are evidenced by students with these conditions are a function of two factors: the specific nature of the condition and its severity.

Any physical disability affects the expectations that parents and others hold for the development of children. Most psychologists agree that the development of healthy social and emotional behaviors depends to a large extent on children's participation in positive interactions with and positive feedback from caretakers. What happens, then, to children with neurological disorders, who are hyperirritable or nonresponsive? How do they interact positively with caretakers?

Motor impairment creates special problems too. Most psychologists recognize the importance of motor activity in the development of social and emotional behaviors. Young children must move about to learn to be independent and to interact with other young children. Limited motor skills and self-help and self-care skills can limit students' social interactions. Being restricted from social and school activities also can impede the social and emotional development of students with other health impairments.

Disrupted social development is one of the distinctive features of autism. Individuals with autism often repeat verbatim what others say to them or carry on elaborate conversations that have little or nothing to do with the social context they are in; and they exhibit aggressive behaviors, self-injurious behaviors, temper tantrums, and repetitive stereotyped behaviors (head rocking, ritualized routines). These behaviors tend to isolate autistic students, limiting their social interaction and development.

Many of those who have orthopedic and other health impairments also have limited language and communication skills, which can restrict their social and emotional interactions with others.

Finally, these students, like other exceptional students, have to deal with the expectations of others. When those expectations are low, they can inhibit social and emotional development. Many students with physical or other health impairments demonstrate atypical or retarded behavior in response to the expectations of those around them. Those who experience chronic pain can develop emotional reactions to the pain. Those who are very ill must deal with the anxiety of death.

Communication

The language and communication behaviors associated with orthopedic handicaps and other health impairments are open to few generalizations. Think for a moment about the different forms of cerebral palsy and the degrees of severity within them. Many individuals with cerebral palsy have little language involvement; their speech and language skills are normal. Others are unable to communicate through normal channels. They must use special devices like Bliss boards (large lap-held or wheelchair-held boards that display letters, words, and symbols) to communicate with others (see Chapter 11).

Individuals who are autistic usually develop language very slowly. Many never develop functional speech, and those who do show various disturbances—echolalia, saying words or phrases out of context, and voice disorders. And they have poor language comprehension, difficulty following instructions and answering questions.

Checkpoint

- *An orthopedic handicap is an impairment caused by a birth defect, disease, cerebral palsy, amputation, fracture, or burn that adversely affects movement and mobility.*

- *Another health impairment is autism or a chronic or acute health problem that limits the individual's strength or alertness.*

- *Neurological disorders affect the brain or spinal cord.*

- *The characteristics of students with orthopedic handicaps or other health impairments are specific to their particular disorder or disease.*

STUDENTS WHO ARE MULTIHANDICAPPED
Definition

Multiple handicap means

concomitant impairments (such as mentally retarded-blind, mentally retarded-orthopedically impaired, etc.), the combination of which causes such severe educational problems that they cannot be accommodated in special education programs solely for one of the impairments. The term does not include deaf-blind. (*Federal Register,* August 23, 1977, p. 42478)

The category multihandicapped is used to identify two types of students: those with several equally handicapping conditions and those with a primary handicapping condition and other secondary conditions. Some of these students exhibit such a complex array of symptoms and conditions that it is impossible to identify a primary handicapping condition. Others demonstrate a primary handicapping condition and a set of other conditions that are severe enough to interfere with placement in classes with other students of the primary type. For example, a student might have cerebral palsy and at the same time demonstrate mental retardation as a symptom of the cerebral palsy. The mental retardation might be severe enough to limit participation in classes with physically handicapped students who are not retarded. A student who is both blind and mentally retarded may be difficult to teach in classes with other retarded children but also difficult to teach in a class with those who have visual impairments but are not retarded. Students are called multihandicapped when they demonstrate a combination of handicaps that make it nearly impossible to teach them in general education classes or in classes designed for students with a single handicapping condition.

History

Before the 1978–79 academic year, students were not classified as multiply handicapped. Although students with multiple handicaps received special education services, they typically were classified as having one or the other handicapping condition. In 1977, the category multihandicapped was added to federal legislation and formally defined.

Prevalence

During the 1987–88 academic year, 79,132 students were classified as multihandicapped. About 1.9 percent of handicapped students are multihandicapped. This was the fastest growing category between 1985–86 and 1986–87, when about 95,000 were served. Over that one-year period the number of students classified multihandicapped increased 10.8 percent. This compares to an increase of 2.9 percent in the category learning disabled during the same timeframe. Between 1986–87 and 1987–88, there was about a 20 percent decrease in the number of students served. Why do the numbers in this category change so much from year to year? One explanation is that states do not consistently use the same procedures in reporting the number of students who are considered multihandicapped.

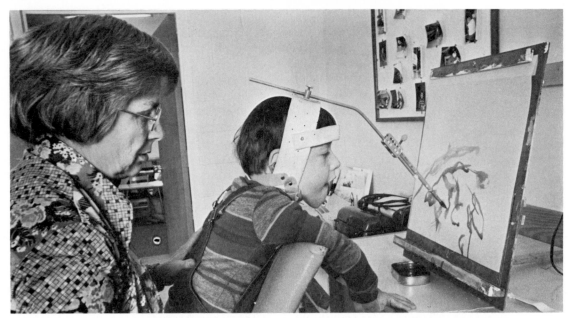

Students are called multihandicapped when a combination of handicaps makes it very challenging to teach them in general education classes or in classes for students with a single handicapping condition.

(© George Bellerose/Stock, Boston)

Another attributes the fluctuation to the ways in which students are classified who demonstrate learning disabilities in combination with another condition. Where at one time it was common practice to identify students who had a physical handicap and who had learning problems as multiply handicapped, in the last two years those same students have been labeled *learning disabled.* For example, regulations in the state of Washington specify that "students who are classified as specific learning disability in combination with another handicapping condition shall not be eligible to be counted for state funding purposes as multihandicapped" (chap. 392, 171 WAC, p. 22). We suspect that there may have been major changes over the past few years in the criteria used by the various states for identifying students as multihandicapped.

The number of individuals with multiple handicaps has increased due to advances in medicine and medical technology. Improved prenatal care, lower infant mortality rates, and early diagnosis and treatment all have contributed to the growing number of students with multiple handicaps. Medical advances save lives, in the process prolonging the lives of those whose functioning is significantly limited by multiple handicaps.

Characteristics

The cognitive, academic, physical, social/emotional/behavioral, and communication characteristics associated with multiple handicaps are associated with the specific conditions that make up the multiple handicaps. For example, students said to be both hearing impaired and learning disabled are expected to demonstrate the characteristics associated with hearing impairment and learning disabilities, but they might demonstrate at least some of those characteristics at a greater level of severity than those who have only one handicap.

Those who demonstrate multiple handicaps usually are more severely impaired than those who demonstrate a single handicap. That is, a student who is both blind and cognitively retarded would tend to demonstrate severe or profound retardation. And a student who is both emotionally disturbed and physically impaired would tend to show severe behavior problems and severe physical problems.

Checkpoint

- *Students are identified as multiply handicapped when they demonstrate a combination of handicapping conditions and do not profit to the extent thought necessary and possible from special education services for one of the conditions.*

- *Special education services for students who are multiply handicapped were not mandated until 1977.*

- *There are no characteristics universal to those who are multiply handicapped; the characteristics they evidence are specific to their handicapping conditions.*

- *A handicap that appears in combination with another disability tends to be more severe than the same handicap appearing by itself.*

STUDENTS WHO ARE HARD OF HEARING AND DEAF
Definition

There is little consensus on terminology used to describe students who demonstrate hearing handicaps. Moores (1987) reports that

> For most, the term hearing impaired covers the entire range of auditory impairment, encompassing both the deaf person and the one with a very mild loss, who may understand speech without difficulty. For others, the term hearing impaired refers to the smaller class better known as the hard

of hearing. Although one person's concept of hard of hearing may overlap with another's concept of deafness, hard of hearing is usually used to distinguish individuals whose auditory channel is affected but functional from those for whom the sense of hearing is nonfunctional as the primary modality for the development of language. However, no satisfactory definition other than a behavioral one has been developed. The difficulties lie in (1) trying to categorize hearing losses into discrete levels when, in actuality, they exist on a continuum and (2) attempting to generalize from an audiogram alone, when so many other factors also may influence the behavior of an acoustically handicapped child. (Moores, 1987, p. 8)

The federal definitions of deaf and hard of hearing are very brief and stress impact on educational performance. **Deafness** is defined as

a hearing impairment which is so severe that the child is impaired in processing linguistic information through hearing, with or without amplification, which adversely affects educational performance. (*Federal Register,* August 23, 1977, p. 42478)

Hard of hearing is defined as

a hearing impairment, whether permanent or fluctuating, which adversely affects a child's educational performance but which is not included under the definition of "deaf." (*Federal Register,* August 23, 1977, p. 42478)

Eligibility for services under the category deaf and hearing impaired is determined in terms of degree of hearing loss. People with normal hearing can understand speech without a hearing aid. People who are deaf are unable to understand speech, even with the help of a hearing aid. Between normal hearing and deafness are various degrees of hearing loss.

We measure the ability to hear—**auditory acuity**—using two dimensions: intensity and frequency. People hear sounds at certain levels of loudness, or intensity. Loudness is expressed in decibels (dB); the greater the decibels, the louder the sound. Frequency, or pitch, is measured in hertz (Hz), or cycles per second. The frequency range for conversational speech is between 500 and 2,000 Hz. Both intensity and frequency can be measured with an **audiometer**.

Moores (1987) defines deaf and hard of hearing in terms of the degree of hearing loss:

A "deaf person" is one whose hearing is disabled to an extent (usually 70 dB or greater) that precludes the understanding of speech through the ear alone, without or with the use of a hearing aid.

A "hard of hearing person" is one whose hearing is disabled to an extent (usually 35 to 69 dB) that makes difficult but does not preclude, the understanding of speech through the ear alone, without or with a hearing aid. (p. 9)

For practical purposes, you should know that deafness means the absence of hearing in both ears and that individuals who are hard of hearing experience significant difficulties hearing.

History

Moores (1987) notes that

> although occasional references to education of the deaf may be found, no evidence exists of any organized attempt to provide for the deaf in the United States before the nineteenth century. Parents with the financial resources would send their deaf children to Europe to be educated. (pp. 56–57)

The first permanent school for deaf students in the United States—the American Asylum for the Education and Instruction of the Deaf and Dumb—was established by Thomas Hopkins Gallaudet in Connecticut in 1817. In 1818 the New York Institution for the Instruction of the Deaf and Dumb was established, and in 1820 the Pennsylvania Institution for the Deaf and Dumb was founded. Between 1820 and 1840, Kentucky, Ohio, Missouri, and Virginia each established a school; twenty other schools were established in various states between 1840 and 1860.

In 1857 the Columbian Institution for the Deaf and Dumb was founded in Washington, D.C. This school eventually developed a collegiate and later a university unit. Today that school is known as Gallaudet University, the only liberal arts university for deaf students in the world.

In 1869 day classes were started for deaf students in Boston. These were the first public school classes for any kind of exceptional students.

Prevalence

During the 1987–88 academic year, 56,937 students were classified and served in the category hard of hearing and deaf. This represents about 0.14 percent of the school-age population and 1.4 percent of students who are handicapped. Table 6.1 lists the percentage of students identified as hard of hearing and deaf in each of the states. The prevalence ranges from 0.02 percent in Wisconsin to 0.28 percent in Massachusetts.

Characteristics

Many traits or characteristics are attributed to deaf people in the professional literature. Unfortunately, most of them are negative. We say "unfortunately" because the use of negative terminology leads to negative stereotypes about those who are deaf. Moreover, the negative characteristics attributed to deaf people generally are not substantiated in empirical studies. Lane (1988) conducted an extensive review of the literature and identified some of the cognitive, social, emotional, and behavioral traits attributed to those who are deaf. We've listed some of those traits in Table 6.2. Notice how negative they are, and notice how many of them are used to describe students with other exceptional conditions.

Cognitive

There is considerable debate about the extent to which the cognitive development of deaf individuals is limited by hearing disabilities. Moores (1987) notes that the debate is related to ongoing investigations into the relative influence of heredity and environment on intellectual development. The environment of those who are deaf is qualitatively different than that of those who can hear. Much of what we think of as intelligence is developed through hearing and using language. It has been argued that deaf people do not think in an abstract way and that their intellectual functioning is limited.

Moores (1987) puts the theories about the cognitive functioning of deaf students into perspective:

> The available evidence suggests that the condition of deafness imposes no limitations on the cognitive capabilities of individuals. There is no evidence to suggest that deaf persons think in more "concrete" ways than the hearing or that their intellectual functioning is in any way less sophisticated. As a group, deaf people function within the normal range of intelligence, and deaf individuals exhibit the same wide variability as the hearing population. . . . The great difficulty encountered by deaf children in academic subject matter is most likely not caused by cognitive deficiencies. In fact, it is safe to say that educators of the deaf have not capitalized on the cognitive strengths of deaf children in the academic environment. (pp. 164–165)

Academic

The academic success of students who are hearing impaired is a function of four factors (Moores, 1987):

- The severity of the impairment
- The age of the student at the onset of the hearing loss
- The socioeconomic status of the student's family
- The hearing status of the student's parents

Those students who have mild hearing losses generally perform better academically than those with severe losses. Students who are deaf or hear-

Table 6.2
Terms Used in the Professional Literature to Describe Those Who Are Deaf

Cognitive	Suggestible
Cannot think clearly	Unsocialized
Conceptualizes poorly	
Concrete	*Emotional*
Doubting	Depressive
Egocentric	Easily frustrated
Externalizes failure	Emotionally disturbed
Internalizes failure	Emotionally immature
Incapable of introspection	Explosive
Incapable of language	Irritable
Lacks insight	Lacks anxiety
Lacks self-awareness	Lacks empathy
Language poor	Moody
Mechanically poor	Neurotic
Mechanically inept	Paranoid
Naive	Passionate
Reasoning restricted	Psychotic
Shrewd	Serious
Unaware	Temperamental
Unintelligent	Unfeeling
Social	*Behavioral*
Asocial	Aggressive
Clannish	Anrogynous
Competitive	Conscientious
Credulous	Has few interests
Depends on admiration	Has underdeveloped personality
Disobedient	Hedonistic
Conscience weak	Immature
Dependent	Impulsive
Immature	Lacks initiative
Irresponsible	Possessive
Isolated	Rigid
Morally undeveloped	Shows slow motor development
Rigid	Stubborn
Shy	Suspicious
Submissive	Unconfident

Source: Adapted from "Is There a Psychology of the Deaf?," by H. Lane, *Exceptional Children, 55,* 1988 p. 9. Copyright 1988 by The Council for Exceptional Children. Reprinted with permission.

ing impaired from birth tend to have more difficulty acquiring academic skills than do those who hear, then later lose their hearing. Hearing impaired students from families of high socioeconomic status and those who have hearing parents tend to experience fewer academic difficulties than

Academic success of hearing impaired students is a function of severity, age of onset, family socioeconomic status, and parents' hearing status.

(© Paul Conklin/ Monkmeyer Press Photo Service)

students from families of low socioeconomic status or those whose parents are hearing impaired.

We cannot make firm generalizations about the ways in which students who are deaf and hearing impaired function academically. They do not perform as well as hearing students on standardized tests of reading and writing, and research suggests that deaf children have much more difficulty acquiring writing skills than they do acquiring reading skills (Moores, 1987). But research also suggests that the functional reading ability of deaf students is higher than is implied by the scores they earn on standardized achievement tests (Moores, 1987).

Physical

There are no physical characteristics that are specific to those who are deaf or hard of hearing. The widespread belief that the individual compensates for deficiencies in one sense by developing extraordinary abilities in another is unfounded. People who are deaf or hard of hearing have senses of sight and smell like those who are not handicapped.

Social/Emotional/Behavioral

Generalizations about the social, emotional, and behavioral functioning of students who are deaf are based on the performance of these students on standardized tests. But most of these tests are inappropriate for use with this group. Moores (1987) describes two perspectives on the social, emotional, and behavioral functioning of those who are deaf or hearing impaired: One is that deaf people are deviant and evidence many problems (like those listed in Table 6.2); the other is that deaf people are different and need access to services that encourage their optimal development. Based on a review of the research on the social and emotional functioning of deaf individuals, he concludes that

> the evidence suggests that the social-emotional adjustment of the deaf is similar to that of the hearing, with great individual variation. Most deaf individuals cope with the reality of deafness as a life-long condition and lead normal, productive lives. This fact supports the contention that deafness itself has no direct impact, either negative or positive, on the development of a mentally healthy individual. (p. 180)

Another interesting point: Recent evidence suggests that those who are deaf prefer to be with others who are deaf, that adults who are deaf tend to cluster in groups, socialize, and marry. Although there is considerable debate about the effect on social development of integrating deaf and hearing individuals, most of the research supports that integration.

Communication

Communication problems can seriously interfere with interpersonal relationships for hearing impaired students who have been mainstreamed. Their inability to communicate with other students can delay their language development. And the fact that they communicate in ways that are different from those around them can inhibit their social interaction and development.

As Meadow (1980) noted, the basic deprivation of deafness is not the loss of sound; it is the deprivation of language (McAnally, Rose & Quigley, 1987). Interaction is essential to language development, and much of language development and communication skills comes from the interactions of young children and their mothers. The hearing mothers of deaf children interact differently with their children than do the hearing mothers of hearing impaired children. McAnally, Rose, and Quigley (1987) report that deaf children are often passive participants in communication, that their mothers bombard them with language stimulation and dominate the communication process. These authors also conclude that the vocabulary and syntax of deaf children grow slowly.

For teachers, it is useful to know the onset of deafness or hearing impairment. Those born deaf or seriously hearing impaired are at a significant disadvantage in learning language.

AT THE AGE OF TWELVE I won the swimming award at the Lions Camp for Crippled Children. When my name echoed over the PA system the girl in the wheelchair next to me grabbed the box speaker of my hearing aid and shouted, "You won!" My ear quaking, I took the cue. I stood up straight—the only physically unencumbered child in a sea of braces and canes—affixed a pained but brave grin on my face, then limped all the way to the stage.

Later, after the spotlight had dimmed, I was overcome with remorse, but not because I'd played the crippled heroine. The truth was that I was ashamed of my handicap. I wanted to have something more visibly wrong with me. I wanted to be in the same league as the girl who'd lost her right leg in a car accident; her artificial leg attracted a bevy of awestruck campers. I, on the other hand, wore an unwieldy box hearing aid buckled to my body like a dog halter. It attracted no one. Deafness wasn't, in my eyes, a blue-ribbon handicap. Mixed in with my envy, though, was an overwhelming sense of guilt; at camp I was free to splash in the swimming pool, while most of the other children were stranded at the shallow end, where lifeguards floated them in lazy circles. But seventeen years of living in the "normal" world has diminished my guilt considerably, and I've learned that every handicap has its own particular hell.

I'm something of an anomaly in the deaf world. Unlike most deaf people, who were either born deaf or went deaf in infancy, I lost my hearing in chunks over a period of twelve years. Fortunately I learned to speak before my loss grew too profound, and that ability freed me from the most severe problem facing the deaf—the terrible difficulty of making themselves understood. My opinion of deafness was just as biased as that of a person who can hear. I had never met a deaf child in my life, and I didn't know how to sign. I imagined deaf people to be like creatures from beyond: animallike because their language was so physical, threatening because they were unable to express themselves with sophistication—that is, through speech. I *could* make myself understood, and because I had a talent for lipreading it was easy for me to pass in the wider world. And for most of my life that is exactly what I did—like a black woman playing white, I passed for something other than what I was. But in doing so I was avoiding some very painful facts. And for many years I was inhibited not only by my deafness but my own idea of what it meant to be deaf. . . .

For the first few years my parents were as bewildered as I was. Nothing had prepared them for a handicapped child on the brink of adolescence. They sensed a whole other world of problems, but in those early stages I still seemed so normal that they just couldn't see me in a school for the deaf. They felt that although such schools were there to help, they also served to isolate. I have always been grateful for their decision. Because of it, I had to contend with public schools, and in doing so I developed two methods of survival: I learned to read not just lips but the whole person, and I learned the habit of clear speech by taking every speech and drama course I could.

That is not to say my adolescent years were easy going—they were misery. The lack of sound cast a pall on everything. Life seemed less fun than it had been before. I didn't associate that lack of fun with the lack of sound. I didn't begin to make the connection between the failings of my body and the failings of the world until I was well out of college. I simply did not admit to myself that deafness caused certain problems—or even that I was deaf.

From the time I was twelve until I was twenty-four, the loss of my hearing was erratic. I would lose a decibel or two of sound and then my hearing would stabilize. A week or a year later there would be another slip and then I'd have to adjust all over again. I never knew when I would hit bottom. I remember going to bed one night still being able to make out the reassuring purr of the refrigerator and the late-night conversation of my parents, then waking up the next morning to nothing—even my own voice was gone. These fits and starts continued until my hearing finally dropped to the last rung of amplifiable sound. I was a college student at the time, and whenever anyone asked about my hearing aid, I admitted to being only slightly hard of hearing.

My professors were frequently alarmed by my almost maniacal intensity in class. I was petrified that I'd have to ask for special privileges just to achieve marginal understanding. My pride was in flames. I became increasingly bitter and isolated. I was terrified of being marked a deaf woman, a label that made me sound dumb and cowlike, enveloped in a protective silence that denied me my complexity. . . . I lied about the extent of my deafness so I could avoid the stigma of being thought "different" in a pathetic way.

It was not surprising that in my senior year I suffered a nervous collapse and spent three days in a hospital crying like a baby. When I stopped crying I knew it was time to face a few things—I had to start asking for help when I needed it because I couldn't handle my deafness alone,

and I had to quit being ashamed of my handicap so I could begin to live with its consequences and discover what (if any) were its rewards.

When I began telling people that I was *really* deaf I did so with grim determination. Some were afraid to talk to me at any length, fearing perhaps that they were talking into a void; others assumed that I was somehow an unsullied innocent and always inquired in carefully enunciated sentences; "Doooooooo youuuuuuuuu driiinnk liquor?" But most people were surprisingly sympathetic—they wanted to know the best way to be understood, they took great pains to talk directly to my face, and they didn't insult me by using only words of one syllable.

It was, in part, that gentle acceptance that made me more curious about my own deafness. Always before it had been an affliction to wrestle with as one would with angels, but when I finally accepted it as an inevitable part of my life, I relaxed enough to do some exploring. I would take off my hearing aid and go through a day, a night, an hour or two—as long as I could take it—in absolute silence. I felt as if I were indulging in a secret vice because I was perceiving the world in a new way—stripped of sound. . . .

Silence is not empty; it is simply more sobering than sound. At times I prefer the sobriety. I can still "hear" with a hearing aid—that is, I can discern noise, but I can't tell you where it's coming from or if it is laughter or a faulty drain. When there are many people talking together I hear a strange music, a distant rumbling in my consciousness. But when I take off my hearing aid at night and lie in bed surrounded by my fate, I wonder, "What is this—a foul subtraction or a blessing in disguise?" For despite my fears there is a kind of peace in

(continued)

the silence—albeit an uneasy one. There is, after all, less to distract me from my thoughts.

But I know what I've lost. The process of becoming deaf has at times been frightening, akin perhaps to dying, and early in life it took away my happy confidence in the image of a world where things always work right. When I first came back from the Lions Camp that summer I cursed heaven and earth for doing such terrible wrong to me and to my friends. My grandmother tried to comfort me by promising, "Honey, God's got something special planned for you."

But I thought, "Yes. He plans to make me deaf."

Source: *From Terry Galloway, "I'm Listening as Hard as I Can," Texas Monthly, April 1981. © 1981 by Texas Monthly. Adapted and reprinted with permission.*

Checkpoint

- *Federal definitions of deafness and hard of hearing do not include standards for identifying students who are deaf or hard of hearing.*

- *Students who are deaf or hard of hearing demonstrate the same variation in cognitive, academic, physical, and socioemotional characteristics as do students who are not handicapped.*

- *The basic deprivation of deafness is the deprivation of language.*

STUDENTS WHO ARE VISUALLY HANDICAPPED
Definition

According to federal regulations, a **visual handicap** is

a visual impairment which, even with correction, adversely affects a child's educational performance. The term includes both partially seeing and blind children. (*Federal Register*, August 23, 1977, p. 42479)

Despite the simplicity of this definition, it has generated little consensus. "Definitions of blindness and visual impairment vary depending on the discipline or agency providing the services" (Scholl, 1986, p. 26).

Blindness and visual impairment are defined in terms of **visual acuity**—the ability to see things at specified distances. Visual acuity usually is measured by having people read letters or discriminate objects at a distance of 20 feet. Those who are able to read the letters correctly have normal vision. Visual acuity usually is expressed as a ratio, which tells us how well the individual sees. The expression *20/20 vision* describes perfect (normal) vision; it means that the person can see at 20 feet what people with normal

Orientation and mobility training is a major part of the curriculum for students who are visually handicapped.
(© Karen R. Preuss)

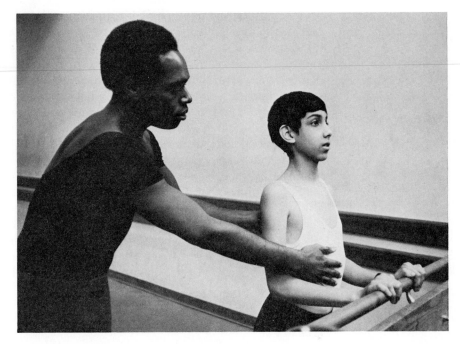

vision see at 20 feet. A person with 20/90 vision can read letters or discriminate objects at 20 feet that a person with normal vision can read or discriminate at 90 feet.

How bad does visual acuity have to be before a person is considered blind? The American Medical Association adopted a legal definition of blindness in 1934 that is still used today. According to that definition, the criterion for blindness is

> central visual acuity of 20/200 or less in the better eye with corrective glasses or central visual acuity of more than 20/200 if there is a visual field defect in which the peripheral field is contracted to such an extent that the widest diameter of the visual field subtends an angular distance no greater than 20 degrees in the better eye. (Koestler, 1976, p. 45)

A person who can see at 20 feet what a person with normal vision can see at 200 feet or more is considered blind. The second part of the AMA definition is included so that people with a severely restricted visual field are also considered blind. People with restricted visual fields are said to have tunnel vision.

Individuals who are visually impaired but not blind are also eligible for special education services. These are people with visual acuity greater than 20/200 but not greater than 20/70 in the better eye with correction.

Actually, students who fall within five levels of visual impairment are recognized as eligible for special education services: total blindness, legal blindness, vision between 20/200 and 20/60, blindness in one eye, and other visual limitations (DE-OSERS, 1975). For all practical purposes, any student who has visual acuity with correction of less than 20/70 is eligible for special education services for visually handicapped students. In all cases, the standard is employed "with correction." This means that if the condition can be corrected with glasses or contact lenses, the student is not eligible for special education services.

In recent years, educators have begun to place more emphasis on visual functioning than on visual acuity as measured by vision tests. This shift in focus recognizes that all blind students and all partially sighted are not alike. It is more common now for blind and partially sighted students to be classified in terms of the kinds of instructional approaches that are effective for them. Blind students, then, are those who must be educated through channels other than sight (using braille or audiotapes, for example). Partially sighted students can use print materials, but the print must be enlarged.

History

Students who are blind or visually impaired were among the first to receive special education services in the United States. The first institutional programs for blind students—the New England Asylum for the Blind and the New York Institution for the Blind—began in 1832. Five years later, the first residential school for blind students opened in Ohio. It was not until 1900 that the first day school classes for blind students were held in Chicago. In 1911 New York became the first state to make education for blind students compulsory. And in 1913 Boston and Cleveland started classes for partially sighted students.

Early programs for partially sighted students were called "sight conservation programs"; they actually discouraged students from using residual vision. Apparently educators believed that to use residual vision was to lose it (Roberts, 1986). Robert Irwin was the first to encourage partially sighted students to read print. In 1914 he conducted research to identify the size and style of type that would be easiest for partially sighted students to read and had the first large-print books printed.

Legislation played an important role in the development of programs and services for students who are blind or visually impaired. Some of the very first special education laws pertained to these students (see Table 2.1). In 1899 Connecticut enacted the first law requiring vision testing in schools, and in 1930 Congress passed the Pratt-Smoot Act, which provided books to blind adults. In 1931 the Library of Congress began distributing braille materials and phonograph records to blind people, and in 1932 the

American Printing House for the Blind began developing and distributing talking books.

Until recently, it was common to place blind students in residential settings and day schools. Today, more and more of these students are being accommodated in general education classes.

Prevalence

During the 1987–88 academic year 22,864 students with visual handicaps received special education services. This represents 0.06 percent of school-age children and adolescents and 0.6 percent of students who are handicapped. There is very little variation in the percentage of students identified in each of the states (see Table 6.1).

Characteristics
Cognitive

Cognition is largely a matter of developing concepts. Because many concepts are learned entirely through visual means, students with visual handicaps have difficulty learning concepts. Think for a minute about the difficulty of learning concepts like orange, circle, bigger, perpendicular, bright, and foggy without sight. Students who have visual handicaps are not necessarily intellectually retarded, but they may perform poorly on most standard intelligence tests. The reason? The nature of those tests. Look at these items from intelligence tests:

- What is a collar?
- What is a pagoda?
- Tell me another word for luminate?
- In what way are a radio tower and a police car alike?

Moreover, many of the subtests and items on intelligence tests require that students see the stimuli and responses: Students are shown pictures and asked to identify them; they are shown bead patterns and asked to reproduce them; they are shown visual stimulus arrays and asked to find the one stimulus that differs from the others.

Academic

Newland (1986) reported that "with the exception of unique problems of input and possibly a greater demand in processing, the fundamental learning procedures of blind children do not differ from those of nonimpaired children" (p. 576).

The impact of visual handicaps on academic performance is very much a function of the severity of the condition and the age at which the student became blind. There are three major groups of students with visual impairments: those who have a moderate correctable impairment, those who are partially sighted, and those who are blind.

The learning situation for students with moderate impairments is not markedly different from that of other students. Moderate impairments generally can be corrected with glasses. Younger children need help getting used to their glasses, need to be encouraged to use them, and often need help taking care of them. Teachers also should take into account lighting and seating arrangements to maximize the vision of these students. Those who are partially sighted need large-print materials, magnifiers, large-print typewriters, and other devices. Those who are blind need compensatory modes of communication, like braille. These students experience the greatest academic difficulty.

Students who are born blind or lose their sight before the age of 5 lack visual imagery. They are unable to picture in their mind things they have not seen or experienced.

Physical

In terms of size and appearance, individuals who are visually handicapped are no different from those who are not handicapped. But there are physical mannerisms that are typical of blind people. These behaviors include rocking, eye poking, head rolling, and hand waving.

Students who are visually handicapped have difficulty with orientation and mobility. **Orientation** refers to the ability to know where one is in relation to the environment; **mobility** is the ability to move safely and efficiently from one place to another. Orientation and mobility training is a major part of the curriculum for students who are visually handicapped.

Social/Emotional/Behavioral

In contrast to those who are deaf, individuals who are blind do not cluster in groups. The difference is primarily related to the way they communicate. Those who are deaf communicate by lip reading or signing, methods that are much easier to use when others are using them too. Communication by braille, on the other hand, is a pretty solitary act.

The manneristic behaviors that are common to individuals who are visually handicapped can lead others to avoid them. Just the fact that they are blind may cause others to avoid them. This exclusion can inhibit the development of socially appropriate behaviors and lead to social and emotional difficulties. Otherwise, there are no social and emotional characteristics specific to visual handicaps.

Communication

This is the major area in which students with visual handicaps experience difficulty. To "read," for example, they have to use large-print books and magnifiers, braille, or recorded materials and readers. Also, they cannot see nonverbal forms of communication, so they miss out on the information and feelings imparted through a look, a nod, a smile, a frown, a shrug.

Checkpoint

- *Students are considered visually handicapped when their impairment interferes with their academic performance.*
- *The federal definition of visual handicap does not include standards for identifying students as blind or partially sighted. The standards generally used are those of the American Medical Association.*
- *Students who are visually handicapped exhibit the same variation in characteristics as do those who are not visually handicapped, with one exception: They cannot input and process visual information in the same way.*

STUDENTS WHO ARE DEAF AND BLIND

In 1968 the federal government began funding programs for students who are both deaf and blind. In 1977 the condition was formally defined in federal rules and regulations.

> "Deaf-blind" means concomitant hearing and visual impairments, the combination of which causes such severe communication and other developmental and educational problems that they cannot be accommodated in special education programs solely for deaf or blind children. (*Federal Register*, August 23, 1977, p. 42478)

The common view of students who are deaf and blind is that they are totally deaf and totally blind. This is not the case. To be considered deaf-blind, a student must meet the criteria for being considered deaf as well as the criteria for being considered blind. Many students who meet these criteria have some functional hearing and vision.

History

You probably know the story of Helen Keller, a deaf-blind student who was taught by Anne Sullivan. To put the history of development of school programs into perspective, you should know that Sullivan began teaching Keller in 1887. Keller received her college degree in 1904, the first deaf-blind person to do so, some sixty-four years before the federal government began funding programs for students who are both deaf and blind.

Prevalence

During the 1987–88 academic year, 1,472 students were identified as deaf and blind and received special education services. This number is very small, less than 0.01 percent of the school-age population, and it may be far from accurate. We don't have a firm count of these students for two reasons: "Parents of such children tend to keep them out of circulation, and . . . once they are located, diagnosis of them is often ambiguous" (Newland, 1986, p. 577).

Formal identification has increased over the years with the development of **child-find programs** (formal community and public school programs to locate young children who are handicapped) and services for students who are deaf and blind.

Characteristics

The characteristics of students who are deaf and blind are a combination of those we've described for students who are deaf and students who are blind. In addition, these students exhibit more severe academic, social, and communication problems than do students with a single impairment. This is especially evident in communication skills. Students who are blind can profit from verbal and tactile (touch) stimulation: Those who are deaf can profit from visual and tactile input. But students who are both blind and deaf essentially rely only on tactile stimulation.

Checkpoint

■ *Students are identified as deaf and blind when they demonstrate both conditions and when their needs cannot be met in classes for students who are deaf or classes for students with visual handicaps.*

PRACTICAL CONSIDERATIONS IN TEACHING STUDENTS IN LOW-PREVALENCE CATEGORIES

When the Rehabilitation Act of 1973 and the Education for All Handicapped Children Act of 1975 were passed, I believed wonderful things would happen for people with disabilities. I pictured disabled children finally going to school with nondisabled students of their age and grade. I pictured disabled and nondisabled children taking the same classes, reading the same books, and taking the same tests. I pictured them participating in the same clubs, sometimes becoming friends and other times not, getting into the same scrapes, and learning how to solve the same problems. I believed that the integrated education that had been atypical for me and other blind students of New Jersey in the 1950s and 1960s would be standard and unremarkable for this generation of disabled students. I assumed that today's high school graduates and college students would have experiences comparable to or better than my own of many years ago. . . . In the 1980s, I find that my expectations are only sometimes met. (Asch, 1989, p. 181)

We believe that Adrienne Asch's dreams are important. We believe they are being met in schools across the country and will continue to be met if people who work with exceptional students treat them as much like normal as possible. Toward this goal, students in low-prevalence categories can best be helped by teachers who can eliminate barriers, improve communication, and foster independence.

Eliminate Barriers

Architectural obstacles that cause students who are blind or mobility impaired to be dependent on other people should be removed or at least rendered manageable. For example, Kim ordered a specially designed desk for a student in her room who needed a wheelchair to get around. Until it arrived, she placed the student's desk on concrete blocks to raise it to a comfortable level. Greer, Allsop, and Greer (1980) provided a brief checklist (see Table 6.3) for deciding whether schools and other public buildings are accessible to students with physical and health handicaps.

When Larry works with a student who is blind, he provides an orientation to his classroom. He points out the location of his desk, the student's desk, the learning centers, the computer, the pencil sharpener, and all the other places and things the student needs to know or asks about. He has found that it is helpful to introduce a few new things each day and to always start the student at his own desk as a point of reference for the orientation. Larry has found that introducing students with vision problems to the classroom environment and school space in a systematic manner helps them to "cognitively map" the physical space and function more effectively in it.

In working with students with physical disabilities, Kim has found it helpful to keep the classroom arrangement of desks, work areas, and material as constant as possible. She tries to notify students of any changes in the physical structure of her room. She allows students to move freely within the room to find the best view during instructional activities and also places students with physical disabilities at the end of tables or rows of desks to make movement easier for them. When she teaches students with hearing impairments, she becomes familiar with their special equipment (such as hearing aids) and periodically checks to be sure the equipment is working properly.

Table 6.3
Checklist for Evaluating Accessibility

Area of Concern	Questions of Interest
Sidewalks	Do curb cuts provide access? Is the walkway at least 48 inches wide? Are the surfaces level and free of obstructions?
Ramps	Are 32-inch-high handrails present? Is the grade of the rise more than 1 inch in every 12 foot distance? Does it have nonslip surface appropriate for all types of weather?
Doors and Elevators	Is there a 5 foot by 5 foot level area in the direction the door opens? Is the opening at least 32 inches when the door is open? Are thresholds nonobstructive (e.g., 1/2 inch or less)?
Floors	Do hallways, stairs, and class areas have carpeting or other nonslip surfaces?
Toilets	Is at least one stall 3 feet wide by 4 feet 8 inches deep with 33-inch-high handrails? Is the toilet seat 20 inches high and urinals 19 inches from the floor? Are sinks, towel dispensers, soap dispensers, and mirrors no higher than 40 inches from the floor?
Water Fountains	Are controls hand operated? Is the spout in front of the unit? Are they mounted 26 to 30 inches from the floor?

Source: B. B. Greer, J. Allsop, & J. G. Greer. (1980). Environmental alternatives for the physically handicapped. In J. W. Schifani, R. M. Anderson & S. J. Odle (Eds.), *Implementing Learning in the Least Restrictive Environment*, pp. 128–129. Austin, TX: PRO-ED, Inc.

Improve Communication

Teaching is an act of communication. Effective teachers of exceptional students consider how the students' special needs may affect instruction and adjust their presentations accordingly. We have found that considering the following suggestions related to classroom instruction helps teachers work more effectively with students in low-prevalence categories:

- When presenting written materials and pictures on blackboards, overhead projectors, and other visually dependent forms, verbalize written instructions and written material as much as necessary.

- Seat students with vision problems with their backs to windows or other sources of light to avoid glare on instructional materials. Have these students seated near the blackboard or other sources of demonstrations. Students with hearing problems should be seated near the teacher and the center of desk arrangements.

- Use face-to-face contact as much as possible. Don't turn away from students with hearing impairments during a conversation or instructional lesson.
- Use complete sentences when talking to students with hearing problems. This provides more context for understanding what has been said during conversation.
- Because large-print materials slow reading rate, they should be used only when absolutely necessary. It is preferable to have students read regular print by bringing it closer or by magnifying it for easier reading.
- Dark-lined paper and soft pencils (or felt-tipped pens) create the best contrast for students with vision problems; computer word processors and typewriters also can be useful.
- Use visual cues when referring to objects in the room and during instructional units (such as the outline of a lesson written on the board or a handout).
- Have students take notes for a classmate with a hearing problem and have the hearing impaired student transcribe the notes after the oral presentation.
- Arrange seating so that distracting noises are kept to a minimum for students with hearing aids.

Foster Independence

Students with physical disabilities have a wide range of personal and social characteristics that can make them very dependent on others. Effective teachers encourage independent activities from these students. They teach social skills and listening skills as needed to foster a realistic balance between dependency and overdependency. They might allow extra time for completion of tasks and use group activities to encourage socialization among regular and special students. They might learn to use special materials such as manual alphabets, sign language systems, and oral/manual communication activities so they can communicate effectively with their students. They might work with other teachers who have suggestions for alternative classroom activities, materials, and instructional units. These teachers are aware of the delicate balance that exists between needing special assistance and wanting to be normal. They are concerned with the impressions a student's special learning needs create, and they try to minimize the extent to which a student is treated negatively because of them.

WHAT WE THINK ABOUT LOW-PREVALENCE CONDITIONS

Several of the low-prevalence conditions described in this chapter have serious educational implications. Students who are blind and deaf have unique educational needs that are difficult, but not impossible, to accommodate in general education classes.

In Chapters 4 and 5, we said that there are no characteristics specific to the conditions of learning disabilities, speech and language handicaps, mental retardation, and emotional disturbance. And we said that there are no educational implications specific to these conditions. Instead we stressed the fact that implications for education need to be drawn from the behaviors students demonstrate rather than from the names assigned to them.

Things are different with sensory handicaps. There are characteristics specific to these conditions, and the conditions themselves have specific educational implications. Students who are visually handicapped input and process visual stimuli in unique ways. Those who are deaf input and process verbal or auditory stimuli in unique ways. Knowing that a student is blind or partially sighted, or deaf or hard of hearing allows us to plan instruction for that student.

The kinds of accommodations educators and schools must make for students who demonstrate sensory handicaps are a function of the severity of those handicaps. For example, we can help visually handicapped students improve their orientation and mobility in schools by putting horizontal bars on major exit doors and vertical bars on major entrance doors. We can design tactile instructional materials. We can see that lighting is adequate for students who are partially sighted, and we can seat those students in the front of the room or close to their work. We can give them large-print books and special output materials, like wide-lined paper and felt-tip pens.

Major technological advances are changing the ways in which and the extent to which students with sensory and physical impairments are able to participate in and profit from schooling. The future is bright. We believe that over the next ten years, new technology, especially in the computer industry, will enable larger numbers of those with sensory and physical handicaps to participate fully in educational programs.

Summary

1. About 5 percent of the students who are handicapped are orthopedically handicapped, other health impaired, multiply handicapped, hearing impaired and deaf, visually handicapped, or deaf and blind.
2. Orthopedic handicaps and other health impairments are caused by disease or defect.

3. The characteristics of individuals who are classified orthopedically handicapped or other health impaired are specific to the condition.
4. Cerebral palsy, epilepsy, paralysis, spina bifida, and brain injury due to trauma are among the common neurological disorders.
5. Students are identified as multiply handicapped when they exhibit a combination of impairments that causes such severe educational problems that they cannot be accommodated in special education programs designed for one of the conditions alone.
6. Recent advances in medicine and technology have increased the prevalence of students with multiple handicaps.
7. Deafness means the absence of hearing in both ears; hard of hearing refers to significant difficulties in hearing.
8. The academic success of students who are hearing impaired is a function of four factors: the severity of the impairment, the age of the student at the onset of the hearing loss, the socioeconomic status of the student's family, and the hearing status of the student's parents.
9. Research suggests that those who are deaf prefer to socialize with other nonhearing people.
10. The category visually handicapped includes both blind and partially sighted children.
11. With the exception of their unique problems of inputting and processing information, students who are visually handicapped learn much like other students.
12. Students are identified as deaf and blind when they demonstrate the two conditions in combination and when they cannot be accommodated in special education programs solely for deaf or blind students.
13. Sensory handicaps do have specific educational implications.

Activities

1. Go to any of the general textbooks on orthopedic impairments, other health impairments, multiple handicaps, hearing impairments, visual impairments, and deafness and blindness, and make a list of the characteristics said to be demonstrated by students who are members of each category.
2. Visit an Easter Seal facility and observe the teaching methods used with students who are physically handicapped or multiply handicapped. Describe the different strategies used with preschool children versus elementary school children. Include in your report a description of the kinds of services offered and any special equipment used by occupational therapists, physical therapists, speech and language pathologists, and teachers.

3. Look through the yellow pages of your phone book for a social service agency that serves individuals who are either deaf or blind. Contact the agency and ask about the kinds of services it provides.

Suggested Readings

Batshaw, M.L., & Perret, Y.M. (1981). *Children with handicaps: A medical primer.* Baltimore: Brookes.
> *Much of the terminology in physical disabilities is unfamiliar to school personnel. This text gives educators an understanding of the nature of common medical conditions experienced by students.*

Blackman, J. A. (Ed.) (1983). *Medical aspects of developmental disabilities in children birth to three: A resource for special-service providers in the educational setting.* Iowa City: University of Iowa.
> *A handy reference for those who are involved in providing services to very young children with special needs. This text includes chapters on most of the orthopedic, physical, and health impairments described briefly in this chapter.*

Bleck, E., & Nagel, D. (1982). *Physically handicapped children: A medical atlas for teachers* (2nd ed.) New York: Grune & Stratton.
> *The authors describe each of the most common physical disabilities in terms that are relatively easy for educators to understand. The text includes sections on educational implications for each of the disabilities described and discussed.*

Moores, D. (1987). *Educating the deaf: Psychology, principles, and practices* (3rd ed.) Boston: Houghton Mifflin.
> *A comprehensive survey of the practices and issues in the education of students who are deaf and hard of hearing.*

Newland, T.E. (1986). Children with auditory and visual impairment. In R.T. Brown & C.R. Reynolds (Eds.), *Psychological perspectives on childhood exceptionality: A handbook.* New York: Wiley.
> *Newland describes psychological, sociological, and educational considerations about children who have auditory and/or visual impairments. In a section entitled "The Learning Locales" he describes the kinds of settings in which these students are educated.*

Rynders, J.E., & Stealy, D. S. (1985). Early education: A strategy for producing a less (least) restrictive environment for young children with severe handicaps. In K.C. Lakin & R.H. Bruininks (Eds.), *Strategies for achieving community integration of developmentally disabled citizens.* Baltimore: Brookes.
> *An analysis of the effectiveness of early intervention programs for very young severely handicapped children and their families.*

Scholl, G. (Ed.) (1986). *Foundations of education for blind and visually handicapped children and youth.* New York: American Foundation for the Blind.

> *A comprehensive overview of practice in educating children who are blind and visually handicapped.*

Van Hasselt, V. B., Strain, P., & Hersen, M. (Eds.). (1988). *Handbook of developmental and physical disabilities.* New York: Pergamon Press.

> *A detailed examination of sixteen developmental and physical disabilities, including asthma, cerebral palsy, hearing impairment, and musculoskeletal disorders.*

three

Practicing Special Education

Now that you know something about the foundations of special education and the categories of people who are exceptional, it is time to turn to the "hows" and "wheres" of providing services to them. We discuss classification practices because students are categorized before they are eligible for special education. We also talk about the ways parents, teachers, and program administrators deliver services in settings that are as much as possible like those in which nonexceptional students are taught. We describe classification practices and efforts to organize special education programs in Chapter 7. Since current practices in special education are shaped by people who work with exceptional students and by members of professional organizations who advocate for the needs of people who are exceptional, we describe the professionals and organizations involved with exceptional individuals in Chapter 8.

7

Delivering Services to Students with Special Needs

FOCUSING QUESTIONS

■ Why do we classify exceptional students?

■ How do different definitions and criteria affect the classification of exceptional students?

■ What are the components of educational programs that meet the least restrictive environment provision of Public Law 94–142?

■ How has mainstreaming become an objective of special education programs?

■ What are the assumptions on which categorical, noncategorical, and cross-categorical (or multicategorical) pull-out programs are based?

■ What are the six basic types of stay-put programs?

■ What is a cascade system of special education services?

■ What effect is the regular education initiative having on special education today?

■ What special services are being offered today to preschool children and to secondary school students?

ALEXANDER IS A NINE-YEAR-OLD WHO RECEIVES SPECIAL education services in the Philadelphia public schools. He is formally classified as severely mentally retarded and attends a special class in which all of the other students are identified as mentally retarded. He spends his entire school day in that class. If you spoke to the principal in Alexander's school, she would tell you that special education services in the school are organized "categorically." Students who are identified as mentally retarded attend classes for mentally retarded students; those who are identified as emotionally disturbed attend classes for emotionally disturbed students.

Brenda is a sixteen-year-old who receives special education services in the Amherst, Massachusetts, schools. Although she is identified as eligible for special education services, she has not been formally labeled. She spends most of her school day in general education classes, but is pulled out of these classes to attend a resource room program. If you spoke to the principal in Brenda's school, he would tell you that special education services there are "noncategorical." Students are not formally tested and labeled, but are grouped on the basis of their instructional needs.

José is an eight-year-old who receives special education services in the Minneapolis public schools. The principal in José's school would tell you that José is enrolled in a "cross-categorical" or "multicategorical" program. He spends most of his day in a self-contained pull-out program, but there are all different kinds of students in that class: Some are labeled mentally retarded, some emotionally disturbed, and some learning disabled.

Special education looks different in different states and even in different districts within states. This has to do with the way the state departments of education decide to organize the delivery of special education services. In this chapter we describe two ways in which special education services are organized: pull-out programs, in which students are removed from general education classes for all or part of the school day, and stay-put programs, in which special education services are delivered in general education classes.

Classification is an important part of special education today. In this chapter we also examine the reasons why we classify exceptional students and look at current classification practices. And we describe two major concepts—least restrictive environment and mainstreaming—that guide our decisions about where to place exceptional students. We end the chapter with a discussion of some of the major issues that influence the delivery of special education services.

CLASSIFICATION IN SPECIAL EDUCATION

The process of grouping people, places, or things into categories is called **classification**. Since early times, people have classified things to give order to them. Although the process of classification probably has always gone on, Aristotle (384–322 B.C.) usually is credited with the first scientific classification. He developed a "ladder of nature," in which he classified people and things on a continuum from nonliving to human. The plant and animal species were included as intermediate classes. Aristotle's system of classifying things into groups according to their permanent and visible differences is still followed in most classification schemes.

Classification plays a major role in special education today. By law, only students with identified handicaps are eligible for special education services. In most states, students are grouped for instruction on the basis of the kind of handicaps they demonstrate (see Table 1.1). Federal and state laws, rules, and regulations governing the education of handicapped students usually define the kinds of handicapped students who can receive special education. Because classification is fundamental to the practice of special education today, it is important that you understand its objectives and current practices.

Objectives

The primary purpose of classification is to give order to everyday life. The practice of classifying people, places, and things is all around us.

A RECENT MOVIE FOR television, *A Bridge to Silence*, brings to the forefront issues relevant to the hearing-impaired population. In one scene of the movie, the character portrayed by Marlee Matlin, the hearing-impaired actress who won an Academy Award for her role in *Children of a Lesser God*, and several of her friends are having dinner and discussing their childhood experiences in "hearing" schools. One friend remembered that she did not know much of what was going on and relied on "following the other kids around." She remarked, "I don't know how I survived." The other characters agreed that similar situations were remedied when their parents placed them in special schools for the deaf where they became successful.

The question of where their children should be educated is just one of the difficult decisions parents of children with hearing impairments must face. Today, many of these parents elect to place their children in local public schools. Thought to be the least restrictive environment, home school placement may, in reality, severely restrict a hearing impaired student's opportunity for a successful education.

From the vantage point of an educational interpreter who works with students on a one-to-one basis, seven hours a day, 180 days a year, I can offer insight to the value of placing hearing impaired students at the junior high level into central programs rather than into their home schools. The students with whom I work are all trying to overcome the negative experience, emotionally and academically, of having "failed to make it" in their home school. You can imagine their attitude toward school in general after a year of frustration trying to cope with the new experience of junior high with very little support. In contrast, my previous position was in a central program consisting of twenty-five hearing-impaired students, three teachers, and seven interpreters. All hearing-impaired students in a three-county radius were served at this central location along with all the hearing students in that area. The one negative aspect of a long bus ride to and from school was offset by the many benefits of central placement that created a positive environment conducive to learning.

Central placement supplies a network of support services that cannot be matched in home school placement. The most important elements in this network are the on-staff certified teachers of the hearing impaired who have received training and insight into the special educational needs of deaf students. They are available on a daily basis to provide intensive resources to hearing-impaired students. This normally is accomplished in one class period a day and involves personalized tutoring in trouble areas, specific instruction in study skills, vocabulary building, reading improvement, and auditory training. In a special classroom, the resource teacher has access to materials designed for the deaf to augment mainstreamed instruction.

The resource teacher addresses specific academic needs of hearing-impaired students and also guides and monitors their overall progress. He or she can design a tailored schedule specifically to fit students' needs. For instance, the resource teacher can see to it that students are mainstreamed in their stronger subjects and attend self-contained classes for their weaker subjects. He or she will be responsible, as well, for writing students' IEPs and will see to it that standardized testing is administered to hearing-impaired students in a small-group setting and that appropriate portions are interpreted. Generally speaking, this teacher is an advocate for hearing-impaired students, looking out for their best interests and making sure they do not fall through the cracks of the bureaucracy.

On the other hand, a hearing-impaired student placed in the local public school is served by an itinerant teacher an hour a day for two or three days a week depending on the number of assigned schools. In the absence of a teacher who works with the student on a consistent basis and monitors the student's progress, it is likely that problems and issues arise that are not adequately handled. When compared to the dependable daily availability of the resource teacher in the central program, the home school/itinerant teacher arrangement is less effective.

The on-staff certified teacher of the hearing impaired not only serves as a resource person to the student, but also serves as a resource to the school's teachers and staff. He or she is available to confer with teachers who may be apprehensive about having a hearing-impaired student in their regular classroom, and offers guidelines for proper teaching strategies to meet deaf students' needs. Moreover, the resource teacher can promote deaf awareness through in-service training to mainstream teachers and school staff members. A smooth working relationship is continually being promoted by the resource teacher on behalf of the student.

Finally, central placement offers the hearing-impaired student an opportunity for social interaction with both hearing-impaired peers and hearing peers. Large numbers of hearing-impaired students can constitute a voice in school activities. Extracurricular activities such as sign language clubs have done much to increase understanding and acceptance among both hearing and hearing-impaired students.

Alternately, home school placement advocates a lone wolf principle where a ratio exists of one hearing-impaired student to hundreds of hearing students. The hearing-impaired student needs to be a very secure individual and to possess a great deal of self-confidence and self-esteem to deal with this kind of isolation. As we know, teenage students are not exactly well known for their ability to cope with being different. Their desire is to look, dress, and act like their peers and to be accepted by them. In home school placement no opportunity exists for the hearing-impaired student to experience the camaraderie of students who share his disability nor the opportunity to know that others share the same fears, anxieties, and experiences. To their own detriment, students I have served who came from home schools spent most of their time denying and downplaying their impairment in an effort not to appear different.

The controversy of central versus home school placement may not be resolved in the near future. However, movies by Marlee Matlin and others can only help expose the issues of the hearing-impaired population to the general public. This increased awareness may bring about improvements and change in the educational struggles of hearing-impaired students. We can only hope.

Janice Luckey is an interpreter/tutor at Randolph Junior High School in Charlotte, North Carolina. She spends her days translating verbal presentations and lessons while sitting with a hearing-impaired student who spends all but one period in regular junior high school classrooms.

Advertisements are classified in newspapers; supermarkets classify their goods into aisles and shelves; colleges and universities classify their courses into departments and programs.

In most states, classification is fundamental to the process of delivering special education services to students who are exceptional. Remember, these students must be declared eligible for services. In most states, the process of declaring students eligible involves classifying or categorizing them.

Classification practices in special education today developed from the belief that students with similar special needs could be taught more easily and more effectively if they were grouped for instructional purposes. Over time, laws, rules, and regulations were passed mandating that students who experience academic and behavioral difficulties in school be sorted into different categories. Then names were assigned to the categories (*visually impaired*, *mentally retarded*, and so on), and definitions of the categories were written.

Classification also helps government agencies develop social policy. Each year school personnel must report the number of students served in each category to their state department of education. These departments complete annual reports for the Office of Special Education and Rehabilitative Services in the U.S. Department of Education. State and federal officials use this information—**child count data**—to allocate funds for special education services. These data also form the basis of annual reports to Congress. As the number of students who receive services increases or decreases, Congress decides whether to allocate more money for special education, to insist that eligibility criteria be reviewed or rewritten, or to develop new social policies on the education of exceptional students.

Classification practices and social policy are clearly interrelated. Classification tells us how many people exhibit a certain condition. This information is used by government officials to formulate social policy. Once people are classified, government officials develop policies on their treatment. The policies that are developed can have positive or negative effects: They can enhance individual development and expand life opportunities, or, as has happened in the past, they can lead to the institutionalization of those who are handicapped and deprive them of their fundamental rights.

When government officials develop social policies on the services or treatments to be provided handicapped students, they establish criteria to determine precisely who is eligible for services or treatment. Some of those criteria are objective (for example, the distance at which a target can be seen). Others are subjective (for example, imperfect ability to read). When relatively lenient standards are used to make eligibility decisions, large numbers of students are eligible for services; when restrictive standards are used, few individuals are eligible for services.

Finally, classification practices in special education also are designed to help researchers. Researchers typically study specific categories of students. To the extent that students in various parts of the country are classified on the basis of similar criteria, research findings can be translated across individuals and across geographic locations.

A Brief History of Classification Practices

Current classification practices evolved from early efforts to classify exceptional individuals. As you consider the development of classification practices, think about how terminology has become more positive over time, and remember that changes in terminology are a result of changes in how people view the various conditions.

Mental Retardation

Current classification practices in mental retardation can be traced to the middle of the nineteenth century. At that time, very derogatory terms—like *idiot* and *imbecile*—were used to classify retarded persons. Blanton (1976) indicates that the first clear definition of mental retardation was given by J. E. D. Esquirol, who stated,

> Idiocy is not a disease, but a condition in which the intellectual faculties are never manifested, or have never been developed sufficiently to enable the idiot to acquire such amount of knowledge as persons of his own age and placed in similar circumstances with himself are capable of receiving. (Esquirol, 1845, p. 446)

Based on this definition, identification and classification practices required the collection of information on the relative amounts of knowledge the person had acquired.

In the mid-1800s, retarded people were classified as idiots, simpletons, or fools. In 1910, Goddard coined the term *moron* to classify certain feeble-minded individuals. He did so because he thought the terms previously used were not "practical."

Intelligence testing brought an objectivity (that is, a number reflecting ability) to measuring differences among people, and Goddard was the first popularizer of the practice in this country. In his work at the Vineland Training School, Goddard was the first professional to link numbers associated with performance on tests to diagnostic classification labels for conditions.

Mental Disorders

The classification system used for mental retardation is thought to be the most objective. An individual who scores 18 on an intelligence test will be classified as profoundly retarded; someone scoring 30 will be called severe-ly retarded. Although that system is based on the most specific criteria, it is not the most elaborate. Classification practices in psychology and psychia-try are based on criteria agreed upon by professionals. The Diagnostic and Statistical Manuals (DSM) of the American Psychiatric Association (APA) provide diagnostic criteria for use in classifying mental disorders. The first volume (*DSM-I*, APA, 1952) listed eight major categories of disorders. "Mental deficiencies" (for example, mental retardation) was but one of them, the other seven being categories of "mental disorders." The second *Diagnostic and Statistical Manual of Mental Disorders* (APA, 1968) con-tained ten categories, and the most recent revision (*DSM-III-R*, APA, 1988) contains seventeen types of disorders. Over three hundred types of prob-lems can be identified using the criteria presented in the third manual.

Exceptional Students

In the first textbook dealing with the "education of exceptional children," Horn (1924) argued for a set of "general principles for inclusion or exclu-sion [read classification] which may guide the school in the recognition of those children who are properly entitled to demand and to receive special educational provision adapted to their case" (p. 13). He offers the following "complete classification" to assist the service delivery process:

> I. Children who are exceptional for reasons primarily mental.
>   1. The most highly endowed group.
>   2. The most poorly endowed group.
> II. Children who are exceptional for reasons primarily temperamental.
>   3. Incorrigibles and truants.
>   4. Speech defectives.
> III. Children who are exceptional for reasons primarily physical.
>   5. The deaf.
>   6. The blind.
>   7. The crippled.   (p. 16)

The similarities between Horn's first system for classifying exception-al children and the one currently adopted by most professionals in special education are striking. The "most highly endowed" are today called gifted and talented. They are exceptional because of their superior performance on intelligence tests and their unusual skills in specific areas, such as art, music, and so on. The "most poorly endowed" are today called mentally retarded. They are exceptional because of their inferior performance on intelligence tests and their lack of facility with fundamental tasks, such as eating, dressing, reading, writing, and so on. The "incorrigibles and truants" of yesterday are the emotionally disturbed students of today. Their behavior is the source of their problems. The parallels in the catego-

Some students are classified as gifted and talented because of their superior performance on intelligence tests and their unusual skills in specific areas such as art, music, mathematics, and science.

(© Michael Weisbrot and Family)

ries of speech defectives, deaf, blind, and crippled are clear. In fact, the only difference in the list of categories recognized in Horn's first classification system for exceptional students and the current list in use is the absence of learning disabilities from the former.

Current Classification Practices

Classification enables school personnel to secure funding and to provide special education services to exceptional students. The process makes use of the definitions of and criteria for handicapping conditions. When society's attitudes about who should receive services change, the definitions and criteria also can change. Classification, then, depends on how the state defines a handicapping condition at a given time; it depends on where we live and when we live.

In most states, the department of education uses the classification system specified in Public Law 94–142. But some states use different criteria for meeting certain conditions. These differences make the classification process an arbitrary one.

In our research at the University of Minnesota's Institute for Research on Learning Disabilities, we gathered test data on students identified as learning disabled by the schools, low-achieving students, and normal stu-

Researchers have found that all school-identified learning disabled students, all low-achieving students, and more than 80 percent of normal students can be called learning disabled on the basis of at least one set of criteria.

(© Alan Carey/ The Image Works)

dents. We examined the extent to which students in these three groups met the criteria for being called learning disabled.

We started with the federal criteria (see Chapter 4). Those criteria are not very specific. For example, one criterion is that students must demonstrate a "severe discrepancy between achievement and intellectual ability." But *severe* is not defined. Does it mean a two-year discrepancy? A one-year discrepancy? A two-month discrepancy? When we searched the literature, we found more than forty sets of criteria for identifying students with learning disabilities.

We took seventeen of these different sets of criteria and used them to classify groups of students that the schools had identified as learning disabled, low achieving, and normal. We found that all school-identified learning disabled students, all low-achieving students, and more than 80 percent of the normal students could be called learning disabled on the basis of at least one set of criteria. And we found that no students met all criteria.

To understand the impact of this variation on the eligibility decision, look at Table 7.1. The table lists the diagnostic decision for eighteen students, using six different definitions and sets of criteria. It is not necessary to know what the definitions and criteria are. What you should recognize is that different definitions and criteria exist, and that when they are applied, they lead to different decisions.

If school personnel used Definition 1, four of the six students currently identified as learning disabled would still be identified as learning disabled, but so would two of the low-achieving students and two of the nor-

Table 7.1
Classification of Three Groups of Students as Learning Disabled or Not
Learning Disabled on the Basis of Six Different Sets of Definitions and Criteria

| Student Groups | Definition/Criteria | | | | | |
	1	*2*	*3*	*4*	*5*	*6*
School-identified Learning Disabled Students						
Mel	x		x	x		x
Ellen	x	x		x	x	
Ruth		x	x			x
John	x				x	
Ivan	x	x	x	x		
Zeke		x	x	x		x
Low-achieving Students						
Sue		x	x			
Judy		x	x	x		
Ray	x				x	
Bob		x			x	
Amy	x	x				
Mark			x			
Normal Students						
Phil	x	x			x	
Matt			x	x		
Chuck						
Martha	x					x
Jim		x	x	x		
Joan		x				

mal students. On the other hand, if the school used Definition 2, four students in the learning disabled and low-achieving groups would be called learning disabled, as would three in the normal group.

Look at the decisions for individual students. Mel and Zeke are both currently identified as learning disabled. Under Definition 1, Mel still would be eligible for services, but Zeke would not. But under Definition 2, Zeke would be eligible for services and Mel would not. Only one student in Table 7.1, Chuck, would not receive services under any criteria, yet he could be failing in school.

The point here is that the subjective nature of the definitions and criteria used in deciding eligibility make classification an arbitrary process. The particular criteria used by any one school district are a function of what school personnel believe and of how much money society is willing to pay for the education of handicapped students. When there is plenty of money available, school personnel tend to use relatively lenient criteria, criteria by which many students are eligible for service. When funds get tight, school personnel use more rigid criteria.

At this time, there is a movement away from the practice of classifying students as handicapped and educating them in separate environments. Educators increasingly are advocating the placement and instruction of handicapped students in the regular classroom. Lipsky and Gartner (1989) describe this trend as part of a "progressive inclusion of an ever broader range of students—girls, children of color, children of noncitizens, those whose parents were not property owners, and, most recently, children who are labeled handicapped, including those who are the most severely impaired" (p. xxii). Factors that have contributed to this trend are extensive litigation to establish the right to a free appropriate education for students who are handicapped; the virtual end of suspensions and exclusions; the movement of students from residential treatment centers into public school settings; the development of interventions for students at one time thought to be uneducable; and the serious objections of parents and advocacy groups to classification practices. Although classification is still a necessary prerequisite to receiving special education, many are arguing against it.

Checkpoint
- *Classification is the process of grouping people, places, and things.*
- *The process of classifying exceptional students stemmed from the belief that these students could be taught more easily and effectively in homogeneous groups.*
- *Today classification helps government agencies develop social policy.*
- *Undermining the utility of the classification process is the variation in the definitions and criteria used by the different states to determine students' eligibility for special services.*

CONCEPTS GUIDING PLACEMENT DECISIONS

Two major concepts or principles guide the process of deciding where students who are exceptional should be educated. These concepts—least restrictive environment and mainstreaming—are closely related. The right of students with handicapping conditions to be educated in the least restrictive environment is affirmed in Public Law 94–142, the Education for

All Handicapped Children Act. When professionals talk about educating students in the least restrictive environment, they often talk about mainstreaming, the practice of providing educational services to students with handicaps in regular schools and regular classrooms.

Least Restrictive Environment

The educational placement of exceptional students is governed both by the needs of the students and by the legal requirement that students be educated in the least restrictive environment (LRE). Public Law 94–142 requires that state and local education agencies "to the maximum extent appropriate," offer "children and youth with handicaps . . . academic, non-academic, and extra-curricular services in conjunction with their nonhandicapped peers." (Liles, 1988, p. 9) In short, students with handicaps must be given opportunities to be educated in the same schools as nonhandicapped students and, within those schools, opportunities to interact with their nonhandicapped peers.

What criteria do federal, state, and local officials use to judge the extent to which the intent of the law is met? Typically they consider three major criteria:

- The proximity of the educational program to the regular education environment
- The proximity of the educational program to the student's home
- The degree of opportunity the student has to interact with non-handicapped peers

It is presumed that school personnel will "remove students from regular education environments only when absolutely necessary and only so far as absolutely necessary to meet individual needs" (Bellamy, 1987).

Although it is relatively easy to talk about the concept of least restrictive environment, it is not that easy to implement it or to demonstrate that the placement of all students with handicaps meets the letter and intent of the law. Adding to the problem here is the conflict among educators, administrators, parents, and advocacy groups over what *least restrictive environment* means (Table 7.2).

At the heart of the concept of least restrictive environment is the belief that segregation in classrooms is inappropriate. In Chapter 2 we talked about a landmark court case, *Brown* v. *Board of Education* (1954), in which the Supreme Court declared that separate or segregated educational facilities are inherently unequal. In its decision in *Brown*, the Court recognized the long-term negative social consequences of not allowing black children and white children to attend the same schools and to interact academically and socially. In much the same way, Public Law 94–142 recognizes that

---

Table 7.2
Understanding the Meaning of Least Restrictive Environment

Least restrictive environment does not mean

- dumping students with disabilities into regular programs without adequate preparation or support.
- locating special education classes in separate wings of a school building.
- grouping students with a wide range of disabilities and needs in the same program.
- ignoring students' individual needs.
- exposing students to unnecessary hazards or risks.
- placing unreasonable demands on teachers and administrators.
- ignoring parents' concerns.
- isolating students with disabilities in regular schools.
- placing older students with disabilities in schools for younger students.
- maintaining separate schedules for special education and regular students.

Least restrictive environment does mean

- educating students with disabilities in regular schools.
- providing special services within regular schools.
- supporting regular teachers and administrators.
- having students with disabilities follow the same schedules as other students.
- having students with disabilities in as many academic classes and extracurricular activities as possible, including music, art, gym, field trips, assemblies, and graduation exercises.
- arranging for students with disabilities to use the school cafeteria, library, playground, and other facilities at the same time as other students.
- encouraging helper and buddy relationships between nonhandicapped students and those with disabilities.
- teaching all students to understand and accept human differences.
- placing students with disabilities in the same schools they would attend if they were not disabled.
- taking parents' concerns seriously.
- providing an appropriate, individualized education program.

Source: Adapted from C. M. Liles (1988), *Determining Placement in the Least Restrictive Environment* (Plantation, FL: South Atlantic Regional Resource Center, 1988), adapted from S.J. Taylor, D. Biklen, and S.J. Searle, Jr., *Preparing for LIfe: A Manual for Parents on the Least Restrictive Environment*, vol. 1 (Boston: TAPP Project, Federation for Children with Special Needs, 1985). Reprinted with permission.

there are negative social consequences of educating students with handicaps in separate facilities and classes. A fundamental concept underlies the principle of least restrictive environment: the constitutional guarantee of

Window on Practice

EAMON SHANNON IS A twelve-year-old student who happens to have Down syndrome. Eamon attends a self-contained special education class in a regular public school outside his community. While his family feels very positively about his program and the involvement Eamon has with regular education students, they were asked to comment about the impact the availability of a neighborhood school program would have for Eamon.

Heather Shannon, Eamon's sister, offered the following: "As much as we (my family) love Eamon and try to give him a 'normal' childhood, there is one thing that he is missing: *friends*. Every day he comes home and plays by himself. He has a wonderful personality and would love to have friends. One way in which this is evident is that Eamon has an avid interest in the relationship I have with my friends. When I go out, a stream of questions follows. *Where are you going? Who with? When are you coming back?* There are hardly any kids in the neighborhood Eamon knows, much less to be friends with.

"I attended a dance at Eamon's school (I was chaperoning). The other kids were very nice, but Eamon looked extremely uncomfortable. Being with kids his age in a social activity was a foreign experience for Eamon, and he didn't know how to handle it. I feel that if Eamon were to attend a neighborhood school it would help him greatly to feel comfortable in social situations. Suddenly, he would see other boys his age outside his classroom and would be able to develop more long-lasting friendships that would help him to really 'belong' in the community in which he lives."

Anne Shannon, Eamon's mother, says: "Having our son in his neighborhood school would indeed change our family lifestyle. First and foremost, our son would immediately expand the spectrum of his horizons. Not only would there be imminent opportunities for building friendships and fitting in the neighborhood, there would also be future benefits because the community would get to know Eamon as they get to know every other child in the community. Secondly, things most families take for granted like car pools, bike riding, and shooting 'hoops' with other kids after school would become the norm.

"Today, Mom and Dad or older siblings must drive at least twenty minutes, wait, or devote an entire afternoon or evening so that their son or brother may fit in. Others might say, 'Big deal!' It is a big deal for us! The ordinary give and take of car pools, after school activities, and 'my house,' 'your house,' and 'their house' neighborhood routines is absent when your child does not attend the neighborhood school. Kids belong at home. Kids belong in their neighborhood. Kids belong in their community. Try as we may, we can't make an unnatural situation natural, another community our community, a school away from the neighborhood our neighborhood school.

Source: *Heather Shannon and Anne Shannon, "A Family Perspective," Total Integration Neighborhood Schools, 1989, p. 8. Published by La Grange Area Department of Special Education, 1301 West Cossitt Avenue, La Grange, IL 60525. Reprinted with permission.*

equal opportunity. To exclude students with handicaps from public schools and from the opportunity to learn and interact with nonhandicapped students is to deny them equal opportunity.

Today most students who are exceptional receive all or part of their education in regular classes. But simply including students with handicaps in educational programs along with students who are not handicapped does not meet the intent of the LRE provision of Public Law 94–142. Some integrated programs are good; and some are not. Taylor, Biklen, and Searl (1986) described the components of good programs:

- Students with disabilities are taught in the same school they would attend if they were not disabled.

- Decisions about educational programs are based on each student's needs; that is, not all students with the same disabilities are placed in the same program.

- Each student's educational needs are outlined in an individualized education program (IEP) developed jointly by the student's parents and school personnel. Placement decisions are reviewed at least once a year to ensure that programs are meeting students' needs.

- Whenever possible, students with disabilities are taught in regular classes with their nondisabled peers, and students and teachers are given the necessary support to make the placement successful.

- Special services, including physical therapy, speech and language therapy, and training in sign language or braille, are provided in regular schools.

- Students who cannot be fully integrated into regular classes are integrated to the extent possible. Any separate classes are located near regular classes, not in a separate area of the school, and are not given special labels (like "the ED class").

- Positive attitudes and social integration are promoted actively.

- Junior high students are provided career planning and counseling services and prevocational skill training.

- Secondary students are provided opportunities to learn practical vocational and community living skills at community training sites.

Mainstreaming

Least restrictive environment is largely a legal principle; it is mandated by law. The concept of mainstreaming is a social principle. It was derived in part from the principle of **normalization**, the idea that individuals with handicaps ought to be allowed to live (indeed encouraged to live) as normal a life as possible. The principle of normalization in school settings becomes mainstreaming, the practice of educating students with handicaps

Mainstreaming is a social principle derived in part from the principle of normaliza- tion—the idea that individuals with handicaps should be encouraged to live as normal a life as possible.

(© Michael Weisbrot and Family)

in regular schools, regular education environments, and regular education classrooms alongside students who are not handicapped.

It was largely through court action in the 1970s that the concept of mainstreaming was defined. Parents and advocacy groups went to court to argue that students with handicaps had a right to be educated along with nonhandicapped students, that their development would be impeded if they did not have that opportunity. Birch (1974) listed the following rea- sons or motives for mainstreaming.

1. The capability to deliver special education anywhere has improved. Specialized equipment and special techniques can now be used or im- plemented in regular classroom settings.
2. Parental concerns are being expressed more directly and forcefully.
3. The rejection of the labeling of children is growing.
4. Court actions have accelerated changes in special education proce- dures.
5. The fairness and accuracy of psychological testing has been questioned.
6. Too many children were classified psychometrically as mentally retarded.
7. Civil rights actions against segregation uncovered questionable special education placement practices.
8. Non-handicapped children are deprived if they are not allowed to asso- ciate with handicapped children.

9. The effectiveness of conventional special education was questioned.
10. Financial considerations foster mainstreaming.
11. American philosophical foundations encourage diversity in the same educational setting. (pp. 3–7)

In *Department of Education* v. *Katherine*, the parents of an 8-year-old girl with cystic fibrosis brought suit against a public school that refused to accept her as a student. The school argued that it did not have personnel with the training to suction the child's lungs several times a day. The court awarded the parents the cost of placing the child in a private school. Later, when the school district developed an IEP for the child that accommodated her instructional and medical needs in the public school, the court ruled that the parents would no longer receive compensation if they chose to keep their daughter in a private school. The decision argued that placement in a public school setting, in which the youngster would have an opportunity to interact with other children, was appropriate.

decided this because it was the LRE →

In *Mallory* v. *Drake* (1981), the parents of a severely retarded child sued the school system for placing their daughter in a separate school. They demanded placement in one of two public schools. When the school district refused to allow the child to attend one of the two public schools and assigned the child to a state school for retarded individuals, the parents withdrew the child from the institution. A special hearing panel ruled that the school district did not demonstrate that placement in the state school was the least restrictive environment, and recommended that the child be grouped with other children in a class located in the public school. The panel stated as its primary reason for its ruling the access the student would have to social interaction with students who were less handicapped.

won on LRE →

The courts regularly test the concept of providing educational services to handicapped students in mainstream environments. For example, in *Community High School District 155* v. *Denz* (1984), the appellate court of Illinois considered the question of the appropriate placement of a severely retarded child with Down syndrome who also was a carrier of infectious hepatitis. The child had been excluded from school, school personnel arguing that the appropriate placement was in a homebound setting in which she would not transmit the disease to other children. The plaintiff argued that the chance of spreading the disease was remote and that placement in a homebound setting denied the child equal opportunity. The court decided in favor of the child, arguing that the primary goal of placement in a regular school environment is socialization. The school was ordered to accept the child, following appropriate sanitary procedures. Today, one of the burning issues being addressed in the courts is the extent to which students with AIDS ought to be educated in mainstream environments. The decisions the courts make on this issue will refine the definition of *mainstreaming* and will affect all students with handicaps.

Fundamental to the principles of least restrictive environment and mainstreaming is the argument that students with handicaps develop optimally when they are given opportunities to interact with and learn from students who are not handicapped. We said above that least restrictive environment means different things to different professionals; so it is with the concept of mainstreaming. To some, mainstreaming means full integration into regular schools and classes of all students who are handicapped, regardless of the severity of their handicaps. To others, mainstreaming means giving students with handicaps an opportunity to interact with those who are not handicapped. The term *mainstreaming* is not used in Public Law 94–142, and there is no legal definition of it. Mainstreaming is a moral concept, a social ideal:

> The question of whether or not to promote mainstreaming is not essentially a question for science. It is a moral question. It is a goal, indeed a value, we decide to pursue or reject on the basis of what we want our society to look like. (Biklen, 1985)

Has mainstreaming made a difference? Yes and no. Asch (1989) gathered firsthand accounts of students with special needs who were being educated in general education classes. Pat, Wendy, and Michelle all have mobility impairments; they attend different high schools in New York City. The three students told of being penalized for school absences or lateness caused by their impairments.

> Pat and Wendy received low grades when they were late for classes because elevators packed with teachers and nondisabled students failed to stop for them. Michelle failed to get credit for a semester of school because the special education bus was irregular in picking her up, and she was frequently absent. (Asch, 1989, p. 184)

But mainstreaming was a very different experience for Annee, a senior from a small rural district in Washington State, whose blindness did not stop her from conducting laboratory work in chemistry or from participating in a student exchange program in Latin America. And Asch describes April, a high school senior whose blindness did not stop her from taking part in much of her school's physical education program.

Checkpoint   ■   *Three criteria are used to determine whether the LRE provision of Public Law 94–142 is being met: proximity of the educational program to the regular education environment; proximity of the program to the student's home; and the degree of opportunity given the student to interact with nonhandicapped peers.*

■ *Mainstreaming is a social principle that has become part of special education primarily through court decisions.*

SPECIAL EDUCATION PROGRAMS

Students with special needs are educated in a variety of settings. Schools organize the delivery of special education services differently. At the beginning of this chapter, we described three exceptional students who are being educated in different settings, under different administrative arrangements. Here we describe the kinds of settings in which students are educated and the major ways of organizing the delivery of services to students who are exceptional.

Settings and Services

Over 70 percent of students with special needs spend a substantial amount of the school day in a regular classroom. Current estimates indicate that 26 percent of students receiving special education services are educated primarily in regular classrooms. Regular classroom teachers select materials or adapt instruction to meet the needs of these students. Some plan instruction or teach their exceptional students with the help of instructional consultants. And some rely on itinerant teachers, who come into the classroom to help exceptional students in very specialized areas. (We talk more about those who teach and work with exceptional students in Chapter 8.)

When exceptional students need more help than can be provided in the regular classroom, they usually leave the classroom for part of the day to receive instruction in a **resource room**, a classroom that is staffed by a special education teacher. Typically, only a few students with special needs go to a resource room at one time, to be taught individually or in small groups. The content covered in a resource room depends on the needs of the students.

Some students receive their *primary* instruction in one or more subjects in the resource room. Reading or math may be taught to a student only in the resource room, and the student may not receive instruction in those subject areas in the regular classroom. Instruction is *supplemental* when the resource teacher provides extra or supplementary instruction in a particular subject area but primary instruction occurs in the regular classroom. Instruction is *remedial* when the resource teacher assists the student in overcoming deficits or deficiencies in past learning; the teacher helps remedy learning problems. Instruction is *compensatory* when the resource teacher provides instruction that compensates for deficits or deficiencies.

Those exceptional students who require more intensive attention are assigned to self-contained classes, separate classes within the school. They may spend most of the school day receiving instruction in these classes, participating in regular classroom activities as much as they are able. Some students spend all their school time in a self-contained class, but socialize with nonhandicapped peers during class breaks or at lunch.

In some cases the public school or school system cannot provide services for certain students who are exceptional. **Special schools** are day schools that have the staff, facilities, and programs to meet the needs of students with handicaps. **Residential schools** offer the same facilities and programs found in special schools, but students live at these schools while they are being served. Some exceptional students require twenty-four-hour care, which can be provided in a residential or hospital setting.

An alternative to a residential or hospital setting for students who are too sick or disabled to travel to school is **home-based instruction**. Generally, special education teachers travel to the student's home to provide instruction or tutoring. When it was first developed, home-based instruction was intended for students whose absence was temporary or periodic due to a chronic condition, to help them keep up with their classmates during convalescence. Increasingly, school districts are offering home-based instruction for preschool children who are handicapped. Here, parents provide intervention for their children. One advantage of this program is that children are taught in a familiar setting by a familiar person.

Organizing Programs

Students can be "pulled out" of regular classrooms and provided education in special settings. Or they can "stay put" in regular classrooms and special education services can be brought to them.

Pull-out Programs

The most common approach to educating students who are handicapped is to provide services in **pull-out programs**, programs that remove students from the regular classroom. As we discussed in the last section, most of the settings in which students receive special education are removed from the regular classroom. Resource rooms and self-contained classes (in schools or institutions) are both pull-out programs.

Categorical Programs   Most pull-out programs are organized according to categories of exceptionality. Students are formally classified, then receive services with others who are in the same category as they are. The classes are formally identified as classes for those who are hearing

Some students who are handicapped receive services in pull-out programs like resource rooms and self-contained classes.

(© MacDonald Photography/The Picture Cube)

impaired, learning disabled, mentally retarded, and so on. Students are declared eligible for these services by a placement team or child-study team made up of professionals from many different disciplines who assess them and plan instructional programs for them. According to Morsink, Chase-Thomas, and Smith-Davis (1987), "categorical approaches to the delivery of services to . . . students are theoretically based on the assumptions that all students with similar labels have similar characteristics and abilities/disabilities and that, consequently, these students can be expected to respond similarly to the same types of educational programs" (p. 287).

Noncategorical Programs   The vast majority of the states organize their special education services along categorical lines (see Table 1.1). Only Massachusetts and South Dakota use a noncategorical model, although New Jersey currently is experimenting with the use of a noncategorical model in ten school districts. These noncategorical programs include children who are mildly handicapped and who would in other instances be considered mentally retarded, learning disabled, or emotionally disturbed.

Even for noncategorical programs, formal accounting may be made on a categorical basis:

Reports may be made to state and federal offices showing that certain numbers of the students might be considered educable mentally retarded, learn-

ing disabled, behaviorally disordered, and so on, but, in noncategorical programs there is a denial that such classifications are important for instructional purposes. Children with specific speech problems are usually treated
separately, but to the extent that problems are language related, they tend
also to be encompassed in large part by the noncategorical rubric.
(Reynolds, 1987, p. 251)

Morsink, Chase-Thomas, and Smith-Davis (1987) add that "noncategorical approaches are based on the rationale that these types of students
(students who are variously labeled) cannot be separated precisely and accurately into categories and that such separations are not useful in pre-
scribing educational practices with differential probabilities of success" (p.
287).

Decisions about assigning students to noncategorical programs typically are made by teams of educators who meet and must agree on a response to one question: Can this student's instructional needs be met in
the regular education setting? If the answer is yes, the student stays in the
regular classroom. If the answer is no, the student is pulled out of the regular classroom for all or part of the school day and grouped with other students who have similar instructional needs.

Cross-categorical or Multicategorical Programs   Cross-categorical or
multicategorical programs enroll students from several categories of exceptionality in a single program. For example, a resource room program
might serve students who have been classified learning disabled, mentally
retarded, and emotionally disturbed. The important distinction between
noncategorical programs and cross-categorical programs is that in
cross-categorical programs "it is assumed that the classifications are instructionally meaningful but that programming for the students can be
cross-categorical" (Reynolds, 1987, p. 251). When school districts use a
noncategorical model, they typically do so because they assume that
knowledge of a student's category does not help in teaching the student.

Stay-put Programs
Increasingly, students with special needs are being educated in regular
classrooms. In **stay-put programs**, exceptional students receive special
education services without being removed from the regular classroom.
There are six basic types of stay-put programs:

- Using special educators in the regular classroom
- Team teaching
- Using staff support teams or intervention assistance teams
- Using special educators as instructional consultants

■ Peer networks
■ Using special education assistants

The Special Educator in the Regular Classroom   When pull-out programs are used, exceptional students go to special education classes. It is also possible to bring special education personnel and services into the regular classroom. This usually is done in two ways. Special education teachers may come into a regular classroom and take over the teaching responsibilities for one or more exceptional students. For example, Ms. Ribbens, a certified special education teacher, may come into Kim's fifth-grade class to teach reading to Donald and Sam, two students who are exceptional. Or the special education teacher may demonstrate rather than actually teach. For example, Ms. Ribbens might go into Kim's class and demonstrate how to teach Donald and Sam in the context of the regular instructional program. Ms. Ribbens would take over instruction for the entire class while Kim observes how she instructs all of the students, including Donald and Sam, in reading.

Lincoln County School District in Oregon has integrated all students, including those with both mild and severe disabilities, those who are developmentally disabled, and students who are emotionally disturbed. Each school building within the district contains a student service center, which is used for small-group instruction. Students attend the center according to their instructional needs. Many of the students do not have disabilities. In the Central School District in Oregon, special education teachers supplement lessons to some students (both those who are handicapped and some who are not) in small groups in the regular classroom. Both the special education teacher and general education teacher work with students in small groups. For some students the objective of instruction is enrichment; for others, remediation.

One other way in which special educators work directly in general education classrooms is through **preteaching**. For example, in Oregon's Central School District special education teachers preteach vocabulary and objectives the day before they are used in a lesson. This helps prepare students who are handicapped to participate in science or social studies lessons. The purpose of preteaching is to give students extra time and opportunity to learn new content before it is used in the classroom.

Team Teaching   In special education, **team teaching** usually consists of a regular education teacher and a special education teacher working together to instruct students who are exceptional. Recently, the practice has been called "professional peer collaboration" (Pugach & Johnson, 1988). But peer collaboration usually involves two or three teachers working together to solve students' instructional or behavioral problems; it can involve some team teaching, but does not necessarily do so.

Robert Slavin and his colleagues at Johns Hopkins University have been setting up cooperative elementary schools, using team teaching at each site. In the Central School District in Oregon, special education and general education teachers plan and team-teach a subject to all students in the regular classroom.

Intervention Assistance Teams   An **intervention assistance team** is a group of teachers and related services personnel who help regular educators solve problems with individual students. A number of names are used in the professional literature to describe intervention assistance teams: *schoolwide assistance teams, school resource committees, mainstream assistance teams, staff support teams, teacher assistance teams,* and *prereferral intervention teams.* In New Jersey, for example, where the state department of education is experimenting with a noncategorical model of delivering services to exceptional students, school resource committees are teams of professionals whose role is to help teachers resolve difficult instructional and behavioral problems. Hawaii has begun using prereferral intervention teams as a first step in dealing with students who experience academic and behavioral problems. James Chalfant and Margaret Pysh for seventeen years have been training teachers in forty-four states to participate in teacher assistance teams (Chalfant, 1980; Chalfant, Pysh, & Moultrie, 1979). And in a federally funded project at Vanderbilt University, special and regular educators work together on mainstream assistance teams (Fuchs & Fuchs, 1988). Carter and Sugai (1989) report that these kinds of teams are required in twenty-three states and recommended in eleven.

Intervention assistance teams operate differently in different settings. Sometimes the teams provide crisis intervention. They might move in to help a teacher with a student who is suicidal, or they might relieve a classroom teacher for a period of time so that he or she can deal with a student who is exhibiting an emotional outburst. Intervention assistance teams also provide short-term consultation in instances in which school problems can be solved relatively quickly; they provide longer-term assistance and continuous support for difficult students. In some instances, intervention assistance teams do not work directly with students, but provide information, resources, or training to teachers. They also may help teachers monitor the progress that is being made by individual students who are handicapped. The focus of intervention assistance teams is on problem solving.

Carter and Sugai (1989) describe considerable variation in team activities among the states. In most cases, intervention involves modifying a student's instruction. In others, it involves the development of behavior management procedures, parent training, counseling, staff development, or tutoring.

In North Carolina, regulations require two levels of regular education intervention for the identification of students with learning disabilities and behavioral or emotional handicaps. Team members help regular classroom teachers develop interventions for students before referral and train regular classroom teachers in intervention strategies. This training gives teachers a greater array of strategies to use with their students and also reduces inappropriate referrals.

Chalfant and Pysh did some of the very early work on the development of intervention assistance teams. They called their teams *teacher assistance teams*, and they laid out a model for team functioning (Figure 7.1). A teacher who is having difficulty with an individual student contacts the teacher assistance team. The team leader (coordinator) reviews the case and either asks for additional information or schedules a member of the team to visit the classroom. The team meets, usually with the classroom teacher present, to go over the case and to try to solve the problem. The team develops a set of recommendations for the teacher, refers the student elsewhere, or gathers more information on the problem by means of assessment.

One problem with the teacher assistance team model is that it takes time. Teachers tell us that the time they spend meeting with and explaining to a group of experts the difficulties they have with individual students could be spent solving the problem. An alternative, the Student Learning

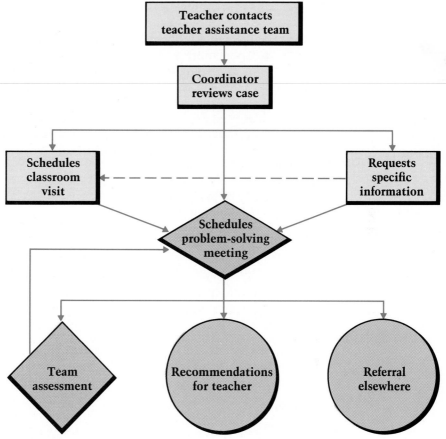

Figure 7.1
The Teacher Assistance Team
Source: From J. C. Chalfant, M. V. Pysh, and R. Moultrie (1979), Teacher assistance teams: A model for within building problem-solving, *Learning Disability Quarterly*, 2, 85–96. Reprinted with permission.

in Context model, brings team members into classrooms to help teachers solve problems (Ysseldyke, Christenson, & Thurlow, 1989).

Special Educators as Instructional Consultants   Special educators sometimes work as part of intervention assistance teams to help regular classroom teachers develop interventions for students who have special needs (see Chapter 8). They also work individually as instructional consultants, working collaboratively with regular educators to solve student problems (DeBoer, 1986; in press). Notice that we use the term *collaboratively*. Special educators provide two kinds of consultation: expert and collaborative.

Expert consultation means giving advice—the specialist advises the regular teacher on methods or techniques to use. *Collaborative consultation* means the specialist works along with the regular teacher to try to solve problems. Collaborative consultation is much more effective than expert consultation in helping teachers solve difficult problems.

Idol (1988) described consultation this way:

> It is indirect in that the special education teacher does not provide the instructional service to the student(s), . . . collaborative in that all individuals involved in the process are assumed to have expertise to contribute and responsibility to share for instructional outcomes, . . . voluntary in that all parties are willing participants in the process, and . . . problem solving oriented in that the goal of consultation is to prevent or resolve student problems. (p. 48)

Ponti, Zins, and Graden (1988) studied the implementation of instructional consultation in an elementary school. Through that implementation, the number of students referred for assessment fell but the number of referrals for consultation increased. Teachers who took advantage of the services of consultants said the process greatly improved their problem-solving skills.

Peer Networks   In the Northwest Suburban Special Education Organization in Palatine, Illinois, regular education teachers are trained in teaching techniques as well as in collaborative consultation methods. These teachers act as peer consultants in their schools, helping their colleagues devise strategies to work with students who are handicapped and others who are difficult to teach.

Special Education Assistants   Special education assistants are professionals or paraprofessionals who are assigned to general education classrooms as needed throughout a school. They may work with students individually or in groups, reviewing lessons or working on follow-up assignments. Some school districts train volunteers to work in this capacity.

Checkpoint

- *Most students receiving special education services today are being taught primarily in the regular classroom.*

- *Pull-out programs remove students for some or all of the time from the regular classroom. These programs can be organized along categorical, noncategorical, cross-categorical, and multicategorical lines.*

- *Stay-put programs bring special education services into the regular classroom, through the use of special educators there, team teach-*

ing, intervention assistance teams, instructional consultants, peer networks, and special education assistants.

ISSUES IN ORGANIZING THE DELIVERY OF SERVICES

Various movements have directly affected the settings and approaches we've just discussed, and ongoing debates in the field continue to have a major impact on how special education services are organized and delivered. Where at one time there was regular education and special education, and virtually nothing in between, today students are educated in a series of placements, varying in intensity and in the extent to which the services are removed from the regular classroom.

Cascade of Services

In 1970 Evelyn Deno described a cascade system of special education services (Figure 7.2). "The tapered design indicates the considerable difference in numbers involved at the different levels and calls attention to the fact that the system serves as a diagnostic filter" (Deno, 1970, p. 235). According to Deno, the system makes available whatever kind of setting is necessary to provide appropriate services to students. Unlike systems that sort out students to fit group standards, this system makes it easy to tailor treatment to individual needs. It acknowledges that the school system is a giant intelligence test, in which performance is judged on the basis of highly variable criteria. It is designed to facilitate modification as conditions and assumptions change.

Today, most students with handicaps attend regular classes, though they may receive supportive services. This is by far the largest number of students with handicaps. The next largest group of students with handicaps attend regular classes but receive special help from an itinerant teacher. At the next level, students spend most of the school day in the regular classroom, leaving for just part of the time to go to a resource room. As we move down the cascade, notice that fewer students attend special classes full time, while even fewer attend special schools or stations controlled by the school district. The width of the level reflects the number of students served in each setting.

Some students with handicaps do not attend public schools; they receive special education and related services outside the school system, in a hospital, at home, or in a special treatment or detention center. Deno

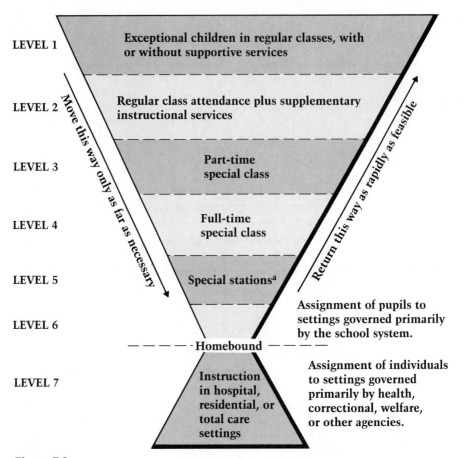

Figure 7.2
Deno's Cascade System of Special Education Services

a. Special schools in the public school system.

Source: From "Special Education as Developmental Capital," by E. Denos, *Exceptional Children*, 37, 1970 229–237. Copyright 1970 by The Council for Exceptional Children. Reprinted with permission.

(1970) argues that movement through the cascade should be based on performance at each level and on information about the student in each of the respective placements.

Maynard Reynolds and Jack Birch (1977) refined Deno's cascade. In the Reynolds-Birch Cascade (Figure 7.3), most exceptional students receive special education services in diverse regular education environments. Many different kinds of students (including those who are handicapped and those who are gifted) receive instruction designed to meet their unique

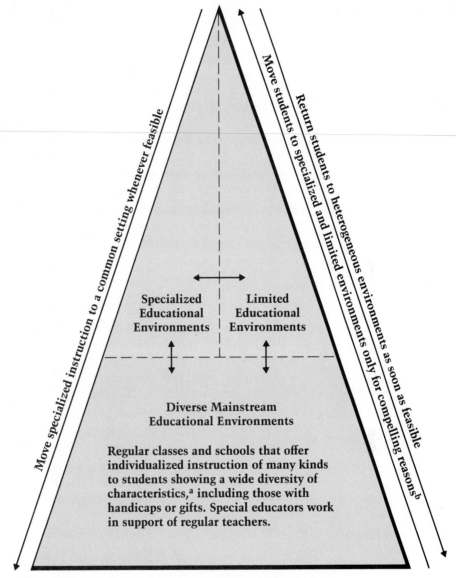

Move specialized instruction to a common setting whenever feasible

Return students to heterogeneous environments as soon as feasible

Move students to specialized and limited environments only for compelling reasons[b]

Specialized Educational Environments

Limited Educational Environments

Diverse Mainstream Educational Environments

Regular classes and schools that offer individualized instruction of many kinds to students showing a wide diversity of characteristics,[a] including those with handicaps or gifts. Special educators work in support of regular teachers.

Figure 7.3
Reynolds-Birch Cascade System of Special Education Services

a. It is assumed that no educational "place" is impervious to change and development and that through good efforts many of the varieties of specialized and intensive forms of education can be moved into a developing mainstream.

b. Here, as in the case of the original cascade, it is assumed that students should be removed from the mainstream only for limited periods and compelling reasons; that their progress should be monitored carefully and regularly; and that they should be returned to the mainstream as soon as feasible. All students start their schooling in the mainstream and have a *place* there at all times, even though they may be located in a special setting for some period of time.

Source: From *Teaching Exceptional Children in All America's Schools*, By M. C. Reynolds and J. Birch Reston, Va.: The Council for Exceptional Children. Copyright 1977 by The Council for Exceptional Children. Reprinted with permission.

needs, and the instruction is delivered in regular education environments. Only those individuals with the most severe handicaps or the most outstanding gifts are educated in special educational environments (like separate classes) or in limited educational environments (like residential schools).

According to the Reynolds-Birch cascade:

- Specialized instruction should occur in a common setting (one including students who are not handicapped) whenever possible.
- Students should be returned from pull-out settings to heterogeneous environments as soon as possible.
- Students should be moved to special and limited environments only for compelling reasons.

The Reynolds-Birch cascade rests on several broad policies:

- A decentralization policy—to develop the capacity to conduct specialized forms of education in many settings, rather than in a few.
- A "give away" policy for educational specialists, that is, the willingness to teach aspects of their specialties to less specialized professionals and sometimes to aides and to parents.
- A joining of responsibilities for assessment, planning, and instruction in a single setting, as opposed to a policy of referral to special centers for child study and prescription.
- Descriptions of students that are made mainly in terms directly relevant to instruction, rather than in terms of abstract categories, such as retarded or disturbed. (Reynolds & Birch, 1977, p. 39)

The Regular Education Initiative

Student: I've been reading recently about something called the regular education initiative. Can you tell me what it's all about?

Professor: First, you should understand a bit about what's been happening in special education. Over time, more and more students are being called handicapped and placed in special education classrooms. When researchers study these students, they find that many of them are no different from nonhandicapped low-achieving students who have been left in the regular classroom. Others are concerned about the labeling process. They argue that calling a student *retarded*, *disturbed*, *learning disabled*, or *multihandicapped* leads to negative stereotypes and stigmatizes the student. Still others contend that we've been unable to demonstrate consistently that special education helps

> students. These findings and arguments seem to indicate that more students with handicaps should be educated in general education.
>
> Student: Is this the position of regular education or of special education?
>
> Professor: The term *regular education initiative* was first used by Madeleine Will, the assistant secretary of special education, in a 1985 paper.
>
> Student: Sounds like a special education initiative to me.
>
> Professor: Either way, the contention is that we should be educating an increasing number of students with handicaps in general education.

As we were writing this text, there was considerable debate in professional journals and at national conferences over what has come to be known as the **regular education initiative (REI)** or *general education initiative (GEI)*. (See Chapter 13 for more on REI.) The REI argues that we should be placing fewer mildly handicapped students in set-aside environments; that more handicapped students belong in regular education classes. Although we call this a *regular education initiative,* the concept had its origins among special educators.

Those who advocate increasing the provision of special education services in regular education environments and a stronger partnership between regular and special educators usually cite as a basis for their views the research on classification. They argue that (1) it is impossible to differentiate handicapped and nonhandicapped students on the basis of test performance, (2) many nonhandicapped students are being identified as handicapped and placed in special education services, (3) identification as handicapped and placement in special education often is stigmatizing, and (4) there is little evidence that students placed in special education benefit from the services they receive, that in fact those services may limit life opportunities.

The regular education initiative was first proposed by Madeleine Will in a speech in which she called for a change in the direction of special education. She noted that of the then 39 million students enrolled in public schools, about 10 percent were eligible for special education services under federal or state laws. Another 10 to 20 percent of students were not handicapped, but demonstrated learning and behavioral problems that interfered with their educational progress. And she estimated that 20 to 30 percent of the students enrolled in public schools were having difficulty making progress. Later she observed: "The numbers alone argue for new strategies to increase the educational success of these students. If allowed to fail in large numbers, these children, as adults, will represent an enormous pool of unused, marginally productive manpower" (Will, 1986b, p. 413). Will called for a partnership between regular and special educators, to work together to assess the educational needs of students with learning problems and to develop strategies for meeting those needs.

Much of the debate over the regular education initiative centers on how that initiative is interpreted. Like the concepts of least restrictive environment and mainstreaming, there are different definitions of and perspectives on REI. Many of the arguments set forth are not specific to the regular education initiative. For example, there's the question of whether too many or too few students are being identified as handicapped, which itself has to do with the validity of research. Another issue is the source of students' difficulties. Some insist that students who demonstrate learning and behavioral problems do so because they are not being taught effectively by regular classroom teachers; others argue that these students' difficulties are a function of students' own deficits and disabilities. A third area of contention is the extent to which teachers can be trained to manage all students with handicaps effectively in the regular classroom, and the corollary concept that if teachers can be educated to teach appropriately, we can cut back the number of students being placed in special education classes.

You should understand that debate about appropriate placement of students who are exceptional is not new. For some time teachers have debated the appropriate placement of students who are exceptional, and they have debated the extent to which regular and special educators are responsible for educating students. Discussion and debate have centered on the kinds of students who can be educated under certain conditions. In 1975 the National Education Association spelled out the circumstances under which mainstreaming should occur.

The NEA will support mainstreaming handicapped students only when

- it provides a favorable learning experience both for handicapped and for regular students.
- regular and special teachers and administrators share equally in its planning and implementation.
- regular and special teachers are prepared for these roles.
- appropriate instructional materials, supportive services, and pupil personnel services are provided for the teacher and the handicapped student.
- modifications are made in class size, scheduling, and curriculum design to accommodate the shifting demands that mainstreaming creates.
- there is a systematic evaluation and reporting of program developments.
- adequate additional funding and resources are provided for mainstreaming and are used exclusively for that purpose. (Adelman, Bellizia, Joslin, McGrath, Manipoli, Farrar, & Yates, 1976, p. 19)

We do find agreement on the regular education initiative, the education in regular education settings of students with handicaps, and the placement of exceptional students. Kauffman, Gerber, and Semmel (1988) list several statements with which few educators would argue:

- We need to work toward better integration and coordination of services for students who have difficulty in school.
- We should seek the most effective and economical methods of serving handicapped students.
- Students should be identified as needing special services only when necessary and should be placed with their nonhandicapped peers to the greatest extent possible, and at the same time the educational interest of all students should be protected.
- Research on instruction and effective schools now suggests guidelines for school reform.
- Special educators should focus their efforts on the students who need the most specialized and extensive services, not on students who have problems but can be taught successfully by general educators.
- Many or most of the teaching practices that are appropriate for one group of students are appropriate for all students.
- Some students fail because of inadequacies of teachers of regular classes.
- A continuum or cascade of special services, ranging from full-time placement of handicapped students in regular classes to instruction in institutional settings, should be maintained and should be matched to the needs of individual students.
- Identification of handicapped students and assessment of their individual needs are difficult and controversial. (p. 6)

Today a number of states are experimenting with alternative methods for providing special education services to students with handicaps in regular education environments. Individual school districts are experimenting with ways to strengthen partnerships between regular and special educators. And the federal government has just funded six universities to work together with six individual school districts to develop models for providing effective instruction to all students with handicaps in regular education. Long after the debate on the regular education initiative has subsided, these efforts to improve instruction for students with handicaps will have moved us forward significantly.

Early Intervention

The interventions that were designed to provide special education services to children and adolescents are now being extended to infants and toddlers. Underlying this activity is recognition of the fact that the earlier we can intervene to alleviate a handicapping condition, the better our chances of success.

Although legislation (PL 99-457) and medical advances have created new interest in early intervention, the concept itself is not new. For example, Project EDGE (Expanding Developmental Growth through Education) was started in 1968 at the University of Minnesota by Professors John Rynders and Margaret Horrobin. The project was a longitudinal early education program for infants with Down syndrome. The program was family centered, beginning in the child's home with daily structured play sessions. A primary objective of these sessions was to promote the child's language development through positive parent-child interaction. At the age of 30 months, children were moved into a preschool program, which focused on concept formation and language development. This program was supplemented at home with daily one-on-one, thirty-minute reading sessions at bedtime.

Vocational Education and Transition Services

Vocational rehabilitation came into being after World War I, when physically disabled veterans had to be integrated into the work force. In the 1950s work-study programs for teenagers with handicaps first emerged. High school students were provided with controlled in-school work, followed by placement in special job situations in the community. Many students with severe handicaps were educated in sheltered workshop settings.

Recently, there has been a shift away from simulated employment or employment in sheltered workshop settings. Parents and advocacy groups are insisting that students receive real employment experiences before they leave school.

> Prevocational, simulated, or other pretend types of work are increasingly in disfavor in many school systems. The segregated adult centers which have been spawned over the past decade and a half are now and will continue to change rather dramatically in the nature of services they offer. Center-based options will be rejected by students and parents, thus forcing local programs to become more industry-based in nature. (Wehman, 1987, pp. 552–553)

The significant social and personal costs associated with the unemployment and underemployment of those who are handicapped have raised this issue to one of national priority. In 1983 Congress passed Public Law 98–199, the Secondary Education and Transitional Services for Handicapped Youth Act. The act authorized the Department of Education to fund grants and programs intended to strengthen and coordinate education, training, and related services to help those in transition to postsecondary education, competitive employment, or adult services. A total of ninety-six demonstration models and programs were funded. In 1984 Congress passed the Carl D. Perkins Vocational Education Act, mandating delivery of assessment, support services, counseling, and transitional services for students identified as handicapped and disadvantaged.

The need for these kinds of services is clear:

> Individuals who are mentally retarded, physically disabled, and/or otherwise disabled, often have not made a successful transition to the community. Most of them either work in sheltered settings, are underemployed, or are unemployed and live with family, relatives, or friends without much hope of participating in their community as most nondisabled persons participate. There is considerable evidence to suggest that these individuals will not make any major gains in the world of work unless there is a concentrated effort to identify and introduce interventions that will lead to their employment. Focusing upon transition from school to work, as a national priority, will begin to impact on efforts to employ youth with handicaps who are conspicuously absent from the workplace. (Rusch & Phelps, 1987, p. 491)

Checkpoint

- *Cascade systems of service delivery tailor those services to the students' needs.*

- *The regular education initiative has led to research into new ways to bring handicapped students into the regular education program.*

- *Early intervention programs are based on the belief that the earlier we intervene to alleviate a handicapping condition, the more successful we can be.*

- *The unemployment and underemployment of those with handicaps has focused attention on vocational education and transition services for exceptional students at the secondary level.*

WHAT WE THINK ABOUT DELIVERING SERVICES TO STUDENTS WITH SPECIAL NEEDS

Where a student is educated probably has little to do with the quality of the instruction the student receives. But when we isolate students who are exceptional, we limit their opportunities to interact and learn with other students. We believe that special education makes good sense. Some students have special needs, and those students profit from efforts on the part of educators to meet those needs. But categorical special education makes very little sense. There is little evidence to suggest that different categories of students learn differently. In fact, there is now good evidence, much of it in our own research, that students who are handicapped benefit from interventions specifically designed to meet their unique needs. Increasingly, those needs can be and are being met in the regular classroom.

Summary

1. Classification is the process of grouping people, places, and things.
2. The process of classifying exceptional students stemmed from the belief that these students could be taught more easily and effectively in homogeneous groups.
3. The classification of exceptional students helps government agencies develop social policies and helps researchers evaluate the effects of those policies.
4. Undermining the utility of the classification process is the variation in the definitions and criteria used by the different states to determine students' eligibility for special services.
5. Three criteria are used to determine whether the LRE provision of Public Law 94–142 is being met: proximity of the educational program to the regular education environment; proximity of the program to the student's home; and degree of opportunity given the student to interact with nonhandicapped peers.
6. Mainstreaming is a social principle that has become part of special education primarily through court decisions.
7. Most students receiving special education services today are being taught primarily in the regular classroom.
8. Pull-out programs remove students for some or all of the time from the regular classroom. These programs can be organized along categorical, noncategorical, cross-categorical, and multicategorical lines.
9. Stay-put programs bring special education services into the regular classroom, through the use of special educators there, team teaching, intervention assistance teams, instructional consultants, peer networks, and special education assistants.
10. Cascade systems of service delivery tailor those services to students' individual needs.
11. The regular education initiative argues that more exceptional students should be taught in the regular classroom.
12. Early intervention programs are based on the belief that the earlier we intervene to alleviate a handicapping condition, the more successful we can be.
13. The unemployment and underemployment of those with handicaps has focused attention on vocational education and transition services for exceptional students at the secondary level.
14. Research shows that students who are handicapped do benefit from interventions specifically designed to meet their needs.

Activities

1. Contact the department of special education in your local school district and obtain a list of the kinds of settings in which students with special needs are educated. If there are several school districts in your local area, divide the class into groups and have each group contact one district. Then engage in a class discussion of the alternative ways in which the delivery of special education services is organized in the various districts.

2. Obtain two research articles on learning disabilities and record the way in which the authors describe the subject populations for the studies.

3. Read the paper by Kauffman, Gerber, and Semmel and list the assumptions underlying the regular education initiative that they challenge.

Suggested Readings

Cromwell, R. L., Blashfield, R. K., & Strauss, J. S. (1975). Criteria for classification systems. In N. Hobbs (Ed.), *Issues in the classification of children* (Vol. 1). San Francisco: Jossey-Bass.

> *In this classic reference the authors describe a valid classification as one in which assessment data have clear implications for prescribing treatments with known outcomes. They raise many questions about the validity of current classification practices.*

Hobbs, N. (Ed.). (1975). *Issues in the classification of children* (2 vols.). San Francisco: Jossey-Bass.

> *A systematic and comprehensive review of the classification and labeling of exceptional students. Ninety-three experts (educators, psychologists, pediatricians, sociologists, parents, and public school administrators) summarize existing knowledge in topical areas.*

Idol, L. (1988). A rationale and guidelines for establishing special education consultation programs. *Remedial and Special Education, 9,* 48–58.

> *The author provides a comprehensive definition of consultation for use in establishing consultation programs. She lists twelve major benefits of using these programs and gives seven guidelines for using them.*

Ysseldyke, J. E., & Algozzine, B. (1982). *Critical issues in special and remedial education.* Boston: Houghton Mifflin.

> *In Chapter 2 the authors describe the problems and the history of classifying and labeling students who are exceptional.*

8

Professionals in Special Education

FOCUSING QUESTIONS

■ What is the educational background of those who teach and work with exceptional students?

■ What are the different roles assumed by special education teachers today?

■ How do we define *collaborative consultation*?

■ What is the difference between itinerant teachers and resource room teachers?

■ What do we mean by *clinical teaching*?

■ There is a tendency today for personnel in related services to have less direct contact with exceptional students. What is responsible for that trend?

■ What roles do administrators play in special education programs?

■ How do an organization's members affect its policies?

K
IM IS A GENERAL EDUCATION TEACHER WHO HAS students with special needs in her class. Larry is a special education teacher who teaches in a resource room. Although Kim is a regular education teacher and Larry is a special education teacher, both work with students who are exceptional. And in the process of teaching those students, both work with psychologists, counselors, social workers, and other professionals.

Those who work with exceptional students do many different jobs. Teachers are responsible for instructional programs. Psychologists, counselors, and other professionals are responsible for testing students to identify those who are eligible for special education services. They also provide therapy for students with special needs, help teachers develop instructional programs for individual students, and serve as liaisons between community service agencies and schools. Administrators hire teachers, arrange schedules, and manage the special education program in their school or district. In this chapter, we talk about the many professionals and organizations working on behalf of individuals who are exceptional. And to help you choose the role you'd like to play, we also look at the supply and demand of professionals who serve students with special needs.

Most of those who work with exceptional students have licenses or certificates that allow them to do so. Requirements for licensure or certification vary from state to state, and we touch on this variation in our descriptions of the professionals who work with exceptional students.

Teachers, counselors, and psychologists are licensed or certified by state departments of education, usually after completing prescribed courses of studies and being recommended by a college or university. In most states teachers must take tests to be licensed (Table 8.1). Even though they have credentials that allow them to do certain kinds of work, the functions of these professionals often overlap. Services provided in one district by a teacher may be provided in another by a school psychologist. The director of special education may be responsible for transportation, program evaluation, and other administrative matters in one district, while the superintendent of schools assumes these same responsiblilities in another. Responsibilities are more a function of the individual's training and experience, and the expectations of a particular setting than of job title.

REGULAR EDUCATION TEACHERS

Although this is a book about the practice of special education, it is important to recognize that about one-fourth of students who are exceptional receive all or most special education services from regular education teachers working in the regular classroom. During the 1986–87 school year (the most recent year for which data were available at the time we were writing this text), 26 percent of those students identified as handicapped received educational services primarily in regular classes. Remember that the LRE provision of Public Law 94–142 means that, to the greatest extent possible, students with handicaps must be educated in the regular classroom.

Until very recently, we could say that regular education teachers had either a bachelor's or master's degree in education and were certified by their state departments of education. Today we find increasing use of five-year programs and professional preparation programs. In some universities, graduates are recommended for certification only after they complete five years of study in which some coursework is in teacher education. Increasingly, those who become teachers complete a bachelor's degree in a content area (like mathematics or children's literature), then spend a fifth year taking education courses for a master's degree. In nearly all states, teacher certification is by grade level—teachers are certified to teach either elementary or secondary students. Some states break down certification levels even further, into preprimary, primary, middle, and secondary levels. In most states, teachers must take coursework in the education of exceptional students.

Regular education teachers participate in the development of individualized education programs for exceptional students assigned to their class. Once a teacher participates in the development of an IEP, he or she may retain primary responsibility for teaching the student, or primary responsibility for the student's instructional program may be assigned to a

Increasingly, special educators are providing indirect services to students and direct services to their teachers by acting as consultants to regular educators.

(© Laimute Druskis/ Jeroboam)

special education teacher. Typically this decision is based on who spends the most time during school with the student, and is made by the IEP planning team, but practices vary from district to district.

SPECIAL EDUCATION TEACHERS

Special education teachers hold at least a bachelor's degree with a major in special education. In addition, most have done advanced work in special education and may have a master's degree. All are certified by state departments of education. The most recent data available indicate that in twenty-seven states or territories certification is completely or primarily categorical; in twenty-six certification is completely or primarily noncategorical or cross-categorical (Smith-Davis, Burke, & Noel, 1984).

The term *special education teacher* is a general one. There are many different kinds of special education teachers. Most of the titles assigned to these individuals reflect the setting in which they are employed or the types of students in their classes. Special education teachers typically are responsible for meeting the specific educational needs of those students assigned to them. They usually participate in the development of IEPs for

Table 8.1
States That Have Enacted Testing Programs for Certifying Teachers, Fall 1987

State	Enacted	Effective	Tests Used*
Alabama	1980	1981	State
Arizona	1980	1980	State
Arkansas	1979	1983	NTE
California	1981	1982	CBEST
Colorado	1981	1983	CAT
Connecticut	1982	1985	State
Delaware	1982	1983	PPST
Florida	1978	1980	State
Georgia	1975	1980	State
Hawaii	1986	1986	NTE
Idaho	1987	1988	NTE
Illinois	1985	1988	State
Indiana	1984	1985	NTE
Kansas	1984	1986	NTE, PPST
Kentucky	1984	1985	NTE
Louisiana	1977	1978	NTE
Maine	1984	1988	NTE
Maryland	1986	1986	NTE
Massachusetts	1985	†	†
Michigan	1986	1991	†
Minnesota	1986	1988	PPST
Mississippi	1975	1977	NTE
Missouri	1985	1988	†
Montana	1985	1988	NTE
Nebraska	1984	1989	†
Nevada	1984	1989	PPST, State
New Hampshire	1984	1985	PPST, NTE
New Jersey	1984	1985	NTE
New Mexico	1981	1983	NTE
New York	1980	1984	NTE
North Carolina	1984	1984	NTE
North Dakota	1986	†	†
Ohio	1986	1987	NTE
Oklahoma	1980	1982	State
Oregon	1984	1985	CBEST
Pennsylvania	1985	1987	State
Rhode Island	1985	1986	NTE
South Carolina	1979	1982	NTE, State
South Dakota	1985	1986	NTE
Tennessee	1980	1981	NTE
Texas	1981	1986	State
Virginia	1979	1980	NTE

Table 8.1 *(continued)*
States That Have Enacted Testing Programs for Certifying Teachers, Fall 1987

State	Enacted	Effective	Tests Used*
Washington	1984	†	†
West Virginia	1982	1985	State
Wisconsin	1986	1990	†

Notes: * CAT = California Achievement Test; CBEST = California Basic Skills Test; NTE = National Teacher Examination; PPST = Pre-Professional Skills Test; State = state-developed test.
† To be determined.
Source: *What's Happening in Teacher Testing—1987*, August 1987, Washington, DC: From U.S. Department of Education, Office of Research.

students and are primarily responsible for working to meet the goals set forth in those programs.

Special education teachers who work at the preschool level may be employed by the school district or a private agency. Those who are employed at the secondary level may teach students full time, or help students in specific subject matter areas for limited parts of the school day.

Below we describe the roles assumed by special education teachers in the schools. Don't expect to find all of them in every school system. Schools organize their delivery of services differently. Some have resource room teachers, some do not. Some have itinerant teachers, some do not.

Instructional Consultant

Increasingly, special educators are providing indirect services to students and direct services to their teachers by acting as consultants to regular educators. In fact, regular educator-special educator collaboration is becoming the primary model for providing services to students who are exceptional. As more students with special needs are educated in the regular classroom, regular educators and special educators work together to determine the nature of the instructional program for the students for whom they share responsibility. Those who provide indirect services are called **instructional consultants**, or *teacher consultants*.

In some states, *instructional consultation* is defined as any type of supportive relationship among professionals that is designed to benefit students who are handicapped. In others, instructional consultation means an expert gives the classroom teacher help.

This distinction is the basis of the distinction between collaborative consultation and *expert* consultation (see Chapter 7). Idol, Paolucci-Whitcomb, and Nevin (1986) defined *collaborative consultation* as an interactive process that enables teams of people with diverse expertise to generate creative solutions to mutually defined problems. The outcome is enhanced, altered, and produces solutions that are different from those that the individual team member would produce independently. The major outcome of collaborative consultation is to provide comprehensive and effective programs for students with special needs within the most appropriate context, thereby enabling them to achieve maximum constructive interaction with their nonhandicapped peers. (p. 1)

Instructional consultants have two major goals: to solve problems that are evidenced by students who are handicapped or gifted, and to give classroom teachers the skills they need to teach preventively and to generalize strategies that are effective with one student to others.

Itinerant Teacher

Itinerant teachers are special education teachers who travel from building to building within a district or, in rural areas, from district to district. Itinerant teachers usually spend just one or two days a week in a given building, so they typically work with individual children less frequently than do resource room teachers. In rural areas, itinerant teachers travel with trunkloads of instructional materials.

Itinerant teachers often are used when the number of handicapped students of particular types in a single school is too small to justify another classroom delivery system. These teachers may have the same caseload as those assigned to resource rooms, but their students are enrolled in different classrooms in different schools, not in the same school.

Resource Room Teacher

The **resource room teacher** is a special education teacher who instructs exceptional students in a resource room. These students are assigned to regular classes, but leave those classes to attend the resource room for a part of the school day. The length of time students are in the resource room is a function of the severity of their academic difficulties. Instruction in the resource room can be primary, supplementary, compensatory, or remedial (see Chapter 7). Increasingly, as more and more students are mainstreamed, resource room teachers are assuming the role of instructional consultants.

Self-contained Special Class Teacher

Some exceptional students are assigned to one classroom and one teacher for most of their academic instruction. The class is called a self-contained class and the teacher is called a **self-contained special class teacher**. This

Itinerant teachers often are used when the number of handicapped students of particular types in a single school is too small to justify another classroom delivery system.

(© Alan Carey/The Image Works)

teacher, who is in charge of all activities, structures the class and plans and carries out all instruction, usually including music, art, and physical education. Students in these classes are almost always assigned by category. They are grouped for instructional efficiency, on the assumption they will profit from similar levels and methods of instruction. Students enrolled in self-contained classrooms usually are severely handicapped. School personnel place these students in such classes because they assume that the severity of the students' difficulties would make it difficult for them to profit from even limited exposure to regular classroom instruction.

Self-contained special class teachers can teach in separate schools. For example, in some districts, they teach in private or state schools that are designed to provide instruction for one or more types of handicapped students.

Clinical Teacher

Clinical teachers either teach in clinical settings (child guidance clinics, classes run in psychiatric treatment centers or correctional institutions) or teach "clinically" in any number of settings. *Clinical teaching* means

MY NAME IS LYNN Wilcox, and I am a speech/language pathology supervisor in rural Nebraska. For approximately half of my time, I am responsible for the professional growth and evaluation of fifteen persons who practice speech/language pathology and audiology in a county area. The other half of my time, I attempt to provide consulting and diagnostic support to those clinicians and to other special education team members working with children from birth to age 21 for the communication problems associated with whatever handicapping conditions we identify.

I love my job. I love the people I work with and work for. Those feelings are not expressed lightly, nor should they represent to you that my job is in any way easy. I could tell you that I have great responsibility to see to it that child change occurs, but that would be an unfortunate exaggeration. Actually, I am a cheerleader. I am a politician. And I am a loving manager. Finally, I strive to be a fair, firm, and friendly evaluator. I attempt to be aware of resources, techniques, materials, programs, services, and on and on. Much more though, it is my responsibility to be able to demonstrate and clearly explain to those I serve the areas I think the child needs help in and what they can do to implement improvement so they can see child change. I am a one-on-one inservice presenter who gets to coach the staff through a problem, direct their thinking a little, and enjoy watching their own excitement and the child's progress in relation to their efforts.

There are different supervisory styles. You may meet a supervisor along the way who functions differently from the way I do. My work is primarily directed toward the excitement of learning, and in that way I act primarily as a consultant to the clinician and very often to the resource teacher and the class teacher as well. I drop little nuggets about communication and how it affects class performance and test performance (particularly intelligence test performance) and offer suggestions about what things can be done to support a communicationally handicapped child in whatever setting to anybody that will listen, either by mandate or by interest. I am not very good at sitting and watching someone work. I have discovered that the people with whom I work appreciate having me participate in activities and sessions with them. Observing is a viable supervisory style. I do it briefly sometimes, although usually my supervision occurs in action.

Sometimes I work as part of the team diagnosing a child's problem. I have to be able to clearly state what the problems are from a communication viewpoint. I have to make that information relevant to the classroom and particularly clear and relevant to the child's parents. Then I either help write or provide ideas for writing educational plans that match the child's problems. I negotiate placement with administrators and other professionals who might see the child's problems differently than the way I see them. Sometimes I sit back while a clinician presents data and does the interpreting — oh, so important, that interpreting. Sometimes I am pleased because a clinician or a resource teacher or a parent really sees and understands how the child's communication fits into the scheme of things. Sometimes I am embarrassed by the lack of ability to interpret. I have to be careful not to wound clinicians and yet find a way to present uncomfortable information to them to make them want to learn instead of squashing their feelings just because

I was embarrassed by their lack of preparation or information.

So, back I go to being a cheerleader for those who really didn't know when they got into this profession just how demanding it really is. What carrot can I find to encourage, motivate, and excite them to go on a little further for the benefit of the kids they serve? Why are some people so threatened by my excitement about changes and growth and ideas that might make a difference for the kids? What happened along the way to kill their enthusiasm for learning (which, in my opinion, kills their enthusiasm for teaching), and is there anything I can do to give support, information, or encouragement to help these stagnant and threatened clinicians to recognize that my appearance or my support isn't a threat but a promise? Fortunately, these frustrating situations occur infrequently. Frankly, if they happened more often, I would be selling candles in a card shop. Or hamburgers.

Did I mention politician? As a supervisor I must be aware of the emotional, attitudinal, physical, and home status of each person I serve. Besides that, I must be aware of the attitudes of the administrators under whom they work directly, because ours is an outside agency and every time I walk in a building, I am an interloper.

A typical day (if there is such a thing in my professional life) involves several activities. Almost always, my day involves a lot of driving. I have a new tape deck in my vehicle so that I can listen to language samples provided by clinicians as I drive down the highway. Sometimes I listen to Cat Stevens. I arrive at a school and usually try to find the building administrator, unless I am really late. I bring with me materials that have been requested and tests that might be applicable to the kids we are seeing that day.

I may do demonstration testing, informal probing, testing, or I may watch. I try to stay awhile and ask the next group of kids to wait a bit while I check to see how things are going with the caseload, with the other professionals in the building, and with the real problem kids (or administrators!). After about two hours or less, I travel on again. Sometimes I carry my video tape equipment, and we tape and view a session to see how the kids are doing. When watching themselves in action that way, clinicians are harder on themselves than I would ever dream of being.

At some time during each day I get near a telephone. I must be very good at relaying information by that instrument; without it my professional life would be impossible. I contact parents. I call administrators. I check on appointments. I coordinate my activities with my supervisor. I call the psychologist to discuss a child. I get an average of six calls each day from people. I supervise, often before 8:00 A.M. and after 6:00 P.M. They ask questions or share information and concerns about kids and programs. I spend an average of two to three hours a day on the telephone. I revise the next day's schedule based on those calls and visits.

About once a week, I get in front of my typewriter. There must be some kind of written record of my activities, and I must write down ideas that have been shared. I must write reports for people. I write little notes of encouragement to people.

All in all, I spend about fifty or more hours every week doing something related to my profession. I am on call to each clinician at any time. In addition, I read, here and there, and call or write to those who replenish my own enthusiasm and my knowledge.

(continued)

Maybe supervision can be done in a way that requires less dedication and less commitment. My personal philosophy is that I am willing to do more than I ask anyone else to do. I must be able to demonstrate any idea I present. I must understand my profession well enough to teach it to others.

Lynn Wilcox is a speech/language pathology supervisor from Hastings, Nebraska.

different things in different places. Some teachers teach clinically by incorporating specific psychotherapeutic methods into their instruction. Others teach prescriptively, trying to match instruction to learners' strengths and weaknesses. Still others teach experimentally, trying different approaches until an effective one is found. Clinical teachers may teach one type of special students (for example, those who are emotionally disturbed) or several types, depending on the school district. There are no clear distinctions between the kinds of services offered by those who are called clinical teachers and special educators who are called other names. It's just that in some settings special educators are called clinical teachers.

Homebound Teacher

Homebound teachers do not stay at home themselves; they teach students who are unable to attend school. The nature of the services they offer varies, from helping students who are injured keep up with their homework to providing a complete instructional program for those who are homebound or hospitalized for long periods of time. The problems that require homebound instruction occur so infrequently that many school districts do not have homebound teachers. They are more common in city school systems with large enrollments.

Checkpoint

- *Both regular and special education teachers may be assigned to work with students who are exceptional.*

- *Responsibility for educating individual students with special needs most often resides with the teacher with whom the student spends most of the day.*

- *Many different kinds of special education teachers serve students who are gifted or handicapped.*

- *The title assigned to teachers (instructional consultant, itinerant teacher, resource room teacher, self-contained special class teacher, clinical teacher, homebound teacher) reflects either the setting in which they work or the kinds of services they provide.*

RELATED SERVICES PERSONNEL

Many other professionals work with students who are exceptional, providing services that are related to the instructional services provided by classroom teachers. Counselors, school psychologists, diagnosticians, therapists, and school social workers are called *related services personnel*. In many states, two-year programs provide training for a number of specific support personnel in special education, including classroom paraprofessionals, interpreters for those with hearing impairments, and drug and alcohol abuse aides.

Counselor

Counselors usually are required to have at least a master's degree in guidance and counseling, counseling psychology, or student personnel psychology, and are licensed or certified by the state in which they work. Many guidance counselors have doctoral degrees.

Guidance counselors work in both elementary and secondary schools. They perform a variety of functions, depending on what the system or the particular school expects of them. Often they advise students on particular courses of study or help them make college and career choices. In some schools, counselors are responsible for administering or supervising the administration of the school's testing program. Often they play a major role in the special education process, coordinating all testing activities during the referral stage and participating in decision-making meetings. They also may counsel individual students who are experiencing academic, behavioral, or personal difficulties, or their parents or families. And especially at the secondary level, counselors are often in charge of curricular content areas. For example, they may coordinate instruction in chemical dependency programs or supervise instruction in a moral education curriculum.

School Psychologist

Most school psychologists hold at least a specialist or other six-year degree and are licensed or certified by the state in which they are employed. And many of them hold doctoral degrees. The particular functions a school psychologist performs depend on the individual's training and the expectations of the system in which he or she works. School psychologists are trained to perform a variety of functions, ranging from assessment and instructional planning for students who are experiencing academic and behavior problems, to individual psychotherapy and behavioral treatment. The specific role of the school psychologist is difficult to describe, precisely because it is so varied.

School psychologists are trained to perform a variety of functions, ranging from assessment and instructional planning for students who are experiencing academic and behaviorial problems, to individual psychotherapy and behavorial treatment.

(© Michael Weisbrot and Family)

If you ask teachers or parents what school psychologists do, chances are good that you will get one of three responses: they will not know what a school psychologist is; they will say that school psychologists give tests to atypical children; or they will describe functions commonly attributed to psychiatrists or clinical psychologists. If you ask clinical or counseling psychologists what school psychologists do, they will most likely talk about testing of children for special education by an assortment of persons certified as school psychometrists. If you ask school psychologists what they do, you can expect to receive detailed information about the many functions school psychologists could perform, given an opportunity to do so. These functions will include virtually everything that can be done by professional psychologists of any kind or persuasion, but with emphasis on their performance in schools or with school-age children and their families. If you press further and insist that you be told what school psychologists actually do rather than what they could do if permitted, your respondents reluctantly will describe functions that are less encompassing than they would like them to be and inevitably involve substantial attention to the administration of individual tests to children referred by school personnel either for special education classification or because of untoward behavior or poor school performance in a classroom. (Bardon, 1982, p. 3)

Of all the individuals who work in the school system, school psychologists are most knowledgeable about learning theory and its application to educational settings. They are the critical link between education and psychology. Although school psychologists are expected to perform a variety of functions, their primary responsibility is intervention in the educational programs of students who are failing to make progress in order to modify either the environment or the student to facilitate learning. More typically, they administer and interpret the results of tests.

Educational Diagnostician

Educational diagnosticians hold at least a master's degree and are licensed or certified by the state in which they work. Only a few states employ educational diagnosticians; in other states, the functions they perform are carried out by counselors or school psychologists. The educational diagnostician assesses students, determining their eligibility for special education services, and works with classroom teachers to plan instructional interventions for individual students.

Occupational Therapist

The registered occupational therapist usually holds a bachelor of arts or bachelor of science degree in occupational therapy and has completed the national certification examination of the American Occupational Therapy Association. Occupational therapists most often are employed in hospitals, clinics, or agencies. They also are employed in schools, specifically where IEPs state the need for occupational therapy. Occupational therapists typically help handicapped students develop self-help skills (feeding themselves, dressing themselves), provide certain kinds of vocational training, and help develop motor and perceptual skills. They also teach parents how to train their children at home.

Physical Therapist

Licensed physical therapists usually hold a bachelor's or master's degree in physical therapy and have passed a state licensing examination. Physical therapists, like occupational therapists, work most often in clinics, hospitals, or agencies, where they provide physical therapy, helping individuals develop or recover their physical strength and endurance. But they also work in school settings (especially in larger districts), developing exercise routines for students with physical disabilities and working with them to improve their mobility.

Speech-Language Pathologist

The speech-language pathologist, or speech therapist, holds a master's degree in speech pathology. Those with one year's experience in speech-

Occupational therapists typically provide vocational training, help students develop motor, perceptual, and self-help skills, and teach parents how to train their children at home.

(© Paul Conklin/ Monkmeyer Press Photo Service)

language therapy beyond the master's degree level are eligible for a certificate of clinical competence from the American Speech-Language-Hearing Association (ASHA) (formerly the American Speech and Hearing Association). Those who work in schools are certified by the department of education in their state. Speech-language pathologists conduct assessments of students thought to evidence speech or language difficulties, and provide therapy for them.

Speech-language pathologists who work in schools may function as itinerant specialists, spending one or two days each week in each building to which they are assigned. In larger districts, a speech-language pathologist may be assigned to just one or two schools. Increasingly speech-language pathologists are providing indirect services to students. They work as consultants to regular education teachers, helping them design instruction for individual students or for an entire class.

Audiologist

Larger school systems often employ an audiologist; smaller systems refer students to audiologists who are employed in clinical or agency settings. Audiologists hold at least a master's degree and must pass a national examination to earn a certificate of clinical competence. Their primary functions are administering hearing tests, determining the degree of hearing loss, and recommending ways of correcting or compensating for the condition.

School Social Worker

Social workers typically hold a master of social work degree. Those who have two years' experience beyond that level are eligible for certification through the Academy of Certified Social Workers of the National Association of Social Workers. Nearly every community service agency employs social workers. Those who work in schools are called *school social workers*. Their functions vary across different school settings. Typically they gather social and developmental histories as part of the special education assessment process. In addition, they work with families to help them acquire social services in the community, serve as liaisons with community agencies, and often counsel families or conduct family therapy.

Checkpoint

- *Counselors, school psychologists, diagnosticians, therapists, speech-language pathologists, audiologists, and school social workers provide services that are related to the services classroom teachers provide exceptional students.*
- *The movement to mainstream exceptional students has changed the function of related services personnel. More and more, they are providing direct services to teachers, not students.*

ADMINISTRATORS

Special education programs involve much more than classroom instruction and the related services provided by counselors, therapists, and other personnel. There are staff to hire, funds to allocate, programs to oversee, transportation and equipment to provide. In larger school districts, administrators devote all of their time to managing special education programs. In smaller districts, one administrator may be responsible for both the regular and the special education program.

Superintendent of Schools

The superintendent of schools holds at least a master's degree in educational administration. Especially in large systems, the superintendent may hold a doctoral degree. The superintendent is responsible for the smooth operation of the entire educational system, and must develop and maintain a system that provides for the educational needs of all students.

MY NAME IS MARGE Goldberg. I am the parent of a young adult with disabilities and am Co-director of PACER Center. A description of PACER and the services we offer will give you a vision of how parent centers can be a valuable source of support for families and can advocate for children and young adults with disabilities.

When parents learn their child has a disability, they experience many different emotions and reactions to the knowledge that "something may be wrong" with their child. These parents may feel very much alone and confused about the future. Parents who have children with disabilities spend a great deal of time and energy seeking appropriate services for their youngsters. They must communicate with professionals from many fields, meet with medical/health providers, educators, school and county social workers, and many people who become significant advisors in their child's development. But a very important source of assistance can be gained only from fellow parents who have experienced the same emotions, struggled to obtain the needed services, and know what resources are available.

In 1976, a training and information center for parents of children with all disabilities was established in Minnesota through the efforts of families representing seventeen disability organizations. The Parent Advocacy Coalition for Educational Rights (PACER) developed its initial program to make parents aware of their rights and responsibilities under special education laws and procedures and to increase their knowledge and skills in working cooperatively with schools to plan the most appropriate and beneficial programs for their sons and daughters. Staffed primarily by parents of youth with disabilities and by individuals with disabilities themselves, PACER car-

ries out the philosophy of "Parents Helping Parents" through workshops, individual assistance, and written information. Our mission—to improve and expand opportunities that enhance the quality of life for children and young adults with disabilities and their families—has guided us to develop many new programs in the past ten years. Through PACER, families have become more knowledgeable about their children's needs and programs, and professionals have learned more about parents' feelings and how to improve their own skills in working with families.

Last year, PACER reached 12,000 individuals through its basic parent training and information project. In addition, 24,000 children and 1,200 teachers attended PACER's puppet shows on handicap awareness ("Count Me In") and prevention of child abuse ("Let's Prevent Abuse"). Workshops and written materials cover other topics such as:

- Early intervention and information on preschool services

- Training people to be surrogate parents (representing children, in the education process, who do not have parents available to help them)

- Transition services (from school to postsecondary education, vocational training, employment, and more independent living in the community)

- Supported employment (community-based, integrated employment programs geared for adults with severe disabilities)

- Special populations (underrepresented parents, minority groups)

- Health/medical services and resources in the community

- Support for families of children with emotional disorders

- The "least restrictive alternative"

- Siblings and their feelings
- Training of parents to assist other parents
- Communication to improve parent skills in representing their child's needs

A computer resource center at PACER allows families to try computers, special software, and adaptive devices to enable children and young adults with disabilities to learn and communicate via computers. Technical assistance is provided to parent training programs in other states on management of parent training centers, parent workshops, and other services.

The *Pacesetter*, a new magazine by and for parents of children and young adults with disabilities, is mailed three times a year to approximately 27,000 individuals in Minnesota and in all other states. Four other newsletters, as well as booklets, extensive written materials, video tapes, and other resources, are available—and most are free for parents. In addition to helping parents individually or at workshops, PACER makes presentations for professionals in schools and university settings, at conferences and other meetings.

PACER has had an impact on parents. A follow-up survey of parents regarding the center's services shows that:

- Ninety percent of the parents indicated they acquired new information or knowledge from PACER.
- Sixty-five percent became more involved in their child's education since attending a PACER workshop.
- Ninety-eight percent gained more confidence as a result of

PACER's services.

- Eighty percent indicated their children received increased or improved services as a result of the training.

PACER receives many letters from parents. One recent letter stated, "Your services have been a lifeline to me as a parent, but, most important, your knowledge has given us hope that we can protect and provide services for our youngster with disabilities." Throughout the nation, there is a network of parent training centers. Some are small projects offering individual assistance and training sessions on special education procedures. Others are larger centers that have many programs similar to those described at PACER. Each of them advocates for families of children with all disabilities. In addition, organizations that represent the needs of persons with specific disabilities such as mental retardation (ARC), cerebral palsy (UCP), learning disabilities (ACLD), and epilepsy (EFA) are available in almost all states.

As a parent of a 26-year-old son, I wish these resources had existed years ago. Now the assistance that a family desires is only a phone call away, and many parent centers have toll-free telephone numbers for parents throughout their state. Because no single individual (teacher, doctor, etc.) can serve all the needs a family may have for a child with disabilities, we must all pull together—to learn about laws and available services, to advocate for improvements, and to put families in touch with other parents and with professionals. Armed with information, families will be empowered to make informed and better choices for the future.

For more information on parent training or parent training centers in the United States, contact PACER Center, Inc., 4826 Chicago Avenue South, Minneapolis, MN 55417, telephone (612) 827-2966, voice and TDD.

As chief school administrator, the superintendent has the ultimate responsibility for the kinds of special education services provided in the school system and for ensuring that procedures and programs comply with state and federal laws and guidelines.

Director or Coordinator of Special Education

The director or coordinator of special education typically holds at least a master's degree in education administration, a categorical area (for example, mental retardation, learning disabilities), or special education. The director of special education, who works under the authority of the superintendent of schools, has administrative responsibility for special education programs. He or she is responsible for ensuring district compliance with legal mandates and regulations, oversees supervisors of specific service components, and has responsibility for staffing and inservice training.

Supervisor of Specific Service Components

Most relatively large school districts, those with sizable numbers of exceptional students, employ supervisors. Supervisors hold at least a bachelor's degree in special education, and most hold a master's degree. Supervisors oversee the delivery of services, usually to specific types or categories of students. For example, a school district may employ a supervisor for students with learning disabilities or a supervisor of programs for those who are physically handicapped. The supervisor's responsibilities are similar to those of the director of special education, but usually in a specific area of exceptionality.

Building Principal

The building principal is the chief administrative officer of a specific school building, responsible for the smooth operation of all programs and services within the building. Principals typically are responsible for supervising the delivery of special education services only insofar as programs or classes exist in their building. We find an exception to this general rule in districts that have special schools—entire schools serving exceptional students. Here, principals have considerable responsibility for administering special education programs.

OTHER PROFESSIONALS

The list of specialists who work with exceptional students goes on and on. Although these professionals do not actually teach students, they may

work with specific children or advise schools how to handle specific problems. For example, medical professionals may become involved in special
education when a physical ailment affects a student's learning. Psychiatrists work with severely disturbed students, consulting with school personnel about their education. Neurologists may work with school personnel on the treatment of students who evidence brain injury or other
neurological problems. Orthopedic specialists often become involved in
the educational planning for students who are physically handicapped.
Ophthalmologists or optometrists may become involved when students
have vision difficulties. School nurses participate in routine decisions that
relate to health and often are members of pupil placement teams. Clinical
psychologists may work with individuals who experience learning and behavioral problems, sometimes in school settings, more often in community agencies. Rehabilitation specialists may provide in-school or
out-of-school services for students to facilitate their vocational and community adjustment.

SUPPLY AND DEMAND

Is there a need for personnel to educate and work with students who are
handicapped? In its tenth annual report to Congress on Public Law 94–142,

the Department of Education lists the number of special education teachers employed and needed, by state. For the 1985–86 school year, the states reported that they employed 291,954 special education teachers, and that they needed 27,474 more teachers. The largest number of teachers was reported for the category learning disabled, also the area of greatest need. In the 1985–86 school year, the states needed close to 11,000 teachers for students with learning disabilities. Those states with the greatest personnel needs were Florida, Louisiana, New York, Texas, Virginia, West Virginia, and Wyoming. The same report also described employment figures and need for related services personnel (Table 8.2).

Checkpoint
- *Administrators coordinate and oversee special education programs within their district or school.*
- *A large number of specialists are drawn into the special education system by the individual needs of exceptional students.*
- *Most special education teachers work with learning disabled students.*

PROFESSIONAL ORGANIZATIONS

In America, people with similar interests tend to band together to form organizations, councils, or associations. Many organizations exist for the purpose of enabling like individuals to share experiences and help one another cope with specific kinds of problems. For example, Goffman (1963) notes that "there are the huddle-together self-help clubs formed by the divorced, the aged, the obese, the physically handicapped, the ileostomied, and the colostomied" (p. 22).

Of course not all organizations are of the self-help experience-sharing sort. For example, the purpose of the Amputee Shoe and Glove Exchange is "to facilitate swaps of unneeded shoes and gloves by amputees. [The Exchange] attempts to match amputees who need the opposite shoe or glove, who are about the same age, and who have reasonably similar taste. All mailings of shoes or gloves are between the amputees matched. The Exchange serves both men and women, children and adults" (Akey, 1983, p. 809).

Organizations also exist to give specific causes or categories of individuals higher visibility. Goffman (1963) observes, "It is important to stress that, in America at least, no matter how small and how badly off a particu-

Table 8.2
Nonteaching Staff Needed for Special Education Programs, 1985–86 School Year

Title	Employed	Needed
All staff	229,872	13,712
School social workers	7,833	542
Occupational therapists	3,120	506
Recreational therapists	367	143
Physical therapists	2,534	454
Teacher aides	122,504	6,939
Physical education teachers	5,931	322
Supervisors/administrators	14,957	691
Other noninstructional staff	31,164	1,325
Psychologists	16,313	997

Source: *Tenth Annual Report to Congress on Implementation* of *the Education of the Handicapped Act* (pp. B-71 B-72), 1987, Washington, DC: U.S. Department of Education.

lar stigmatized category is, the viewpoint of its members is likely to be given public presence" (p. 25).

Many organizations advocate for certain causes or specific groups of individuals. In fact, there's an organization to support nearly any and every cause. For example, the Gorilla Foundation is a 2,300-member organization whose purpose is to "promote conservation, propagation, and behavioral study of apes, particularly gorillas" (Akey, 1983). The organization currently is researching the language potential of the gorilla with the foundation's two gorillas, Koko and Michael. Often organizations take opposite positions on an issue. For example, there are prolife and prochoice groups, and there are smokers' rights and antismoking groups.

Many groups have organized to support the development and maintenance of services to exceptional individuals, to promote research relevant to specific exceptionalities, and to enable professionals who work with exceptional students to come together to share their knowledge. There are several hundred organizations that provide services directly to exceptional individuals or to professionals who work with them. Appendix A lists some of these groups. For each organization, we report the year in which it was established, the approximate number of members, the kinds of people who are members, and its objectives. You can see that there are groups of teachers, school psychologists, guidance counselors, administrators, and other professionals. And there are organizations to serve each group of exceptional individuals of all ages. In general, members work to advance the educational experiences of "their" students.

The largest organization serving exceptional students and the professionals who work with them is the Council for Exceptional Children (CEC). CEC, headquartered in Reston, Virginia, has about 60,000 members, most of whom are teachers of students with special needs. It works with educational and other organizations, school administrators, supervisors, parents, and teachers to promote and improve the education of exceptional students. For example, CEC is working at this time to

- extend special education services to those not presently served.
- improve service delivery systems to ensure that adequate resources are available to professionals who provide special education services.
- establish and promote standards of practice and to help enforce those standards.
- establish and promote a code of professional ethics (see Appendix C).
- develop standards in areas of professional training, certification, and licensing (see Appendix C).

Many organizations work to promote the education and treatment of students with special needs, but often their methods are very different. For example, members of the Learning Disabilities Association, the Council for Learning Disabilities, and the Orton Society all use different criteria to define eligibility for services, and all support different treatments for students in this category. This conflict is a by-product of membership: Different types of people join different types of organizations. Parents may be charter members of one group, advocating for very different things than the university professors who founded another group. This in no way means that one organization is better than another. It simply reflects the variety of perspectives that is common in a field as diverse as special education.

Checkpoint

- *Many organizations are formed to enable their members to share experiences and help one another or some special group with specific problems.*
- *The largest organization serving exceptional students and those who work with them is the Council for Exceptional Students.*
- *Organizations working on behalf of the same group of exceptional students can support very different methods of intervention, reflecting the different concerns and objectives of their members.*

WHAT WE THINK ABOUT PROFESSIONALS IN SPECIAL EDUCATION

Many people and organizations serve exceptional students. Teachers are responsible for their education. Psychologists and counselors test and evaluate them to determine their eligibility and measure their progress. Therapists help them develop the skills they need to adapt to or overcome their conditions. Administrators oversee and coordinate their programs. And organizations speak for them in public forums. It all seems so neat and methodical. But in fact, it is not. In reality, many of these groups share responsibilities and functions.

Many of them also share their basic motivation—to make a difference in the lives of those who are exceptional. Although many professionals and groups do not work directly with exceptional students, their work is every bit as important as the work of those who do. For example, research tells us that good administrators are a necessary ingredient in creating an educational program that works. And it is common knowledge that many of the advances in special education in recent years are a product of the advocacy of different organizations—of people who cared enough to band together and work for change.

Summary

1. Those who work with exceptional students do many different jobs.
2. Over a fourth of exceptional students receive all or most special education services from regular education teachers in the regular classroom.
3. Special education teachers include instructional consultants, itinerant teachers, resource room teachers, self-contained special class teachers, clinical teachers, and homebound teachers. Their titles reflect the settings in which they work and the services they provide.
4. Related services personnel—counselors, school psychologists, diagnosticians, therapists, and school social workers—support the classroom teacher's work with exceptional students.
5. Administrators coordinate and oversee special education programs in their schools or districts.
6. The policies of organizations working for exceptional students reflect the concerns of their members.

Activities

1. As a class project, ask three advocacy groups in your community (like the Learning Disabilities Association, the local Developmental

Disabilities Council, or the Association for the Gifted) to send you brochures that describe the kinds of things they do. Then identify similarities and differences among the groups.

2. Interview two special education teachers. Ask them to describe the kind of setting in which they work, what they do, and their educational and experiential background.

3. Interview a school psychologist. Ask what he or she does specifically in assessment and intervention.

4. Invite a special education administrator to talk to your class about the kinds of personnel employed in his or her district. Ask specifically about the responsibilities of each professional.

Suggested Readings

Blackhurst, A. E., Bott, D. A., & Cross, D. P. (1987). Noncategorical special education personnel preparation. In M. Wang, M. C. Reynolds, & H. Walberg (Eds.), *Handbook of special education: Research and practice* (Vol. 1). New York: Pergamon Press.

The authors describe the rationale for noncategorical training practices, trends in noncategorical teacher certification standards, and the resulting teacher preparation programs. They examine implications of noncategorical practices for the preparation of regular and special education teachers. And they make recommendations for public policy, legislation, service delivery, and research.

Redden, M. R., & Blackhurst, A. E. (1978). Mainstreaming competency specifications for elementary teachers. *Exceptional Children, 45,* 615–617.

Lists and descriptions of techniques professionals think are important in providing educational services to special students in regular classrooms.

Smith-Davis, J., Burke, P. J., & Noel, M. M. (1984). *Personnel to educate the handicapped in America: Supply and demand from a programmatic viewpoint.* College Park, MD: University of Maryland Institute for the Study of Exceptional Children and Youth.

Reports the results of a survey of personnel from the fifty states, Guam, Puerto Rico, the Bureau of Indian Affairs, and the District of Columbia. The authors include data on student-teacher ratios, caseload, preparation programs, personnel shortages, recruitment and staffing, certification patterns, inservice needs, and the impact of Public Law 94–142 on personnel needs.

Stile, S. W., Abernathy, S. M., & Pettibone, T. J. (1986). Training and certification of special education administrators: A 5-year follow-up study. *Exceptional Children, 53,* 209–212.

The authors report the results of a study of requirements for certification as a special education administrator.

Ysseldyke, J. E., & Algozzine, B. (1982). *Critical issues in special and remedial education.* Boston: Houghton Mifflin.

Chapter 3 describes issues in special education teacher training, including teacher burnout, the nature of training, and the nature of teaching.

four

Teaching Exceptional Students

Teaching is systematic presentation of content. Before you teach anything, you should know your students' current levels of performance in the content area being presented. Teaching exceptional students is more similar to than different from teaching their nonexceptional classmates. Students with special learning needs are taught many of the same things all students are taught. We think good teaching, which encompasses assessment and instruction, is essential for exceptional students to be successful in school. We describe assessment and teaching in this part of the book.

In Chapter 9 we describe the kinds of assessment decisions educators make and the kinds of tests, observations, and interviews they use in making them. We also review the behaviors sampled during assessment, the technical considerations that we believe are important when assessing students, and the fundamental assumptions that guide all assessment activities. We end this chapter with some considerations for best practices.

We discuss teaching practices in two chapters. Principles of effective instruction are detailed in Chapter 10. What teachers do when planning, managing, delivering, and evaluating instruction is discussed and related to principles of adaptive instruction that are important to efforts to provide special education in regular classrooms. Special purposes of instruction, components of individualized education programs, special learning needs, special teaching methods, and special instructional adaptations are presented in Chapter 11.

9

Assessment Practices in Special Education

FOCUSING QUESTIONS

- How is assessment used in the different phases of the special education process?
- How are curriculum-based assessment, instructional diagnosis, and academic time analysis used?
- What three methods are used to collect assessment information?
- What are the limitations of any assessment instrument?
- What is an error analysis matrix?
- What are the difficulties inherent in assessing a student's adaptive behavior?
- How are tests, observations, and interviews used in the assessment of students' language development?
- What are some of the problem behaviors published checklists evaluate?
- How do we define *reliability, representativeness,* and *validity*?
- What are some of the major assumptions underlying contemporary assessment practices?
- What is the overall objective of the assessment process?

*I*N SCHOOLS, TEACHERS AND OTHERS COLLECT INFORMAtion to make decisions about students. **Assessment** is the process we use to gather information. Testing is only one part of the process. We also collect data by observing students' behaviors and by interviewing students or those who work with them. Our decisions about students, then, are based on information obtained from tests, observations, and interviews.

Assessment is an important part of schooling for all students. For exceptional students, it is especially critical because it helps educators decide who should receive special education services, the specific nature of instruction, and the extent to which students are progressing. In this chapter, we look at the ways assessment data are used to make decisions about exceptional students, the ways in which information is obtained, and the particular type of information collected from different assessment activities. We also discuss standards for conducting assessment and some guidelines for best practice.

ASSESSMENT FOR DECISION-MAKING PURPOSES

The process of assessing students' special educational needs usually begins when a teacher or parent recognizes a need. Because of the complex system that has evolved in delivering special education services, students must be assessed before they are declared eligible for services. Assessment is the first step in obtaining treatment. Students who are exceptional also are assessed as part of their daily educational programs, to determine what they already know and to keep track of their progress. Assessment is a part of each phase of the special education process. We use the information it gives us to make important decisions about students who have special needs (Figure 9.1).

Screening and Referral

Screening is the process of collecting data to decide whether more intensive assessment is necessary. School personnel have neither the time nor the resources to test all students to see if they have special needs; instead they screen them.

Screening takes place at all levels of education. Children are screened before they enter kindergarten or first grade to determine their "readiness" in language, cognitive, and motor development, and in social and emotional functioning. They are tested, then their performance is compared to standards established by those who make the screening tests. For example, if two-thirds of the children who took the test when it was being developed scored 300 points or better, children who score below 300 could be considered "at risk." Test developers usually provide cut-off scores to help educators make decisions. These scores, called **norms**, are based on the performance of those who took the test sometime during its development.

Screening also is used throughout the school years, to identify students who need extra attention because their performance or progress is markedly different from "normal" or "average." Here, cut-off scores are based on the average performance of students at various ages or grade levels. The scores of the norm group are used in making the decision whether or not more testing is necessary.

When students' scores indicate a special need, they are referred for *psychoeducational assessment*, individually administered psychological and educational tests. These tests are used to determine the specific reasons for a student's performance on a screening measure. Usually they are administered by school psychologists or other professionals working for the school district or service providers (private clinics, hospitals).

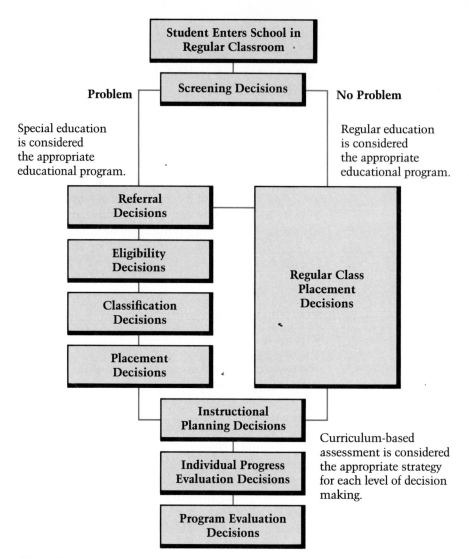

Figure 9.1
Educational Assessment and Decision Making

Performance on a screening test is only one basis for the decision to make a referral. Teachers also use classroom tests and observations and interviews to decide whether a student should undergo more detailed assessment.

Eligibility, Classification, and Placement

In nearly every state, pupils must be declared eligible for special education services before those services can be delivered. Three kinds of decisions must be made:

1. Is the student exceptional?

2. How should the student be classified?
3. Where should services be provided?

Before the Education for All Handicapped Children Act was passed in 1975, eligibility, classification, and placement decisions typically were made by administrators or school psychologists. Members of Congress, acting on the belief that individual decision making was capricious and too often wrong, decided that decisions should be made by a team using multiple sources of information. These teams usually are made up of regular classroom teachers, special education teachers, school psychologists, administrators, and parents (see Chapter 2).

Most state departments of education have published criteria to help child study teams make eligibility and classification decisions. For example, one criterion might be a score below 70 on an individually administered intelligence test for a student to be classified mentally retarded. Most states also have guidelines that list the types of information that should bear on the decision whether a student is exceptional and that describe placement alternatives. How teachers participate in eligibility, classification, and placement decisions is illustrated in Figure 9.2.

Instructional Planning

Regular education teachers are able to take a standard curriculum and plan instruction around it. Although curriculums vary from district to district—largely a function of the values of community and school—they are appropriate for most students at a given age or grade level. But what about those students who need special help to benefit from a standard curriculum? For these students, school personnel must gather data to plan special programs.

Two kinds of decisions are made here: deciding what to teach and how to teach it. Deciding what to teach is a content decision, usually made on the basis of a systematic analysis of the skills that students do and do not have. Scores on tests and other information help teachers decide whether students have specific skills. Teachers also use information gathered from observations and interviews to decide what to teach. And they obtain more information by trying different methods of teaching and monitoring students' progress toward instructional goals. (In Chapters 10 and 11 we examine the topics of effective instruction and teaching exceptional students.)

Progress Evaluation

Teachers use some of the information collected in assessment to decide whether their students are making progress. Parents, teachers, and stu-

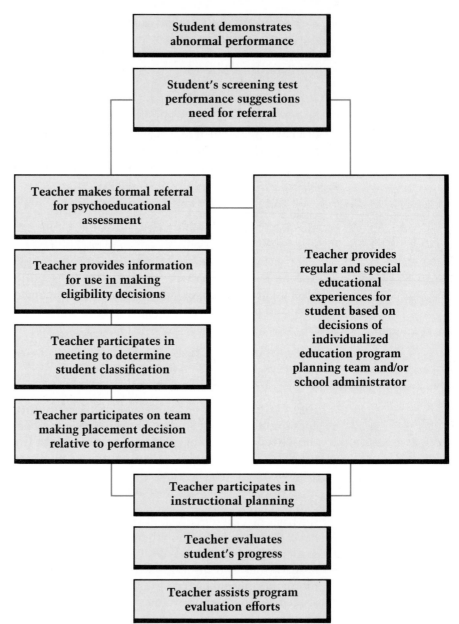

Figure 9.2
How Teachers Participate in Decision-making Activities

dents themselves have a right and a need to know how they are progressing in school. How do we know if students are learning? One way, of course, is

The best way to collect data for evaluating individual students' progress is to sample the skills that are being taught.
(© Michael Weisbrot and Family)

to rely on our observations of a student's behavior, to go with our own feelings and impressions of the student's work. Like the parent who evaluates a child's development on the basis of general impressions or observations, so teachers evaluate students' progress on the basis of subjective general impressions.

The best way to collect data for the purpose of evaluating individual students' progress is to sample the skills that are being taught. This allows teachers to measure the extent to which students have mastered content and to chart their progress toward meeting instructional objectives.

Program Evaluation

Assessment data also are collected to evaluate specific programs. Here the emphasis is on gauging the effectiveness of the curriculum in meeting the goals and objectives of the school. School personnel typically use this information for schoolwide curriculum planning. For example, schools can compare two approaches to teaching in a content area by (1) giving tests at the beginning of the year, (2) teaching two comparable groups two different ways, and (3) giving tests at the end of the year. By comparing students' performances before and after, the schools are able to evaluate the effectiveness of the two competing approaches.

The process of assessing educational programs can be complex if a large number of students is involved and if the criteria for making decisions are written in statistical terms. For example, an evaluation of two instructional programs might involve gathering data from hundreds of students and comparing their performances using statistical tests. Program costs, teacher and student opinions, and the nature of each program's goals and objectives versus those of the curriculum might be compared to determine which program is more effective. This kind of large-scale evaluation probably would be undertaken by a group of administrators working for a school district.

Of course program evaluations can be much less formal. When Kim wants to know the effectiveness of an instructional method that she is using, she does her own evaluation. For example, recently she wanted to know if having students complete activities in their basal readers was as effective as having them use language experience activities. She compared students' written products using both methods and concluded that their language experience stories were better.

Decision-making Practices

The best way to evaluate a curriculum is to directly measure the skills it is supposed to teach. If a basal reading series contains two hundred new words at a particular grade level, we might assess its effectiveness by writing each word on an index card, then having students read all the cards. It also is important to be able to identify the extent to which school problems are a function of instructional variables. Curriculum-based assessment practices and analyses of the learning environment are used to make screening, referral, eligibility, classification, placement, and evaluation decisions.

Curriculum-based Decision Making

Curriculum-based assessment is "a procedure for determining the instructional needs of a student based on the student's ongoing performance within existing course content" (Gickling & Havertape, 1981, p. 55). This kind of assessment includes direct observation and analysis of the learning environment, analysis of the processes students use to approach tasks, examination of students' products, and controlling and arranging tasks for students.

> *Observing the Learning Environment.* In curriculum-based assessment, the teacher or diagnostic specialist evaluates the learning environment in several ways. One involves looking specifically at the kinds of instructional materials being used as well as the basis for their selection and use. And it includes looking at the ways in which instruction is organized and at the sequencing of both con-

tent and concepts within the curriculum. Teachers or diagnosticians look for pitfalls that may be interfering with the student's learning. They also examine how information is presented—that is, the methods (lecture, workbook, programmed instruction) being used to convey information to the students. In curriculum-based assessment, considerable effort is devoted to the systematic analysis of situational variables—the ways in which groups are used to facilitate instruction, the involvement of students in instructing their peers, and the ways in which volunteers are used to work with individual students. Special emphasis is placed on evaluating the structure of the school day. Diagnostic personnel systematically analyze the amount of time allocated to instruction and the amount of time pupils actually spend responding to academic material.

Evaluating Task Approach Strategies.   Rather than immediately assuming that students who perform poorly do so because something is wrong with them, the teacher doing a curriculum-based assessment begins by looking at the ways in which students approach tasks. The teacher evaluates their demeanor, their attention to the task, and the extent to which they read and follow instructions.

Evaluating the Products of Instruction.   The products of instruction are written essays, completed worksheets, and performance on tests or quizzes. In curriculum-based assessments, teachers regularly and systematically examine students' performance and analyze errors. For example, a teacher may examine math worksheets, not only to determine how many problems students solved correctly, but also to identify specific error patterns.

Controlling and Arranging Tasks.   This part of curriculum-based assessment often is called *diagnostic teaching.* Teachers can manipulate the ways in which materials or concepts are presented and feedback strategies are used. Observing the influence of modifications on student performance gives them the information they need to plan future instruction.

Regular education teachers use performance on curriculum-based measures to decide which students are making satisfactory progress and which have special learning needs. According to Gickling and Thompson (1985), since 1973 teachers in Louisiana have had to complete a curriculum-based assessment before making a formal referral. The objective is to determine if problems are due to a lack of knowledge in the content areas being taught, inappropriate instruction, or different learning styles.

Shinn and Marston (1985) argue that the results of curriculum-based assessment can be used as operational criteria in making eligibility, classification, and placement decisions. Unquestionably, assessing current skills is the best way to decide on instructional goals. And periodic monitoring of progress in basic curriculum skills is a straightforward appropriate means of evaluating individuals and programs.

Choate and her colleagues (1987) list several reasons for using curriculum-based assessment:

■ It complies with the procedural requirements of Public Law 94–142 for assessing students in need of special education.

■ It is efficient.

■ It is a valid reliable basis for making decisions.

■ It can be used to make different kinds of decisions (for example, screening, program effectiveness).

■ It increases students' achievement.

■ It helps teachers decide what to teach.

Instructional Diagnosis

The difficulties students experience occur in a context—in an educational setting. At times those difficulties are a response to the expectations their teachers hold for them (see Chapter 3). Because their expectations color teachers' interactions with their students, it makes sense to begin collecting data by looking at the extent to which instruction is appropriate for the learners. "Typically a diagnosis is called for when there is trouble, generally because whatever the teacher is not doing is not working. The learner is not 'growing' 'developing,' 'interacting,' or, 'behaving' in an appropriate manner" (Engelmann, Granzin, & Severson, 1979, p. 355).

Instructional diagnosis identifies both the extent to which a student's poor performance is caused by poor instruction and possible remedies for the problem. It reflects a new perspective. Traditional diagnostic practices look for some basic flaw in the learner. Although placing responsibility on the learner is easier for teachers than accepting it themselves, it limits the possibilities for intervention. Information on a student's motivation or background is of little value. Teachers cannot manipulate neurons or their students' histories. But they can change the teaching process.

Academic Time Analysis

Academic time analysis is the study of how time is allocated in school. Borg (1980) reviewed a series of studies devoted to academic time analysis (Mann, 1928; Payne, 1904; Holmes, 1915). He found that contemporary educators allocate their time very differently from their predecessors (Table 9.1).

The importance of time spent in an activity to performance in that activity was addressed by Reverend Jesse Jackson:

Table 9.1
Percentage of Time Allocated to School Subjects (Grade 2)

Study	Reading	Mathematics	Other Academic Subjects	Nonacademic Subjects
Mann 6 cities 1862–1872	47	16	11	26
Payne 6 cities 1904	55	14	5	26
Holmes 50 cities 1914	42	9	7	42
Mann 444 cities 1926	48	10	7	35
Beginning Teacher Evaluation Study 1977–1978	28	12	3	57

Source: Adapted from W. R. Borg, "Time and School Learning." In C. Denham and A. Lieberman, *Time to Learn.* Washington, D.C.: U.S. Department of Education, 1980.

We keep saying Johnny can't read because he's deprived, because he's hungry, because he's discriminated against. We say Johnny can't read because his daddy is not in the home. Well, Johnny learns to play basketball without daddy.

We do best what we do most, and for many of our children that is playing ball. One of the reasons Johnny does not read well is that Johnny doesn't practice reading. (Cited in Raspberry, 1976, p. A19)

Think about something you do well. You probably spend a lot of time doing it. The time you set aside for the activity is *allocated time*; the time you spend doing the activity is *engaged time*. For example, a jogger who spends fifteen minutes warming up, five minutes running, ten minutes cooling down, and thirty minutes getting ready for another activity may have allocated sixty minutes to physical exercise. Of course, only a small percentage of the time is actually spent in physical exercise. The benefits of this individual's exercise program are related more directly to the engaged time than to the allocated time. Put another way, five minutes of running is better than forty minutes spent talking about running or not running. When we examine a student's performance in reading, for example, we must also look at the time spent reading.

<table>
<tr>
<td>

Checkpoint

</td>
<td>

- *Assessment is the process we use to gather information about students and programs.*

- *We use the information gathered in the assessment process in every phase of special education: screening, referral, determining eligibility, classification, placement, instructional planning, and progress and program evaluations.*

- *Curriculum-based assessment is the process of determining students' instructional needs in a specified content area.*

- *Instructional diagnosis identifies both the extent to which a student's poor performance is due to poor instruction and what teachers can do about it.*

- *Critical to an understanding of students' performance is an understanding of how they spend their time in school.*

</td>
</tr>
</table>

COLLECTING ASSESSMENT DATA

Educational assessment is the process of gathering information about individual students for the purpose of making decisions about their education. Teachers use this information to plan and evaluate instruction, and, together with other team members, to determine the eligibility of students for special education services and the nature of those services. Whether you teach or work with students in regular or special education programs, assessment will be a large part of what you do each day. It makes sense, then, to know something about the methods used to gather educational information and the behaviors sampled in the process of that assessment.

Methods for Collecting Data

We use three processes to gather information about exceptional students:

- **Testing** is the process of administering a set of items to obtain a score. A *test* is a collection of items designed to measure knowledge in a content area.

- **Observing** is the process of watching an individual perform a set of behaviors to obtain information about the rate or duration of those behaviors. An *observation* is a record of performance.

- **Interviewing** is the process of asking questions to obtain information about an individual's background, current levels of performance, and plans. An *interview* is a set of questions designed to provide information about a content area of interest.

Teachers and other professionals use tests, observations, and interviews to make decisions about students. There are no hard-and-fast rules for deciding which assessment method to use. We choose the method that gives us the best information for the decision we are making. Suppose we are gathering data to decide whether a student is eligible for special education. Most states require that an individual test of intelligence be administered. Here, then, we'd use a test. To evaluate a student's ongoing progress, we might use daily or weekly observations. And in making screening and referral decisions, we might use rating scales or other types of interviews.

Tests

You've taken hundreds of tests over the years, so varied in form and content that they probably would confuse even the most able classifier. When confronted with large amounts of information, we find it helpful to use categories to organize what we know. For example, grouping tests into formal and informal measures is a practical way to organize them. Or we can group them by the way they are given, their format, their purpose, or their content.

Formal tests have standardized administration procedures and usually are produced by test development companies. They often are designed for use with large groups of people, but some are primarily for testing individuals. Tests taken at the end of the school year during elementary, middle, and high school are good examples of formal tests. *Informal tests* often are developed by teachers to measure knowledge in an area that was recently taught. Unit tests in science or social studies, weekly spelling tests, 15- to 20-item math tests, all are used by teachers to assign grades in academic content areas. Because these tests vary from year to year, usually are produced by the teacher right before they are given, and are administered without strict adherence to standardized procedures, they are thought of as informal measures.

Another way to describe tests is according to the way in which they are administered. They can be group administered, given to an entire class at once, or individually administered, given to one student at a time. The primary advantage of group administration is that data can be obtained on an entire class in a relatively short time. Individual administration gives the examiner an opportunity to observe the student being tested more closely and to gather data on how the student earns his or her score.

We also can categorize tests according to the way the items are presented and responses are obtained. For example, on most tests, items are read to the students or the students are required to read the items themselves. Some tests require written responses in multiple-choice form; others require short answers or essays. Students give verbal answers on some tests; on others, they "perform" their answers, by choosing one item from several items, by putting puzzles together, or by performing some other physical action.

Tests differ in their intended use. *Screening tests* are used to spot pupils who are making too little or too much progress compared to others or to the objectives of the curriculum. *Diagnostic tests* are designed to provide more specific information, usually in the form of a description of strengths and weaknesses in the development of a specific skill.

Tests also are either *norm referenced* or *criterion referenced*, names that describe the way in which test results are used more than the actual format of the test. When norm-referenced interpretations are made, the student's performance is compared to the performance of other students. **Norm-referenced tests** are standardized at the time they are developed; that is, they are given to a large number of students in order to provide an index of "typical" or "average" performance. An individual's performance on the test is compared to that of a national or local sample of students of the same age or grade level. By definition, students who earn significantly higher or lower scores than their agemates or grademates are said to perform "abnormally." Students who perform very poorly on a test relative to others their age are said to be deficient in the area of poor performance; those who do much better than their agemates are said to be exceptionally proficient.

Criterion-referenced tests give teachers a measure of the extent to which individuals or groups have mastered specific curriculum content. These tests also are called *objective-referenced tests* or *curriculum-based tests*, names that reflect what the tests are designed to do. These tests are developed by specifying the objectives or criteria to be mastered, usually in basic skill areas like reading and mathematics, then writing items to assess mastery of those objectives or criteria. The results indicate the degree to which the content or skill representing a particular instructional objective has been mastered; they are used to describe what each pupil has learned and needs to learn in a specific content area.

We also can describe tests according to the content of the items. In special education, tests commonly are used to assess intelligence, achievement, sensory acuity, perceptual-motor abilities, adaptive behavior, language functioning, and personality development. (See Appendix B for a list of widely used tests.) Scores on these and other measures can be found in the school records of virtually every student who receives special education services.

Observations

Observations vary in the way information is collected. *Active observations* record ongoing behavior. When Kim sits beside Bobby and watches him do his math problems, she is using active observation. She also uses it when she records the amount of time he is out of his seat or the number of times he raises his hand to ask for help. When she looks at a product he produced last week, at test records, or at information in his cumulative folder, she is using *passive observation*.

Another way to describe observations is in terms of the action or product being observed. Classroom behaviors, academic tasks, vocational skills, interpersonal skills, and athletic performance are examples of actions or products that are observed in school settings. Like tests, observations also can be formal (using systematic procedures) or informal (using spontaneous data collection procedures).

Teachers, other school professionals, and parents make observations as part of the educational process, to gather the information needed to make decisions about students and programs. Observations provide different information than that available from tests and interviews. They are used when information is not available from other assessment sources or to verify information collected from those other sources. For example, there are no tests of hyperactivity currently available, and interviews tell us little about whether a student is hyperactive. If we want to know a student's level of activity, we have to observe his or her behavior. We use our observations to confirm and support information gathered from other sources (rating scales, interviews).

Interviews

Interviews can be given to a group of people or to one person. They can be given to people who know the person about whom information is being collected or administered to the target individual directly. For example, Kim asks the parents of new students and the students themselves to complete a survey about attitudes toward school. She compares the responses of the parents with those of the student, then uses the information to decide how to motivate and teach the student.

We also can describe interviews in terms of their form. Like tests and observations, interviews can be formal (predetermined, written down, and administered the same way each time) or informal (developed as the interview proceeds from initial questions). They also can be structured or unstructured. In a structured interview, we ask the same set of questions in the same way each time we use them. In an unstructured interview, the

One method of collecting data is the interview—the process of asking questions to obtain information about an individual's background, current levels of performance, and plans.

(© *Meri Houtchens-Kitchens/The Picture Cube)*

exact nature of the interview is not known before it is administered. We ask a question, then, depending on the student's answer, we ask another question related to it. In all interviews, students respond orally or in writing.

Interviews can touch on any topic—from name, address, and phone number to opinions about parents and pets. Kim asks each of her students the following questions during the first days of the school year:

- What is your most favorite subject in school?
- What is your least favorite subject in school?
- When some students complete a project, they still want to work on it to make it better. How about you?
- When some students receive a low grade, they try to improve it. How about you?
- Some students try different ways to solve problems before giving up. How about you?
- Some students really like school. How about you?

She uses the information from this brief survey to make decisions about what students to put together for group projects. She also thinks it helps her get to know the students a little better early in the school year.

Checkpoint

- *Teachers and other school professionals use tests, observations, and interviews to make decisions about exceptional students.*

- *Testing is the process of administering a set of items to an individual to obtain a score.*
- *Observing is the process of watching an individual perform a set of behaviors to obtain information about the rate or duration of those behaviors.*
- *Interviewing is the process of asking questions to obtain information about an individual's background, current levels of performance, and plans.*

Behaviors Sampled by Assessment

Any test, observation, or interview is just a sampling of the items that could be used to assess an ability, skill, or characteristic. For example, there are literally hundreds of items that could be used to assess the math achievement of fifth-grade students. Any test just contains a sample of these items. When we observe a student, we select what to observe and when to observe it. Obviously, we can't watch everything a student does at all times during the school day; any observation is a sample of the student's behavior. In the same way, the questions in an interview are just samples of those that could be asked. Remember this when you are collecting and evaluating information about students: What you collect is a sample of behavior, and the way you collect it controls the answers you get.

Intelligence tests are used as measures of general ability. They can sample many kinds of behaviors and are used as a criterion for determining how an individual should be classified. Observations, interviews, and tests of academic achievement in reading, mathematics, spelling, and other content areas are used to monitor general progress in schools. Tests and observations help identify sensory disabilities; interviews help treat them. Adaptive behavior rating scales, language tests, and personality interviews are used to keep track of social functioning, communication skills, and psychological development. Perceptual-motor tests are used to assess students' ability to translate sensory information into action. On the basis of these assessments, we determine students' eligibility for special education, the nature of their programs, and their progress.

Recent legislation requires that eligibility and classification decisions be based on multiple sources of information. Even before they were required in the assessment process, observations and interviews were important sources of information in educational decision making.

Intellectual Abilities
School personnel regularly use intelligence tests to identify the extent to which students demonstrate normal thinking and problem-solving skills.

They are looking for discrepant scores, scores that are significantly lower or higher than the norm. Students who demonstrate lower levels of intelligence are thought to learn more slowly than their agemates; those who demonstrate higher levels of intelligence are thought to learn more quickly than their agemates. These students are a challenge for regular classroom teachers. They do not fit into the organization, goals, and activities of the typical classroom.

Different intelligence tests sample different behaviors. The particular behaviors sampled by a specific test depend on the kinds of behaviors the test author thinks best reflect the performance being measured. Table 9.2 lists thirteen kinds of behaviors sampled by intelligence tests.

Observations also are used to assess intellectual abilities. As part of a psychoeducational evaluation, Kim was asked to record the number of four types of questions that one of her students asked during reading over a week's time. She also was asked to supply previously written products as evidence of the student's higher levels of thinking.

Informal observations gathered during the administration of a test can be very revealing. Kim told us about a school psychologist's experience testing one of her students. When asked general information questions on the intelligence test, the student consistently gave very expansive answers. For example, when asked who discovered America, he answered: "Some people say Christopher Columbus, some say Amerigo Vespucci, some people say Leif Erikson; actually, nobody really knows." When asked the sum of two numbers, the student supplied the answer and gave five more number sentences like it. When the testing was over, the psychologist commented that the student was the smartest child he had ever tested. His opinion was based, not only on the student's score on the test, but also on his informal observations of the student's performance.

Interviews are another source of information about a student's intellectual abilities. Many school districts use screening checklists to identify students who may need special educational enrichment or acceleration. These rating scales usually are administered to parents or teachers, and contain items like these:

> Use the following scale (1 = strongly disagree, 2 = disagree, 3 = unsure, 4 = agree, 5 = strongly agree) to indicate the extent to which you agree with each of the following statements.
> This student (My child) . . .
> 1. demonstrates superior thinking abilities.   1 2 3 4 5
> 2. demonstrates excellent memory for details.   1 2 3 4 5
> 3. demonstrates creative problem-solving skills.   1 2 3 4 5

Academic Achievement

We mentioned earlier that students, teachers, and parents need to know if progress is being made in academic subject areas of instruction. Achieve-

Table 9.2
Kinds of Behaviors Sampled by Intelligence Tests

Nature of Task	Performance Required
Discrimination	Given a set of stimuli, the student is required to find the one that differs from all the others. The stimuli may be figures, symbols, or words.
Generalization	Given a stimulus, the student must select from among a number of response alternatives the one that is most like the stimulus. Both the stimulus and response alternatives may be figures, symbols, or words.
Sequencing	Given a series, the pupil must identify the one that comes next in the series.
Analogies	The individual must respond to an item of an A:B:C:? nature. The student must first identify a relationship between A and B, then identify from several alternative response items the one that has the same relationship to C as A does to B.
Motor behavior	The student may be required to walk, place geometric forms in a recessed form board, copy geometric designs, trace paths through a maze, and so on.
General information	The student is required to answer specific factual questions.
Vocabulary	The student is required to define words or to point to pictures that illustrate words read by the examiner.
Induction	The student is presented with a series of examples and required to induce a governing principle.
Comprehension	The student must give evidence of understanding directions, printed material, or societal customs and mores.
Detail recognition	Students are judged on the extent to which they recognize details in drawing pictures, find hidden objects in pictures, or recall details of a story.
Abstract reasoning	Students are required to state the meaning of proverbs, solve arithmetic story problems, and so on.
Memory	Several different kinds of tasks are used to assess pupil skill in remembering items, objects, details of stories, sequences of digits, and so on.
Pattern completion	Given a pattern, students must select from among response items the one that completes the pattern.

ment tests often are used to provide this information. There are literally hundreds of published achievement tests; we've listed some of them in Table 9.3.

Table 9.3
Categories of Achievement Tests

Screening Devices

		Norm-referenced		Criterion-referenced	
		Single Skill	Multiple Skill	Single Skill	Multiple Skill
Group Administered		Gates-MacGinitie	California Achievement Test Iowa Tests of Basic Skills Metropolitan Achievement Tests (Survey Battery) SRA Achievement Series Stanford Achievement Test Series	None	California Achievement Test Iowa Tests of Basic Skills Metropolitan Achievement Tests (Instructional Batteries) SRA Achievement Series Stanford Achievement Test Series
Individually Administered		Test of Mathematical Abilities	Kaufman Test of Educational Achievement Peabody Individual Achievement Test Wide Range Achievement Test–Revised Woodcock-Johnson Psychoeducational Battery Kaufman Assessment Battery for Children Basic Academic Skills Individual Screener	None	Basic Academic Skills Individual Screener

Source: J. Salvia and J. E. Ysseldyke, *Assessment in Special and Remedial Education* (4th ed.). Boston: Houghton Mifflin Company, 1988, pp. 310–311. Reproduced with permission.

Achievement tests measure skill development in academic content areas. Some measure skill development in multiple content areas (say math and reading); others concentrate on one content area (for example, spelling). Any achievement test can be described using the framework in Table 9.3. For example, the Metropolitan Achievement Tests are group-administered, norm-referenced or criterion-referenced screening tests that assess skill development in several content areas. The Gray Oral Reading Test is an individually administered, norm-referenced diagnostic measure that provides specific information on skill development in oral reading.

Table 9.3 *(cont.)*
Categories of Achievement Tests

Diagnostic Devices

	Norm-referenced		Criterion-referenced	
	Single Skill	Multiple Skill	Single Skill	Multiple Skill
Group Administered	Stanford Diagnostic Reading Test Stanford Diagnostic Mathematics Test	None	Prescriptive Reading Inventory Diagnostic Mathematics Inventory Stanford Diagnostic Mathematics Test	None
Individually Administered	Gray Oral Reading Test–Revised Durrell Analysis of Reading Difficulty Diagnostic Reading Scales Gates-McKillop-Horowitz Reading Diagnostic Tests Gilmore Oral Reading Test Woodcock Reading Mastery Tests–Revised Test of Written Language Test of Written Spelling 2 Test of Reading Comprehension Formal Reading Inventory Test of Language Development Test of Adolescent Language	None	KeyMath Stanford Diagnostic Reading Test Standardized Reading Inventory	BRIGANCE® Diagnostic Inventories

Teachers use observations gathered while tests are being administered to help them understand a student's performance. They also use analyses of permanent products. For example, two students may earn exactly the same score on a mathematics achievement test, but demonstrate very different math skills on more detailed analysis of their written products. Consider the test performances in Figure 9.3. Bob and Jim each performed seven items correctly. Their score could be represented as 47 percent correct or 53 percent incorrect. Similarly, if Bob and Jim were the same age, the number of items correct could be converted to age-equivalent scores, grade-equivalent scores, percentiles, quotients, standard scores, or other derived scores that are exactly the same.

But even though Bob and Jim would receive the same score, Bob's performance on the test was different from Jim's. He seems to have mastered

BOB

Wide Range Achievement Test (WRAT) $\frac{7}{15}$ CORRECT

Level 1 — Arithmetic (5–0 to 11–11 Years) $\frac{8}{15}$ INCORRECT
Written Part

$$1 + 1 = \underline{2} \qquad 6 \qquad 5 \qquad \begin{array}{r} 32 \\ 24 \\ +40 \end{array} \qquad 4 \times 2 = \underline{8} \qquad \begin{array}{r} 23 \\ \times\ 3 \end{array} \qquad \begin{array}{r} 29 \\ -18 \end{array} \qquad \begin{array}{r} 75 \\ +\ 8 \end{array}$$

$$4 - 1 = \underline{5}\ \checkmark \qquad \begin{array}{r} +2\ \checkmark \\ \hline 12 \end{array} \qquad \begin{array}{r} -3 \\ \hline 2 \end{array} \qquad \begin{array}{r} \\ \hline 90\ \checkmark \end{array} \qquad \qquad \begin{array}{r} \\ \hline 69 \end{array} \qquad \begin{array}{r} \\ \hline 11 \end{array} \qquad \begin{array}{r} \\ \hline 1513\ \checkmark \end{array}$$

$$\begin{array}{r} {}^{6\,4} \\ 452 \\ 137 \\ +245 \\ \hline 1211\ \checkmark \end{array} \qquad 6 \div 2 = \underline{3} \qquad \begin{array}{r} {}^{1\,1} \\ \$62.04 \\ -\ 5.30 \\ \hline 57.74\ \checkmark \end{array} \qquad 1\ 1/2\ \text{hr.} = \underline{190}\ \text{min.}\checkmark \qquad \begin{array}{r} 16\,r2 \\ 6\overline{)968} \\ 6 \\ \hline 36 \\ 36 \\ \hline 08 \\ 6 \\ \hline 2 \end{array}$$

$$1/3 + 1/3 = \underline{2/6}\ \checkmark$$

JIM

Wide Range Achievement Test (WRAT) $\frac{7}{15}$ CORRECT

Level 1 — Arithmetic (5–0 to 11–11 Years) $\frac{8}{15}$ INCORRECT
Written Part

$$1 + 1 = \underline{2} \qquad 6 \qquad 5 \qquad \begin{array}{r} 32 \\ 24 \\ +40 \end{array} \qquad 4 \times 2 = \underline{6} \qquad \begin{array}{r} \checkmark \\ 23 \\ \times\ 3 \end{array} \qquad \begin{array}{r} \checkmark \\ 29 \\ -18 \end{array} \qquad \begin{array}{r} \checkmark \\ 75 \\ +\ 8 \end{array}$$

$$4 - 1 = \underline{3} \qquad \begin{array}{r} +2 \\ \hline 8 \end{array} \qquad \begin{array}{r} -3 \\ \hline 2 \end{array} \qquad \begin{array}{r} \\ \hline 96 \end{array} \qquad {}^{\checkmark} \qquad \begin{array}{r} \\ \hline 56 \end{array} \qquad \begin{array}{r} \\ \hline 31 \end{array} \qquad \begin{array}{r} \\ \hline 163 \end{array}$$

$$\begin{array}{r} \checkmark \\ 452 \\ 137 \\ +245 \\ \hline 254 \end{array} \qquad 6 \div 2 = \underline{8} \qquad \begin{array}{r} \checkmark \\ \$62.04 \\ -\ 5.30 \\ \hline 63.34 \end{array} \qquad 1\ 1/2\ \text{hr.} = \underline{90}\ \text{min.} \qquad \begin{array}{r} \checkmark \\ 123 \\ 6\overline{)968} \\ 600 \\ \hline 68 \end{array}$$

$$1/3 + 1/3 = \underline{2/3}$$

Figure 9.3

Math Performance of Two Students

Source: Test items from Level 1 Arithmetic Subtest of the Wide Range Achievement Test (1978 Rev. ed.) by J. F. Jastak and S. Jastak. Wilmington, Del.: Jastak Associates, 1978. Copyright © 1978 by Jastak Associates, Inc. Reprinted with permission.

multiplication, for example; Jim has not. This kind of analysis gives us more data for making decisions about a student's academic abilities.

To make these kinds of observations, we can watch a student perform a task or examine the test record. Test record booklets usually are provided

1. **Foundations**
1.1 **Number Discrimination**   -1-2-3-4-12-15-17-25-33-
1.2 **Size Discrimination**   -5-6-
1.3 **Shape Discrimination**   -11-22-41-
1.4 **General Information**   -19-21-28-35-40-53-69-
2. **Basic Facts**
2.1 **Addition**   -7-9-10-23-26-
2.2 **Subtraction**   -8-14-24-27-
2.3 **Money**   -16-18-29-42-43-
2.4 **Multiplicaiton**   -30-34-36-46-
2.5 **Division**   -31-32-38-39-52
3. **Applications**
3.1 **Fractions**   -13-20-47-55-
3.2 **Numerical Relationships**   -37-44-48-51-54-60-62-65-72-
3.3 **Word Problems**   -45-49-50-58-59-61-63-66-78
3.4 **Geometry**   -56-57-64-68-73-74-76-79-81-84-
3.5 **Algebra**   -67-70-71-75-77-80-82-83-

Summary

Foundations	Basic Facts	Applications
/ = % correct	/ = % correct	/ = % correct
/ = % incorrect	/ = % incorrect	/ = % incorrect

Figure 9.4
Error Analysis Matrix for Subsections and Subgroups within the PIAT Mathematics Subtest

Source: From "Diagnostic Testing in Mathematics: An Extension of the PIAT?," by B. Algozzine and K. McGraw, *Teaching Exceptional Children, 12*, 1980, 71–77. Copyright 1980 by The Council for Exceptional Children. Reprinted with permission.

for group-administered tests. Using this record, it's easy to prepare a form to analyze a student's performance on any test. This is what Algozzine and McGraw (1980) did with the Peabody Individual Achievement Test (PIAT) Mathematics Subtest. The eighty-four items on the subtest represent fourteen subgroups of behavioral activities in three main areas of mathematics (foundations, basic facts, and applications). Each subgroup contains different numbers of items and measures different skills (for example, number discrimination, addition, money). Algozzine and McGraw described the content of each item and created an *error analysis matrix* to use in analyzing students' performance on the subtest (Figure 9.4). To use the matrix, they suggest underlining items that are sampled within a subgroup, circling correct ones, and crossing out wrong ones, then analyzing the pattern of performance within the set of items.

1.   **Foundations**

1.1 **Number**
     Discrimination   -1-2-3-4-12-15-17-25-(33)-   100%*
1.2 **Size Discrimination**   -5-6-
1.3 **Shape Discrimination** -11-22-(41)-   100%
1.4 **General Information**   -19-21-28-36-(40)(53)-69-   67%
2.   **Basic Facts**
2.1 **Addition**   -7-9-10-23-26-
2.2 **Subtraction**   -8-14-24-27-
2.3 **Money**   -16-18-29-42-(43)-   50%
2.4 **Multiplicaiton**   -(30)(34)(36)-46-   ⁻5%
2.5 **Division**   -(31)(32)-38-(39)(52)   80%
3.   **Applications**
3.1 **Fractions**   -13-20-47-55- 0%
3.2 **Numerical**
     Relationships   -(37)(44)(48)-51-54-60-62-65-72- 60%
3.3 **Word Problems**   -(45)-49-(50)-58-59-61-63-66-78- 50%
3.4 **Geometry**   -56-57-64-68-73-74-76-79-81-84- 0%
3.5 **Algebra**   -67-70-71-75-77-80-82-83-
                               *% correct within subgroup

Summary

Foundations	Basic Facts	Applications
4/5 = 80% correct	8/11 = 73% correct	5/13 = 39% correct
1/5 = 20% incorrect	3/11 = 27% incorrect	8/13 = 62% incorrect

Figure 9.5

Example of Error Analysis Matrix Application

Source: From "Diagnostic Testing in Mathematics: An Extension of the PIAT?," by B. Algozzine and K. McGraw, *Teaching Exceptional Children, 12*, 1980, 71–77. Copyright 1980 by The Council for Exceptional Children. Reprinted with permission.

In an example, Algozzine and McGraw used the matrix to analyze the performance of Charles, a sixth-grader (Figure 9.5). Based on the scoring procedures in the test manual, Charles received these scores:

Raw score: 45
Grade equivalent: 5.3
Percentile: 33
Standard score: 95

The matrix indicates that Charles performed seventeen of twenty-nine items correctly. Most of these were in the foundation skills and certain basic facts (for example, 75 percent of multiplication items and 80 percent of division items). He had difficulty with fractions, word problems, and geometry. This kind of information tells a teacher much more about how Charles is doing in mathematics than a score of 5.3 or 95.

More information about what students know in various content areas can be obtained from informal observations of their work. Three sets of

KATE

27	33	55	88	29
+33	+69	+55	+88	+29
510	912	1010	1316	1118

Note: Number facts correct, disregard for place value is obvious.

FAYE

623	657	847	893	543
−419	−294	−693	−186	−289
216	443	254	713	346

Note: Number facts correct, disregard for number placement is obvious.

JIM

73	39	57	53	93
+48	+29	+38	−26	−61
112	716	18	28	22

Note: Inadequate basic number facts skill demonstrated.

Figure 9.6
Work Samples for Three Students

Source: Adapted from *Problem Behavior Management: Educator's Resource Service* by B. Algozzine, p. 3:6, with permission of Aspen Publishers, Inc., © 1982.

simple mathematics problems are shown in Figure 9.6. Each tells us something different about the way the student does his or her work. For example, both Kate and Faye have a similar problem. They know their basic facts (addition and subtraction of single-digit numbers), but they apply inappropriate algorithms when asked to do higher-level operations (addition and subtraction of two- or three-digit numbers). (An *algorithm* is a rule or procedure that is repeatedly applied to solve a problem.) Kate's rule for solving two-digit addition problems is to add the single-digit combinations together without thinking about the effects each has on the other (she ignores place value effects). When Faye solves a three-digit subtraction problem that requires regrouping, she subtracts the smaller number from the larger one regardless of the effect on place value in the original number. She probably makes the same mistake in two-digit subtraction problems. Jim's work shows a different error pattern. He simply has not mastered the basic number facts. If we asked him to work on similar problems for practice, his performance probably would not improve. In fact, he'd be practicing errors.

It is possible to analyze performance on any test and develop teaching plans from that analysis. There may come a time when performance on exams like the Scholastic Aptitude Test (SAT) and Graduate Record Exam (GRE) is used for prescriptive programming, not just to determine eligibility. It's possible to envision an educational corporation guaranteeing college entrance by teaching students to perform items that give them difficulty on entrance exams.

Observations also can be valuable in deciding what to teach. For example, by observing how students read, teachers can uncover the errors they make and identify the factors that may be limiting their reading performance. Ekwall (1981) describes over twenty types of errors that students often make in reading and recommends ways to correct them. By recognizing and correcting specific types of reading errors, teachers are more likely to see improvement in reading scores than if they simply ask students to read without regard to the quality of the effort.

Kim uses an informal interview to gain insight into factors that influence her students' performances in mathematics. She asks their opinions about the work in the textbook and their preferences for doing workbook assignments, teacher-made worksheets, or homework. She also asks questions designed to assess their fears of math. She uses the last questions in the interview to estimate students' mastery of number facts, computation, problem solving, fractions, and other mathematics skills. Other teachers in her school use informal interviews to gain insight into the factors that facilitate or inhibit students' performance in reading. They find that students' answers indicate that they often are bored by basal reading activities, are confused by new words, and prefer to read silently. Kim asks her students to rank their word recognition skills when reading in science, social studies, health, and other content areas. She also asks them to rank the ways they remember words (sounding them out, using word parts, using meanings). Larry keeps a record of his students' responses to questions about their learning patterns and reading methods that have been effective in the past.

Sensory Acuity

Poor academic performance is sometimes caused by problems with seeing and hearing. Although severe sensory impairments are almost always diagnosed before a child begins school, tests of visual and auditory acuity

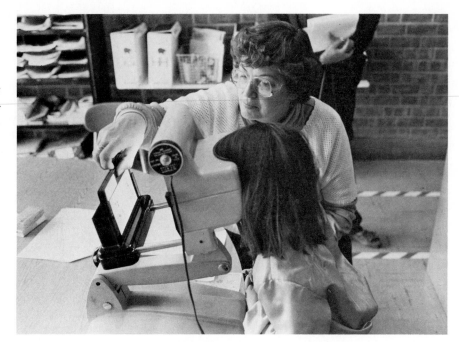

Although severe sensory impairments are almost always diagnosed before a child begins school, tests of visual and auditory acuity are used regularly in assessments of students who are having difficulties in school.
(© Michael Weisbrot and Family)

are used regularly in assessments of students who are having difficulties in school. The simplest test of visual acuity uses the Snellen Chart. The individual being tested stands 20 feet away from the chart and tries to read it. An adaptation of the Snellen Chart, the Snellen E, is used to assess preschool students and those who are unable to read. The Titmus Vision Tester also is used to screen school-age children. An audiometer is used to assess hearing acuity (see Chapter 6). A pure-tone audiometer generates pure tones at different frequencies and at varying degrees of loudness.

Teachers also make informal assessments of sensory acuity by watching how students read and how they act when asked questions, and by asking them about how they approach tasks. Kim watches her students to answer these questions:

- Can they see the chalkboard from their seats, or do they need to be closer to it to see or hear better?
- Do they tilt their heads or squint when reading from textbooks and other printed materials?
- Do they complain about itchy eyes or squint when focusing on different objects?

■   Do their visual skills differ in the classroom, on the playground, or in other areas of school?

■   Do they often ask for directions to be repeated?

Kim and Larry have developed an interview for use with students with special learning needs. They ask parents to complete a questionnaire about their child's visual and auditory abilities as a way of learning more about how to help the child succeed in school. A section of their interview form is shown in Figure 9.7.

Adaptive Behavior

There was a time when students were classified mentally retarded solely on the basis of their performance on an intelligence test. In 1969, a report from the President's Committee on Mental Retardation indicated that many of these students demonstrated very normal behaviors outside of school. The phrase *six-hour retarded child* was coined to describe students who had been labeled mentally retarded in school but who were functioning normally out of school, in other environments. Because so much of performance on intelligence tests is based on general knowledge gained in school, it was reasoned that other criteria should be used as well in the decision to classify a student as mentally retarded.

In 1973 the American Association on Mental Deficiency (AAMD) modified its definition of mental retardation to include both subaverage intellectual functioning and deficits in adaptive behavior. It defined adaptive behavior as "the effectiveness or degree with which the individual meets the standards of personal independence and social responsibility expected of his age and social group" (Grossman, 1973, p. 11) (See Chapter 5). That definition was "legitimized" with the enactment of Public Law 94–142 in 1975.

There are no tests of adaptive behavior. Instead we use interviews with parents, teachers, or others familiar with the student to assess his or her behavior. For example, many adaptive behavior scales provide information about the student's self-help skills (eating, dressing, toileting), communication skills (imitating sounds, following directions), and occupational and social skills (using money, doing chores, playing games).

A common measure of adaptive behavior is the AAMD Adaptive Behavior Scale (ABS) (Nihira, Foster, Shellhass, & Leland, 1975). It is in two parts (Table 9.4). Part 1 lists items in ten domains and twenty-one subdomains of daily living skills. Part 2 assesses the individual's level of maladaptive behavior in fourteen domains.

Assessing adaptive behavior is not an easy process. To evaluate the extent to which someone's behavior is "adaptive"—that is, normal in an environment—we have to identify the environment and understand the

Visual Abilities

1. Does your child require any special considerations relative to the use of vision in the classroom? ___ If yes, what are they?

_____

_____

_____

2. Does your child have trouble reading from the chalkboard? ___ If yes, what helps?

_____

_____

3. Does your child require special reading materials (for example, large-print books)? ___ If yes, what are they and do you have access to them?

_____

_____

4. Does your child wear glasses or use a magnifying glass or other visual aids? _____

Auditory Abilities

1. Does your child require any special considerations relative to the use of hearing in the classroom? ___ If yes, what are they?

_____

_____

2. Does your child use alternative communication systems (sign language, lip reading)? ___ If yes, which one(s)?

_____

_____

3. Does your child require special adaptations from speakers (slower pace, alterations of loudness)? ___ If yes, what are they?

_____

_____

4. Does your child wear a hearing aid? ____ If yes, is there anything special that I should know about it?

_____

_____

_____

Figure 9.7
Sample Items from an Interview Form

Table 9.4
Areas Covered by the AAMD Adaptive Behavior Scale

Part 1
I. Independent Functioning
   A. Eating
   B. Toilet use
   C. Cleanliness
   D. Appearance
   E. Care of clothing
   F. Dressing and undressing
   G. Travel
   H. General independent functioning
II. Physical Development
   A. Sensory development
   B. Motor development
III. Economic Activity
   A. Money handling and budgeting
   B. Shopping skills
IV. Language Development
   A. Expression
   B. Comprehension
   C. Social language development
V. Numbers and Time
VI. Domestic Activity
   A. Cleaning
   B. Kitchen duties
   C. Other

VII. Vocational Activity
VIII. Self-direction
   A. Initiative
   B. Perseverance
   C. Leisure time
IX. Responsibility
X. Socialization

Part 2
I. Violent and Destructive Behavior
II. Antisocial Behavior
III. Rebellious Behavior
IV. Untrustworthy Behavior
V. Withdrawal
VI. Stereotyped Behavior/Odd
VII. Inappropriate Manners
VIII. Unacceptable Vocal Habits
IX. Unacceptable or Eccentric Habits
X. Self-abusive Behavior
XI. Hyperactive Tendencies
XII. Sexually Aberrant
XIII. Psychological Disturbances
XIV. Use of Medications

Source: From *AAMD Adaptive Behavior Scale* (pp. 6–7), by K. Nihira, R. Foster, M. Shellhaas, & H. Leland, 1975 (Washington, DC: American Association on Mental Deficiency). Reprinted by permission of the American Association on Mental Retardation.

kinds of behaviors that are socially acceptable in that environment. There are two frames of reference for deciding whether a behavior is conforming: Is it deemed acceptable by most people, by a majority or public culture? Or, is it deemed acceptable by a few people, by a minority or private culture? It is difficult to develop a standardized measure of adaptive behavior simply because people's tolerance for particular behaviors depends on the type of behavior, the context in which it is exhibited, the status of the individual exhibiting the behavior, and the orientation (and indeed presence) of the observer.

Language Development

For many students, poor academic performance is a function of immature or deficient language development. Tests exist for all levels of language development and functioning. They measure four components of language: phonology, morphology, syntax, and semantics (see Chapter 4).

Tests that are designed specifically to assess aspects of language require the student to provide language samples, which are then evaluated. Some tests also evaluate comprehension, with items that require the student to follow simple directions or to imitate words, phrases, and sentences. Language functioning also is a part of other tests, especially tests of intelligence and academic achievement.

Teachers also assess the language development of their students through formal and informal observation. They can count the number of specific classes of speech problems (part-word repetitions, whole-word repetitions) under a variety of conditions (reading, conversation), or they can assess fluency by counting syllables or words produced during a timed speech sample. They also can keep track of articulation errors (*wabbit* for "rabbit"), distortions (*bulu* for "blue"), and omissions (*pay* for "play"). Some teachers use videotapes, audiotapes, or written transcriptions to study their students' speech.

Background information about a student's language development generally is collected from parents using a structured-interview approach. A good interview does more than ask questions like "Does your child talk?" or "When did your child start to talk?"; it addresses how the child uses language. For example, the speech therapist in Kim's school gave her an interview form that contained the following questions:

1. Is speech easy to understand?	Yes	No
2. Is speech pleasant to hear?	Yes	No
3. Is speech linguistically appropriate?	Yes	No
4. Is speech labored in production?	Yes	No
5. Is content and manner of speech appropriate?	Yes	No

In assessing language development, usually a background interview comes first. Next, observations of the components of language development are completed as a basis for understanding how a student uses language in natural settings. Finally, standardized tests are used to provide information on selected aspects of language ability and to provide corroborative evidence for the strengths and weaknesses identified through other methods of assessment.

Psychological Development

Psychological development is assessed by having students draw family pictures or self-portraits, answer open-ended questions about themselves, or respond to ambiguous pictures, drawings, or situations. These responses are evaluated for evidence of clinical or diagnostic pathology (for example, excessive fear of death, aggressiveness, inadequacy). The use of personality tests in schools has diminished over the years. But in some schools, these tests are used extensively and may even be required to classify students as emotionally disturbed. In some districts, school psychologists conduct personality tests; in others, professionals in private practice are contracted by the school to assess a student's psychological development.

Observations play an important part in the assessment of psychological development because inappropriate behavior is seen as an indicator of abnormal development. Any action can be the target of a formal or informal observation. The procedure is straightforward. First the class of problem behavior to be observed is described in terms that can be counted. For example, the category of inappropriate behavior might include counts for not sitting in an assigned seat, looking out the window instead of at an assignment, talking without permission, and not completing worksheets. Next a system for measuring each target behavior is selected and applied. Finally, the counts are tallied and reported.

Counts can be recorded in different ways:

- *Interval recording* measures the number of time blocks in which a behavior or response occurs. For example, when Kim uses this method, she divides her observation period (say ten minutes) into smaller intervals (say thirty seconds), and checks whether the behavior she is watching for occurs at any time during an interval.
- *Time sample recording* measures the number of times a behavior or response occurs after a preset observation period (for example, ten seconds or two minutes). When using time samples, Kim sets an observation period (say every two minutes), then records whether or not the target behavior occurs at that time.
- *Event recording* measures the number of times a behavior or response occurs during a preset observation period. For example, Kim used event recording to count the number of times a student raised her hand during a thirty-minute observation period.
- *Duration recording* measures the length of time over which a behavior or response occurs. When Kim and Larry use this method, they record the time a behavior starts and stops. Then they calculate the cumulative total time (for example, forty-eight minutes) for the observation period (say sixty minutes) as a record of how long the behavior occurred.
- *Latency recording* measures the time between a request for behavior and an actual response. When Kim and Larry use this method, they

record the time they ask a student to perform a behavior and the time the student starts doing it.

Teachers' and parents' ratings also are used extensively in assessing students who are thought to have emotional problems. These interviews vary considerably in form and content. For example, some require yes or no answers to questions about specific behaviors exhibited by the student being evaluated. Others use a Likert-type response format (1 = strongly agree . . . 5 = strongly disagree) to indicate the extent to which an item reflects the problems of the student being assessed. Most of the scales contain several dimensions of problem behaviors. The Revised Behavior Problem Checklist contains six: conduct disorders, socialized aggression, attention problems/immaturity, anxiety/withdrawal, psychotic behavior, and motor excesses (Quay, 1983). The Walker Problem Behavior Identification Checklist contains five (Walker, 1976):

- *Acting out.* The student complains about discrimination or unfairness and becomes upset when things don't go the way he or she would like.
- *Withdrawal.* The student has few friends, does not initiate interpersonal interactions, and does not engage in group activities.
- *Distractibility.* The student is restless, continually moves, seeks attention more than other students, and easily loses interest in tasks and learning activities.
- *Disturbed peer relations.* The student makes negative self-statements and comments that nobody likes him or her.
- *Immaturity.* The student reacts to stress with physical complaints (stomach hurts, head aches) and cries easily.

Perceptual-motor Development

Many educators believe that being able to translate sensory information into meaningful actions is important for success in school. For example, some special educators argue that a student who cannot copy a geometric design (a square, a diamond) has difficulty copying letters and numbers when working on academic tasks. Tests of perceptual-motor development require students to copy designs or perform other actions after being told or shown what to do.

The Bender Visual Motor Gestalt Test is a good example of a perceptual-motor assessment device. It consists of nine geometric shapes that the student is asked to copy on a plain sheet of white paper. The reproductions are scored relative to four types of errors: shape distortions, perseveration, integration, and rotation. Errors are scored as *shape distortions* when a student's design is distorted to the extent that a representation of the original figure is lost. *Perseveration errors* are scored when a student fails to stop after completing the required picture. *Integration errors* result when parts of a design overlap or fail to meet. *Rotation errors* are scored when a student shifts a design more than 45 degrees from the way it was presented.

Kim uses observations to assess her students' perceptual-motor development. On the playground she keeps track of the way they walk, skip, and run around, and of their catching and throwing skills. When the students are working on art projects, she watches how well they color within the lines and use scissors. Many teachers also ask parents, other teachers, and students themselves about perceptual-motor skills. Students who lack these skills often are assigned to training programs. This practice is common with students classified as learning disabled, mentally retarded, physically impaired, or multihandicapped.

Checkpoint	■ *Any test, observation, or interview can contain only a sample of the items that could be used to assess an ability, skill, or characteristic.*
	■ *The assessment of intellectual abilities identifies the extent to which students demonstrate normal thinking and problem-solving skills.*
	■ *Achievement tests measure skill development in academic content areas.*
	■ *Error analysis tells teachers much more about a student's academic abilities than can a simple score.*
	■ *Because poor academic performance is sometimes caused by vision and hearing problems, assessments of visual and auditory acuity are used regularly in schools.*
	■ *With the recognition that many students who were classified mentally retarded in school were functioning normally in other environments, an adaptive behavior criterion was added to the definition of mental retardation.*
	■ *For many students, poor academic performance is a function of immature or deficient language development.*
	■ *We assess psychological development by having students draw family pictures or self-portraits, answer open-ended questions about themselves, or respond to ambiguous pictures, drawings, or situations.*
	■ *Tests of perceptual-motor development require students to copy designs or perform other actions after being told or shown what to do.*

STANDARDS FOR GOOD ASSESSMENT PRACTICES

In addition to the kinds of behaviors sampled by tests, observations, and interviews and the ways in which assessment data are used, you should understand the technical aspects of assessment practices—reliability, representativeness of performance, and validity.

Reliability: Is Performance Consistent?

Tests, observations, and interviews should provide consistent measures of pupil performance. This means that different examiners, each using the same procedures with a student, should be able to obtain comparable results. It means that students should earn comparable scores on repeated administrations. Of course inconsistent performance can reflect different responses to different examiners or illness during one of the testing sessions, not just a problem with the test itself. But the value of a measure is very much a product of its reliability.

Reliability is an index of consistency in measurement. Test, observation, and interview scores that fluctuate considerably on repeated measurement, either by different examiners over time or by separate administrations of the same measure, may not be reliable. Authors are supposed to include information in their technical manuals on the reliability of their instruments. Reliability is expressed as a coefficient, an index of the degree of relationship between scores earned on two administrations of a test. Reliability coefficients range from .00 to .99.

How high should reliability be? It depends on how we are using the scores. Two standards of reliability generally are accepted for use in educational decision making:

- *Group data.* When scores are being used for general purposes and are reported for groups, they should have a reliability of at least .60.
- *Individual data.* When scores are used to make placement decisions about individual students, the minimum standard is .90. When a referral decision is being made, .80 is the accepted standard.

Representativeness: Does the Instrument Adequately Sample the Behavior?

An assessment instrument should include adequate samples of the behavior being tested. The more extensively an instrument samples the behavior, the better it is. Of course tests, observations, and interviews cannot sample all aspects of a behavior, but they must sample enough to be repre-

WOULD YOU LIKE TO DEvelop a test? A test that could be published and then used by others? In most areas of human endeavor, whether art or technology, the product appears deceptively simple to accomplish. This is often the case with test development. If you try it, you may find the work arduous, but you can also find it interesting and stimulating.

Most professional test developers have had advanced training in a special branch of statistics called measurement theory. Your task of developing a test is facilitated by special training but also by the presence of certain character traits: Since your task will require attention to detail over a long period of time, it will help if you can become a compulsive neurotic. It will also help if you can develop a taste for delayed gratification, for the fruits of your labor may not be seen for years. Finally, you should strive to become a bit sadistic. This will be especially helpful when it is necessary to test young children for hours in order to gather important data.

Of course, you must have an idea for a test. Opportunities do exist. In the field of special education there are many potential areas of measurement for which no one has developed a good test. Your test might be the one that will be helpful to others. What would you like to measure better? An aspect of school achievement? Adaptive behavior? Cognitive ability? Perhaps motivation or attention?

After you identify the area, other decisions remain. Is your test to be a clinical procedure that will be administered to one subject at a time, or a group test that can be administered to an entire classroom? With what age range is the test to be

used? Is the interpretation of an examinee's performance to be normreferenced (compared to peers) or criterion-referenced (compared to curriculum objectives)?

Given the prerequisite personality characteristics for test development and an idea, what is next? The steps followed in test development are fairly standard and, in a sense, a form of engineering. First, the test design and specifications are prepared. Several more questions must be answered. How are the test questions to be presented (orally, read by the examinee, by pantomime)? What kinds of responses do you want from the examinees (written, oral, pointing)? What kinds of derived scores will the users of your test need (grade equivalents, age equivalents, standard scores, percentile ranks)?

Once you have designed the test, your next step is to prepare a pool of potential test items, usually at least twice as many as you expect to use in the final form of the test. (You will be surprised how many of your favorite items prove inadequate once they are given a trial.) Keep in mind that your item pool is only a sampling of the knowledge or skills you want to measure; therefore, you must carefully analyze the area to be measured and then prepare a pool of items that represents a good crosssection.

Next, you will conduct a series of small-scale tryouts, at first with only a small group of subjects. These tryouts allow you to polish the test administration procedures, improve item content and wording, and detect potential scoring problems. One outcome of this step is likely to be the realization that you need to develop even more items. Perhaps you notice that you do not have enough easy items, or perhaps you decide you should measure one aspect in your test more thoroughly.

After this revision step, it is time to repeat the process of evaluating and editing your fledgling test again. This cycle will be repeated three or four times before you are satisfied that a good draft of your test has been created. Then you are ready to begin the process of standardizing the test.

Two goals are involved in standardizing a norm-referenced test. First, the test is administered under controlled, documented conditions that will be followed by subsequent test users.

The second goal is to obtain normative data. The normative data provide the information that will allow future users to compare the scores they obtain to the scores obtained by the subjects in your norming sample. The user of a standardized test usually wants to compare a person's performance on a test to the performance of others at the same age or grade placement. The people included in your norming sample must be carefully selected so that they provide a good cross-section of the population to which your test users want to compare their scores. This requires careful attention to factors such as a geographic distribution of your sample and personal characteristics such as race, sex, and socioeconomic variables. Finally, the test items are arranged in the final form from the easiest to the most difficult. The data from your norming study tell you that sequence.

Your users will expect you to provide information about the reliability and validity of your test. The reliability information tells how precisely your test measures. The validity information tells how well your test measures what it is intended to measure.

Your last step is to prepare the testing materials, including the manuals that your users need. This step makes all your efforts useful to others. The better you complete this part of your project, the easier it is for others to use your test in the way you intended.

And that's about all there is to it. That is, until it is time to revise your test.

Source: *Richard W. Woodcock is an educational consultant and developer of the Woodcock-Johnson Psychoeducational Battery and the Woodcock Reading Mastery Tests.*

sentative. At the same time, procedures must be manageable in terms of time and costs.

Representativeness also has to do with item content. To be technically adequate, an assessment instrument must sample the appropriate kinds of behaviors. This means math tests should include math items, and reading tests should include reading items. It also means that observations should include different types of acceptable actions (for example, sitting in an assigned seat, maintaining eye contact when talking to another person, raising a hand before asking or answering a question). And it means that rating scales of adaptive behavior must contain more than a couple of items about independent living skills.

Validity: Does a Procedure Measure What It Is Supposed to Measure?

Suppose Kim developed a test to measure her students' skills in volleyball. If we wanted to use her test, how would we know whether it measures what she says it measures? It is Kim's responsibility to give us evidence of the test's **validity**. Validity can be demonstrated in many ways. For example:

■ Pupil performance on a measure of word recognition is shown to be highly related to performance on other measures of word recognition. Pupils who do well on one test of reading do well on other reading tests or just read well.

■ People who earn high scores on a test of mechanical aptitude and who choose to become mechanics are shown to become successful mechanics; those who earn low scores do not.

■ Successful typists are shown to earn high scores on a measure of typing speed; bad typists do poorly.

■ People who have the best understanding of the content of this chapter earn the highest scores on a measure of understanding of the content of this chapter.

Observations made during atypical or insuffcient time periods on unrepresentative behaviors by untrained or biased people are not considered valid measures of a student's performance. Similarly, interview information obtained from people with little knowledge of the student being evaluated or from people with biased opinions are not appropriate sources of information for making important decisions.

Checkpoint

■ *Tests, observations, and interviews must be reliable: They should provide consistent measures of pupil performance.*

■ *A technically adequate measure of performance includes representative samples of the behavior being assessed.*

■ *A technically adequate assessment instrument is valid; it measures what it is supposed to measure.*

When students are assessed, it is assumed that the examiner is trained to establish rapport with students and knows how to administer, score, and interpret the instrument used to collect the assessment information.

(© Bob Daemmrich/ The Image Works)

ASSUMPTIONS UNDERLYING ASSESSMENT PRACTICES

Assessment is a common practice in America's schools. Each year, more than 250 million standardized tests are administered to the nation's 44 million students. Assessment is the basis on which professionals decide who should receive special education services, where and by whom those services will be delivered, the specific nature of instructional treatments, and the criteria used in evaluating the effectiveness of those treatments.

Major Assumptions

Teachers and psychologists gather information about students to make decisions about them. Parents expect the assessments to be completed by competent, well-trained people. Professionals who monitor assessment practices are guided by a set of assumptions that help define what assessment should be.

The Examiner Is Trained

When students are assessed, it is assumed that the person doing the assessment is trained to establish rapport with the students and knows how to administer, score, and interpret the instrument used to collect the assessment information. The amount and type of training needed vary with the type of assessment being conducted and its purpose. Special training is needed to administer, score, and interpret most individually administered tests. For many group tests and most other types of assessment, just reading the test manual is enough. To the extent that rapport is not adequately established and the instrument is administered, scored, and interpreted incorrectly, the results are not valid.

Establishing rapport means making the student feel comfortable in the test situation and motivated to do her or his best. Suppose you want to remove Pat from a third-grade classroom to give him a reading test. It probably isn't a good idea to enter the classroom and shout "Next victim." And you certainly wouldn't march Pat down the hall to the testing room and say "Read." Instead you would talk to him about hobbies or television shows or some other interest. Once you enter the testing room, you might have Pat draw pictures or tell a story to relax. Your task is to make the student feel comfortable. There are no rules for doing that; different techniques work with different students. Remember too that you do want to test the student. Some examiners spend far too long getting the student ready for testing, so that by the time they get to the test itself, the student has lost interest.

Second, an examiner must know how to administer an instrument. Obviously if a test is not administered correctly, the student's performance has little meaning. Some tests can be administered with little formal training; others require extensive training and practice. Similarly, some observation instruments require formal training and others can be completed simply by counting target behaviors. Very few interviews require extensive training, but most commercially available rating scales provide administration guidelines in their technical manuals.

Third, the examiner must be able to score the assessment instrument. In this age of machine scoring, teachers seldom have to worry about scoring group-administered intelligence and achievement tests, though they should check machine scoring when the results are suspect (e.g., a gifted student's scores are below average or the best reader in the class performs poorly). Most individually administered tests are scored by the examiner. All tests should include information about scoring in the test manual. Extra care should be taken when compiling scores on observations. Inaccurate counts of observed behaviors can result in misinterpretation of the extent of a student's skills or problems.

Finally, the examiner must know how to interpret the student's performance. For some procedures this simply means reporting the student's scores. For others, it means learning how to interpret the score.

Present Behavior Is Observed, Future Behavior Is Inferred

The second assumption underlying any assessment is that present behavior is measured and future behavior is inferred. We said above that all tests, observations, and interviews are samples of behavior. If we are trying to predict performance on the assembly line in an automobile plant, for example, the best assessment would be to watch the individual working on the assembly line. In most instances, this isn't possible, so we sample the target behavior in different ways. We choose a form of assessment that we believe will predict future performance on the target task. To predict performance on an assembly line, we would not use a spelling test, but we could use a manual-dexterity test. Future behavior can never be observed, so any prediction about future behavior is an inference. Inferences have different degrees of plausibility, depending on the similarity between the behavior sampled and the kind of behavior being predicted.

Assessment Is Imperfect

A third basic assumption is that measurement is not precise. Educational, psychological, and behavioral tests, observations, and interviews are not perfect measures of skills, characteristics, or abilities. On any day, a student can make a careless mistake, or an answer may simply be a guess. The student's scores are inaccurate to the extent that careless mistakes are made and some answers are guesses. The scores that students earn on tests always are made up of two components: true score and error. To the extent that error is present, the true score is inaccurate.

In observations and interviews, we also must be concerned about the extent of error present in scores. After Kim observes a student, she asks herself if the performance she recorded is typical of the student's behavior. Brown (1981) describes the following types of common errors in rating scales:

- *Errors of central tendency.* Raters tend to avoid extreme points on a continuum, overusing the middle categories.
- *Errors of leniency.* Raters often are generous in their ratings.
- *Severity errors.* Raters also can be too stringent in their ratings.
- *Halo effect errors.* Raters sometimes allow their general impressions and opinions to influence their ratings.
- *Logical errors.* Raters sometimes assume characteristics or behaviors are related when they are not.

Obviously, what people say about another person is not always what the other person does. Be mindful that inaccurate information can easily be gathered using the interview form simply because the respondent is the sole source of the answers or ratings used to score the "performance" of another person.

Students Have Comparable Acculturation

Acculturation means background experiences and opportunities. The fourth major assumption in assessment is that the student being assessed has comparable, not necessarily identical, acculturation to those with whom the student is being compared—that the student being assessed has had experiences and opportunities to learn like those in the norm group. According to standards specified by a joint committee of the American Psychological Association, the American Educational Research Association, and the National Council on Measurement in Education, information is supposed to be included in technical manuals that tells users precisely the nature of the group on whom an instrument was standardized. Sufficient information should be provided on the age, gender, grade level, socioeconomic status, and geographic region of the norm group so that others can judge the extent to which the student being assessed is like those to whom he or she is being compared. To the extent that students differ from the norm group, judgments based on comparisons are invalid.

The Behavior Sampled Is Adequate and Representative

The fifth assumption concerns the nature of the behavior sample. It should be adequate in amount and representative in area. Again, any test, observation, or interview is a sample of behavior. But that sample must provide adequate information about the ability or skill being assessed, and it must be representative of the behaviors so that a student's performance on the measure can be generalized to performance in the behavior. It would be difficult to evaluate a student's skill in addition on the basis of a sample of two addition problems. And it would be difficult to predict a student's performance in mathematics on the basis of performance on a reading test or on a test that only assesses skill in adding single-digit numbers.

Checkpoint

- *When students are assessed, it is assumed that the person doing the assessment is trained to establish rapport with the students and knows how to administer, score, and interpret the instrument used to collect the assessment information.*

- *Assessment measures present behavior and infers future behavior.*

- *Assessment is not precise.*

- *Students being evaluated should have experiences and opportunities to learn comparable to those with whom they are being compared.*

- *All tests, observations, and interviews are samples of behavior. They should be adequate in amount and representative in area.*

Further Considerations

Assessment is central to special education because students cannot receive special services or leave special programs without it. And it is the basis of planning, implementation, and evaluation decisions. Given the importance of assessment in the lives of exceptional students, we believe you should know something about "best practices." Here are some guidelines.

There Is No One Way to Do It Right

There is no recipe for assessment—no single battery of tests, form of observation, or specific rating scale that can tell us everything we want to know about any student. Remember that assessment is the process of collecting data for the purpose of making decisions about students. Only if all students had the same kinds of problems could there be one right way to assess them. Assessment activities must be tailored to the individual and to the nature of the instructional setting.

There Is No One Cause of School Problems

We think one of the major failings of current assessment practices is that many of those practices are driven by a "search for pathology." Students with academic and behaviorial problems are assessed because somebody thinks there's something wrong with them. And of course sometimes there is. Students do have sensory, communication, physical, emotional, and intellectual difficulties that are significant enough to interfere with learning. And sometimes those problems are so evident that assessors can assume they are the primary problem.

But often the problems students experience in school have to do with instruction and the goals or demands of the school. And most students who come to the attention of special educators do not exhibit problems that are evident. Less than 10 percent of the students receiving services in regular or special education have severe handicaps. So assessors need to operate from a broader perspective, to look beyond the student.

Assessment Must Do More Than Describe Problems

Sometimes school personnel spend far too much time searching for and describing students' problems. They gather extensive information, develop elaborate profiles, and write lengthy descriptions of students' dysfunctions, defects, deficits, and disabilities. Then they share these descriptions with parents, colleagues, and school administrators. This process seldom benefits students. It is our job to solve problems, to do what we can to develop competence in students. Unless assessment practices facilitate the development of competence in students, they are of limited value.

Assessment Should Be Directed at Improving Instruction

We think the ultimate goal of assessment is to improve instruction, to indicate problems, and to lead to treatment. Frankly, a good share of assessment activities today consist of meddling. Many professionals gather data simply because they find those data interesting. This isn't enough. We have to be able to use assessment data to improve instruction.

Assessment Should Occur Often During Teaching

Good teachers are constantly assessing students and programs. It is impossible to know for sure how best to teach students, so teachers choose an approach (their best guess), then measure the extent to which progress is being made. The only way to determine the effectiveness of instruction is to collect data.

Assessment Should Concentrate on Relevant Variables

For whatever reasons, much of the assessment being done today is irrelevant to instructional decision making. Diagnostic personnel regularly administer intelligence tests, achievement tests, and other tests without thinking about the reasons why students are being tested. They conduct comprehensive interviews that bear little relation to the problem they are trying to solve. These practices are inappropriate and unnecessary. We don't always need information on cognitive functioning, general achievement, or personality functioning to improve instruction for students who are failing in school. We think the most relevant variable to look at when students have problems is the extent to which teaching is occurring. When students fail to read adequately, it may be because they have had little instruction in reading. Large numbers of students may fail to do well in mathematics because they seldom practice doing numbers. And although it is important to sometimes assess the learner and to almost always assess the nature of instruction, the way to begin any assessment is by evaluating the extent to which instruction has occurred and the extent to which the learner has played an active part in it.

Many teachers and school psychologists think that they must look at literally every area of functioning in order to "uncover" a child's problem. They are wrong. Assessment should be directed toward identifying factors that can improve instruction. And what goes on in the classroom is clearly the place to start.

Assessment Should Occur Where the Behavior Occurs

To the extent possible, data on student performance should be collected in the environment where that performance occurs. If a student's performance in mathematics is of concern, math performance should be assessed in the classroom where it is a problem, with the materials the student uses in that classroom. There is much less room for inference this way than

To the extent possible, data on student performance should be collected in the environment where the performance occurs.

(© Alan Carey/The Image Works)

when the youngster is removed from the class and assessed using a math test that is not related to the curriculum.

One of the authors of this textbook was once a school psychologist and, having been trained to do so, often tested students. As was common practice in those days, he would remove students from the classroom, then administer a number of reading tests. Later, when he would describe a student's "reading" to the classroom teacher, more often than not he would be told that the measure overestimated or underestimated the student's actual ability. Students perform differently in different settings with different people. This means that the best place to assess performance is in the environment where a behavior occurs.

Checkpoint	■ *There is no one way to do an assessment.*
	■ *There is no one cause of school problems.*
	■ *Assessment should do more than describe a student's problems.*
	■ *Assessment should be directed at improving instruction.*
	■ *Assessment should occur often during instruction.*
	■ *Assessment should concentrate on relevant variables.*
	■ *Assessment should occur where the target behavior occurs.*

WHAT WE THINK ABOUT ASSESSMENT

Many teachers have been taught that it is their job to spot students who are having difficulty, and that they or someone else ought to spend time and effort identifying deficits or disabilities. Often they don't know what they are looking for, but the search itself is exciting. We think there is a kind of test mania in many schools. Parents and teachers worry too much about overlooking students' problems. They worry that a problem left uncovered may irreparably damage a student. We don't agree. We think that serious problems are obvious early on, usually well before a child begins school. The real danger, then, is not in overlooking a problem, but in identifying a disorder where one does not exist.

Assessment is an ongoing part of the special education process. Assessment data are used to determine eligibility, the special education program, and the effectiveness of that program. We think the best place to collect assessment data is in the classroom, and we encourage you to make regular use of tests, observations, and interviews when you teach. We also encourage you to use the information you gather as a record of students' present level of functioning, not as an indicator of underlying problems.

Summary

1. Assessment is the collection of information about a student for the purpose of making decisions.
2. Assessment information is used to make screening, referral, eligibility, classification, placement, instructional planning, and evaluation decisions.
3. Curriculum-based assessment is the process of determining students' instructional needs in a specified content area.
4. Instructional diagnosis identifies both the extent to which a student's performance is tied to poor instruction and what teachers can do about it.
5. Critical to an understanding of students' performance is an understanding of how they spend their time in school.
6. Tests, observations, and interviews are methods used to gather assessment information across a range of behaviors, skills, abilities, and characteristics.
7. The information collected in the assessment process is just a sample, and it is controlled by the way in which it is collected.
8. Error analysis tells teachers much more about a student's academic abilities than can a simple score.
9. Tests of visual and auditory acuity are used regularly in assessments of students who are having difficulty in school.
10. To evaluate adaptive behavior, we must understand the students' environment and the kinds of behavior that are acceptable within that environment.

11. The process of assessing language development usually begins with interviews, then observations, and ends with standardized testing.
12. Technical considerations—reliability, representativeness, and validity—are important in evaluating tests and other assessment instruments.
13. A set of fundamental assumptions underlies current assessment practices; when those assumptions are violated, the results of the assessment are invalid.

Activities

1. Obtain any commercial test. Write down five test items, then state the kind of behavior each samples.
2. List five kinds of behaviors that could be sampled in an assessment of intelligence.
3. Ask a school psychologist to meet with your class and to describe the steps used to assess students in his or her school. Also ask the psychologist to describe situations in which data have been collected through testing, observation, and interviewing.
4. State two reasons why you believe tests should be reliable.
5. List the assumptions underlying psychological assessment.
6. Interview a classroom teacher who has referred at least one student for evaluation within the last two years. Ask the teacher to explain why he or she referred the student and to tell you what happened to the student.
7. Visit an elementary school classroom. Pick any student at random and observe the student for three hours. Keep a tally of the number of twenty-second intervals in which the student is (a) actively engaged in responding to academic materials and (b) doing something else. Write a summary of your observations.
8. Visit a local elementary school classroom. Pick a student at random and observe the student for two hours. During that time, record (a) the amount of time the teacher is showing or telling the student what to do, (b) the amount of time the student spends demonstrating that he or she understands what is being taught, and (c) the amount of time the student is tested on mastery of what has been taught. Write a summary of your observations.

Suggested Readings

Algozzine, B., & Ysseldyke, J. E. (1981). Special education services for normal students: Better safe than sorry? *Exceptional Children, 48,* 238–243.

An analysis of practices used to classify students as handicapped. The authors report the results of a computer-simulated study of decision making, and show that in more than 50 percent of cases, normal students are identified as handicapped.

Hammill, D. D., Brown, L., & Bryant, B. R. (1989). *A consumer's guide to tests in print.* Austin, TX: PRO-ED.

> *A compilation of objective information about the technical characteristics of norm-referenced tests. Each test in the guide was reviewed by two experts using a standard evaluation form.*

Mitchell, J. V. (Ed.) (1987). *Buros' mental measurements yearbook.* Lincoln, NB: University of Nebraska Press.

> *A compilation of reviews of published and unpublished tests, inventories, and rating scales. For most, two experts provide a detailed review of what the instrument measures and a critical appraisal of its adequacy.*

Newland, T. E. (1979). Psychological assessment of exceptional children and youth. In W. Cruickshank (Ed.), *Psychology of exceptional children and youth* (pp. 115–174). Englewood Cliffs, NJ: Prentice-Hall.

> *Newland describes the fundamental assumptions that underlie the assessment of handicapped students and examines assessment as a behavior-sampling process.*

Poland, S. F., Thurlow, M. L., Ysseldyke, J. E., & Mirkin, P. K. (1982). Current psychoeducational assessment and decision-making practices as reported by directors of special education. *Journal of School Psychology, 20,* 171–179.

> *The authors analyze questionnaire data from one hundred directors of special education, to characterize the way in which decisions are made about students. The results indicate that although most directors agree on some components of the decision-making process, there is considerable variation in how the process is carried out.*

Salvia, J., & Ysseldyke, J. E. (1988). *Assessment in special and remedial education* (4th ed.). Boston: Houghton Mifflin.

> *Chapter 1 describes factors that should be considered in assessment, various kinds of assessment information, and the process of assessment. The authors provide comprehensive coverage of psychoeducational assessment practices and review many popular tests.*

10

Effective Instruction

FOCUSING QUESTIONS

- What are the four major components of instruction?
- How is task analysis used in planning and delivering instruction?
- Deciding what to teach is a diagnostic process; deciding how to teach it is a prescriptive process. What does this statement mean?
- What is the first step in presenting instruction?
- How do we teach thinking skills?
- How should feedback be used in the process of monitoring instruction?
- Why is task-specific praise important?
- What are three ways in which teachers can adjust instruction to meet individual students' needs?
- What is the difference between formative and summative evaluation?

A FUNDAMENTAL GOAL OF TEACHERS IS TO HELP STUdents develop to their fullest potential by giving them the necessary skills to function in society. This goal is no different for students who are exceptional. A big part of teaching is deciding which skills to develop and how to teach those skills.

Does special education involve a unique set of teaching practices? Yes and no. For the most part, the things we do to plan, manage, deliver, and evaluate instruction for students who are exceptional are the same as those we do for nonexceptional students. But at times it is necessary to modify teaching practices. Certain exceptional students require specialized methods of instruction or instructional materials that have been adapted to their special learning needs. For example, specialized instructional methods using touch and hearing are necessary for students who have profound visual impairments, and their teachers use modified instructional materials (large-type books, raised-line paper, cassette recordings). But the basic principles of instruction—principles that are critical for effective teaching—continue to apply.

Phyllis is a student in Kim's class. She has a profound visual impairment. To meet her special learning needs, in language arts, Kim asked a student in a friend's class to tape-record reading assignments so that Phyllis would be able to participate in class discussions. She also had the student record daily quizzes, to evaluate Phyllis's understanding of the content. When a unit is complete, Kim evaluates the overall level of Phyllis's knowledge by giving her an oral test, the same as the written test she prepares for the rest of the class.

We've already discussed the various settings in which exceptional students can be taught, and we've looked at assessment practices that help teachers make decisions about the learning needs of exceptional students. In this chapter, we describe the components of effective instruction, the principles that make education work for all students. In the next chapter, we examine some of the instructional variables that make special education different from regular education.

COMPONENTS OF EFFECTIVE INSTRUCTION

Teaching is the systematic presentation of content assumed necessary for mastery within a general area of instruction. When Kim teaches, she first plans her presentations. Based on her knowledge of what her students currently know, she decides what to teach. For example, if the target area of instruction is addition of whole numbers, Kim uses information from formal and informal tests, observations, and interviews to determine her students' present levels of performance. She then decides how to improve their performance using instructional methods she believes will work. She might decide to use basal texts or worksheets, manipulatives, games, or workbooks as her primary instructional materials. She also decides how and when to evaluate the efforts of her instruction and when to modify it based on the results of her evaluations. And she anticipates how she will manage the instruction and any disruptions that occur during her presentations. As she teaches, these various activities overlap and come into play at different times.

The many components of effective instruction can be grouped into four broad areas: planning instruction, managing instruction, delivering instruction, and evaluating instruction. Whether they teach gifted, non-handicapped, mildly handicapped, or severely handicapped students, teachers must plan, manage, deliver, and evaluate instruction.

Planning Instruction

If all students in a class were at the same instructional level and if the goals and objectives of schooling were clearly prescribed and the same for all students, then instruction would consist of doing the same things with all students, being certain to do them in the right order and at the right time. But all students are not alike, and the goals and objectives of instruction are not the same for all students. This is why instructional planning is such an important part of teaching.

MY NAME IS KAREN Richards, and I was a student intern from the University of Florida assigned to a public school for the trainable mentally retarded in Gainesville, Florida. For eleven weeks, I taught social skills, reading, and math, and assumed all of the responsibilities of my supervising teacher, with the exception of collecting the paycheck.

Student teaching: THE final exam. You are finally ready to put those hours of lectures, notes, theories, lesson plans, and materials to the test. But you start doubting yourself and you begin asking yourself things like, "Do I really know enough about teaching to take over a whole class? Did I need to learn all that stuff? Do I really want to be a special educator?" Soon you realize that everyone else is asking themselves the same questions and you feel relieved.

Your student teaching experience begins with paperwork—lots of paperwork. The application I had to fill out looked like a small novel. It included three copies each of a biographical sketch, resume, picture, letters of reference, career center registration cards, and the classic essay, "Why do you want to be a teacher?" You ought to pass your internship for being able to fill out your application correctly! Could this really be preparing us for the field of special education?

The next step is waiting. You hope and pray that you won't be assigned to a "bad" school or to a "slavedriver" teacher. It is usually close to the month before your internship is to begin that you receive your assignment. I found that visiting the classroom before I began teaching was a big help. It gave me a chance to meet my supervising teacher and aide, to see the class in action, and best of all, it gave the kids a chance to meet me and get accustomed to my being in the classroom. Because of these early visits, I felt very comfortable around all these people when my internship began and I was able to jump right into action.

The real test of your ability comes when you actually take over the classroom, usually in the third or fourth week of your internship. You become the planner, the decision maker, the clock watcher, the audio-visual genius, the cheerleader, and whatever else it takes to fill your supervising teacher's shoes. You discover that nobody has the time to write the kind of lesson plans you learned to write in college. You discover that adequate classroom materials are nonexistent. You discover that parents are not always cooperative. You discover that paperwork takes up a lot of good teaching time. You discover that a lot of teachers are getting by with minimum effort. And, after all this discovering, you realize that college has prepared you to teach the ideal class in the ideal classroom, one that you seldom, if ever, get assigned to as an intern. Welcome to the real world. You will learn, you will make mistakes, and you will learn more. Once you accept this fact, you can start to enjoy yourself.

The success of your internship will be strongly influenced by your supervising teacher. He or she can be an invaluable resource or a threatening observer, depending on how you wish to view the situation. Your specific responsibilities will vary depending on your teacher. After taking over my supervising teacher's responsibilities, I realized how much more there is to teaching than just teaching. I can honestly say I spent more time performing nonteaching duties than actually teaching. I happened to have a teacher who was extremely active in the school's projects and in outside activities involving her students, and I was expected to become involved in these same activities. Although interns are not required to go beyond school responsibilities, I feel that my involvement in outside activities greatly improved my relationship with my supervising teacher. I never felt intimidated or threatened by her, and she became an excellent role model. I didn't always agree with her ideas, but this made me realize how I would do things differently in my own classroom. An important thing to remember is that an intern is only temporary, and as much as you would like to, you can't make drastic changes in a classroom in eleven weeks. It will only frustrate your teacher, your students, and yourself.

Every internship experience is different. Having a roommate and many friends who were also student teaching made it impossible for me not to compare. We would talk about our experiences and realize that some of us had to do much more planning, while others had to spend much more time with extracurricular activities, and some seemed to have it much too easy. But one thing we all had in common was the kids. We loved the kids. After all, that's why we chose this profession. Probably the most useful statement I ever heard in college was, "Be a teacher to your students, not a buddy." I found this out the hard way. You want so much for your students to like you that it becomes very hard to enforce your rules. Enjoy your kids, but remember why you are there.

At the end of eleven weeks I hated to leave. Fortunately, I had been applying for jobs while interning and landed a position before graduation. I now teach a class of emotionally handicapped students in an elementary school in Virginia Beach, Virginia. My internship experience has greatly enhanced my ability to teach. Oh, there are still days when I ask myself, "Do I really want to be a special educator?" But then there are many more days when I wouldn't trade my job for anything.

Karen Richards is a teacher of emotionally handicapped students in Virginia Beach, Virginia.

Instructional planning means making decisions—about what content to present, what materials or other activities to use, how to present information, and how to determine if students are learning. In deciding what to teach and how to teach it, teachers set goals and expectations for their students. These goals and expectations help students learn. Instuctional planning, then, has three main components: deciding what to teach, deciding how to teach it, and communicating realistic expectations (Figure 10.1). We talk about each of these components in the sections that follow.

Deciding What to Teach

In making decisions about what to teach, teachers have to assess their students' skill levels. They have to identify those skills students have and those they do not have. As we discussed in Chapter 9, teachers gather

Instructional planning means making decisions—about what content to present, what materials or other activities to use, how to present information, and how to determine whether students are learning.

(© Rick Kopstein/ Monkmeyer Press Photo Service)

assessment information using tests, observations, and interviews. Much of this assessment goes on during instruction. Teachers sample students' performance by asking them to read aloud from their books, spell the words on their spelling lists, or do the kinds of math problems that are in their math texts. Larry uses this kind of informal assessment along with formal testing to plan instruction in his resource room. For example, standardized achievement tests tell him what his students know in broad content areas (science, social studies, mathematics). Using norm-referenced tests, he can make judgments about their relative knowledge and estimate the grade levels at which they are performing. Using criterion-referenced tests, he can identify the specific skills his students have and do not have. With an understanding of his students' academic and behavioral strengths and weaknesses, Larry is able to modify his instructional methods to meet the needs of individual students in his classes.

Another part of deciding what to teach is analyzing the instructional task. **Task analysis** consists of breaking down a complex task into its com-

DECIDING WHAT TO TEACH	DECIDING HOW TO TEACH	COMMUNICATING REALISTIC EXPECTATIONS

Figure 10.1
Main Components of Instructional Planning

ponent parts. For example, to do the problem 105 ÷ 3, a student must understand numerals, know the meaning of the division sign, and have a basic understanding of subtraction and multiplication. It's not enough to know what students are able to do; we also must know exactly what it is we want them to do. Only then can we match activities to their level of skill development.

Task analysis also helps teachers plan a logical sequence of instruction. Students are more likely to learn if teachers present material in a clear, logical sequence. This is especially true when the acquisition of new skills depends on the learning of lower-level skills.

Contextual variables also play a part in deciding what to teach. Where will instruction take place? How long will the lesson(s) be? Who will be in the room during instructional presentations? In planning what to teach, Kim considers the instructional groupings that work best in her classroom. Usually she teaches students in a group, but sometimes she teaches them individually. She also considers her students' performances, behaviors, and skills when they are in particular instructional arrangements. And she thinks about the physical space and the ways in which students interact in it. For example, if Darryl and Bobby are not getting along and their behavior is interfering with their learning, Kim figures it makes good sense to teach them in different groups. At another time, she would work with the boys on their social relationship.

Finally, in deciding what to teach, teachers must identify any gaps that exist between a student's actual level of performance and the level of performance a student is expected to achieve. By recognizing the difference between actual performance and expected performance, teachers are able to keep instructional goals and objectives realistic, neither too low nor too high.

The elements we've described here—analyzing students' skills, examining the instructional task, establishing a logical sequence of instruction, considering relevant classroom variables, identifying gaps between students' actual and expected performance—are all a part of planning known as *diagnosis* (Figure 10.2). Diagnosis is a critical part of instructional planning because it allows us to match what we teach to each student's level of skill development.

Deciding How to Teach

It's difficult to know ahead of time how best to teach. Teaching is an experimental process: Teachers try alternative approaches and materials until they find an approach or combination of approaches that works best in moving students toward instructional objectives. You may have thought, or even been told in courses, that the way to decide how to teach a student is to give a battery of tests, identify the student's strengths and weaknesses, then remediate weaknesses or build up strengths. But this is not enough.

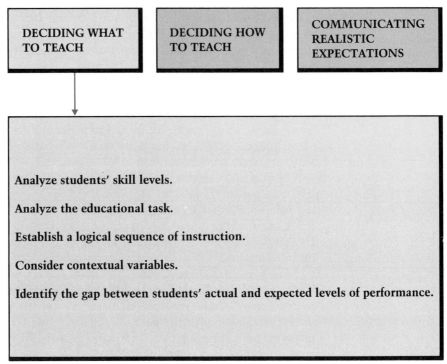

Figure 10.2
Deciding What to Teach

Yes, it's important to take into account a pupil's level of skill development and to identify learning and behavioral strengths and weaknesses, but simply knowing a student's score on a test cannot help you decide how to teach the student.

In making decisions about how to teach, teachers must make an "educated guess" about the kinds of approaches that will work, then try those approaches and monitor the results. That educated guess is based on experience, either with a particular student or with others like that student.

The only way to decide how to teach is to teach, then to gather data to determine the effectiveness of the approach. This does not mean that we teach blindly. Our experience gives us a basic understanding of what works and what doesn't work. Also, the literature is filled with guidelines for instruction (cf. Wittrock, 1986). For example:

- Beginning with an overview or using advance organizers or lists of objectives to set the stage for a presentation
- Signalling transitions between parts of a lesson and reviewing or summarizing subparts as the lesson proceeds

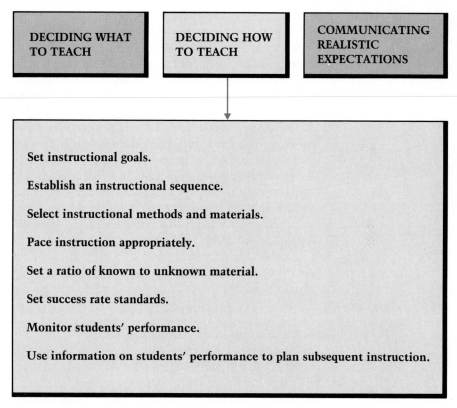

Figure 10.3
Deciding How to Teach

- Asking questions of varying levels of difficulty throughout a presentation
- Controlling the pace and continuity of lessons by regulating the time allowed for students to ask or answer questions

The process of deciding how to teach is shown in Figure 10.3. It begins with setting instructional goals for individual students, then establishing an instructional sequence. Most complex skills consist of combinations of simpler or lower-level skills; these skills must be taught in a logical sequence.

The next step is to choose appropriate methods and materials. This is a relatively easy task that can become complicated when students are exceptional. These students may need special methods (using sign language, acceleration). Or they may need special instructional materials (tape-recorded lessons, advanced reading materials, high interest–low vocabulary reading books). Some of Larry's students have learning disabilities. In the regular classroom they are reading *Macbeth*. In the resource room, Larry has them read from the *Illustrated Macbeth*, then tests their comprehension using verbal quizzes and discussions after each scene of the play.

Pacing instruction is also part of the process, as are setting a ratio of known to unknown material and setting standard rates of success. We believe that effective instruction should include about 75 percent known and 25 percent unknown material, and that students should be expected to demonstrate about 80 percent mastery of such material.

Probably the most important activities here are monitoring students' performance and using that information to plan subsequent instruction. (We talk more about this later in the chapter.)

Deciding what to teach is a form of diagnosis; deciding how to teach is a prescription, a treatment. If that treatment is not appropriate to the individual's needs, it actually can produce educational problems.

Communicating Realistic Expectations

An important component of instructional planning is setting realistic expectations for students and communicating those expectations to them. In Chapter 3 we talked about expectations and the impact they have on learning. When teachers do not expect much from their students, they are shortchanging them. If they have the skills to do so, over time students learn to perform at the level of expectation teachers hold for them (Good & Brophy, 1984). When those expectations are realistically high, students succeed; when they are unrealistically low, students fail.

Figure 10.4 lists some of the things teachers must do to communicate realistic expectations to their students. First, they have to get students active and involved in learning. Students who do not take part in learning activities cannot be expected to demonstrate high levels of performance on classroom quizzes and tests. This is particularly important when students are handicapped. Too often, teachers decide that these students cannot handle the same assignments as other students. By using separate standards in deciding what and how to teach handicapped students, teachers are setting separate standards for those students' education.

> Unanimously, disabled students and parents of students in every educational setting complain that adapting or accommodating to disability all too often results in lowered expectations and partronization. Instead, they contend that disability sometimes requires modification and adaptation but never patronization. Accommodating without patronizing requires students, their parents, fellow classmates, and professionals to adopt a

DECIDING WHAT TO TEACH	DECIDING HOW TO TEACH	COMMUNICATING REALISTIC EXPECTATIONS

Get students to be active and involved learners.

Teach students to understand the consequences of failure.

State expectations explicitly.

Figure 10.4
Communicating Realistic Expectations

standard of inclusion in activities and of expectations of meeting norms of performance set for an activity. (Asch, 1989, p. 184)

Another part of communicating realistic expectations is teaching students to understand the consequences of failure. Finally, there's the communication itself, the process of telling students (and being sure they understand) what it is they are expected to learn and what they have to do to learn it.

Managing Instruction

Few of us are comfortable in chaos. We need a certain order around us. Students, too, need an orderly environment in which to learn. They need rules to follow; they need an understanding of those rules and the consequences of not following them; and they need to see that those rules are enforced (Figure 10.5). These elements are all part of managing instruction.

In order to manage instruction effectively, teachers must establish and communicate rules for behavior in the classroom early in the school year. Students must understand the importance of following rules and the

SETTING CLASSROOM RULES	COMMUNI-CATING RULES CLEARLY	INFORMING STUDENTS OF THE CONSEQUENCES OF BREAKING RULES	HANDLING DISRUPTIONS PROMPTLY AND CONSIS-TENTLY

Figure 10.5
Managing Instruction

In a well-managed instructional environment, time is used productively, transitions between activities are short, few interruptions break the flow of classroom activities, the classroom has an academic, task-oriented focus, and sufficient time is allocated to academic activities.
(© David C. Phillips)

consequences of not following them. When disruptions occur, it is important to handle them quickly, as soon as possible after they happen, and consistently. Prompt, consistent action helps the class settle back down and refocus its attention on the work at hand.

One factor that limits the integration of students with handicaps into general education settings is that teachers can become overwhelmed with managing problem behaviors (Algozzine, 1989). One solution is to teach students to manage their own behavior. There are several easy-to-use procedures for doing this. Kim places an index card on some of her students' desks. At the top of each card, she writes a question that is appropriate for the student. Sandy has this question: *Am I paying attention?* Pat's is *Did I raise my hand?* Kim has taught Sandy and Pat to periodically check their own behavior and record their performance by making a mark on their card if they are doing what they are supposed to be doing. She checks the card during the day and gives the students feedback on their self-monitoring and their behavior.

Teachers must teach; they must present academic content and other instructional material. But they also must manage learning environments so that students are able to learn. What does a well-managed instructional environment look like?

- Time is used productively.
- Transitions between activities are short.
- Few interruptions break the flow of classroom activities.
- The classroom has an academic, task-oriented focus.
- Sufficient time is allocated to academic activities.

Students are more motivated to learn when teachers accept their individual differences, interact positively with them, and create a supportive, cooperative classroom atmosphere. Students feel better about school and about learning when their teachers demonstrate acceptance and caring.

Checkpoint	■ *A fundamental goal of teaching is to help students develop to their fullest potential by giving them the necessary skills to function in society.*
	■ *Planning instruction is one of the components of effective instruction. It involves deciding what to teach, deciding how to teach it, and communicating realistic expectations to students.*
	■ *In order to manage instruction effectively, teachers must establish rules, communicate their expectations to students, inform students of the consequences of breaking rules, and enforce rules promptly and consistently.*

Delivering Instruction

Delivering instruction is a three-stage process in which teachers present, monitor, then adjust instruction (Figure 10.6).

Presenting Instruction

Presenting instruction has to do with presenting content, teaching cognitive skills, motivating students, and providing practice (Figure 10.7).

PRESENTING INSTRUCTION	MONITORING INSTRUCTION	ADJUSTING INSTRUCTION

Figure 10.6
Delivering Instruction

| PRESENTING INSTRUCTION | MONITORING INSTRUCTION | ADJUSTING INSTRUCTION |

Presenting Content

Get students' attention.
Review earlier lessons or skills.
Tell students the goals of instruction.
Make lessons relevant.
Maintain students' attention.
Be enthusiastic.
Organize lessons.
Use a brisk pace.
Interact positively with students.
Communicate instructional demands and intent.
Check that students understand.

Teaching Thinking Skills

Model thinking skills.
Teach learning strategies directly.
Check that students understand.

Motivating Students

Show enthusiasm and interest.
Get students to understand the importance of assigned tasks.
Use rewards sparingly.
Get students to believe they can do their work.

Providing Relevant Practice

Make tasks and materials relevant.
Give students ample time.
Teach skills that students can master.
Help students develop automaticity.
Vary instructional materials.

Figure 10.7
Presenting Instruction

Making lessons relevant is one way to maintain students' attention; others are for students to be enthusiastic, to be organized, and to pace instruction.

(© Laimute Druskis/ Jeroboam)

Presenting Content   The first thing teachers must do when they present content is to get their students' attention. Students cannot learn unless they pay attention and get involved in the instructional process. Effective instruction begins with a review of skills students already have or of material they already have learned. New material should be introduced within the context of material with which students are familiar. Those skills necessary to complete new lessons should be reviewed and reinforced. Another important factor early is a statement of instructional goals and their importance. When Larry teaches, he tells students the goals of instruction and the reasons each lesson is important. He also tells students why what they are being asked to do is important and shows them how to carry out assigned tasks.

Teachers also should make lessons relevant to individual students. To do this, they have to be knowledgeable about their students and the social environment in which their students live. Students in rural North Dakota have different frames of reference from students in inner-city classrooms. It makes sense, then, to use different examples when teaching them.

Making lessons relevant is one way to maintain students' attention; others are to be enthusiastic, to be organized, and to pace instruction. It's also important that teachers and students interact positively, that teachers be supportive of their students, that they avoid negative comments, put-downs, and criticism.

Another component of presenting instruction is clear communication of instructional demands and intent. This means that written or oral directions should be easy to understand, complete, and in order.

Finally, it's important to check that students understand what's being taught. The best way to do this is to check students' understanding *before* they start to practice a new skill. This keeps them from practicing incorrectly.

Teaching Thinking Skills   Students should be taught more than how to do something by rote. Most studies of effective instruction contend that the thinking skills used in completing assignments should also be explained to students. There are a number of ways to do this. First, teachers can model thinking skills; that is, they can show students how to do what they expect them to do. They also can teach learning strategies directly, explaining how and why students' responses are right or wrong, and the processes that must be used to complete a task. Here, too, it's important to check that students understand what they are supposed to do. Kim does this by having students go through the steps they will use to solve a problem before they actually do the work. We watched the process in a math lesson. Kim asked her students to describe how they would do a sheet of two-digit addition problems before working on them. Each student described the process he or she would use. Some said they would start at the upper-left-hand corner and work across the first line; others said they would start in different places. Kim told them she didn't mind where they started as long as they did each problem by adding the right column together before going to the left. She also carefully monitored what the students said about what they would do when the sum of the first column was greater than 9.

Motivating Students   Students learn better when they are motivated. How do we motivate students? First, we have to show enthusiasm and interest in the material we present. Second, we have to get students to understand the importance of assigned tasks. One way to do this is to design work to reflect individual students' interests and experiences. Rewards can motivate students, but they should be used sparingly. Students who are constantly rewarded for what they do soon lose interest. Instead, rewards should be administered intermittently to maintain attention and behavior. Another strategy we use to motivate students is to make them believe they can do the work. Two simple methods work here: maintaining a warm, supportive atmosphere, and selecting and using instructional activities at which we know students can succeed.

Providing Relevant Practice   Students learn better when they have an opportunity to practice. Whether they practice under the teacher's direction or independently, it's important that the tasks they work on and the materials they work with be relevant to achieving instructional goals. Time is important here; students should have ample time to practice skills independently. It's also important to teach skills that students can master 90 to 100 percent of the time. With relevant practice over adequate time periods and with high levels of success, students develop *automaticity*; they complete tasks and demonstrate skills automatically.

Finally, teachers should vary instructional materials. Having students engage in extensive relevant practice is important; but if instructional materials are not varied, then practice becomes boring and interferes with instructional goals.

Monitoring Instruction

The second part of delivering instruction is monitoring students' learning (Figure 10.8). **Feedback**—information about a student's performance—is very important here. Good teachers give students immediate, frequent, explicit feedback on their performance or behavior. When students do something correctly, they should be told so. When they do something incorrectly, they should be corrected.   It's important to use praise and encouragement, tying them to a specific task. "I like the way you used your number line to add your numbers correctly" tells the student what he or she did right; diffuse praise leaves the student wondering. One way to provide corrective feedback is to explain the material again. Especially for students with learning difficulties, it is often necessary to explain over and over how to accomplish a specific task. Teachers also can model correct performance. It is often necessary, and almost always helpful, to show students specifically how to complete academic tasks.

Students should be actively involved in responding to instruction. One way to do this is to use their names during instructional sessions or to move around the room during a presentation. Another is to teach students to be active learners. When we described a well-managed classroom, we talked about strategies that increase the time students spend on tasks. This is an important part of monitoring instruction too. Teachers should keep an eye out for students who are not busy and redirect them. And they should work individually with students who finish tasks early. Students should not spend a lot of time waiting for things to happen.

Finally, teachers should establish mechanisms for students to get needed help. For example, students who need help can be asked to sit quietly at their desk with a hand raised until the teacher is able to help them. Or they can be asked to move to a special workstation, where help is provided by the teacher, a paraprofessional, or a peer.

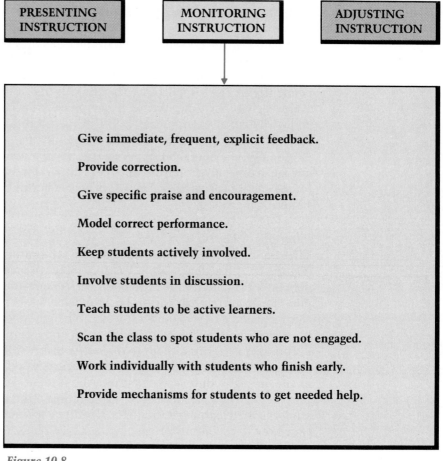

Figure 10.8
Monitoring Instruction

Adjusting Instruction

All students do not learn in the same way, at the same pace. So teachers have to adjust instruction for individual learners (Figure 10.9). We cannot give you specific rules how to modify lessons to meet all students' needs. The process usually is one of trial and error. We try alternative approaches until we identify one that works. An example: We recently observed Larry teaching a lesson on the characteristics of dinosaurs. During the lesson, he noticed Tim was not paying attention, Susan asked to go to the bathroom, and Marty started drumming on his desk with two pencils. Larry later told us it was clear to him that the students were not interested in the lesson, so he modified it, assigning to each dinosaur the name of one of the students.

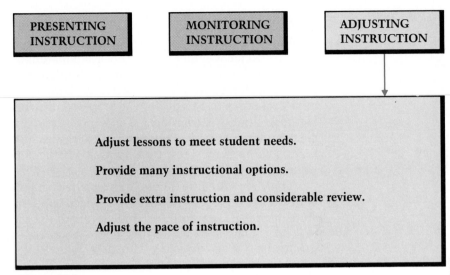

Figure 10.9
Adjusting Instruction

He saved the most powerful, tyrannosaurus rex, to the end of the lesson and named him Larry. He said this slight change was enough to interest the students in the lesson, and he was right.

Another way teachers can adjust instruction is to use different methods and materials. This increases the chances of meeting individual students' needs. Also, teachers can provide extra instruction and review for students who are having difficulty. Or they can adjust the pace of instruction.

Checkpoint

- *Delivering instruction involves presenting, monitoring, and adjusting lessons to meet the needs of students.*

- *The components of presenting instruction are presenting content, teaching thinking skills, motivating students, and providing relevant practice.*

- *Teachers monitor instruction by giving students supportive and corrective feedback and by keeping them actively involved.*

- *To adjust instruction to meet the needs of individual students, teachers may use different methods and materials, provide extra review, or adjust the pace of instruction.*

Evaluating Instruction

Evaluation is an important part of teaching. It is the process by which teachers decide whether the methods and materials they are using are effective based on individual students' performance. There are two kinds of evaluation: formative and summative. Both involve data collection. **Formative evaluation** occurs during the process of instruction: The teacher collects data during instruction and uses those data to make instructional decisions. **Summative evaluation** occurs at the end of instruction, when the teacher administers a test to determine whether a pupil has met instructional objectives.

There are six components in the evaluation process: monitoring students' understanding, monitoring engaged time, maintaining records of students' progress, informing students about their progress, using data to make decisions, and making judgments about students' performance (Figure 10.10).

Monitoring Students' Understanding

Students must understand what teachers expect them to do in the classroom, which means teachers must monitor the extent to which they understand directions. This involves more than asking a student, "Do you understand what you are supposed to do?" It's too easy for students to say "yup" without having the foggiest idea of what's expected. Instead, ask students to tell you or show you what they are going to do.

Second, students must understand the process they need to go through to complete classroom assignments. You can check this out by asking them to show you what they are going to do, to describe the process of responding to questions or doing problems.

Finally, a handy method to use in monitoring students' understanding is simply to check their success rate. Think about it for a moment. If you were to show a student how to solve double-digit addition problems, send her off to solve a page of twenty problems, and find out that she got eight of twenty correct, what would you conclude? You probably would conclude that she did not have a good understanding of the task. If, on the other hand, she got nineteen of twenty correct, you could assume that she did understand the process. Data on student success rate tells us a great deal about the extent to which students understand what we ask them to do.

Monitoring Engaged Time

Students who answer direct questions and participate in discussions during instruction learn more in school. Teachers can monitor the amount of time their students are actively involved in lessons by noting the extent to which individuals are participating in classroom activities. For example, Kim wanted to know whether Mark was actively participating in the class

MONITORING STUDENTS' UNDERSTANDING

Monitor students' understanding of directions.
Monitor the process students use to do their work.
Check students' success rate.

MONITORING ENGAGED TIME

Monitor active engagement in instruction.
Teach students to monitor their own participation.
Scan the classroom to spot unengaged students.

MAINTAINING RECORDS OF STUDENTS' PROGRESS

Maintain records.
Teach students to chart their own progress.

INFORMING STUDENTS OF PROGRESS

Inform students regularly.
Give frequent feedback.
Correct errors quickly.
Use task-specific praise.
Have students correct their mistakes.

USING DATA TO MAKE DECISIONS

MAKING JUDGMENTS ABOUT STUDENTS' PERFORMANCE

Figure 10.10
Evaluating Instruction

discussion on various types of trees. As an index of involvement and participation, she kept track of the number of times Mark raised his hand and the number of times he asked questions.

Keeping track of students' participation can be a time-consuming task. One way to deal with this is to teach students to monitor their own participation. Kim has a chart in her room that lists each student's name. At the end of every math class, Kim has the students record the number of times they asked a question during the day's lesson. She also has them place a plus sign, minus sign, or equal sign after the number to indicate if they did better (+), worse (–), or about the same (=) as the day before. At the end of the week, she has them evaluate their overall performance and write a note to take home describing how they did in math during the week.

Teachers also can gather data on student engagement by scanning the classroom to see who is actively involved in instruction. Periodically, they record the results of these observations and award free time or other prizes to students who meet criteria they have set for expected levels of involvement.

Maintaining Records of Students' Progress

To know the extent to which students are profiting from instruction, teachers must keep records of their progress. Record keeping can be informal or formal. Kim keeps relatively informal records of some students' progress in math, simply writing down the number of problems completed and the number or percentage completed correctly. In other subjects she keeps more formal records. Figure 10.11 shows a chart on which Kim keeps track of Bobby's performance in reading words correctly. Along the bottom of the chart are the days she has been graphing his behavior. Along the left side of the chart are numbers of words read correctly. The line in the middle of the chart shows progress in the number of words read correctly. Both a student's performance and goals can be recorded on the same chart. The chart then can be used as a visual aid in making decisions about the student's rate of progress toward meeting specific objectives.

Charting, like monitoring engaged time, can be a lot of work, particularly in a large class. Here, too, students can learn to keep track of their own performance. For instance, Kim taught Bobby how to chart the percentage of math problems he solves correctly each day. This frees up Kim's time, but, more important, keeps Bobby actively involved in his own learning and gives him a sense of accomplishment.

Informing Students of Progress

Regular feedback is one way to keep students informed about their progress. It helps students know what is expected of them and the extent to which they are meeting expectations. Here, too, feedback should be frequent and quick. Students learn better when they know how they are doing and when errors are corrected quickly, before they can become habits.

Again, task-specific praise is most effective. It's not enough to simply tell Manuel that he did a good job; we have to tell him what we mean when we say "Good job." For example: "Manuel, you did a very nice job of filling in the names of the countries on your map; you got them all correct."

When students make mistakes, it's good practice to have them correct the mistakes immediately. Both Kim and Larry are very concerned that students do not practice errors. Kim told us about something that happened when she was student teaching. She had students do a math work-

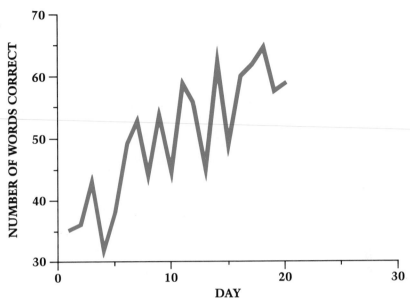

Figure 10.11
Bobby's Reading Performance

sheet, while she worked individually with a boy who was having trouble completing the worksheet. She didn't pay much attention to the other students. She figured that because they were quiet and busy, the activity must be instructionally appropriate. Later, when she reviewed the students' work, she found that one student had done all the problems on the sheet using the wrong algorithm (27 + 43 = 610). She realized that she should have monitored the student's work.

Using Data to Make Decisions

Records are important, not only for charting students' progress, but also for making decisions about their educational programs. For example, suppose the child study team is considering placing Bill in a self-contained class. Before they make that decision, members of the team want to know what has been done instructionally with Bill in the regular classroom and the extent to which he has profited from instruction there. If his teacher has kept good records or better yet charted Bill's progress, the data are readily accessible. The decision to discontinue special education services also rests on information about the student with special needs and about the student's agemates. If teachers have kept track of the student's progress, and if they know the progress of students in the general education classroom, they can make *normative peer comparisons*, judgments about the

Students learn better when they know how they are doing and when errors are corrected quickly, before they become habits. Task-specific praise is the most effective.

(© David C. Phillips)

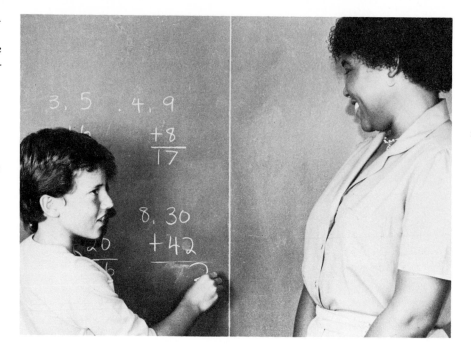

performance of the individual student relative to the average performance of his or her peers.

In Figure 10.12 we show the ways in which direct frequent data on pupil performance can be used to make instructional decisions. We've plotted the average number of words read correctly by one of the reading groups in Kim's classroom. We also show the rate of reading for three of Kim's students: Rodney, Raleigh, and Ralph. Notice that Rodney's rate of progress is above average for the group, Raleigh's performance is about the same as the average for the group, and Ralph's rate of progress is below average for the group. Using this information, Kim decided to move Rodney and Raleigh to another reading group; she decided to keep Ralph in the group until his rate improves.

Direct frequent data on student performance also can be used to make instructional decisions. By keeping track of students' progress, teachers can decide whether the approach or materials they are using are effective. Although monitoring a student's progress does not tell a teacher how to teach that student, it does tell the teacher the extent to which the student is making the kind of progress expected.

Making Judgments About Students' Performance

By regularly measuring students' performance, teachers are able to make judgments about their progress. To do this, teachers must specify their

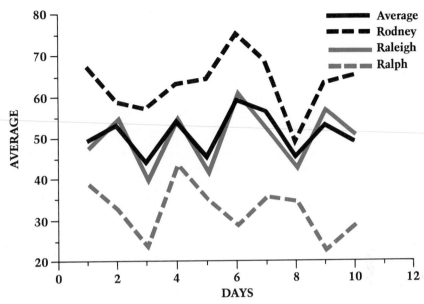

Figure 10.12
Reading Group Performance

goals for individual students, then plot what we call an *aim line*. An aim line shows the rate of ongoing progress that is necessary for a student to achieve a particular goal. Notice that teachers still have to make a critical judgment about the goal. Does Larry want or expect Courtney to achieve the same instructional goals that are held for all students in the school? Or does he want Courtney to achieve goals that are specific for her?

In Figure 10.13 we've shown Courtney's progress relative to a goal that Larry has set. The solid straight line is the aim line. It denotes the rate of progress necessary for Courtney to achieve the instructional goal. Her actual progress is slower. Larry can use this information to make instructional or placement decisions about Courtney.

Checkpoint	■ *Formative evaluation goes on during instruction; summative evaluation occurs at the end of instruction.*
	■ *Teachers evaluate students by monitoring their understanding and engaged time, and maintaining records of and informing them about their progress. They use evaluation data to make instructional decisions about students.*

AS A RESOURCE ROOM teacher, I work with high school students who have learning disabilities. The students in my school come from a very poor economic environment. Many have no parental support and they haven't been taught social and moral ethics. Their academic needs often come second to their social needs. Along with meeting the academic and vocational needs of my students, I spend a great deal of time addressing their social needs and counseling them.

I teach my students to think for themselves, believe in themselves, and always be in tune with themselves. Throughout the year we take class time and have heart-to-heart talks about whatever they want to discuss. Some of the topics we've addressed this year include drugs, sex, the service, college, abuse, peer pressure, and cheating. My students call me "The Preacher" because they say I preach to them about everyday things of life that no one has sat down and discussed with them before. I don't mind the name—I think it's quite fitting. One of my students last year told me that I was the first teacher to care about him as a person, not just as a student.

The only difference I see between my job and that of a regular classroom teacher is I sometimes spend more time counseling than teaching because my students' social needs are so great. Don't get the idea that I skimp on covering the academic competencies I'm required to teach: I spend a great deal of time preparing my students so that they can do as well in their mainstreamed classes as in their resource room classes. But a lot of times I think educators overlook the social needs of students. If I need to address them during class time, then I'll do that because in the long run I know

that my counseling is going to be just as helpful to them as my teaching. The way I see it, a child can't be taught new tricks until he or she understands the old tricks—or, another way of putting it, a child can't understand where he's going until he understands where he comes from.

Some of the major concerns I have about educating exceptional students center on their teachers' willingness to listen to them and to help them make their own decisions. Many exceptional students are not informed about postsecondary opportunities, and those who are often get the information too late. They may find out that they can go to college and receive financial aid, but if this information is not available to them until late in their secondary education, there may not be enough time for them to prepare for a college program right after graduation. Teachers need to spend time ensuring that students are adequately informed about opportunities. Moreover, teachers need to listen more carefully to exceptional students expressing their career preferences and to work with them in selecting a course of study that will help them reach their goals.

Anthony Wolfe is one student who has helped me learn a lot this year. He has helped me understand that even I need to work on listening to students more. At the beginning of the past school year, Anthony wanted to take an Algebra I course and I talked him out of it, saying, "No, you go ahead and take the Competency Math course." Halfway through the year I started to think that I hadn't made the best choice for Anthony. At the end of the year I knew I'd made a mistake. Anthony was talking about going to college and he had discovered that math requirements for college include Algebra I, Algebra II, and Geometry.

Anthony will have to attend summer school to pick up the math he needs for college. I limited Anthony by not listening to what he was trying to tell me. I realize that my students and I can learn a lot from each other. I usually tell them this at the outset of the school year because I want them to feel comfortable with me. I want to be of help to them in any way they need.

Students with learning disabilities can lead successful lives—they can go on to college if that is what they want to do. One of my primary goals as a teacher of exceptional students is to help them realize that it is okay to have a learning disability and to have to learn information differently. I hope they will learn to see that this disability does not have to control them, that they can use strategies to help them control it.

Mabel Hines is a resource room teacher of students with learning disabilities at Terry Sanford Senior High School, Fayetteville, North Carolina.

APPLICATION OF EFFECTIVE INSTRUCTION

We know a good deal today about effective instruction. The principles of effective instruction and improved methods of teaching are being included in teacher training programs.

The principles of effective instruction apply to all students—exceptional and nonexceptional. The methods we use for students who are exceptional are much the same as those we use for nonexceptional students.

Teaching exceptional students is a decision-making process in which school personnel decide what to teach, the approach to use (developmental, enrichment, acceleration, remediation, compensation, prevention), and whether or not adaptive devices are needed. Once these fundamental decisions are made, the principles of effective instruction come into play. Teachers still have to plan, manage, deliver, and monitor instruction.

More than ever before, regular and special class teachers are working together to accommodate students with special learning needs in classroom environments that are as much like normal as possible. Through combinations of individualized instruction, small- and large-group instruction, and teacher- and student-directed instruction, teachers are adapting learning experiences for all students.

Wang (1989) describes several ways in which instruction is adapted to the exceptional student:

- Instruction is based on the assessed capabilities of each student. Teachers provide varying amounts of instruction and use a variety of approaches to work with students individually or in groups.

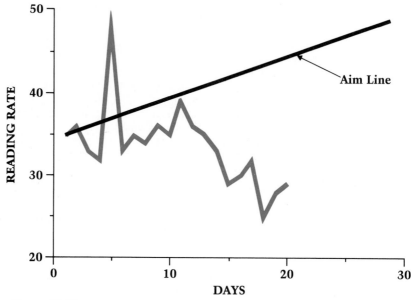

Figure 10.13
Courtney's Progress Relative to a Goal

- Materials and procedures permit each student to progress in the mastery of instructional content at a pace suited to his or her abilities and interests.
- Periodic and systematic evaluations of student progress serve to inform individual students of their mastery of academic skills and content.
- Each student undertakes, with teacher assistance and coaching, increasing responsibility for identifying his or her learning needs, as well as the resources required to perform tasks, plan learning activities, and evaluate his or her mastery.
- Alternate activities and materials are available to aid students in the acquisition of essential academic skills and content.
- Students have opportunities to make choices and decisions about their individual learning goals, their specific learning activities, and consequently, their own learning outcomes.
- Students assist each other in pursuing individual goals, and they cooperate in achieving group goals. (p. 102)

Clearly, adaptive instruction is no more than the principles of instruction that have been shown to be effective with all students. You should be able to trace the relationship beween the material presented in this chapter and the principles of effective adaptive instruction outlined by Wang.

More than ever before, regular and special class teachers are working together to accommodate students with special learning needs in classroom environments that are as much like normal as possible.
(© Alan Carey/The Image Works)

Checkpoint	■	*For the most part, principles of effective instruction for students who are exceptional are no different from those for nonexceptional students.*
	■	*More and more, regular and special educators are working together to accommodate students with special needs in classroom environments that are as much like normal as possible.*

WHAT WE THINK ABOUT EFFECTIVE INSTRUCTION

We have been in special education for more than twenty years. Over that time, some of our beliefs about teaching exceptional students have stayed the same and others have changed. We have always believed in a simple axiom: Good teaching is good teaching. We think the principles of instruction are more clearly articulated today than ever before, plus there is more and more robust research on good teaching, so we continue to hold to this belief.

We think you will be better teachers if you use a simple teaching model based on what is known about effective instruction. It goes like this: First, *demonstrate* what the student is expected to do. This demonstration can be in the form of a verbal presentation or actual performance of the expected behavior. Next, have the student *demonstrate* that he or she can do what is expected. Your job during student demonstrations is to provide supportive or corrective feedback. *Supportive feedback* lets the student know that he or she did what was expected; it supports the performance by letting the student know that what was done was done correctly ("Yes, that's great. When we add two numbers together, we . . . "). *Corrective feedback* lets the student know that he or she did not do what was expected; it corrects the performance by letting the student know that what was done was done incorrectly and it provides a corrective demonstration from the teacher ("No, this is how we do two-digit addition"). Once students have demonstrated that they can perform the expected behaviors at 80 percent accuracy, we release them to independent *practice.* During the practice stage of our teaching model, teachers monitor the performances of their students and again provide corrective or supportive feedback. This stage provides a final opportunity for the teacher to correct misconceptions and errors. It also gives students a chance to use new skills in different activities (e.g., games, problem solving, enrichment activities) in preparation for the final step of the model, which is providing *proof* they have learned the new skill. We believe performance on a mastery test should be 90 percent accurate before a student proceeds to new material within an instructional sequence.

This demonstrate-demonstrate-practice-prove teaching model can be used when teaching in different content areas. We believe it is an effective way to approach instruction of exceptional as well as nonexceptional students. We would like to see this model or something like it tried before any student is referred or removed from a regular classroom in search of an alternative educational enviornment designed to meet his or her unique educational needs.

Summary

1. A teacher's primary goal is to help students develop to their fullest potential by teaching the necessary skills to function in society.
2. Whether their students are exceptional or not, effective teachers plan, manage, deliver, and evaluate instruction.
3. Planning decisions include deciding what to teach (diagnosis) and how to teach (prescription), and communicating realistic expectations to students.
4. Task analysis is the process of breaking down a complex task into its component parts.

5. In order to manage instruction effectively, teachers need to establish and communicate rules for behavior in the classroom early in the school year, then enforce them promptly and consistently.
6. When delivering instruction, teachers present, monitor, and adjust lessons to meet the needs of their students.
7. The four components of presenting instruction are presenting content, teaching thinking skills, motivating students, and providing relevant practice.
8. Teachers monitor instruction by providing supportive and corrective feedback and keeping students actively involved.
9. Offering different instructional options, providing extra instruction and review, and changing the pace of work are three ways in which teachers adjust instruction to meet the needs of individual students.
10. Evaluation is the process by which teachers decide whether the methods and materials they are using are effective based on individual students' performance.
11. When teachers collect data during instruction and use those data to make instructional decisions, they are undertaking formative evaluation. Summative evaluation occurs at the end of instruction, when teachers administer a test to determine whether students have met instructional objectives.
12. Today more than ever before, regular and special class teachers are working together to accommodate students with special learning needs in classroom environments that are as much like normal as possible.

Activities

1. Interview a regular classroom teacher who is currently teaching special needs students. Ask him or her to describe how he or she plans, manages, delivers, and evaluates instruction for different groups of students in his or her classroom.
2. Interview several special education teachers. Ask them to describe how they plan, manage, deliver, and evaluate instruction for different groups of students in their classrooms.
3. Observe elementary, middle, and high school teachers working with exceptional students. Note any similarities and differences in what the teachers do during instructional presentations.
4. Observe regular class and special class teachers teaching an exceptional student at different times during the school day. Note any similarities and differences in what each of these teachers do.

Suggested Readings

Bijou, S. (1970). What psychology has to offer education—now. *Journal of Applied Behavior Analysis, 3,* 65–71.

The author argues that functional analysis of behavior has more to offer education than do test-based approaches. At the kindergarten level psychologists can help children make the transition from home to school and at the later elementary level they can help teachers manage students' behavior problems. These principles illustrate selected effective teaching behaviors related to managing classroom instruction.

Brophy, J. E. (1982). How teachers influence what is taught and learned in classrooms. *Elementary School Journal, 83,* 1–13.

Brophy reviews research on how teachers determine what they teach. He shows how teachers' decisions, along with their unplanned actions, influence what students learn.

Stainback, S., Stainback, W., & Forest, M. (1989). *Educating all students in the mainstream of regular education.* Baltimore, MD: Brookes.

This is a compilation of the latest thinking on methods and practices for accomplishing the goal of merging special and regular education into an integrated service delivery system to meet the needs of all students.

Wang, M. C. (1989). Adaptive instruction: An alternative for accommodating student diversity through the curriculum. In D. K. Lipsky & A. Gartner (Eds.), *Beyond separate education: Quality education for all* (pp. 99–119). Baltimore, MD: Brookes.

Wang points out that many principles of special education are being challenged as ineffective and duplicative relative to the education provided in regular classrooms. The author believes that adaptive instructional techniques founded on the principles of effective instruction derived from process-product research can improve the education provided to many students with special learning needs. This chapter offers a positive set of guidelines for adapting instructional methods for exceptional students.

Wittrock, M. C. (1986). *Handbook of research on teaching* (3rd ed.). New York: Macmillan.

This is a compilation of the latest knowledge on effective teaching theories, techniques, and practices. Academic content areas as well as special education instructional techniques are discussed in great detail.

11

Teaching
Exceptional Students

FOCUSING QUESTIONS

- What is special about special education?

- The broad goals of instruction in special education are the same as they are in regular education; the specific goals are different. What does this statement mean?

- What is the difference between remedial and compensatory instruction?

- What kinds of information should be included in every individualized education program?

- How are the principles of respondent and operant conditioning tied to behavior therapy?

- What are two ways in which ability training can be used?

- What are the key components of crisis therapy?

- What are some of the roles computers are playing in special education today?

- How are modifications in testing practices being used to allow students with handicaps to demonstrate their achievement on standardized tests?

WE HAVE WORKED IN SPECIAL EDUCATION MOST OF our adult lives. We often are asked to talk about our research and about teaching exceptional students at local, state, and national conferences. We believe in the principles of effective instruction that were discussed in Chapter 10. We believe that good teaching is good teaching. We believe that there are more similarities than differences between students in special and regular education classes, and that there are more similarities than differences between what teachers do in special and regular education classes. At conferences and meetings, when we say that special education is more like regular education than it is different from it, someone usually asks us this question: What's special about special education?

We believe five factors make teaching students with special needs different from teaching students who are not exceptional:

- Although most educational objectives are universal, special education does have certain unique goals.

- Although many of their educational experiences are like those of their agemates, special education students have individualized education programs; their agemates do not.
- Some exceptional students receive instruction in skills that their agemates develop without special instruction.
- Although teachers in regular and special education do many of the same things, certain instructional techniques are used more with exceptional students than with nonexceptional students.
- Finally, some students need special instructional adaptations to grow, develop, and prosper from schooling.

In this chapter, we talk about these aspects of teaching exceptional students. As you're reading, remember: The purpose of instruction, specific educational plans, the content of instruction, the methods used, and instructional modifications may be different in special education, but the students are not. And most of what we do for these students can be and should be going on in the regular classroom.

SPECIAL PURPOSES FOR INSTRUCTION

The fundamental goal of schooling is to help students develop the skills they need to function in society. Those skills relate to content areas (reading, mathematics, science, language arts), to specific kinds of jobs, and to affective or social behaviors (developing trust, building relationships, handling joint decisions and interpersonal conflicts, working for delayed gratification). Teachers and other people who work in schools help students develop these skills.

Within any classroom some students already have developed the skills being taught, others need help developing those skills, and still others need to be taught a set of prerequisite skills before they can learn the content others are learning. Put simply, students develop skills at different rates. Instruction in all classrooms must be adjusted to accommodate these individual differences. Teachers try to match the level of instruction to the level of skill development of different learners in their classes. They modify and adapt the prescribed curriculum to meet the unique needs of their students.

When teachers need help accommodating a student with special learning needs, they can turn to special education. Why? Because the objectives of instruction in special education focus on meeting the needs of exceptional students. That instruction serves six purposes: development, enrichment, acceleration, remediation, compensation, and prevention. And it is guided by an individualized education program that clearly defines the special learning needs of each student.

To meet the special needs of students who make exceptional progress in regular classes, classroom teachers enhance their educational experiences by adding materials and activities to the curriculum; the educational setting remains the same.
(© David Phillips)

Instruction in regular education is designed to help students achieve competence in a variety of broad areas of knowledge. The goals and objectives of regular education reflect society's values. For example, children are told they have to go to school so they can learn to read, write, and do math, so they will grow up to be independent productive citizens. When parents, teachers or other professionals, or students themselves believe students need help to meet broad educational goals, special education is one option. The broad goals of instruction in special education are the same as they are in regular education; the specific goals are different.

An extensive knowledge base has been derived from research in the psychology of learning and development on how individuals develop skills. The component skills students must learn and demonstrate in order to perform complex behaviors have been studied, and the merits of learning skills in different sequences have been compared. The process of teaching students a set of skills that are progressively more difficult in order to enable them to demonstrate the complex skills or abilities necessary to meet instructional objectives is called **developmental instruction**.

Some students make exceptional progress in regular classes. They are able to read earlier than many of their peers. Their arithmetic, writing, and language skills are more developed than those of their classmates. To meet their special needs, their teachers adjust instruction (see Chapter 4). **Enrichment** is the simplest approach. Classroom teachers enhance the educational experiences of these students by adding materials and activities to the curriculum; the educational setting remains the same. **Acceleration** is another way to meet the needs of students who are gifted and talented. In accelerated programs, students progress through a curriculum at a faster pace than their peers. They may spend less time drilling and practicing, or they may skip one or more grades to accommodate their heightened academic skills.

When students don't make expected progress in regular classes, many receive **remediation**—instruction that is designed to repair or correct basic problems or difficulties. In much the same way that doctors treat patients with medication, teachers give their students remedial instruction. A student can be taught specific skills (reading skills, math skills) to remediate deficiencies in skill development. Or specific deficits in abilities (memory, perception of sounds) can be addressed in remediation.

By the time they are in high school, most students have learned to do basic math with high degrees of accuracy. But many of Larry's students have trouble with multiplication. Fred was having difficulty multiplying two-digit numbers. In watching the way Fred did his calculations, Larry noticed that he had not developed the skills to add the interim products together to produce the correct answer. Larry knew that trying to teach Fred to multiply two-digit numbers would be unproductive until he taught him to add the intermediate products correctly. This process of going back to remedy skill deficits is the kind of remedial instruction that takes place in resource rooms and in the regular classroom. One of Kim's students who was having trouble reading proved to have deficits in prerequisite reading skills. So Kim did some special remedial training with him before trying to teach him to read new material.

Instruction also can be **compensatory**. The word comes from *compensate*, which means "to make up for." If you don't own a car, you may compensate for it by taking buses, riding a bike, or getting rides from friends who do own cars. People who do not have the use of their legs compensate by getting around in wheelchairs; some of those who have lost the use of their voice compensate by writing down what they want to "say." Usually, compensatory treatments are used only when it's impossible to remediate a condition or when it's easier to compensate for the condition than try to remediate it. Many educational methods are compensatory. Most are used in the treatment of sensory or physical handicaps, but some also are used with mildly handicapped students. Teaching blind students to communicate using braille, teaching students without arms to write holding a pencil in their toes, teaching deaf students to communicate using sign language and finger spelling—all are forms of compensatory instruction. Arranging for students who have difficulty reading or writing to take oral examinations, using "talking books" with students who have visual impairments, and tape recording lectures for students who have difficulty taking notes also are forms of compensatory instruction. Compensatory instruction is designed to help students overcome the effects of handicaps that cannot be corrected.

A final objective of instruction is **prevention.** Researchers have spent a lot of time studying why students fail to achieve. They have identified individual students' characteristics, home and family characteristics, the ways in which schools are organized, and teaching procedures as factors associated with student failure. They also have identified instructional practices that, if taken into consideration in teaching, might foster the development of skills and competencies in more students. When school personnel know the kinds of academic skills and social behaviors students must have in order to acquire more complex skills and behaviors, and when they know the kinds of things that interfere with skill development, they are in a position to develop curriculums and interventions to prevent failure in school.

A good example of a preventive intervention is the Head Start program, which was instituted in the United States in the 1960s. Head Start was a preschool program for children from low-income families. It was developed in response to the high incidence of school difficulties and failure among these children. It was hoped that intensive preschool instruction with as many children as possible from poor families would alleviate later problems.

Do preventive programs work? In 1987 the Committee for Economic Development issued a report entitled *Children in Need: Investment Strategies for the Educationally Disadvantaged*. In that report, the committee concluded that "quality preschool programming for disadvantaged children is a sound investment in which the benefits far outweigh the costs." The U.S. House of Representatives Select Committee on Children, Youth, and Families found that every dollar invested in preschool intervention returns $4.75 in savings on special education, welfare costs, and higher worker productivity. The federal law that funds early intervention for preschool students is a Catch 22, however. In order to enrich their experience, it labels the children *handicapped*. One way around the labeling stigma is to provide day care and instruction for all preschool children of working parents.

Faced with deciding why to teach, teachers have many options. They can teach to foster the development of skills, to enrich or to accelerate the learning of content and skills, to correct or to make up for skills that have not been learned, and to prevent learning problems. These objectives are not unique to special education, but they are more evident in the instructional experiences of exceptional students than they are in the educational lives of nonexceptional students.

- *Developmental instruction is the process of teaching students progressively more difficult skills to enable them to demonstrate the complex skills or abilities necessary to meet instructional objectives.*

- *Enrichment and acceleration are the objectives of instruction for students who are gifted and talented.*

- *Remediation is instruction that is designed to repair or correct students' basic problems or difficulties.*

- *Compensatory instruction helps students overcome the effects of handicaps that cannot be corrected.*

- *Preventive intervention is used with students who are at risk for academic problems, to stop those problems from becoming a reality.*

- *These objectives are not unique to special education, but they are more evident in special education programs than in regular education programs.*

INDIVIDUALIZED EDUCATION PROGRAMS

How are all of these different kinds of instruction organized and delivered to students with special learning needs? An *individualized education program (IEP)* is a written statement that describes what teachers and other professionals will do to meet the special learning needs of an exceptional student. An IEP is written for one particular student, and at any time only one IEP is used to guide the special education of that student.

Kim uses an IEP to plan daily lessons and activities for managing, delivering, and evaluating Phyllis's instruction. She finds it helpful when sharing information with other teachers who work with Phyllis. The IEP is also a source of information for Phyllis's parents and other professionals who provide services at school and at home. Her parents use it to know which teachers to talk to about their child, to get ideas about things they might work on at home, to have a record of the kinds of program and services Phyllis is receiving at school, and to help them know what to look for or what questions to ask when they visit Phyllis's school. The information in Table 11.1 will help you understand what an IEP is.

Table 11.1
Individualized Education Program: A Closer Look

An individualized education program is

- a written statement that describes the special education program for an exceptional student.
- a written statement that describes in general terms what an exceptional student can do (his or her present level of functioning).
- a written statement that describes the specific direct and indirect services the student will receive while in the special education program.
- a written statement that describes how much time a student will spend in special and regular education classes.
- a written statement that lists the dates on which special education will begin, end, and be reviewed.
- a written statement that describes what an exceptional student is expected to learn and how progress will be evaluated.
- a written statement that lists the people who developed the plan and indicates their agreement with its content.

An individualized education program is not

- a daily lesson plan that describes each little thing that will happen to a student while in a special program.
- a report written by a psychologist or educational diagnostician to describe a student's strengths and weaknesses.
- an agreement that promises all services that are needed will be provided or that guarantees that services that are provided will work.
- a ticket to unlimited mainstreaming or to full-time placement in a special education program.
- inflexible.
- a substitute for a report card or other daily, weekly, or monthly progress reports.
- a formal contract that places legal obligations on the people who develop it or the parents and professionals who agree to it.

Most school districts have forms that are used for individualized education programs. The forms may differ from district to district, but the following information should be a part of all IEPs:

- The special education program and any related services
- The extent of participation in the regular education program
- Beginning, ending, and review dates
- A statement of present levels of functioning

- A statement of annual goals and short-term objectives
- A statement of evaluation procedures and criteria
- The signatures of participants at meetings

Special Education and Related Services. An IEP must list the student's special education program (a program for students with hearing impairments, a resource room program for those who are emotionally handicapped, a gifted resource program). It also should list the name(s) of the person(s) responsible for the program and the school where the program(s) is held. Related services (readers for a visually handicapped student, counseling for an emotionally handicapped student, special transportation for a student with health impairments) and the names of the people responsible for them also should be listed on the IEP if they are part of a student's special education program.

Participation in Regular Education. Exceptional students should be educated in environments that are as much like normal as possible. How much time a student will spend in regular education classes and the subjects that will be studied there should be listed on the student's IEP, along with teachers' names.

Special Education Dates. The date the program or service will begin (the initiation date), the length of time the program will continue (the anticipated duration), and the month and year the program will be reviewed (the review date) should be listed on the IEP. Most IEPs have a place to indicate the date the program was written and a place to indicate the date parents and teachers and other professionals agreed to the information in the document.

Present Levels of Functioning. The IEP should identify areas of special learning needs. Included here is a description of current levels of performance and the source of that information (for example, a score of 115 on the WISC-R). An IEP should describe what a student can do (Bobby read 47 words a minute with 80 percent accuracy in his basal reader) and may describe what a student cannot do (five days of independent observations indicate that Phyllis is unable to move freely around school without the help of a classmate). Sometimes present levels of performance are simply listed as test scores.

Goals and Objectives of the Special Education Program. One or more general statements describing what is expected in each area of special learning need should be included in the IEP. Annual goals describe what a student is expected to do after a year in the special education program. For example, these are the annual goals listed in the IEPs of some of Larry's students:

William will be able to read and comprehend a story written at the sixth-grade reading level.

Marsha will be able to complete at least 30 two-step word problems with 90 percent accuracy.

Kerry will be able to write a hundred-word paragraph using proper sentence structure with less than 10 percent spelling errors.

Short-term objectives identify the steps that should be mastered to reach an annual goal. Suppose an annual goal is "Mary will be able to dress herself without help." These short-term objectives would be appropriate:

1. Mary will select appropriate clothes based on weather conditions.
2. Mary will put clothes on with help.
3. Mary will button, zipper, snap, or otherwise fasten clothes with help.
4. Mary will select appropriate shoes and put them on correctly with help.
5. Mary will put clothes on without help.
6. Mary will button, zipper, snap, or otherwise fasten clothes without help.
7. Mary will select appropriate shoes and put them on correctly without help.

Evaluation Procedures and Criteria. By the end of the year or periodically during the year (for example, after a specified number of short-term objectives have been mastered), Kim decides how well her exceptional students are doing. All IEPs describe how progress will be measured and specify how much or how well a student must do. Evaluation procedures identify specific tests, observations, and interviews that will be used to measure progress (for example, the Reading Recognition Subtest of the Peabody Individual Achievement Test, five-minute time sampling on ten consecutive days, Informal Perfectionism Inventory). Evaluation criteria define standards that are used to measure progress (80 percent of the time, ten minutes each day of the week, 90 percent accuracy).

Signatures. When an IEP is complete, parents (or guardians) must give their permission for the special services described in it to begin. Teachers and other professionals who prepare the IEP, parents, and the student usually sign it to indicate that they were at the meeting where it was developed or that they agree with its content.

Other Information. This information is required by law. Teachers and administrators can include other kinds of information too, information that makes the IEP even more useful:

■ How parents are expected to participate
■ The language spoken in the student's home

- Health or medical information
- Management programs being used to control the student's behavior
- Special testing considerations
- Special requirements related to graduation from high school
- The student's daily or weekly class schedule
- Emergency information for use in contacting parents

Providing an individualized education program to guide an exceptional student's educational experiences is one way special education is different from regular education. Having an IEP does not mean a student must be educated in a special environment. In fact, the better the program, the more likely instruction can and will be delivered in an environment as much like normal as possible.

SPECIAL LEARNING NEEDS

IEPs are used to guide the special education of exceptional students. Students who receive special education want to learn and should be taught the same content as their friends and peers in regular education. The goals and objectives contained in IEPs provide an indication of the areas in which exceptional students have special learning needs. Because special learning needs are a minor part of a student's life, they should be viewed only as a small indicator of how special and regular students and education are different. Primary areas of special learning needs, sample instructional goals, and examples of IEP objectives are shown in Table 11.2. As you look at the table, remember that all students need to learn the skills identified in each of the areas listed. What makes some students special is that their current levels of functioning indicate that they have not learned the skills on their own or under ordinary conditions of instruction, or that they have special learning needs that require special instruction. Special education helps them learn the skills that they have not or would not learn without the help of special teaching methods.

Checkpoint	■ *An individualized education program is a written statement that describes a student's current level of functioning, special needs, and the educational program that's been developed to meet those needs.*
	■ *It is not a daily lesson plan or a substitute for regular progress reports; not is it a formal contract.*

Table 11.2
Special Learning Needs of Exceptional Students

Area	Sample Instructional Goals	Examples of IEP Objectives
Preacademic skills	Visual tracking Auditory discrimination Visual discrimination Visual memory	. . . will identify similarities and differences in visually presented stimuli . . . will demonstrate 90% accuracy on Frostig worksheets assigned
Academic skills	Reading, writing arithmetic, science, social studies, civics, calculus, computers	. . . will pass all tests at Basic 4 level with 80% or better score . . . will complete Units 1–9 of the seventh grade science program
Social skills	Self-management Peer interactions Disruptiveness Verbal/nonverbal noises	. . . will sit attentively and listen for five consecutive three-minute time periods . . . will raise hand to ask questions during class lessons
Language skills	Nonverbal communication Verbal communication Speech production Sentence structure Grammar/syntax	. . . will complete Units 4–9 of fourth-grade language program . . . will complete supplemental units of *Language Step by Step*
Mobility skills	Physical independence Obstacle detection Cognitive maps	. . . will travel independently from homeroom to lunchroom . . . will identify three critical points for unaided trip to library
Independent living skills	Dining out Checkbook balancing Dressing	. . . will put boot on correct foot with assistance from Freddie . . . will calculate daily balance with 95% accuracy for one month
Vocational skills	Preemployment interview Employment interview Arrive at work on time Use machines safely	. . . will complete job application without assistance . . . will identify appropriate job listings in classified ads
Leisure skills	Dancing, singing, bicycling, swimming, softball, fishing, camping, hiking, board games, computer games	. . . will play electronic bowling for ten minutes with Phyllis . . . will complete "Scrabble" game with three other students without having a temper tantrum

- *The short-term goals in an IEP identify the steps that must be taken to meet long-term goals.*

- *An IEP must identify both the procedures for evaluation (specific means of measuring performance) and the criteria for evaluation (specific standards for measuring performance).*

SPECIAL TEACHING METHODS

The actual content of an IEP depends on the special learning needs of the student being served. If you looked at one hundred IEPs, you'd find many similarities in the information in them. And if you watched regular and special education teachers working with exceptional students, you'd notice many similarities in the ways they put the information in the IEPs into practice. The special teaching methods we describe below illustrate the diversity of approaches that are used to meet the special learning needs of exceptional students in regular and special classrooms. But, there is no magic in these methods. They are simply used more often when teaching exceptional students because special education is needed to help these students learn what they could not learn without it.

Behavior Therapy

Behavior therapy is the process of systematically arranging environmental events to influence behavior. It assumes that stimuli and consequences can be used to increase, decrease, or maintain behaviors. And it is commonly used in working with exceptional students.

Behavior therapy is based on the principles of respondent and operant conditioning. **Respondent conditioning** ties a reflex response to a new stimulus.

- Innate responses (reflexes) follow specific eliciting stimuli. For example, a puff of air near your eyes causes you to blink. The frequency of the response is directly related to the frequency of the eliciting stimulus.

- New stimuli can come to elicit innate responses through the process of *conditioning.* By continually pairing a stimulus that elicits a response with a new stimulus that does not normally elicit the response, the new stimulus comes to elicit the response when presented alone.

Teachers use many different respondent and operant techniques to meet the learning needs of exceptional students. Teaching desensitization can help students overcome test anxiety.

(© Laima Druskis/ Jeroboam)

Operant conditioning is the systematic application and removal of rewards and punishments to increase wanted behaviors and to reduce unwanted behaviors. Behavior therapy approaches based on operant conditioning typically follow five steps:

1. Specifying a target behavior and a plan for measuring it
2. Identifying levels of the behavior before intervention
3. Selecting reinforcers (rewards or punishments) and formulating a plan for systematically applying them
4. Implementing the plan
5. Evaluating the effects of the intervention

Teachers use many different respondent and operant techniques to meet the learning needs of exceptional students. For example, Larry uses **desensitization** to help students overcome test anxiety. At the beginning of the year, he noticed that Marsha, Pat, and Andrea became very nervous right before tests and quizzes. Now before an exam, he has them do some relaxation exercises, in which they alternately tense and relax the muscles in their hands, arms, legs, and feet. He also has them do some deep breathing and some "positive self-talk" ("If I mess this up, I can always make it up on the next quiz," "This only counts for 5 percent of my total grade"). His records of their performance before and after the desensitization exercises indicate that the technique has improved the students' performance on tests and quizzes.

Another teacher at Larry's high school designed a **token system** to improve students' behavior on bus trips. She identified target behaviors that her students needed to change (entering the bus screaming at the driver, shouting across people to talk to a friend). Then she listed the target behaviors and dollar amounts that could be earned for them on the first page of a checkbook. She gave each student a checklist that had the behaviors on the left side of the page and the days of the week across the top. She talked to the bus driver, who agreed to check the students' behaviors after each trip. Just before lunch each day, she had the students calculate the money they had earned and gave each of them a personal check in that amount. The students kept track of their earnings in their own checkbooks (which gave them needed practice in basic mathematics). Periodically, they were allowed to write checks in exchange for coupons that could be used at off-campus restaurants for lunch.

Kim uses **contingency contracts** with many of her students. She wrote a formal agreement for Bobby that specified the consequences of completing and not completing his homework. She described the behavior she wanted him to change (not completing homework assignments) and identified things that she wanted to use as reinforcers (discount coupons for a fast-food restaurant). Then she wrote up a contract that stated that Bobby would earn 1 point for each homework problem he completed. When he earned 20 points, he could trade them for a coupon for a free order of french fries. It wasn't long before Bobby started asking for his homework assignments right after lunch.

Another fifth-grade teacher in Kim's school uses **response cost** to improve behavior during art class. Her students had asked if they could listen to music while they work on their projects. She identified a set of appropriate and inappropriate behaviors and posted them on a chart in the front of the room, and made the music contingent on the students' behavior. Now she tunes a radio to an FM "rock" station and plays it softly while students work on their projects. If a student misbehaves, she gives the student a warning. After three warnings, she turns off the radio. When six students demonstrate appropriate behaviors, she turns it on again.

Precision Teaching

Precision teaching is one of the ways in which teachers plan, use, and analyze the effects of instructional methods to improve a student's performance. The approach involves continuous evaluation of students' progress toward meeting instructional objectives and always focuses on improving skills. It is a five-step process:

1. The teacher pinpoints the target behavior.
2. The teacher or student counts and records the baseline rate of the behavior, a measure of performance before teaching begins.
3. Using this baseline information, the teacher writes a short-term objective.
4. The teacher tries an instructional method, recording and evaluating changes in the student's behavior.
5. If the evaluation indicates that the student's performance is inadequate, the teacher changes the instuctional method.

Teachers who use precision teaching usually record each student's progress on a special record called a *standard behavior chart*, but some just use graph paper to keep track of changes in behavior.

Ability Training

When students need instruction in preacademic skills (for example, differentiating visual or auditory stimuli and remembering them), their teachers use **ability training** to organize their special education experiences. For example, if a student has a problem seeing the differences among geometric shapes, letters, or numbers, the teacher would assign worksheets that require matching a figure with one like it. If a student has a problem differentiating the *sh* and *th* consonant blends or the vowel sounds of *a* and *e*, the teacher might assign tape-recorded activities to give the student practice. Often ability training involves this kind of practice in an area where a student has difficulty. But it is also an effective way to teach students to use their own strengths to compensate for their ability deficits. For example, a child with poor auditory discrimination could be taught using a sight-word approach.

Direct Instruction

Larry believes that his actions are directly and functionally related to the goals of instruction. For example, if a student has not mastered math skills involving division or is not able to use tools to assemble a product, he arranges teaching activities to provide systematic, guided instruction in division facts or tool use. This approach is called **direct instruction**, and it relies on task analysis to identify the component steps of the skill that needs teaching.

Attack strategy training is a form of direct instruction in which students are taught small steps of a skill and rules for putting the steps together, so that they can use the strategy for any problem like those they have solved (Lloyd, 1980). For example, in solving a multiplication problem like 2×4, students might be taught to read the problem and say "Count by 2, four times ("2" "4" "6" "8"), then to say the last number in the sequence as the solution to the problem." Once learned, the same strategy can be used to attack similar problems (3×4, 4×2, and so on).

The process works like this:

1. Analyze the curriculum content to determine the class of skills to be taught.
2. Devise a strategy for attacking problems that require the application of the skill being taught.
3. Analyze the attack strategy to decide how to teach it.
4. Teach the attack strategy and evaluate performance.

Cognitive behavior modification teaches students to use self-statements to improve their performance on academic and other skills. For example, Kim and Larry have taught students to evaluate whether they are paying attention to an assigned task by using simple checklists taped to their desk. Each student has a personal question (*Am I paying attention? Am I doing what I'm supposed to be doing?*) on top of the sheet and a place to make marks to represent affirmative answers to the question. Research shows that students who have been taught to evaluate their performance by "talking to themselves" this way have improved their performance in academic skill areas.

Cognitive Skills Training

Some of the IEPs for students in Kim's class contain objectives in areas like critical thinking, reasoning, and convergent and divergent thinking. Many teachers believe that students should be taught thinking skills as part of their schooling. The most widely recognized grouping (taxonomy) of educational objectives in the cognitive domain was developed by Benjamin Bloom and his colleagues (1956). Bloom's taxonomy identifies six levels of cognitive skills—knowledge, comprehension, application, analysis, synthesis, and evaluation—each more complex than the one before it (Clark, 1983). To teach *knowledge* skills, teachers expose students to aesthetic, economic, political, educational, and social aspects of the environment and to people with similar interests, and give them experience doing needs assessments (i.e., determining necessary information or principles for successful completion of a project) and organizing data. *Comprehension* and *application* skills include collecting information to use in decision making, working with people who share common interests, and developing original products. *Analysis* and *synthesis* skills include examining creative products, changing ways of thinking, comparing thinking patterns with others, and integrating knowledge using convergent and divergent thinking strategies (see Chapter 4). Identifying standards for making comparisons, developing decision-making skills, and making choices are *evaluation* skills.

Teaching students to think should be a goal of all teachers. Critical-thinking objectives are central to the IEPs of many exceptional students because they have enormous potential to improve students' lives and the lives of those who live and work with them.

Counseling Therapy

Some teachers and many related services professionals focus on students' interpersonal problems. Many of them structure classroom activities to accommodate the social and emotional problems of their students with techniques called **counseling therapy**.

A number of different practices are used in this approach. For example, in *reality therapy,* the initial objective is to help students identify the problem and ways to rectify it (Glaser, 1965). In *client-centered therapy,* the teacher creates a warm, permissive environment that encourages students to express themselves and to develop their own problem-solving strategies (C. Rogers, 1951). In this kind of interaction, the teacher avoids making evaluative statements of any type. *Transactional analysis (TA)* identifies communication patterns between individuals, then changes them to improve interpersonal relationships. TA teaching techniques include contracts, discussions, and specific assignments on how to interact.

One of the most widely discussed approaches to counseling therapy is called **crisis therapy** (Redl, 1959). Like other therapies, the focus here is on building supportive therapeutic relationships, but the point at which the therapy begins is an actual life event, not a structured or unstructured therapy session removed from the real world. A key element of crisis therapy is the **life space interview**, which Redl describes as "the type of therapy-like interview that a child may need around an incident of stealing from the 'kitty' in his club group but that would be held right around the event itself by the group worker in charge of that club, rather than by the child's therapist—even though the same material would probably later come up in therapy too" (1959, pp. 40–41). The nature of the life space interview depends on its objective. If a teacher simply wants to help a student get through a critical event or crisis, then emotional first aid on the spot is the appropriate strategy; if the intervention target is longer-term learning, then a clinical exploitation of life events is appropriate. The student's willingness to take part in the interview as well as the time frame in which it can occur also help determine which strategy a teacher can use.

To deal with the crisis immediately, the teacher should be sympathetic to and understanding of the student's fears, anger, and guilt, but firm about the need for rules and standards of behavior. The objective here is to bring the student back to the task at hand. In clinical therapy, the details of the critical incident are used to teach new behaviors or ways of reacting in similar situations. For example, by pointing out that each time Mark calls Sally a certain name, he is likely to get the same reaction, Larry helps Mark regulate the future consequences of his behavior. And by offering or having Mark suggest new ways to talk to Sally, Larry helps Mark develop more appropriate interpersonal skills.

Learning Strategies Training

Exceptional students sometimes are trained to follow a step-by-step procedure to acquire teacher-presented content. Learning strategies training teaches students how to learn content and how to demonstrate their knowledge. For example, Larry taught several of his students to use a three-step paraphrasing procedure represented by the mnemonic *RAP* (Schumaker, Denton, & Deshler, 1984). They *r*ead a paragraph, *a*sk themselves about the main idea and two supporting details, then *p*ut (or paraphrase) the information into their own words. The focus of learning strategies is learning content to complete teacher-assigned tasks. They are taught to students using direct instructional techniques (Deshler & Schumaker, 1986; Schumaker, Deshler, Alley, & Warner, 1983).

Cooperative Learning

Teachers can structure school activities cooperatively, competitively, or individually. In cooperative learning structures, a small group of students, usually less than six to a group, works together on an instructional task. *Positive interdependence* (goals are achieved through the participation of all group members), *individual accountability* (each participant makes unique contributions to the group's goals), and *collaborative skills* (communication and decision making) are essential parts of all cooperative learning activities (Johnson & Johnson, 1976).

Larry uses this technique to teach social studies to some of his students. First he breaks an academic unit (say the Civil War) into several component parts (biographies of key people, major historical events). He then assigns each member of a cooperative learning team one section of the total project (for example, a ten-page written report, an oral report, a play). Students work independently gathering information, then meet to share their contributions with other team members and to plan the final product. Sometimes Larry assigns final grades to each student independently; at other times he awards the same grade to all group members.

Peer-directed Learning

For many years, questions like "Why can't Johnny read?" have motivated teachers to search for something within their students that causes them to

In cooperative learning structures, a few students work together on an instructional task. Positive interdependence, individual account-ability, and collaborative skills are essential parts of all cooperative learning activities.
(© Michael Weisbrot and Family)

fail. Recently, the concept of opportunity to learn has shifted the blame for academic failure from the student to interactions within the classroom. Research findings that students typically spend little time actively engaged in academic tasks support the development of instructional methods that can increase opportunities to learn (Delquadri, Greenwood, Whorton, Carta, & Hall, 1986).

One of those methods is **peer tutoring**: A student is assigned to teach a classmate or peer under the supervision of a teacher. One resource room teacher incorporated peer tutoring into his sixth-grade instructional program. His objectives were to review and practice basic math facts and increase the self-confidence, responsibility, and interpersonal interaction skills of his students. He matched up students from regular third and fourth grades who were having difficulties remembering their number facts, with special class students who needed review on the same academic content. The tutors spent two weeks practicing effective teaching techniques (planning lessons, providing supportive or corrective feedback) before they worked with their "students." On Monday and Wednesday of each week, the older students planned their lessons. On Tuesday and Thursday, they tutored for thirty minutes. On Friday, they evaluated their own performance and that of the student they had tutored. Periodically, the classroom teacher evaluated the progress of all the participating students and changed the program as needed.

Classwide peer tutoring is an instructional alternative in which students supervise one another's responses to academic tasks. Kim uses this approach twice a week during math. She divides the class into two teams, then pairs the students on each team. Each pair of students creates a set of flashcards by copying single-digit number facts onto a set of index cards. The problem goes on one side of the card, the answer on the other. Then the students actively practice the facts for twenty minutes. During the first ten-minute session, the "teacher" shows the problem sides of the index cards and the "student" provides the answers. During the second ten-minute session, the students change roles. During both sessions, the "teacher" provides corrective ("No, two plus two equals four") or supportive ("Yes, three plus two equals five") feedback. After the tutoring sessions, Kim tallies the total points for each team and records the results on a graph in the front of the room.

Social Skills Training

Some teachers take a direct instructional approach to improving students' interpersonal relationships. Critical elements of social skills training are a definition of the problem or target behavior, an assessment of the current levels of the problem, and the development and implementation of systematic procedures for teaching new behaviors or improving old ones (Hughes & Ruhl, 1989). Friendship skills (greetings, joining and leaving activities), social maintenance skills (helping, cooperating), and conflict resolution skills (compromising, persuasion) are common goals of social skills training. And principles of direct instruction—task analysis, modeling expected behavior, corrective and supportive feedback, and independent practice—are central to the process.

Checkpoint

- *Behavior therapy uses the principles of respondent and operant conditioning to increase, decrease, or maintain students' behaviors.*

- *Precision teaching uses the continuous evaluation of students' progress to assess the effectiveness of instructional methods.*

- *Ability training focuses on students' development of preacademic skills.*

- *Attack strategy training and cognitive behavior modification are forms of direct instruction.*

- *Many teachers believe that students should be taught thinking skills as part of their schooling.*

- *Counseling therapy is directed toward students' interpersonal problems.*

- *Like other therapies, crisis therapy focuses on building supportive therapeutic relationships; unlike other therapies, it is initiated in response to an actual crisis.*

- *Learning strategies training teaches students how to learn content and how to demonstrate their knowledge.*

- *Positive interdependence, individual accountability, and collaborative skills are essential to cooperative learning.*

- *In peer tutoring, a student "teaches" another student, with the teacher's supervision.*

- *Common goals of social skills training are the development of friendship skills, social maintenance skills, and conflict resolution skills.*

SPECIAL INSTRUCTIONAL ADAPTATIONS

Four years ago, Marc Buoniconti was paralyzed from the neck down in a football accident. Today the twenty-two-year-old is a dean's list student at the University of Miami, using a voice-operated computer that manages everything, from answering the telephone to turning on the lights. He exercises daily at the university's medical center, using a high-tech bicycle that electrically stimulates his legs. Buoniconti has proved there is life after football (M. Rogers, 1989).

Voice-operated computers and other instructional adaptations are things exceptional students use to modify the way they participate in instruction and other activities of daily living. Even though many of these modifications help exceptional students succeed in regular classrooms, their number and variety are evidence of another way special and regular education are different.

In this section we describe some of the instructional adaptations that are commonly used with exceptional students to improve their communication and mobility. We talk about these adaptations here instead of in the chapters describing conditions of exceptionality to give you a picture of the range of devices that are available, and to demonstrate that many of them are used by students with different handicapping conditions.

For Communication

To be successful in school a student must be able to communicate with teachers and other students. Many exceptional people have special learning needs in the area of communication. For example, some need large-print books to read. Others need special equipment on their telephones to "talk." Still others need some sort of modification to take tests. We discuss these and other specific communication adaptations below.

Communication Boards. Communciation boards are used by students who cannot speak. These boards have letters and symbols on them. The students point to the letters and symbols in order to communicate. You probably have seen a student in a wheelchair with a board, much like a large tray, mounted on the chair.

Hearing Aids. Perhaps the most widely known adaptive device is the modern hearing aid, a device that amplifies sound. Hearing aids can be worn behind the ear, in the ear, on the body, or in eyeglass frames. Technological advances have made hearing aids smaller, lighter, and more powerful. Audiologists or other specialists usually recommend the type of device that is best suited to meet the needs of a particular individual.

Classroom amplification systems also are used to increase the communication abilities of groups of exceptional students. Most of the systems use a microphone to link the teacher to the students, who wear receivers that often double as personal hearing aids. We recently observed a self-contained class of preschool children with hearing impairments. Each child had a small receiver attached unobstructively around his or her neck; the receiver was connected to a small earplug in one or both ears. The teacher talked to the children using what looked like a regular microphone that hung around her neck. When she spoke to a particular child, she often would get his or her attention by touching a shoulder or arm. Both teacher and children seemed to have adjusted very well to their adapted form of communication. Systems like this also are used when students with hearing impairments are integrated in regular classrooms.

Telecommunication Devices. Another way those who are deaf communicate is by translating verbal messages into written form. The simplest method, of course, is pencil and paper; closed captioning on television and telecommunication devices that allow people who are deaf to talk on the telephone are more sophisticated methods. Although you probably have seen the closed-caption symbol on television, you may not have seen a program on a television equipped to receive and transmit closed captions. The captions—a band of words running across the screen much like subtitles in a foreign language film—summarize dialogue or plot.

Telecommunication devices are small typewriters and a transmitter/receiver that are connected to a normal telephone by an acoustic coupler. To make a call, you hook your phone to the device and call another person with a similar device. When the connection is established, a message appears on a small screen or mechanical printer on your machine. Then you type your conversation, which is translated and printed on the printer connected to the other person's phone. Telecommunication devices have

Window on Practice

DR. LANCE MEAGHER HAD a busy medical practice when he came down with a degenerative nerve disease 12 years ago that left him paralyzed. Today, confined to a wheelchair and with virtually no muscle control except his eyes, he has a dream. He dreams of piloting an airplane around the world.

He may get his wish.

Ingenious new technology, involving a computer connected to electrodes implanted in his head, has already restored Meagher's ability to speak with a synthesized voice and to use a computer for word processing. It will soon allow him to control home appliances, giving him back a measure of independence.

Once he has practiced enough to operate it smoothly, Meagher said through an interpreter in a telephone interview last week, "I will use it 24 hours a day for speaking and writing."

The same technology may eventually allow him to realize his dream of flying. "I am hoping for this spring or summer," said Meagher, 41, after "my plane . . . has been painted and flight tested, and then I will put my special controls in,"

Meanwhile, he continues to practice some medicine, treating patients who have his disease (amyotrophic lateral sclerosis, or Lou Gehrig's disease) with an experimental drug he found helpful in his own case.

Meagher's story is just one example of how computer technology is making it possible for people with the most profound disabilities to talk, work and regain some control in ways not dreamed possible a few years ago.

Computers have become "equalizers," said Deborah Gilden of Smith–Kettlewell Eye Research Foundation. Now, "adults who couldn't talk can have a voice, children who couldn't read or write can do their school work. The quality of life for disabled people has improved by putting them in the mainstream of the real world."

Some of the most dramatic inventions were demonstrated recently in San Francisco at the annual meeting of the American Association for the Advancement of Science.

Among the new technologies being developed:

- Systems that translate sign language into spoken English and vice-versa will allow people who are deaf and blind to converse, in ordinary spoken English, with anyone at any time, unaided.

- People who are losing their sight may be able to read and recognize faces with electronic glasses that use image-processing techniques developed by the space agency to produce computer-enhanced video images. Eventually, the whole system might be mounted on a sort of helmet using tiny TV screens.

- People with all manner of disabilities may be able to tap into the power of computers to write, speak and gather information using specialized keyboards, display systems that generate braille, speech synthesizing devices and mechanical hands for sign language.

New worlds are opening up, and old limitations are crumbling.

People paralyzed by spinal cord injuries or degenerative disease often lose the ability to speak, and restoring the ability to communicate has been a major technical challenge.

Most attempts have involved a "keyboard"—a grid on a computer screen containing letters or words and a movable cursor. The user selects words or letters by moving the cursor with a switch controlled by the hand, the chin or any other muscles that retain mobility, or by blowing or sucking through a straw-like tube.

In other systems, tiny cameras monitor eye movements to determine where on the grid the user is looking. Because eye control usually survives even in people who have no other muscle control, this method has great potential. It also has serious problems.

The cameras are easily confused by head movements, which makes the system impractical for those with cerebral palsy or nerve diseases that produce uncontrollable tremors. The cameras are also fooled by reflections from eyeglasses and can be thrown off by poor lighting. They are too bulky to be mounted on a wheelchair.

The system Lance Meagher is field-testing, developed by scientist Erich Sutter of Smith-Kettlewell and called the Brain Response Interface, may overcome those problems.

Instead of monitoring Meagher's eyes, it directly monitors his brainwaves to determine what square on the grid he is looking at. Each square on the grid contains a particular letter or word and is coded by flashing patterns or changing colors. Focusing the eyes on that distinctive pattern produces unique brain waves that can be picked up by sensors taped to the back of the head—or, in Meagher's case, implanted through the skull.

As the eyes move around the grid picking out letters or words, the brain waves can drive a speech synthesizer to provide a voice or a word processor to produce writing.

The signals can also control a television set or other appliances or steer a wheelchair. Eventually, the system could give people who retain only eye control a remarkable degree of independence and the ability to communicate easily.

Meagher, who lives in a small town in Oregon, volunteered to be a guinea pig for the system. But, like many who have tried it, he grew frustrated trying to get it to work consistently.

In the morning, he could get a response rate of one keystroke per second, but as the day wore on, muscle spasms in his head and neck overwhelmed the faint brain signals and caused more errors.

The skull, unfortunately, is an electrical insulator that shields the weak brainwave signals. So Meagher volunteered (in fact, he insisted) to have electrodes implanted permanently through his skull, where they could pick up the signals much more reliably.

The electrodes do not penetrate the brain—they do not even touch it—so the surgery was relatively safe. So far, it seems to work well, allowing him to use the system reliably for hours on end.

"It was about 60 percent accurate before," Meagher said, "because of muscle artifacts. Now it can be 100 percent, but I am not there yet."

Gilden, associate director of Smith-Kettlewell's rehabilitation engineering center, said even hours of staring at the flashing screen did not prove to be a strain: "If you've been locked in and have had no way of communicating or controlling your environment, boy, you'd stare at flashing lights all day!"

So far, Meagher can use the system to converse and do word processing. He has equipment, which has not yet been hooked up to allow him to control his television set, VCR and other appliances. Soon, it will be linked to the telephone,

(continued)

allowing him to make and receive calls with his computerized voice.

And someday, if he has his way, it will be hooked up to the controls of his airplane.

Sutter, the system's creator, "is reluctant to have me use it [in the plane] since it is not known how reliable it is." Meagher said. "But I am working on him."

Source: *David L. Chandler, "Breaking the Shackles of Disability," The Boston Globe, February 6, 1989, pp. 31–32. Reprinted courtesy of The Boston Globe.*

broken down long-standing barriers in employment and social interaction for those who have trouble hearing through normal channels.

Braille. In the early 1800s, Louis Braille developed a system of reading and writing that uses arrangements of six raised dots to represent letters, words, and numbers. Almost two hundred years later, that is still being used by people who are blind or severely visually handicapped. Although the braille system is complex, blind students can read much faster using it than they can using raised letters of the standard alphabet.

Most youngsters who need braille are introduced to it very early in school. They usually are taught a set of contractions rather than letter-by-letter representations of the words they read. Generally it takes students a couple of years to become proficient readers of braille; of course, it usually takes nonexceptional students a couple of years to become proficient readers of print. Children who read braille learn to write using a *brailler*, a six-keyed device that creates raised-dot words. Older students use a slate and stylus to punch out braille dots because they are smaller and quieter than a brailler.

Optacon. This device translates written materials to tactual representations, enabling students who are visually handicapped to read. A miniature camera is moved along a line of print with one hand, while a tactile representation of the letters is felt with the other. The reading rate with the Optacon is slow, although some students can read as many as ninety words a minute using the device.

Kurzweil Reading Machine. Many students with visual handicaps use a computer-based device that converts printed words into synthetic English speech. A popular form of this device is the Kurzweil Personal Reader. It has brought independence and self-confidence to many people who have trouble reading any other way. Stevie Wonder uses this kind of machine. In an issue of *Sports Illustrated for Kids,* he is shown with a Kurzweil Personal Reader produced by Xerox (see page 413).

Calculators. Solar and other portable calculators are common aids for students who have not mastered basic math facts and operations. They can motivate younger students and provide a vocational link for older

Communication boards are used by students who cannot speak but who can point to the letters and symbols on these boards in order to communicate.

(© MacDonald Photography/ The Picture Cube)

students, who typically come across some form of "adding machine" in their jobs.

Computers   Computers are being used increasingly to overcome visual, hearing, and physical handicaps. Cartwright, Cartwright, and Ward (1989) identify several ways in which computers are being used to help students with visual impairments. They read print and produce synthetic speech; produce hard-copy braille; read braille, which enables students to do word processing, then output the product in braille; and produce large-print displays.

Computers are helping exceptional people do almost anything (M. Rogers, 1989). A professional musician who is paralyzed, unable to speak or swallow, uses a computer music system to compose and play his work. An architect with severe cerebral palsy who cannot use his arms and legs produces elaborate maps using a mouth stick for computer-assisted drafting. For those with extremely limited physical mobility, there are computers that can be operated just by moving the eyes. Also, computers are powerful teaching machines and rewards for all students.

Test Modifications.   Both the Education for All Handicapped Children Act and Section 504 of the Rehabilitation Act assure all handicapped people the right to a free appropriate education. This right implies that exceptional students will have the opportunity to complete their education, graduate, and receive a diploma signifying their achievement. Exceptional students are exempted from some statewide testing programs for graduation and promotion purposes. But the idea is not to create second-class degrees; it is to modify testing instruments and procedures so that students with handicaps or disabilities can demonstrate their achievement (Grise, 1980). To this end, some states currently allow flexible scheduling, flexible settings, alternative response recording options, revised test formats, and the use of auditory or visual aids for students taking standardized tests.

Flexible scheduling means administering a test during several brief sessions rather than in a single lengthy one. Flexible settings mean administering standardized tests to an individual or small group in a resource room or classroom rather than an auditorium. Alternatives for recording answers include marking in the actual test booklet, typing answers, and indicating answers to a test proctor for later transcription to a computer-scored answer sheet. Large-print test booklets and braille tests are used with some exceptional students. Although no portion of a test designed to measure reading skills can be read to a student, narrators and tape-recorded versions of some tests are used with students with seeing problems. Magnifying glasses are another modification for students with visual problems.

For Mobility

In recent years, society has demonstrated an increased awareness of the special needs of it's citizens. It is almost impossible to go anywhere without seeing some evidence of this. Special parking places for people with handicaps are one example. College and university campuses as well as most public buildings and city streets have been changed bu the addition of travel ramps and curb cuts that make them more accessible to people in wheelchairs. As a result of these changes, exceptional people today are where they should be, participating in life with the rest of us. We discuss other adaptations that help them get around below.

Animals. Guide dogs are used by people who are blind to help them move around. They generally are not available to people under age 16. (Most guide dog schools require that owners be 16 years old because of the responsibility of caring for an animal.) Less than 2 percent of those with visual handicaps use guide dogs. Hill (1986) suggests that they walk too fast for visually handicapped people who are also elderly or physically handicapped, that most visually handicapped people have enough vision to enable them to get about, and that many blind people either do not like dogs or prefer another means of mobility. Dogs also are used to help those who are hearing impaired.

Canes. Several types of canes are used by people with visual handicaps to help them get around: long canes, laser canes, orthopedic canes, and folding canes. The most common are long canes—aluminum canes that have a rubber grip, a nylon tip, and a crook. By systematically tapping the cane from side to side to keep track of sidewalks and steps and walls, people who have difficulty seeing can tell where they are. C-5 Laser (light by stimulated emission of radiation) Canes emit three narrow beams of infrared light. One of the beams detects objects that are immediately in front of the person; a second, objects at head height; the third, holes and stairs. The cane emits tones that tell the user where objects and holes are in the person's path.

Electronic Travel Aids. The Lindsay Russell Model E Pathsounder, Mowat Sensor, and Sonicguide are electronic travel aids, devices that send out signals that sense the environment within a certain range or distance, then translate the information received for the user.

The Pathsounder is a boxlike device that weighs about a pound; it is chest mounted, supported by a neck strap. The device emits and receives sonar waves that detect objects in the line of travel. It is used along with the long cane as an aid to mobility.

The Mowat Sensor is another device that is used as a supplement to guide dogs and long canes in helping those with visual handicaps to get around. It is a small hand-held box that locates objects in the person's path of travel. The device vibrates when an object is present; the closer the object, the more the device vibrates.

The Sonicguide operates much like the Pathsounder and the Mowat Sensor, but the device is mounted in a set of eyeglasses. The individual wears an earpiece like the one worn with a transistor radio. The device emits pitches and tones that give the user information about distance from and the direction of an object. The Sonicguide is used for concept development activities with children because it can be used to teach spatial concepts.

Wheelchairs. When people's mobility is limited because they cannot rise from a sitting to a standing position or when those who use crutches need to carry things and move around, they generally use wheelchairs. Modern wheelchairs are made of lightweight metal, and have a durable seat and four wheels. The large back wheels have a special rim that helps make the chair move.

Adults who use wheelchairs to get around work in many different professions and can do most anything people who don't use wheelchairs can do. One of the teachers in Kim's school uses a wheelchair. He can't run up a flight of stairs, but he can and does play the guitar, lead an active social life with his family and colleagues, and teach fifth-grade students. Kim says that he has replaced the "can'ts" that handicap many people with the "cans" that many able-bodied people never achieve. Ron Anderson, a colleague of ours, uses a wheelchair to get around the university campus where he teaches an introductory course to undergraduate students planning to be teachers. Richard Simmons recently hosted the Seventeenth Annual Ms. Wheelchair America Pageant in Mobile, Alabama. The duties of the winner are numerous: "She will travel, visit advocacy groups, make public appearances and conduct television, radio, and print interviews. These include promoting awareness of the need to eliminate architectural and attitudinal barriers, informing the able-bodied public of the achievements of physically challenged people across the nation" (Simmons, 1988, pp. 10–11).

Prostheses. Some people with physical disabilities use special devices to increase their mobility. Artificial replacements for missing body parts are known as *prostheses* or *prosthetic devices.* These devices allow those with physical handicaps to function fully in society.

> Several years ago, Ivy Hunter was inducted into the International Models Hall of Fame, joining such modeling legends as Wilhelmina, Naomi Sims, and Cybill Shephard. The honor was in recognition of her personal and professional achievements, achievements in personal courage, and professional commitment which far exceed those usually demanded of a fashion model: Ivy Hunter's right leg has been amputated.
>
> With a state-of-the-art natural-looking prosthetic leg . . . Ivy continues to model everything from swimwear and lingerie to daytime fashions and evening gowns at photo sessions, runway fashion shows, and in television commercials. . . . Ivy has learned to snow ski [and] has garnered several gold and bronze medals in the National Handicapped Sports and Recreation Association competitions. She also plays tennis, golfs, and water skis. ("Profile," 1988, p. 14)

Checkpoint	■ *Special instructional adaptations are helping exceptional students communicate and move around.*
	■ *Modifications in test schedules, placement, recording processes, and forms are allowing students with disabilities to demonstrate their achievement on standardized tests.*
	■ *Computers allow those with all kinds of handicaps to participate in all kinds of activities; they also are very effective teaching machines and motivators.*

WE REMEMBER TEACHERS

We said earlier that good teaching is good teaching, whatever the special needs of the students. And this is true. Regular educators and special edu-

Teachers may capture students' attention through innovative media or through the spoken word; they may be egalitarians (giving equal time to all students), randomizers (keeping students on their toes by selecting them in no special order), or humanitarians (choosing only students who know the answers).
(© Michael Weisbrot and Family)

cators do the same things: They plan instruction and teach academic or nonacademic subjects, they manage classroom activities, and they spend a portion of the school day involved in other activities (lunch, recess).

Although their functions are the same, studies tell us that different teachers do different things. Think of your own school experiences. You probably remember some teachers who structured their class presentations around a brilliant selection of supportive media. They knew the best films and filmstrips, had the right guest lecturers, and made use of well-prepared overheads, slides, and visual aids. Some probably used the spoken word to capture content and your attention. They spun tales of intrigue and mystery about advanced algebra, social studies, and art.

Teachers structure their presentations in ways they believe are interesting. They also use different ways of having students demonstrate their understanding of new material. Some teachers are *egalitarians*: They divide their time equally among subjects and students. Watching them, you'd see them diligently going around the room carefully asking each student to read four sentences or recite three lines of a poem or do five multiplication facts at the board. The teaching behaviors of egalitarians are predictable. And students know exactly what they are going to have to do during group instruction.

Of course, not all teachers structure classroom experiences so that each student has a precisely controlled turn. Others keep students on their toes by selecting them to read, recite, write, spell, or otherwise demonstrate a skill in no special order. We call these teachers *randomizers*. With uncanny precision, they are able to duplicate a table of random numbers in their heads and use it as a sequence for calling on students. A particular version of this type of teacher is the one who never calls on students twice (randomization without replacement). You remember the feeling of relief once you'd performed for a randomizer, the knowledge that you wouldn't be called on again. Both the egalitarian and the randomizer provide an opportunity for each member of the class to take part during a period, but they do so in different ways.

Then there's the *humanitarian*, the teacher who chooses only those students who know the answers. This gives "the rich" an opportunity to demonstrate their wealth and "the poor" an opportunity not to be embarrassed.

Good teaching is good teaching. And good teachers are good teachers. But all teaching and all teachers are not alike. Yes, teachers share objectives and perform the same basic functions, but they, like the students they teach, are individuals. They have their own ways of delivering instruction, of evaluating instruction, and of interacting with their students. This, too, is evidence of the diversity that makes the field of education so exciting. It is also the one intangible that makes teaching so rewarding. We all remember those wonderful people who made a difference in our educational lives. We all remember teachers for what they did, how they taught, and the effects they had on our lives.

WHAT WE THINK ABOUT TEACHING EXCEPTIONAL STUDENTS

What's special about special education? This question has plagued us throughout our professional careers. We have never believed that the students in special education were very different from their friends in regular education. When we observed teachers in special and regular classrooms, we noticed that much of what they did was very similar. They all plan instructional units, deal with classroom disruptions, present content, monitor their students' performances, and worry that there is not enough time in the day to "get everything done." Since the similarities between regular education and special education teachers, students, or practices outweigh the differences between them, we began to wonder whether special education could be provided in a more efficient and productive manner.

Sometimes, when we are playing with alternatives to current practices, we think about what it would be like if regular teachers' first and foremost responsibility was to teach all students—if their primary goal was to take students where they are and move them forward, to reduce their need for special educational experiences. If students needed special help their classroom teacher would provide remedial or compensatory instruction. If any students performed beyond expectations, their classroom teacher would enrich or accelerate their educational experiences.

Special instructional techniques (learning strategies, social skills training) would be considered appropriate for all students, and would be provided as an academic content area by a specially trained teacher. If these techniques can help students learn, we'd like all students to have access to them.

In the same way, it would be wonderful if all students had individualized education programs, both to improve instruction and to eliminate the stigma of being "different." Even though IEPs represent a positive difference between regular and special education, they sometimes reinforce stereotypes that operate contrary to the best interests of exceptional students. Having an IEP is like wearing a freshman cap, eating in a separate dining room, riding a special bus, going to a special class, and having a special teacher. It's a white flag, a badge that reads "I am different." Most exceptional people that we know tell us they do everything they can to convey another message to people: I AM NOT DIFFERENT.

The only legitimate obstacle to using special instructional methods in the regular classroom is the size of classes in most schools today. We would like to see an educational system in which the typical grade (120 students) is divided among five, not four, teachers. With fewer students, all teachers can spend more time on specialized instruction. We know they can; many are doing it in regular classes already.

We think special adaptations should become content areas of instruction, not methods for keeping exceptional students away from their peers. Why not teach second-graders braille so they can read what some of their exceptional friends have to say? Why not teach sign language to seventh-graders so they can communicate with a classmate who is deaf? Why not illustrate early on the importance of keeping schools, libraries, and other public places accessible to all people who what to use them?

What we're saying is that all education should be special. We would like to eliminate the differences that exist between special and regular education; we want our children and our children's children to learn in a single educational system where all education is special. The reasons for not doing things differently are becoming less and less easy to articulate and justify. And we are doing our part to make the dream a reality.

Summary

1. Five elements make special education different from regular education: the objectives of instruction, individualized education programs, content areas, instructional techniques, and instructional adaptations.

2. Special education is appropriate for some students because the objectives of instruction in special education programs more closely match their needs.
3. Development, enrichment, acceleration, remediation, compensation, and prevention are six objectives of instruction in special education programs.
4. An individualized education program is a written statement that describes what teachers and other professionals will do to meet the special learning needs of an exceptional student.
5. The IEP describes the skills that require special instruction.
6. The methods used to teach students with special needs are not special in themselves; it is just that they are more evident in special education programs than in regular education programs.
7. Instructional adaptations make it possible for students with disabilities to communicate and move around.
8. Teachers share objectives and functions, but have their own individual styles of teaching.

Activities

1. Obtain a copy of an individualized education program. Identify the long-term goals, short-term objectives, levels of current functioning, and procedures to be used in evaluating progress.
2. Interview a classroom teacher. Ask what special methods he or she uses to meet the special learning needs of exceptional students.

Suggested Readings

Alberto, P. A., & Troutman, A. C. (1986). *Applied Behavior Analysis for Teachers.* Columbus, OH: Merrill.
 Systematic, organized presentations of fundamentals of applied behavior analysis are provided in this easy–to–read textbook. Concepts and principles guiding the application and analysis of behavioral techniques in classrooms are provided. Each aspect of planning, implementing, and evaluating applied behavior analysis programs is clearly described.

Algozzine, B., & Maheady, L. (1986). When all else fails, teach! *Exceptional Children, 52,* 487–488.
 This was an introduction to a special issue of Exceptional Children. *In it, precision teaching, classwide peer tutoring, learning strategies approaches, and other effective techniques for teaching exceptional students are described by experts in the field.*

Arter, J., & Jenkins, J. (1979). Differential diagnosis-prescriptive teaching: A critical appraisal. *Review of Educational Research, 49,* 517–555.

An extensive review of the research on diagnostic-prescriptive teaching. The authors conclude that there is little support for the practice of designing individualized programs for students on the basis of their performance on tests.

Jenkins, J. R., Deno, S. L., & Mirkin, P. K. (1979). Measuring pupil progress toward the least restrictive alternative. *Learning Disability Quarterly, 2,* 81–92.

The authors contend that IEPs must include specific objectives and timelines for monitoring progress. They outline the characteristics of measurement systems, and evaluate the adequacy of data systems.

Mangrum, C. T., III., & Strichart, S. S. (1984). *College and the Learning Disabled Student.* New York: Grune and Stratton.

Meeting the special learning needs of older students has become a prominent concern for teachers, counselors, and other professionals. This book contains valuable information about selecting, developing, and implementing higher education programs for students classified as learning disabled. The material in it will be valuable to anyone concerned with meeting the special learning needs of older exceptional people.

Reynolds, M. C. (1971). Trends in special education: Implications for measurement. In W. Hively & M. C. Reynolds (Eds.), *Domain-referenced testing in special education.* Reston, VA: Council for Exceptional Children.

Reynolds points out that major changes in public policy on the education of students who are handicapped make norm-referenced assessment nonproductive. He describes the ways in which educators can assess students to produce most effectively.

Schloss, P. J., & Sedlak, R. A. (1986). *Instructional Methods for Students with Learning and Behavior Problems.* Boston: Allyn & Bacon.

This is a book about general methods of instruction for students with special learning needs. Individual assessment, instructional planning, and educational procedures are discussed with direct application to problems faced by those who teach exceptional students. Theoretical practices and related research are translated nicely into classroom activities that teachers can use.

Wittrock, M. C. (1986). *Handbook of research on teaching* (3rd ed.). New York: Macmillan.

This is a compilation of research on effective teaching theories, techniques, and practices. The author examines academic content areas as well as special education instructional techniques.

Ysseldyke, J. E., & Algozzine, B. A. (1983). Where to begin in diagnosing reading problems. *Topics in Learning and Learning Disabilities, 2,* 60–69.

Two different diagnostic models are described. In one, the focus is on finding out what is wrong with the learner. In the other, the emphasis is on diagnosing instruction. The authors lay out a step-by-step approach for diagnosis that begins with in-house class observation of students' participation in instruction.

five

The Social Context of Special Education

We have described the foundations, categories, and important practices of special education. Social, political, and economic factors regularly interact with these educational factors to place limits on what happens in special education, influencing decisions about which students will be served, and how, where, and by whom they will be served. We discuss the influence of these external factors on the day-to-day practices of special education and exceptional people in society in the final part of the text.

Relationships among social, political, and economic factors and their relations to policy and practice are described in Chapter 12. We address such questions as how social class and treatment are related, how social values influence policies, how political values influence policy, how people with handicaps achieve rights, and how categories and eligibility criteria are determined. We also review such economic considerations as who pays for special education, how monies are allocated, and the costs of special education.

Chapter 13 examines the key areas in which changes are occurring in the lives of exceptional individuals and in the practice of special education. This final section includes discussion of parents and families, early childhood intervention, cultural diversity, technology, and regular education partnerships, and also considers transition programs to prepare exceptional individuals for life after school and living arrangements for exceptional adults.

12

The Social, Political, and Economic Realities of Special Education

FOCUSING QUESTIONS

■ How do social values influence educational policy?

■ How do political values influence educational policy?

■ What role does the federal government play in setting the research agenda for special education?

■ Decisions about how to allocate monies among special education programs are guided by public perceptions of the different disabilities. What does this statement mean?

■ Who pays for special education programs?

■ What are three ways in which funds are allocated to special education programs?

■ How does the availability of funds at any given time affect the special education process?

■ Why is cost-benefit analysis an inappropriate means of evaluating the effectiveness of special education programs?

*T*HE NATIONAL CENTER FOR EDUCATION STATISTICS collects, collates, and reports statistics on the condition of education in the United States. Since 1986, those statistics have been in the form of "indicators," reflecting the "health" of education and current trends (Elliot, 1988). Issues related to these indicators "have serious implications, not only for the effective operation of schools, but for future individual employment and U.S. economic competitiveness, and ultimately the kind of society that is emerging" (Stern, 1988, p. 1). They are a good place to start our examination of the social, political, and economic realities that affect special education.

THE CONDITION OF EDUCATION

Student enrollment is a basic component of any educational system. After a period of relative stability in the early 1980s, elementary school enrollment is projected to rise to almost 31 million students by 1997. Secondary enrollment is expected to fall for several years, then reach 13 million near the end of this century. Private school enrollments have remained relatively stable since 1970; about 10 percent of K through 12 students attend private schools. The total number of special education students rose between the 1978–79 school year and the 1986–87 school year, from 3.9 million to over 4.4 million. This increase was due primarily to growth in the number of students classified learning disabled, which exceeded the growth of all other groups combined (see Chapter 4).

Education costs money. Between the 1949–50 and 1985–86 school years, per student expenditures in the public schools more than tripled, from $960 to $3,752. Parochial schools are funded by religious organizations; other private schools are funded by tuition fees and independent sources. Public schools are funded by local, state, and federal governments. The share each contributes is determined by many factors: the perception of its role in supporting education, its tax base and the extent to which it taxes itself, and competing demands on tax revenues.

Although the cost of education has risen, apparently we are getting better value today for our tax dollars. The data tell us that average students receive more today relative to what typical taxpayers pay (Stern, 1988).

The number of teachers employed in public schools has grown substantially in recent years, from 1.4 million to 2.2 million. But the proportion of teachers in total staff has fallen, from 65 to 53 percent since 1960. Teachers' salaries have increased by almost 18 percent during this same period. Pupil/teacher ratios went from 22.3 in 1971 to 17.7 in 1988; when school size and level are taken into account, these ratios are no different for public and private schools. Demand for new teachers is expected to swell more than 35 percent by 1995. In a survey of public and private high school principals, more than half reported difficulty hiring fully qualified teachers in physics, chemistry, computer science, mathematics, and foreign languages, and 37 percent reported difficulty hiring special education teachers (Stern, 1988).

Safety in the schools and general attitudes toward school have a large impact on conditions for learning and support for education. Research indicates that a safe, orderly environment is necessary to promote academic success (Stern, 1988). Apparently in many classrooms, conditions are neither safe nor orderly. Almost one-third of the teachers recently surveyed said that they had considered leaving teaching because of students' misbehavior. The factors that contribute to students' difficulties in school are being left alone after school, living in poverty, having single-parent families or families in which both parents work, and teachers' not adapting to meet the needs of individual students (Stern, 1988).

Americans believe that education is an important investment. They hope the money, time, and energy spent on educating young people will produce adults who can lead productive lives and contribute to society. The long-term effects of schooling are difficult to measure. But recent indicators raise questions about the value of that investment (Stern, 1988):

- Average reading proficiency is lower for minority students, disadvantaged students, and males than for nonminority students, advantaged urban students, and females.

- All students have difficulty with tasks that require them to elaborate on or defend their judgments and interpretations of something they have read.

- Average math achievement remains low; many students in junior and senior high school are unable to perform basic operations (adding, subtracting, multiplying, dividing) adequately, solve problems using appropriate arithmetic, or use tables and charts to obtain comparative information.

- Most eleventh-graders know something about pioneers in technology, colonial history, economic history, geography, World War II, slavery, and the Bill of Rights; few can answer questions correctly about the approximate dates of historical events, recent history, or the women's movement.

- Students in grades 3, 7, and 11 average less than 50 percent correct on test items assessing computer competence.

- Students attending parochial high schools obtain an average Scholastic Aptitude Test (SAT) verbal score of 440; students attending independent private high schools score an average of 473; students attending public high schools average 428.

- Students attending parochial high schools obtain an average SAT math score of 469; students attending independent private high schools score an average of 519; students attending public high schools average 476.

There is a wide range of factors that contribute to the condition of education, and their interactions are complex. Of special concern today are declining academic performance, teachers' qualifications and training, violence in the schools, the declining involvement of parents, and increasing enrollments in special education classes. Professionals are responding to these concerns by renewing their commitment to "excellence" and "educational reform." Governments at all levels, the schools themselves, and colleges and universities are addressing these concerns by expanding academic programs, increasing requirements for high school graduation, developing new approaches to attract good teachers, and restructuring special education (Pugach, 1987; Stern, 1988; Will, 1986a).

The social, political, and economic factors that bear on educational practice also influence the practice of special education. Students participate in special education programs because their needs are not being met in regular education programs and because a long time ago members of society decided that these students should receive special services to help them profit from schooling. Some of these students have severe handicaps that make learning difficult for them. Others fail academic subjects, then are assigned a handicap by the schools. Still others just are not performing up to their potential. Identification, assessment, and instruction are complex activities. We cannot simply say that students who act one way are exceptional and students who act another way are not exceptional. It's not surprising that we sometimes have difficulty discussing public policy on the education of handicapped students. Not only do the factors that shape policy interact in complex ways, but they are constantly changing. And they often defy analysis because of inconsistencies in the ways in which services are delivered to students with special needs. The complex interrelationships among agencies, bureaus, divisions, professional associations, advocacy groups, teachers and other professionals, administrators, parents, and students sometimes obscure the roles of the many people other than teachers who work with and help exceptional students.

An example: Kim has several exceptional students in her class. In addition to five local supervisors of special education programs and a local director of special education, she periodically is called on by representatives of social service agencies, physicians, psychiatrists, and psychologists who are working with these students. Each of them has an agenda for what Kim "should" be doing to meet the special learning needs of particular students. And she has daily, weekly, or monthly progress reports to prepare for the state agencies that monitor professional practices.

The point is that when we teach exceptional students, the process involves much more than the interaction of teachers and students. It is always influenced, and at times controlled, by social, political, and economic factors.

SOCIAL FACTORS AND SPECIAL EDUCATION

Before we look at the individual factors that shape the practice of special education today, it's important to recognize that these factors do not operate independently; they interact and influence one another. In Chapter 11 we talked about the Head Start program, a program of intervention for preschool children that was created in 1965. Was Head Start a social, political, or economic innovation? Clearly the program had social origins and benefits: Providing educational opportunities for disadvantaged preschoolers improves their chances for success in later schooling and reduces the likelihood of their needing other special services. It also had political origins and benefits: Members of Congress and other political organizations fought to establish the program and continue to support it. And it was influenced by economic factors. The costs of prevention have reduced the costs of later special services; moreover, the program has added "producers" to society.

As you read this section and those that follow it, bear this in mind: There are no clear distinctions among the factors that influence special

Window on Practice

AN EDUCATION DEPARTment study released in 1988 documents a small but sudden jump in the number of students enrolled in special education programs nationwide.

The 1.2 percent increase in enrollments for the 1986–87 school year is the largest annual increase in the special education population since 1982, according to the report.

It follows three years in which the number of such students had appeared to level off, after rising steadily for nearly a decade.

The figures are contained in the *10th Annual Report of Congress on the Implementation of the Education of the Handicapped Act*. Published each year by the department's Office of Special Education and Rehabilitative Services, the study provides a statistical portrait of the status of special education programs.

Among its other findings—some of which were compiled for the first time—the study noted that:

- Most special education students are being served in school settings with their nonhandicapped classmates. The report indicates that more than 26 percent of the students received special education services in their regular classes; 41 percent were served in nearby resource rooms; and 24 percent were taught entirely in separate classrooms within their schools.

- Although most handicapped students graduate from high school with a diploma or a certificate of completion, the dropout rate among special education students increased by 5 percent, to 26 percent, in 1987. An average of 312 handicapped students drop out of school each day.

- Federal compliance reviews of programs in 29 states indicate that states are still having problems with some of the most basic provisions of the 12-year-old federal law.

Some of the areas that have proved most troublesome include: monitoring local special education programs; ensuring that children are placed in the "least restrictive" educational environment possible; managing complaints; and generally supervising special education programs.

- While the number of special education teachers employed nationwide increased by 6 percent during 1985–86, an additional 27,474 teachers were still needed to fill vacancies and replace uncertified instructors.

Education Department statisticians said they were at a loss to explain the increase in the total number of special education students.

"The atypically large increase," the report says, "could not be attributed to just a few states."

Among the various special education categories, the greatest increase occurred in the number of children classified as learning disabled—the most common of all handicapping conditions.

The number of students in that category increased by 2.9 percent last year, to 53,758, according to the report. Such children represent 43.7 percent of the total special education population.

"Learning disabled is a soft category, subject to variable interpretations," Judith Singer, one expert who has studied the increase, said.

"There is some evidence to suggest that special education has been used to provide supplemental services to kids in need when other federal monies are drying up, such as Chapter 1 or bilingual education funding," added Ms. Singer, an assistant professor at the Harvard University Graduate School of Education. In addition, she said, the learning disabled "label" is less stigmatizing than those of other categories.

"In some ways, it's much easier to classify an inner-city black kid as learning disabled when there are white kids in the suburbs who are also learning disabled," she said. In recent years, the increase in that category has been accompanied by significant decreases in the number of students classified as mentally retarded.

That trend continued in 1987, according to the report, which notes that 3.2 percent fewer children were labeled mentally retarded in 1986–87 than in the previous year.

While many experts have reasoned that children are being shifted from the mentally retarded to the learning disabled classification, the report suggests that such shifts were not widespread.

For example, the report points out that only two states reported both a substantial increase in the number of learning disabled students and a substantial decrease in the number of mentally retarded pupils.

"While some children may have been reclassified, the increase in the number of learning disabled children and the decrease in mentally retarded occurred for the most part in different places," the report says.

As another possible reason for the rise in learning disabled students, the report cites research linking such increases to reform measures that have strengthened academic requirements in recent years.

"Higher standards in the name of educational reform seem to be exaggerating the tendency to refer difficult children to special education," the report states, referring to a 1987 study.

The study, conducted by North Carolina's Research Triangle Institute, also found that "teachers engaged in fewer supportive activities because they needed to achieve higher overall goals by year's end."

Source: *Debra Viadero, "Study Documents Jump in Special Education Enrollments," Education Week, March 2, 1988. Reprinted by permission of the publisher.*

education. They work together to affect the ways in which special education is practiced.

How Do Social Values Influence Policy?

Many of society's resources are limited. People hold social values, opinions and beliefs that influence how those limited resources are distributed. These social values affect who receives special education services, who pays for them, which services are provided, where they are delivered, when they are delivered, and how they are delivered. Social values are not absolute. Different people hold different values or hold the same values in different degrees. For some, education is a critically important social value;

for others, it is less important than a new civic center, good roads, or a strong system of national defense. We voice our social values by voting in local, state, and national elections for candidates who believe as we do, and by forming or joining advocacy groups.

Why do we have schools? Why does society value education? The social value of education is the contribution those who are educated make to the general social welfare. In recognition of that contribution, education has become a right of all people in the United States, including those with handicaps. But there is a difference between the recognition of a right and its implementation. In principle, society agrees that handicapped students have a right to a free appropriate education; conflict arises, however, when it comes to defining what that means. In large part, the issues are economic. Special equipment, special treatment, and transportation are all costly. By deciding to provide special services, we are forced to decide who receives them, how they are delivered, who provides them, and how they are paid for.

Social values are always changing. The general social climate, national and international, has a strong impact on educational policy. Social attitudes toward education in general and toward specific aspects of special education shifted radically, for example, after the Soviets launched Sputnik in 1957. The event led to new programs to educate young handicapped children, disadvantaged students, and gifted students. More recently, we've seen a change in classification practices: The number of students classified mentally retarded has decreased; the number of students classified learning disabled has increased dramatically (see Chapters 4 and 5). Cure rates have not improved for mental retardation, and epidemic illnesses have not caused more students to be learning disabled. The change is a response to society's willingness to provide services for students with learning disabilities and to the legal actions in recent years surrounding decisions to label students *mentally retarded.*

The influence of social factors on special education is probably no more apparent than in the education of very young children (cf. Ysseldyke & Algozzine, 1982). Early intervention has become the fastest growing area in special education. During the first part of the twentieth century, the education of very young children with special needs was a concern of a small dedicated group of educators. Initially, private monies were used to finance this effort, and preschool programs for children with handicaps were operated largely by independent agencies or parent organizations (like the United Cerebral Palsy Association). Designed to provide relief for parents, these agencies were the first to make available educational services of direct benefit to young children. Interest in early childhood education revived during the 1960s—partly because Americans had entered a fierce scientific rivalry with the Soviet Union and partly because, as the post–World War II economy slackened, large numbers of women were en-

In 1973 revised federal regulations stipulated that at least 10 percent of all children served by Head Start must be identified as handicapped, marking the first time that the education of handicapped and nonhandicapped preschoolers was required to take place in one setting.

(© Michael D. Sullivan/ Texastock)

tering the work force and needed child care for infants, toddlers, and preschoolers.

Another factor was that an increasing number of students were not meeting the academic and behavioral standards of public schools. The Head Start program was a response to this, a way to help disadvantaged children adapt to the educational program by giving them learning readiness skills. In 1973, the program's regulations were modified to stipulate that at least 10 percent of all children served by Head Start must be identified as handicapped (LaVor & Harvey, 1976). For the first time, the education of handicapped and nonhandicapped preschoolers was required to take place in the same setting.

How Are Ethnic Origin and Treatment Related?

In 1968 Dunn published an article in *Exceptional Children* challenging the labeling of socioculturally disadvantaged students as mentally retarded. Although probably not as a direct consequence of this article but certainly in response to social pressure about the status of those labeled *retarded*, the American Association on Mental Deficiency changed its criteria for mental retardation (see Chapter 5). Before 1973, a score below 85 on an individually administered intelligence test was used to classify a student mentally retarded; in 1973, the AAMD lowered the cut-off score to 70. In reacting to the change, Blatt (1981) noted that "the most recent, little appreciated but astonishing revision of the American Association on Mental Deficiency [AAMD] definition of mental retardation . . . literally revolutionized the incidence, prevalence, and concept of mental retardation, all with the simple stroke of Herbert Grossman's pen [Grossman was then president of the AAMD]" (p. 27).

In a study of classification practices used with black, white, and Mexican-American students over a seven-year (1970–1977) period, Tucker (1980) uncovered the following facts:

■ From 1970 to 1977, the percentage of the total school population enrolled in special education grew rapidly.

■ From 1970 to 1977 the proportion of students from all three racial groups enrolled in special education increased significantly. By 1977, 15.2 percent of all black students were enrolled in special classes, versus 11.1 percent of white students and 11.5 percent of Mexican-American students.

■ From 1970 to 1977, the number of students labeled *learning disabled* increased significantly, and the overall number of students labeled *educable mentally retarded* fell correspondingly.

■ From 1973 to 1977, the largest proportional increase in enrollment was of black students in classes for those with learning disabilities. The number of black students classified educable mentally retarded significantly decreased, but overall the number of black students enrolled in special education increased.

He concluded:

> It does not take much imagination to infer that there is at least the possibility that when it was no longer socially desirable to place black students in EMR [educable mentally retarded] classes, it became convenient to place them in the newly provided LD [learning disabled] category. (Tucker, 1980, pp. 103–104)

Recent government statistics offer further support for relations between student characteristics and educational experiences. For example, in discussing school dropouts in the United States, Pallas (1987) presented the following observations:

■ Students in urban areas are more likely to drop out of school than those in rural or suburban areas.

■ Students in public schools drop out more than those in Catholic schools.

- Blacks (17 percent) and Hispanics (18 percent) are more likely to drop out than whites (12 percent).
- Dropout rates are highest for American Indians and Alaskan natives (29 percent) and lowest for Asian Americans (3 percent).
- Males are more likely to leave school before graduation than females.
- Students from lower socioeconomic backgrounds are more likely to drop out.

Information provided in the 1987 edition of *The Condition of Education* (Stern & Chandler, 1987) is also revealing:

- The number of students receiving special education rose from 9.1 percent of all students in 1978 to 11 percent in 1984.
- The reasons for the rise are specific to each condition, and growth did not characterize all categories.
- The greatest increase occurred in gifted and talented classes where the proportion more than doubled.
- The proportion of Asian and Pacific Islanders in gifted programs was about twice the average for all students.
- The percentage of specific learning disabled students nearly doubled during the same time period.
- The proportion of white, black, and hispanic students all rose by more than 70 percent.

Other relations between special education classifications for members of different racial and ethnic groups are illustrated in Table 12.1. Participation of students from different ethnic groups approximates their distribution in the general population most closely in the learning disability, emotional disturbance, and speech impaired categories, although Asian students are underrepresented in each of these groups. Within the mental retardation category, white and Asian students appear to be underrepresented and black students are overrepresented. Asian students are overrepresented in gifted and talented programs, whereas black, hispanic, and American Indian students are underrepresented.

In some of our own research, we examined the extent to which parental social status influences classification decisions (Algozzine & Ysseldyke, 1981; Ysseldyke & Algozzine, 1982). We gave more than two hundred decision makers identical data on a student referred for evaluation. All data were indicative of normal or average performance. In half the cases, we said the child's father was a bank vice president and the mother was a real estate agent. In the rest, decision makers were told the child's father was a janitor

Table 12.1
Participation of Racial and Ethnic Groups in Special Education

	Racial/Ethnic Group				
	White	*Black*	*Hispanic*	*Asian*	*Indian*
Learning disabled (LD):					
Percent LD	4.20	4.50	4.50	1.60	5.20
Percent of LD	71.24	17.35	9.77	0.96	1.14
Percent of general population	71.20	16.20	9.10	2.50	0.90
Mentally retarded (MR):					
Percent MR	1.20	3.50	1.50	0.50	1.70
Percent of MR	56.99	37.79	9.12	0.84	1.04
Percent of general population	71.20	16.20	9.10	2.50	0.90
Emotionally disturbed (ED):					
Percent ED	0.60	0.80	0.40	0.10	0.50
Percent of ED	71.24	21.59	6.08	0.42	0.77
Percent of general population	71.20	16.20	9.10	2.50	0.90
Speech impaired (SI):					
Percent SI	2.70	2.40	2.00	1.70	2.50
Percent of SI	76.94	15.55	7.30	1.71	0.92
Percent of general population	71.20	16.20	9.10	2.50	0.90
Gifted and talented (GT):					
Percent GT	4.70	2.20	2.10	8.30	2.00
Percent of GT	79.92	8.48	4.56	4.98	0.44
Percent of general population	71.20	16.20	9.10	2.50	0.90

Source: Derived from information provided in J. D. Stern & M. O. Chandler, (1987). *The condition of education: A statistical report.* Washington, DC: Office of Educational Research and Improvement, Center for Education Statistics, pp. 64, 66.

at the bank and the mother was a check-out clerk at a local supermarket. Different classification and placement decisions were made for the child on the basis of the different social environments.

The effects of parental socioeconomic status also are evident in a study of differential procedures and outcomes for upper-class versus lower-class parents at due process hearings. Budoff and Orenstein (1981) found that the issue for most upper-class parents was getting schools to pay the costs of sending their handicapped children to private schools. (In 70 percent of the cases that came to hearings, the child already had been enrolled in a private school at the parents' expense, and parents were seeking reimbursement.) The issue at hearings involving lower-status parents was typically one of trying to get appropriate services for their children in public school settings.

Significant numbers of mentally retarded students were not "cured" when eligibility criteria changed. Instead, social perceptions of the condition changed, and the condition itself, as reflected in its new definition, changed. And significant numbers of black students once labeled *mentally retarded* did not become learning disabled. Instead, the learning disabled category became available and was socially acceptable (Tucker, 1980). We think these data illustrate vividly that social attitudes and perceptions influence what happens in special education, and that what happens in special education influences the way members of society think about it.

Checkpoint	■ *Identifying whether a particular trend in public policy for the education of exceptional students has a social, economic, or political cause is difficult because of the interaction of these factors.*
	■ *People's opinions and beliefs are their social values, and those values influence every aspect of special education.*
	■ *The general social climate, national and international, affects public policy on the education of students with handicaps.*
	■ *Many recent changes in special education were a response to the overrepresentation of minority and culturally disadvantaged students in special classes.*

POLITICAL FACTORS AND SPECIAL EDUCATION

A variety of political factors, closely related to social and economic factors, have significant (some would say profound) effects on public policy for the education of students who are handicapped. Changes in that public policy come about through political action. That action stems from shifts in social attitudes and values, and is influenced by and has an impact on economic factors.

How Do Political Values Influence Policy?

First, the general political climate influences public policy in special education (Burrello & Sage, 1979). In a liberal or progressive political climate, special education services tend to become more available; the resources for delivering services are greater. In a conservative political climate, efforts are made to limit services. During the 1960s, a liberal period, many new

Window on Practice

SOMETIMES I LET THE snow get to me and 'long about March I become cynical. I am anxious to move out and about: I look at my calendar and get excited about the arrival of spring, but when I do finally leave my barrier-free home, the diminishing snow reveals so many STEPS . . . . Help—help! Society is shunning me. What shall I do?

It's easy to let yourself be discriminated against when you are disabled. I hear references all the time to the disabled as "special" people with "special" needs. I always ask myself, "What's so special about having to go to the bathroom or wanting to cross the street?" Steps discriminate against anyone who uses a wheelchair to get around in this world. Yet building with fewer of them does not lessen the problem. It only takes one step to discriminate.

After coping with the steps in my former house, I moved four years ago to a house where I occupied the lower flat. No steps—no problem. Did I have it made in the shade? I had a ramp built to act as my bridge from the sidewalk to my front door. It turns and slopes over four steps, is three feet wide, and is built pier style (so the wood can breathe in the summer) out of treated lumber (which can be textured with sand in the sealer to prevent wheels from slipping).

I soon learned that mere elimination of steps was not the total solution to my problems. I thought I could call this house "home" because my wheelchair could fit in the bathroom, unlike the bathroom at my previous house. But very soon I realized that, once in the bathroom, there was not enough space to do anything. Once again the cry rings out . . . **HELP!**

Further, the apartment's pea-green carpet had inches of padding. Maneuvering through the rooms was exhausting—I felt like I was in the middle of an Easter basket.

Usually, most residential doors are too narrow to qualify as barrier-free. My chair is 24" wide, but with my hands on the push-rims, the measure is 26 1/2" knuckle to knuckle. There were two 27" doorways on either side of my kitchen sink—ouch!!!—and the sink itself was totally unapproachable.

I got mad, and then I made a lot of changes.

The carpet went. Hardwood floors and mop boards and elimination of thresholds and door jambs make the best surface for moving around. Any door that was not absolutely needed came off. Doors needed to cover closets and close bathrooms and bedrooms were changed to sliding doors. These can slide open to the desired width without creating the clearance problem common to all conventional, hinged swing-out doors.

The unapproachable sink went next, being replaced by a double-basin corner sink mounted not in the corner but facing straight out from a flat wall at its normal height. A swiveling, high goose-necked faucet was used and the two together resulted in success. The sink, mounted in the wall and not to the floor, provides access for the wheelchair and makes the room look more spacious.

My stove, mounted at tabletop height, also provides access for the wheelchair with its accommodating wall mount. And the kitchen table itself is mounted in the wall. Of course, changes such as the ones I've made cost money. A safe and functional barrier-free environment can be expensive. I've kept costs down somewhat by retrofitting with standard products.

There is customizing involved here, but most of it is done by application. I install appliances in a different way, rendering them functional, such as eliminating legs from the kitchen sink, stove, and table to create room for my wheelchair.

Designers, investors, and builders complain of the high cost of remodeling to achieve accessible environments. Everyone learns from hindsight. I suggest more foresight is needed. As long as barrier-free environments are dealt with as an aftersight in the design process, there is great expense involved.

How can we qualify the psychological trauma that comes from trying to function in an unsafe environment? It is easy and cost effective to make changes with a pencil and eraser at the blueprint stage, rather than making changes with the sledge hammer and crow bar after a house has been built.

In the fall of 1988, Congress passed the Fair Housing Act. This means that both children and disabled people will be included in new housing plans. The law gives the disabled a needed legal platform (unprecedented to date), which will initiate some changes including an increase in construction of barrier-free housing. Why not go one better than the new fair housing law and begin to design and build all housing for everyone? Let's stop discriminating.

Source: *Patty Hayes, "Creating the Barrier-Free Environment,"* Habitat World, *June 1989. Reprinted with permission of Habitat for Humanity International.*

federal programs were initiated for handicapped and disadvantaged students. In the late 1970s and 1980s, a conservative period, fiscal restraint was evident. Major questions were raised about the benefits of special education services, funding for programs was cut, and proposals to abolish the U.S. Department of Education were made.

Burrello and Sage (1979) also identify legislatures and courts as external forces that contribute to public policy on the education of handicapped students (see Chapter 2). Since the early 1970s, there has been a kind of quiet revolution taking place in these two policy arenas. In 1972, only 70 percent of the states had mandatory legislation requiring the education of handicapped students; by 1975, all but two states had this kind of legislation (Abeson, 1979). In the courts, a series of decisions has redefined the educational rights of handicapped students. Those with handicaps also have won protections from unusual and cruel treatment in institutions, from employment in institutions without reimbursement or rehabilitative purpose; and from involuntary institutionalization, and the rights to vote, to marry and procreate, to travel on public transportation, and to have access to public buildings (Weintraub, Abeson, Ballard, & LaVor, 1976).

How Do People Who Are Handicapped Achieve Rights?

Significant and obvious parallels exist between the ways in which handicapped individuals and members of other disenfranchised groups have

Individuals with handicaps have used court decisions to redefine their rights to public education and to vote, marry and procreate, travel on public transportation, and have access to public buildings; they also have won protection from economic exploitation, cruel and unusual treatment, and involuntary institutionalization.

(© Sarah Putnam/The Picture Cube)

achieved, and are continuing to achieve, constitutional rights. The process typically begins with the organization of a formal advocacy group. The National Organization for Women (NOW), for example, advocates for women's rights, and the National Association for the Advancement of Colored People (NAACP) advocates for the rights of blacks. In the same way, parents formed the National Association for Retarded Citizens and the Learning Disabilities Association (LDA) to advocate for their children.

Advocacy groups tend to focus their efforts on state and federal legislation. Most employ lobbyists and their constituents' votes to sway lawmakers. When it is difficult or impossible to influence legislation, efforts shift to litigation. State departments of education and local school districts have been sued for failing to meet the rights of students with handicaps. The class action suit has played a special role here. In Chapter 5 we talked about *PARC* v. *Commonwealth of Pennsylvania*, (1971). A consent decree in that case guaranteed all mentally retarded children in Pennsylvania the right to a free and appropriate public education. The decision in *Larry P.* v. *Riles* (1979) forced the San Francisco school district and the California Department of Education to stop using intelligence tests to place black students in classes for the mentally retarded (see Chapter 2).

Sometimes a government agency protects or furthers the rights of handicapped individuals. For example, both the U.S. Office of Civil Rights and the Bureau of Indian Affairs often influence the provision of services for those with handicaps.

Table 12.2
AFT Guidelines for the Implementation of Least Restrictive Environment Placements

1. Not all handicapped children benefit from being placed in the "mainstream." So-called restrictive environments such as residential institutions, resource centers, and self-contained special education classrooms in many cases offer the child developmental opportunities that would be impossible to achieve in a "less restrictive" setting.
2. Placement of handicapped children should be decided on an individual basis, based on the readiness of the special student and the preparedness of the receiving classroom to meet individual children's special needs.
3. Placement decisions should take into consideration a child's social and emotional developmental opportunities, as well as intellectual and physical development.
4. Teachers should be involved in placement decisions to ensure acceptance of the exceptional child in the classroom and to evaluate the capability of the classroom to accommodate the individual child's special needs. Regular teachers should be informed of special placements in their classes.
5. Transitional periods are often necessary to prepare both handicapped and nonhandicapped students to adjust to new situations.
6. Staff development programs to prepare teachers to work with exceptional children in their classes must be available prior to such placements, and continuous support and training are necessary to meet problems as they arise. It is often overlooked that special education teachers specialize in certain areas and may require in-service training when assigned children with disabilities in which they have little or no expertise. In-service training also is needed for paraprofessionals and other support personnel.
7. Class sizes must be kept low in special education whether in a "restrictive" environment or in the regular classroom to ensure the necessary individualization of instruction.
8. Certified special education teachers must be retained to continue to meet the needs of children in special classes and to work with regular teachers in developing appropriate instructional programs for exceptional children.
9. Counselors, psychologists, psychiatrists, and other auxiliary personnel must be readily available to special and regular teachers.
10. Teachers should have regularly scheduled release time for consultations with support personnel.
11. Instructional materials, equipment, and facilities must be adapted to the needs of exceptional children in the regular classroom and throughout the school.
12. Scheduling of the educational program and buses should conform to the needs of exceptional children rather than vice versa.
13. Safeguards should exist to see that funds designated for special education follow the child, even if in a less restrictive environment, including the regular classroom.

Source: From "What Can Be Expected of the Regular Teacher? Ideals and Realities" by M. Rauth, 1981, *Exceptional Education Quarterly, 2*, pp. 32–33. Reprinted by permission.

Finally, the Council for Exceptional Children and other professional organizations also advocate for people who are handicapped. The American Federation of Teachers (AFT) has published a set of guidelines for the implementation of least restrictive environment placements for handicapped students (Table 12.2). When a powerful political association like the AFT sets guidelines, and when regular education teachers, through collective action, advocate the use of those guidelines, there is an impact on the policy of educating exceptional students.

How Are Categories and Eligibility Criteria Determined?

School personnel somehow must decide which students of the many with academic problems should receive special help. Today they rely primarily on the classification systems we described in Chapter 7. Students are declared eligible for special services by showing evidence of certain conditions. Although all classification systems use criteria to establish eligibility, those criteria are not universal and often are difficult to understand and implement.

Ultimately, society provides special education services to whomever it wants. When students need learning help, new categories are created. When providing services to these students becomes difficult or unrealistic, the categories are modified. Eligibility decisions are clearly political. Policymakers at all levels decide what definitions and criteria are used, and their decisions often are made in response to pressure from different advocacy groups. For example, in the early 1960s, founders of the Learning Disabilities Association (then called the Association for Children with Learning Disabilities) lobbied for legislation to fund model programs, teacher training programs, information dissemination, and research to develop services for students with learning disabilities.

Eligibility decisions are made at the school district level. At one time these decisions were made by individual psychologists or administrators. Now, the law mandates that these decisions be made by teams of educators and special education service personnel. The teams try to follow local, state, or federal classification criteria. But in reality, the decisions they make are political. They serve certain students because teachers, parents, and advocacy groups want these students served or because there are resources available to serve them. They don't serve certain students because teachers, parents, and advocacy groups do not want these students served or because there are no resources to serve them.

Checkpoint

■ *A number of political factors, closely interrelated with social and economic factors, have significant, even profound, effects on public policy for the education of handicapped students.*

■ *Advocacy groups have played an enormous role in securing and protecting the rights of exceptional people; these groups focus their efforts on state and federal legislation.*

■ *Eligibility decisions reflect both the influence of teachers, parents, and advocacy groups, and the availability of resources.*

Education—general and special—is a social service that must compete for dollars with highways, sanitation, and other services. To the extent that members of society value special education more than other services, special education is financed more heavily.

(© George Bellerose/ Stock, Boston)

ECONOMIC FACTORS AND SPECIAL EDUCATION

As a social service, education in general and special education in particular must compete for dollars with highways, sanitation, and other services. To the extent that members of society value special education more than other services, special education is financed more heavily. Special education also competes with regular education for financial resources. From all the funds provided for education, monies must be allocated between general and special education. When a state increases the percentage of monies allocated to special education, monies allocated to general education typically go down.

Government spending patterns influence public policy on the education of handicapped students, although we also could argue that those spending patterns reflect public policy. If you want to know where the most research activity in special education will take place over the next five years, look at the research priorities established by the U.S. Department of Education. During the 1950s and 1960s, the federal government made mental retardation a priority, and centers for research on mental retardation were established across the country. As funding priorities changed, new centers were established and old ones changed their names and expanded their missions. During the middle and late 1970s, institutes were funded to conduct research on learning disabilities and on early intervention. In the 1980s there was less federal support for research on learning disabilities. Instead, support shifted to research on students with severe handicaps and transition services for older students with handicaps. In the 1990s, emphasis will be on early childhood education. Decisions to shift research efforts often are motivated by economics: Researchers go "where the money is."

The overall pool of monies available to provide special education services must be divided among all exceptional students. This creates competition for resources among the various categorical programs. If a fixed amount of money is available to educate handicapped students, and if school personnel decide to spend a greater proportion of that money on educating students who are deaf, then less money is available for educating students with other exceptionalities.

Decisions about where to put monies are guided by public perceptions of disabilities (Hahn, 1989). For example, if people think about a disability in terms of its medical effects, then they want to spend money on finding a cure and improving methods of prevention. A sociopolitical perspective focuses on the interactions between people and their environments; it traces the problems of a disability to external obstacles. Section 504 of the Rehabilitation Act of 1973 was a response to the sociopolitical perspective. The law made it illegal to discriminate against a person because of a disability and guaranteed equal access to public buildings and means of transportation (see Chapter 2).

One of the most widely endorsed perspectives on disability has to do with the individual's ability to perform a productive role in society. We can see this perspective at work in the way the Census Bureau assesses disability: Does this person have a physical, mental, or other health condition that has lasted six or more months and that limits the kind or amount of work this person can do at a job, or prevents this person from working at a job? (Haber & McNeil, 1983). Definitions of disability that use ability to work as an indicator of productivity are economic. When they are dominant, we see monies funneled into transition programs and vocational education. We also see schools criticized for not teaching "functional" (work-oriented) skills and for not producing citizens who can contribute to society through gainful employment.

Who Pays for Special Education Services?

Special education services cost money. Who pays for them? In a few instances, parents, private industry, or private organizations do, especially when services are provided in private schools or private residential facilities. More generally, the public—through federal, state, and local tax dollars—pays the cost of educating exceptional students.

Dollars for education in general, and for special education in particular, come from federal, state, and local governments. It is difficult to esti-

Sometimes parents, private industry, or private organizations pay for special education services, especially when services are provided by private facilities, such as project RIDE, but federal, state, and local tax dollars pay the cost of educating most exceptional students.

(© Randolph Falk/Jeroboam)

mate the proportion available from each source because the amount of money spent on education varies from state to state. In the 1970–71 academic year, about 53 percent of funding for all education came from local sources, 39 percent came from state governments, and 8 percent came from the federal government. In the 1978–79 school year, the states' share of revenues rose above the local share for the first time (Stern, 1988). Table 12.3 and Figure 12.1 illustrate trends in revenue receipts of public elementary and secondary schools from federal, state, and local sources.

These data indicate that state and local governments are the primary source of revenues for public schools. However, in areas where state and local support is low, federal sources may provide as much as 20 to 30 percent of the monies spent on education. According to information presented in the Tenth Annual Report to Congress (USDE, 1988), federal contribution through state grant programs to support education of handicapped students has increased from $251,770,000 in FY 1977 to $1,338,000,000 in FY 1987. Accordingly, the per child allocation has increased from $72 per student to $315 during that same period. Despite this increase, the relative percentage of federal support remains around 12 percent of the total cost of educating students with handicaps.

The question of who is responsible for funding programs is actively debated among and within the different levels of government. Debate is especially intense when federal laws mandate services that state or local education agencies are expected to pay for. Ultimately, the schools are responsible for providing all services that students need, including related services (speech and language therapy, counseling, physical therapy, medical services). They must work with local agencies to determine who pays for each service. What happens if they can't raise needed money? They have to pay for related services themselves. This process has serious implications: When funds are limited, administrative personnel may discourage teachers and others from recommending needed related services.

Table 12.3
Revenue Receipts of Public Elementary and Secondary Schools from Federal, State, and Local Sources, 1919–20 School Year to 1984–85 School Year

	Percentage Distribution		
School Year	*Federal*	*State*	*Local (including intermediate)* *
1919–20	0.3	16.5	83.2
1929–30	0.4	16.9	82.7
1939–40	1.8	30.3	68.0
1941–42	1.4	31.4	67.1
1943–44	1.4	33.0	65.6
1945–46	1.4	34.7	63.9
1947–48	2.8	38.9	58.3
1949–50	2.9	39.8	57.3
1951–52	3.5	38.6	57.9
1953–54	4.5	37.4	58.1
1955–56	4.6	39.5	55.9
1957–58	4.0	39.4	56.6
1959–60	4.4	39.1	56.5
1961–62	4.3	38.7	56.9
1963–64	4.4	39.3	56.3
1965–66	7.9	39.1	53.0
1967–68	8.8	38.5	52.7
1969–70	8.0	39.9	52.1
1970–71	8.4	39.1	52.5
1971–72	8.9	38.3	52.8
1972–73	8.7	40.0	51.3
1973–74	8.5	41.4	50.1
1974–75	9.0	42.2	48.8
1975–76	8.9	44.6	46.5
1976–77	8.8	43.4	47.8

Table 12.3 *(cont.)*
Revenue Receipts of Public Elementary and Secondary Schools from Federal, State, and Local Sources, 1919–20 School Year to 1984–85 School Year

	Percentage Distribution		
School Year	*Federal*	*State*	*Local (including intermediate)**
1977–78	9.4	43.0	47.6
1978–79	9.8	45.6	44.6
1979–80	9.8	46.8	43.4
1980–81	9.2	47.4	43.4
1981–82	7.4	47.6	45.0
1982–83[†]	7.1	47.9	45.0
1983–84[†]	6.8	47.8	45.4
1984–85[††]	6.5	48.8	44.7

Note: Because of rounding, details may not add to 100 percent.
* Includes a relatively small amount from nongovernmental sources (gifts and tuition and transportation fees from patrons). These sources accounted for 0.4 percent of total revenue receipts in 1967–68.
[†] Revised from previously published figures.
[††] Preliminary data.
Source: From *Statistics of State School Systems; Revenues and Expenditures for Public Elementary and Secondary Education;* 1986, Washington, DC: U.S. Department of Education, National Center for Education Statistics; and Center for Education Statistics, *Common Core of Data* survey.

How Are the Monies Allocated?

The federal dollars that support the implementation of Public Law 94–142 are distributed in the form of formula grants based on the number of students being served. Different funding mechanisms give districts lots of opportunities to manipulate the identification of students. Biklen (1989) put it this way:

> It is not hard to imagine the programmatic imperatives that can derive from such funding mechanisms. If state reimbursement rates provide more funding for learning disabilities than for "slow learners" or underachievers, for example, the ranks of students labeled "learning disabled" can be expected to expand. Similarly, if a state provides near total funding for certain types of services (e.g., for private or state residential schools), and a far less substantial allotment for serving students in their home districts, local school boards might be tempted to "place" more students outside the district. These effects of fiscal incentives have been well documented. (p. 9)

Most of the funding for special education comes from state and local treasuries. Considerable variation exists, both among and within states, in

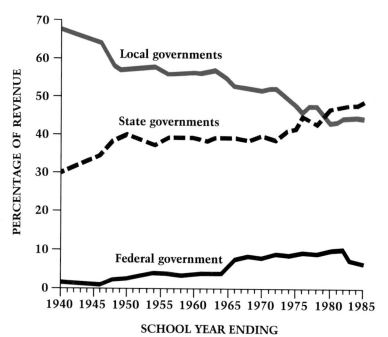

Figure 12.1
Sources of Revenue for Public Elementary and Secondary Schools, 1939–40 School Year to 1984–85 School Year

Source: From *Statistics of State School Systems; Revenues and Expenditures for Public Elementary and Secondary Education;* 1986, Washington, DC: U. S. Department of Education, National Center for Education Statistics; and Center for Education Statistics, *Common Core of Data* survey.

the ways in which special education funds are distributed. But, as Biklen (1989) points out, the "standard state funding mechanisms for special services include one of the following: direct subsidy for special services (e.g., transportation, counseling, resource room programs); funding of types of personnel (e.g., special teachers, itinerant teachers); or per capita student funding" (p. 8).

Special Program Reimbursement

One approach to funding that seems equitable allocates monies to districts on the basis of both the kinds of students served and the kinds of services provided (counseling, resource room programs, special classes). This method recognizes that it is more expensive to serve some categories of students than others, and that within any one category the intensity of service (and so the cost) for certain students varies. It recognizes that students with different degrees of handicap need different intensities of treatment. Some require full-time services in self-contained classrooms; others need only part-time service in a resource room. Different reimbursement formulas are used to reflect this variation. For example, in Florida a multiplier of 4.2 is used to allocate resources for each student who is mentally retarded and one of 7.1 is used for each student who is learning disabled. Within each category, other distinctions are made based on the level of services needed. Burrello and Sage (1979) report that this procedure has led to the establishment of fifteen different funding options in Florida, "with cost factors ranging from 2.3 to 15.0, using the full-time equivalent (FTE) of student time in each program as the basis for revenue allocation" (p. 257).

The special program reimbursement approach gives districts two opportunities to manipulate the identification of students. A district is rewarded not only for "finding" certain kinds of students but also for declaring the students more severely handicapped (that is, in need of more costly services).

Teacher Unit

In some states, monies are allocated to special education according to the number of full-time special education personnel employed by individual districts. State education department personnel make a decision to provide funding for a certain proportion of the salaries of special education personnel. For example, the state might fund 30, 60, or even 90 percent of the salary of each faculty member teaching special students.

For this type of funding to work, the state education department must make assumptions about a reasonable number of personnel for a given district. These assumptions usually are based on community demographics (socioeconomic level, population, per capita income). The department also must monitor districts to be sure that the right students are receiving services.

The teacher-unit method for funding services has one major educational implication: It discourages schools from identifying large numbers of handicapped students. More students mean larger classes, not more money. Under teacher-unit funding, only more teachers means more funds.

Pupil Unit

In some states, funding for special education is based on the numbers of students served. It costs more to educate handicapped than nonhandicapped students. These "excess costs" are the basis for a reimbursement figure that is used in deciding how to distribute monies. State departments of education typically pay districts a per pupil expenditure. They multiply this number by a factor (like 1.25 or 4.0) to pay the costs of educating handicapped students, based on estimates of how much extra it costs to teach certain types of students. Suppose a state typically pays $2,500 per student.

If the multiplier used is 2.3, $5,750 would be allocated for the education of each handicapped student.

A major disadvantage of funding by pupil unit is that it encourages "bounty hunting." The more students of specific types a district declares handicapped and serves, the more money the district receives. Creative administrators can manage their funds very effectively by manipulating child counts and "serving" more students.

In some states, funding is based on the recognition that it is more costly to educate some kinds of handicapped students than others. Funding procedures are like those used in funding on the basis of pupil units, but different multipliers are used for different categories. The state education department might decide that it costs twice as much to educate students who are blind than it does to educate students who are learning disabled. If schools receive 2.3 times the regular per pupil allocation for each learning disabled student, they would receive 4.6 times the regular allocation for blind students. This system has a direct educational implication. It encourages schools to categorize students according to financial return as well as, or instead of, educational need. Classification decisions may be driven more by payoffs to the system than by payoffs to the child when weighted pupil units are used to allocate monies.

What Are the Costs of Special Education?

The "total cost of special education and related services per handicapped child served in 1977–78 was an estimated $3,577." This figure was "2.17 times greater than the comparable cost of regular education per nonhandicapped child" (Kakalik, Furry, Thomas, & Carney, 1981, p. 5). Other studies support the contention that the general cost of educating a special needs student is about twice that of other students (Lipsky & Gartner, 1989; Raphael, Singer, & Walker, 1985).

In nearly all instances, the largest component of cost for educating handicapped students is personnel cost. About 80 percent of the funds for special education are used to pay teachers and other direct service personnel. In addition to personnel costs, schools incur expenses for transportation, food service, health, and rehabilitation services (Figure 12.2). For example, they incur high transportation costs when they must design special buses for students in wheelchairs, especially when only four to six students can be transported at once or when they must be transported over long distances (as they are in some rural areas, where districts combine services). Schools also incur costs for the purchase or modification of equipment for severely handicapped students. In general, the more severely handicapped the student, the more costly the program.

Estimating the cost of providing special education services is difficult (Sage, 1987). The best we can do is cite national averages. Several factors

The largest component (80%) of cost for educating handicapped students is personnel, but schools incur expenses for transportation, food service, health, equipment, and rehabilitation services.

(© Rose Skytta/Jeroboam)

influence our estimates. First, the provision of funds for special education is primarily a responsibility of state and local government agencies. These agencies support special education in different degrees, reflecting the extent to which the state or the individual community values the education of handicapped students.

Community size also contributes to variation in costs. In rural communities, only two or three students may need a particular type of service. The cost of providing that service is high. Typically, rural school districts enter into cooperative arrangements with one another to provide services for students who evidence low-incidence handicapping conditions. But even when cooperative or consortium arrangements are made, money must be spent on transportation and personnel.

The cost of providing special education services also varies as a function of the nature of the handicapping condition. As we said above, it costs more to provide educational and related services to severely handicapped students than to students who are less handicapped. Shell (1981) reports:

> It is not uncommon for one child to require a traveling chair, a stand-in table, a tilt table, and a wheelchair desk built or modified to the chair's specifications. The cost of this equipment can easily exceed $7,000 per child. Many kinds of equipment must be replaced as the child's functional ability changes or as the child's size increases. Special equipment to use in teaching self-feeding skills or for communication with children having limited oral language can also push the equipment cost per child into the thousands. (p. 8)

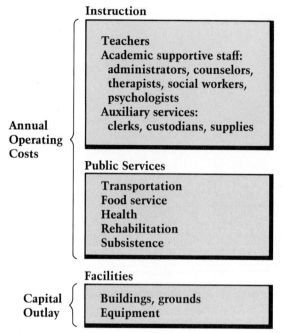

Instruction

Teachers
Academic supportive staff:
   administrators, counselors,
   therapists, social workers,
   psychologists
Auxiliary services:
   clerks, custodians, supplies

Annual Operating Costs

Public Services

Transportation
Food service
Health
Rehabilitation
Subsistence

Facilities

Capital Outlay

Buildings, grounds
Equipment

Figure 12.2
Components of Special Education Costs
Source: From "Alternative Methods of Financing Special Education" by W. P. McClure, 1975, *Journal of Educational Finance, 1,* p. 42. Reprinted by permission.

In 1981 the Rand Corporation conducted a study of "the cost of special education and related services for handicapped children, using information from a national survey taken in 1977–1978" (cf. Kakalik, Furry,Thomas & Carney, 1981, p. iii). The authors used an estimate of $1,650 ($1,500 per elementary school student, $1,782 per secondary school student) as the cost of regular education for nonhandicapped students. Their estimates of total and added costs for different groups of special education students are listed in Table 12.4. And the factors that contribute to the average total cost of special education are listed in Table 12.5. Sage suggests that these figures can be translated to 1986 dollars by adding approximately 90 percent to them. We suggest you double them to obtain estimates of costs today.

Other costs are involved in providing special education. In addition to having to comply with the provisions of federal legislation regulating education of handicapped students, states and local education agencies are faced with having to spend monies to comply with federal court orders that apply only to their state or local area. Similarly, following passage of Public Law 94–142, many federal court cases mandated that the schools provide services for or engage in extensive efforts to locate and identify specific

Table 12.4
Estimated Total and Added Cost of Special Education per Child by Age Level and Type of Handicapping Condition in 1977–78 School Year

| | Age Level and Cost ($) | | | | | | | |
| | *Preschool* | | *Elementary* | | *Secondary* | | *All Ages Combined* | |
Handicapping Condition	Total	Added	Total	Added	Total	Added	Total	Added
Learning disabled	3,392	3,392	4,488	2,838	4,856	2,936	4,525	2,875
Educable mentally retarded	3,465	3,465	3,958	2,308	3,684	2,034	3,795	2,145
Trainable mentally retarded	4,715	4,715	5,078	3,428	6,008	4,358	5,519	3,869
Severely mentally retarded	5,352	5,352	6,013	4,363	5,935	4,285	5,926	4,276
Emotional	3,260	3,260	5,871	4,221	6,845	5,195	6,289	4,639
Deaf	7,676	7,676	8,523	6,873	5,200	3,550	7,311	5,661
Partial hearing	5,853	5,853	4,861	3,211	5,204	3,554	5,091	3,441
Blind	6,603	6,603	11,725	10,075	8,917	7,267	9,664	8,014
Partial sight	3,254	3,254	4,063	2,413	5,253	3,603	4,519	2,869
Orthopedic	5,097	5,097	3,350	1,700	3,545	1,895	3,546	1,896
Other health	2,319	2,319	2,148	498	2,748	1,098	2,502	852
Speech	2,490	2,490	2,214	564	2,580	930	2,253	603
Multiple	9,382	9,382	7,165	5,515	7,773	6,123	7,642	5,992
All	3,526	3,526	3,267	1,167	4,099	2,449	3,577	1,927

Source: From *The Cost of Special Education* (Rand Note N–1972–ED) by J. S. Kakalik, W. S. Furry, M. A. Thomas, and M. F. Carney, November 1981, Santa Monica, CA: The Rand Corporation. Reprinted by permission.

kinds of handicapped students. These activities cost the school districts money.

A tenuous balance exists between society's willingness to provide special education and related services to handicapped students and society's ability to pay for those services. In times of financial prosperity, there are seldom attempts to limit services to students who are handicapped or to limit the number of students declared eligible for services. When school districts have plenty of money to spend on educating handicapped students, diagnostic personnel are encouraged to locate and identify as many handicapped students as possible. When funds are limited, however, concerns grow about the large number of students being declared handicapped. For example, officials in the U.S. Department of Education considered placing a 3 percent cap (that is, 3 percent of school-age children) on the number of students any one district could identify and serve as learning disabled (at one time, there was a 2 percent cap; at other times, no cap). This

Table 12.5
Total Cost of Special Education per Handicapped Child in the 1977–78 School Year

Type of Cost	Cost per Year
Regular education teachers' instructional services	$ 743
Instructional costs of special education teachers	551
Facility operations and maintenance	378
Debt service	245
School administration	209
General district administration	200
Related services	191
Technical assistance to staff members	135
Special transportation	111
Special education aides	106
Admission, placement, IEP development	103
Assessment	100
Food services for handicapped children	88
Special education administrators and secretaries	76
Instructional supplies and texts	66
Regular transportation	48
Facility modification and improvement for general education	44
Staff inservice training	40
Miscellaneous costs	25
Instructional equipment	21
Regular education aides	19
Related services staff and nonclassroom teacher secretaries and clerks	14
Facility modification and improvement for special education	12
Special education nonpersonnel administrative costs	11
Related services staff and nonclassroom teacher supplies	10
Special education program specialists	9
Screening for handicapping conditions	8
Related services staff and nonclassroom teacher equipment	7
Related services staff and nonclassroom teacher administrators	4
Related services staff and nonclassroom teacher transportation	3
Total	$3,577

Source: From *The Cost of Special Education* (Rand Note N–1972–ED) by J. S. Kakalik, W. S. Furry, M. A. Thomas, and M. F. Carney, November 1981, Santa Monica, CA: The Rand Corporation. Reprinted by permission.

was primarily an economic decision. Society simply cannot afford to provide special education to greater and greater numbers of students.

Similarly, before Public Law 94–142 was passed, it was clear who paid for the related services that school personnel recommended. With the exception of speech therapy and some forms of counseling (principally academic guidance), parents did. Schools referred students to external agencies, and parents paid the bills. Parents usually paid for treatment at Easter Seal Society facilities and some other agencies on a sliding scale, based on income. Craig (1981) aptly describes what happened when schools became responsible for the cost of related services:

> Prior to the passage of PL 94–142, schools did not hesitate to recommend such resources as psychological counseling or physical or occupational therapy for students in need of these services. Since the passage of this omnibus act, however, school personnel have become reticent about discussing the need for such resources with parents because of their responsibility for assuring that services are provided; in many schools, informal policies have been established that discourage teachers from initiating discussions with parents about the possible need for noninstructional resources that cannot be provided directly by the school. Thus the intent of the law, which is to enhance and expand the availability and provision of necessary services for the handicapped . . . has actually created disincentives for schools to identify these student needs. (p. 12)

Are We Doing This the Right Way?

Cost-benefit analysis is the systematic assessment of the relative economic efficiency of providing alternative programs. It compares benefits to costs. Special educators seldom conduct cost-benefit analyses. When they do, the costs of special education typically are evaluated by looking at the outcomes for specific kinds of students. For example, if it can be shown that by providing special education services to a mildly handicapped student, the student will eventually be able to work, earn wages, and contribute to the tax base, the monies spent providing those services may be deemed beneficial (both to the individual and to society). This is especially true if the individual ends up contributing more to the tax base than it costs to educate him or her. The costs of educating handicapped students also are evaluated in terms of the alternative: not educating those students. Here people typically consider what it would cost to maintain an individual in a custodial arrangement for the rest of his or her life or the cost to society of a "deviant" individual acting in an uncontrolled fashion versus helping the individual function relatively independently and contribute in some way to society.

When we read about cost-benefit analyses, we wonder why people do them. We believe access to a free appropriate education is every student's right. There is no need to justify it in any other terms.

When we think about the value of special education, we think more about whether we are doing it right: Are special services being provided in the best way possible? Clearly, there are different ways to meet the special learning needs of students. As Biklen (1989) put it, "states could fund the education of all students without identifying any students or programs as special, but they do not. Persistence in funding labeled students or programs may reflect concern that students with disabilities would not receive much needed special services if unlabeled" (p. 9). We would like to see special education freed from the stepchild role it sometimes is forced to play. We would like the future of special education to be different, and we think it will be if people learning about special education today are encouraged to think differently about it. In 1983, Mary Moran wrote that "alternative futures can be imagined, if we free ourselves to question assumptions" (p. 36). Sapon-Shevin (1989) built on Moran's vision of the future of special education:

> In State A, special education continues to grow. Stricter eligibility guidelines are established for special education services, more funds are expended, and quality of education is judged by its effectiveness in preparing the handicapped for employment. As programs grow, however, so does the isolation and segregation of students with handicaps. When economic hard times develop, handicapped students become bitterly resented for their drain on state and local budgets and become targets of discrimination. Soon, programs are cut, advocacy groups battle each other into oblivion, and handicapped students are once more underserved and isolated in society.
>
> In State B, the school population is viewed as an interdependent system and schools are freed from the constraint of having to identify special populations in order to provide services. Schools utilize the dropping birth rate as the occasion to reduce class size instead of reducing teacher staff. People with handicaps are not negatively differentiated from other students or citizens. Schooling and work are integrated and life-long, and all residents (including handicapped citizens) have the opportunity to engage in integrated rotations of schooling, work, and leisure. (p. 102)

Which will it be? The future is yours.

Checkpoint

- *The overall pool of monies available to provide special education services must be divided among all exceptional students.*

- *The public pays the cost of educating exceptional students through federal, state, and local tax dollars.*

- *State and local governments are the primary source of revenues for public schools.*

- *Federal dollars provided to support the implementation of Public Law 94–142 are distributed in the form of formula grants based on the number of handicapped students being served.*

- *Direct subsidies for special services, funding of types of personnel, and funding for types of students are the primary methods states use to finance special education.*

- *The general cost of special education is about twice that of educating nonexceptional students.*

- *It costs more to provide educational and related services to students who are severely handicapped than to students who are less severely handicapped.*

- *A tenuous balance exists between society's willingness to provide special education and related services to handicapped students and society's ability to pay for those services.*

WHAT WE THINK ABOUT THE SOCIAL, POLITICAL, AND ECONOMIC REALITIES OF SPECIAL EDUCATION

Social, political, and economic factors change what happens in special education through their influence on current practice and on one another. When society's attitudes toward the education of handicapped students change, laws may be written or revised and funding patterns may change. When funding patterns change, social attitudes may change, and so on. We can see the relationships among the factors that influence special education by looking at the impact of Public Law 94–142. That law has led to many changes in educational practice, and the effects of some of those changes probably won't be known for years to come.

For decades, special education existed as a parallel system to regular education. With the enactment of Public Law 94–142 and the requirement that handicapped students be educated in the least restrictive environment, special education became part of a continuum of delivering services to students. The law forged a new kind of partnership between special and regular education. For the first time schools were confronted with educating new populations of severely handicapped students, of younger students (ages 3 to 5) and older students (ages 18 to 21). Schools were forced to enter into cooperative arrangements with other agencies to provide related services, and to bear the expense of paying for them.

One area that has felt the impact of this landmark legislation is teacher training. To provide services to new populations of severely handicapped students, schools need specially trained teachers—teachers who can run portable respirators, use Bliss boards to communicate with nonoral children, clean out wounds and bandage children with spina bifida. Regular education teachers, charged with the task of educating handicapped students in the regular classroom, need inservice training. But schools do not have the financial resources to give them that training. When teachers are faced with the task of providing services they are not trained to provide, they develop job-related stress. Many change jobs; others leave the profession.

The enrollment of increasing numbers of severely handicapped students in public education programs has placed a large financial burden on the schools. Buildings and equipment must be modified, and new equipment and facilities must be purchased. Because schools must provide education and related services, they end up paying for communication boards, hearing aids, and other devices. As the financial burden increases, people begin to wonder whether the provision of services to severely handicapped students is worthwhile.

Questions also are asked about the limits of responsibility. Even though the laws seem clear, school personnel have difficulty deciding precisely how services should be paid for, who should deliver them, and where, how, when, and for how long they should be delivered. The schools today are required to serve younger and older handicapped students. The mandate for service is there, but the technology to provide service is not. What usually happens is that schools expand their curriculums upward or downward to educate these new populations of students.

Important decisions about the future of special education have to be made, and many of them will be made by the students of today who will teach the students of tomorrow. This is your challenge, your social responsibility.

Summary

1. The average student receives more today than at any other time in history relative to what the typical taxpayer pays.
2. American citizens hope the money, time, and energy spent on educating young people will produce adults who can lead productive lives and contribute to society.
3. A wide range of factors contribute to the condition of education, and their interactions are complex.
4. Identifying whether a particular trend in public policy for the education of exceptional students has a social, economic, or political cause is difficult because of the way in which these factors interact.
5. The opinions and beliefs members of society hold about education are social values that influence who receives special services, who pays for them, which services are provided, and where, when, and how they are delivered.
6. Social values influence public policy toward special education because members of society support what they value.
7. A variety of political factors, closely related to social and economic factors, have significant effects on public policy for the education of students who are handicapped.

8. The rights of exceptional people were achieved following the formation of advocacy groups that focused their efforts on state and federal legislation.
9. Decisions about eligibility for special education services are made at the school district level.
10. The overall pool of monies available to provide special education services must be divided among all exceptional students.
11. The public pays the cost of educating exceptional students through federal, state, and local tax dollars.
12. State and local governments are the primary source of revenues for public schools.
13. Federal dollars that support the implementation of Public Law 94–142 are distributed in the form of formula grants based on the number of handicapped students being served.
14. The states generally distribute monies to special education through direct subsidies for services, funding of types of personnel, or funding for number and types of students.
15. The general cost of special education is about twice that for other students.
16. It costs more to provide educational and related services to severely handicapped students than to students who are less handicapped.
17. A tenuous balance exists between society's willingness to provide special education and related services to handicapped students and its ability to pay for those services.

Activities

1. Read your local newspaper for stories that indicate how your community values the education of exceptional students. Keep a journal for two or three weeks of the stories and any editorials that follow them.
2. Go to the library and find a summary on two important court cases relevant to special education. Select one that was litigated prior to 1980 and one litigated after 1985. Prepare a report in which you list the plaintiffs, the defendants, and the nature of the complaint brought by the plaintiffs for each case. Then list the major arguments made by the plaintiffs and the defendants, the social, political, or economic issues being contested, and state what the courts decided. Compare the information compiled for the different cases.
3. Contact the director of special education in your local school district to obtain figures on the number of students served in various categories of special education classes. Ask what method of funding is used and what it costs to educate an exceptional student in the district.

4. Contact the local, state, and federal officeholders who represent your district. Ask their opinions about special education.

Suggested Readings

Abeson, A., & Zettel, J. (1977). The end of the quiet revolution: The Education for All Handicapped Children Act of 1975. *Exceptional Children, 44,* 115–128.

The authors review the events leading up to passage of Public Law 94–142 and examine the main provisions of the act.

Ballard, J., & Zettel, J. (1977). Public Law 94–142 and Section 504: What they say about rights and protections. *Exceptional Children, 44,* 177–185.

A review of the similarities and differences between two major pieces of legislation that affect those who are handicapped.

Biklen, D., Ferguson, D., & Ford, A. (Eds.). (1989). *Schooling and disability.* Chicago: National Society for the Study of Education.

The National Society for the Study of Education publishes an annual yearbook that addresses aspects of special education. The most recent is a comprehensive collection of original work that gives the reader a view of the issues that are central to special education today. Several chapters have relevance to the social, political, and economic realities of providing special services to students in America's public schools.

McCarthy, E. F. (1987). The pragmatic press of political reality: Use of P.L. 94–142 discretionary and set-aside funds. *Special Services in the Schools, 4,* 49–62.

The author analyzes two major reports on the financing of special education and the use of discretionary funds, focusing on the impact of federal funds on state and local education agencies. The key factors identified in using these monies are political realities and the legal need for flexibility.

Sage, D. D. (1987). Resource cost analysis: We really need to know. *Special Services in the Schools, 4,* 63–76.

Analyses of costs in delivering special education are completed within the context of the social, political, and economic concerns of various constituencies. The author identifies the problems of making these analyses, offers an alternative cost analysis model, and describes the potential advantages and limitations for local school districts.

Stern, J. D. (1988). *The condition of education: Elementary and secondary education.* Vol. 1. Washington, DC: National Center for Education Statistics.

Data from the most recent administration of the National Assess- ment of Educational Progress, *including indicators of reading skills, knowledge of history and literature, and computer competence, are presented in this report. Analyses of data from public and private surveys also are included.*

13

Exceptional People and Society

FOCUSING QUESTIONS

- How do the responsibilities of a family with an exceptional child change as the child grows and develops?
- What are the differences between home-based and center-based early intervention programs?
- What effect do students' language and cultural differences have on the process of identifying their special educational needs?
- What are the most effective uses of computer technology in the field of special education?
- What are the "obstacles" in the structure and philosophy of special education that limit its effectiveness?
- How do the work and life experiences of adults who are gifted compare with those of other exceptional people?
- What are the differences among sheltered employment, supported employment, and competitive employment?
- What are some of the living arrangements available today for adults who are handicapped and who do not live with their families?

MARLEE MATLIN WON AN OSCAR FROM THE ACADEMY of Motion Picture Arts and Sciences in 1986 for her portrayal of a person who is deaf in *Children of a Lesser God.* The story is about people who are deaf and the problems they face in the hearing world. Marlee Matlin is hearing impaired from an illness she had at eighteen months of age. She is an exceptional actress.

Patti Duke won an award from the Academy in 1962 for her portrayal of a child who is severely handicapped in *The Helen Keller Story*, the story of a teacher's refusal to give up. Patti Duke is not handicapped, but she is a gifted actress and her performance was judged exceptional by her peers. Anne Bancroft, who portrayed the teacher, Anne Sullivan, also won an Oscar for her performance.

Dustin Hoffman recently was selected by the Academy for an award for his portrayal of an autistic person in *Rainman.* Shortly after the picture was released, the popular press ran stories about the amazing feats of autistic people around the country.

Gallaudet University is America's only institution of higher education primarily for individuals who are deaf. In 1986 students at Gallaudet refused to accept the appointment of a hearing individual as their university president. A deaf person who had worked at the university for many years was selected to head this exceptional school.

Exceptional people always have been a part of society. We see more of them today because we are more willing to accept them than ever before. This did not happen overnight. Gaining acceptance has not been easy for people with special needs. And the battle is not over. As recently as 1986, the American Association for Retarded Citizens found it necessary to adopt a position on the use of severe and aversive therapy with individuals who are retarded (Marozas & May, 1988).

Efforts to treat exceptional people better and keep them in the mainstream of society have their origins in the work of pioneering special educators (see Chapter 5). For example, Dorothea Dix's plea in 1843 to the Massachusetts legislature for better treatment of "insane" people was evidence of a need and willingness to change the way people with handicaps were treated. More recently, Burton Blatt (1970, 1976, 1981) described the deplorable conditions that still exist in institutions serving those who are retarded.

Zigler and Baller (1977) summarized twenty-five years of research on the effects of institutional treatment. Some of their conclusions form the basis for current theory and practice. They showed that the level of instruction or functional training that an individual receives before being placed in an institution affects subsequent behavior. Those whose home and school environments and experiences are more favorable are better adjusted after a period of time in a segregated setting than their peers with less positive backgrounds. Zigler and Baller also confirmed that family relations are very important:

> The retarded individuals who maintained contact with their parents or parent surrogates either by being visited at the institution or by going home on vacations were more likely to display the type of autonomous behavior characteristic of nonretarded children. Thus we found clear empirical evidence that an institutional policy of encouraging many contacts with the community does promote psychological growth. (p. 4)

Today people who are exceptional are participating in a small social revolution. Many of the changes they have experienced are the product of parents' and professionals' working to keep families intact and to open educational and transitional opportunities in the mainstream of society.

This revolution is affecting the parents and families of exceptional people. And it is changing the way we provide special education. Services are being mandated and delivered to very young children, and the students being served are more diverse than at any other time in history. Advances in technology make it easier to meet the needs of exceptional students and those who work with them. As the system improves, the lifelong learning needs of older people who are exceptional are being addressed as well. In this chapter, we examine each of these areas, to give you a foundation to live and grow with exceptional people in society.

THE CHANGING ROLES OF PARENTS AND FAMILIES

Not many years ago, parents were encouraged to place children with handicaps in institutions as early as possible. Today, they are being encouraged to keep their children with special needs at home. Parents and families have become active partners in the special education process in ways that were unheard of fifty years ago.

Placing a child in an institution left many families with feelings of guilt and inadequacy. Now that normalization, least restrictive environment, and mainstreaming are available and are the treatments of choice, the families of those with handicaps must address different feelings and concerns. The parents of gifted children also face some of these concerns and others about the social, personal, and educational needs of their children.

Whenever a child is born, the structure of the family changes. All families have to deal with that change. But the families of children with special needs face a special challenge. Some of their problems are unique; others differ only by degree. For example, the family of a child with special medical needs faces certain problems that families with healthy children do not. And although all families must think about their children's future, the families of those who are handicapped have special concerns.

At every stage of their child's life, the families of those who are handicapped must deal with special problems. Parents of a young child who is handicapped need accurate information about their child's condition. They have to decide what and how to tell relatives and friends about their child. They have to locate health and educational services. They worry about what others think about them and their child. And they have to come to grips with their sadness, their guilt, their anxieties. Brothers and sisters have to deal with feelings of jealousy, the loss of their parents' energy and time, new responsibilities, and their fears. They also worry about what their friends will think and say about their handicapped sibling.

Starting school is a change in routine. Most children find it difficult to adjust to that change; exceptional children and their families find it extremely difficult. Parents are expected to participate in the educational program. They need to know about mainstreaming and the special class placement alternatives that are available in their community. Often they have to locate professionals who can give them help at home. And they have to find after-school care and determine the extent to which they want their child to participate in extracurricular activities. Brothers and sisters

LIKE MOST PARENTS, Jeanne Kristaponis and David Seltzer rejoiced when they heard those magic words: 10 fingers, 10 toes. Nine months later, when Ben was diagnosed as having cerebral palsy, the world turned joyless.

They had awful fights, often with David threatening to leave Jeanne and their daughter Alexandra, then three and a half. There were endless rounds of doctors, countless midnight emergency runs to the hospital; there were weeks when Alex regressed, days when Jeanne would be in the bathroom, throwing up from anxiety.

"The world is full of stress and pain and in most cases it goes away with time," says David. "When you are the parent of a handicapped child, it's there every day, every hour." . . .

From birth, Ben had so much trouble sucking that he couldn't nurse, and Jeanne frantically bought every kind of nipple before she found one he could master. Now they know that poor sucking can be a signal of CP; at the time, no one made the connection.

When he was about six months, their day-care provider hinted she thought something was wrong. The next three months were awful, says Jeanne, waiting, anticipating, dreading the diagnosis.

Ben turned two on May 17, 1989. It was a milestone for Jeanne. "I'm really hopeful right now. I don't think I'm as sensitive as I used to be and Ben is starting to crawl and can feed himself. He's happy and responsive and he interacts with his toys. Those are good signs," she says. . . .

Ben has ataxic cerebral palsy, which means he has loose muscle tone, and an accompanying seizure disorder that occurs in 35 to 45 percent of CP children. He also has a developmental delay, which so far means he is nonverbal, and exotropia, which is a wandering eye. He recently had ureter reimplant surgery to correct a kidney problem.

Life has a seemingly normal pattern for Jeanne and David.

David, a chef with a local gourmet store, leaves for work at 6:30 A.M. Jeanne, a communication consultant at Digital, drops Ben at family day care and Alex, now five and a half, at a community day-care facility from which she is bused to kindergarten. David picks them up about 6 P.M. and has dinner started when Jeanne gets home. By the time they eat, play, bathe, and get the children in bed, it is 8:30. David goes to bed almost immediately; Jeanne waits to give Ben medication at 10 P.M.

But there are constant reminders that normalcy is yet to be defined. Two mornings a week, they alternate taking Ben to therapy. He has an average of two scheduled doctor's appointments a week, and in the past eight months, he was hospitalized 15 times, mostly for seizures but also for medical crises revolving around the kidney problem.

That David and Jeanne both work adds another layer of concern. They need the money—even with insurance, they still pay 20 percent of the expenses and some things are not covered. But David worries, "Are we cheating Ben because both of us work? If we eliminate an income, are we cheating Alex? Our basic philosophy is to keep looking at our family as a unit. As a unit, we need two incomes."

Jeanne appears to be the stronger, more optimistic of the two but sometimes it is David who is better able to cope. Always, says David, "There is a strong sense of, 'Why us?' It's a natural question for any parent of a handicapped child."

David seeks an answer in reincarnation: "At first I wondered, what did Ben do in a past life to deserve this? Then I thought, what did I do? Or Jeanne?"

In this life, at least, Jeanne thought she had failed. CP is usually caused by a shortage of oxygen to the brain during pregnancy or birth; statistically, it occurs in one out of every 1,000 births. For months, Jeanne agonized over her pregnancy. "I bled in the first trimester. Was that it? I had the flu. Could it have been that?" She even talked to lawyers but they found no grounds for a lawsuit. Eventually, she gained peace through therapy. "I'm just never going to know," she says.

A vivid memory pops into her mind. She is driving the car, following the ambulance that is carrying Ben to the hospital for yet another seizure. "I thought, it would be better if he died. It's so hard and so painful, would his death be any worse?"

She no longer has feelings like that. "As a mother," she says, "the connections you have with your child, no matter what his needs, get you through a lot. You love him and want the best for him. You just do."

Because Ben is so young, the extent of his handicap is still unknown even though one of his doctors describes his case as moderately to significantly severe. Jeanne hopes he will be able to walk and talk, but she doesn't worry about the future anymore. "There is feedback for you as a parent even if he's not taking his first step or speaking a sentence. My hope for my son is for him to be the best he can be, whatever that is."

Everything is relative, says Jeanne, even parenting: "There is always someone who is worse off than you. For me, if he couldn't relate to me, didn't know I was his mom, couldn't give me his version of hugs and kisses, if I couldn't comfort him just because I'm his mom, then I don't know how I'd make it."

Although David wistfully talks about having a son he could play ball with, his real concerns are more philosophical: "How is he going to survive in a world where people can be so insensitive? What will happen to him when we're old? Will he be able to reproduce? Will he carry on our family name?"

David admits to a wide range of negative feelings—envy, depression, anger, and just plain sadness. But he says, "I'm not consumed by anger." His face lights up when he describes the gigantic smile Ben gives him every morning. "It's wonderful," he says simply. David says Ben has forced him to grow. "Before, I wasn't capable of feeling other people's pain."

David talks in a quiet voice about the scariest day of his life. He and Ben were home alone. Ben suddenly was burning with fever. David put him in the high chair to give him Tylenol when Ben's arms and legs began to move in a rowing-like motion. Ben was having a seizure, his first. He began to turn blue.

David ripped the high chair tray off, cradled Ben, and grabbed the phone. Help arrived quickly. "I was afraid," says David. "I was terrified that he might. . . ."

Jeanne, almost whispering, finishes the thought for him: "Just because there is something wrong with your son, you don't love him less."

Source: *Barbara F. Meltz, "A Family Struggles with Disability,"* The Boston Globe, *June 5, 1989, pp. 31, 33. Reprinted with courtesy of* The Boston Globe.

Parents are expected to participate in the educational program—locating health and education professionals who can help them, learning about placement alternatives, finding after-school care, and determining the extent their child will participate in extracurricular activities.

(© David Wells/The Image Works)

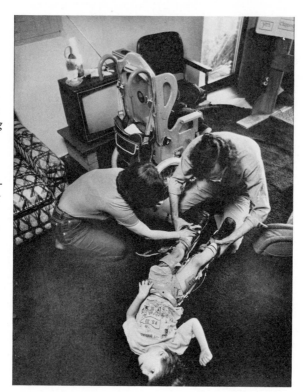

may be embarrassed, frustrated, disappointed, even angry when a sibling who is handicapped is mainstreamed in their own school. Many are expected to participate in special training programs and support groups that compete with other social and school activities. They also have to face the limitations that the handicap may have on their sibling's future.

Adolescents with handicaps encounter increased peer rejection and personal isolation. They also often have special problems adjusting to the normal physical and emotional changes that occur during puberty. Parents may have to help them cope with their feelings and arrange out-of-school activities for them.

Life after school presents a whole new set of problems for the handicapped individual and the family. Finding a job and a place to live can be a special challenge for those with handicaps. For their parents, there is worry about how their child will manage and who will care for them when they are no longer able to do so. Brothers and sisters may face financial responsibilities for their sibling who is handicapped, forced to assume guardianship.

Parents of children who are gifted share many concerns with parents of other exceptional children. Many need help understanding the special needs of their gifted child. They too worry that their children will be isolated, set off by their special abilities. Some need to be convinced that special education is appropriate and necessary for their child. Others seek out special programs for their child. Although parents with unusually high expectations can create problems for their child and the teachers they deal with in school, these same parents can be welcome advocates in the early stages of developing programs for exceptional students.

Parents of children who are gifted can be eager to participate in their child's education. They typically want to know how to broaden their child's experiences, how they can help their child develop a love for learning and a willingness to take intellectual risks, and how they can become actively involved in making more services available to gifted students in their communities. Others worry that they lack the skills and knowledge to meet the special needs of their child, and, like all parents, worry about the effects their mistakes will have on the lives of their children.

Checkpoint

- *Today, parents are being encouraged to keep their exceptional children at home.*
- *Families are active partners in special education in ways that were unheard of fifty years ago.*
- *One of the primary concerns of parents of a young child who is handicapped is getting accurate information about their child's condition.*
- *Today, parents are expected to participate in the educational program of their handicapped child.*
- *Families of adolescents with handicaps must address the problems created by peer rejection and personal isolation.*
- *Finding a job and a place to live is a special challenge for those with handicaps and their families.*
- *The parents of children who are gifted share many concerns with parents of other exceptional children.*

SPECIAL EDUCATION IS CHANGING

We have worked in special education all of our professional lives, as teachers, as counselors, as school psychologists, as administrators. When we started out, the learning disabilities category was just beginning to be recognized and Public Law 94–142 and other federal legislation supporting people with handicaps did not exist. Special education has grown tremendously since we entered the field. It is bigger and better than ever before. And exceptional people are reaping the benefits.

Early Childhood Intervention

Kim recently told us an interesting story. It seems one of the kindergarten teachers in her school was finding that many of the students entering her class already had mastered much of the content she was prepared to present. Checking with some of the parents, she discovered that the local preschool programs had adopted a "firm stance on academics" in response to parents' requests that they better prepare children for kindergarten. Kim's friend was considering restructuring the academic year in response to this new population of students with well-developed skills.

According to the U.S. Census Bureau, more than half of children ages 3 to 5 in the United States were enrolled in nursery school or kindergarten classes in 1986. The total number of children in preschool programs has risen steadily since 1970, and currently totals more than 6 million. By and large, these students are better prepared for school and much more advanced academically than students who started school five to ten years ago.

In 1968 the Handicapped Children's Early Education Assistance Act (Public Law 90–538) was passed. It was the first law that provided federal funds for innovative programs for preschool children with handicaps. By 1973 Head Start and other federally funded programs were required to keep at least 10 percent of their spaces available for handicapped children. Public Law 94–142 mandated services for three- to five-year-olds by 1980, where state law already provided services for nonhandicapped children in that age group. It also provided incentive grants to states for improving early childhood special education programs.

In 1984, Public Law 98–199 made funds available to states to develop comprehensive services for children with special needs from birth to age 5. Two years later, President Reagan signed into law the Amendments to the Education for All Handicapped Children Act (Public Law 99–457). This legislation expanded services to children who are handicapped under age 5. It authorized the distribution of federal funds to help states provide special education to very young children and guaranteed a free appropriate education to all handicapped preschoolers. Public Law 99–457 made special education for young children with handicaps compulsory, and parents are an important part of its educational program.

Some early intervention programs actually are carried out in the child's home. Teachers or other professionals regularly visit with parents to provide direct or indirect services. In some home-based programs, the visits occur weekly and are primarily designed to improve the parents' skills in working with their child. The type of service depends on the type of handicap and the willingness of the parents to teach their child. Parents also receive indirect services in some home-based programs. Specially trained teachers make recommendations for training, organize groups of parents with similar concerns, and help parents monitor the progress of the intervention they are providing.

In other programs, parents bring their child to a center for direct or indirect services. The center may be at a hospital, school, day care center, or other facility. Once there, parents may work with their child under the guidance of specially trained professionals, or they may observe others working with their child. In some center-based programs, groups of parents meet to share concerns and provide support for one another. Other centers are organized primarily as referral sources for services available locally.

Both home-based and center-based intervention programs have advantages and disadvantages. At home, the child learns in a natural environment surrounded by family members, who often can spend more time working with the child at home than they can at a center. Problems associated with transportation, care of other children, and general family disruption are minimized when special education is carried out at home. Home-based programs, however, have several disadvantages: Their success depends heavily on the parents' cooperation, children from poor homes or homes where both parents work are less likely to receive special education at home, and being at home limits opportunities for interaction with other adults and children.

A center-based approach provides varied types of help at a central location. Professionals from several disciplines (medicine, psychology, occupational therapy, speech and language pathology, and education) work together to assess and teach the child. And the program benefits from periodic meetings to discuss progress and plan future interventions. The disadvantages of center-based intervention include the time and expense of transportation, the cost of maintaining a center, and the likelihood of less parent involvement.

Regardless of which approach is taken (and many professionals combine them), the curriculum is pretty much the same. We teach young children who are handicapped to improve their language, motor, self-help, communication, preacademic, and cognitive skills. We also try to improve their self-concepts, creativity, motivation to succeed, and general readiness for social interaction in school.

Twenty years ago, parents of preschool children with handicaps were offered very little help. Today, public special education is available for individuals from birth to age 21, and early childhood programs are one of the fastest growing areas in special education.

Cultural Diversity and Special Education

More than 4 million school-age students speak a language other than English at home, and about three-fourths of them are limited in their ability to use English for academic purposes. The majority of the limited English proficient (LEP) and non–English language background (NELB) students in the United States are Hispanic. Students in the Chicago schools speak as many as thirty-eight different languages and dialects. In Miami, Los Angeles, and New York, teachers may have students from different Latin American countries speaking different dialects of Spanish and students from other countries speaking many different languages. Even in small towns in some states, it is not uncommon for a teacher to have a class with students who speak as many as ten languages other than English.

Historically, students from some cultural groups have not achieved as well as their peers:

- In 1986, 21 percent of white teenagers did not complete high school versus 40 percent of their Hispanic peers.
- High dropout rates also are evident for Native Americans over the last century.
- More than three times as many black students than white students are placed in classes for those who are mentally retarded. Similar patterns exist in classes for disturbed students and in statistics compiled for Hispanic students.
- About 25 percent of the school-age population comes from minority groups, but only about 18 percent of that population is receiving services in gifted programs.

The population of the United States is changing. Although those from birth to age 17 represent 27.6 percent of the total U.S. population, they represent almost 40 percent of the total Hispanic population. Because Hispanic people, as an aggregate group, are young—with a median age of 23.7 compared to 31 for non–Hispanics—they require proportionately more educational and related services than the general population (Bouvier & Davis, 1982; Stern, 1988). This need for educational services will continue and probably increase throughout at least the first part of the next century.

Characteristics of other cultural and ethnic groups also affect special education programs. As a group, Native Americans are very accepting of children who are handicapped or disabled (Stewart, 1977). They are reluctant to have their children removed from the home and often resist efforts to provide special education in places other than a local school. Identifying Native Americans who are gifted is difficult because some of their special abilities—observation, memory, and perception—are not measured in regular screening procedures.

Proportions of minority students in the schools, particularly Asians and Hispanics, have been increasing in recent years (Kaufman, 1987), and yet except for gifted and talented programs, special education is not a common placement for Asian Americans. For example, less than 5 percent of Asian students are in special education classes for students with handicaps. By comparison, 8 to 10 percent of black, Hispanic, and American Indian students are represented in the same programs (Stern, 1987). And while dropout rates for students from minority groups are high (18 percent), they are generally very low for Asian students (3 percent) (Pallas, 1987). Leung (1988) provides a practical frame of reference for understanding similarities and differences among Asian Americans. She discusses immigration and settlement histories as well as acculturation types and notes how the characteristics of these students are related to improving special education practices for them.

Asian Americans have strong familial bonds and are reluctant to pass the treatment of a child who is handicapped to people outside the family. Jerry Arakawa (1981) gives us a picture of what it is like to be Asian and different:

> Being disabled and Asian meant having an additional personality trait that can potentially cause shame to the family. Consequently, the disabled Asian youngster has a less outgoing personality and takes risks less willingly.
>
> In Western culture, individuality is praised. In Asian culture, anything that breaks homogeneity is troubling. And the disabled Asian knows he is different.
>
> The Asian perspective is to minimize the handicap. The emphasis is on adapting and doing as little out of the ordinary as possible. This even means you avoid legal actions against discrimination. To get employment, you tough it out. If busses are inaccessible, you say it doesn't matter.
>
> Consumerism and advocacy are very hard for a disabled Asian to understand. He or she seeks to avoid underscoring a disability and focusing public attention on it. To do otherwise is discomforting.
>
> In the last few years, attitudes about disability in the Asian community have become more Western. But the basic values remain: Be a high achiever and transcend your disability. Asians want to excel. They want to be the best. (p. 1)

Language and cultural differences traditionally have caused difficulties for school personnel working with non–English language background students. A by-product of these difficulties is the under- and overrepresentation of these students in special education programs. Although ethnic minority students represent about 25 percent of the general school-age population, only about 18 percent of them are identified as gifted. For students who have not yet learned English, the risk of misidentification is especially high. Some teachers interpret lack of fluency as a handicapping condition and refer the students for special education services. Other

Language and cultural differences traditionally have caused difficulties for school personnel working with non–English language background students; a byproduct of these difficulties is the under- and over-identification of these students in special education programs.

(© David M. Grossman)

teachers see a lack of fluency as a language learning need when in fact it may be a symptom of a greater learning problem. In both cases, students may be placed inappropriately and fail to receive the educational help they need to benefit from their schooling. Chinn and McCormick (1986) argue that gifted students from minority cultures are underrepresented in special classes because they "possess a variety of talents that are valued and nurtured within their own cultures but are often ignored in school" (p. 103). Until teachers in regular, bilingual, and special education programs learn to collaborate and to share their expertise, misidentification and misplacement will persist.

Technology and Special Education

When we started our careers in special education, computers that did routine data processing were the size of a small room; there were no personal computers. Today, computer technology is changing so quickly that what we write about it here probably will be out of date by the time this book is published.

People who work in special education have been active participants in the computer revolution. Those who work with exceptional students are willing to try anything to help them learn. Computers are being used as teaching machines and communication devices for students with special needs (see Chapter 11). And "thanks to computers and robots the disabled can do almost anything" (M. Rogers, 1989, p. 66). Here are some "profiles in courage, from the high tech age" that appeared in *Time* magazine:

- Kent Cullers has been blind since birth. He is also a key scientist in one of the planet's most farsighted endeavors. A physicist with NASA's Search for Extraterrestrial Intelligence program, Cullers, 39, designs the complex equipment that may someday isolate intelligent signals from the random radio noise of the galaxies. He relies on a computer that reads, writes, and if need be, speaks out loud. "Twenty years ago I could not have held this job," says Cullers. "Now, the fact that I'm blind is incidental."

- John Christensen, 31, has severe cerebral palsy and cannot use his arms or legs. Yet Christensen now does computer-aided drafting at United Cerebral Palsy CAD Productions in Oakland, Calif., producing elaborate digital maps. He's ready to move on: "I have dreams like everyone else. I want to work in an architect's office."

- Herman Briggman, 27, was a professional musician in New York before he was paralyzed by viral encephalitis, unable to even speak or swallow. Now Briggman uses a computer music system to compose and play again, solely by moving his head. (M. Rogers, 1989, p. 66)

And from *A Positive Approach*:

- Shannon Kidder, a teenager from Phoenix, Arizona, was born deaf; she has worn hearing aids since she was 13 years old. In 1987 Shannon was a member of the All American Girls' Basketball Team.

- Mary Kate Hemmerick has replaced the "can'ts" that often immobilize other individuals with a repertoire of "cans" that many able-bodied people never develop. After a spinal cord injury, she was paralyzed from the chest down. Although the accident left her physically challenged (a term she prefers to "disabled"), she completed the requirements for her teaching degree and continues to be a successful educator of people with physical problems. (Lotters, 1988, p.7)

Academic programs for gifted students are being enriched and accelerated by computer-assisted instruction and opportunities for creative expression in word processing and other programming applications. According to Cartwright, Cartwright, and Ward (1989), "technological advances promoting the education and treatment of children with learning disabilities have not emerged" (p. 273), but strides have been made in computer-assisted instructional methods that could be very useful for students with learning problems. For example, many different drill and practice programs for use in reading and mathematics are readily available, and computers have the potential to alter students' performance by promoting active participation, maintaining attention to tasks, and enhancing problem-solving skills (Cartwright, Cartwright, & Ward, 1989; Kneedler, 1984).

Teachers are taking advantage of the tremendous storage and retrieval capacities of computers to plan individualized education programs and monitor their students' progress. Computer programs are available that can

- generate instructional objectives.
- produce records of progress and report cards.
- generate quarterly and semester reports.
- administer, score, and interpret test performances.
- record and analyze classroom observations.
- generate instructional activities.
- manage weekly and monthly meeting schedules.
- store student health, discipline, and academic records.
- store information about community resources.

Administrators use computers to make the routine of monitoring special education programs easier. For example, school districts periodically must report to state and federal agencies the number of students being served in different categories; most have this information on computers. They also keep personnel files and complete student records on their computers so that information can be accessed more easily. Many districts use computers to personalize routine communications with parents and community agencies.

But is special education improved by the use of this technology? Computers reduce off-task behavior and serve as effective rewards for some students, and they do increase students' opportunities for success in certain academic areas. But when traditional lessons are well organized, they are no less effective than computers in most content areas. Computers are excellent tools for students who need drills and practice to improve their basic academic skills. And they are an enormous help in routine record keeping. But computers are no substitute for organized, creative teachers when it comes to planning special education programs.

Regular Education and Special Education

For years, many professionals believed special education was a separate system for educating students who were exceptional. Recently, that belief

Computers reduce off-task behavior, increase opportunities for success, and provide rewards for students who need to improve their basic academic skills— but they are no substitute for organized, creative teachers when it comes to planning special education programs.

(© Julie O'Neil/The Picture Cube)

has been called into question. One of those raising questions was Madeleine Will, then secretary of the Department of Education. In a position paper, she made the following points (1986a):

- She reported that large numbers of students with handicaps have been placed in special classes in recent years and that "another 10–20 percent of the students who are not classified as handicapped, have learning, language, or behavior problems that impede their educational progress" (p. 1).

- Although she believed that much had been accomplished in special education programs, she acknowledged that "problems have emerged which create obstacles to effective education of students with learning problems" (p. 4). She did not use the term *obstacle* to "imply that special programs have failed dismally in their mission to educate children with learning problems," nor to suggest that the "existing general system of education for these children warrants radical reform and redesign" (p. 4). She used the term to "convey the idea that the creation of special programs has produced unintended effects, some of which make it unnecessarily cumbersome for educators to teach—as effectively as they desire—and children to learn—as much and as well as they can" (p. 4).

■ She identified these obstacles:

1. Problems created by a fragmented approach that fails to provide services to many students who are "often not served adequately in the regular classroom and are not 'eligible' for special education or other special programs because they do not meet State or Federal eligibility requirements" (p. 5).
2. Problems created by dual (perhaps dueling) administrative systems for special programs that "contribute to a lack of coordination, raise questions about leadership, cloud areas of responsibility, and obscure lines of accountability within schools" (p. 6).
3. Problems created by segregating students from their peers and attaching labels to them that sometimes result in lowered expectations for success, which "have been fully described in the literature" (p. 7).
4. Problems created by a decision-making process that sometimes turns a valuable partnership between parents and teachers into a series of "adversarial, hit-and-run encounters" (p. 7) that leave everybody tallying points instead of thinking about students' unique learning needs and the most appropriate educational services to meet those needs.

In describing "a solution to the problem," Will qualified her argument: "Although for some students the 'pullout approach' may be appropriate, it is driven by a conceptual fallacy: that poor performance in learning can be understood solely in terms of deficiencies in the student rather than deficiencies in the learning environment" (p. 9). She contended that creating new educational environments as the primary means of improving students' performance is flawed; the alternative she advocated would "adapt the regular classroom to make it possible for the student to learn in that environment" (p. 9).

In closing, she challenged states "to renew their commitment to serve [children with learning problems] effectively" and pointed to the heart of the commitment being a "search for ways to serve as many of these children as possible in the regular classroom by encouraging special education and other special programs to form a partnership with regular education" (p. 19). Finally, she added:

> The basic educational issue for serving this growing group of young people is not finding something to call them so we can put money in a pot with that label on it. The basic issue is providing an educational program that will allow them to learn better.
>
> From that point, we can construct an educational environment that is a broad and rich continuum, rather than a series of discrete programming slots and funding pots. Within that range of available services, we can then pick and choose what we need to construct the program the child needs.

We can deliver the resources and provide the personalized instruction each child must have to achieve to his or her greatest potential. In short, we need to visualize a system that will bring the program to the child rather than one that brings the child to the program. (p. 21)

Will's position on the partnership between special and regular education is not particularly radical. Many professionals agree with her basic premises. For example, Stainback, Stainback, and Bunch (1989) point out that a "growing number of parents and educators are beginning to advocate that all students be integrated into the mainstream of regular education, including those who have traditionally been labeled severely and profoundly handicapped" (p. 3). This interest in sharing the responsibility for meeting the special educational needs of exceptional students has come to be known as the *regular education initiative (REI)* (see Chapter 7).

According to Stainback, Stainback, and Bunch, the rationale for merging regular and special education and sharing the responsibility for educating exceptional students is based on several arguments. First, "the *instructional needs of students do not warrant the operation of a dual system*. Second, *maintaining a dual system is inefficient*. And third, *the dual system fosters an inappropriate and unfair attitude* about the education of students classified as having disabilities" (1989, p. 15).

Others take even stronger positions in support of the need for change. Lipsky and Gartner (1989) contend that "there is little in the current design of special education that makes a difference for students labeled as handicapped" (p. 20). And Forest (1985) writes: "Hopefully, by the year 2000 there will be no more special education but only an educational system that serves all children. . . . *We create our tomorrows by what we dream today*" (p. 40).

Of course, not all professionals agree with Will's assessment of the state of special education or the potential merger of regular and special education. For example, Braaten, Kauffman, Braaten, Polsgrove, and Nelson (1988) argue that "research clearly does not support the assertion that all students can be managed and taught effectively in regular classes" (p. 23) and that "advocates favoring radical restructuring or merging of special and regular education fail to recognize the magnitude of the task, the enormous effort required to achieve the laudable goals of the REI" (p. 24). (See Chapter 7 for more on REI.)

Checkpoint

■ *Public Law 99–457 made special education for young children with handicaps compulsory. Parents are an important part of its educational program.*

■ *In home-based early intervention programs, teachers and other professionals visit the home to teach parents how to work with their child.*

- *Center-based early intervention programs are held outside the home; parents bring their child to a center for direct or indirect services.*

- *More than 4 million school-age students speak a language other than English at home, and about three-fourths of them have only limited use of English.*

- *Language and cultural differences traditionally have caused difficulties for school personnel working with non-English language background students. A by-product of these difficulties is the over- and underrepresentation of these students in special education programs.*

- *People who work in special education have been active participants in the computer revolution, using technology to improve services for exceptional students.*

- *In recent years, there has been a movement to merge special and regular education.*

WHAT HAPPENS AFTER SCHOOL?

What happens to exceptional people when they leave school? How many graduate with diplomas? How many graduate with certificates of attendance? How many drop out? Do they go to college? Do they work? What services do they need when they are no longer in school? How do they support themselves if they don't work? Many people believe these questions are the most critical issues facing special education today.

Who Leaves Special Education?

In the 1980s, more than 200,000 students with handicaps left school each year:

- About 60 percent graduated with some form of certification—either diplomas (43 percent) or certificates of attendance (17 percent).

- About 25 percent dropped out of school between the ages of 16 and 21; the rest left because they reached the maximum age for which services are provided or for other reasons (for example, enrollment in different programs).

- The longer students stay in school after the age of 17, the more likely they are to graduate.

Table 13.1
Number of Handicapped Students Leaving School and Their Reasons for Doing So, 1985–86 School Year

Category	Reason for Leaving School				
	Graduated with Diploma	*Graduated with Certificate*	*Reached Maximum Age*	*Dropped Out*	*Other Reasons for Exit*
Mentally retarded	18,447 (34.4)	15,136 (28.3)	3,018 (5.6)	12,858 (24.0)	4,122 (7.7)
Speech impaired	5,032 (37.4)	3,399 (25.3)	103 (0.8)	2,381 (17.7)	2,530 (18.8)
Visually handicapped	865 (59.7)	174 (12.0)	48 (3.3)	180 (12.4)	181 12.5
Emotionally disturbed	9,691 (33.5)	2,534 (8.8)	657 (2.3)	11,803 (40.7)	4,283 (14.8)
Orthopedically impaired	1,426 (53.9)	492 (18.6)	104 (3.9)	384 (14.5)	241 (9.1)
Other health impaired	1,094 (35.9)	456 (15.0)	132 (4.3)	941 (30.9)	426 (14.0)
Learning disabled	51,628 (49.7)	13,150 (12.7)	590 (0.6)	26,644 (25.6)	11,955 (11.5)
Deaf and blind	32 (17.7)	70 (38.7)	57 (31.5)	13 (7.2)	9 (5.0)
Multihandicapped	640 (24.3)	749 (28.4)	399 (15.2)	466 (17.7)	380 (14.4)
Hard of hearing	2,066 (55.8)	711 (19.2)	74 (2.0)	486 (13.1)	366 (9.8)

Source: Adapted from *Tenth Annual Report to Congress on the Implementation of the Education of the Handicapped Act*, 1988, p. 42. Washington, DC: U.S. Department of Education.

The number of students with various handicapping conditions and the circumstances under which they left school in the 1985–86 school year are listed in Table 13.1. Highest graduation rates are evident among students with visual handicaps, hearing handicaps, and orthopedic handicaps; more than half of the students in these groups graduate with diplomas. The least likely to drop out of school are students who are deaf and blind or visually handicapped. Students who are emotionally disturbed drop out at higher rates than students in all the other categories. In fact, more of these students leave school without finishing than graduate with diplomas.

Table 13.2
Anticipated Need for Selected Employment Services by Adults with Handicaps

Category	Type of Service				
	Vocational Training Services	Vocational Placement Services	Vocational Evaluation Services	Transition Employment Services	Post-employment Services
Mentally retarded	15.95	13.96	12.77	8.61	5.79
Speech impaired	10.89	19.73	16.42	5.11	11.16
Visually handicapped	11.23	8.98	11.47	6.77	3.92
Emotionally disturbed	13.58	13.17	11.71	6.69	4.16
Orthopedically impaired	11.02	10.51	11.21	7.08	2.71
Other health impaired	10.57	9.34	10.22	5.34	2.22
Learning disabled	18.65	15.66	13.47	7.08	7.36
Deaf and blind	11.71	9.67	6.04	5.29	4.98
Multihandicapped	9.44	10.41	8.84	8.07	6.35
Hard of hearing	11.62	11.68	11.25	6.05	4.65
All categories	15.79	14.11	12.62	7.42	5.98

Source: Adapted from *Tenth Annual Report to Congress on the Implementation of the Education of the Handicapped Act*, 1988, pp. 64–65. Washington, DC: U.S. Department of Education.

When students with handicaps leave school, most are unemployed or underemployed. Only a third of the people with handicaps between the ages of 16 and 64 are working, and of those working three-fourths have part-time jobs. Employment is the single most important concern of those who work with older people who are handicapped. Table 13.2 shows differences in the anticipated need of these people for different types of employment services. Most need vocational training, placement, and evaluation services more than they need transition or postemployment services. There is little variation in the need for services across different categories, but the need for vocational placement and evaluation is somewhat greater for older people in high-incidence categories.

Most adults with handicaps say that their greatest wish is to live independently. Most parents of adults with handicaps say that their greatest wish is for their child to live independently. Some of the things that make independent living easier for those with disabilities are modified controls on kitchen appliances; adjustable countertops and furniture; accessible sinks, toilets, and showers; adapted door handles; room-to-room intercoms; and easy access to emergency medical, police, and fire services. There are several different personal and social services for adults with

Table 13.3
Anticipated Need for Selected Personal and Social Services by Adults with Handicaps

| Category | Type of Service | | | | |
	General Counseling Services	*Personal Family Services*	*Independent Living Services*	*Community Transportation Services*	*Residential Living Services*
Mentally retarded	10.84	5.44	6.81	5.83	3.09
Speech impaired	14.96	4.21	2.11	2.17	0.30
Visually handicapped	9.51	3.83	6.26	7.85	2.15
Emotionally disturbed	15.68	11.85	6.54	2.06	3.74
Orthopedically impaired	7.87	3.87	8.94	11.01	2.34
Other health impaired	5.38	6.81	9.55	10.40	4.54
Learning disabled	18.18	3.37	2.89	2.62	0.38
Deaf and blind	8.23	6.57	6.19	7.18	6.87
Multihandicapped	8.20	6.38	5.43	7.98	6.08
Hard of hearing	10.73	3.74	4.31	5.20	1.78
All categories	14.10	5.68	5.22	4.26	2.21

Source: Adapted from *Tenth Annual Report to Congress on the Implementation of the Education of the Handicapped Act*, 1988, pp. 64–65. Washington, DC: U.S. Department of Education.

handicaps (Table 13.3). Those with high-incidence handicaps need more counseling services than do those with other handicaps; those who are disturbed need more family services; and transportation needs are greater for those with physical and health impairments. The need for independent and residential living skills is similar across handicapping conditions.

As people with handicaps grow older, their opportunities for education are restricted. The characteristics that lead them to special services during childhood often become barriers to education in adulthood. Table 13.4 lists differences in the anticipated need of adults with handicaps for additional education or training. If you look at Tables 13.2, 13.3, and 13.4, you can see that the education and training service needs of adults who are handicapped seem to be less important than their employment and personal/social service needs. The need for educational maintenance services, however, is the highest among their education and training needs. Adults with more severe handicaps need more education services after school. For example, people with visual handicaps, orthopedic impairments, other health impairments, and multiple handicaps have twice the need that people who are learning disabled, speech impaired, or emotionally disturbed have. Only individuals with sensory handicaps need professional readers or professional interpreters to any great degree.

Table 13.4
Anticipated Need for Selected Education and Training Services by Adults with Handicaps

Category	Type of Service				
	Educational Maintenance Services	Personal Restoration Services	Technical Aide Services	Professional Reader Services	Professional Interpreter Services
Mentally retarded	5.73	2.35	0.70	0.62	0.11
Speech impaired	2.42	1.38	5.23	0.37	0.30
Visually handicapped	5.78	3.31	8.18	8.07	0.32
Emotionally disturbed	3.07	6.00	0.40	0.19	0.05
Orthopedically impaired	6.42	6.38	6.96	0.61	0.18
Other health impaired	7.70	7.10	6.42	0.96	0.22
Learning disabled	2.42	1.10	1.71	3.01	0.11
Deaf and blind	5.21	4.76	4.76	3.63	4.98
Multihandicapped	7.37	5.59	5.26	1.45	1.64
Hard of hearing	3.28	1.37	9.65	1.36	11.85
All categories	4.04	2.78	1.94	1.38	0.57

Source: Adapted from *Tenth Annual Report to Congress on the Implementation of the Education of the Handicapped Act*, 1988, pp. 64–65. Washington, DC: U.S. Department of Education.

More than ever before, students with handicaps are entering colleges, community colleges, vocational schools, and advanced technical schools with accessible and intensive programs for exceptional students. Many factors have contributed to the emergence of these specialized educational programs (Mangrum & Strichart, 1984):

- Many students with handicaps graduate from high school and are eligible to enter college; the support they received in elementary school and high school has been extended in many college programs.

- The realization that college is a viable goal for students with handicaps has led many parents and professionals to advocate for special programs in colleges and universities.

- The interest of exceptional students in advanced schooling has brought pressure on institutions of higher learning to develop programs to meet these students' unique educational needs.

- There are not enough programs; the need for more is apparent and is a factor that is bringing more programs into existence.

- The movement toward open admission policies has led many students to actively seek enrollment who at one time were hesitant to apply for fear of being rejected.

- Colleges, universities, and other advanced professional schools are being pressured to develop programs to meet the needs of exceptional students by advocacy groups.

- With higher education enrollments dropping, students with handicaps are a potential new consumer of postsecondary education; financial incentives, then, have helped stimulate program development for exceptional college students.

What Happens to Exceptional People in Society?

Most of what we know about the after-school life of gifted students comes from the work of Lewis Terman and his associates. Terman (1954) summarized the career adjustments of eight hundred men who were gifted like this:

> By 1950, when the men had an average age of 40 years, they had published 67 books (46 in the fields of science, arts, and the humanities, and 21 books of fiction). They had published more than 1400 scientific, technical, and professional articles; over 200 short stories, novelettes, and plays and 236 miscellaneous articles on a great variety of subjects. They had also authored more than 150 patents. The figures on publications do not include the hundreds of publications by journalists that classify as news stories, editorials, or newspaper columns, nor do they include the hundreds if not thousands of radio and television scripts.
> . . . The level of education attained by this group was over ten times that expected of the general population. (p. 224)

In a related study, Sears and Barbee (1977) found that gifted women experienced less divorce, were less likely to be housewives, and were more likely to graduate from college than a representative sample of women who were not gifted.

The work and life experiences of adults who are gifted are much more positive than those of other exceptional people. When young adults from special education programs for handicapped students are employed, they often do not work in full-time positions and typically earn very little from their employment—findings that are supported by several studies (Table 13.5).

The most common work experience for people with handicaps is in sheltered and supported employment settings, not competitive employment positions. **Competitive employment** means that the individual's work is valued by the employer and is performed in an integrated setting

Most professionals agree that competitive, not sheltered or supported, employment should be the goal of all young adults with disabilities or handicaps.

(© Sven Martson/ Comstock)

with nonhandicapped coworkers, and that the individual earns at or above the federal minimum wage (Rusch, Chadsey-Rusch, & Lagomarcino, 1987). Despite the low percentage of adults who are handicapped in competitive employment settings, most professionals agree that competitive employment should be the goal of all young adults with disabilities or handicaps.

Sheltered employment is work in a self-contained environment in which exceptional people are trained and paid for their output. Some sheltered workshops provide training for work that is performed outside the special setting. Other sheltered workshops are permanent work settings

Table 13.5
Follow-up Studies of Special Education Students

Study	Sample	Results
Hasazi, Gordon, & Roe (1985)	301 young adults	55% were employed, two-thirds in full-time programs
Mithaugh, Horiuchi, & Fanning (1985)	234 young adults	69% were employed, one-third in full-time positions
Wehman, Kregel, & Seyfarth (1985)	300 young adults	42% were employed, three-fourths earning less than $500 a month

for the exceptional people who work there. In recent years, almost three thousand sheltered workshops across the country served more than 115,000 people with a variety of handicaps, many of whom earned an average of a dollar a day (Victor, 1976; Wills, 1986a).

Supported employment is a relatively new concept that is designed for individuals who are handicapped and who need help finding, performing, and holding a job. Professionals who provide supportive employment assistance to people who are handicapped do one or more of the following things:

- Assist during job placement efforts (plan transportation, identify appropriate jobs, match skills to available jobs, communicate with social service agencies)
- Provide on-the-job training and help (train work skills, provide social skills and job-site training, work with coworkers)
- Monitor job performance (obtain regular feedback from employers, identify levels of performance and need for further training)
- Provide evaluation and follow-up experiences (determine employer's satisfaction, communicate with employee periodically, help with future job placements)

Professionals in supportive employment activities spend most of their time at job sites, where people with handicaps work. Supportive employment specialists also spend time working with parents and exceptional people in training centers or at their homes.

Handicapped people are much more likely to find and keep jobs today than they were even a few years ago—largely because parents and professionals have worked to give them opportunities to become contributing members of society.

Where Do People with Handicaps Live?

The transition from school to work also means dealing with independent living responsibilities and residential needs. Not long ago, people who were moderately and severely handicapped lived primarily in large state hospitals and institutions. In fact, institutional placement of people who were retarded, deaf, blind, or handicapped in other ways was the primary means of intervention for over two hundred years. Today, large numbers of people with handicaps still live in institutional settings, but other options are available for those who do not live at home with their families. In Maryland, for example, there has been a decrease of more than 1,200 people in institutions and an increase of more than 2,400 people in community residences since 1970 (Jones, 1988). Exceptional people are moving out into the world.

Deinstitutionalization is the implementation of the least restrictive environment principle in residential treatment facilities—such as group homes, a fast-growing community-based residential alternative for many people who are handicapped.
(© Michael Weisbrot and Family)

Group Homes

The practice of mainstreaming began when teachers and other professionals implemented the LRE principle of Public Law 94–142 in public school settings and programs. In school settings, least restrictive environment means that exceptional students receive all or part of their educational experiences in classrooms that are as much like normal as possible. **Deinstitutionalization** is the implementation of the LRE principle in residential treatment facilities. It moves exceptional people out of institutions into smaller community-based settings that are as much like normal living arrangements as possible. **Group homes** are a fast-growing community-based residential alternative for many people who are handicapped.

Group homes provide family-style living. They usually are located in residential neighborhoods near shopping and public transportation. The number of people living in each home varies from three or four to as many as fifteen or twenty. Generally, specially trained professionals serve as house parents for residents. Some group homes are primarily long-term residential placements. People in them are expected to develop independent living skills and often work outside the home in sheltered workshops or businesses in the community. Other group homes are intermediate-care facilities, where people who are handicapped are supposed to learn the skills they need to move to more independent living arrangements (foster homes, supervised apartments).

Group homes are a very positive environment for the people who live in them. But they continue to create controversy in communities across the country. Here's how one town in North Carolina reacted to plans for a small group home in the community:

> Some residents of Echo Farms, a golf subdivision in Wilmington off Carolina Beach Road, are trying to stop a home for the mentally retarded from locating in their neighborhood.
> At issue is the intended use of a brick house at 220 Dorchester Place. The owner, Charles Woodard of Goldsboro, plans to build an intermediate care facility for the mentally retarded.
> About 50 residents met Tuesday night for about two hours at the Echo Farms clubhouse. At the end of the meeting, representatives of the Homeowners Association said they were going to check into the situation. They also asked a lawyer who was present to check on whether Woodard had followed proper procedure before starting to work on the facility. . . . Mitwol [the lawyer] said he would make certain that Woodard had followed all procedures correctly.
> "I think it would behoove all of you folks to hold his feet to the fire on this," he said. "If they didn't follow the rules, they're out." (*Wilmington Morning Star*, June 2, 1988, p. 1C)

Controlling this type of stereotyped thinking and discrimination remains a challenge for all of us.

Alternative Living Units
Some states have organized small group homes of two or three residents as an alternative to more costly homes for larger groups of exceptional people. An **alternative living unit (ALU)** is ideal for providing a more personal environment for training and an easier structure for supervision. In Maryland, 80 percent of the people with handicaps participating in the state's community living programs live in ALUs (Jones, 1988).

The amount of service provided in these settings varies with the needs of residents. People with basic living skills may need a counselor to help with specific activities and tasks (like balancing a checkbook). Others may need someone to live in, to help with cooking, cleaning, and other activities.

One advantage of this type of living arrangement is its flexibility: As residents' needs change, the amount and type of support they receive can be changed; they don't have to change facilities. Professionals who support the use of alternative living units also argue that they are easier to set up than group homes and attract less attention from neighbors.

Foster Homes
Some people with handicaps live with families who provide them a temporary home in return for reimbursement of their living expenses. Foster homes offer a number of positive life experiences for exceptional people.

Participating in normal family experiences, receiving personal attention, and developing close relationships with people who are not handicapped are among the advantages. The primary disadvantage of foster homes is the difficulty of monitoring the quality of the experiences provided.

Independent Living

The greatest opportunity for independence and normal social interactions is provided by living in an apartment, mobile home, or other private residence. And a goal of many professionals in special education is the movement of all people with handicaps to these kinds of independent living facilities. They argue that group homes and foster homes are too "institutional" to fit their ideal of normalization.

Institutions

A residential institution can have as many as five hundred people with handicaps living in it and is an environment that provides few opportunities for normal interactions. In recent years, professionals in special education have been critical of the care provided in the nation's residential facilities. They claim that residential placements violate the ideal of "life as much like normal as possible" that is at the core of Public Law 94–142. Parents do not necessarily agree: Surveys of their attitudes toward residential care are generally favorable.

Checkpoint

- *Employment is the single most important concern of those who work with older people who are handicapped.*
- *Adults with handicaps need vocational training, placement, and evaluation services more than they need transition or postemployment services.*
- *Most adults with disabilities and handicaps say that their greatest wish is to live independently.*
- *As people with handicaps grow older, they face restricted opportunities for education.*
- *The work and life experiences of adults who are gifted are more positive than those of other exceptional people.*
- *The most common work experience for people with handicaps is in sheltered and supported employment settings, not competitive employment positions.*
- *People who are handicapped are much more likely to find and keep jobs today than they were even a few years ago—largely because parents and professionals have worked to give them opportunities to become contributing members of society.*

■ *Today, large numbers of people with handicaps still live in institutional settings, but other, less restricted options are available for those who do not live at home with their families.*

WHAT WE HAVE LEARNED ABOUT SPECIAL EDUCATION

When people hear that we are in special education, they often say, "Oh, that's wonderful! You must have so much patience." We usually respond by saying that you don't need patience in special education, you need persistence. You must persist in working with students who haven't learned what their agemates have learned. You must believe and expect that these students will learn when instruction is adapted to meet their individual learning needs. You must persist in efforts to involve parents in the education of their children because they often have been discouraged and disheartened by their efforts to find help for their child. And you must persist in fighting the tendency for professionals to relinquish responsibility for educating exceptional students once they have been formally declared eligible for special education services.

We've reflected on what we have presented in this book and the challenges awaiting people who will work with students who need special education and we offer you some of these reflections on what goes on in special education.

When we teach people about special education, we organize information around topics other than the categories of exceptionality. We do this for a couple of reasons. First and foremost, we think students are more alike than different. When we describe exceptional students and special education today, we spend a lot of time talking about what those similarities mean for people who live and work with people who are exceptional.

We also think it is important to present students with special needs in ways that are not easily stereotyped. We don't want teachers to be handicapped by what they think students will or will not be able to do. We think the greatest disservice we can do for people who are exceptional is to not challenge them to their fullest potential. Unfortunately, the categorical approach often results in stereotypes that work against this goal.

There are many ways to practice special education and help teachers meet the special learning needs of exceptional students. Good teaching is good teaching, and there are no boundaries on where it can occur or by whom it will be provided. In this book we have not tied instructional practices to categories of exceptional students because we simply do not believe it makes sense to do so. We encourage future teachers to experiment with interventions and monitor the effects of their efforts before deciding what works with exceptional and nonexceptional students. We have used this method as a guide to best practice when describing the principles of effective instruction and specialized methods sometimes used with children with special needs.

People with handicaps are people first and disabled, handicapped, or gifted and talented second. We hope we have conveyed this message to the readers of our book. We know people with disabilities who are teachers, architects, bankers, scientists, bakers, and other professionals in many communities. We'd like the readers of our book to help people who are exceptional have lives as much like normal as possible.

Special education is a helping profession, and tremendous rewards are out there for people in this field. Many good people work with exceptional students, but many more are needed. We hope some of what we have presented will motivate others to enter this dynamic and rewarding field.

We feel that several themes will be central to the future of special education. Special education will continue to be provided to children at younger ages and adults at older ages than ever before in history. They will have access to educational opportunities designed to make their lives as much like normal as possible. Special education will be delivered in schools as it has been in the past, but educational experiences will be provided in other environments as well, such as community-based training facilities. The special education will be technology-oriented because computers can do things that they did not do well a short time ago. Finally, concerns about the merging of special and regular education probably will be the central focus of professional debate for some time to come.

Talking about the regular education initiative—the movement to combine special and regular education—reminds us of a story. Two frogs fell into a cream can. They swam around for a while, discussing the fact that it would be nearly impossible to get out of their predicament. One frog, bemoaning their fate, finally gave up, sank to the bottom of the can, and drowned. The other frog worked vigorously, swimming around the can so fast and so hard that the cream turned to butter, giving the frog a "platform" from which he jumped out of the can. Here is our "platform":

- All students are more alike than different.
- All students have unique learning needs.
- Education should be designed to meet the individual learning needs of all students.
- Good teaching is good teaching.
- All students can profit from education provided in regular classroom environments.

■   Members of society have an obligation to treat people who are exceptional in ways as much like normal as possible, respectful of individual differences that are central to all of our lives.

A new beginning unfolds for you as you take an active role in education. We encourage you to develop a platform of beliefs about educating exceptional students. Regardless of where or when or how you participate in education, you will meet and work with people with special needs. You are ending this first part of your trip through special education, and it may be the beginning of a journey that may become something you do for the rest of your life. If we have motivated you to consider such a possibility, welcome to a wonderful profession. If we have only introduced you to special education, we hope you enjoyed the trip.

Summary

1. Today, parents are being encouraged to keep their exceptional children at home and to be active partners in their education.
2. The role of the family with an exceptional child changes as the child grows and develops.
3. Public Law 99–457 made the education of young children with handicaps compulsory and brought their parents into the educational program.
4. Early intervention programs can be home based or center based. Home-based programs focus on the parents, teaching them the skills they need to work with their child. Although parents may take part in center-based programs, the primary focus here is on direct or indirect services for the child.
5. Language and cultural differences have led to the misidentification of non–English language background students.
6. Computer technology is being used to improve services for exceptional students.
7. For years, many professionals believed special education was a separate system for educating students who are exceptional. Today, the regular education initiative is raising important questions about that belief.
8. Employment is the single most important issue for those who work with adults who are handicapped.
9. Handicapped adults need vocational training, placement, and evaluation services more than they need transition or postemployment services.
10. The goal of most adults with disabilities and handicaps is to live independently.

11. As people with handicaps grow older, their educational opportunities are more limited.
12. The work and life experiences of adults who are gifted are more positive than those of other exceptional people.
13. Most adults with handicaps work in sheltered and supported employment settings, not competitive employment positions.
14. Handicapped people are much more likely to find and keep jobs today than they were even a few years ago—largely because parents and professionals have worked to give them opportunities to become contributing members of society.
15. Today, large numbers of people with handicaps still live in institutional settings, but many other options are available for those who do not live at home with their families.

Activities

1. Locate a group home in your community. Find out when it was established, then check back issues of your local newspaper to see how the community responded to the home. Note the tone of the articles and check for editorial comments in the same or later issues of the paper.
2. Contact your local Association for Retarded Citizens (ARC) and arrange to visit a sheltered workshop and group home. Talk to counselors and people working or living at the facility. Take notes on the numbers of adults present and what they are doing. Compare your impressions of each environment to your first impressions of living in a dorm or apartment or working in a local store, restaurant, or university office.
3. Ask a special education and a regular education professor for their impressions of trends that are likely to influence education during the next century. Ask each what they think of the regular education initiative. Compare the information you receive with that of a classmate who interviews different professors.

Suggested Readings

Clark, G. M., & Knowlton, H. E., (Eds). (1987). Special Issue: The transition from school to adult life. *Exceptional Children, 53.*
>   *This entire issue of a professional journal consists of articles addressing models, programs, outcomes, and trends in secondary education and the transition from school to adult life. It should be required reading for anyone interested in working with older people with handicaps.*

Mangrum, C. T. II, & Strichart, S. S. (1984). *College and the learning disabled student.* New York: Grune and Stratton.

Increasingly, teachers are being asked to assist exceptional students in making decisions about higher education. This book provides an overview of comprehensive programs of services for students with learning disabilities after they enter college. It has widespread applicability for other exceptional students as well.

Stainback, S., Stainback, W., & Forest, M. (1989). *Educating all students in the mainstream of regular education.* Baltimore, MD: Paul H. Brookes.

This book addresses approaches to merging special and regular education so that more students will be educated in the mainstream. The introduction and overview are followed by examples of a school system, classroom, and family actively involved in promoting integration. Organizational considerations and strategies are also provided for promoting educational alternatives for keeping exceptional students in regular classes.

Appendix A
Professional Associations Relevant to Special Education

Organization	Established	Number of Members
Alexander Graham Bell Association for the Deaf 3417 Volta Place, N.W. Washington, DC 20007	1890	7,000
American Association on Mental Deficiency 5101 Washington Ave., N.W. Washington, DC 20016	1876	13,000
American Orthopsychiatric Association 1775 Broadway New York, NY 10019	1924	8,000
American Personnel and Guidance Association Two Skyline Place, Suite 400 5203 Leesburg Pike Falls Church, VA 22041	1952	41,000
American Psychological Association 1200 17th St., N.W. Washington, DC 20036 (Especially Divisions of Child and Youth Services, Clinical Psychology, Educational Psychology, School Psychology, Mental Retardation, Counseling Psychology, and Developmental Psychology)	1892	50,000

Members	What They Do
Teachers of the deaf, speech-language pathologists, audiologists, physicians, hearing aid dealers	Promote the teaching of speech, lipreading, and use of residual hearing to the deaf; encourage research; and work to further better education of the deaf.
Physicians, educators, administrators, social workers, psychologists, psychiatrists, and others interested in the general welfare of mentally retarded persons and the study of cause, treatment, and prevention of mental retardation	Work to promote the general welfare of mentally retarded persons; facilitate research and information dissemination relative to causes, treatment, and prevention of mental retardation.
Psychiatrists, psychologists, psychiatric social workers, educators	Provides a common meeting ground for all of those interested in the study of human behavior and especially abnormal behavior.
Guidance counselors and personnel workers	Scientific professional society working to improve effective guidance and counseling services in elementary and secondary schools; advocates for programs for improved mental health; facilitates research and professional development.
Psychologists and educators	Scientific and professional society working to improve mental health services and to advocate for legislation and programs that will promote mental health; facilitate research and professional development.

Organization	Established	Number of Members
American Speech-Language-Hearing Association 10801 Rockville Pike Rockville, MD 20852	1925	35,000
Association for Children and Adults with Learning Disabilities 4156 Library Road Pittsburgh, PA 15234	1964	60,000
Association for the Gifted 1920 Association Drive Reston, VA 22091	1958	2,000
Association for Retarded Citizens 2501 Avenue J Arlington, TX 76011	1950	200,000
Association for the Severely Handicapped 7010 Roosevelt Way, N.E. Seattle, WA 98115	1974	5,500
Council for Children with Behavioral Disorders 1920 Association Drive Reston, VA 22091	1962	4,811
Council for Educational Diagnostic Services 1920 Association Drive Reston, VA 22091	1974	1,342
Council for Exceptional Children 1920 Association Drive Reston, VA 22091	1922	62,000

Members	What They Do
Specialists in speech-language pathology and audiology	Advocate for provision of speech-language and hearing services in school and clinical settings; advocate for legislation relative to the profession; and work to promote effective services and development of the profession.
Parents of children with learning disabilities and interested professionals	Advance the education and general well-being of "children with adequate intelligence who have learning disabilities arising from perceptual, conceptual, or subtle coordinative problems, sometimes accompanied by behavior difficulties."
Members of the Council for Exceptional Children who teach gifted students or educate professionals to work with gifted students	Disseminate information, encourage research and scholarly investigation on education of gifted students, encourage professional development for teachers and others who work with gifted students.
Parents, professionals, and others interested in mentally retarded individuals	Work on local, state, and national levels to promote treatment, research, public understanding, and legislation for mentally retarded persons; provide counseling for parents of mentally retarded children.
Teachers, therapists, parents, administrators, university faculty, and advocates involved in all areas of service to severely handicapped persons	Advocate quality education for handicapped persons, and work to ensure a dignified, autonomous lifestyle for all severely handicapped persons; disseminate information and promote research on education of and service to severely handicapped individuals.
Members of the Council for Exceptional Children who teach children with behavior disorders or who train teachers to work with those children	Promote education and general welfare of children and youth with behavior disorders or serious emotional disturbances. Promote professional growth and research on students with behavior disorders and severe emotional disturbances.
Members of the Council for Exceptional Children who are school psychologists, educational diagnosticians, social workers, etc., and who are involved in diagnosing educational difficulties	Promote the most appropriate education of children and youth through appraisal, diagnosis, educational intervention, implementation, and evaluation of a prescribed educational program. Work to facilitate the professional development of those who assess students. Work for further development of better diagnostic techniques and procedures.
Teachers, administrators, teacher educators, and related service personnel	Advocate for services for handicapped and gifted individuals. A professional organization that addresses service, training, and research relative to handicapped and gifted persons.

Organization	Established	Number of Members
Council for Learning Disabilities Dept. of Special Education University of Louisville Louisville, KY 40292	1983 (originally est. in 1968 as a division of Council for Exceptional Children)	5,000
Council of Administrators of Special Education 1920 Association Drive Reston, VA 22091	1951	3,600
Division for Children with Communication Disorders 1920 Association Drive Reston, VA 22091	1964	1,820
Division for Early Childhood 1920 Association Drive Reston, VA 22091	1973	2,688
Division for the Physically Handicapped 1920 Association Drive Reston, VA 22091	1958	1,603
Division for the Visually Handicapped 1920 Association Drive Reston, VA 22091	1954	851
Division on Career Development 1920 Association Drive Reston, VA 22091	1976	1,289

Members	What They Do
Teachers who work with students with specific learning disabilities, teacher trainers who educate professionals to work with those students, and researchers who conduct research of learning disabled students	Promote the general welfare and education of individuals with specific learning disabilities through improving teacher preparation programs, local special education programs, and research.
Members of the Council for Exceptional Children who are administrators, directors, coordinators, or supervisors of programs, schools, or classes for exceptional children; college faculty who train administrators	Promote professional leadership; provide opportunities for the study of problems common to its members; communicate through discussion and publications information that will facilitate improved services for exceptional children.
Members of the Council for Exceptional Children who are speech-language pathologists, audiologists, teachers of children with communication disorders, or educators of professionals who plan to work with children who have communication disorders	Promote the education of children with communication disorders. Promote professional growth and research.
Members of the Council for Exceptional Children who teach preschool children and infants or educate teachers to work with young children	Promote effective education for young children and infants. Promote professional development of those who work with young children and infants. Promote legislation and research.
Members of the Council for Exceptional Children who work with individuals who have physical handicaps or educate professionals to work with those individuals	Promote closer relationships among educators of students who are physically handicapped or homebound. Facilitate research and encourage development of new ideas, practices, and techniques through professional meetings, workshops, and publications.
Members of the Council for Exceptional Children who work with individuals who have visual handicaps or educate professionals to work with those individuals	Work to advance the education and training of individuals with visual handicaps. Work to bring about better understanding of educational, emotional, or other problems associated with visual impairment. Facilitate research and development of new techniques or ideas in education and training of individuals with vision problems.
Members of the Council for Exceptional Children who teach or in other ways work toward career development and vocational education of exceptional children	Promote and encourage professional growth of all those concerned with career development and vocational education. Promote research, legislation, information dissemination, and technical assistance relevant to career development and vocational education.

Organization	Established	Number of Members
Division on Mental Retardation 1920 Association Drive Reston, VA 22091	1964	6,897
Gifted Child Society P.O. Box 120 Oakland, NJ 07436	1957	3,000
National Association for the Education of Young Children 1834 Connecticut Avenue, N.W. Washington, DC 20009	1926	33,000
National Association of School Psychologists 1929 K St., N.W., Suite 520 Washington, DC 20006	1969	6,000
National Association of Social Workers 1425 H St., N.W., Suite 600 Washington, DC 20005	1955	85,000
National Easter Seal Society 2023 W. Ogden Avenue Chicago, IL 60612	1919	1,000
National Federation of the Blind 1800 Johnson Street Baltimore, MD 21230	1940	50,000

Members	What They Do
Members of the Council for Exceptional Children who work with mentally retarded students or educate professionals to work with those students	Work to advance the education of the mentally retarded, research on mental retardation, and the training of professionals to work with mentally retarded individuals. Promote public understanding of mental retardation and professional development of those who work with mentally retarded persons.
Parents and educators of gifted children	Train educators to meet the needs of gifted students, offer assistance to parents facing special problems in raising gifted children, and seek public recognition of the needs of gifted children.
Teachers and directors of nursery schools, day care centers, cooperatives, church schools, play groups, and others interested in preschool education	Promote service and action on behalf of the needs and rights of young children, with emphasis on provision of educational services and resources.
School psychologists	Serve the mental health and educational needs of all children and youth. Encourage and provide opportunities for professional growth for school psychologists. Inform the public about the services and practice of school psychology. Work to advance the standards of the profession of school psychology.
Persons with a minimum of a bachelor's degree in social work	Promote the quality and effectiveness of social work practice by advancing sound social policies and programs and using the professional knowledge and skills of social work to "alleviate sources of deprivation, distress, and strain"; set professional standards; conduct research; and work to improve professional practice.
State units (49) and local societies (951); no individual members	Establish and run programs for physically handicapped individuals, usually including diagnostic services, speech therapy, preschool services, physical therapy, and occupational therapy.
State and local organizations of blind people	Work to facilitate equality of opportunity for blind people and their integration into society. Monitor legislation affecting the blind, evaluate services for the blind, and work to improve policies toward blind individuals. Conduct leadership training for blind people and work to stimulate research on blindness.

Organization	Established	Number of Members
Orton Society 8415 Bellona Lane, Suite 113 Towson, MD 21204	1949	5,000
Teacher Education Division 1920 Association Drive Reston, VA 22091	1953	1,396

Members	What They Do
Members of the professions of neurology, pediatrics, psychiatry, education, social work, psychology; parents and others interested in study, treatment, and prevention of the problems of specific language disability, often called dyslexia	Provide a focal point for activities and ideas generated in various fields as they relate to problems of language development and learning; specific reference to students with dyslexia.
Members of the Council for Exceptional Children who are teacher educators	Stimulate and actively assist in development of programs to educate professionals who will work with exceptional students. Promote research on teacher education.

Appendix B
Commonly Used Tests

Table B.1
Commonly Used Achievement Tests

Test	Authors	Type of Test	
		Screening	Diagnostic
Basic Achievement Skills Individual Screener	J. L. Sonnenschein	X	
Brigance ® Diagnostic Inventory of Early Development	A. Brigance		X
California Achievement Tests	CTB/McGraw-Hill	X	
Diagnostic Achievement Test for Adolescents	P. Newcomer & B. Bryant	X	
Diagnostic Inventory of Basic Skills	A. Brigance		X
Diagnostic Inventory of Essential Skills	A. Brigance		X
Diagnostic Mathematics Inventory	J. K. Gessell		X
Diagnostic Reading Scales	G. D. Spache		X
Durrell Analysis of Reading Difficulty	D. D. Durrell & J. Catterson		X
Formal Reading Inventory	L. Wiederholt	X	X
Gates-McKillop-Horowitz Reading Diagnostic Tests	A. I. Gates, A. S. McKillop, & R. Horowitz		X
Gray Oral Reading Test Revised	L. Wiederholt & B. Bryant		X
Hudson Educational Skills Inventory	G. F. Hudson, S. E. Colson, D. L. Hudson Welch, A. K. Banikowski & T. A. Mehring	X	

Standardization		Administration		Skills Assessed			
Norm-Referenced	*Criterion-Referenced*	*Individual*	*Group*	*Multiple*	*Single*	Publisher	Date
X		X		X		Psychological Corporation	1983
	X	X				Curriculum Associates	1978
X	X		X	X		CTB/McGraw-Hill	1985
X			X	X		Pro-Ed	1986
	X	X				Curriculum Associates	1977
	X	X				Curriculum Associates	1978
	X	X			X	CTB/McGraw-Hill	1983
X		X			X	CTB/McGraw-Hill	1981
X		X			X	Harcourt Brace Jonanovich	1980
X		X			X	Pro-Ed	1986
X		X			X	Teachers College Press	1981
X		X			X	Pro-Ed	1986
X		X		X		Pro-Ed	1989

Table B.1   *(cont.)*
Commonly Used Achievement Tests

Test	Authors	Type of Test	
		Screening	*Diagnostic*
Iowa Tests of Basic Skills	A. N. Hieronymus, H. D. Hoover, E. F. Lindquist & D. P. Scannell	X	
Kaufman Test of Educational Achievement	A. Kaufman & N. Kaufman	X	
Keymath Diagnostic Arithmetic Test—Revised	A. Connolly, W. Nachtman & E. Pritchett		X
Language Diagnostic Tests	I. H. Balow, T. P. Hogan, R. C. Farr & G. A. Prescott		X
Mathematics Diagnostic Tests	T. P. Hogan, R. C. Farr, G. A. Prescott & I. H. Balow		X
Metropolitan Achievement Tests Survey Battery	G. A. Prescott, I. H. Balow, T. P. Hogan & R. C. Farr	X	
Peabody Individual Achievement Test—Revised	F. C. Markwardt	X	
Prescriptive Reading Inventory	CTB/McGraw-Hill	X	
Reading Diagnostic Tests	R. C. Farr, G. A. Prescott, I. H. Balow & T. P. Hogan		X

Standardization		Administration		Skills Assessed			
Norm-Referenced	Criterion-Referenced	Individual	Group	Multiple	Single	Publisher	Date
X	X		X	X		Riverside Publishing Company	1986
X		X		X		American Guidelines	1985
X	X	X			X	American Guidance Services	1989
X	X		X		X		
X	X		X		X		
X			X	X		Psychological Corporation	1984
X		X		X		American Guidance Services	1989
	X	X			X	CTB/McGraw-Hill	1980
X	X		X		X		

Table B.1 *(cont.)*
Commonly Used Achievement Tests

		Type of Test	
Test	**Authors**	*Screening*	*Diagnostic*
Screening Children for Related Early Educational Needs	W. P. Hresko, D. K. Reid, D. D. Hammill, H. P. Ginsburg & A. J. Baroody	X	
SRA Achievement Series	R. A. Naslund, L. P. Thorpe & D. W. Lefever	X	
Standardized Reading Inventory	P. Newcomer		X
Stanford Achievement Test	E. R. Gardner, H. C. Rudman, B. Karlsen & J. C. Merwin	X	
Stanford Diagnostic Mathematics Test	L. S. Beatty, E. Gardner, R. Madden & B. Karlsen		X
Stanford Diagnostic Reading Test	B. Karlsen & E. Gardner		X
Stanford Early School Achievement Test	R. Madden, E. F. Gardner & C. S. Collins	X	
Test of Academic Skills	R. Callis, J. C. Merwin & H. C. Rudman	X	
Test of Early Reading Ability—2	D. K. Reid, W. P. Hresko & D. D. Hammill	X	
Test of Mathematical Ability	V. Brown & E. McEntire		X

| Standardization | | Administration | | Skills Assessed | | | |
Norm-Referenced	Criterion-Referenced	Individual	Group	Multiple	Single	Publisher	Date
X		X		X		Pro-Ed	1988
X	X		X	X		Science Research Associates	1978
	X	X			X	Pro-Ed	1986
X	X		X		X	Psychological Corporation	1982
X	X		X	X		Psychological Corporation	1985
X			X		X	Psychological Corporation	1985
X	X		X	X		Psychological Corporation	1983
X	X		X	X		Psychological Corporation	1983
X		X		X		Pro-Ed	1989
X		X			X	Pro-Ed	1984

Table B.1 *(cont.)*
Commonly Used Achievement Tests

Test	Authors	Type of Test	
		Screening	*Diagnostic*
Test of Reading Comprehension—Revised	V. Brown, D. Hammill & L. Wiederholt		X
Test of Written Spelling—2	S. Larsen & D. Hammill		X
Tests of Achievement and Proficiency	D. P. Scannell	X	
Wide Range Achievement Test	S. Jastak & G. Wilkinson	X	
Woodcock Reading Mastery Tests—Revised	R. Woodcock	X	X

Table B.2
Commonly Used Achievement Tests

Test	Authors	Behaviors Sampled
Auditory Discrimination Test	J. Wepman	Auditory discrimination of words
Carrow Elicited Language Inventory	E. Carrow	Expressive grammatical competence
Goldman-Fristoe Test of Articulation	R. Goldman & M. Fristoe	Articulation of speech sounds
Northwestern Syntax Screening Test	L. Lee	Comprehension of expressive language
Peabody Picture Vocabulary Test—Revised	L. Dunn & L. Dunn	Receptive vocabulary
Phonological Process Analysis	F. Weiner	Articulation of speech sounds

| Standardization | | Administration | | Skills Assessed | | | |
Norm-Referenced	Criterion-Referenced	*Individual*	*Group*	*Multiple*	*Single*	Publisher	Date
X		X			X	Pro-Ed	1986
X		X			X	Pro-Ed	1986
X	X		X	X		Riverside Publishing Company	1986
X		X		X		Jastak Assessment Systems	1984
X	X	X			X	American Guidance Services	1987

| Administration | | Standardization | | | |
Group	*Individual*	Norm-Referenced	Criterion-Referenced	Publisher	Date
	X	X		Language Research Associates	1973
	X	X	X	Learning Concepts	1974
	X		X	American Guidance Services	1986
	X	X		CTB/McGraw-Hill	1969
	X	X		American Guidance Services	1981
	X		X	University Park Press	1979

Table B.2 *(cont.)*
Commonly Used Achievement Tests

Test	Authors	Behaviors Sampled
Test for Auditory Comprehension of Language	E. Carrow-Wolfolk	Style Receptive vocabulary Language structure: Morphology Syntax Semantics
Test of Adolescent Language	D. D. Hammill, V. Brown, S. Larsen & L. Weiderholt	Listening; Speaking; Reading; Writing; Spoken language; Written language; Vocabulary; Grammar; Receptive language; Expressive language
Test of Early Language Development	W. Hresko K. K. Reid & D. D. Hammill	Semantics and syntax of spoken language
Test of Language Development—Intermediate	D. Hammill & P. Newcomer	Understanding the meaning of spoken words; Sentence combining; Word ordering; Grammatic comprehension
Test of Language Development—Primary	P. Newcomer & D. Hammill	Picture vocabulary; Oral vocabulary; Grammatic understanding; Sentence imitation; Grammatic completion; Word articulation; Word discrimination
Test of Written Language	D. Hammill & S. Larsen	Vocabulary; Thematic maturity; Thought unity; Handwriting; Spelling; Word usage

| Administration | | Standardization | | | |
Group	Individual	Norm-Referenced	Criterion-Referenced	Publisher	Date
	X	X		Learning Concepts	1985
X		X		Pro-Ed	1987
	X	X		Pro-Ed	1981
	X	X		Pro-Ed	1982
	X	X		Pro-Ed	1982
X	X	X		Pro-Ed	1983

Table B.3
Commonly Used Intelligence Tests

Test	Authors	Administration		Publisher	Date
		Group	*Individual*		
Arthur Adaptation of the Leiter International Performance Scale	G. Arthur		X	Stoelting	1950
Blind Learning Aptitude Test	T. E. Newland		X	University of Illinois Press	1969
Cognitive Abilities Test	R. Thorndike & E. Hagen	X		Riverside Publishing Company	1986
Columbia Mental Maturity Scale	B. B. Burgmeister, L. H. Blum & I. Lorge		X	Psychological Corporation	1972
Culture Fair Intelligence Scale	R. Cattell & P. Cattell	X		Institute for Personality and Ability Testing	1950, 1960, 1963
Detroit Test of Learning Aptitude—Primary	D. Hammill & B. Bryant		X	Pro-Ed	1986
Detroit Tests of Learning Aptitude—2	D. Hammill		X	Pro-Ed	1985
Educational Ability Series	T. Thurstone	X		Science Research Associates	1978
Henmon-Nelson Tests of Mental Ability	T. Lamke, M. Nelson & J. L. French	X		Riverside Publishing Company	1973, 1974
Kaufman Assessment Battery for Children	A. Kaufman & N. Kaufman		X	American Guidance Services	1983
McCarthy Scales of Children's Abilities	D. McCarthy		X	Psychological Corporation	1972
Nebraska Test of Learning Aptitude	M. Hiskey		X	Marshall S. Hiskey	1966
Otis-Lennon School Ability Test	A. Otis & R. Lennon	X		Psychological Corporation	1982
Peabody Picture Vocabulary Test—Revised	L. Dunn & L. Dunn		X	American Guidance Services	1981

Table B.3 *(cont.)*
Commonly Used Intelligence Tests

Test	Authors	Administration Group	Individual	Publisher	Date
Pictorial Test of Intelligence	J. L. French		X	Houghton Mifflin Company	1964
Slosson Intelligence Test	R. L. Slosson		X	Slosson Educational Publications	1971
Stanford-Binet Intelligence Scale	R. L. Thorndike, E. Hagen & J. Sattler		X	Riverside Publishing Company	1985
Test of Nonverbal Intelligence	L. Brown, R. J. Sherbenou & S. J. Dollar		X	Pro-Ed	1982
Wechsler Adult Intelligence Scale —Revised	D. Wechsler		X	Psychological Corporation	1981
Wechsler Preschool and Primary Scale	D. Wechsler		X	Psychological Corporation	1967
Wechsler Intelligence Scale for Children —Revised	D. Wechsler		X	Psychological Corporation	1974
Woodcock-Johnson Psychoeducational Battery	R. Woodcock		X	DLM	1989

Table B.4
Commonly Used Measures of Socioemotional Functioning and Behavior Problems

Test	Authors	Administration Group	Individual	Publisher	Date
Behavior Evaluation Scale	S. B. McCarney, J. E. Leigh & J. A. Cornbleet		X	Pro-Ed	1983
Behavior Rating Profile	L. Brown & D. D. Hammill		X	Pro-Ed	1983

Table B.4 *(cont.)*
Commonly Used Measures of Socioemotional Functioning and Behavior Problems

| Test | Authors | Administration | | Publisher | Date |
		Group	Individual		
Peterson-Quay Problem Behavior Checklist—Revised	D. Peterson & H. Quay		X	University of Miami	1983
Self Perception Profile for Children	S. Harter	X	X	University of Denver	1988
Self Perception Profile for Adolescents	S. Harter	X	X	University of Denver	1988
Social Skills Rating Scales	S. Elliott & F. Gresham		X	American Guidance Service	1989
Walker-McConnell Scale of Social Competence and School Adjustment	H. M. Walker		X	Pro-Ed	1988

Table B.5
Commonly Used Measures of Adapted Behavior

Test	Authors	Publisher	Date
AAMD Adaptive Behavior Scale	K. Nihara, R. Foster, M. Shelhass & H. Leland	American Association on Mental Deficiency	1969
AAMD Adaptive Behavior Scale, Public School Version	N. Lambert, M. Windmiller, I. Cole & R. Rigueroa	American Association on Mental Deficiency	1981
Vineland Adaptive Behavior Scale	S. Sparrow, D. Ball & D. Cicchetti	American Guidance Service	1984
Adaptive Behavior Inventory	L. Brown & J. Leigh	Pro-Ed	1986
Scales of Independent Behavior	R. Bruininks, R. Woodcock, R. Weatherman & B. Hill	Teaching Resources/DLM	1984

Appendix C
Council for Exceptional Children Code of Ethics

We declare the following principles to be the Code of Ethics for educators of exceptional persons. Members of the special education profession are responsible for upholding and advancing these principles. Members of the Council for Exceptional Children agree to judge by them in accordance with the spirit and provisions of this Code.

a. Special education professionals are committed to developing the highest educational and quality of life potential of exceptional individuals.

b. Special education professionals promote and maintain a high level of competence and integrity in practicing their profession.

c. Special education professionals engage in professional activities which benefit exceptional individuals, their families, other colleagues, students, or research subjects.

d. Special education professionals exercise objective professional judgment in the practice of their profession.

e. Special education professionals strive to advance their knowledge and skills regarding the education of exceptional individuals.

f. Special education professionals work within the standards and policies of their profession.

g. Special education professionals seek to uphold and improve where necessary the laws, regulations, and policies governing the delivery of special education and related services and the practice of their profession.

h. Special education professionals do not condone or participate in unethical or illegal acts, nor violate professional standards adopted by the Delegate Assembly of CEC.

Source: The Council for Exceptional Children. Copyright © 1983. Reprinted by permission.

Appendix D
Council for Exceptional Children Policy on Standards for Professional Practices in Special Education

A. Requirements for professional practice should be sufficiently flexible to provide for the newly emerging and changing roles of special education professionals and to encourage experimentation and innovation in their preparation.

B. CEC and its divisions should be the lead organizations in establishing minimum standards for entry into the profession of special education. CEC should develop and promote a model that requires no less than a bachelor's degree which encompasses the knowledge and skills consistent with entry level into special education teaching.

   The model will specify knowledge and skills that are (a) common to teaching; (b) related to the practice of special education; (c) unique to specific populations (exceptionalities and infancy through secondary). A special education teacher will be required to demonstrate requisite knowledge and skills in these areas.

C. Each new professional in special education should receive a minimum of a one-year mentorship, during the first year of his/her professional special education practice in a new role. The mentor should be an experienced professional in the same or a similar role, who can provide expertise and support on a continuing basis.

D. State and provincial education agencies should adopt common knowledge and skills as a basis for providing reciprocity for approval of professional practice across state and provincial lines.

E. Approval of individuals for professional practice in the field of special education should be for a limited period of time with periodic renewal.

F. There should be a continuum of professional development for special educators. The continuum for special education teachers should include at a minimum:

1. Knowledge and skills required to practice as a teacher in a particular area of exceptionality/age grouping (infancy through secondary).
2. Knowledge and skills required to excel in the instruction of a particular area of exceptionality/age grouping (infancy through secondary).

G. Each professional in the field of educating exceptional students (e.g., teachers, supervisors, administrators, college/university faculty) should participate in a minimum of 25 clock hours each year of planned, "pre-approved," organized, and recognized professional development activities related to his/her field of professional practice. Such activities may include a combination of professional development units, continuing education units, college/university coursework, professional organization (e.g., CEC federations and chapters, divisions, sub-divisions, and caucuses) service, professional workshops, special projects, or reading professional literature. Employing agencies should provide resources to enable each professional's continuing development.

Source: The Council for Exceptional Children. Copyright © 1983. Reprinted by permission.

References

Abeson, A. (1979). Litigation. In F. Weintraub, A. Abeson, J. Ballard, & M. LaVor (Eds.), *Public policy and the education of exceptional children.* Reston, VA: Council for Exceptional Children.

Adelman, F., Bellizia, J., Joslin, N., McGrath, L., Manipoli, J., Farrar, N., & Yates, N. (1976). Mainstreaming. *Today's Education, 65,* 18–19.

Akey, D. (1983). *Encyclopedia of associations: National organizations of the U.S.* Detroit: Gale Research.

Algozzine, B. (Ed.). (1989). *Problem behavior management: Educator's resource service.* Rockville, MD: Aspen.

Algozzine, B., & McGraw, K. (1980). Diagnostic testing in mathematics: An extension of the PIAT? *Teaching Exceptional Children, 12,* 71–77.

Algozzine, B., & Mercer, C. (1980). Labels and expectancies for handicapped children and youth. In D. Sabatino & L. Mann (Eds.), *Fourth review of special education.* New York: Grune & Stratton.

Algozzine, B., & Ysseldyke, J. (1981). Special education services for normal children: Better safe than sorry? *Exceptional Children, 48,* 238–243.

Aloia, G. (1975). Effects of physical stigmata and labels on judgments of subnormality by preservice teachers. *Mental Retardation, 13,* 17–21.

American Association on Mental Deficiency (AAMD). (1987). The AAMD position statement on aversive therapy. *Mental Retardation, 25,* 18.

American Psychiatric Association. (1952). *Diagnostic and statistical manual of mental disorders.* Washington, DC: APA.

American Psychiatric Association. (1968). *Diagnostic and statistical manual of mental disorders* (2d ed.). Washington, DC: APA.

American Psychiatric Association. (1987). *Diagnostic and statistical manual of mental disorders* (3rd ed., rev.). Washington, DC: APA.

American Speech-Language-Hearing Association. (1976). *Comprehensive assessment and service information system.* Washington, DC: ASHA.

American Speech-Language-Hearing Association. (1982). Definitions:

Communicative disorders and variations. *ASHA, 24,* 949–950.

Anderson, W., Chitwood, S., & Hayden, D. (1982). *Negotiating the special education maze: A guide for parents and teachers.* Englewood Cliffs, NJ: Prentice-Hall.

Arakawa, J. (1981). Minority voices: Neither part of a double disability is the whole person. *Disabled USA, 4,* 1.

Asch, A. (1989). Has the law made a difference? What some disabled students have to say. In D. Lipsky & A. Gartner (Eds.), *Beyond separate education: Quality education for all* (pp. 181–205). Baltimore: Brookes.

Bardon, J. (1982). The psychology of school psychology. In C. Reynolds & J. Gutkin (Eds.), *The handbook of school psychology.* New York: Wiley.

Becker, G., & Jauregui, J. (1985). The invisible isolation of deaf women: Its effect on social awareness. In M. Degan & N. Brooks (Eds.), *Women and disability: The double handicap* (pp. 23–36). New Brunswick, NJ: Transaction Books.

Beers, C. (1908). *A mind that found itself.* New York: Longmans, Green.

Bellamy, T. (1987, May). *The OSEP plan for LRE: Schools are for everybody!* Welcome address to the National Leadership Conference, Indianapolis.

Bersoff, D. (1979). Regarding psychologists testily: Legal regulation of psychological assessment in the public schools. *Maryland Law Review, 39,* 27–120.

Bettelheim, B. (1972). How do you help a child who has a physical handicap? *Ladies Home Journal, 89,* 34–35.

Biklen, D. (1985). Achieving the complete school: Strategies for effective mainstreaming. New York: Teachers College Press.

Biklen, D. (1989). Redefining education. In D. Biklen, D. Ferguson, & A. Ford (Eds.), *Schooling and disability* (pp. 1–24). Chicago: National Society for the Study of Education.

Blanton, R. (1976). Historical perspectives on classification of mental retardation. In N. Hobbs (Ed.), *Issues in the classification of children* (Vol. 1). San Francisco: Jossey-Bass.

Blatt, B. (1970). *Exodus from pandemonium: Human abuse and a reformation of public policy.* Boston: Allyn & Bacon.

Blatt, B. (1976). *Revolt of the idiots: A story.* Glen Ridge, NJ: Exceptional Press.

Blatt, B. (1981). *In and out of mental retardation.* Baltimore: University Park Press.

Bloom, B. (Ed.). (1956). *Taxonomy of educational objectives. Handbook I: Cognitive domain.* New York: McKay.

Bockhoven, J. (1963). *Moral treatment in American psychiatry.* New York: Springer.

Borg, W. (1980). Time and school learning. In C. Denham & A. Lieberman (Eds.), *Time to learn.* Washington, DC: National Institute of Education.

Bouvier, L., and Davis, C. (1982). *The future racial composition of the United States.* Washington, DC: Demographic Information Services Center of Population Reference Bureau.

Braaten, S., Kauffman, J. M., Braaten, B., Polsgrove, L., & Nelson, C. M. (1988). The regular education initiative: Patent medicine for behavioral disorders. *Exceptional Children, 55,* 21–28.

Brown, F. (1981). *Measuring classroom achievement.* New York: Holt, Rinehart & Winston.

Budoff, M., & Orenstein, A. (1981). Special education appeals hearings: Are they fair and are they helping? *Exceptional Education Quarterly, 2,* 37–48.

Burrello, L., & Sage, D. (1979). *Leadership and change in special education.* Englewood Cliffs, NJ: Prentice-Hall.

Carter, J., & Sugai, G. (1989). Survey on prereferral practices: Responses from state departments of education. *Exceptional Children, 55,* 298–302.

Cartwright, G., Cartwright, C., & Ward, M. (1989). *Educating special learners* (3rd ed.). Belmont, CA: Wadsworth.

Chalfant, J. (1980). *A teacher assistance model: Inservice training for teachers and administrators* (Project No. 451 AH 81305). Washington, DC: Bureau of Education for the Handicapped.

Chalfant, J., Pysh, M., & Moultrie, R. (1979). Teacher assistance teams: A model for within building problem-solving. *Learning Disability Quarterly, 2,* 85–96.

Chinn, P., & McCormick, L. (1986). Cultural diversity and exceptionality. In N. Haring & L. McCormick (Eds.), *Exceptional children and youth.* Columbus, OH: Merrill.

Choate, J., Bennett, T., Enright, B., Miller, L., Poteet, J., & Rakes, T. (1987). *Assessing and programming basic curriculum skills.* Boston: Allyn & Bacon.

Clark, B. (1983). *Growing up gifted.* (2d ed.) Columbus, OH: Merrill.

Coleman, M. (1986). *Behavior disorders: Theory and practice.* Englewood Cliffs, NJ: Prentice-Hall.

Coles, G. (1988). *The learning mystique.* New York: Fawcett-Columbine.

Committee for Economic Development. (1987). *Children in need: Investment strategies for the educationally disadvantaged.* Washington, DC: Committee for Economic Development.

Craig, P. (1981). Provision of related services: A good idea gone awry. *Exceptional Education Quarterly, 2,* 11–16.

Creer, T., Marion, R., & Harm, D. (1988). Childhood asthma. In V. Van Hasselt, P. Strain, & M. Hersen (Eds.), *Handbook of developmental and physical disabilities.* New York: Pergamon Press.

Cullinan, D., Epstein, M., & Lloyd, J. (1983). *Behavior disorders of children and adolescents.* Englewood Cliffs, NJ: Prentice-Hall.

DeBoer, A. (1986). *The art of consulting.* Chicago: Arcturus Books.

DeBoer, A. (in press). *A "special" alternative to staff development: A pre-referral consultation process.* Chicago: Arcturus Books.

de Boor, M. (1975). What is to become of Katherine? *Exceptional Children, 41,* 517–518.

Degan, M., & Brooks, N. (1985). Introduction—Women and disability: The double handicap. In M. Degan & N. Brooks (Eds.), *Women and disability: The double handicap* (pp. 1–5). New Brunswick, NJ: Transaction Books.

Delquadri, J., Greenwood, C., Whorton, D., Carta, J., & Hall, V. (1986). *Exceptional Children, 52,* 535–542.

Deno, E. (1970). Special education as developmental capital. *Exceptional Children, 37,* 229–237.

Deshler, D., & Schumaker, J. (1986). Learning strategies: An instructional alternative for low-achieving adolescents. *Exceptional Children, 52,* 583–590.

Dunn, L. (1968). Special education for the mildly retarded—Is much of it justifiable? *Exceptional Children, 35,* 5–22.

Edgerton, R. (1967). *The cloak of competence.* Berkeley, CA: University of California Press.

Edmonson, B. (1988). Disability and sexual adjustment. In V. Van Hasselt, P. Strain, & M. Hersen (Eds.), *Handbook of developmental and physical disabilities.* New York: Pergamon Press.

Ekwall, E. (1981). *Locating and correcting reading difficulties* (3rd ed.). Columbus, OH: Merrill.

Elliot, E. (1988). Commissioner's statement. In J. Stern (Ed.), *The condition of education: Elementary and secondary education.* Washington, DC: National Center for Education Statistics.

Englemann, S., Granzin, A., & Severson, H. (1979). Diagnosing instruction. *Journal of Special Education, 13,* 355–365.

Esquirol, J. (1845). Mental maladies (E. Hunt, Trans.). Philadelphia: Lea & Blanchard. (Original work published 1838)

Ferguson, D., & Asch, A. (1989). Lessons from life: Personal and parental perspectives on school, childhood, and disability. In D. Biklen, D. Ferguson, & A. Ford (Eds.), *Schooling and disability* (pp. 108–140). Chicago: National Society for the Study of Education.

Fischer, C., Berliner, D., Filby, N., Marliave, R., Cohen, L., Deshaw, M., & Moore, J. (1978). *Teaching and learning in elementary schools: A summary of the beginning teacher evaluation study.* San Francisco, CA: Far West Regional Laboratory for Educational Research and Development.

Forest, M. (1985). Education update. *Canadian Journal of Mental Retardation, 35,* 37–40.

Foster, G., & Ysseldyke, J. (1976). Expectancy and halo effects as a result of artificially induced bias. *Contemporary Educational Psychology, 1,* 37–45.

Friedman, J., & Gallo, N. (1988). Steve Largent has caught more passes than anyone, but without his home team he'd be incomplete. *People Weekly, 30*(22), 77–80.

Fuchs, D., & Fuchs, L. (1988). *Mainstream assistance teams.* Nashville: Vanderbilt University.

Furakawa, C., Shapiro, G., DuHamel, T., Weimer, L., Pierson, W., & Bierman, C. (1984). Learning and behavior problems associated with theophylline therapy. *Lancet, 621.*

Gallagher, J. (1985). *Teaching the gifted child* (3rd ed.). Boston: Allyn & Bacon.

Gickling, E., & Havertape, J. (1981). Curriculum-based assessment. In J. Tucker (Ed.), *Non-test-based assessment.* Minneapolis: National School Psychology Inservice Training Network.

Gickling, E., & Thompson, V. (1985). A personal view of curriculum-based assessment. *Exceptional Children, 52,* 205–218.

Glaser, W. (1965). *Reality therapy.* New York: Harper & Row.

Goffman, E. (1963). *Stigma: Notes on the management of spoiled identity.* Englewood Cliffs, NJ: Prentice-Hall.

Goldsmith, L., & Schloss, P. (1986). Diagnostic overshadowing among school psychologists working with hearing impaired learners. *American Annals of the Deaf, 131,* 288–293.

Good, T., & Brophy, J. (1984). *Looking in classrooms* (3rd ed.). New York: Harper & Row.

Gorham, K. (1975). A lost generation of parents. *Exceptional Children, 41*, 268–273.

Gottlieb, J. (1974). Attitudes toward retarded children: Effects of labeling and academic performance. *American Journal of Mental Deficiency, 79*, 268–273.

Greer, B., Allsop, J., & Greer, J. (1980). Environmental alternatives for the physically handicapped. In J. Schifani, R. Anderson, & S. Odle (Eds.), *Implementing learning in the least restrictive environment* (pp. 128–129). Baltimore: University Park Press.

Grise, P. (1980). Florida's minimum competency testing program for handicapped students. *Exceptional children, 47*, 186–193.

Grossman, H. (Ed.). (1973). *Manual on terminology and classification in mental retardation* (rev. ed.). Washington, DC: American Association on Mental Deficiency.

Grossman, H. (Ed.). (1983). *Manual on terminology and classification in mental retardation* (rev. ed.). Washington, DC: American Association on Mental Deficiency.

Guilford, J. (1959). Traits of creativity. In H. Anderson (Ed.), *Creativity and its cultivation*. New York: Harper.

Guilford, J. (1972). *The nature of human intelligence*. New York: McGraw-Hill.

Guskin, S., Bartel, N., & MacMillan, D. (1976). Perspectives of the labeled child. In N. Hobbs (Ed.), *Issues in classification of children* (Vol. 2). San Francisco: Jossey-Bass.

Haber, L., & McNeil, J. (1983). *Methodological questions in the estimation of disability prevalence*. Washington, DC: U.S. Government Printing Office. (Available from the Population Division, Bureau of the Census)

Hahn, H. (1989). The politics of special education. In D. Lipsky & A. Gartner (Eds.), *Beyond separate education: Quality education for all* (pp. 225–241). Baltimore: Brookes.

Hammill, D., Leigh, J., McNutt, G., & Larsen, S. (1981). A new definition of learning disabilities. *Learning Disability Quarterly, 4*(Fall), 336–342.

Hasazi, S., Gordon, L., & Roe, C. (1985). Factors associated with the employment status of handicapped youth exiting high school from 1979 to 1983. *Exceptional Children, 51*, 455–469.

Heber, R. (1959). *Manual on terminology and classification in mental retardation*. Washington, DC: American Association on Mental Deficiency.

Heber, R. (1961). A manual on terminology and classification in mental retardation. Monograph Suppl. *American Journal of Mental Deficiency, 64*.

Heward, W., & Orlansky, M. (1988). *Exceptional children* (3rd ed.). Columbus, OH: Merrill.

Hill, R. (1949). *Families under stress*. New York: Harper & Row.

Hill. (1986). Orientation and mobility. In G. Scholl (Ed.), *Foundations of education for blind and visually handicapped children and youth: Theory and practice* (pp. 315–340). New York: American Foundation for the Blind.

Holmes, H. (1915). Time distributions by subject and grades in representative cities. In S. Parker (Ed.), *The fourteenth yearbook of the National Society for the Study of Education. Part I: Minimum essentials* in elementary-school subjects—standards and current practices. Chicago: University of Chicago Press.

Horn, J. (1924). *The education of exceptional children: A consideration of public school problems and policies in the field of differentiated education.* New York: Century.

Hughes, C., & Ruhl, K. (1989). Social skills training. In B. Algozzine (Ed.), *Problem behavior management: Educator's resource service* (pp. 279–291). Rockville, MD: Aspen.

Idol, L. (1988). A rationale and guidelines for establishing special education consultation programs. *Remedial and Special Education, 9,* 48–58.

Idol, L., Paolucci-Whitcomb, P., & Nevin, A. (1986). *Collaborative consultation.* Rockville, MD: Aspen.

Interagency Committee on Learning Disabilities. (1987). *Learning disabilities: A report to the U.S. Congress.* Washington, DC: U.S. Department of Health and Human Services.

Johnson, D., & Johnson, R. (1976). *Learning together and alone: Cooperation, competition, and individualization.* Englewood Cliffs, NJ: Prentice-Hall.

Jones, B. (1988). Homey housing. *WAYS,* Spring, 11–12.

Kakalik, J., Furry, W., Thomas, M., & Carney, F. (1981). *The cost of special education* (RAND Note N-1792-ED). Santa Monica, CA: RAND.

Kauffman, J. (1985). *Characteristics of children's behavior disorders* (3rd ed.). Columbus, OH: Merrill.

Kauffman, J., Gerber, M., & Semmel, M. (1988). Arguable assumptions underlying the regular education initiative. *Journal of Learning Disabilities, 21,* 6–12.

Kaufman, P. (1987). *Trends in elementary and secondary school enrollment.* Washington, DC: Center for Education Statistics.

Kirk, S., & Chalfant, J. (1984). *Developmental and academic learning disabilities.* Denver: Love.

Kirk, S., & Gallagher, J. (1989). *Educating exceptional children* (6th ed.). Boston: Houghton Mifflin.

Kneedler, R. (1984). *Special education for today.* Englewood Cliffs, NJ: Prentice-Hall.

Koestler, F. (1976). *The unseen minority: A social history of blindness in the United States.* New York: McKay.

La Grange Area Department of Special Education (LADSE). (1989). *Total integration neighborhood schools.* La Grange, IL: LADSE.

Lane, H. (1988). Is there a "psychology of the deaf"? *Exceptional Children, 55,* 7–19.

LaVor, M., & Harvey, J. (1976). Head Start, economic opportunity, Community Partnership Act of 1974. *Exceptional Children, 42,* 227–230.

Lerner, J. (1989). *Learning disabilities: Theories, diagnosis, and teaching strategies* (5th ed.). Boston: Houghton Mifflin.

Leung, E. (1988). Cultural and accultural commonalities and diversities among Asian Americans: Identification and programming issues. In A. Ortiz & B. Ramirez (Eds.), *School and the culturally diverse exceptional student: Promising practices and future directions.* Reston, VA: Council for Exceptional Children.

Lipsky, D., & Gartner, A. (1989a). *Beyond separate education: Quality education for all.* Baltimore: Brookes.

Lipsky, D., & Gartner, A. (1989b). The current situation. In D. Lipsky & A. Gartner (Eds.), *Beyond separate education: Quality education for all* (pp. 3–24). Baltimore: Brookes.

Lloyd, J. (1980). Academic instruction and cognitive behavior modification: The need for attack strategy training. *Exceptional Education Quarterly, 1,* 53–63.

Lottero, J. (1987). Profile: Challenging the can'ts to cans. *A Positive Approach,* November/December, 7–8.

MacMillan, D., Jones, R., & Aloia, G. (1974). The mentally retarded label: A theoretical analysis and review of research. *American Journal of Mental Deficiency, 79,* 241–261.

Mangrum II, C., & Strichart, S. S. (1984). *College and the learning disabled student.* New York: Grune & Stratton.

Mann, C.H. (1928). *How schools use their time: Practice in 444 cities including a study of trends from 1826–1926.* New York: Teachers College Press.

Marinelli, J. (1975). Critical issues in the financing of education for the handicapped. *Journal of Educational Finance, 1,* 259–260.

Marland, S. (Ed.). (1972). *Education of the gifted and talented* (Report to the Congress of the United States by the U.S. Commissioner of Education). Washington, DC: U.S. Government Printing Office.

Marozas, D., & May, D. (1988). *Issues and practices in special education.* New York: Longman.

McAnally, P., Rose, S., & Quigley, S. (1987). *Language learning practices with deaf children.* Boston: College Hill Press.

McKinney, J. (1987). Research on conceptually and empirically derived subtypes of specific learning disabilities. In M. Wang, M. Reynolds, & H. Walberg (Eds.), *Handbook of special*

education: Research and practice. New York: Pergamon Press.

McKinney, J., & Speece, D. (1986). Academic consequences and longitudinal stability of behavioral subtypes of learning disabled children. *Journal of Educational Psychology, 78,* 365–372.

McLoughlin, J., Noll, M., Isaacs, B., Petrosko, J., Karibo, J., & Lindsey, B. (1983). The relationship of allergies and allergy treatment to school performance and student behavior. *Annals of Allergy, 51,* 506–510.

Meadow, K. (1980). *Deafness and child development.* Berkeley, CA: University of California Press.

Minner, S., & Johnson, P. (1987). Referral and placement recommendations of teachers toward gifted and handicapped children. *Roeper Review, 9,* 247–249.

Minnesota standards for services to gifted and talented students. (1988, April 22). St. Paul, MN: Minnesota State Advisory Council for the Gifted and Talented.

Mithaugh, D., Horiuchi, C., & Fanning, P. (1985). A report on the Colorado statewide followup survey of special education students. *Exceptional Children, 51,* 397–404.

Moores, D. (1985). *Educating the deaf: Psychology, principles, and practices* (2d ed.). Boston: Houghton Mifflin.

Moores, D. (1987). *Educating the deaf: Psychology, principles, and practices* (3rd ed.). Boston: Houghton Mifflin.

Moran, M. (1983). Inventing a future for special education: A cautionary tale. *Journal for Special Educators, 19,* 28–36.

Morsink, C., Chase-Thomas, C., & Smith-Davis, J. (1987). Noncategorical special education programs:

Process and outcomes. In M. Wang, M. Reynolds, & H. Walberg (Eds.), *Handbook of special education: Research and practice* (Vol. 1). New York: Pergamon Press.

National Center for Education Statistics. (1988). *The condition of education: Elementary and secondary education.* Washington, DC: National Center for Education Statistics.

Nelson, F. (1983). School district response to labeling cost and programmatic incentives in special education. *Journal of Education Finance, 8,* 380–398.

Newland, T. (1979). *The gifted in socioeducational perspective.* Englewood Cliffs, NJ: Prentice-Hall.

Newland, T. (1986). Children with auditory and visual impairment. In R. Brown & C. Reynolds (Eds.), *Psychological perspectives on childhood exceptionality: A handbook.* New York: Wiley.

Nihira, D., Foster, R., Shellhass, M., & Leland, H. (1975). *AAMD Adaptive Behavior Scale.* Washington, DC: American Association on Mental Deficiency.

Nuffield, E. (1988). Biomedical perspectives. In V. Van Hasselt, P. Strain, & M. Hersen (Eds.), *Handbook of developmental and physical disabilities.* New York: Pergamon Press.

Pallas, A. (1987). *School dropouts in the United States.* Washington, DC: Center for Education Statistics.

Patterson, G. (1964). An empirical approach to the classification of disturbed children. *Journal of Clinical Psychology, 20,* 326–337.

Payne, B. (1905). *Public elementary school curricula.* New York: Silver, Burdett.

Ponti, C., Zins, J., & Graden, J. (1988). Implementing a consultation-based service delivery system to decrease referrals for special education: A case study of organizational considerations. *School Psychology Review, 17,* 89–100.

Profile: Ivy Hunter. (1988). *A Positive Approach,* November/December, 14.

Pugach, M. (1988). The National Education Reports and special education: Implications for teacher preparation. *Exceptional Children, 53,* 308–314.

Pugach, M., & Johnson, L. (1987). Rethinking the relationship between consultation and collaborative problem solving. *Focus on Exceptional Children, 21,* 1–8.

Quay, H. (1983). *Manual for the Revised Behaviors Problem Checklist.* Coral Gables, FL: University of Miami.

Quay, H., & Peterson, D. (1975). *Manual for the Behavior Problem Checklist.* Unpublished manuscript.

Raphael, E., Singer, J., & Walker, D. (1985). Per pupil expenditures on special education in three metropolitan school districts. *Journal of Educational Finance, 11,* 69–88.

Raspbery, W. (1976). Racism and victims. *Washington Post,* March 8, p. A19.

Redl, F. (1959). The concept of the life space interview. *American Journal of Orthopsychiatry, 29,* 1–18.

Renzulli, J. (1979). *What makes giftedness?* (Brief 6). Los Angeles: National/State Leadership Training Institute of the Gifted and Talented.

Reschly, D. (1987). Learning characteristics of mildly handicapped students: Implications for classification, placement, and programming. In M. Wang, M. Reynolds, & H. Walberg (Eds.), *Handbook of special education: Research and practice.* New York: Pergamon Press.

Reynolds, M. (1987). Introduction. In M. Wang, M. Reynolds, & H. Walberg (Eds.), *Handbook of special education: Research and practice* (Vol. 1). New York: Pergamon Press.

Reynolds, M., & Birch, J. (1977). *Educating exceptional children in all America's schools.* Reston, VA: Council for Exceptional Children.

Rizzo, J., & Zabel, R. (1988). *Educating children and adolescents with behavioral disorders: An integrative approach.* Boston: Allyn & Bacon.

Roberts, F. (1986). Education for the visually handicapped: A social and educational history. In G. Scholl (Ed.), *Foundations of education for blind and visually handicapped children and youth: Theory and practice.* New York: American Foundation for the Blind.

Rogers, C. (1951). *Client-centered therapy.* Boston: Houghton Mifflin.

Rogers, M. (1989). Technology: More than wheelchairs. *Newsweek*, April 24, 66–67.

Rotter, J. (1954). *Social learning and clinical psychology.* Englewood Cliffs, NJ: Prentice-Hall.

Rusch, F., Chadsey-Rusch, J., & Lagomarcino, T. (1987). Preparing students for employment. In M. Snell (Ed.), *Systematic instruction of persons with severe handicaps* (3rd ed., pp. 471–490). Columbus, OH: Merrill.

Rusch, F., & Phelps, L. (1987). Secondary special education and transition from school to work: A national priority. *Exceptional Children, 53,* 487–492.

Sage, D. (1987). Resource cost analysis: We really need to know. *Special Services in the Schools, 4,* 63–76.

Sapon-Shevin, M. (1989). Mild disabilities: In and out of special education. In D. Biklen, D. Ferguson, & A. Ford (Eds.), *Schooling and disability* (pp. 77–107). Chicago: National Society for the Study of Education.

Sarason, S., & Doris, J. (1979). *Educational handicap, public policy, and social history: A broadened perspective on mental retardation.* New York: Free Press.

Saxton, M., & Howe, F. (Eds.). (1987). *With wings.* New York: Feminist Press.

Scheerenberger, R. (1983). *A history of mental retardation.* Baltimore: Brookes.

Schloss, P., & Schloss, C. (1984). Job description and handicapping condition: An analysis of employer expectations for training and success of handicapped job applicants. *Journal of Vocational Special Needs Education, 6,* 9–11, 26.

Scholl, G. (1986). *Foundations of education for blind and visually handicapped children and youth: Theory and practice.* New York: American Foundation for the Blind.

Schumaker, J., Denton, P., & Deshler, D. (1984). *The paraphrasing strategy.* Lawrence, KS: University of Kansas Institute for Research on Learning Disabilities.

Schumaker, J., Deshler, D., Alley, G., & Warner, M. (1983). Toward the development of an intervention model for learning disabled adolescents: The University of Kansas Institute. *Exceptional Education Quarterly, 4,* 45–70.

Sears, P., & Barbee, A. (1977). Career and life satisfaction among Terman's gifted women. In J. Stanley, W. George, & C. Solano (Eds.), *The gifted and the creative: A fifty-year perspective.* Baltimore: Johns Hopkins University Press.

Seguin, E. (1846). *Traitement moral, hygiene et education des idiots et des autres enfants arrieres.* Paris: Bailliere.

Severance, L., & Gasstrom, L. (1977). Effects of the label "mentally retarded" on causal explanations for success and failure outcomes. *American Journal of Mental Deficiency, 81,* 547–555.

Shell, P. (1981). Straining the system: Serving low-incidence handicapped students in an urban school system. *Exceptional Education Quarterly, 2,* 1–10.

Shinn, M., & Marston, D. (1985). Differentiating mildly handicapped, low-achieving, and regular education students: A curriculum-based approach. *Remedial and Special Education, 6,* 31–38.

Silver, A. (1987). *Learning disabilities: A report to the U.S. Congress.* Washington, DC: U.S. Department of Health and Human Services, Interagency Committee on Learning Disabilities.

Simmons, R. (1988). Smart, beautiful: Ms. Wheelchair America Pageant. *A Positive Approach,* November/December, 10–11.

Singer, J., & Butler, J. (1987). The Education for All Handicapped Children Act: Schools as agents of social reform. *Harvard Educational Review, 57,* 125–152.

Smith-Davis, J., Burke, P., & Noel, M. (1984). *Personnel to educate the handicapped in America: Supply and demand from a programmatic viewpoint.* College Park, MD: University of Maryland Institute for the Study of Exceptional Children and Youth.

Snyder, T. (1987). *Digest of education statistics: 1987.* Washington, DC: National Center for Education Statistics.

South Atlantic Regional Resource Center. (1988). *Determining placement in the least restrictive environment.* Plantation, FL: South Atlantic Regional Resource Center.

Stainback, D., Stainback, W., & Forest, M. (1989). *Educating all students in the mainstream of regular education.* Baltimore, MD: Brookes.

Stern, J. (1988). *The condition of education: Elementary and secondary education.* Washington, DC: National Center for Education Statistics.

Stern, J., & Chandler, M. (1987). *The condition of education: A statistical report.* Washington, DC: Office of Educational Research and Improvement, Center for Education Statistics.

Stewart, D. (1977). Unique problems of handicapped Native Americans. In *The White House Conference on Handicapped Individuals* (Vol. 1). Washington, DC: U.S. Government Printing Office.

Sutherland, J., & Algozzine, B. (1979). The learning disabilities label as a biasing factor in the visual-motor performance of normal children. *Journal of Learning Disabilities, 12,* 17–23.

Taylor, S., Biklen, D., & Searl, S. (1986). *Preparing for life: A manual for parents on least restrictive environment.* Boston: Federation for Children with Special Needs.

Terman, L. (1954). The discovery and encouragement of exceptional talent. *American Psychologist, 9,* 224.

Terman, L., & Oden, M. (1951). The Stanford studies of the gifted. In P. Witty (Ed.), *The gifted child.* Boston: Heath.

Tredgold, A. (1937). *A textbook on mental deficiency.* Baltimore: Wood.

Tucker, J. (1980). Ethnic proportions in classes for the learning disabled:

Issues in nonbiased assessment. *Journal of Special Education, 14,* 93–105.

U.S. Department of Education. (1980). *To assure the free appropriate public education of all handicapped children: Second annual report to Congress on the implementation of Public Law 94–142: The Education for All Handicapped Children Act.* Washington, DC: U.S. Government Printing Office.

U.S. Department of Education. (1988). *To assure the free appropriate public education of all handicapped children: Tenth annual report to Congress on the implementation of the Education of the Handicapped Act.* Washington, DC: U.S. Government Printing Office.

Van Riper, C., & Emerick, L. (1984). *Speech correction: An introduction to speech pathology and audiology.* Englewood Cliffs, NJ: Prentice-Hall.

Victor. (1976). Some selected findings from the Greenleigh Associates study of sheltered workshops. In *The Auburn conference of the Greenleigh study of sheltered workshops.* Auburn, AL: Auburn University Rehabilitative Services Education Department.

Walker, H. (1976). *Walker Problem Behavior Identification Checklist.* Los Angeles: Western Psychological Services.

Wang, M. (1989). Adaptive instruction: An alternative for accommodating student diversity through the curriculum. In D. Lipsky & A. Gartner (Eds.), *Beyond separate education: Quality education for all* (pp. 99–119). Baltimore, MD: Brookes.

Wehman, P. (1987a). From school to adult living: A forum on issues and trends. *Exceptional Children, 53,* 487–492.

Wehman, P. (1987b). Interview. In G. Clark & E. Knowlton, From school to adult living: A forum on issues and trends. *Exceptional Children, 53,* 546–554.

Wehman, P., Kregel, J., & Seyfarth, J. (1985). Transition from school to work for individuals with severe handicaps: A follow-up study. *Journal for the Association for Persons with Severe Handicaps, 10,* 132–136.

Weintraub, F., Abeson, A., Ballard, J., & LaVor, M. (Eds.). (1976). *Public policy and the education of exceptional children.* Reston, VA: Council for Exceptional Children.

Will, M. (1986a). *Educating children with learning problems: A shared responsibility* (A report to the Secretary). Washington, DC: U.S. Department of Education.

Will, M. (1986b). Let us pause and reflect—but not too long. *Exceptional Children, 52,* 11–16.

Wittrock, M. (1986). *Handbook of research on teaching* (3rd ed.). New York: Macmillan.

Wonder, S. (1986). Ever wonder how Stevie Wonder reads his mail? *Sports Illustrated for Kids,* April, inside back cover.

Yell, M. (in press). *Honig v. Doe:* The Supreme Court addresses the suspension and expulsion of handicapped students. *Exceptional Children.*

Yoshida, R., & Meyers, C. (1975). Effects of labeling as educable mentally retarded on teachers' expectancies for change in a student's performance. *Journal of Educational Psychology, 67,* 521–527.

Ysseldyke, J., & Algozzine, B. (1982). *Critical issues in special and remedial education.* Boston: Houghton Mifflin.

Ysseldyke, J., Christenson, S., & Thurlow, M. (1989). *Student Learning in Context Model.* Unpublished manuscript.

Zigler, E., & Baller, D. (1977). Impact of institutional experience on the behavior and development of retarded persons. *American Journal of Mental Deficiency, 82,* 1–11.

Glossary

ability training Instruction in preacademic skills.

academic learning disability A disorder that interferes with learning in academic areas (reading, writing, spelling, arithmetic).

academic time analysis The systematic observation and recording of the amount of time a student is actively engaged in responding to academic instruction.

acceleration The process of moving students through a curriculum at a faster rate than their peers.

accessibility The process of making buildings and other structures easier to enter and exit for people with handicaps.

adaptive behavior The way in which the individual meets the standards of personal independence and social responsibility expected of his or her age and cultural group.

advancement Changing a gifted student's curriculum or level by changing the student's placement; also called *double promotion* and *skipping a grade.*

algorithm A rule or procedure that can be applied repeatedly to solve a problem.

alternative living unit (ALU) A supervised home for two or three exceptional residents.

aphasia Lack of speech; often but not always refers to an inability to speak as a result of brain damage.

architectural accessibility The removal of steps and other barriers that limit the participation of people with handicaps.

assessment The process of collecting data for the purpose of making decisions about students.

attack strategy training A form of direct instruction in which pupils are taught small steps of a skill and rules for putting the steps together, so they can use the strategy for any problem like those they have solved.

attribution What one thinks is the cause of a certain behavior, characteristic, or performance.

audiometer An instrument used to assess hearing acuity; the device generates pure tones at different frequencies covering the major portion of the auditory range and at varying degrees of loudness.

auditory acuity The ability to hear at specified levels of intensity.

behavior therapy The process of systematically arranging environmental events to influence behavior.

central nervous system The brain and spinal cord.

child count data Information on the number of specific kinds of students enrolled in special education programs.

child-find program A formal community or public school program to locate young children who are handicapped.

civil rights law A law whose implementation is not tied to program funding; see *program law.*

class action suit A legal action brought on behalf of a group of people with similar claims.

classification The process of grouping people, places, or things into categories.

clinical teacher A special education teacher who teaches in a clinical setting or teaches clinically (by incorporating psychotherapeutic methods or by teaching prescriptively or experimentally).

cognitive behavior modification The practice of teaching students to use self-statements to change their behavior.

communication disorder An impairment in articulation, language, voice, or fluency.

compensatory instruction Instruction that teaches a student to compensate for a disability; for example, teaching braille is a form of compensatory instruction.

competitive employment Employment in which the individual's work is valued by the employer and is performed in an integrated setting.

conceptual definitions In defining categories of exceptionality, the generally agreed-on ideas that shape a category.

consultative services See *indirect services.*

contingency contract A formal agreement between a teacher and a student specifying the consequences of the student's demonstrating certain behaviors.

convergent thinking Reasoning, memory, and classification.

counseling therapy Intervention designed to uncover sources of problems or build new approaches to interpersonal relations through supportive relationships between the client and therapist.

crisis therapy Therapeutic intervention that, like other therapies, consists of building a supportive therapeutic relationship, but begins in response to actual life events, usually of a crisis nature.

criterion-referenced test A test in which the individual's performance is interpreted relative to the specific curricular objectives that have been mastered; a test that evaluates a pupil's absolute level of mastery. Also called *objective-referenced test* and *curriculum-based test.*

curriculum-based assessment A procedure for determining the instructional needs of the student based on the student's ongoing performance in a content area.

deafness The absence of hearing in both ears.

deinstitutionalization The implementation of the principle of least restrictive environment in residential treatment facilities.

desensitization A procedure for reducing the effects of anxiety-producing stimuli by gradually introducing relaxation-producing stimuli in their presence.

developmental diagnosis The process of analyzing a student's skills, abilities, and characteristics within and across developmental areas.

developmental instruction The process of teaching students a set of skills that are progressively more difficult in order to enable them to demonstrate the complex skills or abilities necessary to meet instructional objectives.

developmental learning disability A disorder in the processes or abilities necessary to acquire academic skills.

direct instruction Instruction in which teachers' actions are directly and functionally related to the goals of instruction.

direct services Services in which special education personnel (including special education teachers, speech and language pathologists, and physical therapists) work with students themselves to remediate difficulties or to help them accelerate in the regular classroom.

divergent thinking Thinking that shows fluency, flexibility, originality, and foresight.

Down syndrome A congenital condition that causes mental retardation.

early intervention Educational and other treatment provided before a child reaches school age or before school-related problems become serious.

education The process of learning and changing as a result of schooling and other experiences.

Education for All Handicapped Children Act (1975) The first compulsory special education law; mandates a free and appropriate education for all students with handicaps between the ages of 3 and 21. Also called *Public Law 94–142.*

emotional disturbance A condition in which the individual exhibits one or more of the following characteristics over a period of time and to a marked degree: an inability to learn that cannot be explained by other factors, an inability to build or maintain interpersonal relationships, inappropriate behaviors, unhappiness or depression, and physical symptoms or fears related to personal or school problems; also called *behavior disorder.*

enrichment Enhancing the educational experiences of students without changing the setting in which they are educated.

evaluation The process by which teachers decide whether the methods and materials they are using are effective based on individual students' performance.

exceptional students Students, who because of their special learning needs, require special education. Exceptional students can be handicapped or gifted and talented.

expectation A prediction about an event or action.

feedback Information about a student's performance.

formative evaluation Evaluation during the instructional process.

functional impairment A condition with no known cause that has a detrimental effect on the social, cognitive, emotional, or academic functioning of the individual.

gifted and talented Having intellectual or cognitive gifts, or showing outstanding performance in a specific dimension of skill (music, art, athletics).

group home A home that provides family-style living for a group of exceptional people.

guideline A written description of how a procedure should be followed.

hard of hearing Having significant difficulty hearing.

home-based instruction For students who are unable to travel to school, a program of instruction or tutoring in the home.

homebound teacher A special education teacher who serves students who cannot attend school.

indirect services Working with regular classroom teachers and others to help them meet the needs of exceptional students; also called *consultative services.*

individualized education program (IEP) A written document that includes (1) a statement of the student's present level of functioning. (2) a statement of annual goals and short-term objectives for achieving those goals, (3) a statement of services to be provided and the extent of regular programming, (4) the starting date and expected duration of services, and (5) evaluation procedures and criteria for monitoring progress.

individualized family service plan (IFSP) In an early intervention program, a document that details the child's present level of development and the family's needs related to that development, objectives of the program, the specific services that will be provided to the child and family, evaluation procedures, and transition procedures to move the child from early intervention into a preschool program.

instructional consultant A special education teacher who works with the general education teacher in planning and implementing the instruction of students who are exceptional.

instructional diagnosis An effort to identify the extent to which a student's poor performance is caused by poor instruction and possible remedies for the problem.

intervention assistance team A school-based problem-solving group whose purpose is to provide a vehicle for discussing the specific needs of teachers and staff and offering them follow-up help.

interviewing The process of asking questions to obtain information about an individual's background, current levels of performance, and plans.

itinerant teacher A special education teacher who travels from school to school within a district, or from district to district in rural areas.

label A cue that helps organize knowledge, perceptions, and behavior.

least restrictive environment (LRE) An educational setting that is as much like the regular classroom as possible.

life space interview A therapeutic intervention in which actual experiences are used to manage social and emotional crises or to teach new ways to respond in interpersonal relations.

mainstreaming Wherever possible, keeping exceptional students in the regular classroom.

mental retardation Significant subaverage intellectual functioning occurring concurrently with deficits in adaptive behavior and manifested during the developmental period, which adversely affects the individual's academic performance.

mobility The ability to move safely and efficiently from one place to another.

multiple handicap A combination of impairments that cause educational problems so severe that they cannot be accommodated in special education programs solely for one of them.

normalization The process of making the exceptional individual's life as normal as possible.

norm-referenced test A standardized test in which the performance of the individual is interpreted relative to the performance of a group of others who are of the same age or grade level.

norms Standards against which performance is measured.

observing The process of watching an individual perform a set of behaviors to obtain information about the rate or duration of those behaviors.

operant conditioning The process of teaching or controlling behaviors by changing the consequences of those behaviors.

operational criteria In defining categories of exceptionality, the standards used in making judgments about an exceptional behavior.

organic impairment A condition that has a known physical cause.

orientation The ability to know where one is in relation to the environment.

orthopedic handicap An impairment caused by a birth defect, disease, cerebral palsy, amputation, fracture, or burn that adversely affects movement and mobility.

other health impairment Autism or a chronic or acute health problem that limits the individual's strength or alertness.

peer tutoring The use of students to teach classmates or peers, with a teacher's supervision.

pragmatic language disorder A disorder that interferes with one's understanding of language.

precision teaching A way in which teachers plan, use, and analyze the effects of teaching to improve a student's performance of academic or social skills.

prereferral intervention The process of finding ways to keep exceptional students in the regular classroom.

preteaching Teaching students the vocabulary or other content they need to prepare them to understand and participate in a lesson.

prevalence The number of individuals evidencing a condition at a given time.

process disorder A neurological impairment that interferes with a student's ability to learn; the impairment is beyond the individual's control and is not the by-product of inappropriate instruction or lack of opportunity to learn.

program law A law that must be adhered to in order to qualify for program funding; see *civil rights law.*

psychoeducational assessment The process of administering psychological or educational tests to determine the reasons behind a student's performance on a screening measure.

psychosomatic complaint A physical illness that is brought on by or associated with an individual's emotional state.

Public Law 94–142 See *Education for All Handicapped Children Act.*

pull-out program A program that pulls exceptional students out of the regular classroom for special education services. Resource rooms and special classes are pull-out programs.

referral The first step in determining a student's eligibility for special education; the process of requesting information or a professional evaluation to decide whether a student is eligible for special services.

regular education initiative (REI) The contention that more students with handicaps should be educated in the regular classroom; also called *general education initiative.*

regulation A rule, with the force of law, that defines a way in which a school or district must operate.

related services Services provided by trained personnel directly (to a student) or indirectly (to others working with the student); include psychological testing and counseling, occupational therapy, school health services, and transportation.

reliability An index of consistency in measurement.

remediation Instruction to repair or correct deficits in performance by training students in the specific areas in which they show deficits.

residential school A school that has the staff, facilities, and programs to meet the needs of exceptional students on a twenty-four-hour basis.

resource room A room to which a student goes for part of a school day and in which the student receives special instruction or help with regular classroom work.

resource room teacher A special education teacher who offers primary, remedial, supplementary, or compensatory instruction to exceptional students in a resource room.

respondent conditioning The process of teaching a behavior by pairing a new stimulus with a stimulus that automatically evokes a reflex response.

response cost An intervention in which a penalty or fine is used to reduce inappropriate behavior.

screening The process of collecting data to determine whether more intensive assessment is necessary.

self-contained class A class taught by one teacher to which students are assigned for the entire school day.

self-contained special class teacher A special education teacher who is responsible for the full-time academic instruction of exceptional students.

separation Pulling exceptional students out of regular classes and placing them in homogeneous self-contained classes.

sheltered employment Work in a self-contained environment in which the exceptional individual is trained and paid for output.

special education Instruction designed for students with special learning needs.

special school A day school that has the staff, facilities, and programs to meet the needs of exceptional students.

stay-put program A program in which exceptional students receive special education services without being removed from the regular classroom.

summative evaluation Evaluation at the end of the instructional process.

supported employment The use of professionals to help handicapped individuals find, perform, and hold a job.

task analysis The process of breaking down a complex behavior or skill into its component parts or subskills.

team teaching In special education, a regular education teacher and a special education teacher working together to instruct students who are exceptional.

testing The process of administering a set of items to obtain a score.

token system An instructional approach in which students earn tokens, stars, points, or other prizes and are allowed to exchange these for things they want to purchase (like toys, free time, and so on).

validity The extent to which a test measures what it claims to measure.

visual acuity The ability to see things at specified distances.

visual handicap A visual impairment that, even with correction, adversely affects a student's academic performance.

Author Index

Abernathy, S. W., 302
Abeson, A., 73, 441, 462
Adelman, F., 272
Akey, D., 298, 299
Algozzine, B., 89, 90, 91, 158, 187, 277, 303, 329, 330, 331, 354, 366, 422, 434, 437
Algozzine, K., 91
Alley, G., 405
Allsop, J., 229, 230
Aloia, G., 89, 91
American Psychiatric Association (APA), 126, 169
Anderson, R. M., 230
Anderson, W., 110
Arakawa, J., 475
Argulewicz, E., 90
Arter, J., 422
Asch, A., 12, 102, 105, 106, 110, 229, 257, 365

Ballard, J., 73, 441, 462
Baller, D., 466
Balow, B., 37
Barbee, A., 487
Bardon, J., 290
Bartel, N., 89
Baum, D. D., 110
Becker, G., 102, 103
Beers, C., 178
Bellamy, T., 251
Bellizia, J., 272

Bersoff, D., 40, 65, 73
Bettelheim, B., 87
Bijou, S., 385, 422
Biklen, D., 110, 254, 257, 449, 450, 458, 462
Birch, J., 255, 268, 269, 271
Blackhurst, E., 302
Blanton, R., 245
Blashfield, R. K., 277
Blatt, B., 110, 436, 466
Bloom, B., 403
Bockhoven, J., 178
Borg, W., 316, 317
Bott, D. A., 302
Bouvier, L., 474
Braaten, S. and B., 481
Brophy, J. E., 364, 386
Brown, F., 347
Brown, L., 354
Bryant, B. R., 354
Buck, P. S., 110
Budoff, M., 438
Bunch, J., 481
Burke, P. J., 281, 302
Burrello, L., 61, 439, 441, 451
Butler, J., 20
Byrne, A., 98

Carney, M. F., 452, 454, 455, 456
Carroll, R., 96
Carta, J., 406
Carter, J., 264

Cartwright, G. and C., 413, 477, 478
Center for Education Statistics, 449, 450
Chadsey-Rusch, J., 488
Chalfant, J. C., 121, 128, 131, 263, 264, 265
Chandler, D. L., 412
Chandler, M. O., 437, 438
Chase-Thomas, C., 260, 261
Chinn, P., 476
Chitwood, S., 110
Choate, J., 316
Christenson, S., 265
Christy, M., 209
Clark, B., 154, 403
Clark, G. M., 496
Coleman, M., 178
Coles, G., 129
Council of State Directors of Programs for the Gifted, 114, 139
Craig, P., 457
Creer, T., 207
Cromwell, R. L., 277
Cross, D. P., 302
Cruickshank, W., 354
C–2, S., 183
Cullinan, D., 178, 184

Davis, C., 474
DeBoer, A., 265
Delquadri, J., 406
Dembo, C., 90
Denham, C., 317
Deno, E., 267, 268
Deno, S. L., 422
Denton, P., 405
DE–OSERS, 224
Deshler, D., 405
Diagnostic and Statistical Manual of Mental Disorders (APA), 127, 246
Doris, J., 165, 167, 193
Dunn, L., 435

Edgerton, R., 101, 102
Edmonson, B., 199
Ekwall, E., 332
Elliot, E., 90, 428
Engelmann, S., 316
Epstein, M., 178, 184
Esquirol, J. E. D., 245

Fanning, P., 488
Farrar, N., 272
Federal Register (1977), 115, 116, 161, 175, 197, 198, 211, 214, 222, 227
Ferguson, D., 105, 106, 110, 462
Fine, M., 110
Ford, A., 110, 462

Forest, M., 386, 481, 497
Forgnone, C., 37
Forness, S., 158
Foster, G. G., 90
Foster, R., 334, 336
Frank, J. P., 111
Friedman, J., 106
Fuchs, D. and L., 264
Furakawa, C., 207
Furry, W., 452, 454, 455, 456

Gallagher, J., 107, 131, 132, 141, 144, 153, 154
Gallo, N., 106
Galloway, T., 222
Garrett, J. E., 18
Gartner, A., 36, 250, 386, 452, 481
Gasstrom, L., 90
Gerber, M., 273
Gickling, E., 314, 315
Glaser, W., 404
Goffman, E., 93, 298
Goldsmith, L., 90
Good, T., 364
Gordon, L., 488
Gorham, K., 105
Gottlieb, J., 91, 111
Graden, J., 266
Granzin, A., 316
Greenwood, C., 406
Greer, B. B., 229, 230
Greer, J. G., 37, 229, 230
Grossman, H. J., 80, 161, 163, 168, 334
Guilford, J. P., 139
Guskin, S., 89

Haber, L., 446
Hahn, H., 446
Hall, V., 406
Hallahan, D. P., 36
Hammill, D. D., 120, 354
Harm, D., 207
Harvey, J., 435
Hasazi, S., 488
Havertape, J., 314
Hayden, D., 110
Hayes, P., 441
Heber, R., 168
Hersen, M., 234
Heward, W., 144
Hill, R., 86, 87, 416
Hines, M., 381
Hively, W., 422
Hobbs, N., 277
Holmes, H. W., 316
Horiuchi, C., 488
Horn, J., 246, 247
Howe, F., 87

Hughes, C., 407

Idol, L., 266, 277, 283
Institute for Disabilities Studies, University of Minnesota, 15

Jablow, M. M., 111
Jastak, J. F. and S., 328
Jauregui, J., 102, 103
Jenkins, J. R., 422
Jipson, F. J., 193
Johnson, D. and R., 405
Johnson, L., 262
Jones, B., 489, 491
Jones, R., 89, 111
Joslin, N., 272
Juster, N., 94

Kakalik, J. S., 452, 454, 455, 456
Kauffman, J. M., 36, 180, 273, 481
Kaufman, P., 475
Kavale, K., 158
Keller, H., 111
Kirk, S., 121, 128, 131, 132
Kneedler, R., 478
Knowlton, H. E., 496
Koestler, F., 223
Kregel, J., 488

LADSE (La Grange Area Department of Special Education), 22, 165
Lagomarcino, T., 488
Lane, H., 216, 217
Larsen, S., 120
Lavor, M., 435, 441
Leigh, L., 120
Leland, H., 334, 336
Lerner, J., 119, 158
Leung, E., 475
Lewis, D. E., 143
Lieberman, A., 317
Liles, C. M., 251
Lipsky, D. K., 36, 250, 386, 452, 481
Lloyd, J., 178, 184, 402
Lottero, J., 477
Luckey, J., 243

McAnally, P., 219
McCarthy, E. F., 462
McClure, W. P., 454
McCormick, L., 476
McGrath, L., 272
McGraw, K., 329, 330
McKinney, J., 121, 129
MacMillan, D., 89, 192

McNeil, J., 446
McNutt, G., 120
Maheady, L., 422
Mangrum, C. T. II, 486, 497
Manipoli, J., 272
Mann, C. H., 316
Marion, R., 207
Marozas, D., 466
Marston, D., 315
May, D., 466
Meadow, K., 219
Meltz, B. F., 469
Mercer, C. D., 37, 89
Meyers, C., 91
Minner, S., 90
Minnesota Standards for Services to Gifted and Talented Students (1988), 133
Mirkin, P. K., 354, 422
Mitchell, J. V., 354
Mithaugh, D., 488
Moores, D., 213, 214, 215, 216, 218, 219, 234
Moran, M., 458
Morsink, C., 260, 261
Moultrie, R., 263–264, 265

Neisworth, J. T., 37
Nelson, C. M., 481
Nelson, F., 91
Neuffer, E., 61
Nevin, A., 283
Newland, T. E., 137, 144, 158, 225, 228, 354
Nihira, K., 334, 336
Noel, M. M., 281, 302
Nuffield, E., 199

Oden, M., 143
Odle, S. J., 230
Orenstein, A., 438
Orlansky, M., 144

Pallas, A., 436, 475
Paolucci-Whitcomb, P., 283
Patterson, G., 184
Payne, J., 316
Peterson, D., 184
Pettibone, T. J., 302
Phelps, L., 191, 275
Poland, S. F., 354
Polsgrove, L., 481
Ponti, C., 266
"Profile" (Ivy Hunter), 417
Pugach, M., 262, 430
Pysh, M. V., 263, 264, 265

Ouay, H., 184, 339
Quigley, S., 219

Raphael, E., 452
Raspberry, W., 317
Rauth, M., 444
Redden, M. R., 302
Redl, F., 404
Reese, J., 111
Renzulli, J., 139–140, 141
Reschly, D., 189, 193
Reynolds, M. C., 37, 261, 268, 269, 271,
    302, 422
Richards, K., 359
Rizzo, J., 186, 193
Roberts, F., 224
Roe, C., 488
Rogers, C., 404
Rogers, M., 408, 413, 477
Rose, S., 219
Rotter, J. B., 98
Ruhl, K., 407
Rusch, F., 191, 275, 488

Sage, D. D., 61, 439, 441, 451, 452, 454,
    462
Salvia, J., 326, 354
Sapon-Shevin, M., 458
Sarason, S. B., 165, 167, 193
Saxton, M., 87
Scheerenberger, R., 198
Schifani, J. W., 230
Schloss, C. and P., 90
Scholl, G., 222
Schumaker, J., 405
Searl, S., 254
Sears, P., 487
Semmel, M., 273
Severance, L., 90
Severson, H., 316
Seyfarth, J., 488
Shames, G. H., 158
Shannon, H. and A., 253
Shell, P., 453
Shellhaas, M., 334, 336
Shinn, M., 315
Silver, A., 120
Simmons, R., 417
Singer, J., 20, 452
Smith, B., 73
Smith Davis, J., 260, 261, 281, 302
Speece, D., 121
Sports Illustrated for Kids, 413
Stainback, S. and W., 386, 481, 497
Stern, J. D., 428, 429, 430, 437, 438, 447,
    463, 474, 475
Stewart, J., 474
Stile, S. W., 302

Strain, P., 234
Strauss, J. S., 277
Strichart, S. S., 486, 497
Sugai, G., 264
Sutherland, J., 90

Taylor, S., 254
Terman, L., 143, 144, 487
Thomas, M., 452, 454, 455, 456
Thompson, V., 315
Thurlow, M. L., 265, 354
Time magazine, 477
Tredgold, A., 168
Tucker, J., 169, 436, 439
Turnbull, H. and A., 112

U.S. Department of Education (USDE),
    20, 21, 30, 34, 122, 149, 170, 179, 299,
    447, 483–486 *passim*
U.S. Department of Education, National
    Center for Education Statistics, 449,
    450
U.S. Department of Education, Office of
    Research, 283

van Hasselt, V. B., 234
Viadero, D., 433
Victor, J., 489
Vogelsang, C., 167

Walberg, H., 302
Walker, D., 452
Walker, H., 339
Wang, M. C., 302, 381, 382, 386
Ward, M., 413, 477, 478
Warner, M., 405
Wehman, P., 191, 274, 488
Weintraub, F., 441
Whorton, D., 406
Wiig, E. H., 155, 158
Wilcox, L., 288
Will, Madeline, 270, 430, 479–481, 489
Wilmington [N.C.] *Morning Star*, 491
Wittrock, M. C., 362, 386, 422
Wolfe, A., 130
Wolking, W. D., 37
Woodcock, R. W., 343
Yates, N., 272
Yell, M., 70, 73
Yoshida, R., 90, 91
Ysseldyke, J. E., 89, 90, 111, 158, 265,
    277, 303, 326, 354, 434, 437

Zabel, R., 186, 193
Zettel, J., 73, 462
Zigler, E., 466
Zins, J., 266

Subject Index

Abilities
    discrepancy of, *see* Discrepancy of
      abilities
    intellectual, 323–324
Ability grouping, court rulings on, 61, 62*t*
Ability training, 402, 407
Abnormality. *See* Normality/abnormality
Academic learning disabilities, 121
    of emotionally disturbed, 180–181
    of gifted, 140–141
    of learning disabled, 128–129, 152
    of mentally retarded, 172
    of multihandicapped, 213
    of physically impaired, 207, 216–218,
      225–226, 233
    of speech and language impaired, 150
Academic performance. *See* Students'
    progress or performance
Academic time analysis, 316–318. *See
    also* Time
Acceleration programs, 136, 391, 393
Acculturation, and assessment, 348
Achievement tests, 56, 324–332, 340
    categories of, 326*t*–327*t*
    deaf students and, 218
Acting out, 339
Adaptations (special equipment). *See* In-
    structional adaptations
Adaptive behavior, 168, 174, 334, 336
    AAMD definition of, 161

assessing, 344, 353
    importance of criterion, 162, 340
Administrators, 34, 293, 296, 298, 301
    and eligibility decisions, 311, 443
Adolescents, special problems of, 470,
    471
Adults. *See* Handicapped adults; Parents
Advocacy groups, 175, 255, 274, 442–443,
    444, 461
    and advanced education, 487
    and early intervention, 434
    for emotionally disturbed, 177–178
    for mentally retarded, 163 165, 167,
      174
    PACER, 294, 295
    PASE, 64*t*, 67
    and PL 94–142, 47
    rivalry of, 458
    See also Professional organizations
AIDS, and mainstreaming, 256
Alaskan natives, 437
Algorithm, defined, 331
Allocated time, 317. *See also* Time
Alternate living units (ALUs), 491
American Association for Protecting
    Children, 189
American Association for Retarded Citi-
    zens, 164, 466
American Association for the Advance-
    ment of Science, 410

American Association on Mental Deficiency (AAMD), 161, 334, 435–436
  Adaptive Behavior Scale (ABS) of, 334, 336t
American Association on Mental Retardation (AAMR), 161
American Asylum for the Education and Instruction of the Deaf and Dumb, 215
American Educational Research Association, 348
American Federation of Teachers (AFT), 443
  LRE guidelines of, 444t
American Indians. *See* Native Americans
American Medical Association (AMA), 223, 227
American Printing House for the Blind, 48t, 225
American Psychiatric Association (APA), 126, 246
American Psychological Association, 348
American Speech–Language–Hearing Association. *See* ASHA
Amplification systems, 409
Analysis skills, 403
Anderson, Ron, 417
Animals (as aids to visually or hearing impaired), 416
Annual Report to Congress (1988), 122
Aphasia, 117
Application skills, 403
Appropriate education. *See* Education
Architectural accessibility. *See* Mobility
Aristotle, 241
Arthritis, juvenile rheumatoid, 203
Articulation disorders, 146, 151. *See also* Speech and language disorders
ASHA (American Speech–Language–Hearing Association), 145–146, 147, 292
Asian students, 437, 475. *See also* Minority groups
Assessment, 308–353
  assumptions behind, 345–348, 353
  behaviors sampled by, 323–336, 341, 343–344, 346–347, 348
  collecting data for, 311–314, 318–340, 345–350, 377–378, 385
  court rulings on, 67, 72
  curriculum based, 314–316, 318, 320, 352
  for decision-making, 309–318, 319, 350
  defined, 308, 318, 352

guidelines for, 349–351
  irrelevance of, 350
  legislation regarding, 52–53, 57
  norm-referenced, 320, 326t, 327t, 354, 422
  PEP and, 56, 57
  psychoeducational, 309, 354
  reliability of/errors in, 341, 344, 347, 348, 353
  representativeness of, 341, 343–344, 348, 353
  standards for, 341–344, 364
  testing replaced by, 343
  by trained examiner, 345–346, 348
  validity of, 344, 353
  See also Classification; Eligibility decisions; Evaluation; Placement decisions; Tests
Association for Children with Learning Disabilities (ACLD), 119, 443. *See also* Learning Disabilities Association (LDA)
Association for the Severely Handicapped, The, 164
Attack strategy training, 402–403, 407
Attention, 125–126, 369
Attention deficit–hyperactivity disorder (AD–HD), 126, 127t
Attitudinal barriers, 87. *See also* Exceptionality, attitudes toward/reactions to
attorneys' fees, 51t, 65t, 69, 70
Attributions, 101, 107, 109
Audiologists, 292–293, 409
Audiometer, 214, 333
Audiovisual aids. *See* Instructional adaptations
Auditory acuity. *See* Sensory acuity
Autism, 175, 204–205, 209, 210, 465
  as state category, 18t
Automaticity, 371
Auxiliary aids. *See* Instructional adaptations

Bancroft, Anne, 465
Barsch, Ray, 118
Basic skills
  defined, 148
  for mentally retarded, 186
Beattie v. *State Board of Education*, 62t
Behavior
  adaptive, *see* Adaptive behavior
  analysis of, vs. tests, 422

assessment of, *see* Assessment

attributions and, 101

classroom, rules and, 365–367, 385

expectations of, *see* Expectations; Expectations, teacher

future, prediction of, 347, 348

intelligence test sampling of, 325*t*

"normal," 80, 108 (*see also* Normality/abnormality)

observation and recording of, 338–339

problem, environment and, 189–190, 429

social standards for judging, 83–84

student management of, 366, 403, 407

teacher reactions to, 92–93, 95, 157, 429

See also Social/emotional/behavioral problems

Behavior disorders

terminology describing, 176

two major kinds of (environmental conflict, personal disturbance), 184, 185

See also Emotional disturbance; Emotionally disturbed students

Behavior therapy, 399–401, 407

Bender Visual Motor Gestalt Test, 339

Blackman, Dr. Howard, 164

Black students

court cases regarding, 61, 62*t*, 64*t*, 251, 442

dropout rates of, 31, 437

in special education programs, 30–31, 168, 436, 474, 475

See also Minority students

Blindness: What It Is and How to Live With It (Carroll), 96

Blindness and visual handicaps, 13, 222–228

definitions of, 222–224, 227

history of treatment of, 224–225

as state category, 18*t*

testing for, 332, 333

Blind or visually handicapped students, 12, 13

auxiliary aids and special services for, 46, 224, 226, 254, 412–413, 415, 416–417

characteristics of, 225–227, 228

classroom environment of, 33, 225

dropout or graduation rate of, 31, 483

laws and actions benefiting, 48*t*–51*t* *passim*, 224

prevalence of, 32*t*, 225

state-by-state percentage of, 196*t*–197*t*

test performance of, 225

See also Deaf-blind students

Board of Education of Hendrick Hudson School District v. *Rowley*, 64*t*, 68, 73

Bownes, Judge Hugh, 60

Braille, Louis, and braille system, 412

Brain injuries, 117–118, 202, 233

Brain Response Interface, 411

Brennan, Justice William, 70

Bridge to Silence, A (TV program), 242

Briggman, Herman, 477

Brown v. *Board of Education*, 61, 62*t*, 251

Building principal, 296

Bureau of Indian Affairs, 442

Burger, Chief Justice Warren, 68

Burlington School Committee v. *Department of Education*, 65*t*, 68–69

Calculators, 413

Canes (as aids to visually handicapped), 416

Carl D. Perkins vocational Education Act (1984), 275

Carnegie Foundation, 189

Cascade system of services, 267–269, 271 (fig.), 273, 275, 276

Categories. *See* Classification; Exceptionality, categories of

CCBD (Council for Children with Behavior Disorders), 176

CEC. *See* Council for Exceptional Children

Census, U.S. Bureau of, 446, 472

Center-based programs. *See* Intervention, early

Central placement, 242–243. *See also* Placement decisions

Central School District (Oregon), 262, 263

Cerebral palsy, 200–201, 210, 233, 468, 469, 477

Certification of teachers, 280, 282*t*–283*t*, 289, 291–292, 296

Child count data, 244

Child-find programs, 228

Children in Need: Investment Strategies for the Educationally Disadvantaged (Committee for Economic Development), 392

Children of a Lesser God (film), 242, 465

Christensen, John, 477
Civil rights, 40, 44, 61, 62t, 70, 255
U.S. Office of, 442
Civil rights laws, 43, 72
Civil Rights Act, 68
Civil Service Act amendment (1948), 49t
Class action suits, 44, 65, 67, 442. *See
also* Court rulings
Class-graded system, 10
Classification
assessment and, *see* Assessment
current practices, 247–250, 443
and dangers of categorical approach,
493
defined, 241, 250
and eligibility, 310–311, 443 (*see also*
Eligibility decisions)
funding and, *see* Funding, federal
history of practices, 245–247, 434
of levels of blindness, 224
of levels of mental retardation, 162,
174, 191
and misclassification, 37, 61, 62t,
65–67, 255, 270, 354
objectives of, 241, 244–245
of physically handicapped, 206–207
and reclassification of multiply handicapped, 199
for special programs, 259–267
See also Exceptionality, categories of;
Labels
Classroom, regular, 8, 25, 389, 390 (fig.),
478–481
adaptation of (by special equipment),
see Instructional adaptations
assessment in, 352
in cascade system, 267, 269, 271 (fig.),
273
enrichment programs in, *see* Enrichment
good programs described, 254
under IEP, 395, 397
the law and, 52
and least restrictive environment, 25–
26 (*see also* LRE)
mentally retarded or emotionally disturbed in, 164, 190, 192
numbers of exceptional students in,
33, 34t, 258, 301
and stay-put programs, 261–267, 276
trend toward use of, 164, 250, 276,
381, 383, 385, 481

See also Environment, learning: Mainstreaming; Regular education initiative (REI); Segregation
Client-centered therapy, 404
Clinical teacher, 285–286
Cloak of Competence, The (Edgerton),
102
Code of Ethics, 44, 45
Cognitive behavior modification, 403,
407
Cognitive disorders and difficulties
of emotionally disturbed, 180
of learning disabled, 125–128
of mentally retarded, 172, 174
of multihandicapped, 213
of physically impaired, 206–207, 216,
225
of speech and language impaired,
149–150
Cognitive (thinking) skills training, 370,
373, 385, 403–404, 407
Cognitive traits of gifted students, 137,
139–140
Collaborative consultation, defined, 283
284. *See also* Instructional consultant
Collaborative skills, 405, 408
Colleges and vocational schools, 486–487,
497
Columbian Institution for the Deaf and
Dumb and the Blind. *See* Gallaudet
College/University
Committee for Economic Development,
392
Communication
by blind, 226–227
by deaf or hard of hearing, 219
by emotionally disturbed, 185
by gifted, 144–145
by learning disabled, 131
by mentally retarded, 173
by physically impaired, 210
special devices for, 210, 408–414, 460,
476
by speech and language impaired,
151
by teacher, 370, 384, 385
in teaching of deaf-blind, 230–231
See also Speech and language disorders
Communication boards, 210, 409, 460
Communication disorder defined, 145–
146. *See also* Speech and language disorders

Community High School District 155 v. *Denz*, 256

Compensatory instruction, 258, 391–392, 393

Comprehension skills, 403

Compulsory school attendance, 10, 43

Compulsory special education law, 10. *See also* PL 94–142 (Education for All Handicapped Children Act, 1975)

Computers, 410, 412, 413–414, 418, 476 478, 479 (fig.), 494

Conceptual definitions, 80, 84, 108

Conditioning, 399
    respondent and operant, 399, 400–401, 407

Condition of Education, The (Stern and Chandler), 437

Conduct disorders, 187. *See also* Emotional disturbance

Congenital anomaly, 197, 198

Constitution, U.S., 71
    children under, 61, 62t
    Fourteenth Amendment (equal protection), 40, 41–42, 53, 252
    See also Laws and legislation

Constitutions, state, 41, 42

Consultant teacher, 153. *See also* Instructional consultant

Consultation, expert and collaborative, 283
    defined, 266

Consultative (indirect) services, 16, 25, 27

Content of instruction
    deciding on (what to teach), 332, 359–361, 364, 367
    presenting, 369–370
    relevance of, 369, 371

Contingency contracts, 401

Convergent thinking, 139, 403

Cooperative learning, 405, 406 (fig.), 408

Coordinator of special education, 296

Correctional setting, 34t

Cost
    court action, 69
    preschool intervention, 392, 431
    reimbursement of, 51t, 65t, 69, 70, 450–451
    special education, 429, 438, 445–459, 461
    See also Funding, federal; Tuition and fees

Cost-benefit analysis, 457–458

Council for Children with Behavior Disorders (CCBD), 176

Council for Exceptional Children (CEC), 44, 164, 176, 300, 443

Council for Learning Disabilities, 300

Counseling therapy, 254, 404–405, 407

Counselors, 289, 444t

Court rulings, 39, 40, 42, 44, 45, 60, 167
    before and after PL 94–142, 61, 62t–65t, 65–70, 72, 163–164, 251, 454
    on mainstreaming, 256, 258
    on misclassification, 61, 62t, 65–67, 442
    time and cost of, 69
    See also Laws and legislation

Covarrubias v. *San Diego Unified School District*, 62t

Craniofacial anomalies, 205–206

Crime, 190

Crisis therapy, 404, 408

Criteria. *See* Standards in assessment; Standards in determining normality/exceptionality

Criterion-referenced tests, 320, 326t, 327t

Cruickshank, William, 118

Cullers, Kent, 477

Cultural deprivation/disadvantage, 165, 169, 189
    labels rejected by children, 111

Cultural diversity, 474–476
    and fairness of evaluation, 52, 56

Cultural familial retardation, 165. *See also* Mental retardation

Curriculum, 311, 313. *See also* Instructional planning

Curriculum-based assessment, 314–316, 318, 320, 352

Cut-off scores. *See* Norms

Cystic fibrosis, 206

Data collection (for assessment), 311–314, 318–340, 349, 350, 377–378, 385
    assumptions regarding, 345–348
    methods for, 318–322

Deaf-blind students, 13
    characteristics of, 228
    definition of, 227, 233
    dropout rate of, 31
    history of treatment of, 227
    prevalence of, 32t, 228
    as state category, 18t

state-by-state percentage, 196t–197t
Deafness and hearing handicaps, 13, 213
222, 227–228
definitions of, 213–215, 222, 233
history of treatment of, 215
state categories for, 18t
terms describing, 217t
testing for, 332, 333
Deaf or hard of hearing students, 12, 13,
31, 32t
auxiliary aids and special equipment
for, 46, 409, 411, 416
characteristics of, 215–219, 228
classroom environment of, 33
court case regarding, 64t
direct services for, 25, 64, 68, 254
dropout or graduation rate of, 31, 483
expectations of, 102
labeling effects on, 90
laws and actions benefiting, 48t–51t
passim
prevalence of, 32t, 215
special schools for, 242–243
state-by-state percentage of, 196t–197t
test performance of, 218–219
See also Deaf-blind students
Decision-making in assessment, 309–318,
319
curriculum-based, 314–316
and irrelevance of information, 350
parents' participation in, 33, 56
problems created by, 480
screening and referral in, 309–310
three kinds of, 310–311
Decision-making in teaching. *See* Instruction, effective
Deinstitutionalization, 490. *See also* Institutions
Demonstration-practice-proof teaching
model, 384
Demosthenes, 147
Deprivation. *See* Cultural deprivation/
disadvantage
Deprivation of language, deafness and,
222
Desensitization, 400–401
Development
language, assessment of, 337, 340, 353
"normal," 79–80 (*see also* Normality/
abnormality)
perceptual motor, 339–340
psychological, 337–339, 340
of skills, 356, 389, 390

stages of, in mentally retarded, 162
Developmental instruction, 390, 393
Developmental learning disabilities, 121
Diagnosis
instructional, 316, 318, 352
what to teach, 332, 359–361, 367, 384
Diagnostic and Statistical Manuals
(APA), 246
Diagnostician, 291, 314, 315
Diagnostic teaching, 315, 422
Diagnostic tests, 320, 327
Diana v. *State Board of Education,* 62t,
65
Diet, 170. *See also* Malnutrition
Direct instruction, 402–403. *See also* In-
struction, effective
Director of special education, 296
Direct services, 25, 27, 254
cost of, 452
Disabilities
defined, 446
distinguished from handicaps, 86
reactions to, 86–87
women with, 110–111
See also Exceptionality; Impairments:
Learning disabilities; *specific dis-
abilities*
Disabled students. *See* Handicapped stu-
dents; Learning disabled (LD) students
Disadvantaged, as label, and teacher expectations, 111. *See also* Environment
Discipline
harsh, substituted for services, 11
questions on, 70
See also Exclusion/expulsion from
school
Discrepancy of abilities, 116, 117, 172,
180, 248, 324
Discrimination
court rulings on, 63t, 64t
illegality of, 12, 46, 59, 72, 199, 446
Distractibility, 126, 339
Divergent thinking, 139, 403
Dix, Dorothea, 163, 178, 466
Down syndrome, 82, 83, 166–167, 169,
173, 206
early education program for, 274
Dropout rate, 483
age and, 27, 482
of gifted students, 140
of minority groups, 31, 437, 474, 475
in urban schools, 189, 190, 436
Due process, 39, 53, 56, 57, 72

court rulings on, 62*t*, 63*t*, 64*t*, 67
See also Laws and legislation
Duke, Patti, 465
Duration recording, 338
Dyslexia, 117

Early childhood special education, as
state category, 18*t*. *See also* Special
education
Early intervention. *See* Intervention,
early
Easter Seal Society, 457
Economic factors. *See* Cost; Funding,
federal
ED. *See* Emotional disturbance
EDGE (Expanding Developmental
Growth through Education), 274
Educable mentally retarded (EMR). *See*
Mental retardation
Education
appropriate, court definition of, 68, 69,
70
condition of, in U.S., 428–431
"constructive," for handicapped, court
case on, 63*t*
defined, 9
at home, 10
homebound, 18*t*, 25, 34*t*, 259, 288
opportunity for, *see* Opportunity
regular, *see* Classroom, regular
rights to, laws and actions concerning,
48*t*–51*t*, 224 (*see also* Laws and legislation)
teacher, *see* Teachers
See also Instruction, effective; Schools;
Special education; vocational education
Educational diagnostician, 291, 314, 315
Education for All Handicapped Children
Act. *See* PL 94-142
Egalitarians, teachers as, 418, 419
Electronic travel aids, 416–417. *See also*
Mobility; Technology
Eligibility decisions, 23, 27, 57, 444, 461
assessment and, 310–322, 323, 332
criteria used in, 81, 248–250, 311, 439,
443
in early intervention, 58
for emotionally disturbed, 176, 185,
192
hearing loss and, 214
for mentally retarded, 167
in pull-out programs, 260

Embryonic development, 169
Emotional disturbance
change in terminology argued, 176
definitions of, 175–176, 180, 204
environmental conflict, 184, 185
externalized and internalized, 184
history of treatment of, 177–178, 192
personal, 184, 185
See also Social/emotional/behavioral
problems
Emotionally disturbed students, 16, 175–
193
advocacy groups for, 177–178
age of, 179–180
characteristics of, 171, 180–185
court rulings on rights of, 64*t*, 67,
69–70
dropout rate of, 31, 190, 483
effects of labeling on, 90, 91
employment of, 191
environment and, 189–190
exceptionality of, 246
male-female ratio of, 179
minority groups among, 474
prevalence of, 32*t*, 126, 178–180, 191
sanctioned labeling of (for treatment),
176, 185, 192
separate classes for, 33, 192
state categories for, 18*t*
teaching, 185, 186–188, 190, 192
terms describing, 181*t*
Employment, 484, 492, 495
as challenge, 470, 471
competitive, 487–488, 492, 496
of mentally retarded or emotionally
disturbed, 191
service needs of handicapped adults,
484*t*
sheltered, 488–489, 492, 496
supported, 489, 492, 496
in workshop settings, 274, 275
EMR (educable mentally retarded). *See*
Mental retardation
Endogenous retardation, 117. *See also*
Mental retardation
Engaged time, 317
monitoring, 374–376, 379
See also Time
Enrichment, 135–136, 153, 391, 393
Environment
and adaptive behavior, 353
of assessment, 350–351, 352
and behavior problems, 189–190, 429

and deprivation/neglect/abuse, 169, 189

and dropouts, 437

least restrictive, *see* LRE

and mental retardation, 165, 169, 170, 171, 466

and psychosocial disadvantage, 165, 169

and test scores, 165

See also Interpersonal relationships

Environment, learning

different types of, 32–33, 34*t*, 153

need for rules in, 365–367

special settings and services, 258–267

teacher observation of, 314–315

See also Classroom, regular; Home; Mainstreaming

Environmental conflict. *See* Emotional disturbance

Epilepsy, 201, 233

Equal protection or opportunity. *See* Opportunity

Error analysis, 329–330, 340, 353

Errors in assessment, 347, 348

Ethnic origin

and fairness of evaluation, 52, 56

and treatment, 435–439

See also Minority students

Evaluation, 23, 27

of accessibility, 230*t*

court rulings on, 64*t*, 67

error analysis, 329–330, 340, 353

formative, 374, 379, 385

of instruction, 374, 385

procedures and criteria, under IEP, 396, 399

of products of instruction, 315, 327–328

program, 313–314

progress or performance, 311–313, 382, 396, 399

protection in procedures of (PEP), 56–57, 72

racial and cultural fairness of, 52, 56

and reevaluation, 23

summative, 374, 379, 385

of task-approach strategies, 315

training for skills in, 404

vocational, 484

See also Assessment; Tests

Event recording, 338

Exceptional Children (Periodical), 73, 435

Exceptionality, 78–112, 246

causes of, 88–89

context of, 92–93

identification of (child-find programs), 228

perception of, 88, 95–107 (*see also* Expectations)

as relative concept, 108

standards of, *see* Standards in determining normality/exceptionality

See also specific forms of exceptionality

Exceptionality, attitudes toward/reactions to, 85–95

Asian, 475

and attitudinal barriers, 87

public, and funding, 446

recent changes in, 466

of teachers and parents, 103–107, 109, 111, 144

See also Expectations; Expectations, teacher; Labels

Exceptionality, categories of, 13, 16, 17, 32*t*, 35

category defined, 13

conceptual definitions and operational criteria in judging, 80–81, 84, 108, 311

and effect of labels, 37, 89–95, 102, 104, 108, 109, 111

high-prevalence, 114–159

laws concerning, 244

low-prevalence, 195–234

moderate-prevalence, 160–192

and pull-out programs, 259–260

by state/territory, 18*t*–19*t*

uselessness of differentiation among, 189, 190, 261, 275

Exceptional students

advanced schooling for, 486

age of, 26–27

assessment of, *see* Assessment

behavior management by, 366, 403, 407

blacks among, *see* Black students

classification and categories of, *see* Classification; Exceptionality, categories of

definitions of, 13, 43

diversity among, 29–32, 33, 156

eligibility of, *see* Eligibility decisions

goals of, 356, 382

identification of, 21, 43, 228

male-female ratio among, 29–30
placement of, *see* Placement decisions
reactions of, to "special" education,
33–34, 420
reactions to, *see* Exceptionality, attitudes toward/reactions to
in regular classroom, 8 (*see also* Classroom, regular)
relationships of, *see* Interpersonal relationships; Peers, interaction with
rights of, 10–12 (*see also* Court rulings;
Laws and legislation)
special learning needs of (IEP and), 395,
397, 398*t*
special services for, *see* Special education
teaching of, *see* Instruction, effective;
Instructional adaptations; Teachers
See also Exceptionality; Gifted students; Handicapped students; *specific forms of exceptionality*
Exclusion/expulsion from school
court rulings on, 61, 62*t*, 63*t*, 65*t*,
69–70, 167
of emotionally disturbed, 63*t*, 69–70
of mentally retarded, 61, 62*t*, 63*t*, 167
Expectations
defined, 95, 98, 107, 109
general and specific, 100, 107, 109
labels and, 89–92, 102, 480
parents', 107, 144
and performance, 98–102
physical or health impairments and,
210
self, 100–101, 102, 107, 108
and self–fulfilling prophecy, 102, 107,
109
and social behaviors, 102–103, 107
Expectations, teacher, 12, 98, 100, 316
factors influencing (labeling and), 89,
101–102, 108, 109, 111
of gifted children, 144
importance of, 83–84, 85, 107, 108, 364
realistic, communication of, 364–365,
384
See also Feedback
Expert consultation, 283. *See also* Instructional consultant
Explicit rules (of behavior), 83

Family
Asian, 475
changing role of, 467–471, 495

foster home life with, 491–492
importance of medical history of, 83
See also Parents
Feedback, 315, 366, 371, 376, 378 (fig.)
supportive and corrective, 373, 384,
385, 407
Fees. *See* Tuition and fees
Fernald, Grace, 118
Fetal alcohol syndrome, 206
Fluency disorders, 146, 151. *See also*
Speech and language disorders
Ford, Gerald, 10, 47
Formative evaluation. *See* Evaluation
Foster homes, 491–492
Fourteenth Amendment. *See* Constitution, U.S.
Frederick L. v. *Thomas*, 63*t*, 67, 68, 73
Frostig, Marianne, 118
Functional impairments. *See* Impairments
Funding, federal, 51*t*, 273, 274, 429, 444*t*,
448*t*–449*t*, 459, 461
allocation of, 449–452
block grants for gifted students, 132,
157
change in priorities, 445–446
child count data in, 244
classification and, 247, 249–250,
260–261, 452
compliance with law and, 43, 46,
58–59, 72
debate over, 447–448
of early intervention, 58, 392, 472
increase in, 447
and labeling, 91, 392
for speech and language therapy, 148
state requirements for, 115

Gallaudet, Thomas Hopkins, 215
Gallaudet College/University (formerly
Columbian Institution for the Deaf
and Dumb and the Blind), 48*t*, 49*t*, 51*t*,
87, 215, 465–466
Gender. *See* Male-female ratio
General education initiative (GEI). *See*
Regular education initiative (REI)
Genetics. *See* Hereditary factors
German measles and vaccine, 82, 170
Getman, Arnold, 118
Gifted and Talented Children's Education
Act of 1978. *See* PL 95–561
Gifted students, 12, 13, 17, 132–145

category defined, 132–133, 145
characteristics of, 137–145
dropouts among, 140
Education Act benefiting, *see* PL 95-561
enrichment or acceleration programs for, 135–136, 153, 391, 393
exceptionality of, 246, 247 (fig.)
as high-prevalence category, 157
history of treatment of, 135–137
independent study or special classes for, 154
minority groups among, 437, 474, 475, 476
and normal curve, 81
parents of, 471
physically impaired students as, 90
prevalence of, 32t, 137, 138t–139t, 437
as state category, 18t
State Directors of Programs for, 114
teaching, 153–155
terms describing, 140t
"three–ring" conception of, 141 (fig.)
Goddard, H. H., 245
Goldstein, Kurt, 118
Goso v. *Lopez*, 63t
Grade equivalent score, 330
Graduate Record Exam (GRE), 332
Gray Oral Reading Test, 326
Grossman, Herbert, 436
Group administered tests. *See* Test
Group homes, 490–491
Group learning. *See* Cooperative learning
Guidance counselors, 289
Guide dogs, 48t, 49t, 416
Guidelines, 44. *See also* Laws and legislation

Hairston v. *Drosick*, 63t
Handicapped adults
education opportunities for, 485, 492, 495
employment of, 484t, 487–489, 492
living conditions of, 440–441, 484–485, 489–492, 493, 495 (*see also* Mobility)
service needs of, 484t, 485t, 486t, 492, 495
Handicapped Children's Early Education Assistance Act. *See* PL 90–538
Handicapped Children's Protection Act. *See* PL 99-372

Handicapped students
auxiliary aids and special equipment for, 46, 229, 415–418
cost of educating, 447, 452, 453, 455t, 456t, 459, 460 (*see also* Cost)
court cases concerning, 62t–63t, 68
dropouts and graduates among, 27, 31, 189, 190, 482, 483, 483t
employment of, *see* Employment
evaluation of, 23
families of, 467–471 (*see also* Parents)
and Head Start, 435
labeling of, 89–92, 392
laws and actions benefiting, 12, 48t–51t, 224, 466 (*see also* PL 90–538; PL 93–112; PL 94–142; PL 98–199; PL 99–372; PL 99–457)
misclassification of, 354
mobility of, *see* Mobility
multihandicapped, *see* Multihandicapped students
number of, in U.S., 17, 21t, 36, 47, 114, 169, 178
related services for, 68 (*see also* Related services)
rights of, 11, 43, 250
severely handicapped, 16, 32t, 446, 452, 453, 459, 460
test modifications for, 415, 418
tuition and fees for, 68–69
See also Exceptional students; Physical impairment
Handicaps
and constitutional rights, 441–443
disabilities distinguished from, 86
See also specific handicaps
Hansen v. *Hobson*, 62t
Hawking, Stephen, 86, 208
Head Start program, 392, 431, 435, 472
Head trauma, 118, 202, 233
Health impairment. *See* Orthopedically or other health impaired; Physical impairment
Hearing aids, 409
Hearing handicaps. *See* Deafness and hearing handicaps; Deaf or hard of hearing students
Heart disorders, 205
Helen Keller Story, The (film), 465
Hemmerick, Mary Kate, 477
Hemophilia, 206

Hereditary factors (in mental retardation), 82–83, 169, 171 (fig.), 173

High-prevalence exceptionality, 114–159
practical considerations in teaching, 152–156
See also Gifted students; Learning disabilities; Speech and language disorders

Hispanic students, 474, 475
dropout rates of, 31, 437, 474
Mexican-Americans, 436
See also Minority students

Hoffman, Dustin, 465

Home
education at, 10
and home-based early intervention, 259, 472–473, 481, 495

Homebound/hospitalized, 25, 34*t*, 259
and homebound teacher, 288
as state category, 18*t*

Honig v. *Doe*, 65*t*, 69–70, 73

Horrobin, Margaret, 274

Hull, Clark, 98

Humanitarians, teachers as, 419

Humphrey, Hubert H., 164

Hunter, Ivy, 417

Hyperactivity, 126

IEP (individualized education program), 23, 54–55 (fig.), 254, 389, 393–399, 422
court ruling on, 69
defined, 394*t*, 397, 421
goals in, 399
PL 94–142 and, 52–53, 57, 72
and special (medical) needs, 256
teacher participation in, 281

IFSP (individualized family service plan), 59, 72

Illinois Test of Psycholinguistic Abilities, 118

Immaturity, 339

Impairments
functional and organic, 13, 16, 88–89
neurological, 117, 129, 200–202, 210, 233
See also Disabilities; Exceptionality; Handicaps; Learning disabilities; Physical impairment; Speech and language disorders

Implied rules (of behavior), 83

Indirect or consultative services, 16, 25, 27

Individual accountability, 405, 408

Individualized education program, individualized family service plan. *See* IEP; IFSP

Individually administered tests. *See* Tests

Information. *See* Data collection (for assessment)

Institute of Child Health and Human Development, 50*t*

Institutions, 25–26, 489, 492, 493, 496
and deinstitutionalization, 490

Instruction, effective, 356–386
adjusting, 372–373, 385
application of, 381–383
appropriateness of, 273, 363–364
assessment during, 350, 351 (*see also* Assessment)
components of, 357–379, 385
deciding what and how to teach (diagnosis and prescription), 332, 359–364, 367, 384 (*see also* Content of instruction)
delivering, 367–373, 385
demonstration-practice-proof model of, 384
developmental, 390, 393
diagnostic, 315, 422
evaluation of, 374, 385
goal of, 356 (*see also* Special education)
guidelines for, 362–363
of high-prevalence exceptionality, 152–156
home-based, *see* Home
and learning environment, *see* Environment, learning
of low-prevalence exceptionality, 228–231
managing, 365–367, 385, 386
of moderate-prevalence exceptionality, 185–188, 190, 192
monitoring, 371, 373, 374–376, 379, 385
and placement, 377–378 (*see also* Placement decisions)
precision teaching, 401–402, 407, 422
presenting, 367–370, 373, 385
preteaching, 262
primary, supplemental, remedial, or compensatory, 258–259, 391–392, 393
special adaptation of, *see* Instructional adaptations

special methods of, 399–408
special purposes for, 389–393
teaching defined, 357
variation of material and method, 373
See also Products of instruction;
   Schools; Teachers; Team teaching
Instructional adaptations, 389, 444*t*, 480
   audiovisual aids, 46, 152, 153, 224,
      226, 230–231, 254, 412–417
   communication devices, 210, 408–412,
      460
   for gifted students, 153–155
   laws concerning, 48*t*–51*t passim*
   for mobility, 229, 415–417, 421, 452,
      453
Instructional consultant, 261, 265–266,
   267, 283–284
Instructional consultation, defined, 283
Instructional diagnosis, 316, 318, 352
Instructional planning, 311, 357–365,
   367, 384
Integrated programs, 386. *See also* Classroom, regular; Mainstreaming
Integration errors, 340
Intellectual abilities, 323–324
Intelligence tests
   in assessment, 323, 324
   behaviors sampled by, 325*t*
   court rulings regarding, 62*t*, 64*t*
   criticisms of, 119, 342–343
   emotionally disturbed students and,
      180
   and gifted students, 135, 137
   as measure of mental retardation, 67,
      161–165 *passim*, 168–169, 172,
      245–246, 334, 435–436, 442
   and visually handicapped students, 225
   See also Tests
International Models Hall of Fame, 417
Internship, 358–359
Interpersonal relationships
   effects of labels on, 92 (fig.), 93 (*see
      also* Labels)
   emotional disturbance and, 184–185
   expectations and, 100–103
   health impairment and, 209
   teacher-student, 367, 369, 380–381
   therapy and, 404
   See also Communication; Peers, inter-
      action with; Social/emotional/be-
      havioral problems
Interstate Commerce Act amendment
   (1937), 48*t*

Interval recording, 338
Intervention
   need for experiment with, 494
   prereferral and postreferral, 21, 24, 24*t*
   preventive, 392, 393
Intervention, early, 273–274, 275, 276,
   472–473
   center-based, 473, 482, 495
   cost of, 392, 431
   home-based, 259, 472–473, 481, 495
   numbers of children in, 27
   PL 99–457 and, 58–59, 72, 274, 472,
      481, 495
   research on, 445–446
   social factors in, 434–435
   state category for, 18*t*
Intervention assistance teams, 261,
   263–265, 267
Interview, life space, 404
Interviewing, 321–322, 323, 324, 332,
   334, 337
   defined, 319, 323
   Likert-type response format in, 339
   reliability of, 344, 347
   sample form, 335 (fig.)
Irving Independent School District v. *Tatro,* 65*t*, 68, 69, 73
Irwin, Robert, 224
Itard, Jean Marc Gaspard, 163
Itinerant teacher. *See* Teachers

Jackson, Jesse, 316
Johns Hopkins University, 263

Kanner, Leo, 205
Keller, Helen, 227
Kendall School, 51*t*
Kennedy family, 164
Kephart, Newell, 118
Kidder, Shannon, 477
Kirk, Samuel, 118, 119
Klinefelter's syndrome, 173
Knowledge skills, 403. *See also* Skills
Kurzweil Reading Machine, 412–413, 414
   (fig.)

Labels
   advantages and disadvantages of, 93*t*
   effects of, 89–95, 102, 104, 111, 480
      (*see also* Stigma)

emotionally disturbed as sanctioned
  label, 176, 185, 192
federal funding and, 91, 392
LD as label, 90, 91, 124
mental retardation as label, 169, 434,
  435, 439
necessity for, 91, 92, 95, 108, 176, 185,
  192
pejorative, of mentally retarded, 167,
  245
rejection of, 254, 255
terms describing emotional disturbance, 181t
terms describing LD, 125t
See also Classification; Expectations;
  Expectations, teacher; Stereotyping,
  negative
La Grange Area Department of Special
  Education (LADSE), 164
Language
  assessment of development of, 337,
    340, 353
  form, content, and function of, 147,
    151
  limited English proficient (LEP) stu-
    dents, 474, 482
  non-English, testing in, 56, 61, 62t, 65
  non-English language background
    (NELB) students, 474, 475–476, 482,
    495
Language disorders, Language impaired
  students. *See* Speech and language disorders; Speech and language impaired
  students
Largent, Steve, 105
Larry P. v. *Riles,* 64t, 65–67, 73, 442
Latency recording, 338–339
Laws and legislation, 39–72
  benefiting handicapped, 48t–51t, 224,
    434
  change in focus of, 46, 167
  civil rights, 43, 68, 72
  and classification, 244
  compliance with, and funding, 43, 46,
    58–59, 72
  discrimination prohibited by, 12, 46,
    59, 72, 199, 446
  and least restrictive environment, *see*
    LRE
  and legal rights to special education,
    10–12, 442, 461 (*see also* Public
    Laws)
  Pratt-Smoot Act (1930), 224

program laws, 43, 46, 47, 72
teachers and, 45
See also Constitution, U.S.; Court rulings; Due process
Lead poisoning, 83, 169, 171
Learning
  cooperative, 405, 406 (fig.), 408 peer–
    directed, 405–407, 408 *See also* In-
    struction, effective
Learning disabilities
  academic, *see* Academic learning dis-
    abilities
  cognitive, *see* Cognitive disorders and
    difficulties
  communication, 131 (*see also* Com-
    munication; Speech and language
    disorders)
  definitions of, 115–117, 119–121, 129,
    131
  developmental, 121
  as high-prevalence category, 157
  history of, as category of needs,
    117–121
  research on, 445–446
  Research on, University of Minnesota
    Institute for, 247
  specific, defined, 115–116, 120
  See also Learning disabled (LD) stu-
    dents
Learning Disabilities Association (LDA),
  119, 120, 300, 442, 443
Learning disabled students, 13, 16,
  31
  characteristics of, 123–131
  classrooms for, 33 (*see also* Environ-
    ment, learning)
  definitions of, 37, 115–117
  evaluation of, *see* Evaluation
  identification of (criteria for), 116–117,
    131, 248–250
  and LD as label, 90, 91, 124
  number of, in U.S., 32t, 114, 121–123,
    124 (fig.), 429, 434, 436, 437
  special teachers for (numbers needed),
    298
  as state category, 18t
  subtypes of, 121
  teaching, 152–153
  terms describing, 125t
  test performance of, 124
  test performance of, and discrepancy
    between scores, 116, 117, 172
  See also Learning disabilities

Learning strategies training, 405, 408
Least restrictive environment. *See* LRE
Legal rights. *See* Laws and legislation
Legg-Calve-Perthes Disease, 204
Lehtinen, Laura, 118
Lemon v. *Bossier Parish School Board,*
62*t*
LEP (limited English proficient) students.
See Language
Library of Congress, 224
Licensing. *See* Certification of teachers
Life space interview, 404
Likert-type response format (in inter-
views), 339
Lincoln County School District (Oregon),
262
Lindsay Russell Model E Pathsounder,
416
Litigation. *See* Court rulings
Living conditions for handicapped. *See*
Handicapped adults
Lora v. *New York City Board of Educa-
tion,* 64*t,* 67–68, 73
Low-prevalence exceptionality, 195–234
practical considerations in teaching,
228–231
state–by–state list of students with
(1987–1988), 196*t*–197*t*
See also Blindness and visual handicaps; Deafness and hearing handicaps; Multihandicapped students;
Orthopedically or other health impaired
LRE (least restrictive environment)
AFT guidelines for, 444*t*
concept of, 25–26, 251–254
as legal principle, 254–257, 490
PL 94-142 and, 25, 26 (fig.), 32, 57,
250–254, 276, 459, 490
understanding the meaning of, 252*t*
See also Mainstreaming; Peers, interaction with

Mainstreaming, 21, 102, 254–257, 258,
444*t*
of blind students, 225
in cascade system, 271 (fig.)
of mentally retarded, 190
NEA policy regarding, 272
and related services personnel, 293
siblings and, 470

See also Classroom, regular; LRE (least
restrictive environment)
Male-female ratio
of dropouts, 437
of emotionally disturbed students, 179
of reading proficiency, 429
of students receiving special educa-
tion, 29–30
Mallory v. *Drake,* 256
Malnutrition, 83, 169, 170
Marland, Sidney, 135
Martella v. *Kelley,* 63*t*
Massachusetts School for Idiotic and Fee-
ble-minded Youth, 163
Maternal age and health, and mental re-
tardation, 83, 169, 170
Mathematics, difficulty with, 430
Matlin, Marlee, 242, 243, 465
Meagher, Dr. Lance, 410–412
Medical services, 68, 256, 297. *See also*
Related services
Medical standards of normality/excep-
tionality, 82–83, 85, 109
Memory deficits, 125
Mental disorders, classification of,
245–246. *See also* Mental retardation
Mentally retarded students, 13, 31,
161–174, 189
advocacy groups for, 163–165, 167, 174
characteristics of, 171–174
court cases concerning, 61, 62*t,* 63*t,*
65–67, 163–164
educable (EMR). *see* Mental retardation
employment of, 191
exceptionality of, 246
laws and actions benefiting, 49*t,* 50*t,*
434, 442
minority groups among, 168, 436, 437,
442, 474
misclassification of, 37, 67, 255, 434
prevalence of, 32*t,* 169–171, 174, 191
segregation of, 167
state categories for, 18*t*
teaching, 185–186, 190, 192
trainable, 162, 191
Mental retardation
care for, 110
causes of, 82–83, 169–171, 201, 205,
206
change in policies toward, 167, 168,
174, 436, 466

definitions of, 80, 161, 165, 167, 168–169, 245, 334, 436

distinctions among levels of, 162, 174, 191

educable (EMR), 33, 62*t*, 64*t*, 65–67, 91*t*, 111, 162, 436

endogenous, 117

environmental effects on, 466

and expectations, 100–101

history of treatment of, 162–169, 192

as label, 169, 434, 435, 439

labels (MR, EMR) evaluated, 89, 90*t*, 91*t*

and normal curve, 81

operational criteria for, 80

pejorative labels for, 167, 245

President's Committee on, 334

priority of research on, 445

as secondary condition, 171

and "six–hour retarded child," 334

stages of development in, 162

See also Down syndrome

Mentor, 153–154

Meriken v. *Cressman*, 63*t*

Merrill, Maude, 135

Metropolitan Achievement Tests, 326

Mexican-American students, 436. *See also* Hispanic students; Minority students

Microcephaly, 173

Mills v. *Board of Education*, 63*t*

Mind That Found Itself, A (Beers), 178

Minnesota Mental Health Survey, 190

Minority students, 11

dropout rates of, 31, 437, 474, 475

IQ tests and, 342

misclassification of, court actions on, 61, 62*t*, 65–67, 442

reading proficiency of, 429

in special education, 168, 436, 437, 439, 474–476

See also Black students; Ethnic origin

Misclassification. *See* Classification

Missing limb, 204

Mobility

aids for, 415–417, 421, 452, 453

architectural accessibility and, 46, 47, 50*t*, 59, 229, 230*t*, 440–441, 446

defined, 226

Moderate-prevalence exceptionality, 160–192

practical considerations in teaching, 185–188, 190

See also Emotional disturbance; Mental retardation

Monitoring

self–, by student, 366, 403

by teacher, *see* Feedback; Instruction, effective

Moral treatment, 178, 199

Morphology, 147, 337

Motivation, 367, 370, 385, 418

Mowat Sensor, 416

MR. *See* Mental retardation

Multihandicapped students, 16, 210–213

category added, 199, 211

characteristics of, 213

definition of, 210–211, 213, 233

history of treatment of, 211, 213

prevalence of, 32*t*, 211–212, 233

separate classes for, 33

state-by-state percentage of, 196*t*–197*t*

state categories for, 18*t*

See also Handicapped students

Multiple sclerosis, 203–204

Muscular dystrophy, 202–203

National Assessment of Educational Progress, 463

National Association for Retarded Citizens (NARC), 163, 442

National Association of Social Workers, 293

National Association of State Directors of Special Education, 122

National Center for Education Statistics, 428

National Center on Educational Media and Materials for the Handicapped, 50*t*

National Committee for Mental Hygiene, 178

National Council on Measurement in Education, 348

National Defense Education Act (1958), 49*t*

National Education Association, 272

National Handicapped Sports and Recreation Association, 417

National Institute for Neurological and Communicative Disorders, 205

National Institutes of Health (NIH), 120, 129

National Joint Committee for Learning Disabilities (NJCLD), 119, 120

National Society for Autistic Children, 205

National Society for Children and Adults with Autism, 204

National Society for the Study of Education, 110, 462

Native Americans, 31, 437, 474

NELB (non-English language background) students. *See* Language

Neurofibromatosis, 173

Neurological disorders, 117, 129, 200–202, 210, 233

New England Asylum for the Blind, 224

New York Institution for the Blind, 224

New York Institution for the Instruction of the Deaf and Dumb, 215

Normal curve, 81, 82 (fig.)

Normality/abnormality
    defined, 78–81, 84
    labeling effects on, 89–92
    as relative concept, 108
    standards of, *see* Standards in determining normality/exceptionality

Normalization, 254. *See also* Mainstreaming

Normative peer comparisons, 377–378

Norm-referenced tests. *See* Tests

Norms (cut-off scores), 309, 436

Northwest Suburban Special Education Organization (Palatine, IL), 266

Objective-referenced tests, 320

Objectivity, intelligence testing and, 245

Observation, 323, 324, 327, 328, 343
    active and passive, 321
    in deciding what to teach, 332
    defined, 319, 323
    of perceptual-motor development, 340
    of psychological development, 338–339
    validity and reliability of, 344

Occupational therapist. *See* Therapy and therapists

Office of Special Education. *See* U.S. Department of Education

Operant conditioning, 400–401, 407

Operational criteria, 80–81, 84, 108, 311

Opportunity
    access to (court ruling on), 68

educational, of handicapped adult, 485, 492, 495
    equal, 41–42, 44, 64, 252

Optacon, 412

Ordway v. *Hargreaves*, 62t

Organic impairments. *See* Impairments

Organizations. *See* Advocacy groups; Professional organizations

Orientation, defined, 226

Orthopedically or other health impaired, 13, 192–210
    autism as category of, 175 (*see also* Autism)
    causes of handicap, 197–198, 232
    characteristics of, 206–210, 233
    definitions of, 197–198, 210
    graduation rate of, 483
    history of treatment of, 198–199
    major conditions of, 199–206
    prevalence of, 32t, 199, 232
    state-by-state percentage of, 196t–197t
    state categories for, 18t
    See also Physical impairment

Orthopedic disorders, 202–204

Orton, Samuel, 118

Orton Society, 300

Osteogenesis imperfecta, 203

Osteomyelitis, 205

PACER Center, Inc., 294, 295

Pacesetter (magazine), 295

Panitch v. *State of Wisconsin*, 64t

Paralysis, 201, 233

PARC v. *Commonwealth of Pennsylvania*, 63t, 163–164, 442

Parent Advocacy Coalition for Educational Rights (PACER), 294, 295

Parent Network, 167

Parents
    attitudes of, toward exceptional children, 104–107, 109, 111, 144
    and decision-making process, 33, 56
    effect of status of, 437–438
    and home-based instruction, 10, 259, 472–473, 495
    lobbying by, 11
    and mainstreaming, 255
    recovery of fees by, 51t, 65t, 69, 70
    residential care as viewed by, 492
    rights of, 44, 53, 56
    role of, 70–71, 72, 467–471

workshop settings as viewed by, 274
See also Advocacy groups
Parochial schools, 429, 430
PASE v. *Hannon*, 64*t*, 67
Pathsounder (travel aid), 416
Peabody Individual Achievement Test (PIAT), 329
Peckham, Judge Robert F., 66
Peer-directed learning, 405–407
  and peer tutoring, 406–407, 408, 422
Peer networks, 266, 267
Peers, comparison with, 377–378
Peers, interaction with
  of adolescent, 470, 471
  disturbed, 339
  of gifted, 144
  importance of, 35, 57, 256, 257
  of LD, 103, 131
  parent and teacher views on, 14, 15
  See also Interpersonal relationships; Mainstreaming
Pennsylvania Institution for the Deaf and Dumb, 215
PEP (Protection in evaluation procedures), 56–57, 72
Percentile score, 330
Perceptual disorders, 126
Perceptual-motor tests, 323, 339–340
Perseveration errors, 340
Personal disturbance, personality problems. *See* Emotional disturbance
Personality tests
  court ruling on, 63*t*
  decline of use of, 338
Personnel. *See* Professionals; Related services personnel; Teachers
Personnel cost, 452, 453 (fig.). *See also* Cost
Phenylketonuria, 170, 206
Phonology, 147, 337
Physical impairment
  classification of, 206–207
  and classroom environment, 33, 230–231
  disorders acquired in childhood, 169, 197–206
  and gifted programs, 90
  history of treatment of, 198–199
  and independence of student, 232
  and mental retardation, 173, 207
  as state category, 18*t*
  See also Blind or visually impaired students; Deaf-blind students; Deaf or hard of hearing students; Orthopedically or other health impaired
Physical learning disabilities, 129
Physical therapy, physical therapists, 254, 291
PL 90–538 (Handicapped Children's Early Education Assistance Act, 1968), 50*t*, 472
PL 93–112 (Rehabilitation Act, 1973), 51*t*, 199, 228
  Section 504 of, 43, 46–47, 59, 72, 415, 447
  violation of, 63*t*
PL 94–142 (Education for All Handicapped Children Act, 1975), 10–11, 17, 18, 51–52, 228, 334, 415, 459
  amendments to (1986), *see* PL 99–457
  and appropriate education, 68
  classification system specified by, 247, 311, 316
  court rulings before and after, *see* Court rulings
  and definition of LD, 115, 157
  and disincentive to identify needs, 457
  due process under, 53, 56, 72
  and early intervention, 472
  and emotional disturbance as term, 176
  funding of, 449, 459, 461 (*see also* Funding, federal)
  IEP under, 52–53, 57, 72 (*see also* IEP [individualized education program])
  and least restrictive environment, *see* LRE and mainstreaming, 257
  objectives of, 47, 59, 492
  PEP under, 56–57, 72
  as program law, 43, 47
  Section 504 (of 1973 Act) and, 47
  Section 601c of, 68
PL 95–561 (Gifted and Talented Children's Education Act, 1978), 51*t*, 132, 148, 157
PL 98–199 (Secondary Education and Transitional Services for Handicapped Youth Act, 1983), 274, 472
PL 99–372 (Handicapped Children's Protection Act, 1986), 51*t*, 69
PL 99–457 (1986 Amendments to the Education for All Handicapped Children Act of 1975), 18*t*, 51*t*, 69, 87
  and early intervention, 58–59, 72, 274, 472, 481, 495

Placement decisions, 310–311
and central placement (for deaf students), 242–243
concepts guiding, 250–258
court action on, 65–67, 72
debate over, 272
for gifted students, 136
individual needs and, 254, 444t
labeling and, 90–92
parents and, 56
PEP provisions and, 56–57
and regular education initiative (REI), 269–270, 272, 273
review of, 254
teachers' records and, 377–378
See also Classification; Classroom, regular; LRE (least restrictive environment); Mainstreaming
Planning. *See* Instructional planning
Poliomyelitis, 202
Political factors in special education, 439–443, 459–460, 461
Positive Approach, A (Periodical), 477
Positive interdependence, 405, 408
Postreferral intervention, 24t
Practice, 371, 384, 385
Pragmatic language disorders, 131. *See also* Speech and language disorders
Pragmatics, 147
Pratt-Smoot Act (1930), 224. *See also* Laws and legislation
Precision teaching, 401–402, 407, 422
Pregnancy
and exclusion from school, court ruling on, 62t
and prenatal and perinatal problems, 82–83, 169
Prereferral intervention, 21, 24, 24t
Preschool programs, 472. *See also* Intervention, early
Prescription (how to teach), 361–364, 367, 384. *See also* Instruction, effective
Prescriptive programming, 332, 422
President's Committee on Mental Retardation, 334
Preteaching, 262
Prevalence of exceptionality, 32t. *See also* Exceptionality, categories of; *specific form of exceptionality*
Preventive intervention, 392, 393. *See also* Intervention, early
Principal, 296
Private schools, 34t, 429, 438

enrollment in, 428
tuition, court rulings on, 65t, 68–69, 70, 256
Problem solving, problem finding, 154–155
Process disorder, 17, 124
Products of instruction: evaluation of, 315, 327–328
Professional organizations, 298–300, 301, 443. *See also* Advocacy groups
Professionals, 279–303
in center-based intervention programs, 473
medical, 297
tests administered by, 309, 345–346, 348
See also Administrators; Psychiatrists; Psychologists; Related services personnel; Teachers
Program evaluation. *See* Evaluation
Program laws. *See* Laws and legislation
Progress. *See* Evaluation; Students' progress or performance
Prostheses, 417
Protection in evaluation procedures. *See* PEP
Psychiatrists, 297
and APA diagnostic criteria for mental disorders, 126, 246
Psychoeducational assessment, 309, 354
Psychological testing, 309, 337–339, 340
questioned, 255
Psychologists, 289–291, 297, 309, 338, 443, 444t
Psychosocial disadvantage or deprivation, 165, 169
Psychosomatic complaints, 181
Public Health Service Act amendment (1962), 50t
Public Laws, 48t–51t. *See also* PL 90–538; PL 93–112; PL 94–142; PL 95–561; PL 98–199; PL 99–372; PL 99–457
Pull-out programs, 259–261, 266, 269, 276, 480
Pupil-unit funding, 451–452. *See also* Funding, federal

Race. *See* Ethnic origin; Minority students
Rainman (film), 465
Rand Corporation, 454

Randomizers, teachers as, 418–419
Rating scales. *See* Test scores
Raw score, 330
Reading proficiency, 429
Reagan, Ronald, 472
Reality therapy, 404
Recording
  behavior, 338–339
  progress, 376, 377–378, 379
Referral, 21, 309–310, 315
Regular education initiative (REI),
  269–270, 272, 273, 275, 276, 481, 495
  "platform" for, 494–495
  and regular education teachers,
    280–281
  See also Classroom, regular
Regulations, 44. *See also* Laws and legis-
  lation
Rehabilitation Act (1973). *See* PL 93–112
Rehabilitation specialists, 297
Rehnquist, Justice William, 68
Related services, 25, 27, 459
  court ruling on, 65*t*, 70
  for handicapped adults (anticipated
    needs), 485*t*, 486*t*
  IEP listing of, 395
  medical services distinguished from,
    68
  See also Psychological testing;
    Therapy
Related services personnel, 25, 289–293,
  301, 444*t*
  need for, 299*t*
  See also Diagnostician; Professionals
Relationships. *See* Interpersonal relation-
  ships
Relevance of material taught, 369, 371
Reliability of tests, 341, 344, 353
  and errors in scores, 347
Remediation, 258, 391, 393
Representativeness of tests, 341,
  343–344, 348, 353
Research, priorities in, 445–446
Research Triangle Institute (North Caro-
  lina), 433
Residential care. *See* Institutions
Resource room, 34*t*, 153, 258–259
  teacher for, 284
Respondent conditioning, 399, 407
Response cost, 401
"Restrictiveness," 25, 444*t*. *See also* LRE
  (least restrictive environment)
Revised Behavior Problem Checklist, 339

Rhode Island Department of Mental
  Health, Retardation and Hospitals, 69
Rights. *See* Civil rights; Laws and legis-
  lation
Riles, Wilson, 65
Rotation errors, 340
Rules
  explicit and implied, 83
  need for, 365–367, 385
Rynders, John, 274

Salk, Dr. Jonas, 202
Schizophrenia, 83, 175
Scholastic Aptitude Test (SAT), 332, 430
School nurses, 297
School psychologist. *See* Psychologists
Schools
  class-graded system in, 10
  compulsory attendance at, 10, 43
  different types of (for special educa-
    tion), 34*t*
  and dropouts, *see* Dropout rate
  enrollment in, 428–429
  exclusion/expulsion from (court rul-
    ings on), 61, 62*t*, 63*t*, 65*t*, 69–70,
    167
  and funding for special education, *see*
    Funding, federal
  neighborhood, children's views of, 22
  parochial, 429, 430
  residential or institutional, 25–26, 259
  special, 259
  See also Environment, learning; Pri-
    vate schools
School social worker, 293
Scores. *See* Test scores
Screening, screening tests, 309–310, 320,
  326*t*. *See also* Tests
SD (standard deviation) units, 81
Section 504. *See* PL 93–112 (Rehabilita-
  tion Act, 1973)
Segregation
  of handicapped, 12, 167, 274, 466, 486
  racial, court actions on, 61, 62*t*, 67,
    251, 255
Seguin, Edouard, 163
Self-contained classes, 136, 259
  teacher for, 284–285
Self-esteem, 87, 98, 181
Self-fulfilling prophecy. *See* Expectations
Semantics, 147, 337
Sensory acuity

auditory, 214, 332, 333, 353

interview form regarding, 335 (fig.)

testing for, 214, 332–334, 340, 353

visual, 222–224, 332, 353

See also Blindness and visual handicaps; Deafness and hearing handicaps

Separation approach (for gifted students), 136

Services. *See* Special education

Services, related. *See* Related services

Severely handicapped. *See* Handicapped students

Shape distortions, 339

Sheltered employment. *See* Employment

Siblings, 467, 470

Simmons, Richard, 417

Skills

analysis and synthesis, 403

collaborative, 405, 408

comprehension and application, 403

development of, 356, 389, 390 (*see also* Development)

evaluation, 404

knowledge, 403

social, training in, 407, 408

thinking (cognitive), teaching of, 370, 373, 385, 403–404, 407

Slavin, Robert, 263

Smith v. *Robinson*, 65t, 69, 73

Smith-Kettlewell Eye Research Foundation, 410, 411

Snellen Chart, 333

Social/emotional/behavioral problems

of blind, 226

of deaf or hard of hearing, 218–219

of emotionally disturbed, 181, 183–185

of gifted, 144

of learning disabled, 129–130

of mentally retarded, 173

of multihandicapped, 213

of orthopedically or other health impaired, 209–210

of speech and language impaired, 151

Social factors in special education, 431–439, 459–460, 461

Social policies

and classification, 244, 250, 276

and legislation, 40 (*see also* Laws and legislation)

Social Security Act (1935), 48t

Social skills training, 407, 408

Social standards, 83–84, 85, 109

Social worker, school, 293

Sonicguide, 416–417

Soviet Union, 434

Special education

age and, 24, 26–27, 28, 30 (fig.), 58, 72

as alternative program, 10

cascade system of, 267–269, 271 (fig.), 273, 275, 276

categorical, 189, 190, 259–261, 275

changes in, 466, 471–482

classification in, 241–250 (*see also* Classification)

cost of, 429, 438, 445–459, 461

cost of, compared to regular education, 452–454, 459, 461

court rulings on, *see* Court rulings

cultural diversity and, 474–476

dates specified (under IEP), 395

defined, 9, 17

delivering services in, 240–277

director or coordinator of, 296

direct services, 25, 27, 254, 452

diversity in, 28–33

early administrative view of, 10

early childhood, as state category, 18t

and early intervention, *see* Intervention, early

eligibility for, *see* Eligibility decisions

family role in, 467–471 (*see also* Parents)

funding for, *see* Funding, federal

gifted students receiving, 137, 138t–139t

goals and objectives of, 356, 388, 389–390, 393, 395–396, 421

graduation from, 482–483

harsh discipline substituted for, 11

history of, 117–121

IEP and, 395–399 (*see also* IEP [individualized education program])

indirect or consultative services, 16, 25, 27

labeling as necessity for receiving, 91, 92, 95, 176, 185, 192

and learning environment, 32–33, 34t, 153 (*see also* LRE [least restrictive environment]; Mainstreaming; Segregation)

legal basis for, 39–72

male-female ratio of students receiving, 29–30

minority groups in, 30–31, 168, 436, 437, 439, 474–476

need for persistence in, 493

number of students receiving (in U.S.), 9, 17, 114, 121, 428–429, 436, 437

obstacles raised by, 479–480

placement in, *see* Placement decisions

political factors in, 439–443, 459–460, 461

professionals in, *see* Professionals

regular education vs., 420–421, 478–481, 482 (*see also* Classroom, regular)

and regular education initiative (REI), 269–270, 272, 273, 275, 276

and related services, *see* Related services

rights to, 10 (*see also* Laws and legislation)

social factors in, 431–439, 459–460, 461

special adaptations and devices for, *see* Instructional adaptations

special settings and programs, 258–267

student reactions to, 33–34, 420

teachers of, 20 (*see also* Teachers, special education)

technology and, *see* Technology

as three-stage process, 27

transition services, 274–275, 276, 446

variation in services, 27, 36

what happens after students leave, 482–493

See also Instruction, effective; Vocational education

Special education assistants, 266, 267

Special education teachers. *See* Teachers, special education

Special program reimbursement, 450–451. *See also* Funding, federal

Specific learning disabilities. *See* Learning disabilities

Speech and language disorders

defined, 145–147

of emotionally disturbed, 185

health conditions causing, 201, 206

as high-prevalence category, 157

history of treatment of, 147–148

pragmatic language disorders, 131

prevalence of, 148, 149*t*

teaching methods for, 155–156

Speech and language impaired students, 16, 31, 131, 145–152

characteristics of, 148–151

classroom environment of, 33

laws and actions benefiting, 49*t*

number of, in U.S., 32*t*, 114, 148, 149*t*

special equipment for, 409

state categories for, 18*t*

teaching, 155–156

terms used to describe, 150*t*

See also Deaf or hard of hearing students

Speech and language therapy, 254, 457

Speech-language pathologist, 291–292

Spina bifida, 201, 233, 460

Sputnik, 136, 434

Standard behavior chart, 402

Standard deviation (SD) units, 81

Standardized tests. *See* Tests, standardized

Standard score, 330

Standards for Professional Practice, 44, 45

Standards in assessment, 341–344, 364

Standards in determining normality/exceptionality

for eligibility decisions, 81, 248–250, 311, 439, 443

for identifying LD, 116–117, 131, 248–250

importance of adaptive-behavior criterion, 162, 340

medical, 82–83, 85, 109

operational criteria, 80–81, 84, 108, 311

social, 83–84, 85, 109

statistical, 81–82, 84, 109

variations in, 247–250, 276

Standards in evaluation of progress, 396, 399

Stanford-Binet Intelligence Scale, 135. *See also* Intelligence tests

Statistical standards, 81–82, 84, 109

SD (standard deviation) units in, 81

Stay-put programs, 261–267, 276. *See also* Classroom, regular

Stereotyping, negative, 123, 128, 144, 172, 215–216, 269, 491. *See also* Labels

Stigma, 169, 269, 270

teacher management of, 111

See also Labels

Strauss, Alfred, 118, 119

Student Learning Context model, 264–265

Students' progress or performance
  academic, expectations and, 101–102
    (*see also* Expectations; Expecta-
    tions, teacher)
  evaluation of, 311–313, 382, 396, 399
  feedback on, 371, 373, 376–377
  present-day decline of, 430
  records of, 376
  relative to goal, 379, 382 (fig.)
  teachers' judgments about, 378–379
  See also Products of instruction; Tests
Students' understanding, 374, 430. *See
  also* Feedback
Student teaching (internship), 358–359
Stuttering, 146, 147
Subjectivity of classification process,
  249–250
Suicide, 190
Sullivan, Anne, 227, 465
Summative evaluation. *See* Evaluation
Superintendent of schools, 293, 296
Supervisor of specific service compo-
  nents, 296
Supervisors, supervising teacher, 16,
  358–359
Support groups. *See* Advocacy groups
Supreme Court, U.S., 61, 62t, 68–69, 70,
  251
Sutter, Erich, 411, 412
Syntax, 147, 337
Synthesis skills, 403

Talented students. *See* Gifted students
Task analysis, 360–361, 384, 407
Task-approach strategies, evaluation of,
  315
Teacher assistance teams, 264, 265 (fig.).
  See also Team teaching
Teachers
  assessment by, *see* Assessment
  attitudes of, toward exceptionality,
    104, 109, 111
  classroom, as part of special education
    team, 27, 28 (fig.)
  clinical, 285–286
  consultant, 153, 261, 265–266, 267,
    283–284
  and decision-making, 24, 308–316, 319,
    444t (*see also* Instruction, effective)
  differences in, 418–419, 421

education and certification of, 280,
    281, 282t–283t, 289, 291–292, 296,
    460
  and expectations, *see* Expectations,
    teacher
  goal of, 356, 384
  homebound, 288
  itinerant, 258, 284, 285 (fig.), 292
  and the law, 45
  and management of stigma, 111 (*see
    also* Stigma)
  reactions of, to specific behaviors,
    92–93, 95, 157, 429
  regular education, 280–281
  resource room, 284
  self-contained special class, 284–285
  students' performance as judged by,
    378–379
  supervising, 358–359
  and teacher-student relationships, 367,
    369, 380–381
Teachers, special education, 20, 261–266,
    281, 283–288, 301
  AFT guidelines concerning, 444t
  options of, in deciding why to teach,
    392
  supply and demand of, 20, 297–298,
    429, 494
  training of, 460
Teacher-unit funding, 451. *See also*
  Funding, federal
Teaching and teaching methods. *See* Instruction, effective
Team teaching, 261, 262–263, 266–267
  intervention assistance teams, 261,
    263–265, 267
Technology, 418, 476–478, 482, 494, 495
  special equipment for communication,
    210, 408–414, 460, 476
  special equipment for mobility,
    415–417
Telecommunication devices, 409, 411
Terman, Louis, 135, 487
Tests, 319–321
  achievement, *see* Achievement tests
    aptitude, 56
  assessment as replacement for, 343
  behavior analysis vs., 422
  criticisms of, 119, 342–343
  cut-off scores (norms) on, 309, 436
  defined, 318

discrepancy of scores on, *see* Discrepancy of abilities
formal and informal, 319
group administered, 319, 326*t*, 327*t*, 329, 346
individually administered, 319–320, 326*t*, 327*t*
intelligence, *see* Intelligence tests
LD students' performance on, 116, 117, 124, 172
modifications of, for disabled, 415, 418
of Native Americans, 474
norm-referenced, 320, 326*t*, 327*t*, 354, 422
objective-referenced, 320
PEP provisions regarding, 56
personality, 63*t*, 338
psychological, 255, 309, 337–339, 340
reliability and representativeness of, 341, 343–344, 348, 353
Scholastic Aptitude (SAT), 332, 430
of sensory acuity, 332–334
in student's primary language, 56, 61, 62*t*, 65 (*see also* Language)
and testing, defined, 318, 323
and testing programs for teachers, 282*t*–283*t*
validity of, 56, 344, 353
See also Assessment; Evaluation
Tests, standardized, 320, 345, 353
court rulings on, 61, 62*t*, 64*t*, 65–66
modifications of, for disabled, 415, 418
performance of deaf or visually handicapped on, 218–219, 225
Test scores, 330, 341, 346
errors in, 347
Therapy and therapists
aversive, opposition to, 466
behavior, 399–401, 407
client-centered, 404
counseling, 254, 404–405, 407
crisis, 404, 408
moral, 178
occupational, 291, 292 (fig.)
physical, 254, 291
reality, 404
speech and language, 254, 291–292, 457
Thinking
divergent and convergent, 139, 403
teaching skills of, 370, 373, 385, 403–404, 407
Thorndike, Edward L., 98

Time
allocated, 317
engaged, 317, 374–376, 379
management of (in classroom), 316–318, 367, 371, 374–376, 379
Time sample recording (of behavior), 338
Tinker v. *Des Moines Independent School District*, 62*t*
Titmus Vision Tester, 333
Token system, 401
Tracking. *See* Ability grouping
Transactional analysis (TA), 404
Transitional periods, 444*t*
Transition services, 274–275, 276
research on, 446
Tuition and fees, 429, 438
court rulings on, 65*t*, 68–69, 70
See also Cost
Tutoring, peer and classwide peer, 406–407, 422

United Cerebral Palsy Association, 434, 477
University of Minnesota, 274
Institute for Research on Learning Disabilities, 247
U.S. Bureau of the Census, 446, 472
U.S. Department of Education, 114, 116, 123, 204, 274, 298, 456, 479
abolition of, considered, 441
Office of Special Education and Rehabilitative Services, 44, 244, 432
research priorities of, 445
U.S. Department of Education v. *Katherine*, 256
U.S. House of Representatives Select Committee on Children, Youth, and Families, 392

U.S. Office of Civil Rights, 442

Validity of tests, 56, 344, 353
Vanderbilt University, 264
Vineland Training School, 245
Visual acuity. *See* Sensory acuity
Visual handicaps. *See* Blindness and visual handicaps
Vocational education, 186, 254, 274–275, 276, 446, 484, 486
Vocational Education Act (1984), 275
Vocational Rehabilitation Act (1918), 48*t*, 49*t*, 50*t*

Voice disorders, 146, 151. *See also*
    Speech and language disorders
von Recklinghausen's disease, 173

Wagner-O'Day Act (1938), 49*t*
Walker Problem Behavior Identification
    Checklist, 339
Washington v. *Davis*, 63*t*
Watson v. *City of Cambridge*, 62*t*
Wayne County Training School (Detroit),
    118

Werner, Hans, 118
Wheelchairs, 415, 417, 452. *See also* Mo-
    bility
"Wild Boy of Aveyron," 163
Will, Madeline, 270, 479–481
Withdrawal, 339
Wonder, Stevie, 413, 414 (fig.)
Workshop settings. *See* Employment
Wyatt v. *Stickney*, 63*t*